LINUX
DEVICE DRIVERS

LINUX
DEVICE DRIVERS

Second Edition

ALESSANDRO RUBINI & JONATHAN CORBET

O'REILLY®

Beijing • Cambridge • Farnham • Köln • Paris • Sebastopol • Taipei • Tokyo

Linux Device Drivers: Second Edition
by Alessandro Rubini and Jonathan Corbet

Copyright © 2001, 1998 O'Reilly and Associates, Inc. All rights reserved.
Printed in the United States of America.

Published by O'Reilly & Associates, Inc., 101 Morris Street, Sebastopol, CA 95472.

Editor: Andy Oram

Production Editor: Darren Kelly

Cover Designer: Edie Freedman

Printing History:

February 1998:	First Edition.
June 2001:	Second Edition.

Nutshell Handbook, the Nutshell Handbook logo, and the O'Reilly logo are registered trademarks of O'Reilly & Associates, Inc. Many of the designations used by manufacturers and sellers to distinguish their products are claimed as trademarks. Where those designations appear in this book, and O'Reilly & Associates, Inc. was aware of a trademark claim, the designations have been printed in caps or initial caps. The association between the images of the American West and the topic of Linux is a trademark of O'Reilly & Associates, Inc.

While every precaution has been taken in the preparation of this book, the publisher assumes no responsibility for errors or omissions, or for damages resulting from the use of the information contained herein.

This book is freely available under the GNU Free Documentation License, version 1.1. Full license at: *http://www.oreilly.com/catalog/linuxdrive2/chapter/licenseinfo.html* HTML at: *http://www.oreilly.com/catalog/linuxdrive2/chapter/book*; DocBook at: *http://www.oreilly.com/catalog/linuxdrive2/chapter/bookindex.xml*; PDF at: *http://www.oreilly.com/catalog/linuxdrive2/chapter/bookindexpdf.html*.

Library of Congress Cataloging-in-Publication Data

Rubini, Alessandro.
  Linux device drivers/Alessandro Rubini & Jonathan Corbet.--2nd ed. p. cm.
  Includes index.
  ISBN 0-596-00008-1
  1. Linux device drivers (Computer programs) I. Corbet, Jonathan. II. Title.

QA76.76.R92 2001
005.4'32--dc21   2001033172

[M]   [7/02]

TABLE OF CONTENTS

CHAPTER TEN
JUDICIOUS USE OF DATA TYPES _____ 293

CHAPTER ELEVEN
KMOD AND ADVANCED MODULARIZATION _____ 305

CHAPTER TWELVE
LOADING BLOCK DRIVERS _____ 321

CHAPTER THIRTEEN
MMAP AND DMA _____ 370

CHAPTER FOURTEEN
NETWORK DRIVERS _____ 425

CHAPTER FIFTEEN
OVERVIEW OF PERIPHERAL BUSES _____ 470

PREFACE

This is, on the surface, a book about writing device drivers for the Linux system. That is a worthy goal, of course; the flow of new hardware products is not likely to slow down anytime soon, and somebody is going to have to make all those new gadgets work with Linux. But this book is also about how the Linux kernel works and how to adapt its workings to your needs or interests. Linux is an open system; with this book, we hope, it will be more open and accessible to a larger community of developers.

Much has changed with Linux since the first edition of this book came out. Linux now runs on many more processors and supports a much wider variety of hardware. Many of the internal programming interfaces have changed significantly. Thus, the second edition. This book covers the 2.4 kernel, with all of the new features that it provides, while still giving a look backward to earlier releases for those who need to support them.

We hope you'll enjoy reading this book as much as we have enjoyed writing it.

Alessandro's Introduction

As an electronic engineer and a do-it-yourself kind of person, I have always enjoyed using the computer to control external hardware. Ever since the days of my father's Apple IIe, I have been looking for another platform where I could connect my custom circuitry and write my own driver software. Unfortunately, the PC of the 1980s wasn't powerful enough, at either the software or the hardware level: the internal design of the PC is much worse than that of the Apple II, and the available documentation has long been unsatisfying. But then Linux appeared, and I decided to give it a try by buying an expensive 386 motherboard and no proprietary software at all.

At the time, I was using Unix systems at the university and was greatly excited by the smart operating system, in particular when supplemented by the even smarter utilities that the GNU project donates to the user base. Running the Linux kernel on my own PC motherboard has always been an interesting experience, and I could even write my own device drivers and play with the soldering iron once again. I continue to tell people, "When I grow up, I wanna be a hacker," and GNU/Linux is the perfect platform for such dreams. That said, I don't know if I will ever grow up.

As Linux matures, more and more people get interested in writing drivers for custom circuitry and for commercial devices. As Linus Torvalds noted, "We're back to the times when men were men and wrote their own device drivers."

Back in 1996, I was hacking with my own toy device drivers that let me play with some loaned, donated, or even home-built hardware. I already had contributed a few pages to the *Kernel Hacker's Guide*, by Michael Johnson, and began writing kernel-related articles for *Linux Journal*, the magazine Michael founded and directed. Michael put me in touch with Andy Oram at O'Reilly; he expressed an interest in having me write a whole book about device drivers, and I accepted this task, which kept me pretty busy for quite a lot of time.

In 1999 it was clear I couldn't find the energy to update the book by myself: my family had grown and I had enough programming work to keep busy producing exclusively GPL'd software. Besides, the kernel had grown bigger and supported more diverse platforms than it used to, and the API had turned more broad and more mature. That's when Jonathan offered to help: he had just the right skills and enthusiasm to start the update and to force me to stay on track with the schedule—which slipped quite a lot anyway. He's been an invaluable mate in the process, which he pushed forward with good skills and dedication, definitely more than I could put in. I really enjoyed working with him, both on a technical and personal level.

Jon's Introduction

I first started actively playing with Linux early in 1994, when I convinced my employer to buy me a laptop from a company called, then, Fintronic Systems. Having been a Unix user since the beginning of the 1980s, and having played around in the source since about then, I was immediately hooked. Even in 1994, Linux was a highly capable system, and the first truly free system that I had ever been able to work with. I lost almost all my interest in working with proprietary systems at that point.

I didn't ever really plan to get into writing about Linux, though. Instead, when I started talking with O'Reilly about helping with the second edition of this book, I had recently quit my job of 18 years to start a Linux consulting company. As a way of attracting attention to ourselves, we launched a Linux news site, Linux Weekly News (*http://lwn.net*), which, among other things, covered kernel development. As Linux exploded in popularity, the web site did too, and the consulting business was eventually forgotten.

But my first interest has always been systems programming. In the early days, that interest took the form of "fixing" the original BSD Unix paging code (which has to have been a horrible hack job) or making recalcitrant tape drives work on a VAX/VMS system (where source was available, if you didn't mind the fact that it was in assembly and Bliss, and came on microfiche only). As time passed, I got to hack drivers on systems with names like Alliant, Ardent, and Sun, before moving into tasks such as deploying Linux as a real-time radar data collection system or, in the process of writing this book, fixing the I/O request queue locking in the Linux floppy driver.

So I welcomed the opportunity to work on this book for several reasons. As much as anything, it was a chance to get deeply into the code and to help others with a similar goal. Linux has always been intended to be fun as well as useful, and playing around with the kernel is one of the most fun parts of all—at least, for those with a certain warped sense of fun. Working with Alessandro has been a joy, and I must thank him for trusting me to hack on his excellent text, being patient with me as I came up to speed and as I broke things, and for that jet-lagged bicycle tour of Pavia. Writing this book has been a great time.

Audience of This Book

On the technical side, this text should offer a hands-on approach to understanding the kernel internals and some of the design choices made by the Linux developers. Although the main, official target of the book is teaching how to write device drivers, the material should give an interesting overview of the kernel implementation as well.

Although real hackers can find all the necessary information in the official kernel sources, usually a written text can be helpful in developing programming skills. The text you are approaching is the result of hours of patient grepping through the kernel sources, and we hope the final result is worth the effort it took.

This book should be an interesting source of information both for people who want to experiment with their computer and for technical programmers who face the need to deal with the inner levels of a Linux box. Note that "a Linux box" is a wider concept than "a PC running Linux," as many platforms are supported by our operating system, and kernel programming is by no means bound to a specific platform. We hope this book will be useful as a starting point for people who want to become kernel hackers but don't know where to start.

The Linux enthusiast should find in this book enough food for her mind to start playing with the code base and should be able to join the group of developers that is continuously working on new capabilities and performance enhancements. This book does not cover the Linux kernel in its entirety, of course, but Linux device driver authors need to know how to work with many of the kernel's subsystems. It thus makes a good introduction to kernel programming in general. Linux is still a work in progress, and there's always a place for new programmers to jump into the game.

If, on the other hand, you are just trying to write a device driver for your own device, and you don't want to muck with the kernel internals, the text should be modularized enough to fit your needs as well. If you don't want to go deep into the details, you can just skip the most technical sections and stick to the standard API used by device drivers to seamlessly integrate with the rest of the kernel.

The main target of this book is writing kernel modules for version 2.4 of the Linux kernel. A *module* is object code that can be loaded at runtime to add new functionality to a running kernel. Wherever possible, however, our sample code also runs on versions 2.2 and 2.0 of the kernel, and we point out where things have changed along the way.

Organization of the Material

The book introduces its topics in ascending order of complexity and is divided into two parts. The first part (Chapters 1 to 10) begins with the proper setup of kernel modules and goes on to describe the various aspects of programming that you'll need in order to write a full-featured driver for a char-oriented device. Every chapter covers a distinct problem and includes a "symbol table" at the end, which can be used as a reference during actual development.

Throughout the first part of the book, the organization of the material moves roughly from the software-oriented concepts to the hardware-related ones. This organization is meant to allow you to test the software on your own computer as far as possible without the need to plug external hardware into the machine. Every chapter includes source code and points to sample drivers that you can run on any Linux computer. In Chapter 8 and Chapter 9, however, we'll ask you to connect an inch of wire to the parallel port in order to test out hardware handling, but this requirement should be manageable by everyone.

The second half of the book describes block drivers and network interfaces and goes deeper into more advanced topics. Many driver authors will not need this material, but we encourage you to go on reading anyway. Much of the material found there is interesting as a view into how the Linux kernel works, even if you do not need it for a specific project.

Background Information

In order to be able to use this book, you need to be confident with C programming. A little Unix expertise is needed as well, as we often refer to Unix commands and pipelines.

At the hardware level, no previous expertise is required to understand the material in this book, as long as the general concepts are clear in advance. The text isn't based on specific PC hardware, and we provide all the needed information when we do refer to specific hardware.

Several free software tools are needed to build the kernel, and you often need specific versions of these tools. Those that are too old can lack needed features, while those that are too new can occasionally generate broken kernels. Usually, the tools provided with any current distribution will work just fine. Tool version requirements vary from one kernel to the next; consult *Documentation/Changes* in the source tree of the kernel you are using for exact requirements.

Sources of Further Information

Most of the information we provide in this book is extracted directly from the kernel sources and related documentation. In particular, pay attention to the *Documentation* directory that is found in the kernel source tree. There is a wealth of useful information there, including documentation of an increasing part of the kernel API (in the *DocBook* subdirectory).

There are a few interesting books out there that extensively cover related topics; they are listed in the bibliography.

There is much useful information available on the Internet; the following is a sampling. Internet sites, of course, tend to be highly volatile while printed books are hard to update. Thus, this list should be regarded as being somewhat out of date.

http://www.kernel.org
ftp://ftp.kernel.org
> This site is the home of Linux kernel development. You'll find the latest kernel release and related information. Note that the FTP site is mirrored throughout the world, so you'll most likely find a mirror near you.

http://www.linuxdoc.org
> The Linux Documentation Project carries a lot of interesting documents called "HOWTOs"; some of them are pretty technical and cover kernel-related topics.

http://www.linux-mag.com/depts/gear.html

The "Gearheads only" section from *Linux Magazine* often runs kernel-oriented articles from well-known developers.

http://www.linux.it/kerneldocs

This page contains many kernel-oriented magazine articles written by Alessandro.

http://lwn.net

At the risk of seeming self-serving, we'll point out this news site (edited by one of your authors) which, among other things, offers regular kernel development coverage.

http://kt.zork.net

Kernel Traffic is a popular site that provides weekly summaries of discussions on the Linux kernel development mailing list.

http://www.atnf.csiro.au/~rgooch/linux/docs/kernel-newsflash.html

The Kernel Newsflash site is a clearinghouse for late-breaking kernel news. In particular, it concentrates on problems and incompatibilities in current kernel releases; thus, it can be a good resource for people trying to figure out why the latest development kernel broke their drivers.

http://www.kernelnotes.org

Kernel Notes is a classic site with information on kernel releases, unofficial patches, and more.

http://www.kernelnewbies.org

This site is oriented toward new kernel developers. There is beginning information, an FAQ, and an associated IRC channel for those looking for immediate assistance.

http://lksr.org

The Linux Kernel Source Reference is a web interface to a CVS archive containing an incredible array of historical kernel releases. It can be especially useful for finding out just when a particular change occurred.

http://www.linux-mm.org

This page is oriented toward Linux memory management development. It contains a fair amount of useful information and an exhaustive list of kernel-oriented web links.

http://www.conecta.it/linux

This Italian site is one of the places where a Linux enthusiast keeps updated information about all the ongoing projects involving Linux. Maybe you already know an interesting site with HTTP links about Linux development; if not, this one is a good starting point.

Online Version and License

The authors have chosen to make this book freely available under the GNU Free Documentation License, version 1.1.

Full license
    http://www.oreilly.com/catalog/linuxdrive2/chapter/licenseinfo.html;

HTML
    http://www.oreilly.com/catalog/linuxdrive2/chapter/book;

DocBook
    http://www.oreilly.com/catalog/linuxdrive2/chapter/bookindex.xml;

PDF
    http://www.oreilly.com/catalog/linuxdrive2/chapter/bookindexpdf.html.

Conventions Used in This Book

The following is a list of the typographical conventions used in this book:

Italic	Used for file and directory names, program and command names, command-line options, URLs, and new terms
`Constant Width`	Used in examples to show the contents of files or the output from commands, and in the text to indicate words that appear in C code or other literal strings
`Constant Italic`	Used to indicate variable options, keywords, or text that the user is to replace with an actual value
`Constant Bold`	Used in examples to show commands or other text that should be typed literally by the user

Pay special attention to notes set apart from the text with the following icons:

This is a tip. It contains useful supplementary information about the topic at hand.

This is a warning. It helps you solve and avoid annoying problems.

We'd Like to Hear from You

We have tested and verified the information in this book to the best of our ability, but you may find that features have changed (or even that we have made mistakes!). Please let us know about any errors you find, as well as your suggestions for future editions, by writing to:

O'Reilly & Associates, Inc.
101 Morris Street
Sebastopol, CA 95472
(800) 998-9938 (in the United States or Canada)
(707) 829-0515 (international/local)
(707) 829-0104 (fax)

We have a web page for the book, where we list errata, examples, or any additional information. You can access this page at:

http://www.oreilly.com/catalog/linuxdrive2

To comment or ask technical questions about this book, send email to:

bookquestions@oreilly.com

For more information about our books, conferences, software, Resource Centers,and the O'Reilly Network, see our web site at:

http://www.oreilly.com

Acknowledgments

This book, of course, was not written in a vacuum; we would like to thank the many people who have helped to make it possible.

I (Alessandro) would like to thank the people that made this work possible. First of all, the incredible patience of Federica, who went as far as letting me review the first edition during our honeymoon, with a laptop in the tent. Giorgio and Giulia have only been involved in the second edition of the book, and helped me stay in touch with reality by eating pages, pulling wires, and crying for due attention. I must also thank all four grandparents, who came to the rescue when the deadlines were tight and took over my fatherly duties for whole days, letting me concentrate on code and coffee. I still owe a big thanks to Michael Johnson, who made me enter the world of writing. Even though this was several years ago, he's still the one that made the wheel spin; earlier, I had left the university to avoid writing articles instead of software. Being an independent consultant, I have no employer that kindly allowed me to work on the book; on the other hand, I owe due acknowledgment to Francesco Magenta and Rodolfo Giometti, who are helping me as "dependent consultants." Finally, I want to acknowledge the free-software authors who actually taught me how to program without even knowing me; this includes both kernel and user-space authors I enjoyed reading, but they are too many to list.

I (Jon) am greatly indebted to many people; first and foremost I wish to thank my wife, Laura, who put up with the great time demands of writing a book while simultaneously trying to make a "dotcom" business work. My children, Michele and Giulia, have been a constant source of joy and inspiration. Numerous people on the linux-kernel list showed great patience in answering my questions and setting me straight on things. My colleagues at LWN.net have been most patient with my distraction, and our readers' support of the LWN kernel page has been outstanding. This edition probably would not have happened without the presence of Boulder's local community radio station (appropriately named KGNU), which plays amazing music, and the Lake Eldora ski lodge, which allowed me to camp out all day with a laptop during my kids' ski lessons and served good coffee. I owe gratitude to Evi Nemeth for first letting me play around in the early BSD source on her VAX, to William Waite for *really* teaching me to program, and to Rit Carbone of the National Center for Atmospheric Research (NCAR), who got me started on a long career where I learned almost everything else.

We both wish to thank our editor, Andy Oram; this book is a vastly better product as a result of his efforts. And obviously we owe a lot to the smart people who pushed the free-software idea and still keep it running (that's mainly Richard Stallman, but he's definitely not alone).

We have also been helped at the hardware level; we couldn't study so many platforms without external help. We thank Intel for loaning an early IA-64 system, and Rebel.com for donating a Netwinder (their ARM-based tiny computer). Prosa Labs, the former Linuxcare-Italia, loaned a pretty fat PowerPC system; NEC Electronics donated their interesting development system for the VR4181 processor—that's a palmtop where we could put a GNU/Linux system on flash memory. Sun-Italia loaned both a SPARC and a SPARC64 system. All of those companies and those systems helped keep Alessandro busy in debugging portability issues and forced him to get one more room to fit his zoo of disparate silicon beasts.

The first edition was technically reviewed by Alan Cox, Greg Hankins, Hans Lermen, Heiko Eissfeldt, and Miguel de Icaza (in alphabetic order by first name). The technical reviewers for the second edition were Allan B. Cruse, Christian Morgner, Jake Edge, Jeff Garzik, Jens Axboe, Jerry Cooperstein, Jerome Peter Lynch, Michael Kerrisk, Paul Kinzelman, and Raph Levien. Together, these people have put a vast amount of effort into finding problems and pointing out possible improvements to our writing.

Last but certainly not least, we thank the Linux developers for their relentless work. This includes both the kernel programmers and the user-space people, who often get forgotten. In this book we chose never to call them by name in order to avoid being unfair to someone we might forget. We sometimes made an exception to this rule and called Linus by name; we hope he doesn't mind, though.

## CHAPTER ONE

AN INTRODUCTION TO DEVICE DRIVERS

As the popularity of the Linux system continues to grow, the interest in writing Linux device drivers steadily increases. Most of Linux is independent of the hardware it runs on, and most users can be (happily) unaware of hardware issues. But, for each piece of hardware supported by Linux, somebody somewhere has written a driver to make it work with the system. Without device drivers, there is no functioning system.

Device drivers take on a special role in the Linux kernel. They are distinct "black boxes" that make a particular piece of hardware respond to a well-defined internal programming interface; they hide completely the details of how the device works. User activities are performed by means of a set of standardized calls that are independent of the specific driver; mapping those calls to device-specific operations that act on real hardware is then the role of the device driver. This programming interface is such that drivers can be built separately from the rest of the kernel, and "plugged in" at runtime when needed. This modularity makes Linux drivers easy to write, to the point that there are now hundreds of them available.

There are a number of reasons to be interested in the writing of Linux device drivers. The rate at which new hardware becomes available (and obsolete!) alone guarantees that driver writers will be busy for the foreseeable future. Individuals may need to know about drivers in order to gain access to a particular device that is of interest to them. Hardware vendors, by making a Linux driver available for their products, can add the large and growing Linux user base to their potential markets. And the open source nature of the Linux system means that if the driver writer wishes, the source to a driver can be quickly disseminated to millions of users.

This book will teach you how to write your own drivers and how to hack around in related parts of the kernel. We have taken a device-independent approach; the programming techniques and interfaces are presented, whenever possible, without being tied to any specific device. Each driver is different; as a driver writer, you will need to understand your specific device well. But most of the principles and basic techniques are the same for all drivers. This book cannot teach you about your device, but it will give you a handle on the background you need to make your device work.

As you learn to write drivers, you will find out a lot about the Linux kernel in general; this may help you understand how your machine works and why things aren't always as fast as you expect or don't do quite what you want. We'll introduce new ideas gradually, starting off with very simple drivers and building upon them; every new concept will be accompanied by sample code that doesn't need special hardware to be tested.

This chapter doesn't actually get into writing code. However, we introduce some background concepts about the Linux kernel that you'll be glad you know later, when we do launch into programming.

The Role of the Device Driver

As a programmer, you will be able to make your own choices about your driver, choosing an acceptable trade-off between the programming time required and the flexibility of the result. Though it may appear strange to say that a driver is "flexible," we like this word because it emphasizes that the role of a device driver is providing *mechanism*, not *policy*.

The distinction between mechanism and policy is one of the best ideas behind the Unix design. Most programming problems can indeed be split into two parts: "what capabilities are to be provided" (the mechanism) and "how those capabilities can be used" (the policy). If the two issues are addressed by different parts of the program, or even by different programs altogether, the software package is much easier to develop and to adapt to particular needs.

For example, Unix management of the graphic display is split between the X server, which knows the hardware and offers a unified interface to user programs, and the window and session managers, which implement a particular policy without knowing anything about the hardware. People can use the same window manager on different hardware, and different users can run different configurations on the same workstation. Even completely different desktop environments, such as KDE and GNOME, can coexist on the same system. Another example is the layered structure of TCP/IP networking: the operating system offers the socket abstraction, which implements no policy regarding the data to be transferred, while different servers are in charge of the services (and their associated policies).

Moreover, a server like *ftpd* provides the file transfer mechanism, while users can use whatever client they prefer; both command-line and graphic clients exist, and anyone can write a new user interface to transfer files.

Where drivers are concerned, the same separation of mechanism and policy applies. The floppy driver is policy free—its role is only to show the diskette as a continuous array of data blocks. Higher levels of the system provide policies, such as who may access the floppy drive, whether the drive is accessed directly or via a filesystem, and whether users may mount filesystems on the drive. Since different environments usually need to use hardware in different ways, it's important to be as policy free as possible.

When *writing* drivers, a programmer should pay particular attention to this fundamental concept: write kernel code to access the hardware, but don't force particular policies on the user, since different users have different needs. The driver should deal with making the hardware available, leaving all the issues about *how* to use the hardware to the applications. A driver, then, is flexible if it offers access to the hardware capabilities without adding constraints. Sometimes, however, some policy decisions must be made. For example, a digital I/O driver may only offer byte-wide access to the hardware in order to avoid the extra code needed to handle individual bits.

You can also look at your driver from a different perspective: it is a software layer that lies between the applications and the actual device. This privileged role of the driver allows the driver programmer to choose exactly how the device should appear: different drivers can offer different capabilities, even for the same device. The actual driver design should be a balance between many different considerations. For instance, a single device may be used concurrently by different programs, and the driver programmer has complete freedom to determine how to handle concurrency. You could implement memory mapping on the device independently of its hardware capabilities, or you could provide a user library to help application programmers implement new policies on top of the available primitives, and so forth. One major consideration is the trade-off between the desire to present the user with as many options as possible and the time in which you have to do the writing as well as the need to keep things simple so that errors don't creep in.

Policy-free drivers have a number of typical characteristics. These include support for both synchronous and asynchronous operation, the ability to be opened multiple times, the ability to exploit the full capabilities of the hardware, and the lack of software layers to "simplify things" or provide policy-related operations. Drivers of this sort not only work better for their end users, but also turn out to be easier to write and maintain as well. Being policy free is actually a common target for software designers.

Many device drivers, indeed, are released together with user programs to help with configuration and access to the target device. Those programs can range from simple utilities to complete graphical applications. Examples include the *tunelp* program, which adjusts how the parallel port printer driver operates, and the graphical *cardctl* utility that is part of the PCMCIA driver package. Often a client library is provided as well, which provides capabilities that do not need to be implemented as part of the driver itself.

The scope of this book is the kernel, so we'll try not to deal with policy issues, or with application programs or support libraries. Sometimes we'll talk about different policies and how to support them, but we won't go into much detail about programs using the device or the policies they enforce. You should understand, however, that user programs are an integral part of a software package and that even policy-free packages are distributed with configuration files that apply a default behavior to the underlying mechanisms.

Splitting the Kernel

In a Unix system, several concurrent *processes* attend to different tasks. Each process asks for system resources, be it computing power, memory, network connectivity, or some other resource. The *kernel* is the big chunk of executable code in charge of handling all such requests. Though the distinction between the different kernel tasks isn't always clearly marked, the kernel's role can be split, as shown in Figure 1-1, into the following parts:

Process management
> The kernel is in charge of creating and destroying processes and handling their connection to the outside world (input and output). Communication among different processes (through signals, pipes, or interprocess communication primitives) is basic to the overall system functionality and is also handled by the kernel. In addition, the scheduler, which controls how processes share the CPU, is part of process management. More generally, the kernel's process management activity implements the abstraction of several processes on top of a single CPU or a few of them.

Memory management
> The computer's memory is a major resource, and the policy used to deal with it is a critical one for system performance. The kernel builds up a virtual addressing space for any and all processes on top of the limited available resources. The different parts of the kernel interact with the memory-management subsystem through a set of function calls, ranging from the simple *malloc/free* pair to much more exotic functionalities.

Filesystems
> Unix is heavily based on the filesystem concept; almost everything in Unix can be treated as a file. The kernel builds a structured filesystem on top of unstructured hardware, and the resulting file abstraction is heavily used

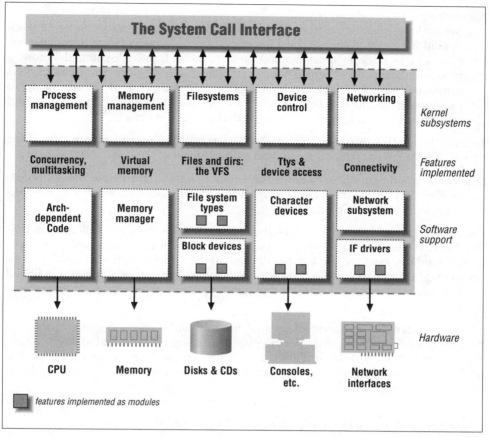

Figure 1-1. A split view of the kernel

throughout the whole system. In addition, Linux supports multiple filesystem types, that is, different ways of organizing data on the physical medium. For example, diskettes may be formatted with either the Linux-standard ext2 filesystem or with the commonly used FAT filesystem.

Device control

Almost every system operation eventually maps to a physical device. With the exception of the processor, memory, and a very few other entities, any and all device control operations are performed by code that is specific to the device being addressed. That code is called a *device driver*. The kernel must have embedded in it a device driver for every peripheral present on a system, from the hard drive to the keyboard and the tape streamer. This aspect of the kernel's functions is our primary interest in this book.

5

Networking

> Networking must be managed by the operating system because most network operations are not specific to a process: incoming packets are asynchronous events. The packets must be collected, identified, and dispatched before a process takes care of them. The system is in charge of delivering data packets across program and network interfaces, and it must control the execution of programs according to their network activity. Additionally, all the routing and address resolution issues are implemented within the kernel.

Toward the end of this book, in Chapter 16, you'll find a road map to the Linux kernel, but these few paragraphs should suffice for now.

One of the good features of Linux is the ability to extend at runtime the set of features offered by the kernel. This means that you can add functionality to the kernel while the system is up and running.

Each piece of code that can be added to the kernel at runtime is called a *module*. The Linux kernel offers support for quite a few different types (or classes) of modules, including, but not limited to, device drivers. Each module is made up of object code (not linked into a complete executable) that can be dynamically linked to the running kernel by the *insmod* program and can be unlinked by the *rmmod* program.

Figure 1-1 identifies different classes of modules in charge of specific tasks—a module is said to belong to a specific class according to the functionality it offers. The placement of modules in Figure 1-1 covers the most important classes, but is far from complete because more and more functionality in Linux is being modularized.

Classes of Devices and Modules

The Unix way of looking at devices distinguishes between three device types. Each module usually implements one of these types, and thus is classifiable as a *char module*, a *block module*, or a *network module*. This division of modules into different types, or classes, is not a rigid one; the programmer can choose to build huge modules implementing different drivers in a single chunk of code. Good programmers, nonetheless, usually create a different module for each new functionality they implement, because decomposition is a key element of scalability and extendability.

The three classes are the following:

Character devices

> A character (char) device is one that can be accessed as a stream of bytes (like a file); a char driver is in charge of implementing this behavior. Such a driver usually implements at least the *open*, *close*, *read*, and *write* system calls. The

text console (*/dev/console*) and the serial ports (*/dev/ttyS0* and friends) are examples of char devices, as they are well represented by the stream abstraction. Char devices are accessed by means of filesystem nodes, such as */dev/tty1* and */dev/lp0*. The only relevant difference between a char device and a regular file is that you can always move back and forth in the regular file, whereas most char devices are just data channels, which you can only access sequentially. There exist, nonetheless, char devices that look like data areas, and you can move back and forth in them; for instance, this usually applies to frame grabbers, where the applications can access the whole acquired image using *mmap* or *lseek*.

Block devices

Like char devices, block devices are accessed by filesystem nodes in the */dev* directory. A block device is something that can host a filesystem, such as a disk. In most Unix systems, a block device can be accessed only as multiples of a block, where a block is usually one kilobyte of data or another power of 2. Linux allows the application to read and write a block device like a char device—it permits the transfer of any number of bytes at a time. As a result, block and char devices differ only in the way data is managed internally by the kernel, and thus in the kernel/driver software interface. Like a char device, each block device is accessed through a filesystem node and the difference between them is transparent to the user. A block driver offers the kernel the same interface as a char driver, as well as an additional block-oriented interface that is invisible to the user or applications opening the */dev* entry points. That block interface, though, is essential to be able to *mount* a filesystem.

Network interfaces

Any network transaction is made through an interface, that is, a device that is able to exchange data with other hosts. Usually, an interface is a hardware device, but it might also be a pure software device, like the loopback interface. A network interface is in charge of sending and receiving data packets, driven by the network subsystem of the kernel, without knowing how individual transactions map to the actual packets being transmitted. Though both Telnet and FTP connections are stream oriented, they transmit using the same device; the device doesn't see the individual streams, but only the data packets.

Not being a stream-oriented device, a network interface isn't easily mapped to a node in the filesystem, as */dev/tty1* is. The Unix way to provide access to interfaces is still by assigning a unique name to them (such as `eth0`), but that name doesn't have a corresponding entry in the filesystem. Communication between the kernel and a network device driver is completely different from that used with char and block drivers. Instead of *read* and *write*, the kernel calls functions related to packet transmission.

Other classes of driver modules exist in Linux. The modules in each class exploit public services the kernel offers to deal with specific types of devices. Therefore, one can talk of universal serial bus (USB) modules, serial modules, and so on. The most common nonstandard class of devices is that of SCSI* drivers. Although every peripheral connected to the SCSI bus appears in */dev* as either a char device or a block device, the internal organization of the software is different.

Just as network interface cards provide the network subsystem with hardware-related functionality, so a SCSI controller provides the SCSI subsystem with access to the actual interface cable. SCSI is a communication protocol between the computer and peripheral devices, and every SCSI device responds to the same protocol, independently of what controller board is plugged into the computer. The Linux kernel therefore embeds a SCSI *implementation* (i.e., the mapping of file operations to the SCSI communication protocol). The driver writer has to implement the mapping between the SCSI abstraction and the physical cable. This mapping depends on the SCSI controller and is independent of the devices attached to the SCSI cable.

Other classes of device drivers have been added to the kernel in recent times, including USB drivers, FireWire drivers, and I2O drivers. In the same way that they handled SCSI drivers, kernel developers collected class-wide features and exported them to driver implementers to avoid duplicating work and bugs, thus simplifying and strengthening the process of writing such drivers.

In addition to device drivers, other functionalities, both hardware and software, are modularized in the kernel. Beyond device drivers, filesystems are perhaps the most important class of modules in the Linux system. A filesystem type determines how information is organized on a block device in order to represent a tree of directories and files. Such an entity is not a device driver, in that there's no explicit device associated with the way the information is laid down; the filesystem type is instead a software driver, because it maps the low-level data structures to higher-level data structures. It is the filesystem that determines how long a filename can be and what information about each file is stored in a directory entry. The filesystem module must implement the lowest level of the system calls that access directories and files, by mapping filenames and paths (as well as other information, such as access modes) to data structures stored in data blocks. Such an interface is completely independent of the actual data transfer to and from the disk (or other medium), which is accomplished by a block device driver.

If you think of how strongly a Unix system depends on the underlying filesystem, you'll realize that such a software concept is vital to system operation. The ability to decode filesystem information stays at the lowest level of the kernel hierarchy and is of utmost importance; even if you write a block driver for your new CD-ROM, it is useless if you are not able to run *ls* or *cp* on the data it hosts. Linux supports the concept of a filesystem module, whose software interface declares the different operations that can be performed on a filesystem inode, directory,

---

* SCSI is an acronym for Small Computer Systems Interface; it is an established standard in the workstation and high-end server market.

file, and superblock. It's quite unusual for a programmer to actually need to write a filesystem module, because the official kernel already includes code for the most important filesystem types.

Security Issues

Security is an increasingly important concern in modern times. We will discuss security-related issues as they come up throughout the book. There are a few general concepts, however, that are worth mentioning now.

Security has two faces, which can be called *deliberate* and *incidental*. One security problem is the damage a user can cause through the misuse of existing programs, or by incidentally exploiting bugs; a different issue is what kind of (mis)functionality a programmer can deliberately implement. The programmer has, obviously, much more power than a plain user. In other words, it's as dangerous to run a program you got from somebody else from the root account as it is to give him or her a root shell now and then. Although having access to a compiler is not a security hole per se, the hole can appear when compiled code is actually executed; everyone should be careful with modules, because a kernel module can do anything. A module is just as powerful as a superuser shell.

Any security check in the system is enforced by kernel code. If the kernel has security holes, then the system has holes. In the official kernel distribution, only an authorized user can load modules; the system call *create_module* checks if the invoking process is authorized to load a module into the kernel. Thus, when running an official kernel, only the superuser,* or an intruder who has succeeded in becoming privileged, can exploit the power of privileged code.

When possible, driver writers should avoid encoding security policy in their code. Security is a policy issue that is often best handled at higher levels within the kernel, under the control of the system administrator. There are always exceptions, however. As a device driver writer, you should be aware of situations in which some types of device access could adversely affect the system as a whole, and should provide adequate controls. For example, device operations that affect global resources (such as setting an interrupt line) or that could affect other users (such as setting a default block size on a tape drive) are usually only available to sufficiently privileged users, and this check must be made in the driver itself.

Driver writers must also be careful, of course, to avoid introducing security bugs. The C programming language makes it easy to make several types of errors. Many current security problems are created, for example, by *buffer overrun* errors, in which the programmer forgets to check how much data is written to a buffer, and data ends up written beyond the end of the buffer, thus overwriting unrelated

---

* Version 2.0 of the kernel allows only the superuser to run privileged code, while version 2.2 has more sophisticated capability checks. We discuss this in "Capabilities and Restricted Operations" in Chapter 5.

data. Such errors can compromise the entire system and must be avoided. Fortunately, avoiding these errors is usually relatively easy in the device driver context, in which the interface to the user is narrowly defined and highly controlled.

Some other general security ideas are worth keeping in mind. Any input received from user processes should be treated with great suspicion; never trust it unless you can verify it. Be careful with uninitialized memory; any memory obtained from the kernel should be zeroed or otherwise initialized before being made available to a user process or device. Otherwise, information leakage could result. If your device interprets data sent to it, be sure the user cannot send anything that could compromise the system. Finally, think about the possible effect of device operations; if there are specific operations (e.g., reloading the firmware on an adapter board, formatting a disk) that could affect the system, those operations should probably be restricted to privileged users.

Be careful, also, when receiving software from third parties, especially when the kernel is concerned: because everybody has access to the source code, everybody can break and recompile things. Although you can usually trust precompiled kernels found in your distribution, you should avoid running kernels compiled by an untrusted friend—if you wouldn't run a precompiled binary as root, then you'd better not run a precompiled kernel. For example, a maliciously modified kernel could allow anyone to load a module, thus opening an unexpected back door via *create_module.*

Note that the Linux kernel can be compiled to have no module support whatsoever, thus closing any related security holes. In this case, of course, all needed drivers must be built directly into the kernel itself. It is also possible, with 2.2 and later kernels, to disable the loading of kernel modules after system boot, via the capability mechanism.

Version Numbering

Before digging into programming, we'd like to comment on the version numbering scheme used in Linux and which versions are covered by this book.

First of all, note that *every* software package used in a Linux system has its own release number, and there are often interdependencies across them: you need a particular version of one package to run a particular version of another package. The creators of Linux distributions usually handle the messy problem of matching packages, and the user who installs from a prepackaged distribution doesn't need to deal with version numbers. Those who replace and upgrade system software, on the other hand, are on their own. Fortunately, almost all modern distributions support the upgrade of single packages by checking interpackage dependencies; the distribution's package manager generally will not allow an upgrade until the dependencies are satisfied.

To run the examples we introduce during the discussion, you won't need particular versions of any tool but the kernel; any recent Linux distribution can be used to run our examples. We won't detail specific requirements, because the file *Documentation/Changes* in your kernel sources is the best source of such information if you experience any problem.

As far as the kernel is concerned, the even-numbered kernel versions (i.e., 2.2.*x* and 2.4.*x*) are the stable ones that are intended for general distribution. The odd versions (such as 2.3.*x*), on the contrary, are development snapshots and are quite ephemeral; the latest of them represents the current status of development, but becomes obsolete in a few days or so.

This book covers versions 2.0 through 2.4 of the kernel. Our focus has been to show all the features available to device driver writers in 2.4, the current version at the time we are writing. We also try to cover 2.2 thoroughly, in those areas where the features differ between 2.2 and 2.4. We also note features that are not available in 2.0, and offer workarounds where space permits. In general, the code we show is designed to compile and run on a wide range of kernel versions; in particular, it has all been tested with version 2.4.4, and, where applicable, with 2.2.18 and 2.0.38 as well.

This text doesn't talk specifically about odd-numbered kernel versions. General users will never have a reason to run development kernels. Developers experimenting with new features, however, will want to be running the latest development release. They will usually keep upgrading to the most recent version to pick up bug fixes and new implementations of features. Note, however, that there's no guarantee on experimental kernels,* and nobody will help you if you have problems due to a bug in a noncurrent odd-numbered kernel. Those who run odd-numbered versions of the kernel are usually skilled enough to dig in the code without the need for a textbook, which is another reason why we don't talk about development kernels here.

Another feature of Linux is that it is a platform-independent operating system, not just "a Unix clone for PC clones" anymore: it is successfully being used with Alpha and SPARC processors, 68000 and PowerPC platforms, as well as a few more. This book is platform independent as far as possible, and all the code samples have been tested on several platforms, such as the PC brands, Alpha, ARM, IA-64, M68k, PowerPC, SPARC, SPARC64, and VR41xx (MIPS). Because the code has been tested on both 32-bit and 64-bit processors, it should compile and run on all other platforms. As you might expect, the code samples that rely on particular hardware don't work on all the supported platforms, but this is always stated in the source code.

---

* Note that there's no guarantee on even-numbered kernels as well, unless you rely on a commercial provider that grants its own warranty.

License Terms

Linux is licensed with the GNU General Public License (GPL), a document devised for the GNU project by the Free Software Foundation. The GPL allows anybody to redistribute, and even sell, a product covered by the GPL, as long as the recipient is allowed to rebuild an exact copy of the binary files from source. Additionally, any software product derived from a product covered by the GPL must, if it is redistributed at all, be released under the GPL.

The main goal of such a license is to allow the growth of knowledge by permitting everybody to modify programs at will; at the same time, people selling software to the public can still do their job. Despite this simple objective, there's a never-ending discussion about the GPL and its use. If you want to read the license, you can find it in several places in your system, including the directory */usr/src/linux*, as a file called *COPYING*.

Third-party and custom modules are not part of the Linux kernel, and thus you're not forced to license them under the GPL. A module *uses* the kernel through a well-defined interface, but is not part of it, similar to the way user programs use the kernel through system calls. Note that the exemption to GPL licensing applies only to modules that use only the published module interface. Modules that dig deeper into the kernel must adhere to the "derived work" terms of the GPL.

In brief, if your code goes in the kernel, you must use the GPL as soon as you release the code. Although personal use of your changes doesn't force the GPL on you, if you distribute your code you must include the source code in the distribution—people acquiring your package must be allowed to rebuild the binary at will. If you write a module, on the other hand, you are allowed to distribute it in binary form. However, this is not always practical, as modules should in general be recompiled for each kernel version that they will be linked with (as explained in Chapter 2, in the section "Version Dependency," and Chapter 11, in the section "Version Control in Modules"). New kernel releases—even minor stable releases—often break compiled modules, requiring a recompile. Linus Torvalds has stated publicly that he has no problem with this behavior, and that binary modules should be expected to work only with the kernel under which they were compiled. As a module writer, you will generally serve your users better by making source available.

As far as this book is concerned, most of the code is freely redistributable, either in source or binary form, and neither we nor O'Reilly & Associates retain any right on any derived works. All the programs are available through FTP from *ftp://ftp.ora.com/pub/examples/linux/drivers/*, and the exact license terms are stated in the file *LICENSE* in the same directory.

When sample programs include parts of the kernel code, the GPL applies: the comments accompanying source code are very clear about that. This only happens for a pair of source files that are very minor to the topic of this book.

Joining the Kernel Development Community

As you get into writing modules for the Linux kernel, you become part of a larger community of developers. Within that community, you can find not only people engaged in similar work, but also a group of highly committed engineers working toward making Linux a better system. These people can be a source of help, of ideas, and of critical review as well—they will be the first people you will likely turn to when you are looking for testers for a new driver.

The central gathering point for Linux kernel developers is the *linux-kernel* mailing list. All major kernel developers, from Linus Torvalds on down, subscribe to this list. Please note that the list is not for the faint of heart: traffic as of this writing can run up to 200 messages per day or more. Nonetheless, following this list is essential for those who are interested in kernel development; it also can be a top-quality resource for those in need of kernel development help.

To join the linux-kernel list, follow the instructions found in the linux-kernel mailing list FAQ: *http://www.tux.org/lkml*. Please read the rest of the FAQ while you are at it; there is a great deal of useful information there. Linux kernel developers are busy people, and they are much more inclined to help people who have clearly done their homework first.

Overview of the Book

From here on, we enter the world of kernel programming. Chapter 2 introduces modularization, explaining the secrets of the art and showing the code for running modules. Chapter 3 talks about char drivers and shows the complete code for a memory-based device driver that can be read and written for fun. Using memory as the hardware base for the device allows anyone to run the sample code without the need to acquire special hardware.

Debugging techniques are vital tools for the programmer and are introduced in Chapter 4. Then, with our new debugging skills, we move to advanced features of char drivers, such as blocking operations, the use of *select*, and the important *ioctl* call; these topics are the subject of Chapter 5.

Before dealing with hardware management, we dissect a few more of the kernel's software interfaces: Chapter 6 shows how time is managed in the kernel, and Chapter 7 explains memory allocation.

Next we focus on hardware. Chapter 8 describes the management of I/O ports and memory buffers that live on the device; after that comes interrupt handling, in Chapter 9. Unfortunately, not everyone will be able to run the sample code for these chapters, because some hardware support *is* actually needed to test the software interface to interrupts. We've tried our best to keep required hardware support to a minimum, but you still need to put your hands on the soldering iron to build your hardware "device." The device is a single jumper wire that plugs into the parallel port, so we hope this is not a problem.

Chapter 10 offers some additional suggestions about writing kernel software and about portability issues.

In the second part of this book, we get more ambitious; thus, Chapter 11 starts over with modularization issues, going deeper into the topic.

Chapter 12 then describes how block drivers are implemented, outlining the aspects that differentiate them from char drivers. Following that, Chapter 13 explains what we left out from the previous treatment of memory management: *mmap* and direct memory access (DMA). At this point, everything about char and block drivers has been introduced.

The third main class of drivers is introduced next. Chapter 14 talks in some detail about network interfaces and dissects the code of the sample network driver.

A few features of device drivers depend directly on the interface bus where the peripheral fits, so Chapter 15 provides an overview of the main features of the bus implementations most frequently found nowadays, with a special focus on PCI and USB support offered in the kernel.

Finally, Chapter 16 is a tour of the kernel source: it is meant to be a starting point for people who want to understand the overall design, but who may be scared by the huge amount of source code that makes up Linux.

CHAPTER TWO

BUILDING AND RUNNING MODULES

It's high time now to begin programming. This chapter introduces all the essential concepts about modules and kernel programming. In these few pages, we build and run a complete module. Developing such expertise is an essential foundation for any kind of modularized driver. To avoid throwing in too many concepts at once, this chapter talks only about modules, without referring to any specific device class.

All the kernel items (functions, variables, header files, and macros) that are introduced here are described in a reference section at the end of the chapter.

For the impatient reader, the following code is a complete "Hello, World" module (which does nothing in particular). This code will compile and run under Linux kernel versions 2.0 through 2.4.*

```
#define MODULE
#include <linux/module.h>

int init_module(void)  { printk("<1>Hello, world\n"); return 0; }
void cleanup_module(void) { printk("<1>Goodbye cruel world\n"); }
```

The *printk* function is defined in the Linux kernel and behaves similarly to the standard C library function *printf.* The kernel needs its own printing function because it runs by itself, without the help of the C library. The module can call *printk* because, after *insmod* has loaded it, the module is linked to the kernel and can access the kernel's public symbols (functions and variables, as detailed in the next section). The string <1> is the priority of the message. We've specified a high priority (low cardinal number) in this module because a message with the default priority might not show on the console, depending on the kernel version you are

---

* This example, and all the others presented in this book, is available on the O'Reilly FTP site, as explained in Chapter 1.

running, the version of the *klogd* daemon, and your configuration. You can ignore this issue for now; we'll explain it in the section "printk" in Chapter 4.

You can test the module by calling *insmod* and *rmmod*, as shown in the screen dump in the following paragraph. Note that only the superuser can load and unload a module.

The source file shown earlier can be loaded and unloaded as shown only if the running kernel has module version support disabled; however, most distributions preinstall versioned kernels (versioning is discussed in "Version Control in Modules" in Chapter 11). Although older *modutils* allowed loading nonversioned modules to versioned kernels, this is no longer possible. To solve the problem with *hello.c*, the source in the *misc-modules* directory of the sample code includes a few more lines to be able to run both under versioned and nonversioned kernels. However, we strongly suggest you compile and run your own kernel (without version support) before you run the sample code.*

```
root# gcc -c hello.c
root# insmod ./hello.o
Hello, world
root# rmmod hello
Goodbye cruel world
root#
```

According to the mechanism your system uses to deliver the message lines, your output may be different. In particular, the previous screen dump was taken from a text console; if you are running *insmod* and *rmmod* from an *xterm*, you won't see anything on your TTY. Instead, it may go to one of the system log files, such as */var/log/messages* (the name of the actual file varies between Linux distributions). The mechanism used to deliver kernel messages is described in "How Messages Get Logged" in Chapter 4.

As you can see, writing a module is not as difficult as you might expect. The hard part is understanding your device and how to maximize performance. We'll go deeper into modularization throughout this chapter and leave device-specific issues to later chapters.

Kernel Modules Versus Applications

Before we go further, it's worth underlining the various differences between a kernel module and an application.

Whereas an application performs a single task from beginning to end, a module registers itself in order to serve future requests, and its "main" function terminates immediately. In other words, the task of the function *init_module* (the module's

---

* If you are new to building kernels, Alessandro has posted an article at *http://www.linux.it/kerneldocs/kconf* that should help you get started.

entry point) is to prepare for later invocation of the module's functions; it's as though the module were saying, "Here I am, and this is what I can do." The second entry point of a module, *cleanup_module*, gets invoked just before the module is unloaded. It should tell the kernel, "I'm not there anymore; don't ask me to do anything else." The ability to unload a module is one of the features of modularization that you'll most appreciate, because it helps cut down development time; you can test successive versions of your new driver without going through the lengthy shutdown/reboot cycle each time.

As a programmer, you know that an application can call functions it doesn't define: the linking stage resolves external references using the appropriate library of functions. *printf* is one of those callable functions and is defined in *libc*. A module, on the other hand, is linked only to the kernel, and the only functions it can call are the ones exported by the kernel; there are no libraries to link to. The *printk* function used in *hello.c* earlier, for example, is the version of *printf* defined within the kernel and exported to modules. It behaves similarly to the original function, with a few minor differences, the main one being lack of floating-point support.*

Figure 2-1 shows how function calls and function pointers are used in a module to add new functionality to a running kernel.

Because no library is linked to modules, source files should *never* include the usual header files. Only functions that are actually part of the kernel itself may be used in kernel modules. Anything related to the kernel is declared in headers found in *include/linux* and *include/asm* inside the kernel sources (usually found in */usr/src/linux*). Older distributions (based on *libc* version 5 or earlier) used to carry symbolic links from */usr/include/linux* and */usr/include/asm* to the actual kernel sources, so your *libc* include tree could refer to the headers of the actual kernel source you had installed. These symbolic links made it convenient for user-space applications to include kernel header files, which they occasionally need to do.

Even though user-space headers are now separate from kernel-space headers, sometimes applications still include kernel headers, either before an old library is used or before new information is needed that is not available in the user-space headers. However, many of the declarations in the kernel header files are relevant only to the kernel itself and should not be seen by user-space applications. These declarations are therefore protected by `#ifdef __KERNEL__` blocks. That's why your driver, like other kernel code, will need to be compiled with the `__KERNEL__` preprocessor symbol defined.

The role of individual kernel headers will be introduced throughout the book as each of them is needed.

---

* The implementation found in Linux 2.0 and 2.2 has no support for the L and Z qualifiers. They have been introduced in 2.4, though.

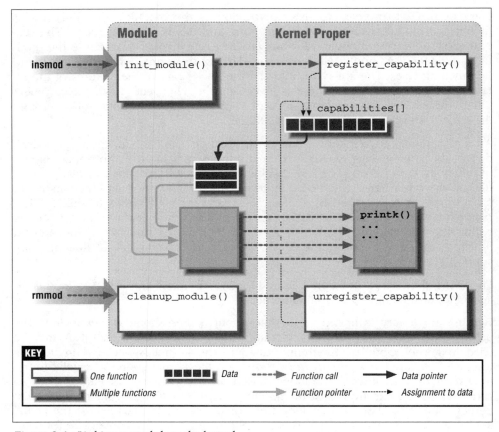

Figure 2-1. Linking a module to the kernel

Developers working on any large software system (such as the kernel) must be aware of and avoid *namespace pollution*. Namespace pollution is what happens when there are many functions and global variables whose names aren't meaning-ful enough to be easily distinguished. The programmer who is forced to deal with such an application expends much mental energy just to remember the "reserved" names and to find unique names for new symbols. Namespace collisions can cre-ate problems ranging from module loading failures to bizarre failures—which, per-haps, only happen to a remote user of your code who builds a kernel with a different set of configuration options.

Developers can't afford to fall into such an error when writing kernel code because even the smallest module will be linked to the whole kernel. The best approach for preventing namespace pollution is to declare all your symbols as `static` and to use a prefix that is unique within the kernel for the symbols you leave global. Also note that you, as a module writer, can control the external visibility of your symbols, as described in "The Kernel Symbol Table" later in this chapter.*

Using the chosen prefix for private symbols within the module may be a good practice as well, as it may simplify debugging. While testing your driver, you could export all the symbols without polluting your namespace. Prefixes used in the kernel are, by convention, all lowercase, and we'll stick to the same convention.

The last difference between kernel programming and application programming is in how each environment handles faults: whereas a segmentation fault is harmless during application development and a debugger can always be used to trace the error to the problem in the source code, a kernel fault is fatal at least for the current process, if not for the whole system. We'll see how to trace kernel errors in Chapter 4, in the section "Debugging System Faults."

User Space and Kernel Space

A module runs in the so-called *kernel space*, whereas applications run in *user space*. This concept is at the base of operating systems theory.

The role of the operating system, in practice, is to provide programs with a consistent view of the computer's hardware. In addition, the operating system must account for independent operation of programs and protection against unauthorized access to resources. This nontrivial task is only possible if the CPU enforces protection of system software from the applications.

Every modern processor is able to enforce this behavior. The chosen approach is to implement different operating modalities (or levels) in the CPU itself. The levels have different roles, and some operations are disallowed at the lower levels; program code can switch from one level to another only through a limited number of gates. Unix systems are designed to take advantage of this hardware feature, using two such levels. All current processors have at least two protection levels, and some, like the x86 family, have more levels; when several levels exist, the highest and lowest levels are used. Under Unix, the kernel executes in the highest level (also called *supervisor mode*), where everything is allowed, whereas applications execute in the lowest level (the so-called *user mode*), where the processor regulates direct access to hardware and unauthorized access to memory.

We usually refer to the execution modes as *kernel space* and *user space*. These terms encompass not only the different privilege levels inherent in the two modes, but also the fact that each mode has its own memory mapping—its own address space—as well.

---

* Most versions of *insmod* (but not all of them) export all non-static symbols if they find no specific instruction in the module; that's why it's wise to declare as static all the symbols you are not willing to export.

Unix transfers execution from user space to kernel space whenever an application issues a system call or is suspended by a hardware interrupt. Kernel code executing a system call is working in the context of a process—it operates on behalf of the calling process and is able to access data in the process's address space. Code that handles interrupts, on the other hand, is asynchronous with respect to processes and is not related to any particular process.

The role of a module is to extend kernel functionality; modularized code runs in kernel space. Usually a driver performs both the tasks outlined previously: some functions in the module are executed as part of system calls, and some are in charge of interrupt handling.

Concurrency in the Kernel

One way in which device driver programming differs greatly from (most) application programming is the issue of concurrency. An application typically runs sequentially, from the beginning to the end, without any need to worry about what else might be happening to change its environment. Kernel code does not run in such a simple world and must be written with the idea that many things can be happening at once.

There are a few sources of concurrency in kernel programming. Naturally, Linux systems run multiple processes, more than one of which can be trying to use your driver at the same time. Most devices are capable of interrupting the processor; interrupt handlers run asynchronously and can be invoked at the same time that your driver is trying to do something else. Several software abstractions (such as kernel timers, introduced in Chapter 6) run asynchronously as well. Moreover, of course, Linux can run on symmetric multiprocessor (SMP) systems, with the result that your driver could be executing concurrently on more than one CPU.

As a result, Linux kernel code, including driver code, must be *reentrant*—it must be capable of running in more than one context at the same time. Data structures must be carefully designed to keep multiple threads of execution separate, and the code must take care to access shared data in ways that prevent corruption of the data. Writing code that handles concurrency and avoids race conditions (situations in which an unfortunate order of execution causes undesirable behavior) requires thought and can be tricky. Every sample driver in this book has been written with concurrency in mind, and we will explain the techniques we use as we come to them.

A common mistake made by driver programmers is to assume that concurrency is not a problem as long as a particular segment of code does not go to sleep (or "block"). It is true that the Linux kernel is nonpreemptive; with the important exception of servicing interrupts, it will not take the processor away from kernel code that does not yield willingly. In past times, this nonpreemptive behavior was enough to prevent unwanted concurrency most of the time. On SMP systems, however, preemption is not required to cause concurrent execution.

If your code assumes that it will not be preempted, it will not run properly on SMP systems. Even if you do not have such a system, others who run your code may have one. In the future, it is also possible that the kernel will move to a preemptive mode of operation, at which point even uniprocessor systems will have to deal with concurrency everywhere (some variants of the kernel already implement it). Thus, a prudent programmer will always program as if he or she were working on an SMP system.

The Current Process

Although kernel modules don't execute sequentially as applications do, most actions performed by the kernel are related to a specific process. Kernel code can know the current process driving it by accessing the global item `current`, a pointer to `struct task_struct`, which as of version 2.4 of the kernel is declared in `<asm/current.h>`, included by `<linux/sched.h>`. The `current` pointer refers to the user process currently executing. During the execution of a system call, such as *open* or *read*, the current process is the one that invoked the call. Kernel code can use process-specific information by using `current`, if it needs to do so. An example of this technique is presented in "Access Control on a Device File," in Chapter 5.

Actually, `current` is not properly a global variable any more, like it was in the first Linux kernels. The developers optimized access to the structure describing the current process by hiding it in the stack page. You can look at the details of `current` in `<asm/current.h>`. While the code you'll look at might seem hairy, we must keep in mind that Linux is an SMP-compliant system, and a global variable simply won't work when you are dealing with multiple CPUs. The details of the implementation remain hidden to other kernel subsystems though, and a device driver can just include `<linux/sched.h>` and refer to the `current` process.

From a module's point of view, `current` is just like the external reference *printk*. A module can refer to `current` wherever it sees fit. For example, the following statement prints the process ID and the command name of the current process by accessing certain fields in `struct task_struct`:

```
printk("The process is \"%s\" (pid %i)\n",
  current->comm, current->pid);
```

The command name stored in `current->comm` is the base name of the program file that is being executed by the current process.

Compiling and Loading

The rest of this chapter is devoted to writing a complete, though typeless, module. That is, the module will not belong to any of the classes listed in "Classes of Devices and Modules" in Chapter 1. The sample driver shown in this chapter is called *skull*, short for Simple Kernel Utility for Loading Localities. You can reuse the *skull* source to load your own local code to the kernel, after removing the sample functionality it offers.*

Before we deal with the roles of *init_module* and *cleanup_module*, however, we'll write a makefile that builds object code that the kernel can load.

First, we need to define the _ _KERNEL_ _ symbol in the preprocessor before we include any headers. As mentioned earlier, much of the kernel-specific content in the kernel headers is unavailable without this symbol.

Another important symbol is MODULE, which must be defined before including <linux/module.h> (except for drivers that are linked directly into the kernel). This book does not cover directly linked modules; thus, the MODULE symbol is always defined in our examples.

If you are compiling for an SMP machine, you also need to define _ _SMP_ _ before including the kernel headers. In version 2.2, the "multiprocessor or uniprocessor" choice was promoted to a proper configuration item, so using these lines as the very first lines of your modules will do the task:

```
#include <linux/config.h>
#ifdef CONFIG_SMP
# define __SMP__
#endif
```

A module writer must also specify the −*O* flag to the compiler, because many functions are declared as `inline` in the header files. *gcc* doesn't expand inline functions unless optimization is enabled, but it can accept both the −*g* and −*O* options, allowing you to debug code that uses inline functions.† Because the kernel makes extensive use of inline functions, it is important that they be expanded properly.

You may also need to check that the compiler you are running matches the kernel you are compiling against, referring to the file *Documentation/Changes* in the kernel source tree. The kernel and the compiler are developed at the same time, though by different groups, so sometimes changes in one tool reveal bugs in the

---

* We use the word *local* here to denote personal changes to the system, in the good old Unix tradition of */usr/local*.

† Note, however, that using any optimization greater than −*O2* is risky, because the compiler might inline functions that are not declared as `inline` in the source. This may be a problem with kernel code, because some functions expect to find a standard stack layout when they are called.

other. Some distributions ship a version of the compiler that is too new to reliably build the kernel. In this case, they will usually provide a separate package (often called *kgcc*) with a compiler intended for kernel compilation.

Finally, in order to prevent unpleasant errors, we suggest that you use the *−Wall* (all warnings) compiler flag, and also that you fix all features in your code that cause compiler warnings, even if this requires changing your usual programming style. When writing kernel code, the preferred coding style is undoubtedly Linus's own style. *Documentation/CodingStyle* is amusing reading and a mandatory lesson for anyone interested in kernel hacking.

All the definitions and flags we have introduced so far are best located within the `CFLAGS` variable used by *make*.

In addition to a suitable `CFLAGS`, the makefile being built needs a rule for joining different object files. The rule is needed only if the module is split into different source files, but that is not uncommon with modules. The object files are joined by the *ld -r* command, which is not really a linking operation, even though it uses the linker. The output of *ld -r* is another object file, which incorporates all the code from the input files. The *−r* option means "relocatable;" the output file is relocatable in that it doesn't yet embed absolute addresses.

The following makefile is a minimal example showing how to build a module made up of two source files. If your module is made up of a single source file, just skip the entry containing *ld -r*.

```
# Change it here or specify it on the "make" command line
KERNELDIR = /usr/src/linux

include $(KERNELDIR)/.config

CFLAGS = -D__KERNEL__ -DMODULE -I$(KERNELDIR)/include \
  -O -Wall

ifdef CONFIG_SMP
 CFLAGS += -D__SMP__ -DSMP
endif

all: skull.o

skull.o: skull_init.o skull_clean.o
  $(LD) -r $^ -o $@

clean:
  rm -f *.o *~ core
```

If you are not familiar with *make*, you may wonder why no *.c* file and no compilation rule appear in the makefile shown. These declarations are unnecessary because *make* is smart enough to turn *.c* into *.o* without being instructed to, using the current (or default) choice for the compiler, `$(CC)`, and its flags, `$(CFLAGS)`.

After the module is built, the next step is loading it into the kernel. As we've already suggested, *insmod* does the job for you. The program is like *ld*, in that it links any unresolved symbol in the module to the symbol table of the running kernel. Unlike the linker, however, it doesn't modify the disk file, but rather an in-memory copy. *insmod* accepts a number of command-line options (for details, see the manpage), and it can assign values to integer and string variables in your module before linking it to the current kernel. Thus, if a module is correctly designed, it can be configured at load time; load-time configuration gives the user more flexibility than compile-time configuration, which is still used sometimes. Load-time configuration is explained in "Automatic and Manual Configuration" later in this chapter.

Interested readers may want to look at how the kernel supports *insmod*: it relies on a few system calls defined in *kernel/module.c*. The function *sys_create_module* allocates kernel memory to hold a module (this memory is allocated with *vmalloc*; see "vmalloc and Friends" in Chapter 7). The system call *get_kernel_syms* returns the kernel symbol table so that kernel references in the module can be resolved, and *sys_init_module* copies the relocated object code to kernel space and calls the module's initialization function.

If you actually look in the kernel source, you'll find that the names of the system calls are prefixed with `sys_`. This is true for all system calls and no other functions; it's useful to keep this in mind when grepping for the system calls in the sources.

Version Dependency

Bear in mind that your module's code has to be recompiled for each version of the kernel that it will be linked to. Each module defines a symbol called `__module_kernel_version`, which *insmod* matches against the version number of the current kernel. This symbol is placed in the `.modinfo` Executable Linking and Format (ELF) section, as explained in detail in Chapter 11. Please note that this description of the internals applies only to versions 2.2 and 2.4 of the kernel; Linux 2.0 did the same job in a different way.

The compiler will define the symbol for you whenever you include `<linux/module.h>` (that's why *hello.c* earlier didn't need to declare it). This also means that if your module is made up of multiple source files, you have to include `<linux/module.h>` from only one of your source files (unless you use `__NO_VERSION__`, which we'll introduce in a while).

In case of version mismatch, you can still try to load a module against a different kernel version by specifying the –*f* ("force") switch to *insmod*, but this operation isn't safe and can fail. It's also difficult to tell in advance what will happen. Loading can fail because of mismatching symbols, in which case you'll get an error message, or it can fail because of an internal change in the kernel. If that happens, you'll get serious errors at runtime and possibly a system panic—a good reason to be wary of version mismatches. Version mismatches can be handled more gracefully by using versioning in the kernel (a topic that is more advanced and is introduced in "Version Control in Modules" in Chapter 11).

If you want to compile your module for a particular kernel version, you have to include the specific header files for that kernel (for example, by declaring a different KERNELDIR) in the makefile given previously. This situation is not uncommon when playing with the kernel sources, as most of the time you'll end up with several versions of the source tree. All of the sample modules accompanying this book use the KERNELDIR variable to point to the correct kernel sources; it can be set in your environment or passed on the command line of *make*.

When asked to load a module, *insmod* follows its own search path to look for the object file, looking in version-dependent directories under */lib/modules*. Although older versions of the program looked in the current directory, first, that behavior is now disabled for security reasons (it's the same problem of the PATH environment variable). Thus, if you need to load a module from the current directory you should use *./module.o*, which works with all known versions of the tool.

Sometimes, you'll encounter kernel interfaces that behave differently between versions 2.0.*x* and 2.4.*x* of Linux. In this case you'll need to resort to the macros defining the version number of the current source tree, which are defined in the header <linux/version.h>. We will point out cases where interfaces have changed as we come to them, either within the chapter or in a specific section about version dependencies at the end, to avoid complicating a 2.4-specific discussion.

The header, automatically included by *linux/module.h*, defines the following macros:

UTS_RELEASE
> The macro expands to a string describing the version of this kernel tree. For example, "2.3.48".

LINUX_VERSION_CODE
> The macro expands to the binary representation of the kernel version, one byte for each part of the version release number. For example, the code for 2.3.48 is 131888 (i.e., 0x020330).* With this information, you can (almost) easily determine what version of the kernel you are dealing with.

KERNEL_VERSION(major,minor,release)
> This is the macro used to build a "kernel_version_code" from the individual numbers that build up a version number. For example, KERNEL_VERSION(2,3,48) expands to 131888. This macro is very useful when you

---

* This allows up to 256 development versions between stable versions.

need to compare the current version and a known checkpoint. We'll use this macro several times throughout the book.

The file *version.h* is included by *module.h*, so you won't usually need to include *version.h* explicitly. On the other hand, you can prevent *module.h* from including *version.h* by declaring `__NO_VERSION__` in advance. You'll use `__NO_VERSION__` if you need to include `<linux/module.h>` in several source files that will be linked together to form a single module—for example, if you need preprocessor macros declared in *module.h*. Declaring `__NO_VERSION__` before including *module.h* prevents automatic declaration of the string `__module_kernel_version` or its equivalent in source files where you don't want it (*ld -r* would complain about the multiple definition of the symbol). Sample modules in this book use `__NO_VERSION__` to this end.

Most dependencies based on the kernel version can be worked around with preprocessor conditionals by exploiting `KERNEL_VERSION` and `LINUX_VERSION_CODE`. Version dependency should, however, not clutter driver code with hairy `#ifdef` conditionals; the best way to deal with incompatibilities is by confining them to a specific header file. That's why our sample code includes a *sysdep.h* header, used to hide all incompatibilities in suitable macro definitions.

The first version dependency we are going to face is in the definition of a "`make install`" rule for our drivers. As you may expect, the installation directory, which varies according to the kernel version being used, is chosen by looking in *version.h*. The following fragment comes from the file *Rules.make*, which is included by all makefiles:

```
VERSIONFILE = $(INCLUDEDIR)/linux/version.h
VERSION  = $(shell awk -F\" '/REL/ {print $$2}' $(VERSIONFILE))
INSTALLDIR = /lib/modules/$(VERSION)/misc
```

We chose to install all of our drivers in the *misc* directory; this is both the right choice for miscellaneous add-ons and a good way to avoid dealing with the change in the directory structure under */lib/modules* that was introduced right before version 2.4 of the kernel was released. Even though the new directory structure is more complicated, the *misc* directory is used by both old and new versions of the *modutils* package.

With the definition of `INSTALLDIR` just given, the install rule of each makefile, then, is laid out like this:

```
install:
        install -d $(INSTALLDIR)
        install -c $(OBJS) $(INSTALLDIR)
```

Platform Dependency

Each computer platform has its peculiarities, and kernel designers are free to exploit all the peculiarities to achieve better performance in the target object file.

Unlike application developers, who must link their code with precompiled libraries and stick to conventions on parameter passing, kernel developers can dedicate some processor registers to specific roles, and they have done so. Moreover, kernel code can be optimized for a specific processor in a CPU family to get the best from the target platform: unlike applications that are often distributed in binary format, a custom compilation of the kernel can be optimized for a specific computer set.

Modularized code, in order to be interoperable with the kernel, needs to be compiled using the same options used in compiling the kernel (i.e., reserving the same registers for special use and performing the same optimizations). For this reason, our top-level *Rules.make* includes a platform-specific file that complements the makefiles with extra definitions. All of those files are called `Makefile.plat-form` and assign suitable values to *make* variables according to the current kernel configuration.

Another interesting feature of this layout of makefiles is that cross compilation is supported for the whole tree of sample files. Whenever you need to cross compile for your target platform, you'll need to replace all of your tools (*gcc*, *ld*, etc.) with another set of tools (for example, *m68k-linux-gcc*, *m68k-linux-ld*). The prefix to be used is defined as `$(CROSS_COMPILE)`, either in the *make* command line or in your environment.

The SPARC architecture is a special case that must be handled by the makefiles. User-space programs running on the SPARC64 (SPARC V9) platform are the same binaries you run on SPARC32 (SPARC V8). Therefore, the default compiler running on SPARC64 (*gcc*) generates SPARC32 object code. The kernel, on the other hand, must run SPARC V9 object code, so a cross compiler is needed. All GNU/Linux distributions for SPARC64 include a suitable cross compiler, which the makefiles select.

Although the complete list of version and platform dependencies is slightly more complicated than shown here, the previous description and the set of makefiles we provide is enough to get things going. The set of makefiles and the kernel sources can be browsed if you are looking for more detailed information.

The Kernel Symbol Table

We've seen how *insmod* resolves undefined symbols against the table of public kernel symbols. The table contains the addresses of global kernel items—

functions and variables—that are needed to implement modularized drivers. The public symbol table can be read in text form from the file */proc/ksyms* (assuming, of course, that your kernel has support for the */proc* filesystem—which it really should).

When a module is loaded, any symbol exported by the module becomes part of the kernel symbol table, and you can see it appear in */proc/ksyms* or in the output of the *ksyms* command.

New modules can use symbols exported by your module, and you can stack new modules on top of other modules. Module stacking is implemented in the mainstream kernel sources as well: the *msdos* filesystem relies on symbols exported by the *fat* module, and each input USB device module stacks on the *usbcore* and *input* modules.

Module stacking is useful in complex projects. If a new abstraction is implemented in the form of a device driver, it might offer a plug for hardware-specific implementations. For example, the video-for-linux set of drivers is split into a generic module that exports symbols used by lower-level device drivers for specific hardware. According to your setup, you load the generic video module and the specific module for your installed hardware. Support for parallel ports and the wide variety of attachable devices is handled in the same way, as is the USB kernel subsystem. Stacking in the parallel port subsystem is shown in Figure 2-2; the arrows show the communications between the modules (with some example functions and data structures) and with the kernel programming interface.

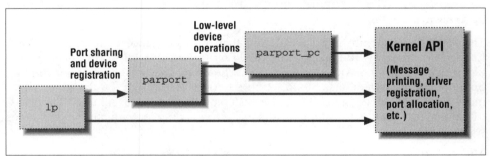

Figure 2-2. Stacking of parallel port driver modules

When using stacked modules, it is helpful to be aware of the *modprobe* utility. *modprobe* functions in much the same way as *insmod*, but it also loads any other modules that are required by the module you want to load. Thus, one *modprobe* command can sometimes replace several invocations of *insmod* (although you'll still need *insmod* when loading your own modules from the current directory, because *modprobe* only looks in the tree of installed modules).

Layered modularization can help reduce development time by simplifying each layer. This is similar to the separation between mechanism and policy that we discussed in Chapter 1.

In the usual case, a module implements its own functionality without the need to export any symbols at all. You will need to export symbols, however, whenever other modules may benefit from using them. You may also need to include specific instructions to avoid exporting all non-`static` symbols, as most versions (but not all) of *modutils* export all of them by default.

The Linux kernel header files provide a convenient way to manage the visibility of your symbols, thus reducing namespace pollution and promoting proper information hiding. The mechanism described in this section works with kernels 2.1.18 and later; the 2.0 kernel had a completely different mechanism, which is described at the end of the chapter.

If your module exports no symbols at all, you might want to make that explicit by placing a line with this macro call in your source file:

```
EXPORT_NO_SYMBOLS;
```

The macro expands to an assembler directive and may appear anywhere within the module. Portable code, however, should place it within the module initialization function (*init_module*), because the version of this macro defined in *sysdep.h* for older kernels will work only there.

If, on the other hand, you need to export a subset of symbols from your module, the first step is defining the preprocessor macro `EXPORT_SYMTAB`. This macro must be defined *before* including *module.h*. It is common to define it at compile time with the *–D* compiler flag in *Makefile*.

If `EXPORT_SYMTAB` is defined, individual symbols are exported with a couple of macros:

```
EXPORT_SYMBOL (name);
EXPORT_SYMBOL_NOVERS (name);
```

Either version of the macro will make the given symbol available outside the module; the second version (`EXPORT_SYMBOL_NOVERS`) exports the symbol with no versioning information (described in Chapter 11). Symbols must be exported outside of any function because the macros expand to the declaration of a variable. (Interested readers can look at `<linux/module.h>` for the details, even though the details are not needed to make things work.)

Initialization and Shutdown

As already mentioned, *init_module* registers any facility offered by the module. By *facility*, we mean a new functionality, be it a whole driver or a new software abstraction, that can be accessed by an application.

Modules can register many different types of facilities; for each facility, there is a specific kernel function that accomplishes this registration. The arguments passed to the kernel registration functions are usually a pointer to a data structure describing the new facility and the name of the facility being registered. The data structure usually embeds pointers to module functions, which is how functions in the module body get called.

The items that can be registered exceed the list of device types mentioned in Chapter 1. They include serial ports, miscellaneous devices, */proc* files, executable domains, and line disciplines. Many of those registrable items support functions that aren't directly related to hardware but remain in the "software abstractions" field. Those items can be registered because they are integrated into the driver's functionality anyway (like */proc* files and line disciplines for example).

There are other facilities that can be registered as add-ons for certain drivers, but their use is so specific that it's not worth talking about them; they use the stacking technique, as described earlier in "The Kernel Symbol Table." If you want to probe further, you can grep for EXPORT_SYMBOL in the kernel sources and find the entry points offered by different drivers. Most registration functions are prefixed with `register_`, so another possible way to find them is to grep for `register_` in */proc/ksyms*.

Error Handling in init_module

If any errors occur when you register utilities, you must undo any registration activities performed before the failure. An error can happen, for example, if there isn't enough memory in the system to allocate a new data structure or because a resource being requested is already being used by other drivers. Though unlikely, it might happen, and good program code must be prepared to handle this event.

Linux doesn't keep a per-module registry of facilities that have been registered, so the module must back out of everything itself if *init_module* fails at some point. If you ever fail to unregister what you obtained, the kernel is left in an unstable state: you can't register your facilities again by reloading the module because they will appear to be busy, and you can't unregister them because you'd need the same pointer you used to register and you're not likely to be able to figure out the address. Recovery from such situations is tricky, and you'll be often forced to reboot in order to be able to load a newer revision of your module.

Error recovery is sometimes best handled with the `goto` statement. We normally hate to use `goto`, but in our opinion this is one situation (well, the *only* situation) where it is useful. In the kernel, `goto` is often used as shown here to deal with errors.

The following sample code (using fictitious registration and unregistration functions) behaves correctly if initialization fails at any point.

```
int init_module(void)
{
int err;

    /* registration takes a pointer and a name */
    err = register_this(ptr1, "skull");
    if (err) goto fail_this;
    err = register_that(ptr2, "skull");
    if (err) goto fail_that;
    err = register_those(ptr3, "skull");
    if (err) goto fail_those;

    return 0; /* success */

    fail_those: unregister_that(ptr2, "skull");
    fail_that: unregister_this(ptr1, "skull");
    fail_this: return err; /* propagate the error */
}
```

This code attempts to register three (fictitious) facilities. The `goto` statement is used in case of failure to cause the unregistration of only the facilities that had been successfully registered before things went bad.

Another option, requiring no hairy `goto` statements, is keeping track of what has been successfully registered and calling *cleanup_module* in case of any error. The cleanup function will only unroll the steps that have been successfully accomplished. This alternative, however, requires more code and more CPU time, so in fast paths you'll still resort to `goto` as the best error-recovery tool. The return value of *init_module*, `err`, is an error code. In the Linux kernel, error codes are negative numbers belonging to the set defined in `<linux/errno.h>`. If you want to generate your own error codes instead of returning what you get from other functions, you should include `<linux/errno.h>` in order to use symbolic values such as `-ENODEV`, `-ENOMEM`, and so on. It is always good practice to return appropriate error codes, because user programs can turn them to meaningful strings using *perror* or similar means. (However, it's interesting to note that several versions of *modutils* returned a "Device busy" message for any error returned by *init_module*; the problem has only been fixed in recent releases.)

Obviously, *cleanup_module* must undo any registration performed by *init_module*, and it is customary (but not mandatory) to unregister facilities in the reverse order used to register them:

```
void cleanup_module(void)
{
unregister_those(ptr3, "skull");
unregister_that(ptr2, "skull");
unregister_this(ptr1, "skull");
return;
}
```

If your initialization and cleanup are more complex than dealing with a few items, the `goto` approach may become difficult to manage, because all the cleanup code must be repeated within *init_module*, with several labels intermixed. Sometimes, therefore, a different layout of the code proves more successful.

What you'd do to minimize code duplication and keep everything streamlined is to call *cleanup_module* from within *init_module* whenever an error occurs. The cleanup function, then, must check the status of each item before undoing its registration. In its simplest form, the code looks like the following:

```
struct something *item1;
struct somethingelse *item2;
int stuff_ok;

void cleanup_module(void)
{
  if (item1)
        release_thing(item1);
  if (item2)
    release_thing2(item2);
  if (stuff_ok)
    unregister_stuff();
  return;
}

int init_module(void)
{
  int err = -ENOMEM;

  item1 = allocate_thing(arguments);
  item2 = allocate_thing2(arguments2);
  if (!item2 || !item2)
    goto fail;
  err = register_stuff(item1, item2);
  if (!err)
    stuff_ok = 1;
  else
    goto fail;
  return 0; /* success */

fail:
  cleanup_module();
  return err;
}
```

As shown in this code, you may or may not need external flags to mark success of the initialization step, depending on the semantics of the registration/allocation function you call. Whether or not flags are needed, this kind of initialization scales well to a large number of items and is often better than the technique shown earlier.

The Usage Count

The system keeps a usage count for every module in order to determine whether the module can be safely removed. The system needs this information because a module can't be unloaded if it is busy: you can't remove a filesystem type while the filesystem is mounted, and you can't drop a char device while a process is using it, or you'll experience some sort of segmentation fault or kernel panic when wild pointers get dereferenced.

In modern kernels, the system can automatically track the usage count for you, using a mechanism that we will see in the next chapter. There are still times, however, when you will need to adjust the usage count manually. Code that must be portable to older kernels must still use manual usage count maintenance as well. To work with the usage count, use these three macros:

MOD_INC_USE_COUNT
>   Increments the count for the current module

MOD_DEC_USE_COUNT
>   Decrements the count

MOD_IN_USE
>   Evaluates to true if the count is not zero

The macros are defined in <linux/module.h>, and they act on internal data structures that shouldn't be accessed directly by the programmer. The internals of module management changed a lot during 2.1 development and were completely rewritten in 2.1.18, but the use of these macros did not change.

Note that there's no need to check for MOD_IN_USE from within *cleanup_module*, because the check is performed by the system call *sys_delete_module* (defined in *kernel/module.c*) in advance.

Proper management of the module usage count is critical for system stability. Remember that the kernel can decide to try to unload your module at absolutely any time. A common module programming error is to start a series of operations (in response, say, to an *open* request) and increment the usage count at the end. If the kernel unloads the module halfway through those operations, chaos is ensured. To avoid this kind of problem, you should call MOD_INC_USE_COUNT *before* doing almost anything else in a module.

You won't be able to unload a module if you lose track of the usage count. This situation may very well happen during development, so you should keep it in mind. For example, if a process gets destroyed because your driver dereferenced a NULL pointer, the driver won't be able to close the device, and the usage count won't fall back to zero. One possible solution is to completely disable the usage count during the debugging cycle by redefining both MOD_INC_USE_COUNT and

MOD_DEC_USE_COUNT to no-ops. Another solution is to use some other method to force the counter to zero (you'll see this done in the section "Using the ioctl Argument" in Chapter 5). Sanity checks should never be circumvented in a production module. For debugging, however, sometimes a brute-force attitude helps save development time and is therefore acceptable.

The current value of the usage count is found in the third field of each entry in */proc/modules*. This file shows the modules currently loaded in the system, with one entry for each module. The fields are the name of the module, the number of bytes of memory it uses, and the current usage count. This is a typical */proc/modules* file:

```
parport_pc     7604 1 (autoclean)
lp        4800 0 (unused)
parport     8084 1 [parport_probe parport_pc lp]
lockd     33256 1 (autoclean)
sunrpc      56612 1 (autoclean) [lockd]
ds       6252 1
i82365      22304 1
pcmcia_core   41280 0 [ds i82365]
```

Here we see several modules in the system. Among other things, the parallel port modules have been loaded in a stacked manner, as we saw in Figure 2-2. The (autoclean) marker identifies modules managed by *kmod* or *kerneld* (see Chapter 11); the (unused) marker means exactly that. Other flags exist as well. In Linux 2.0, the second (size) field was expressed in pages (4 KB each on most platforms) rather than bytes.

Unloading

To unload a module, use the *rmmod* command. Its task is much simpler than loading, since no linking has to be performed. The command invokes the *delete_module* system call, which calls *cleanup_module* in the module itself if the usage count is zero or returns an error otherwise.

The *cleanup_module* implementation is in charge of unregistering every item that was registered by the module. Only the exported symbols are removed automatically.

Explicit Initialization and Cleanup Functions

As we have seen, the kernel calls *init_module* to initialize a newly loaded module, and calls *cleanup_module* just before module removal. In modern kernels, however, these functions often have different names. As of kernel 2.3.13, a facility exists for explicitly naming the module initialization and cleanup routines; using this facility is the preferred programming style.

Consider an example. If your module names its initialization routine *my_init* (instead of *init_module*) and its cleanup routine *my_cleanup*, you would mark them with the following two lines (usually at the end of the source file):

```
module_init(my_init);
module_exit(my_cleanup);
```

Note that your code must include `<linux/init.h>` to use *module_init* and *module_exit*.

The advantage of doing things this way is that each initialization and cleanup function in the kernel can have a unique name, which helps with debugging. These functions also make life easier for those writing drivers that work either as a module or built directly into the kernel. However, use of *module_init* and *module_exit* is not required if your initialization and cleanup functions use the old names. In fact, for modules, the only thing they do is define *init_module* and *cleanup_module* as new names for the given functions.

If you dig through the kernel source (in versions 2.2 and later), you will likely see a slightly different form of declaration for module initialization and cleanup functions, which looks like the following:

```
static int __init my_init(void)
{
    ....
}

static void __exit my_cleanup(void)
{
    ....
}
```

The attribute `__init`, when used in this way, will cause the initialization function to be discarded, and its memory reclaimed, after initialization is complete. It only works, however, for built-in drivers; it has no effect on modules. `__exit`, instead, causes the omission of the marked function when the driver is not built as a module; again, in modules, it has no effect.

The use of `__init` (and `__initdata` for data items) can reduce the amount of memory used by the kernel. There is no harm in marking module initialization functions with `__init`, even though currently there is no benefit either. Management of initialization sections has not been implemented yet for modules, but it's a possible enhancement for the future.

Using Resources

A module can't accomplish its task without using system resources such as memory, I/O ports, I/O memory, and interrupt lines, as well as DMA channels if you use old-fashioned DMA controllers like the Industry Standard Architecture (ISA) one.

As a programmer, you are already accustomed to managing memory allocation; writing kernel code is no different in this regard. Your program obtains a memory area using *kmalloc* and releases it using *kfree*. These functions behave like *malloc* and *free*, except that *kmalloc* takes an additional argument, the priority. Usually, a priority of GFP_KERNEL or GFP_USER will do. The GFP acronym stands for "get free page." (Memory allocation is covered in detail in Chapter 7.)

Beginning driver programmers may initially be surprised at the need to allocate I/O ports, I/O memory,* and interrupt lines explicitly. After all, it is possible for a kernel module to simply access these resources without telling the operating system about it. Although system memory is anonymous and may be allocated from anywhere, I/O memory, ports, and interrupts have very specific roles. For instance, a driver needs to be able to allocate the exact ports it needs, not just *some* ports. But drivers cannot just go about making use of these system resources without first ensuring that they are not already in use elsewhere.

I/O Ports and I/O Memory

The job of a typical driver is, for the most part, writing and reading I/O ports and I/O memory. Access to I/O ports and I/O memory (collectively called *I/O regions*) happens both at initialization time and during normal operations.

Unfortunately, not all bus architectures offer a clean way to identify I/O regions belonging to each device, and sometimes the driver must guess where its I/O regions live, or even probe for the devices by reading and writing to "possible" address ranges. This problem is especially true of the ISA bus, which is still in use for simple devices to plug in a personal computer and is very popular in the industrial world in its PC/104 implementation (see PC/104 and PC/104+ in Chapter 15).

Despite the features (or lack of features) of the bus being used by a hardware device, the device driver should be guaranteed exclusive access to its I/O regions in order to prevent interference from other drivers. For example, if a module probing for its hardware should happen to write to ports owned by another device, weird things would undoubtedly happen.

The developers of Linux chose to implement a request/free mechanism for I/O regions, mainly as a way to prevent collisions between different devices. The mechanism has long been in use for I/O ports and was recently generalized to manage resource allocation at large. Note that this mechanism is just a software

---

* The memory areas that reside on the peripheral device are commonly called *I/O memory* to differentiate them from system RAM, which is customarily called memory).

abstraction that helps system housekeeping, and may or may not be enforced by hardware features. For example, unauthorized access to I/O ports doesn't produce any error condition equivalent to "segmentation fault"—the hardware can't enforce port registration.

Information about registered resources is available in text form in the files */proc/ioports* and */proc/iomem*, although the latter was only introduced during 2.3 development. We'll discuss version 2.4 now, introducing portability issues at the end of the chapter.

Ports

A typical */proc/ioports* file on a recent PC that is running version 2.4 of the kernel will look like the following:

```
0000-001f : dma1
0020-003f : pic1
0040-005f : timer
0060-006f : keyboard
0080-008f : dma page reg
00a0-00bf : pic2
00c0-00df : dma2
00f0-00ff : fpu
0170-0177 : ide1
01f0-01f7 : ide0
02f8-02ff : serial(set)
0300-031f : NE2000
0376-0376 : ide1
03c0-03df : vga+
03f6-03f6 : ide0
03f8-03ff : serial(set)
1000-103f : Intel Corporation 82371AB PIIX4 ACPI
  1000-1003 : acpi
  1004-1005 : acpi
  1008-100b : acpi
  100c-100f : acpi
1100-110f : Intel Corporation 82371AB PIIX4 IDE
1300-131f : pcnet_cs
1400-141f : Intel Corporation 82371AB PIIX4 ACPI
1800-18ff : PCI CardBus #02
1c00-1cff : PCI CardBus #04
5800-581f : Intel Corporation 82371AB PIIX4 USB
d000-dfff : PCI Bus #01
  d000-d0ff : ATI Technologies Inc 3D Rage LT Pro AGP-133
```

Each entry in the file specifies (in hexadecimal) a range of ports locked by a driver or owned by a hardware device. In earlier versions of the kernel the file had the same format, but without the "layered" structure that is shown through indentation.

The file can be used to avoid port collisions when a new device is added to the system and an I/O range must be selected by moving jumpers: the user can check what ports are already in use and set up the new device to use an available I/O range. Although you might object that most modern hardware doesn't use jumpers any more, the issue is still relevant for custom devices and industrial components.

But what is more important than the *ioports* file itself is the data structure behind it. When the software driver for a device initializes itself, it can know what port ranges are already in use; if the driver needs to probe I/O ports to detect the new device, it will be able to avoid probing those ports that are already in use by other drivers.

ISA probing is in fact a risky task, and several drivers distributed with the official Linux kernel refuse to perform probing when loaded as modules, to avoid the risk of destroying a running system by poking around in ports where some yet-unknown hardware may live. Fortunately, modern (as well as old-but-well-thought-out) bus architectures are immune to all these problems.

The programming interface used to access the I/O registry is made up of three functions:

```
int check_region(unsigned long start, unsigned long len);
struct resource *request_region(unsigned long start,
unsigned long len, char *name);
void release_region(unsigned long start, unsigned long len);
```

check_region may be called to see if a range of ports is available for allocation; it returns a negative error code (such as -EBUSY or -EINVAL) if the answer is no. *request_region* will actually allocate the port range, returning a non-NULL pointer value if the allocation succeeds. Drivers don't need to use or save the actual pointer returned—checking against NULL is all you need to do.* Code that needs to work only with 2.4 kernels need not call *check_region* at all; in fact, it's better not to, since things can change between the calls to *check_region* and *request_region*. If you want to be portable to older kernels, however, you must use *check_region* because *request_region* used to return void before 2.4. Your driver should call *release_region*, of course, to release the ports when it is done with them.

The three functions are actually macros, and they are declared in `<linux/ioport.h>`.

The typical sequence for registering ports is the following, as it appears in the *skull* sample driver. (The function *skull_probe_hw* is not shown here because it contains device-specific code.)

---

* The actual pointer is used only when the function is called internally by the resource management subsystem of the kernel.

```
#include <linux/ioport.h>
#include <linux/errno.h>
static int skull_detect(unsigned int port, unsigned int range)
{
 int err;

 if ((err = check_region(port,range)) < 0) return err; /* busy */
 if (skull_probe_hw(port,range) != 0) return -ENODEV; /* not found */
 request_region(port,range,"skull");        /* "Can't fail" */
 return 0;
}
```

This code first looks to see if the required range of ports is available; if the ports cannot be allocated, there is no point in looking for the hardware. The actual allocation of the ports is deferred until after the device is known to exist. The *request_region* call should never fail; the kernel only loads a single module at a time, so there should not be a problem with other modules slipping in and stealing the ports during the detection phase. Paranoid code can check, but bear in mind that kernels prior to 2.4 define *request_region* as returning void.

Any I/O ports allocated by the driver must eventually be released; *skull* does it from within *cleanup_module*:

```
static void skull_release(unsigned int port, unsigned int range)
{
 release_region(port,range);
}
```

The request/free approach to resources is similar to the register/unregister sequence described earlier for facilities and fits well in the `goto`-based implementation scheme already outlined.

Memory

Similar to what happens for I/O ports, I/O memory information is available in the */proc/iomem* file. This is a fraction of the file as it appears on a personal computer:

```
00000000-0009fbff : System RAM
0009fc00-0009ffff : reserved
000a0000-000bffff : Video RAM area
000c0000-000c7fff : Video ROM
000f0000-000fffff : System ROM
00100000-03feffff : System RAM
  00100000-0022c557 : Kernel code
  0022c558-0024455f : Kernel data
20000000-2fffffff : Intel Corporation 440BX/ZX - 82443BX/ZX Host bridge
68000000-68000fff : Texas Instruments PCI1225
68001000-68001fff : Texas Instruments PCI1225 (#2)
e0000000-e3ffffff : PCI Bus #01
e4000000-e7ffffff : PCI Bus #01
  e4000000-e4ffffff : ATI Technologies Inc 3D Rage LT Pro AGP-133
```

```
    e6000000-e6000fff : ATI Technologies Inc 3D Rage LT Pro AGP-133
    fffc0000-ffffffff : reserved
```

Once again, the values shown are hexadecimal ranges, and the string after the colon is the name of the "owner" of the I/O region.

As far as driver writing is concerned, the registry for I/O memory is accessed in the same way as for I/O ports, since they are actually based on the same internal mechanism.

To obtain and relinquish access to a certain I/O memory region, the driver should use the following calls:

```
int check_mem_region(unsigned long start, unsigned long len);
int request_mem_region(unsigned long start, unsigned long len,
    char *name);
int release_mem_region(unsigned long start, unsigned long len);
```

A typical driver will already know its own I/O memory range, and the sequence shown previously for I/O ports will reduce to the following:

```
if (check_mem_region(mem_addr, mem_size)) { printk("drivername:
  memory already in use\n"); return -EBUSY; }
  request_mem_region(mem_addr, mem_size, "drivername");
```

Resource Allocation in Linux 2.4

The current resource allocation mechanism was introduced in Linux 2.3.11 and provides a flexible way of controlling system resources. This section briefly describes the mechanism. However, the basic resource allocation functions (*request_region* and the rest) are still implemented (via macros) and are still universally used because they are backward compatible with earlier kernel versions. Most module programmers will not need to know about what is really happening under the hood, but those working on more complex drivers may be interested.

Linux resource management is able to control arbitrary resources, and it can do so in a hierarchical manner. Globally known resources (the range of I/O ports, say) can be subdivided into smaller subsets—for example, the resources associated with a particular bus slot. Individual drivers can then further subdivide their range if need be.

Resource ranges are described via a *resource* structure, declared in `<linux/ioport.h>`:

```
struct resource {
  const char *name;
  unsigned long start, end;
  unsigned long flags;
  struct resource *parent, *sibling, *child;
};
```

Top-level (root) resources are created at boot time. For example, the resource structure describing the I/O port range is created as follows:

```
struct resource ioport_resource =
    { "PCI IO", 0x0000, IO_SPACE_LIMIT, IORESOURCE_IO };
```

Thus, the name of the resource is `PCI IO`, and it covers a range from zero through `IO_SPACE_LIMIT`, which, according to the hardware platform being run, can be `0xffff` (16 bits of address space, as happens on the x86, IA-64, Alpha, M68k, and MIPS), `0xffffffff` (32 bits: SPARC, PPC, SH) or `0xffffffffffffffff` (64 bits: SPARC64).

Subranges of a given resource may be created with *allocate_resource*. For example, during PCI initialization a new resource is created for a region that is actually assigned to a physical device. When the PCI code reads those port or memory assignments, it creates a new resource for just those regions, and allocates them under `ioport_resource` or `iomem_resource`.

A driver can then request a subset of a particular resource (actually a subrange of a global resource) and mark it as busy by calling *__request_region*, which returns a pointer to a new `struct resource` data structure that describes the resource being requested (or returns `NULL` in case of error). The structure is already part of the global resource tree, and the driver is not allowed to use it at will.

An interested reader may enjoy looking at the details by browsing the source in *kernel/resource.c* and looking at the use of the resource management scheme in the rest of the kernel. Most driver writers, however, will be more than adequately served by *request_region* and the other functions introduced in the previous section.

This layered mechanism brings a couple of benefits. One is that it makes the I/O structure of the system apparent within the data structures of the kernel. The result shows up in */proc/ioports*, for example:

```
e800-e8ff : Adaptec AHA-2940U2/W / 7890
e800-e8be : aic7xxx
```

The range `e800-e8ff` is allocated to an Adaptec card, which has identified itself to the PCI bus driver. The *aic7xxx* driver has then requested most of that range—in this case, the part corresponding to real ports on the card.

The other advantage to controlling resources in this way is that it partitions the port space into distinct subranges that reflect the hardware of the underlying system. Since the resource allocator will not allow an allocation to cross subranges, it can block a buggy driver (or one looking for hardware that does not exist on the system) from allocating ports that belong to more than range—even if some of those ports are unallocated at the time.

Automatic and Manual Configuration

Several parameters that a driver needs to know can change from system to system. For instance, the driver must know the hardware's actual I/O addresses, or memory range (this is not a problem with well-designed bus interfaces and only applies to ISA devices). Sometimes you'll need to pass parameters to a driver to help it in finding its own device or to enable/disable specific features.

Depending on the device, there may be other parameters in addition to the I/O address that affect the driver's behavior, such as device brand and release number. It's essential for the driver to know the value of these parameters in order to work correctly. Setting up the driver with the correct values (i.e., configuring it) is one of the tricky tasks that need to be performed during driver initialization.

Basically, there are two ways to obtain the correct values: either the user specifies them explicitly or the driver autodetects them. Although autodetection is undoubtedly the best approach to driver configuration, user configuration is much easier to implement. A suitable trade-off for a driver writer is to implement automatic configuration whenever possible, while allowing user configuration as an option to override autodetection. An additional advantage of this approach to configuration is that the initial development can be done without autodetection, by specifying the parameters at load time, and autodetection can be implemented later.

Many drivers also have configuration options that control other aspects of their operation. For example, drivers for SCSI adapters often have options controlling the use of tagged command queuing, and the Integrated Device Electronics (IDE) drivers allow user control of DMA operations. Thus, even if your driver relies entirely on autodetection to locate hardware, you may want to make other configuration options available to the user.

Parameter values can be assigned at load time by *insmod* or *modprobe*; the latter can also read parameter assignment from a configuration file (typically */etc/modules.conf*). The commands accept the specification of integer and string values on the command line. Thus, if your module were to provide an integer parameter called *skull_ival* and a string parameter *skull_sval*, the parameters could be set at module load time with an *insmod* command like:

```
insmod skull skull_ival=666 skull_sval="the beast"
```

However, before *insmod* can change module parameters, the module must make them available. Parameters are declared with the **MODULE_PARM** macro, which is defined in *module.h*. **MODULE_PARM** takes two parameters: the name of the variable, and a string describing its type. The macro should be placed outside of any function and is typically found near the head of the source file. The two parameters mentioned earlier could be declared with the following lines:

```
int skull_ival=0;
char *skull_sval;

MODULE_PARM (skull_ival, "i");
MODULE_PARM (skull_sval, "s");
```

Five types are currently supported for module parameters: b, one byte; h, a short (two bytes); i, an integer; l, a long; and s, a string. In the case of string values, a pointer variable should be declared; *insmod* will allocate the memory for the user-supplied parameter and set the variable accordingly. An integer value preceding the type indicates an array of a given length; two numbers, separated by a hyphen, give a minimum and maximum number of values. If you want to find the author's description of this feature, you should refer to the header file <linux/module.h>.

As an example, an array that must have at least two and no more than four values could be declared as:

```
int skull_array[4];
MODULE_PARM (skull_array, "2-4i");
```

There is also a macro MODULE_PARM_DESC, which allows the programmer to provide a description for a module parameter. This description is stored in the object file; it can be viewed with a tool like *objdump*, and can also be displayed by automated system administration tools. An example might be as follows:

```
int base_port = 0x300;
MODULE_PARM (base_port, "i");
MODULE_PARM_DESC (base_port, "The base I/O port (default 0x300)");
```

All module parameters should be given a default value; *insmod* will change the value only if explicitly told to by the user. The module can check for explicit parameters by testing parameters against their default values. Automatic configuration, then, can be designed to work this way: if the configuration variables have the default value, perform autodetection; otherwise, keep the current value. In order for this technique to work, the "default" value should be one that the user would never actually want to specify at load time.

The following code shows how *skull* autodetects the port address of a device. In this example, autodetection is used to look for multiple devices, while manual configuration is restricted to a single device. The function *skull_detect* occurred earlier, in "Ports," while *skull_init_board* is in charge of device-specific initialization and thus is not shown.

```
/*
 * port ranges: the device can reside between
 * 0x280 and 0x300, in steps of 0x10. It uses 0x10 ports.
 */
#define SKULL_PORT_FLOOR 0x280
#define SKULL_PORT_CEIL 0x300
#define SKULL_PORT_RANGE 0x010
```

```
/*
 * the following function performs autodetection, unless a specific
 * value was assigned by insmod to "skull_port_base"
 */

static int skull_port_base=0; /* 0 forces autodetection */
MODULE_PARM (skull_port_base, "i");
MODULE_PARM_DESC (skull_port_base, "Base I/O port for skull");


static int skull_find_hw(void) /* returns the # of devices */
{
  /* base is either the load-time value or the first trial */
  int base = skull_port_base ? skull_port_base
         : SKULL_PORT_FLOOR;
  int result = 0;

  /* loop one time if value assigned; try them all if autodetecting */
  do {
        if (skull_detect(base, SKULL_PORT_RANGE) == 0) {
          skull_init_board(base);
          result++;
        }
        base += SKULL_PORT_RANGE; /* prepare for next trial */
  }
  while (skull_port_base == 0 && base < SKULL_PORT_CEIL);

  return result;
}
```

If the configuration variables are used only within the driver (they are not published in the kernel's symbol table), the driver writer can make life a little easier for the user by leaving off the prefix on the variable names (in this case, skull_). Prefixes usually mean little to users except extra typing.

For completeness, there are three other macros that place documentation into the object file. They are as follows:

MODULE_AUTHOR (name)
    Puts the author's name into the object file.

MODULE_DESCRIPTION (desc)
    Puts a description of the module into the object file.

MODULE_SUPPORTED_DEVICE (dev)
    Places an entry describing what device is supported by this module. Comments in the kernel source suggest that this parameter may eventually be used to help with automated module loading, but no such use is made at this time.

Doing It in User Space

A Unix programmer who's addressing kernel issues for the first time might well be nervous about writing a module. Writing a user program that reads and writes directly to the device ports is much easier.

Indeed, there are some arguments in favor of user-space programming, and sometimes writing a so-called user-space device driver is a wise alternative to kernel hacking.

The advantages of user-space drivers can be summarized as follows:

- The full C library can be linked in. The driver can perform many exotic tasks without resorting to external programs (the utility programs implementing usage policies that are usually distributed along with the driver itself).

- The programmer can run a conventional debugger on the driver code without having to go through contortions to debug a running kernel.

- If a user-space driver hangs, you can simply kill it. Problems with the driver are unlikely to hang the entire system, unless the hardware being controlled is *really* misbehaving.

- User memory is swappable, unlike kernel memory. An infrequently used device with a huge driver won't occupy RAM that other programs could be using, except when it is actually in use.

- A well-designed driver program can still allow concurrent access to a device.

An example of a user-space driver is the X server: it knows exactly what the hardware can do and what it can't, and it offers the graphic resources to all X clients. Note, however, that there is a slow but steady drift toward frame-buffer-based graphics environments, where the X server acts only as a server based on a real kernel-space device driver for actual graphic manipulation.

Usually, the writer of a user-space driver implements a server process, taking over from the kernel the task of being the single agent in charge of hardware control. Client applications can then connect to the server to perform actual communication with the device; a smart driver process can thus allow concurrent access to the device. This is exactly how the X server works.

Another example of a user-space driver is the *gpm* mouse server: it performs arbitration of the mouse device between clients, so that several mouse-sensitive applications can run on different virtual consoles.

Sometimes, though, the user-space driver grants device access to a single program. This is how *libsvga* works. The library, which turns a TTY into a graphics display, gets linked to the application, thus supplementing the application's capabilities without resorting to a central authority (e.g., a server). This approach usually gives you better performance because it skips the communication overhead, but it requires the application to run as a privileged user (this is one of the problems being solved by the frame buffer device driver running in kernel space).

But the user-space approach to device driving has a number of drawbacks. The most important are as follows:

- Interrupts are not available in user space. The only way around this (on the x86) is to use the *vm86* system call, which imposes a performance penalty.*

- Direct access to memory is possible only by *mmap*ping */dev/mem*, and only a privileged user can do that.

- Access to I/O ports is available only after calling *ioperm* or *iopl*. Moreover, not all platforms support these system calls, and access to */dev/port* can be too slow to be effective. Both the system calls and the device file are reserved to a privileged user.

- Response time is slower, because a context switch is required to transfer information or actions between the client and the hardware.

- Worse yet, if the driver has been swapped to disk, response time is unacceptably long. Using the *mlock* system call might help, but usually you'll need to lock several memory pages, because a user-space program depends on a lot of library code. *mlock*, too, is limited to privileged users.

- The most important devices can't be handled in user space, including, but not limited to, network interfaces and block devices.

As you see, user-space drivers can't do that much after all. Interesting applications nonetheless exist: for example, support for SCSI scanner devices (implemented by the *SANE* package) and CD writers (implemented by *cdrecord* and other tools). In both cases, user-level device drivers rely on the "SCSI generic" kernel driver, which exports low-level SCSI functionality to user-space programs so they can drive their own hardware.

In order to write a user-space driver, some hardware knowledge is sufficient, and there's no need to understand the subtleties of kernel software. We won't discuss user-space drivers any further in this book, but will concentrate on kernel code instead.

One case in which working in user space might make sense is when you are beginning to deal with new and unusual hardware. This way you can learn to manage your hardware without the risk of hanging the whole system. Once you've

---

* The system call is not discussed in this book because the subject matter of the text is kernel drivers; moreover, *vm86* is too platform specific to be really interesting.

done that, encapsulating the software in a kernel module should be a painless operation.

Backward Compatibility

The Linux kernel is a moving target—many things change over time as new features are developed. The interface that we have described in this chapter is that provided by the 2.4 kernel; if your code needs to work on older releases, you will need to take various steps to make that happen.

This is the first of many "backward compatibility" sections in this book. At the end of each chapter we'll cover the things that have changed since version 2.0 of the kernel, and what needs to be done to make your code portable.

For starters, the `KERNEL_VERSION` macro was introduced in kernel 2.1.90. The *sysdep.h* header file contains a replacement for kernels that need it.

Changes in Resource Management

The new resource management scheme brings in a few portability problems if you want to write a driver that can run with kernel versions older than 2.4. This section discusses the portability problems you'll encounter and how the *sysdep.h* header tries to hide them.

The most apparent change brought about by the new resource management code is the addition of *request_mem_region* and related functions. Their role is limited to accessing the I/O memory database, without performing specific operations on any hardware. What you can do with earlier kernels, thus, is to simply not call the functions. The *sysdep.h* header easily accomplishes that by defining the functions as macros that return 0 for kernels earlier than 2.4.

Another difference between 2.4 and earlier kernel versions is in the actual prototypes of *request_region* and related functions.

Kernels earlier than 2.4 declared both *request_region* and *release_region* as functions returning `void` (thus forcing the use of *check_region* beforehand). The new implementation, more correctly, has functions that return a pointer value so that an error condition can be signaled (thus making *check_region* pretty useless). The actual pointer value will not generally be useful to driver code for anything other than a test for `NULL`, which means that the request failed.

If you want to save a few lines of code in your drivers and are not concerned about backward portability, you could exploit the new function calls and avoid using *check_region* in your code. Actually, *check_region* is now implemented on top of *request_region*, releasing the I/O region and returning success if the request is fulfilled; the overhead is negligible because none of these functions is ever called from a time-critical code section.

If you prefer to be portable, you can stick to the call sequence we suggested earlier in this chapter and ignore the return values of *request_region* and *release_region*. Anyway, *sysdep.h* declares both functions as macros returning 0 (success), so you can both be portable and check the return value of every function you call.

The last difference in the I/O registry between version 2.4 and earlier versions of the kernel is in the data types used for the `start` and `len` arguments. Whereas new kernels always use `unsigned long`, older kernels used shorter types. This change has no effect on driver portability, though.

Compiling for Multiprocessor Systems

Version 2.0 of the kernel didn't use the `CONFIG_SMP` configuration option to build for SMP systems; instead, choice was made a global assignment in the main kernel *makefile*. Note that modules compiled for an SMP machine will not work in a uniprocessor kernel, and vice versa, so it is important to get this one right.

The sample code accompanying this book automatically deals with SMP in the makefiles, so the code shown earlier need not be copied in each module. However, we do not support SMP under version 2.0 of the kernel. This should not be a problem because multiprocessor support was not very robust in Linux 2.0, and everyone running SMP systems should be using 2.2 or 2.4. Version 2.0 is covered by this book because it's still the platform of choice for small embedded systems (especially in its no-MMU implementation), but no such system has multiple processors.

Exporting Symbols in Linux 2.0

The Linux 2.0 symbol export mechanism was built around a function called *register_symtab*. A Linux 2.0 module would build a table describing all of the symbols to be exported, then would call *register_symtab* from its initialization function. Only symbols that were listed in the explicit symbol table were exported to the kernel. If, instead, the function was not called at all, all global symbols were exported.

If your module doesn't need to export any symbols, and you don't want to declare everything as `static`, just hide global symbols by adding the following line to *init_module*. This call to *register_symtab* simply overwrites the module's default symbol table with an empty one:

```
register_symtab(NULL);
```

This is exactly how *sysdep.h* defines `EXPORT_NO_SYMBOLS` when compiling for version 2.0. This is also why `EXPORT_NO_SYMBOLS` must appear within *init_module* to work properly under Linux 2.0.

If you do need to export symbols from your module, you will need to create a symbol table structure describing these symbols. Filling a Linux 2.0 symbol table structure is a tricky task, but kernel developers have provided header files to simplify things. The following lines of code show how a symbol table is declared and exported using the facilities offered by the headers of Linux 2.0:

```
static struct symbol_table skull_syms = {

#include <linux/symtab_begin.h>
  X(skull_fn1),
  X(skull_fn2),
  X(skull_variable),
#include <linux/symtab_end.h>
        };


  register_symtab(&skull_syms);
```

Writing portable code that controls symbol visibility takes an explicit effort from the device driver programmer. This is a case where it is not sufficient to define a few compatibility macros; instead, portability requires a fair amount of conditional preprocessor code, but the concepts are simple. The first step is to identify the kernel version in use and to define some symbols accordingly. What we chose to do in *sysdep.h* is define a macro **REGISTER_SYMTAB()** that expands to nothing on version 2.2 and later and expands to *register_symtab* on version 2.0. Also, **__USE_OLD_SYMTAB__** is defined if the old code must be used.

By making use of this code, a module that exports symbols may now do so portably. In the sample code is a module, called *misc-modules/export.c*, that does nothing except export one symbol. The module, covered in more detail in "Version Control in Modules" in Chapter 11, includes the following lines to export the symbol portably:

```
#ifdef __USE_OLD_SYMTAB__
  static struct symbol_table export_syms = {
   #include <linux/symtab_begin.h>
   X(export_function),
   #include <linux/symtab_end.h>
  };
#else
  EXPORT_SYMBOL(export_function);
#endif

int export_init(void)
{
  REGISTER_SYMTAB(&export_syms);
  return 0;
}
```

If `__USE_OLD_SYMTAB__` is set (meaning that you are dealing with a 2.0 kernel), the *symbol_table* structure is defined as needed; otherwise, `EXPORT_SYMBOL` is used to export the symbol directly. Then, in *init_module*, `REGISTER_SYMTAB` is called; on anything but a 2.0 kernel, it will expand to nothing.

Module Configuration Parameters

`MODULE_PARM` was introduced in kernel version 2.1.18. With the 2.0 kernel, no parameters were declared explicitly; instead, *insmod* was able to change the value of any variable within the module. This method had the disadvantage of providing user access to variables for which this mode of access had not been intended; there was also no type checking of parameters. `MODULE_PARM` makes module parameters much cleaner and safer, but also makes Linux 2.2 modules incompatible with 2.0 kernels.

If 2.0 compatibility is a concern, a simple preprocessor test can be used to define the various `MODULE_` macros to do nothing. The header file *sysdep.h* in the sample code defines these macros when needed.

Quick Reference

This section summarizes the kernel functions, variables, macros, and */proc* files that we've touched on in this chapter. It is meant to act as a reference. Each item is listed after the relevant header file, if any. A similar section appears at the end of every chapter from here on, summarizing the new symbols introduced in the chapter.

`__KERNEL__`
`MODULE`
> Preprocessor symbols, which must both be defined to compile modularized kernel code.

`__SMP__`
> A preprocessor symbol that must be defined when compiling modules for symmetric multiprocessor systems.

`int init_module(void);`
`void cleanup_module(void);`
> Module entry points, which must be defined in the module object file.

`#include <linux/init.h>`
`module_init(init_function);`
`module_exit(cleanup_function);`
> The modern mechanism for marking a module's initialization and cleanup functions.

```
#include <linux/module.h>
```
Required header. It must be included by a module source.

```
MOD_INC_USE_COUNT;
MOD_DEC_USE_COUNT;
MOD_IN_USE;
```
Macros that act on the usage count.

/proc/modules

The list of currently loaded modules. Entries contain the module name, the amount of memory each module occupies, and the usage count. Extra strings are appended to each line to specify flags that are currently active for the module.

```
EXPORT_SYMTAB;
```
Preprocessor macro, required for modules that export symbols.

```
EXPORT_NO_SYMBOLS;
```
Macro used to specify that the module exports no symbols to the kernel.

```
EXPORT_SYMBOL (symbol);
EXPORT_SYMBOL_NOVERS (symbol);
```
Macro used to export a symbol to the kernel. The second form exports without using versioning information.

```
int register_symtab(struct symbol_table *);
```
Function used to specify the set of public symbols in the module. Used in 2.0 kernels only.

```
#include <linux/symtab_begin.h>
X(symbol),
#include <linux/symtab_end.h>
```
Headers and preprocessor macro used to declare a symbol table in the 2.0 kernel.

```
MODULE_PARM(variable, type);
MODULE_PARM_DESC (variable, description);
```
Macros that make a module variable available as a parameter that may be adjusted by the user at module load time.

```
MODULE_AUTHOR(author);
MODULE_DESCRIPTION(description);
MODULE_SUPPORTED_DEVICE(device);
```
Place documentation on the module in the object file.

`#include <linux/version.h>`
Required header. It is included by `<linux/module.h>`, unless `__NO_VERSION__` is defined (see later in this list).

`LINUX_VERSION_CODE`
Integer macro, useful to `#ifdef` version dependencies.

`char kernel_version[] = UTS_RELEASE;`
Required variable in every module. `<linux/module.h>` defines it, unless `__NO_VERSION__` is defined (see the following entry).

`__NO_VERSION__`
Preprocessor symbol. Prevents declaration of `kernel_version` in `<linux/module.h>`.

`#include <linux/sched.h>`
One of the most important header files. This file contains definitions of much of the kernel API used by the driver, including functions for sleeping and numerous variable declarations.

`struct task_struct *current;`
The current process.

`current->pid`
`current->comm`
The process ID and command name for the current process.

`#include <linux/kernel.h>`
`int printk(const char * fmt, ...);`
The analogue of *printf* for kernel code.

`#include <linux/malloc.h>`
`void *kmalloc(unsigned int size, int priority);`
`void kfree(void *obj);`
Analogue of *malloc* and *free* for kernel code. Use the value of GFP_KERNEL as the priority.

`#include <linux/ioport.h>`
`int check_region(unsigned long from, unsigned long extent);`
`struct resource *request_region(unsigned long from, unsigned long extent, const char *name);`
`void release_region(unsigned long from, unsigned long extent);`
Functions used to register and release I/O ports.

```
int check_mem_region (unsigned long start, unsigned long
    extent);
struct resource *request_mem_region (unsigned long start,
    unsigned long extent, const char *name);
void release_mem_region (unsigned long start, unsigned long
    extent);
```
Macros used to register and release I/O memory regions.

/proc/ksyms

The public kernel symbol table.

/proc/ioports

The list of ports used by installed devices.

/proc/iomem

The list of allocated memory regions.

## CHAPTER THREE

CHAR DRIVERS

The goal of this chapter is to write a complete char device driver. We'll develop a character driver because this class is suitable for most simple hardware devices. Char drivers are also easier to understand than, for example, block drivers or network drivers. Our ultimate aim is to write a *modularized* char driver, but we won't talk about modularization issues in this chapter.

Throughout the chapter, we'll present code fragments extracted from a real device driver: *scull*, short for Simple Character Utility for Loading Localities. *scull* is a char driver that acts on a memory area as though it were a device. A side effect of this behavior is that, as far as *scull* is concerned, the word *device* can be used interchangeably with "the memory area used by *scull*."

The advantage of *scull* is that it isn't hardware dependent, since every computer has memory. *scull* just acts on some memory, allocated using *kmalloc*. Anyone can compile and run *scull*, and *scull* is portable across the computer architectures on which Linux runs. On the other hand, the device doesn't do anything "useful" other than demonstrating the interface between the kernel and char drivers and allowing the user to run some tests.

The Design of scull

The first step of driver writing is defining the capabilities (the mechanism) the driver will offer to user programs. Since our "device" is part of the computer's memory, we're free to do what we want with it. It can be a sequential or random-access device, one device or many, and so on.

To make *scull* be useful as a template for writing real drivers for real devices, we'll show you how to implement several device abstractions on top of the computer memory, each with a different personality.

The *scull* source implements the following devices. Each kind of device implemented by the module is referred to as a *type*:

scull0 to *scull3*

Four devices each consisting of a memory area that is both global and persistent. Global means that if the device is opened multiple times, the data contained within the device is shared by all the file descriptors that opened it. Persistent means that if the device is closed and reopened, data isn't lost. This device can be fun to work with, because it can be accessed and tested using conventional commands such as *cp*, *cat*, and shell I/O redirection; we'll examine its internals in this chapter.

scullpipe0 to *scullpipe3*

Four FIFO (first-in-first-out) devices, which act like pipes. One process reads what another process writes. If multiple processes read the same device, they contend for data. The internals of *scullpipe* will show how blocking and nonblocking *read* and *write* can be implemented without having to resort to interrupts. Although real drivers synchronize with their devices using hardware interrupts, the topic of blocking and nonblocking operations is an important one and is separate from interrupt handling (covered in Chapter 9).

scullsingle
scullpriv
sculluid
scullwuid

These devices are similar to *scull0*, but with some limitations on when an *open* is permitted. The first (*scullsingle*) allows only one process at a time to use the driver, whereas *scullpriv* is private to each virtual console (or X terminal session) because processes on each console/terminal will get a different memory area from processes on other consoles. *sculluid* and *scullwuid* can be opened multiple times, but only by one user at a time; the former returns an error of "Device Busy" if another user is locking the device, whereas the latter implements blocking *open*. These variations of *scull* add more "policy" than "mechanism;" this kind of behavior is interesting to look at anyway, because some devices require types of management like the ones shown in these *scull* variations as part of their mechanism.

Each of the *scull* devices demonstrates different features of a driver and presents different difficulties. This chapter covers the internals of *scull0* to *skull3*; the more advanced devices are covered in Chapter 5: *scullpipe* is described in "A Sample Implementation: scullpipe" and the others in "Access Control on a Device File."

Major and Minor Numbers

Char devices are accessed through names in the filesystem. Those names are called special files or device files or simply nodes of the filesystem tree; they are conventionally located in the */dev* directory. Special files for char drivers are identified by a "c" in the first column of the output of *ls –l*. Block devices appear in */dev* as well, but they are identified by a "b." The focus of this chapter is on char devices, but much of the following information applies to block devices as well.

If you issue the *ls –l* command, you'll see two numbers (separated by a comma) in the device file entries before the date of last modification, where the file length normally appears. These numbers are the major device number and minor device number for the particular device. The following listing shows a few devices as they appear on a typical system. Their major numbers are 1, 4, 7, and 10, while the minors are 1, 3, 5, 64, 65, and 129.

```
crw-rw-rw- 1 root    root     1,  3  Feb 23 1999   null
crw------- 1 root    root    10,  1  Feb 23 1999   psaux
crw------- 1 rubini  tty      4,  1  Aug 16 22:22  tty1
crw-rw-rw- 1 root    dialout  4, 64  Jun 30 11:19  ttyS0
crw-rw-rw- 1 root    dialout  4, 65  Aug 16 00:00  ttyS1
crw------- 1 root    sys      7,  1  Feb 23 1999   vcs1
crw------- 1 root    sys      7, 129 Feb 23 1999   vcsa1
crw-rw-rw- 1 root    root     1,  5  Feb 23 1999   zero
```

The major number identifies the driver associated with the device. For example, */dev/null* and */dev/zero* are both managed by driver 1, whereas virtual consoles and serial terminals are managed by driver 4; similarly, both *vcs1* and *vcsa1* devices are managed by driver 7. The kernel uses the major number at *open* time to dispatch execution to the appropriate driver.

The minor number is used only by the driver specified by the major number; other parts of the kernel don't use it, and merely pass it along to the driver. It is common for a driver to control several devices (as shown in the listing); the minor number provides a way for the driver to differentiate among them.

Version 2.4 of the kernel, though, introduced a new (optional) feature, the device file system or *devfs*. If this file system is used, management of device files is simplified and quite different; on the other hand, the new filesystem brings several user-visible incompatibilities, and as we are writing it has not yet been chosen as a default feature by system distributors. The previous description and the following instructions about adding a new driver and special file assume that *devfs* is not present. The gap is filled later in this chapter, in "The Device Filesystem."

When *devfs* is not being used, adding a new driver to the system means assigning a major number to it. The assignment should be made at driver (module) initialization by calling the following function, defined in **<linux/fs.h>**:

```
int register_chrdev(unsigned int major, const char *name,
    struct file_operations *fops);
```

The return value indicates success or failure of the operation. A negative return code signals an error; a 0 or positive return code reports successful completion. The `major` argument is the major number being requested, `name` is the name of your device, which will appear in */proc/devices*, and `fops` is the pointer to an array of function pointers, used to invoke your driver's entry points, as explained in "File Operations," later in this chapter.

The major number is a small integer that serves as the index into a static array of char drivers; "Dynamic Allocation of Major Numbers" later in this chapter explains how to select a major number. The 2.0 kernel supported 128 devices; 2.2 and 2.4 increased that number to 256 (while reserving the values 0 and 255 for future uses). Minor numbers, too, are eight-bit quantities; they aren't passed to *register_chrdev* because, as stated, they are only used by the driver itself. There is tremendous pressure from the developer community to increase the number of possible devices supported by the kernel; increasing device numbers to at least 16 bits is a stated goal for the 2.5 development series.

Once the driver has been registered in the kernel table, its operations are associated with the given major number. Whenever an operation is performed on a character device file associated with that major number, the kernel finds and invokes the proper function from the `file_operations` structure. For this reason, the pointer passed to *register_chrdev* should point to a global structure within the driver, not to one local to the module's initialization function.

The next question is how to give programs a name by which they can request your driver. A name must be inserted into the */dev* directory and associated with your driver's major and minor numbers.

The command to create a device node on a filesystem is *mknod*; superuser privileges are required for this operation. The command takes three arguments in addition to the name of the file being created. For example, the command

```
mknod /dev/scull0 c 254 0
```

creates a char device (`c`) whose major number is 254 and whose minor number is 0. Minor numbers should be in the range 0 to 255 because, for historical reasons, they are sometimes stored in a single byte. There are sound reasons to extend the range of available minor numbers, but for the time being, the eight-bit limit is still in force.

Please note that once created by *mknod*, the special device file remains unless it is explicitly deleted, like any information stored on disk. You may want to remove the device created in this example by issuing *rm /dev/scull0*.

Dynamic Allocation of Major Numbers

Some major device numbers are statically assigned to the most common devices. A list of those devices can be found in *Documentation/devices.txt* within the kernel source tree. Because many numbers are already assigned, choosing a unique number for a new driver can be difficult—there are far more custom drivers than available major numbers. You could use one of the major numbers reserved for "experimental or local use,"* but if you experiment with several "local" drivers or you publish your driver for third parties to use, you'll again experience the problem of choosing a suitable number.

Fortunately (or rather, thanks to someone's ingenuity), you can request dynamic assignment of a major number. If the argument `major` is set to 0 when you call *register_chrdev*, the function selects a free number and returns it. The major number returned is always positive, while negative return values are error codes. Please note the behavior is slightly different in the two cases: the function returns the allocated major number if the caller requests a dynamic number, but returns 0 (not the major number) when successfully registering a predefined major number.

For private drivers, we strongly suggest that you use dynamic allocation to obtain your major device number, rather than choosing a number randomly from the ones that are currently free. If, on the other hand, your driver is meant to be useful to the community at large and be included into the official kernel tree, you'll need to apply to be assigned a major number for exclusive use.

The disadvantage of dynamic assignment is that you can't create the device nodes in advance because the major number assigned to your module can't be guaranteed to always be the same. This means that you won't be able to use loading-on-demand of your driver, an advanced feature introduced in Chapter 11. For normal use of the driver, this is hardly a problem, because once the number has been assigned, you can read it from */proc/devices*.

To load a driver using a dynamic major number, therefore, the invocation of *insmod* can be replaced by a simple script that after calling *insmod* reads */proc/devices* in order to create the special file(s).

A typical */proc/devices* file looks like the following:

```
Character devices:
  1 mem
  2 pty
  3 ttyp
  4 ttyS
  6 lp
  7 vcs
 10 misc
 13 input
 14 sound
 21 sg
180 usb
```

---

* Major numbers in the ranges 60 to 63, 120 to 127, and 240 to 254 are reserved for local and experimental use: no real device will be assigned such major numbers.

```
Block devices:
 2 fd
 8 sd
11 sr
65 sd
66 sd
```

The script to load a module that has been assigned a dynamic number can thus be written using a tool such as *awk* to retrieve information from */proc/devices* in order to create the files in */dev*.

The following script, *scull_load*, is part of the *scull* distribution. The user of a driver that is distributed in the form of a module can invoke such a script from the system's *rc.local* file or call it manually whenever the module is needed.

```sh
#!/bin/sh
module="scull"
device="scull"
mode="664"

# invoke insmod with all arguments we were passed
# and use a pathname, as newer modutils don't look in . by default
/sbin/insmod -f ./$module.o $* || exit 1

# remove stale nodes
rm -f /dev/${device}[0-3]

major=`awk "\\$2==\"$module\" {print \\$1}" /proc/devices`

mknod /dev/${device}0 c $major 0
mknod /dev/${device}1 c $major 1
mknod /dev/${device}2 c $major 2
mknod /dev/${device}3 c $major 3

# give appropriate group/permissions, and change the group.
# Not all distributions have staff; some have "wheel" instead.
group="staff"
grep '^staff:' /etc/group > /dev/null || group="wheel"

chgrp $group /dev/${device}[0-3]
chmod $mode /dev/${device}[0-3]
```

The script can be adapted for another driver by redefining the variables and adjusting the *mknod* lines. The script just shown creates four devices because four is the default in the *scull* sources.

The last few lines of the script may seem obscure: why change the group and mode of a device? The reason is that the script must be run by the superuser, so newly created special files are owned by root. The permission bits default so that only root has write access, while anyone can get read access. Normally, a device node requires a different access policy, so in some way or another access rights must be changed. The default in our script is to give access to a group of users, but your needs may vary. Later, in the section "Access Control on a Device File" in Chapter 5, the code for *sculluid* will demonstrate how the driver can enforce its own kind of authorization for device access. A *scull_unload* script is then available to clean up the */dev* directory and remove the module.

As an alternative to using a pair of scripts for loading and unloading, you could write an init script, ready to be placed in the directory your distribution uses for these scripts.* As part of the *scull* source, we offer a fairly complete and configurable example of an init script, called *scull.init*; it accepts the conventional arguments—either "start" or "stop" or "restart"—and performs the role of both *scull_load* and *scull_unload*.

If repeatedly creating and destroying */dev* nodes sounds like overkill, there is a useful workaround. If you are only loading and unloading a single driver, you can just use *rmmod* and *insmod* after the first time you create the special files with your script: dynamic numbers are not randomized, and you can count on the same number to be chosen if you don't mess with other (dynamic) modules. Avoiding lengthy scripts is useful during development. But this trick, clearly, doesn't scale to more than one driver at a time.

The best way to assign major numbers, in our opinion, is by defaulting to dynamic allocation while leaving yourself the option of specifying the major number at load time, or even at compile time. The code we suggest using is similar to the code introduced for autodetection of port numbers. The *scull* implementation uses a global variable, `scull_major`, to hold the chosen number. The variable is initialized to `SCULL_MAJOR`, defined in *scull.h*. The default value of `SCULL_MAJOR` in the distributed source is 0, which means "use dynamic assignment." The user can accept the default or choose a particular major number, either by modifying the macro before compiling or by specifying a value for `scull_major` on the *insmod* command line. Finally, by using the *scull_load* script, the user can pass arguments to *insmod* on *scull_load*'s command line.†

Here's the code we use in *scull*'s source to get a major number:

```
result = register_chrdev(scull_major, "scull", &scull_fops);
if (result < 0) {
 printk(KERN_WARNING "scull: can't get major %d\n",scull_major);
 return result;
}
if (scull_major == 0) scull_major = result; /* dynamic */
```

---

* Distributions vary widely on the location of init scripts; the most common directories used are */etc/init.d*, */etc/rc.d/init.d*, and */sbin/init.d*. In addition, if your script is to be run at boot time, you will need to make a link to it from the appropriate run-level directory (i.e., *.../rc3.d*).

† The init script *scull.init* doesn't accept driver options on the command line, but it supports a configuration file because it's designed for automatic use at boot and shutdown time.

Removing a Driver from the System

When a module is unloaded from the system, the major number must be released. This is accomplished with the following function, which you call from the module's cleanup function:

```
int unregister_chrdev(unsigned int major, const char *name);
```

The arguments are the major number being released and the name of the associated device. The kernel compares the name to the registered name for that number, if any: if they differ, -EINVAL is returned. The kernel also returns -EINVAL if the major number is out of the allowed range.

Failing to unregister the resource in the cleanup function has unpleasant effects. */proc/devices* will generate a fault the next time you try to read it, because one of the **name** strings still points to the module's memory, which is no longer mapped. This kind of fault is called an *oops* because that's the message the kernel prints when it tries to access invalid addresses.*

When you unload the driver without unregistering the major number, recovery will be difficult because the *strcmp* function in *unregister_chrdev* must dereference a pointer (**name**) to the original module. If you ever fail to unregister a major number, you must reload both the same module and another one built on purpose to unregister the major. The faulty module will, with luck, get the same address, and the **name** string will be in the same place, if you didn't change the code. The safer alternative, of course, is to reboot the system.

In addition to unloading the module, you'll often need to remove the device files for the removed driver. The task can be accomplished by a script that pairs to the one used at load time. The script *scull_unload* does the job for our sample device; as an alternative, you can invoke *scull.init stop*.

If dynamic device files are not removed from */dev*, there's a possibility of unexpected errors: a spare */dev/framegrabber* on a developer's computer might refer to a fire-alarm device one month later if both drivers used a dynamic major number. "No such file or directory" is a friendlier response to opening */dev/framegrabber* than the new driver would produce.

dev_t and kdev_t

So far we've talked about the major number. Now it's time to discuss the minor number and how the driver uses it to differentiate among devices.

Every time the kernel calls a device driver, it tells the driver which device is being acted upon. The major and minor numbers are paired in a single data type that the driver uses to identify a particular device. The combined device number (the major

---

* The word *oops* is used as both a noun and a verb by Linux enthusiasts.

and minor numbers concatenated together) resides in the field `i_rdev` of the `inode` structure, which we introduce later. Some driver functions receive a pointer to `struct inode` as the first argument. So if you call the pointer `inode` (as most driver writers do), the function can extract the device number by looking at `inode->i_rdev`.

Historically, Unix declared `dev_t` (device type) to hold the device numbers. It used to be a 16-bit integer value defined in `<sys/types.h>`. Nowadays, more than 256 minor numbers are needed at times, but changing `dev_t` is difficult because there are applications that "know" the internals of `dev_t` and would break if the structure were to change. Thus, while much of the groundwork has been laid for larger device numbers, they are still treated as 16-bit integers for now.

Within the Linux kernel, however, a different type, `kdev_t`, is used. This data type is designed to be a black box for every kernel function. User programs do not know about `kdev_t` at all, and kernel functions are unaware of what is inside a `kdev_t`. If `kdev_t` remains hidden, it can change from one kernel version to the next as needed, without requiring changes to everyone's device drivers.

The information about `kdev_t` is confined in `<linux/kdev_t.h>`, which is mostly comments. The header makes instructive reading if you're interested in the reasoning behind the code. There's no need to include the header explicitly in the drivers, however, because `<linux/fs.h>` does it for you.

The following macros and functions are the operations you can perform on `kdev_t`:

`MAJOR(kdev_t dev);`
   Extract the major number from a `kdev_t` structure.

`MINOR(kdev_t dev);`
   Extract the minor number.

`MKDEV(int ma, int mi);`
   Create a `kdev_t` built from major and minor numbers.

`kdev_t_to_nr(kdev_t dev);`
   Convert a `kdev_t` type to a number (a `dev_t`).

`to_kdev_t(int dev);`
   Convert a number to `kdev_t`. Note that `dev_t` is not defined in kernel mode, and therefore `int` is used.

As long as your code uses these operations to manipulate device numbers, it should continue to work even as the internal data structures change.

File Operations

In the next few sections, we'll look at the various operations a driver can perform on the devices it manages. An open device is identified internally by a `file` structure, and the kernel uses the `file_operations` structure to access the driver's functions. The structure, defined in `<linux/fs.h>`, is an array of function pointers. Each file is associated with its own set of functions (by including a field called `f_op` that points to a `file_operations` structure). The operations are mostly in charge of implementing the system calls and are thus named *open*, *read*, and so on. We can consider the file to be an "object" and the functions operating on it to be its "methods," using object-oriented programming terminology to denote actions declared by an object to act on itself. This is the first sign of object-oriented programming we see in the Linux kernel, and we'll see more in later chapters.

Conventionally, a `file_operations` structure or a pointer to one is called `fops` (or some variation thereof); we've already seen one such pointer as an argument to the *register_chrdev* call. Each field in the structure must point to the function in the driver that implements a specific operation, or be left `NULL` for unsupported operations. The exact behavior of the kernel when a `NULL` pointer is specified is different for each function, as the list later in this section shows.

The `file_operations` structure has been slowly getting bigger as new functionality is added to the kernel. The addition of new operations can, of course, create portability problems for device drivers. Instantiations of the structure in each driver used to be declared using standard C syntax, and new operations were normally added to the end of the structure; a simple recompilation of the drivers would place a `NULL` value for that operation, thus selecting the default behavior, usually what you wanted.

Since then, kernel developers have switched to a "tagged" initialization format that allows initialization of structure fields by name, thus circumventing most problems with changed data structures. The tagged initialization, however, is not standard C but a (useful) extension specific to the GNU compiler. We will look at an example of tagged structure initialization shortly.

The following list introduces all the operations that an application can invoke on a device. We've tried to keep the list brief so it can be used as a reference, merely summarizing each operation and the default kernel behavior when a `NULL` pointer is used. You can skip over this list on your first reading and return to it later.

The rest of the chapter, after describing another important data structure (the `file`, which actually includes a pointer to its own `file_operations`), explains the role of the most important operations and offers hints, caveats, and real code examples. We defer discussion of the more complex operations to later chapters because we aren't ready to dig into topics like memory management, blocking operations, and asynchronous notification quite yet.

The following list shows what operations appear in `struct file_operations` for the 2.4 series of kernels, in the order in which they appear. Although there are minor differences between 2.4 and earlier kernels, they will be dealt with later in this chapter, so we are just sticking to 2.4 for a while. The return value of each operation is 0 for success or a negative error code to signal an error, unless otherwise noted.

`loff_t (*llseek) (struct file *, loff_t, int);`
> The *llseek* method is used to change the current read/write position in a file, and the new position is returned as a (positive) return value. The `loff_t` is a "long offset" and is at least 64 bits wide even on 32-bit platforms. Errors are signaled by a negative return value. If the function is not specified for the driver, a seek relative to end-of-file fails, while other seeks succeed by modifying the position counter in the `file` structure (described in "The file Structure" later in this chapter).

`ssize_t (*read) (struct file *, char *, size_t, loff_t *);`
> Used to retrieve data from the device. A null pointer in this position causes the *read* system call to fail with −EINVAL ("Invalid argument"). A non-negative return value represents the number of bytes successfully read (the return value is a "signed size" type, usually the native integer type for the target platform).

`ssize_t (*write) (struct file *, const char *, size_t, loff_t *);`
> Sends data to the device. If missing, −EINVAL is returned to the program calling the *write* system call. The return value, if non-negative, represents the number of bytes successfully written.

`int (*readdir) (struct file *, void *, filldir_t);`
> This field should be NULL for device files; it is used for reading directories, and is only useful to filesystems.

`unsigned int (*poll) (struct file *, struct poll_table_struct *);`
> The *poll* method is the back end of two system calls, *poll* and *select*, both used to inquire if a device is readable or writable or in some special state. Either system call can block until a device becomes readable or writable. If a driver doesn't define its *poll* method, the device is assumed to be both readable and writable, and in no special state. The return value is a bit mask describing the status of the device.

`int (*ioctl) (struct inode *, struct file *, unsigned int, unsigned long);`
> The *ioctl* system call offers a way to issue device-specific commands (like formatting a track of a floppy disk, which is neither reading nor writing). Additionally, a few *ioctl* commands are recognized by the kernel without referring

to the `fops` table. If the device doesn't offer an *ioctl* entry point, the system call returns an error for any request that isn't predefined (-`ENOTTY`, "No such ioctl for device"). If the device method returns a non-negative value, the same value is passed back to the calling program to indicate successful completion.

`int (*mmap) (struct file *, struct vm_area_struct *);`
mmap is used to request a mapping of device memory to a process's address space. If the device doesn't implement this method, the *mmap* system call returns -`ENODEV`.

`int (*open) (struct inode *, struct file *);`
Though this is always the first operation performed on the device file, the driver is not required to declare a corresponding method. If this entry is NULL, opening the device always succeeds, but your driver isn't notified.

`int (*flush) (struct file *);`
The *flush* operation is invoked when a process closes its copy of a file descriptor for a device; it should execute (and wait for) any outstanding operations on the device. This must not be confused with the *fsync* operation requested by user programs. Currently, *flush* is used only in the network file system (NFS) code. If *flush* is NULL, it is simply not invoked.

`int (*release) (struct inode *, struct file *);`
This operation is invoked when the `file` structure is being released. Like *open*, *release* can be missing.*

`int (*fsync) (struct inode *, struct dentry *, int);`
This method is the back end of the *fsync* system call, which a user calls to flush any pending data. If not implemented in the driver, the system call returns -`EINVAL`.

`int (*fasync) (int, struct file *, int);`
This operation is used to notify the device of a change in its `FASYNC` flag. Asynchronous notification is an advanced topic and is described in Chapter 5. The field can be NULL if the driver doesn't support asynchronous notification.

`int (*lock) (struct file *, int, struct file_lock *);`
The *lock* method is used to implement file locking; locking is an indispensable feature for regular files, but is almost never implemented by device drivers.

`ssize_t (*readv) (struct file *, const struct iovec *,`
`    unsigned long, loff_t *);`
`ssize_t (*writev) (struct file *, const struct iovec *,`
`    unsigned long, loff_t *);`

---

* Note that *release* isn't invoked every time a process calls *close*. Whenever a `file` structure is shared (for example, after a *fork* or a *dup*), *release* won't be invoked until all copies are closed. If you need to flush pending data when any copy is closed, you should implement the *flush* method.

These methods, added late in the 2.3 development cycle, implement scatter/gather read and write operations. Applications occasionally need to do a single read or write operation involving multiple memory areas; these system calls allow them to do so without forcing extra copy operations on the data.

`struct module *owner;`

This field isn't a method like everything else in the `file_operations` structure. Instead, it is a pointer to the module that "owns" this structure; it is used by the kernel to maintain the module's usage count.

The *scull* device driver implements only the most important device methods, and uses the tagged format to declare its `file_operations` structure:

```
struct file_operations scull_fops = {
  llseek:  scull_llseek,
  read:    scull_read,
  write:   scull_write,
  ioctl:   scull_ioctl,
  open:    scull_open,
  release: scull_release,
};
```

This declaration uses the tagged structure initialization syntax, as we described earlier. This syntax is preferred because it makes drivers more portable across changes in the definitions of the structures, and arguably makes the code more compact and readable. Tagged initialization allows the reordering of structure members; in some cases, substantial performance improvements have been realized by placing frequently accessed members in the same hardware cache line.

It is also necessary to set the `owner` field of the `file_operations` structure. In some kernel code, you will often see `owner` initialized with the rest of the structure, using the tagged syntax as follows:

```
owner: THIS_MODULE,
```

That approach works, but only on 2.4 kernels. A more portable approach is to use the **SET_MODULE_OWNER** macro, which is defined in `<linux/module.h>`. *scull* performs this initialization as follows:

```
SET_MODULE_OWNER(&scull_fops);
```

This macro works on any structure that has an `owner` field; we will encounter this field again in other contexts later in the book.

The file Structure

`struct file`, defined in `<linux/fs.h>`, is the second most important data structure used in device drivers. Note that a `file` has nothing to do with the

FILEs of user-space programs. A FILE is defined in the C library and never appears in kernel code. A `struct file`, on the other hand, is a kernel structure that never appears in user programs.

The `file` structure represents an *open file*. (It is not specific to device drivers; every open file in the system has an associated `struct file` in kernel space.) It is created by the kernel on *open* and is passed to any function that operates on the file, until the last *close*. After all instances of the file are closed, the kernel releases the data structure. An open file is different from a disk file, represented by `struct inode`.

In the kernel sources, a pointer to `struct file` is usually called either `file` or `filp` ("file pointer"). We'll consistently call the pointer `filp` to prevent ambiguities with the structure itself. Thus, `file` refers to the structure and `filp` to a pointer to the structure.

The most important fields of `struct file` are shown here. As in the previous section, the list can be skipped on a first reading. In the next section though, when we face some real C code, we'll discuss some of the fields, so they are here for you to refer to.

`mode_t f_mode;`
> The file mode identifies the file as either readable or writable (or both), by means of the bits `FMODE_READ` and `FMODE_WRITE`. You might want to check this field for read/write permission in your *ioctl* function, but you don't need to check permissions for *read* and *write* because the kernel checks before invoking your method. An attempt to write without permission, for example, is rejected without the driver even knowing about it.

`loff_t f_pos;`
> The current reading or writing position. `loff_t` is a 64-bit value (`long long` in *gcc* terminology). The driver can read this value if it needs to know the current position in the file, but should never change it (*read* and *write* should update a position using the pointer they receive as the last argument instead of acting on `filp->f_pos` directly).

`unsigned int f_flags;`
> These are the file flags, such as O_RDONLY, O_NONBLOCK, and O_SYNC. A driver needs to check the flag for nonblocking operation, while the other flags are seldom used. In particular, read/write permission should be checked using `f_mode` instead of `f_flags`. All the flags are defined in the header `<linux/fcntl.h>`.

```
struct file_operations *f_op;
```
The operations associated with the file. The kernel assigns the pointer as part of its implementation of *open*, and then reads it when it needs to dispatch any operations. The value in `filp->f_op` is never saved for later reference; this means that you can change the file operations associated with your file whenever you want, and the new methods will be effective immediately after you return to the caller. For example, the code for *open* associated with major number 1 (*/dev/null*, */dev/zero*, and so on) substitutes the operations in `filp->f_op` depending on the minor number being opened. This practice allows the implementation of several behaviors under the same major number without introducing overhead at each system call. The ability to replace the file operations is the kernel equivalent of "method overriding" in object-oriented programming.

```
void *private_data;
```
The *open* system call sets this pointer to NULL before calling the *open* method for the driver. The driver is free to make its own use of the field or to ignore it. The driver can use the field to point to allocated data, but then must free memory in the *release* method before the `file` structure is destroyed by the kernel. `private_data` is a useful resource for preserving state information across system calls and is used by most of our sample modules.

```
struct dentry *f_dentry;
```
The directory entry (*dentry*) structure associated with the file. Dentries are an optimization introduced in the 2.1 development series. Device driver writers normally need not concern themselves with dentry structures, other than to access the `inode` structure as `filp->f_dentry->d_inode`.

The real structure has a few more fields, but they aren't useful to device drivers. We can safely ignore those fields because drivers never fill `file` structures; they only access structures created elsewhere.

open and release

Now that we've taken a quick look at the fields, we'll start using them in real *scull* functions.

The open Method

The *open* method is provided for a driver to do any initialization in preparation for later operations. In addition, *open* usually increments the usage count for the device so that the module won't be unloaded before the file is closed. The count, described in "The Usage Count" in Chapter 2, is then decremented by the *release* method.

In most drivers, *open* should perform the following tasks:

• Increment the usage count

• Check for device-specific errors (such as device-not-ready or similar hardware problems)

• Initialize the device, if it is being opened for the first time

• Identify the minor number and update the `f_op` pointer, if necessary

• Allocate and fill any data structure to be put in `filp->private_data`

In *scull*, most of the preceding tasks depend on the minor number of the device being opened. Therefore, the first thing to do is identify which device is involved. We can do that by looking at `inode->i_rdev`.

We've already talked about how the kernel doesn't use the minor number of the device, so the driver is free to use it at will. In practice, different minor numbers are used to access different devices or to open the same device in a different way. For example, */dev/st0* (minor number 0) and */dev/st1* (minor 1) refer to different SCSI tape drives, whereas */dev/nst0* (minor 128) is the same physical device as */dev/st0*, but it acts differently (it doesn't rewind the tape when it is closed). All of the tape device files have different minor numbers, so that the driver can tell them apart.

A driver never actually knows the name of the device being opened, just the device number—and users can play on this indifference to names by aliasing new names to a single device for their own convenience. If you create two special files with the same major/minor pair, the devices are one and the same, and there is no way to differentiate between them. The same effect can be obtained using a symbolic or hard link, and the preferred way to implement aliasing is creating a symbolic link.

The *scull* driver uses the minor number like this: the most significant nibble (upper four bits) identifies the type (personality) of the device, and the least significant nibble (lower four bits) lets you distinguish between individual devices if the type supports more than one device instance. Thus, *scull0* is different from *scullpipe0* in the top nibble, while *scull0* and *scull1* differ in the bottom nibble.[*] Two macros (**TYPE** and **NUM**) are defined in the source to extract the bits from a device number, as shown here:

```
#define TYPE(dev) (MINOR(dev) >> 4) /* high nibble */
#define NUM(dev)  (MINOR(dev) & 0xf) /* low nibble */
```

---

[*] Bit splitting is a typical way to use minor numbers. The IDE driver, for example, uses the top two bits for the disk number, and the bottom six bits for the partition number.

For each device type, *scull* defines a specific `file_operations` structure, which is placed in `filp->f_op` at open time. The following code shows how multiple `fops` are implemented:

```
struct file_operations *scull_fop_array[]={
 &scull_fops,  /* type 0 */
 &scull_priv_fops, /* type 1 */
 &scull_pipe_fops, /* type 2 */
 &scull_sngl_fops, /* type 3 */
 &scull_user_fops, /* type 4 */
 &scull_wusr_fops /* type 5 */
};
#define SCULL_MAX_TYPE 5

/* In scull_open, the fop_array is used according to TYPE(dev) */
 int type = TYPE(inode->i_rdev);

  if (type > SCULL_MAX_TYPE) return -ENODEV;
  filp->f_op = scull_fop_array[type];
```

The kernel invokes *open* according to the major number; *scull* uses the minor number in the macros just shown. `TYPE` is used to index into `scull_fop_array` in order to extract the right set of methods for the device type being opened.

In *scull*, `filp->f_op` is assigned to the correct `file_operations` structure as determined by the device type, found in the minor number. The *open* method declared in the new `fops` is then invoked. Usually, a driver doesn't invoke its own `fops`, because they are used by the kernel to dispatch the right driver method. But when your *open* method has to deal with different device types, you might want to call `fops->open` after modifying the `fops` pointer according to the minor number being opened.

The actual code for *scull_open* follows. It uses the `TYPE` and `NUM` macros defined in the previous code snapshot to split the minor number:

```
int scull_open(struct inode *inode, struct file *filp)
{
 Scull_Dev *dev; /* device information */
 int num = NUM(inode->i_rdev);
 int type = TYPE(inode->i_rdev);

 /*
  * If private data is not valid, we are not using devfs
  * so use the type (from minor nr.) to select a new f_op
  */
 if (!filp->private_data && type) {
  if (type > SCULL_MAX_TYPE) return -ENODEV;
  filp->f_op = scull_fop_array[type];
  return filp->f_op->open(inode, filp); /* dispatch to specific open */
 }
```

```
/* type 0, check the device number (unless private_data valid) */
dev = (Scull_Dev *)filp->private_data;
if (!dev) {
 if (num >= scull_nr_devs) return -ENODEV;
 dev = &scull_devices[num];
 filp->private_data = dev; /* for other methods */
}

MOD_INC_USE_COUNT; /* Before we maybe sleep */
/* now trim to 0 the length of the device if open was write-only */
if ( (filp->f_flags & O_ACCMODE) == O_WRONLY) {
 if (down_interruptible(&dev->sem)) {
  MOD_DEC_USE_COUNT;
  return -ERESTARTSYS;
 }
 scull_trim(dev); /* ignore errors */
 up(&dev->sem);
}

return 0;   /* success */
}
```

A few explanations are due here. The data structure used to hold the region of memory is Scull_Dev, which will be introduced shortly. The global variables scull_nr_devs and scull_devices[] (all lowercase) are the number of available devices and the actual array of pointers to Scull_Dev.

The calls to *down_interruptible* and *up* can be ignored for now; we will get to them shortly.

The code looks pretty sparse because it doesn't do any particular device handling when *open* is called. It doesn't need to, because the *scull0-3* device is global and persistent by design. Specifically, there's no action like "initializing the device on first open" because we don't keep an open count for *sculls*, just the module usage count.

Given that the kernel can maintain the usage count of the module via the **owner** field in the file_operations structure, you may be wondering why we increment that count manually here. The answer is that older kernels required modules to do all of the work of maintaining their usage count—the **owner** mechanism did not exist. To be portable to older kernels, *scull* increments its own usage count. This behavior will cause the usage count to be too high on 2.4 systems, but that is not a problem because it will still drop to zero when the module is not being used.

The only real operation performed on the device is truncating it to a length of zero when the device is opened for writing. This is performed because, by design, overwriting a *pscull* device with a shorter file results in a shorter device data area. This is similar to the way opening a regular file for writing truncates it to zero length. The operation does nothing if the device is opened for reading.

We'll see later how a real initialization works when we look at the code for the other *scull* personalities.

The release Method

The role of the *release* method is the reverse of *open*. Sometimes you'll find that the method implementation is called `device_close` instead of `device_release`. Either way, the device method should perform the following tasks:

- Deallocate anything that *open* allocated in `filp->private_data`

- Shut down the device on last close

- Decrement the usage count

The basic form of *scull* has no hardware to shut down, so the code required is minimal:*

```
int scull_release(struct inode *inode, struct file *filp)
{
 MOD_DEC_USE_COUNT;
 return 0;
}
```

It is important to decrement the usage count if you incremented it at *open* time, because the kernel will never be able to unload the module if the counter doesn't drop to zero.

How can the counter remain consistent if sometimes a file is closed without having been opened? After all, the *dup* and *fork* system calls will create copies of open files without calling *open*; each of those copies is then closed at program termination. For example, most programs don't open their *stdin* file (or device), but all of them end up closing it.

The answer is simple: not every *close* system call causes the *release* method to be invoked. Only the ones that actually release the device data structure invoke the method—hence its name. The kernel keeps a counter of how many times a `file` structure is being used. Neither *fork* nor *dup* creates a new `file` structure (only *open* does that); they just increment the counter in the existing structure.

The *close* system call executes the *release* method only when the counter for the `file` structure drops to zero, which happens when the structure is destroyed. This relationship between the *release* method and the *close* system call guarantees that the usage count for modules is always consistent.

---

* The other flavors of the device are closed by different functions, because *scull_open* substituted a different `filp->f_op` for each device. We'll see those later.

Note that the *flush* method *is* called every time an application calls *close*. However, very few drivers implement *flush*, because usually there's nothing to perform at close time unless *release* is involved.

As you may imagine, the previous discussion applies even when the application terminates without explicitly closing its open files: the kernel automatically closes any file at process exit time by internally using the *close* system call.

scull's Memory Usage

Before introducing the *read* and *write* operations, we'd better look at how and why *scull* performs memory allocation. "How" is needed to thoroughly understand the code, and "why" demonstrates the kind of choices a driver writer needs to make, although *scull* is definitely not typical as a device.

This section deals only with the memory allocation policy in *scull* and doesn't show the hardware management skills you'll need to write real drivers. Those skills are introduced in Chapter 8, and in Chapter 9. Therefore, you can skip this section if you're not interested in understanding the inner workings of the memory-oriented *scull* driver.

The region of memory used by *scull*, also called a *device* here, is variable in length. The more you write, the more it grows; trimming is performed by overwriting the device with a shorter file.

The implementation chosen for *scull* is not a smart one. The source code for a smart implementation would be more difficult to read, and the aim of this section is to show *read* and *write*, not memory management. That's why the code just uses *kmalloc* and *kfree* without resorting to allocation of whole pages, although that would be more efficient.

On the flip side, we didn't want to limit the size of the "device" area, for both a philosophical reason and a practical one. Philosophically, it's always a bad idea to put arbitrary limits on data items being managed. Practically, *scull* can be used to temporarily eat up your system's memory in order to run tests under low-memory conditions. Running such tests might help you understand the system's internals. You can use the command *cp /dev/zero /dev/scull0* to eat all the real RAM with *scull*, and you can use the *dd* utility to choose how much data is copied to the *scull* device.

In *scull*, each device is a linked list of pointers, each of which points to a `Scull_Dev` structure. Each such structure can refer, by default, to at most four million bytes, through an array of intermediate pointers. The released source uses an array of 1000 pointers to areas of 4000 bytes. We call each memory area a *quantum* and the array (or its length) a *quantum set*. A *scull* device and its memory areas are shown in Figure 3-1.

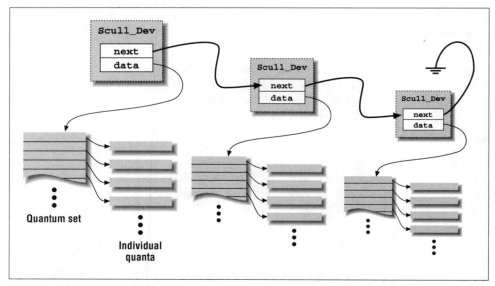

Figure 3-1. The layout of a scull device

The chosen numbers are such that writing a single byte in *scull* consumes eight or twelve thousand bytes of memory: four thousand for the quantum and four or eight thousand for the quantum set (according to whether a pointer is represented in 32 bits or 64 bits on the target platform). If, instead, you write a huge amount of data, the overhead of the linked list is not too bad. There is only one list element for every four megabytes of data, and the maximum size of the device is limited by the computer's memory size.

Choosing the appropriate values for the quantum and the quantum set is a question of policy, rather than mechanism, and the optimal sizes depend on how the device is used. Thus, the *scull* driver should not force the use of any particular values for the quantum and quantum set sizes. In *scull*, the user can change the values in charge in several ways: by changing the macros SCULL_QUANTUM and SCULL_QSET in *scull.h* at compile time, by setting the integer values scull_quantum and scull_qset at module load time, or by changing both the current and default values using *ioctl* at runtime.

Using a macro and an integer value to allow both compile-time and load-time configuration is reminiscent of how the major number is selected. We use this technique for whatever value in the driver is arbitrary, or related to policy.

The only question left is how the default numbers have been chosen. In this particular case, the problem is finding the best balance between the waste of memory resulting from half-filled quanta and quantum sets and the overhead of allocation, deallocation, and pointer chaining that occurs if quanta and sets are small.

Additionally, the internal design of *kmalloc* should be taken into account. We won't touch the point now, though; the innards of *kmalloc* are explored in "The Real Story of kmalloc" in Chapter 7.

The choice of default numbers comes from the assumption that massive amounts of data are likely to be written to *scull* while testing it, although normal use of the device will most likely transfer just a few kilobytes of data.

The data structure used to hold device information is as follows:

```
typedef struct Scull_Dev {
  void **data;
  struct Scull_Dev *next; /* next list item */
  int quantum;     /* the current quantum size */
  int qset;       /* the current array size */
  unsigned long size;
  devfs_handle_t handle; /* only used if devfs is there */
  unsigned int access_key; /* used by sculluid and scullpriv */
  struct semaphore sem;  /* mutual exclusion semaphore  */
} Scull_Dev;
```

The next code fragment shows in practice how `Scull_Dev` is used to hold data. The function *scull_trim* is in charge of freeing the whole data area and is invoked by *scull_open* when the file is opened for writing. It simply walks through the list and frees any quantum and quantum set it finds.

```
int scull_trim(Scull_Dev *dev)
{
  Scull_Dev *next, *dptr;
  int qset = dev->qset; /* "dev" is not null */
  int i;

  for (dptr = dev; dptr; dptr = next) { /* all the list items */
   if (dptr->data) {
    for (i = 0; i < qset; i++)
     if (dptr->data[i])
      kfree(dptr->data[i]);
    kfree(dptr->data);
    dptr->data=NULL;
   }
   next=dptr->next;
   if (dptr != dev) kfree(dptr); /* all of them but the first */
  }
  dev->size = 0;
  dev->quantum = scull_quantum;
  dev->qset = scull_qset;
  dev->next = NULL;
  return 0;
}
```

A Brief Introduction to Race Conditions

Now that you understand how *scull*'s memory management works, here is a scenario to consider. Two processes, A and B, both have the same *scull* device open for writing. Both attempt simultaneously to append data to the device. A new quantum is required for this operation to succeed, so each process allocates the required memory and stores a pointer to it in the quantum set.

The result is trouble. Because both processes see the same *scull* device, each will store its new memory in the same place in the quantum set. If A stores its pointer first, B will overwrite that pointer when it does its store. Thus the memory allocated by A, and the data written therein, will be lost.

This situation is a classic *race condition*; the results vary depending on who gets there first, and usually something undesirable happens in any case. On uniprocessor Linux systems, the *scull* code would not have this sort of problem, because processes running kernel code are not preempted. On SMP systems, however, life is more complicated. Processes A and B could easily be running on different processors and could interfere with each other in this manner.

The Linux kernel provides several mechanisms for avoiding and managing race conditions. A full description of these mechanisms will have to wait until Chapter 9, but a beginning discussion is appropriate here.

A *semaphore* is a general mechanism for controlling access to resources. In its simplest form, a semaphore may be used for *mutual exclusion*; processes using semaphores in the mutual exclusion mode are prevented from simultaneously running the same code or accessing the same data. This sort of semaphore is often called a *mutex*, from "mutual exclusion."

Semaphores in Linux are defined in <asm/semaphore.h>. They have a type of struct semaphore, and a driver should only act on them using the provided interface. In *scull*, one semaphore is allocated for each device, in the Scull_Dev structure. Since the devices are entirely independent of each other, there is no need to enforce mutual exclusion across multiple devices.

Semaphores must be initialized prior to use by passing a numeric argument to *sema_init*. For mutual exclusion applications (i.e., keeping multiple threads from accessing the same data simultaneously), the semaphore should be initialized to a value of 1, which means that the semaphore is available. The following code in *scull*'s module initialization function (*scull_init*) shows how the semaphores are initialized as part of setting up the devices.

```
for (i=0; i < scull_nr_devs; i++) {
  scull_devices[i].quantum = scull_quantum;
  scull_devices[i].qset = scull_qset;
  sema_init(&scull_devices[i].sem, 1);
}
```

A process wishing to enter a section of code protected by a semaphore must first ensure that no other process is already there. Whereas in classical computer science the function to obtain a semaphore is often called *P*, in Linux you'll need to call *down* or *down_interruptible*. These functions test the value of the semaphore to see if it is greater than 0; if so, they decrement the semaphore and return. If the semaphore is 0, the functions will sleep and try again after some other process, which has presumably freed the semaphore, wakes them up.

The *down_interruptible* function can be interrupted by a signal, whereas *down* will not allow signals to be delivered to the process. You almost always want to allow signals; otherwise, you risk creating unkillable processes and other undesirable behavior. A complication of allowing signals, however, is that you always have to check if the function (here *down_interruptible*) was interrupted. As usual, the function returns 0 for success and nonzero in case of failure. If the process is interrupted, it will not have acquired the semaphores; thus, you won't need to call *up*. A typical call to invoke a semaphore therefore normally looks something like this:

```
if (down_interruptible (&sem))
        return -ERESTARTSYS;
```

The `-ERESTARTSYS` return value tells the system that the operation was interrupted by a signal. The kernel function that called the device method will either retry it or return `-EINTR` to the application, according to how signal handling has been configured by the application. Of course, your code may have to perform cleanup work before returning if interrupted in this mode.

A process that obtains a semaphore must always release it afterward. Whereas computer science calls the release function *V*, Linux uses *up* instead. A simple call like

```
up (&sem);
```

will increment the value of the semaphore and wake up any processes that are waiting for the semaphore to become available.

Care must be taken with semaphores. The data protected by the semaphore must be clearly defined, and *all* code that accesses that data must obtain the semaphore first. Code that uses *down_interruptible* to obtain a semaphore must not call another function that also attempts to obtain that semaphore, or deadlock will result. If a routine in your driver fails to release a semaphore it holds (perhaps as a result of an error return), any further attempts to obtain that semaphore will stall. Mutual exclusion in general can be tricky, and benefits from a well-defined and methodical approach.

In *scull*, the per-device semaphore is used to protect access to the stored data. Any code that accesses the `data` field of the `Scull_Dev` structure must first have obtained the semaphore. To avoid deadlocks, only functions that implement device methods will try to obtain the semaphore. Internal routines, such as *scull_trim* shown earlier, assume that the semaphore has already been obtained. As long as these invariants hold, access to the `Scull_Dev` data structure is safe from race conditions.

read and write

The *read* and *write* methods perform a similar task, that is, copying data from and to application code. Therefore, their prototypes are pretty similar and it's worth introducing them at the same time:

```
ssize_t read(struct file *filp, char *buff,
    size_t count, loff_t *offp);
ssize_t write(struct file *filp, const char *buff,
    size_t count, loff_t *offp);
```

For both methods, `filp` is the file pointer and `count` is the size of the requested data transfer. The `buff` argument points to the user buffer holding the data to be written or the empty buffer where the newly read data should be placed. Finally, `offp` is a pointer to a "long offset type" object that indicates the file position the user is accessing. The return value is a "signed size type;" its use is discussed later.

As far as data transfer is concerned, the main issue associated with the two device methods is the need to transfer data between the kernel address space and the user address space. The operation cannot be carried out through pointers in the usual way, or through *memcpy*. User-space addresses cannot be used directly in kernel space, for a number of reasons.

One big difference between kernel-space addresses and user-space addresses is that memory in user-space can be swapped out. When the kernel accesses a user-space pointer, the associated page may not be present in memory, and a page fault is generated. The functions we introduce in this section and in "Using the ioctl Argument" in Chapter 5 use some hidden magic to deal with page faults in the proper way even when the CPU is executing in kernel space.

Also, it's interesting to note that the x86 port of Linux 2.0 used a completely different memory map for user space and kernel space. Thus, user-space pointers couldn't be dereferenced at all from kernel space.

If the target device is an expansion board instead of RAM, the same problem arises, because the driver must nonetheless copy data between user buffers and kernel space (and possibly between kernel space and I/O memory).

Cross-space copies are performed in Linux by special functions, defined in `<asm/uaccess.h>`. Such a copy is either performed by a generic (*memcpy*-like) function or by functions optimized for a specific data size (`char`, `short`, `int`, `long`); most of them are introduced in "Using the ioctl Argument" in Chapter 5.

The code for *read* and *write* in *scull* needs to copy a whole segment of data to or from the user address space. This capability is offered by the following kernel functions, which copy an arbitrary array of bytes and sit at the heart of every *read* and *write* implementation:

```
unsigned long copy_to_user(void *to, const void *from,
        unsigned long count);
unsigned long copy_from_user(void *to, const void *from,
        unsigned long count);
```

Although these functions behave like normal *memcpy* functions, a little extra care must be used when accessing user space from kernel code. The user pages being addressed might not be currently present in memory, and the page-fault handler can put the process to sleep while the page is being transferred into place. This happens, for example, when the page must be retrieved from swap space. The net result for the driver writer is that any function that accesses user space must be reentrant and must be able to execute concurrently with other driver functions (see also "Writing Reentrant Code" in Chapter 5). That's why we use semaphores to control concurrent access.

The role of the two functions is not limited to copying data to and from user-space: they also check whether the user space pointer is valid. If the pointer is invalid, no copy is performed; if an invalid address is encountered during the copy, on the other hand, only part of the data is copied. In both cases, the return value is the amount of memory still to be copied. The *scull* code looks for this error return, and returns -EFAULT to the user if it's not 0.

The topic of user-space access and invalid user space pointers is somewhat advanced, and is discussed in "Using the ioctl Argument" in Chapter 5. However, it's worth suggesting that if you don't need to check the user-space pointer you can invoke *__copy_to_user* and *__copy_from_user* instead. This is useful, for example, if you know you already checked the argument.

As far as the actual device methods are concerned, the task of the *read* method is to copy data from the device to user space (using *copy_to_user*), while the *write* method must copy data from user space to the device (using *copy_from_user*). Each *read* or *write* system call requests transfer of a specific number of bytes, but the driver is free to transfer less data—the exact rules are slightly different for reading and writing and are described later in this chapter.

Whatever the amount of data the methods transfer, they should in general update the file position at *offp to represent the current file position after successful completion of the system call. Most of the time the offp argument is just a pointer to filp->f_pos, but a different pointer is used in order to support the *pread* and *pwrite* system calls, which perform the equivalent of *lseek* and *read* or *write* in a single, atomic operation.

Figure 3-2 represents how a typical *read* implementation uses its arguments.

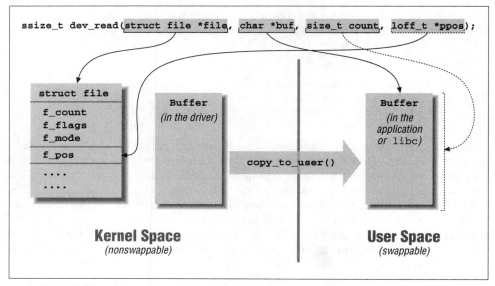

Figure 3-2. The arguments to read

Both the *read* and *write* methods return a negative value if an error occurs. A return value greater than or equal to 0 tells the calling program how many bytes have been successfully transferred. If some data is transferred correctly and then an error happens, the return value must be the count of bytes successfully transferred, and the error does not get reported until the next time the function is called.

Although kernel functions return a negative number to signal an error, and the value of the number indicates the kind of error that occurred (as introduced in Chapter 2 in "Error Handling in init_module"), programs that run in user space always see −1 as the error return value. They need to access the `errno` variable to find out what happened. The difference in behavior is dictated by the POSIX calling standard for system calls and the advantage of not dealing with `errno` in the kernel.

The read Method

The return value for *read* is interpreted by the calling application program as follows:

- If the value equals the `count` argument passed to the *read* system call, the requested number of bytes has been transferred. This is the optimal case.

- If the value is positive, but smaller than `count`, only part of the data has been transferred. This may happen for a number of reasons, depending on the device. Most often, the application program will retry the read. For instance, if you read using the *fread* function, the library function reissues the system call till completion of the requested data transfer.

- If the value is 0, end-of-file was reached.

- A negative value means there was an error. The value specifies what the error was, according to `<linux/errno.h>`. These errors look like `-EINTR` (interrupted system call) or `-EFAULT` (bad address).

What is missing from the preceding list is the case of "there is no data, but it may arrive later." In this case, the *read* system call should block. We won't deal with blocking input until "Blocking I/O" in Chapter 5.

The *scull* code takes advantage of these rules. In particular, it takes advantage of the partial-read rule. Each invocation of *scull_read* deals only with a single data quantum, without implementing a loop to gather all the data; this makes the code shorter and easier to read. If the reading program really wants more data, it reiterates the call. If the standard I/O library (i.e., *fread* and friends) is used to read the device, the application won't even notice the quantization of the data transfer.

If the current read position is greater than the device size, the *read* method of *scull* returns 0 to signal that there's no data available (in other words, we're at end-of-file). This situation can happen if process A is reading the device while process B opens it for writing, thus truncating the device to a length of zero. Process A suddenly finds itself past end-of-file, and the next *read* call returns 0.

Here is the code for *read*:

```
ssize_t scull_read(struct file *filp, char *buf, size_t count,
    loff_t *f_pos)
{
 Scull_Dev *dev = filp->private_data; /* the first list item */
 Scull_Dev *dptr;
 int quantum = dev->quantum;
 int qset = dev->qset;
 int itemsize = quantum * qset; /* how many bytes in the list item */
 int item, s_pos, q_pos, rest;
 ssize_t ret = 0;

 if (down_interruptible(&dev->sem))
   return -ERESTARTSYS;
 if (*f_pos >= dev->size)
  goto out;
 if (*f_pos + count > dev->size)
  count = dev->size - *f_pos;
 /* find list item, qset index, and offset in the quantum */
 item = (long)*f_pos / itemsize;
 rest = (long)*f_pos % itemsize;
```

```
    s_pos = rest / quantum; q_pos = rest % quantum;

    /* follow the list up to the right position (defined elsewhere) */
    dptr = scull_follow(dev, item);

    if (!dptr->data)
     goto out; /* don't fill holes */
    if (!dptr->data[s_pos])
     goto out;
    /* read only up to the end of this quantum */
    if (count > quantum - q_pos)
     count = quantum - q_pos;

    if (copy_to_user(buf, dptr->data[s_pos]+q_pos, count)) {
     ret = -EFAULT;
          goto out;
    }
    *f_pos += count;
    ret = count;

    out:
    up(&dev->sem);
    return ret;
  }
```

The write Method

write, like *read*, can transfer less data than was requested, according to the following rules for the return value:

- If the value equals `count`, the requested number of bytes has been transferred.

- If the value is positive, but smaller than `count`, only part of the data has been transferred. The program will most likely retry writing the rest of the data.

- If the value is 0, nothing was written. This result is not an error, and there is no reason to return an error code. Once again, the standard library retries the call to *write*. We'll examine the exact meaning of this case in "Blocking I/O" in Chapter 5, where blocking *write* is introduced.

- A negative value means an error occurred; like for *read*, valid error values are those defined in `<linux/errno.h>`.

Unfortunately, there may be misbehaving programs that issue an error message and abort when a partial transfer is performed. This happens because some programmers are accustomed to seeing *write* calls that either fail or succeed completely, which is actually what happens most of the time and should be supported by devices as well. This limitation in the *scull* implementation could be fixed, but we didn't want to complicate the code more than necessary.

The *scull* code for *write* deals with a single quantum at a time, like the *read* method does:

```
ssize_t scull_write(struct file *filp, const char *buf, size_t count,
    loff_t *f_pos)
{
 Scull_Dev *dev = filp->private_data;
 Scull_Dev *dptr;
 int quantum = dev->quantum;
 int qset = dev->qset;
 int itemsize = quantum * qset;
 int item, s_pos, q_pos, rest;
 ssize_t ret = -ENOMEM; /* value used in "goto out" statements */

 if (down_interruptible(&dev->sem))
   return -ERESTARTSYS;

 /* find list item, qset index and offset in the quantum */
 item = (long)*f_pos / itemsize;
 rest = (long)*f_pos % itemsize;
 s_pos = rest / quantum; q_pos = rest % quantum;

 /* follow the list up to the right position */
 dptr = scull_follow(dev, item);
 if (!dptr->data) {
  dptr->data = kmalloc(qset * sizeof(char *), GFP_KERNEL);
  if (!dptr->data)
   goto out;
  memset(dptr->data, 0, qset * sizeof(char *));
 }
 if (!dptr->data[s_pos]) {
  dptr->data[s_pos] = kmalloc(quantum, GFP_KERNEL);
  if (!dptr->data[s_pos])
   goto out;
 }
 /* write only up to the end of this quantum */
 if (count > quantum - q_pos)
  count = quantum - q_pos;

 if (copy_from_user(dptr->data[s_pos]+q_pos, buf, count)) {
  ret = -EFAULT;
      goto out;
 }
 *f_pos += count;
 ret = count;

 /* update the size */
 if (dev->size < *f_pos)
  dev-> size = *f_pos;
```

```
    out:
    up(&dev->sem);
    return ret;
    }
```

readv and writev

Unix systems have long supported two alternative system calls named *readv* and *writev*. These "vector" versions take an array of structures, each of which contains a pointer to a buffer and a length value. A *readv* call would then be expected to read the indicated amount into each buffer in turn. *writev*, instead, would gather together the contents of each buffer and put them out as a single write operation.

Until version 2.3.44 of the kernel, however, Linux always emulated *readv* and *writev* with multiple calls to *read* and *write*. If your driver does not supply methods to handle the vector operations, they will still be implemented that way. In many situations, however, greater efficiency is achieved by implementing *readv* and *writev* directly in the driver.

The prototypes for the vector operations are as follows:

```
    ssize_t (*readv) (struct file *filp, const struct iovec *iov,
        unsigned long count, loff_t *ppos);
    ssize_t (*writev) (struct file *filp, const struct iovec *iov,
        unsigned long count, loff_t *ppos);
```

Here, the `filp` and `ppos` arguments are the same as for *read* and *write*. The `iovec` structure, defined in `<linux/uio.h>`, looks like this:

```
    struct iovec
    {
     void *iov_base;
     _ _kernel_size_t iov_len;
    };
```

Each `iovec` describes one chunk of data to be transferred; it starts at `iov_base` (in user space) and is `iov_len` bytes long. The `count` parameter to the method tells how many `iovec` structures there are. These structures are created by the application, but the kernel copies them into kernel space before calling the driver.

The simplest implementation of the vectored operations would be a simple loop that just passes the address and length out of each `iovec` to the driver's *read* or *write* function. Often, however, efficient and correct behavior requires that the driver do something smarter. For example, a *writev* on a tape drive should write the contents of all the `iovec` structures as a single record on the tape.

Many drivers, though, will gain no benefit from implementing these methods themselves. Thus, *scull* omits them. The kernel will emulate them with *read* and *write*, and the end result is the same.

Playing with the New Devices

Once you are equipped with the four methods just described, the driver can be compiled and tested; it retains any data you write to it until you overwrite it with new data. The device acts like a data buffer whose length is limited only by the amount of real RAM available. You can try using *cp*, *dd*, and input/output redirection to test the driver.

The *free* command can be used to see how the amount of free memory shrinks and expands according to how much data is written into *scull*.

To get more confident with reading and writing one quantum at a time, you can add a *printk* at an appropriate point in the driver and watch what happens while an application reads or writes large chunks of data. Alternatively, use the *strace* utility to monitor the system calls issued by a program, together with their return values. Tracing a *cp* or an *ls -l > /dev/scull0* will show quantized reads and writes. Monitoring (and debugging) techniques are presented in detail in the next chapter.

The Device Filesystem

As suggested at the beginning of the chapter, recent versions of the Linux kernel offer a special filesystem for device entry points. The filesystem has been available for a while as an unofficial patch; it was made part of the official source tree in 2.3.46. A backport to 2.2 is available as well, although not included in the official 2.2 kernels.

Although use of the special filesystem is not widespread as we write this, the new features offer a few advantages to the device driver writer. Therefore, our version of *scull* exploits *devfs* if it is being used in the target system. The module uses kernel configuration information at compile time to know whether particular features have been enabled, and in this case we depend on `CONFIG_DEVFS_FS` being defined or not.

The main advantages of *devfs* are as follows:

- Device entry points in */dev* are created at device initialization and removed at device removal.

- The device driver can specify device names, ownership, and permission bits, but user-space programs can still change ownership and permission (but not the filename).

- There is no need to allocate a major number for the device driver and deal with minor numbers.

As a result, there is no need to run a script to create device special files when a module is loaded or unloaded, because the driver is autonomous in managing its own special files.

To handle device creation and removal, the driver should call the following functions:

```
#include <linux/devfs_fs_kernel.h>

devfs_handle_t devfs_mk_dir (devfs_handle_t dir,
    const char *name, void *info);

devfs_handle_t devfs_register (devfs_handle_t dir,
    const char *name, unsigned int flags,
    unsigned int major, unsigned int minor,
    umode_t mode, void *ops, void *info);

    void devfs_unregister (devfs_handle_t de);
```

The *devfs* implementation offers several other functions for kernel code to use. They allow creation of symbolic links, access to the internal data structures to retrieve **devfs_handle_t** items from inodes, and other tasks. Those other functions are not covered here because they are not very important or easily understood. The curious reader could look at the header file for further information.

The various arguments to the register/unregister functions are as follows:

dir
> The parent directory where the new special file should be created. Most drivers will use **NULL** to create special files in */dev* directly. To create an owned directory, a driver should call *devfs_mk_dir*.

name
> The name of the device, without the leading /**dev**/. The name can include slashes if you want the device to be in a subdirectory; the subdirectory is created during the registration process. Alternatively, you can specify a valid **dir** pointer to the hosting subdirectory.

flags
> A bit mask of *devfs* flags. **DEVFS_FL_DEFAULT** can be a good choice, and **DEVFS_FL_AUTO_DEVNUM** is the flag you need for automatic assignment of major and minor numbers. The actual flags are described later.

major
minor
> The major and minor numbers for the device. Unused if **DEVFS_FL_AUTO_DEVNUM** is specified in the flags.

mode
> Access mode of the new device.

ops
> A pointer to the file operation structure for the device.

`info`

> A default value for `filp->private_data`. The filesystem will initialize the pointer to this value when the device is opened. The `info` pointer passed to *devfs_mk_dir* is not used by *devfs* and acts as a "client data" pointer.

`de` A "*devfs* entry" obtained by a previous call to *devfs_register*.

The flags are used to select specific features to be enabled for the special file being created. Although the flags are briefly and clearly documented in `<linux/devfs_fs_kernel.h>`, it's worth introducing some of them.

`DEVFS_FL_NONE`
`DEVFS_FL_DEFAULT`

> The former symbol is simply 0, and is suggested for code readability. The latter macro is currently defined to `DEVFS_FL_NONE`, but is a good choice to be forward compatible with future implementations of the filesystem.

`DEVFS_FL_AUTO_OWNER`

> The flag makes the device appear to be owned by the last uid/gid that opened it, and read/write for anybody when no process has it opened. The feature is useful for tty device files but is also interesting for device drivers to prevent concurrent access to a nonshareable device. We'll see access policy issues in Chapter 5.

`DEVFS_FL_SHOW_UNREG`
`DEVFS_FL_HIDE`

> The former flag requests not to remove the device file from */dev* when it is unregistered. The latter requests never to show it in */dev*. The flags are not usually needed for normal devices.

`DEVFS_FL_AUTO_DEVNUM`

> Automatically allocate a device number for this device. The number will remain associated with the device name even after the *devfs* entry is unregistered, so if the driver is reloaded before the system is shut down, it will receive the same major/minor pair.

`DEVFS_FL_NO_PERSISTENCE`

> Don't keep track of this entry after it is removed. This flags saves some system memory after module removal, at the cost of losing persistence of device features across module unload/reload. Persistent features are access mode, file ownership, and major/minor numbers.

It is possible to query the flags associated with a device or to change them at runtime. The following two functions perform the tasks:

```
int devfs_get_flags (devfs_handle_t de, unsigned int *flags);
int devfs_set_flags (devfs_handle_t de, unsigned int flags);
```

Using devfs in Practice

Because *devfs* leads to serious user-space incompatibilities as far as device names are concerned, not all installed systems use it. Independently of how the new feature will be accepted by Linux users, it's unlikely you'll write *devfs*-only drivers anytime soon; thus, you'll need to add support for the "older" way of dealing with file creation and permission from user space and using major/minor numbers in kernel space.

The code needed to implement a device driver that only runs with *devfs* installed is a subset of the code you need to support both environments, so we only show the dual-mode initialization. Instead of writing a specific sample driver to try out *devfs*, we added *devfs* support to the *scull* driver. If you load *scull* to a kernel that uses *devfs*, you'll need to directly invoke *insmod* instead of running the *scull_load* script.

We chose to create a directory to host all *scull* special files because the structure of *devfs* is highly hierarchical and there's no reason not to adhere to this convention. Moreover, we can thus show how a directory is created and removed.

Within *scull_init*, the following code deals with device creation, using a field within the device structure (called `handle`) to keep track of what devices have been registered:

```
/* If we have devfs, create /dev/scull to put files in there */
scull_devfs_dir = devfs_mk_dir(NULL, "scull", NULL);
if (!scull_devfs_dir) return -EBUSY; /* problem */

for (i=0; i < scull_nr_devs; i++) {
  sprintf(devname, "%i", i);
  devfs_register(scull_devfs_dir, devname,
      DEVFS_FL_AUTO_DEVNUM,
      0, 0, S_IFCHR | S_IRUGO | S_IWUGO,
      &scull_fops,
      scull_devices+i);
}
```

The previous code is paired by the two lines that are part of the following excerpt from *scull_cleanup*:

```
if (scull_devices) {
  for (i=0; i<scull_nr_devs; i++) {
    scull_trim(scull_devices+i);
    /* the following line is only used for devfs */
    devfs_unregister(scull_devices[i].handle);
  }
  kfree(scull_devices);
}

/* once again, only for devfs */
devfs_unregister(scull_devfs_dir);
```

Part of the previous code fragments is protected by `#ifdef CONFIG_DEVFS_FS`. If the feature is not enabled in the current kernel, *scull* will revert to *register_chrdev*.

The only extra task that needs to be performed in order to support both environments is dealing with initialization of `filp->f_ops` and `filp->private_data` in the *open* device method. The former pointer is simply not modified, since the right file operations have been specified in *devfs_register*. The latter will only need to be initialized by the *open* method if it is NULL, since it will only be NULL if *devfs* is not being used.

```
/*
 * If private data is not valid, we are not using devfs
 * so use the type (from minor nr.) to select a new f_op
 */
if (!filp->private_data && type) {
  if (type > SCULL_MAX_TYPE) return -ENODEV;
  filp->f_op = scull_fop_array[type];
  return filp->f_op->open(inode, filp); /* dispatch to specific open */
}

/* type 0, check the device number (unless private_data valid) */
dev = (Scull_Dev *)filp->private_data;
if (!dev) {
  if (num >= scull_nr_devs) return -ENODEV;
  dev = &scull_devices[num];
  filp->private_data = dev; /* for other methods */
}
```

Once equipped with the code shown, the *scull* module can be loaded to a system running *devfs*. It will show the following lines as output of *ls -l /dev/scull*:

```
crw-rw-rw- 1 root   root    144,  1 Jan 1 1970 0
crw-rw-rw- 1 root   root    144,  2 Jan 1 1970 1
crw-rw-rw- 1 root   root    144,  3 Jan 1 1970 2
crw-rw-rw- 1 root   root    144,  4 Jan 1 1970 3
crw-rw-rw- 1 root   root    144,  5 Jan 1 1970 pipe0
crw-rw-rw- 1 root   root    144,  6 Jan 1 1970 pipe1
crw-rw-rw- 1 root   root    144,  7 Jan 1 1970 pipe2
crw-rw-rw- 1 root   root    144,  8 Jan 1 1970 pipe3
crw-rw-rw- 1 root   root    144, 12 Jan 1 1970 priv
crw-rw-rw- 1 root   root    144,  9 Jan 1 1970 single
crw-rw-rw- 1 root   root    144, 10 Jan 1 1970 user
crw-rw-rw- 1 root   root    144, 11 Jan 1 1970 wuser
```

The functionality of the various files is the same as that of the "normal" *scull* module, the only difference being in device pathnames: what used to be */dev/scull0* is now */dev/scull/0*.

Portability Issues and devfs

The source files of *scull* are somewhat complicated by the need to be able to compile and run well with Linux versions 2.0, 2.2, and 2.4. This portability requirement brings in several instances of conditional compilation based on CONFIG_DEVFS_FS.

Fortunately, most developers agree that #ifdef constructs are basically bad when they appear in the body of function definitions (as opposed to being used in header files). Therefore, the addition of *devfs* brings in the needed machinery to completely avoid #ifdef in your code. We still have conditional compilation in *scull* because older versions of the kernel headers can't offer support for that.

If your code is meant to only be used with version 2.4 of the kernel, you can avoid conditional compilation by calling kernel functions to initialize the driver in both ways; things are arranged so that one of the initializations will do nothing at all, while returning success. The following is an example of what initialization might look like:

```
#include <devfs_fs_kernel.h>

int init_module()
{
 /* request a major: does nothing if devfs is used */
 result = devfs_register_chrdev(major, "name", &fops);
 if (result < 0) return result;

 /* register using devfs: does nothing if not in use */
 devfs_register(NULL, "name", /* .... */ );
 return 0;
}
```

You can resort to similar tricks in your own header files, as long as you are careful not to redefine functions that are already defined by kernel headers. Removing conditional compilation is a good thing because it improves readability of the code and reduces the amount of possible bugs by letting the compiler parse the whole input file. Whenever conditional compilation is used, there is the risk of introducing typos or other errors that can slip through unnoticed if they happen in a place that is discarded by the C preprocessor because of #ifdef.

This is, for example, how *scull.h* avoids conditional compilation in the cleanup part of the program. This code is portable to all kernel versions because it doesn't depend on *devfs* being known to the header files:

```
#ifdef CONFIG_DEVFS_FS /* only if enabled, to avoid errors in 2.0 */
#include <linux/devfs_fs_kernel.h>
#else
 typedef void * devfs_handle_t; /* avoid #ifdef inside the structure */
#endif
```

Nothing is defined in *sysdep.h* because it is very hard to implement this kind of hack generically enough to be of general use. Each driver should arrange for its own needs to avoid excessive #ifdef statements in function code. Also, we chose not to support *devfs* in the sample code for this book, with the exception of *scull*. We hope this discussion is enough to help readers exploit *devfs* if they want to; *devfs* support has been omitted from the rest of the sample files in order to keep the code simple.

Backward Compatibility

This chapter, so far, has described the kernel programming interface for version 2.4 of the Linux kernel. Unfortunately, this interface has changed significantly over the course of kernel development. These changes represent improvements in how things are done, but, once again, they also pose a challenge for those who wish to write drivers that are compatible across multiple versions of the kernel.

Insofar as this chapter is concerned, there are few noticeable differences between versions 2.4 and 2.2. Version 2.2, however, changed many of the prototypes of the file_operations methods from what 2.0 had; access to user space was greatly modified (and simplified) as well. The semaphore mechanism was not as well developed in Linux 2.0. And, finally, the 2.1 development series introduced the directory entry (dentry) cache.

Changes in the File Operations Structure

A number of factors drove the changes in the file_operations methods. The longstanding 2 GB file-size limit caused problems even in the Linux 2.0 days. As a result, the 2.1 development series started using the loff_t type, a 64-bit value, to represent file positions and lengths. Large file support was not completely integrated until version 2.4 of the kernel, but much of the groundwork was done earlier and had to be accommodated by driver writers.

Another change introduced during 2.1 development was the addition of the f_pos pointer argument to the *read* and *write* methods. This change was made to support the POSIX *pread* and *pwrite* system calls, which explicitly set the file offset where data is to be read or written. Without these system calls, threaded programs can run into race conditions when moving around in files.

Almost all methods in Linux 2.0 received an explicit inode pointer argument. The 2.1 development series removed this parameter from several of the methods, since it was rarely needed. If you need the inode pointer, you can still retrieve it from the filp argument.

The end result is that the prototypes of the commonly used file_operations methods looked like this in 2.0:

```
int (*lseek) (struct inode *, struct file *, off_t, int);
```
Note that this method is called *lseek* in Linux 2.0, instead of *llseek*. The name change was made to recognize that seeks could now happen with 64-bit offset values.

```
int (*read) (struct inode *, struct file *, char *, int);
int (*write) (struct inode *, struct file *, const char *,
        int);
```
As mentioned, these functions in Linux 2.0 had the `inode` pointer as an argument, and lacked the position argument.

```
void (*release) (struct inode *, struct file *);
```
In the 2.0 kernel, the *release* method could not fail, and thus returned `void`.

There have been many other changes to the `file_operations` structure; we will cover them in the following chapters as we get to them. Meanwhile, it is worth a moment to look at how portable code can be written that accounts for the changes we have seen so far. The changes in these methods are large, and there is no simple, elegant way to cover them over.

The way the sample code handles these changes is to define a set of small wrapper functions that "translate" from the old API to the new. These wrappers are only used when compiling under 2.0 headers, and must be substituted for the "real" device methods within the `file_operations` structure. This is the code implementing the wrappers for the *scull* driver:

```
/*
 * The following wrappers are meant to make things work with 2.0 kernels
 */
#ifdef LINUX_20
int scull_lseek_20(struct inode *ino, struct file *f,
    off_t offset, int whence)
{
 return (int)scull_llseek(f, offset, whence);
}

int scull_read_20(struct inode *ino, struct file *f, char *buf,
    int count)
{
 return (int)scull_read(f, buf, count, &f->f_pos);
}

int scull_write_20(struct inode *ino, struct file *f, const char *b,
    int c)
{
 return (int)scull_write(f, b, c, &f->f_pos);
}

void scull_release_20(struct inode *ino, struct file *f)
{
```

```
    scull_release(ino, f);
}

/* Redefine "real" names to the 2.0 ones */
#define scull_llseek scull_lseek_20
#define scull_read scull_read_20
#define scull_write scull_write_20
#define scull_release scull_release_20
#define llseek lseek
#endif /* LINUX_20 */
```

Redefining names in this manner can also account for structure members whose names have changed over time (such as the change from *lseek* to *llseek*).

Needless to say, this sort of redefinition of the names should be done with care; these lines should appear before the definition of the `file_operations` structure, but after any other use of those names.

Two other incompatibilities are related to the `file_operations` structure. One is that the *flush* method was added during the 2.1 development cycle. Driver writers almost never need to worry about this method, but its presence in the middle of the structure can still create problems. The best way to avoid dealing with the *flush* method is to use the tagged initialization syntax, as we did in all the sample source files.

The other difference is in the way an `inode` pointer is retrieved from a `filp` pointer. Whereas modern kernels use a `dentry` (directory entry) data structure, version 2.0 had no such structure. Therefore, *sysdep.h* defines a macro that should be used to portably access an `inode` from a `filp`:

```
#ifdef LINUX_20
# define INODE_FROM_F(filp) ((filp)->f_inode)
#else
# define INODE_FROM_F(filp) ((filp)->f_dentry->d_inode)
#endif
```

The Module Usage Count

In 2.2 and earlier kernels, the Linux kernel did not offer any assistance to modules in maintaining the usage count. Modules had to do that work themselves. This approach was error prone and required the duplication of a lot of work. It also encouraged race conditions. The new method is thus a definite improvement.

Code that is written to be portable, however, must be prepared to deal with the older way of doing things. That means that the usage count must still be incremented when a new reference is made to the module, and decremented when that reference goes away. Portable code must also work around the fact that the **owner** field did not exist in the `file_operations` structure in earlier kernels.

The easiest way to handle that is to use `SET_MODULE_OWNER`, rather than work-ing with the `owner` field directly. In *sysdep.h*, we provide a null `SET_FILE_OWNER` for kernels that do not have this facility.

Changes in Semaphore Support

Semaphore support was less developed in the 2.0 kernel; support for SMP systems in general was primitive at that time. Drivers written for only that kernel version may not need to use semaphores at all, since only one CPU was allowed to be running kernel code at that time. Nonetheless, there may still be a need for semaphores, and it does not hurt to have the full protection needed by later kernel versions.

Most of the semaphore functions covered in this chapter existed in the 2.0 kernel. The one exception is *sema_init*; in version 2.0, programmers had to initialize semaphores manually. The *sysdep.h* header file handles this problem by defining a version of *sema_init* when compiled under the 2.0 kernel:

```
#ifdef LINUX_20
# ifdef MUTEX_LOCKED /* Only if semaphore.h included */
   extern inline void sema_init (struct semaphore *sem, int val)
   {
    sem->count = val;
    sem->waking = sem->lock = 0;
    sem->wait = NULL;
   }
# endif
#endif /* LINUX_20 */
```

Changes in Access to User Space

Finally, access to user space changed completely at the beginning of the 2.1 devel-opment series. The new interface has a better design and makes much better use of the hardware in ensuring safe access to user-space memory. But, of course, the interface is different. The 2.0 memory-access functions were as follows:

```
void memcpy_fromfs(void *to, const void *from, unsigned long count);
void memcpy_tofs(void *to, const void *from, unsigned long count);
```

The names of these functions come from the historical use of the `FS` segment reg-ister on the i386. Note that there is no return value from these functions; if the user supplies an invalid address, the data copy will silently fail. *sysdep.h* hides the renaming and allows you to portably call *copy_to_user* and *copy_from_user*.

Quick Reference

This chapter introduced the following symbols and header files. The list of the fields in `struct file_operations` and `struct file` is not repeated here.

`#include <linux/fs.h>`
> The "file system" header is the header required for writing device drivers. All the important functions are declared in here.

`int register_chrdev(unsigned int major, const char`
`    *name, struct file_operations *fops);`
> Registers a character device driver. If the major number is not 0, it is used unchanged; if the number is 0, then a dynamic number is assigned for this device.

`int unregister_chrdev(unsigned int major, const char *name);`
> Unregisters the driver at unload time. Both `major` and the `name` string must contain the same values that were used to register the driver.

`kdev_t inode->i_rdev;`
> The device "number" for the current device is accessible from the `inode` structure.

`int MAJOR(kdev_t dev);`
`int MINOR(kdev_t dev);`
> These macros extract the major and minor numbers from a device item.

`kdev_t MKDEV(int major, int minor);`
> This macro builds a `kdev_t` data item from the major and minor numbers.

`SET_MODULE_OWNER(struct file_operations *fops)`
> This macro sets the `owner` field in the given `file_operations` structure.

`#include <asm/semaphore.h>`
> Defines functions and types for the use of semaphores.

`void sema_init (struct semaphore *sem, int val);`
> Initializes a semaphore to a known value. Mutual exclusion semaphores are usually initialized to a value of 1.

`int down_interruptible (struct semaphore *sem);`
`void up (struct semaphore *sem);`
> Obtains a semaphore (sleeping, if necessary) and releases it, respectively.

`#include <asm/segment.h>`
`#include <asm/uaccess.h>`
> *segment.h* defines functions related to cross-space copying in all kernels up to and including 2.0. The name was changed to *uaccess.h* in the 2.1 development series.

```
unsigned long __copy_from_user (void *to, const void *from,
        unsigned long count);
unsigned long __copy_to_user (void *to, const void *from,
        unsigned long count);
```
Copy data between user space and kernel space.

```
void memcpy_fromfs(void *to, const void *from, unsigned long
        count);
void memcpy_tofs(void *to, const void *from, unsigned long
        count);
```
These functions were used to copy an array of bytes from user space to kernel space and vice versa in version 2.0 of the kernel.

```
#include <linux/devfs_fs_kernel.h>
devfs_handle_t devfs_mk_dir (devfs_handle_t dir, const char
        *name, void *info);
devfs_handle_t devfs_register (devfs_handle_t dir, const
        char *name, unsigned int flags,
  unsigned int major, unsigned int minor, umode_t mode, void
        *ops, void *info);
void devfs_unregister (devfs_handle_t de);
```
These are the basic functions for registering devices with the device filesystem (*devfs*).

## CHAPTER FOUR

DEBUGGING TECHNIQUES

One of the most compelling problems for anyone writing kernel code is how to approach debugging. Kernel code cannot be easily executed under a debugger, nor can it be easily traced, because it is a set of functionalities not related to a specific process. Kernel code errors can also be exceedingly hard to reproduce and can bring down the entire system with them, thus destroying much of the evidence that could be used to track them down.

This chapter introduces techniques you can use to monitor kernel code and trace errors under such trying circumstances.

Debugging by Printing

The most common debugging technique is monitoring, which in applications programming is done by calling *printf* at suitable points. When you are debugging kernel code, you can accomplish the same goal with *printk*.

printk

We used the *printk* function in earlier chapters with the simplifying assumption that it works like *printf*. Now it's time to introduce some of the differences.

One of the differences is that *printk* lets you classify messages according to their severity by associating different *loglevels*, or priorities, with the messages. You usually indicate the loglevel with a macro. For example, KERN_INFO, which we saw prepended to some of the earlier print statements, is one of the possible loglevels of the message. The loglevel macro expands to a string, which is concatenated to the message text at compile time; that's why there is no comma between the priority and the format string in the following examples. Here are two examples of *printk* commands, a debug message and a critical message:

```
printk(KERN_DEBUG "Here I am: %s:%i\n", __FILE__, __LINE_&_);
printk(KERN_CRIT "I'm trashed; giving up on %p\n", ptr);
```

There are eight possible loglevel strings, defined in the header `<linux/kernel.h>`:

KERN_EMERG
Used for emergency messages, usually those that precede a crash.

KERN_ALERT
A situation requiring immediate action.

KERN_CRIT
Critical conditions, often related to serious hardware or software failures.

KERN_ERR
Used to report error conditions; device drivers will often use **KERN_ERR** to report hardware difficulties.

KERN_WARNING
Warnings about problematic situations that do not, in themselves, create serious problems with the system.

KERN_NOTICE
Situations that are normal, but still worthy of note. A number of security-related conditions are reported at this level.

KERN_INFO
Informational messages. Many drivers print information about the hardware they find at startup time at this level.

KERN_DEBUG
Used for debugging messages.

Each string (in the macro expansion) represents an integer in angle brackets. Integers range from 0 to 7, with smaller values representing higher priorities.

A *printk* statement with no specified priority defaults to **DEFAULT_MESSAGE_LOGLEVEL**, specified in *kernel/printk.c* as an integer. The default loglevel value has changed several times during Linux development, so we suggest that you always specify an explicit loglevel.

Based on the loglevel, the kernel may print the message to the current console, be it a text-mode terminal, a serial line printer, or a parallel printer. If the priority is less than the integer variable `console_loglevel`, the message is displayed. If both *klogd* and *syslogd* are running on the system, kernel messages are appended to */var/log/messages* (or otherwise treated depending on your *syslogd* configuration), independent of `console_loglevel`. If *klogd* is not running, the message won't reach user space unless you read */proc/kmsg*.

The variable `console_loglevel` is initialized to DEFAULT_CON-SOLE_LOGLEVEL and can be modified through the *sys_syslog* system call. One way to change it is by specifying the *–c* switch when invoking *klogd*, as specified in the *klogd* manpage. Note that to change the current value, you must first kill *klogd* and then restart it with the *–c* option. Alternatively, you can write a program to change the console loglevel. You'll find a version of such a program in *misc-progs/setlevel.c* in the source files provided on the O'Reilly FTP site. The new level is specified as an integer value between 1 and 8, inclusive. If it is set to 1, only messages of level 0 (KERN_EMERG) will reach the console; if it is set to 8, all messages, including debugging ones, will be displayed.

You'll probably want to lower the loglevel if you work on the console and you experience a kernel fault (see "Debugging System Faults" later in this chapter), because the fault-handling code raises the `console_loglevel` to its maximum value, causing every subsequent message to appear on the console. You'll want to raise the loglevel if you need to see your debugging messages; this is useful if you are developing kernel code remotely and the text console is not being used for an interactive session.

From version 2.1.31 on it is possible to read and modify the console loglevel using the text file */proc/sys/kernel/printk*. The file hosts four integer values. You may be interested in the first two: the current console loglevel and the default level for messages. With recent kernels, for instance, you can cause all kernel messages to appear at the console by simply entering

```
# echo 8 > /proc/sys/kernel/printk
```

If you run 2.0, however, you still need the *setlevel* tool.

It should now be apparent why the *hello.c* sample had the `<1>` markers; they are there to make sure that the messages appear on the console.

Linux allows for some flexibility in console logging policies by letting you send messages to a specific virtual console (if your console lives on the text screen). By default, the "console" is the current virtual terminal. To select a different virtual terminal to receive messages, you can issue `ioctl(TIOCLINUX)` on any console device. The following program, *setconsole*, can be used to choose which console receives kernel messages; it must be run by the superuser and is available in the *misc-progs* directory.

This is how the program works:

```
int main(int argc, char **argv)
{
    char bytes[2] = {11,0}; /* 11 is the TIOCLINUX cmd number */

    if (argc==2) bytes[1] = atoi(argv[1]); /* the chosen console */
    else {
        fprintf(stderr, "%s: need a single arg\n",argv[0]); exit(1);
    }
```

```
    if (ioctl(STDIN_FILENO, TIOCLINUX, bytes)<0) {     /* use stdin */
        fprintf(stderr,"%s: ioctl(stdin, TIOCLINUX): %s\n",
                argv[0], strerror(errno));
        exit(1);
    }
    exit(0);
}
```

setconsole uses the special *ioctl* command `TIOCLINUX`, which implements Linux-specific functions. To use `TIOCLINUX`, you pass it an argument that is a pointer to a byte array. The first byte of the array is a number that specifies the requested subcommand, and the following bytes are subcommand specific. In *setconsole*, subcommand 11 is used, and the next byte (stored in `bytes[1]`) identifies the virtual console. The complete description of `TIOCLINUX` can be found in *drivers/char/tty_io.c*, in the kernel sources.

How Messages Get Logged

The *printk* function writes messages into a circular buffer that is `LOG_BUF_LEN` (defined in *kernel/printk.c*) bytes long. It then wakes any process that is waiting for messages, that is, any process that is sleeping in the *syslog* system call or that is reading */proc/kmsg*. These two interfaces to the logging engine are almost equivalent, but note that reading from */proc/kmsg* consumes the data from the log buffer, whereas the *syslog* system call can optionally return log data while leaving it for other processes as well. In general, reading the */proc* file is easier, which is why it is the default behavior for *klogd*.

If you happen to read the kernel messages by hand, after stopping *klogd* you'll find that the */proc* file looks like a FIFO, in that the reader blocks, waiting for more data. Obviously, you can't read messages this way if *klogd* or another process is already reading the same data because you'll contend for it.

If the circular buffer fills up, *printk* wraps around and starts adding new data to the beginning of the buffer, overwriting the oldest data. The logging process thus loses the oldest data. This problem is negligible compared with the advantages of using such a circular buffer. For example, a circular buffer allows the system to run even without a logging process, while minimizing memory waste by overwriting old data should nobody read it. Another feature of the Linux approach to messaging is that *printk* can be invoked from anywhere, even from an interrupt handler, with no limit on how much data can be printed. The only disadvantage is the possibility of losing some data.

If the *klogd* process is running, it retrieves kernel messages and dispatches them to *syslogd*, which in turn checks */etc/syslog.conf* to find out how to deal with them. *syslogd* differentiates between messages according to a facility and a priority; allowable values for both the facility and the priority are defined in

<sys/syslog.h>. Kernel messages are logged by the LOG_KERN facility, at a priority corresponding to the one used in *printk* (for example, LOG_ERR is used for KERN_ERR messages). If *klogd* isn't running, data remains in the circular buffer until someone reads it or the buffer overflows.

If you want to avoid clobbering your system log with the monitoring messages from your driver, you can either specify the *–f* (file) option to *klogd* to instruct it to save messages to a specific file, or modify */etc/syslog.conf* to suit your needs. Yet another possibility is to take the brute-force approach: kill *klogd* and verbosely print messages on an unused virtual terminal,* or issue the command *cat /proc/kmsg* from an unused *xterm*.

Turning the Messages On and Off

During the early stages of driver development, *printk* can help considerably in debugging and testing new code. When you officially release the driver, on the other hand, you should remove, or at least disable, such print statements. Unfortunately, you're likely to find that as soon as you think you no longer need the messages and remove them, you'll implement a new feature in the driver (or somebody will find a bug) and you'll want to turn at least one of the messages back on. There are several ways to solve both issues, to globally enable or disable your debug messages and to turn individual messages on or off.

Here we show one way to code *printk* calls so you can turn them on and off individually or globally; the technique depends on defining a macro that resolves to a *printk* (or *printf*) call when you want it to.

- Each print statement can be enabled or disabled by removing or adding a single letter to the macro's name.

- All the messages can be disabled at once by changing the value of the CFLAGS variable before compiling.

- The same print statement can be used in kernel code and user-level code, so that the driver and test programs can be managed in the same way with regard to extra messages.

The following code fragment implements these features and comes directly from the header *scull.h*.

```
#undef PDEBUG              /* undef it, just in case */
#ifdef SCULL_DEBUG
#  ifdef __KERNEL__
     /* This one if debugging is on, and kernel space */
#    define PDEBUG(fmt, args...) printk( KERN_DEBUG "scull: " fmt, \
                                    ## args)
```

---

* For example, use *setlevel 8; setconsole 10* to set up terminal 10 to display messages.

```
#   else
      /* This one for user space */
#     define PDEBUG(fmt, args...) fprintf(stderr, fmt, ## args)
#   endif
#else
#   define PDEBUG(fmt, args...) /* not debugging: nothing */
#endif

#undef PDEBUGG
#define PDEBUGG(fmt, args...) /* nothing: it's a placeholder */
```

The symbol **PDEBUG** depends on whether or not **SCULL_DEBUG** is defined, and it displays information in whatever manner is appropriate to the environment where the code is running: it uses the kernel call *printk* when it's in the kernel, and the *libc* call *fprintf* to the standard error when run in user space. The **PDEBUGG** symbol, on the other hand, does nothing; it can be used to easily "comment" print statements without removing them entirely.

To simplify the process further, add the following lines to your makefile:

```
# Comment/uncomment the following line to disable/enable debugging
DEBUG = y

# Add your debugging flag (or not) to CFLAGS
ifeq ($(DEBUG),y)
  DEBFLAGS = -O -g -DSCULL_DEBUG # "-O" is needed to expand inlines
else
  DEBFLAGS = -O2
endif

CFLAGS += $(DEBFLAGS)
```

The macros shown in this section depend on a *gcc* extension to the ANSI C preprocessor that supports macros with a variable number of arguments. This *gcc* dependency shouldn't be a problem because the kernel proper depends heavily on *gcc* features anyway. In addition, the makefile depends on GNU's version of *make*; once again, the kernel already depends on GNU *make*, so this dependency is not a problem.

If you're familiar with the C preprocessor, you can expand on the given definitions to implement the concept of a "debug level," defining different levels and assigning an integer (or bit mask) value to each level to determine how verbose it should be.

But every driver has its own features and monitoring needs. The art of good programming is in choosing the best trade-off between flexibility and efficiency, and we can't tell what is the best for you. Remember that preprocessor conditionals (as well as constant expressions in the code) are executed at compile time, so you must recompile to turn messages on or off. A possible alternative is to use C conditionals, which are executed at runtime and therefore permit you to turn messaging on and off during program execution. This is a nice feature, but it requires additional processing every time the code is executed, which can affect performance even when the messages are disabled. Sometimes this performance hit is unacceptable.

The macros shown in this section have proven themselves useful in a number of situations, with the only disadvantage being the requirement to recompile a module after any changes to its messages.

Debugging by Querying

The previous section described how *printk* works and how it can be used. What it didn't talk about are its disadvantages.

A massive use of *printk* can slow down the system noticeably, because *syslogd* keeps syncing its output files; thus, every line that is printed causes a disk operation. This is the right implementation from *syslogd*'s perspective. It tries to write everything to disk in case the system crashes right after printing the message; however, you don't want to slow down your system just for the sake of debugging messages. This problem can be solved by prefixing the name of your log file as it appears in */etc/syslogd.conf* with a minus.* The problem with changing the configuration file is that the modification will likely remain there after you are done debugging, even though during normal system operation you do want messages to be flushed to disk as soon as possible. An alternative to such a permanent change is running a program other than *klogd* (such as *cat /proc/kmsg*, as suggested earlier), but this may not provide a suitable environment for normal system operation.

More often than not, the best way to get relevant information is to query the system when you need the information, instead of continually producing data. In fact, every Unix system provides many tools for obtaining system information: *ps, netstat, vmstat*, and so on.

Two main techniques are available to driver developers for querying the system: creating a file in the */proc* filesystem and using the *ioctl* driver method. You may use *devfs* as an alternative to */proc*, but */proc* is an easier tool to use for information retrieval.

Using the /proc Filesystem

The */proc* filesystem is a special, software-created filesystem that is used by the kernel to export information to the world. Each file under */proc* is tied to a kernel function that generates the file's "contents" on the fly when the file is read. We

---

* The minus is a "magic" marker to prevent *syslogd* from flushing the file to disk at every new message, documented in *syslog.conf(5)*, a manual page worth reading.

have already seen some of these files in action; */proc/modules*, for example, always returns a list of the currently loaded modules.

/proc is heavily used in the Linux system. Many utilities on a modern Linux distribution, such as *ps*, *top*, and *uptime*, get their information from */proc*. Some device drivers also export information via */proc*, and yours can do so as well. The */proc* filesystem is dynamic, so your module can add or remove entries at any time.

Fully featured */proc* entries can be complicated beasts; among other things, they can be written to as well as read from. Most of the time, however, */proc* entries are read-only files. This section will concern itself with the simple read-only case. Those who are interested in implementing something more complicated can look here for the basics; the kernel source may then be consulted for the full picture.

All modules that work with */proc* should include `<linux/proc_fs.h>` to define the proper functions.

To create a read-only */proc* file, your driver must implement a function to produce the data when the file is read. When some process reads the file (using the *read* system call), the request will reach your module by means of one of two different interfaces, according to what you registered. We'll leave registration for later in this section and jump directly to the description of the reading interfaces.

In both cases the kernel allocates a page of memory (i.e., `PAGE_SIZE` bytes) where the driver can write data to be returned to user space.

The recommended interface is *read_proc*, but an older interface named *get_info* also exists.

```
int (*read_proc)(char *page, char **start, off_t offset, int
        count, int *eof, void *data);
```
> The `page` pointer is the buffer where you'll write your data; `start` is used by the function to say where the interesting data has been written in `page` (more on this later); `offset` and `count` have the same meaning as in the *read* implementation. The `eof` argument points to an integer that must be set by the driver to signal that it has no more data to return, while `data` is a driver-specific data pointer you can use for internal bookkeeping.* The function is available in version 2.4 of the kernel, and 2.2 as well if you use our *sysdep.h* header.

```
int (*get_info)(char *page, char **start, off_t offset, int
        count);
```
> *get_info* is an older interface used to read from a */proc* file. The arguments all have the same meaning as for *read_proc*. What it lacks is the pointer to report end-of-file and the object-oriented flavor brought in by the `data` pointer. The

---

* We'll find several of these pointers throughout the book; they represent the "object" involved in this action and correspond somewhat to `this` in C++.

function is available in all the kernel versions we are interested in (although it had an extra unused argument in its 2.0 implementation).

Both functions should return the number of bytes of data actually placed in the `page` buffer, just like the *read* implementation does for other files. Other output values are `*eof` and `*start`. `eof` is a simple flag, but the use of the `start` value is somewhat more complicated.

The main problem with the original implementation of user extensions to the */proc* filesystem was use of a single memory page for data transfer. This limited the total size of a user file to 4 KB (or whatever was appropriate for the host platform). The `start` argument is there to implement large data files, but it can be ignored.

If your *proc_read* function does not set the `*start` pointer (it starts out NULL), the kernel assumes that the `offset` parameter has been ignored and that the data page contains the whole file you want to return to user space. If, on the other hand, you need to build a bigger file from pieces, you can set `*start` to be equal to `page` so that the caller knows your new data is placed at the beginning of the buffer. You should then, of course, skip the first `offset` bytes of data, which will have already been returned in a previous call.

There has long been another major issue with */proc* files, which `start` is meant to solve as well. Sometimes the ASCII representation of kernel data structures changes between successive calls to *read*, so the reader process could find inconsistent data from one call to the next. If `*start` is set to a small integer value, the caller will use it to increment `filp->f_pos` independently of the amount of data you return, thus making `f_pos` an internal record number of your *read_proc* or *get_info* procedure. If, for example, your *read_proc* function is returning information from a big array of structures, and five of those structures were returned in the first call, `start` could be set to 5. The next call will provide that same value as the offset; the driver then knows to start returning data from the sixth structure in the array. This is defined as a "hack" by its authors and can be seen in *fs/proc/generic.c*.

Time for an example. Here is a simple *read_proc* implementation for the *scull* device:

```
int scull_read_procmem(char *buf, char **start, off_t offset,
                   int count, int *eof, void *data)
{
    int i, j, len = 0;
    int limit = count - 80; /* Don't print more than this */

    for (i = 0; i < scull_nr_devs && len <= limit; i++) {
        Scull_Dev *d = &scull_devices[i];
        if (down_interruptible(&d->sem))
                return -ERESTARTSYS;
        len += sprintf(buf+len,"\nDevice %i: qset %i, q %i, sz %li\n",
                    i, d->qset, d->quantum, d->size);
        for (; d && len <= limit; d = d->next) { /* scan the list */
```

```
                    len += sprintf(buf+len, "   item at %p, qset at %p\n", d,
                                        d->data);
                if (d->data && !d->next) /* dump only the last item
                                            - save space */
                    for (j = 0; j < d->qset; j++) {
                        if (d->data[j])
                            len += sprintf(buf+len,"    % 4i: %8p\n",
                                                j,d->data[j]);
                    }
            }
        up(&scull_devices[i].sem);
    }
    *eof = 1;
    return len;
}
```

This is a fairly typical *read_proc* implementation. It assumes that there will never be a need to generate more than one page of data, and so ignores the **start** and **offset** values. It is, however, careful not to overrun its buffer, just in case.

A */proc* function using the *get_info* interface would look very similar to the one just shown, with the exception that the last two arguments would be missing. The end-of-file condition, in this case, is signaled by returning less data than the caller expects (i.e., less than **count**).

Once you have a *read_proc* function defined, you need to connect it to an entry in the */proc* hierarchy. There are two ways of setting up this connection, depending on what versions of the kernel you wish to support. The easiest method, only available in the 2.4 kernel (and 2.2 too if you use our *sysdep.h* header), is to simply call *create_proc_read_entry*. Here is the call used by *scull* to make its */proc* function available as */proc/scullmem*:

```
create_proc_read_entry("scullmem",
                0    /* default mode */,
                NULL /* parent dir */,
                scull_read_procmem,
                NULL /* client data */);
```

The arguments to this function are, as shown, the name of the */proc* entry, the file permissions to apply to the entry (the value 0 is treated as a special case and is turned to a default, world-readable mask), the **proc_dir_entry** pointer to the parent directory for this file (we use **NULL** to make the driver appear directly under */proc*), the pointer to the *read_proc* function, and the data pointer that will be passed back to the *read_proc* function.

The directory entry pointer can be used to create entire directory hierarchies under */proc*. Note, however, that an entry may be more easily placed in a subdirectory of */proc* simply by giving the directory name as part of the name of the entry—as long as the directory itself already exists. For example, an emerging convention says that */proc* entries associated with device drivers should go in the subdirectory *driver/*; *scull* could place its entry there simply by giving its name as *driver/scullmem.*

Entries in */proc*, of course, should be removed when the module is unloaded. *remove_proc_entry* is the function that undoes what *create_proc_read_entry* did:

```
remove_proc_entry("scullmem", NULL /* parent dir */);
```

The alternative method for creating a */proc* entry is to create and initialize a `proc_dir_entry` structure and pass it to *proc_register_dynamic* (version 2.0) or *proc_register* (version 2.2, which assumes a dynamic file if the inode number in the structure is 0). As an example, consider the following code that *scull* uses when compiled against 2.0 headers:

```
static int scull_get_info(char *buf, char **start, off_t offset,
                int len, int unused)
{
    int eof = 0;
    return scull_read_procmem (buf, start, offset, len, &eof, NULL);
}

struct proc_dir_entry scull_proc_entry = {
        namelen:     8,
        name:        "scullmem",
        mode:        S_IFREG | S_IRUGO,
        nlink:       1,
        get_info:    scull_get_info,
};

static void scull_create_proc()
{
    proc_register_dynamic(&proc_root, &scull_proc_entry);
}

static void scull_remove_proc()
{
    proc_unregister(&proc_root, scull_proc_entry.low_ino);
}
```

The code declares a function using the *get_info* interface and fills in a `proc_dir_entry` structure that is registered with the filesystem.

This code provides compatibility across the 2.0 and 2.2 kernels, with a little support from macro definitions in *sysdep.h*. It uses the *get_info* interface because the 2.0 kernel did not support *read_proc*. Some more work with `#ifdef` could have made it use *read_proc* with Linux 2.2, but the benefits would be minor.

The ioctl Method

ioctl, which we show you how to use in the next chapter, is a system call that acts on a file descriptor; it receives a number that identifies a command to be performed and (optionally) another argument, usually a pointer.

As an alternative to using the */proc* filesystem, you can implement a few *ioctl* commands tailored for debugging. These commands can copy relevant data structures from the driver to user space, where you can examine them.

Using *ioctl* this way to get information is somewhat more difficult than using */proc*, because you need another program to issue the *ioctl* and display the results. This program must be written, compiled, and kept in sync with the module you're testing. On the other hand, the driver's code is easier than what is needed to implement a */proc* file

There are times when *ioctl* is the best way to get information, because it runs faster than reading */proc*. If some work must be performed on the data before it's written to the screen, retrieving the data in binary form is more efficient than reading a text file. In addition, *ioctl* doesn't require splitting data into fragments smaller than a page.

Another interesting advantage of the *ioctl* approach is that information-retrieval commands can be left in the driver even when debugging would otherwise be disabled. Unlike a */proc* file, which is visible to anyone who looks in the directory (and too many people are likely to wonder "what that strange file is"), undocumented *ioctl* commands are likely to remain unnoticed. In addition, they will still be there should something weird happen to the driver. The only drawback is that the module will be slightly bigger.

Debugging by Watching

Sometimes minor problems can be tracked down by watching the behavior of an application in user space. Watching programs can also help in building confidence that a driver is working correctly. For example, we were able to feel confident about *scull* after looking at how its *read* implementation reacted to read requests for different amounts of data.

There are various ways to watch a user-space program working. You can run a debugger on it to step through its functions, add print statements, or run the program under *strace*. Here we'll discuss just the last technique, which is most interesting when the real goal is examining kernel code.

The *strace* command is a powerful tool that shows all the system calls issued by a user-space program. Not only does it show the calls, but it can also show the arguments to the calls, as well as return values in symbolic form. When a system call fails, both the symbolic value of the error (e.g., **ENOMEM**) and the corresponding string (**Out of memory**) are displayed. *strace* has many command-line options; the most useful of which are *−t* to display the time *when* each call is executed, *−T* to display the time *spent in* the call, *−e* to limit the types of calls traced, and *−o* to redirect the output to a file. By default, *strace* prints tracing information on **stderr**.

strace receives information from the kernel itself. This means that a program can be traced regardless of whether or not it was compiled with debugging support (the *−g* option to *gcc*) and whether or not it is stripped. You can also attach tracing to a running process, similar to the way a debugger can connect to a running process and control it.

The trace information is often used to support bug reports sent to application developers, but it's also invaluable to kernel programmers. We've seen how driver code executes by reacting to system calls; *strace* allows us to check the consistency of input and output data of each call.

For example, the following screen dump shows the last lines of running the command *strace ls /dev > /dev/scull0*:

```
[...]
open("/dev", O_RDONLY|O_NONBLOCK)       = 4
fcntl(4, F_SETFD, FD_CLOEXEC)           = 0
brk(0x8055000)                          = 0x8055000
lseek(4, 0, SEEK_CUR)                   = 0
getdents(4, /* 70 entries */, 3933)     = 1260
[...]
getdents(4, /* 0 entries */, 3933)      = 0
close(4)                                = 0
fstat(1, {st_mode=S_IFCHR|0664, st_rdev=makedev(253, 0), ...}) = 0
ioctl(1, TCGETS, 0xbffffa5c)            = -1 ENOTTY (Inappropriate ioctl
                                             for device)
write(1, "MAKEDEV\natibm\naudio\naudio1\na"..., 4096) = 4000
write(1, "d2\nsdd3\nsdd4\nsdd5\nsdd6\nsdd7"..., 96) = 96
write(1, "4\nsde5\nsde6\nsde7\nsde8\nsde9\n"..., 3325) = 3325
close(1)                                = 0
_exit(0)                                = ?
```

It's apparent in the first *write* call that after *ls* finished looking in the target directory, it tried to write 4 KB. Strangely (for *ls*), only four thousand bytes were written, and the operation was retried. However, we know that the *write* implementation in *scull* writes a single quantum at a time, so we could have expected the partial write. After a few steps, everything sweeps through, and the program exits successfully.

As another example, let's *read* the *scull* device (using the *wc* command):

```
[...]
open("/dev/scull0", O_RDONLY)           = 4
fstat(4, {st_mode=S_IFCHR|0664, st_rdev=makedev(253, 0), ...}) = 0
```

```
read(4, "MAKEDEV\natibm\naudio\naudio1\na"..., 16384) = 4000
read(4, "d2\nsdd3\nsdd4\nsdd5\nsdd6\nsdd7"..., 16384) = 3421
read(4, "", 16384)                             = 0
fstat(1, {st_mode=S_IFCHR|0600, st_rdev=makedev(3, 7), ...}) = 0
ioctl(1, TCGETS, {B38400 opost isig icanon echo ...}) = 0
write(1, "   7421 /dev/scull0\n", 20)   = 20
close(4)                                = 0
_exit(0)                                = ?
```

As expected, *read* is able to retrieve only four thousand bytes at a time, but the total amount of data is the same that was written in the previous example. It's interesting to note how retries are organized in this example, as opposed to the previous trace. *wc* is optimized for fast reading and thus bypasses the standard library, trying to read more data with a single system call. You can see from the `read` lines in the trace how *wc* tried to read 16 KB at a time.

Linux experts can find much useful information in the output of *strace*. If you're put off by all the symbols, you can limit yourself to watching how the file methods (*open*, *read*, and so on) work.

Personally, we find *strace* most useful for pinpointing runtime errors from system calls. Often the *perror* call in the application or demo program isn't verbose enough to be useful for debugging, and being able to tell exactly which arguments to which system call triggered the error can be a great help.

Debugging System Faults

Even if you've used all the monitoring and debugging techniques, sometimes bugs remain in the driver, and the system faults when the driver is executed. When this happens it's important to be able to collect as much information as possible to solve the problem.

Note that "fault" doesn't mean "panic." The Linux code is robust enough to respond gracefully to most errors: a fault usually results in the destruction of the current process while the system goes on working. The system *can* panic, and it may if a fault happens outside of a process's context, or if some vital part of the system is compromised. But when the problem is due to a driver error, it usually results only in the sudden death of the process unlucky enough to be using the driver. The only unrecoverable damage when a process is destroyed is that some memory allocated to the process's context is lost; for instance, dynamic lists allocated by the driver through *kmalloc* might be lost. However, since the kernel calls the *close* operation for any open device when a process dies, your driver can release what was allocated by the *open* method.

We've already said that when kernel code misbehaves, an informative message is printed on the console. The next section explains how to decode and use such messages. Even though they appear rather obscure to the novice, processor dumps are full of interesting information, often sufficient to pinpoint a program bug without the need for additional testing.

Oops Messages

Most bugs show themselves in NULL pointer dereferences or by the use of other incorrect pointer values. The usual outcome of such bugs is an oops message.

Any address used by the processor is a virtual address and is mapped to physical addresses through a complex structure of so-called page tables (see "Page Tables" in Chapter 13). When an invalid pointer is dereferenced, the paging mechanism fails to map the pointer to a physical address and the processor signals a *page fault* to the operating system. If the address is not valid, the kernel is not able to "page in" the missing address; it generates an oops if this happens while the processor is in supervisor mode.

It's worth noting that the first enhancement introduced after version 2.0 was automatic handling of invalid address faults when moving data to and from user space. Linus chose to let the hardware catch erroneous memory references, so that the normal case (where the addresses are correct) is handled more efficiently.

An oops displays the processor status at the time of the fault, including the contents of the CPU registers, the location of page descriptor tables, and other seemingly incomprehensible information. The message is generated by *printk* statements in the fault handler (*arch/*/kernel/traps.c*) and is dispatched as described earlier, in the section "printk."

Let's look at one such message. Here's what results from dereferencing a NULL pointer on a PC running version 2.4 of the kernel. The most relevant information here is the instruction pointer (EIP), the address of the faulty instruction.

```
Unable to handle kernel NULL pointer dereference at virtual address \
      00000000
 printing eip:
c48370c3
*pde = 00000000
Oops: 0002
CPU:    0
EIP:    0010:[<c48370c3>]
EFLAGS: 00010286
eax: ffffffea   ebx: c2281a20   ecx: c48370c0   edx: c2281a40
esi: 4000c000   edi: 4000c000   ebp: c38adf8c   esp: c38adf8c
ds: 0018   es: 0018   ss: 0018
Process ls (pid: 23171, stackpage=c38ad000)
Stack: 0000010e c01356e6 c2281a20 4000c000 0000010e c2281a40 c38ac000 \
        0000010e
      4000c000 bffffc1c 00000000 00000000 c38adfc4 c010b860 00000001 \
        4000c000
      0000010e 0000010e 4000c000 bffffc1c 00000004 0000002b 0000002b \
```

```
        00000004
Call Trace: [<c01356e6>] [<c010b860>]
Code: c7 05 00 00 00 00 00 00 00 00 31 c0 89 ec 5d c3 8d b6 00 00
```

This message was generated by writing to a device owned by the *faulty* module, a module built deliberately to demonstrate failures. The implementation of the *write* method of *faulty.c* is trivial:

```
ssize_t faulty_write (struct file *filp, const char *buf, size_t count,
            loff_t *pos)
{
    /* make a simple fault by dereferencing a NULL pointer */
    *(int *)0 = 0;
    return 0;
}
```

As you can see, what we do here is dereference a NULL pointer. Since 0 is never a valid pointer value, a fault occurs, which the kernel turns into the oops message shown earlier. The calling process is then killed.

The *faulty* module has more interesting fault conditions in its *read* implementation:

```
char faulty_buf[1024];

ssize_t faulty_read (struct file *filp, char *buf, size_t count,
            loff_t *pos)
{
    int ret, ret2;
    char stack_buf[4];

    printk(KERN_DEBUG "read: buf %p, count %li\n", buf, (long)count);
    /* the next line oopses with 2.0, but not with 2.2 and later */
    ret = copy_to_user(buf, faulty_buf, count);
    if (!ret) return count; /* we survived */

    printk(KERN_DEBUG "didn't fail: retry\n");
    /* For 2.2 and 2.4, let's try a buffer overflow  */
    sprintf(stack_buf, "1234567\n");
    if (count > 8) count = 8; /* copy 8 bytes to the user */
    ret2 = copy_to_user(buf, stack_buf, count);
    if (!ret2) return count;
    return ret2;
}
```

It first reads from a global buffer without checking the size of the data, and then performs a buffer overrun by writing to a local buffer. The first situation results in an oops only in version 2.0 of the kernel, because later versions automatically deal with user copy functions. The buffer overflow results in an oops with all kernel versions; however, since the return instruction brings the instruction pointer to nowhere land, this kind of fault is much harder to trace, and you can get something like the following:

```
EIP:     0010:[<00000000>]
[...]
Call Trace: [<c010b860>]
Code:   Bad EIP value.
```

The main problem with users dealing with oops messages is in the little intrinsic meaning carried by hexadecimal values; to be meaningful to the programmer they need to be resolved to symbols. A couple of utilities are available to perform this resolution for developers: *klogd* and *ksymoops*. The former tool performs symbol decoding by itself whenever it is running; the latter needs to be purposely invoked by the user. In the following discussion we use the data generated in our first oops example by dereferencing a NULL pointer.

Using klogd

The *klogd* daemon can decode oops messages before they reach the log files. In many situations, *klogd* can provide all the information a developer needs to track down a problem, though sometimes the developer must give it a little help.

A dump of the oops for *faulty*, as it reaches the system log, looks like this (note the decoded symbols on the EIP line and in the stack trace):

```
Unable to handle kernel NULL pointer dereference at virtual address \
      00000000
 printing eip:
c48370c3
*pde = 00000000
Oops: 0002
CPU:    0
EIP:     0010:[faulty:faulty_write+3/576]
EFLAGS: 00010286
eax: ffffffea  ebx: c2c55ae0  ecx: c48370c0  edx: c2c55b00
esi: 0804d038  edi: 0804d038  ebp: c2337f8c  esp: c2337f8c
ds: 0018   es: 0018   ss: 0018
Process cat (pid: 23413, stackpage=c2337000)
Stack: 00000001 c01356e6 c2c55ae0 0804d038 00000001 c2c55b00 c2336000 \
      00000001
      0804d038 bffffbd4 00000000 00000000 bffffbd4 c010b860 00000001 \
      0804d038
      00000001 00000001 0804d038 bffffbd4 00000004 0000002b 0000002b \
      00000004
Call Trace: [sys_write+214/256] [system_call+52/56]
Code: c7 05 00 00 00 00 00 00 00 00 31 c0 89 ec 5d c3 8d b6 00 00
```

klogd provides most of the necessary information to track down the problem. In this case we see that the instruction pointer (EIP) was executing in the function *faulty_write*, so we know where to start looking. The 3/576 string tells us that the processor was at byte 3 of a function that appears to be 576 bytes long. Note that the values are decimal, not hex.

The developer must exercise some care, however, to get useful information for errors that occur within loadable modules. *klogd* loads all of the available symbol information when it starts, and uses those symbols thereafter. If you load a module after *klogd* has initialized itself (usually at system boot), *klogd* will not have your module's symbol information. To force *klogd* to go out and get that information, send the *klogd* process a SIGUSR1 signal after your module has been loaded (or reloaded), and before you do anything that could cause it to oops.

It is also possible to run *klogd* with the *–p* ("paranoid") option, which will cause it to reread symbol information anytime it sees an oops message. The *klogd* man-page recommends against this mode of operation, however, since it makes *klogd* query the kernel for information after the problem has occurred. Information obtained after an error could be plain wrong.

For *klogd* to work properly, it must have a current copy of the *System.map* symbol table file. Normally this file is found in */boot*; if you have built and installed a kernel from a nonstandard location you may have to copy *System.map* into */boot*, or tell *klogd* to look elsewhere. *klogd* refuses to decode symbols if the symbol table doesn't match the current kernel. If a symbol is decoded on the system log, you can be reasonably sure it is decoded correctly.

Using ksymoops

At times *klogd* may not be enough for your tracing purposes. Usually, you need to get both the hexadecimal address and the associated symbol, and you often need offsets printed as hex numbers. You may need more information than address decoding. Also, it is common for *klogd* to get killed during the fault. In such situations, a stronger oops analyzer may be called for; *ksymoops* is such a tool.

Prior to the 2.3 development series, *ksymoops* was distributed with the kernel source, in the *scripts* directory. It now lives on its own FTP site and is maintained independently of the kernel. Even if you are working with an older kernel, you probably should go to *ftp://ftp.ocs.com.au/pub/ksymoops* and get an updated version of the tool.

To operate at its best, *ksymoops* needs a lot of information in addition to the error message; you can use command-line options to tell it where to find the various items. The program needs the following items:

A System.map file
>   This map must correspond to the kernel that was running at the time the oops occurred. The default is */usr/src/linux/System.map*.

A list of modules
>   *ksymoops* needs to know what modules were loaded when the oops occurred, in order to extract symbolic information from them. If you do not supply this list, *ksymoops* will look at */proc/modules*.

A list of kernel symbols defined when the oops occurred
The default is to get this list from */proc/ksyms*.

A copy of the kernel image that was running
Note that *ksymoops* needs a straight kernel image, not the compressed version (*vmlinuz*, *zImage*, or *bzImage*) that most systems boot. The default is to use no kernel image because most people don't keep it. If you have the exact image handy, you should tell the program where it is by using the *-v* option.

The locations of the object files for any kernel modules that were loaded
ksymoops will look in the standard directories for modules, but during development you will almost certainly have to tell it where your module lives using the *-o* option

Although *ksymoops* will go to files in */proc* for some of its needed information, the results can be unreliable. The system, of course, will almost certainly have been rebooted between the time the oops occurs and when *ksymoops* is run, and the information from */proc* may not match the state of affairs when the failure occurred. When possible, it is better to save copies of */proc/modules* and */proc/ksyms* prior to causing the oops to happen.

We urge driver developers to read the manual page for *ksymoops* because it is a very informative document.

The last argument on the tool's command line is the location of the oops message; if it is missing, the tool will read `stdin` in the best Unix tradition. The message can be recovered from the system logs with luck; in the case of a very bad crash you may end up writing it down off the screen and typing it back in (unless you were using a serial console, a nice tool for kernel developers).

Note that *ksymoops* will be confused by an oops message that has already been processed by *klogd*. If you are running *klogd*, and your system is still running after an oops occurs, a clean oops message can often be obtained by invoking the *dmesg* command.

If you do not provide all of the listed information explicitly, *ksymoops* will issue warnings. It will also issue warnings about things like loaded modules that define no symbols. A warning-free run of *ksymoops* is rare.

Output from *ksymoops* tends to look like the following:

```
>>EIP; c48370c3 <[faulty]faulty_write+3/20>   <=====
Trace; c01356e6 <sys_write+d6/100>
Trace; c010b860 <system_call+34/38>
Code;  c48370c3 <[faulty]faulty_write+3/20>
00000000 <_EIP>:
Code;  c48370c3 <[faulty]faulty_write+3/20>   <=====
   0:   c7 05 00 00 00    movl   $0x0,0x0   <=====
Code;  c48370c8 <[faulty]faulty_write+8/20>
   5:   00 00 00 00 00
```

```
Code;   c48370cd <[faulty]faulty_write+d/20>
   a:   31 c0              xorl    %eax,%eax
Code;   c48370cf <[faulty]faulty_write+f/20>
   c:   89 ec              movl    %ebp,%esp
Code;   c48370d1 <[faulty]faulty_write+11/20>
   e:   5d                 popl    %ebp
Code;   c48370d2 <[faulty]faulty_write+12/20>
   f:   c3                 ret
Code;   c48370d3 <[faulty]faulty_write+13/20>
  10:   8d b6 00 00 00     leal    0x0(%esi),%esi
Code;   c48370d8 <[faulty]faulty_write+18/20>
  15:   00
```

As you can see, *ksymoops* provides EIP and kernel stack information much like *klogd* does, but more precisely and in hexadecimal. You'll note that the *faulty_write* function is correctly reported to be 0x20 bytes long. This is because *ksymoops* reads the object file of your module and extracts all available information.

In this case, moreover, you also get an assembly language dump of the code where the fault occurred. This information can often be used to figure out exactly what was happening; here it's clearly an instruction that writes a 0 to address 0.

One interesting feature of *ksymoops* is that it is ported to nearly all the platforms where Linux runs and exploits the *bfd* (binary format description) library in order to support several computer architectures at the same time. To step outside of the PC world, let's see how the same oops message appears on the *SPARC64* platform (several lines have been broken for typographical needs):

```
Unable to handle kernel NULL pointer dereference
tsk->mm->context = 0000000000000734
tsk->mm->pgd = fffff80003499000
                \/  ____
                "@'/ .. \`@"
                /_| \__/ |_\
                   \__U_/
ls(16740): Oops
TSTATE: 0000004400009601 TPC: 0000000001000128 TNPC: 0000000000457fbc \
Y: 00800000
g0: 000000007002ea88 g1: 0000000000000004 g2: 0000000070029fb0 \
g3: 0000000000000018
g4: fffff80000000000 g5: 0000000000000001 g6: fffff8000119c000 \
g7: 0000000000000001
o0: 0000000000000000 o1: 000000007001a000 o2: 0000000000000178 \
o3: fffff8001224f168
o4: 0000000001000120 o5: 0000000000000000 sp: fffff8000119f621 \
ret_pc: 0000000000457fb4
l0: fffff800122376c0 l1: ffffffffffffffea l2: 000000000002c400 \
l3: 000000000002c400
l4: 0000000000000000 l5: 0000000000000000 l6: 0000000000019c00 \
l7: 0000000070028cbc
i0: fffff8001224f140 i1: 000000007001a000 i2: 0000000000000178 \
```

```
i3: 000000000002c400
i4: 000000000002c400 i5: 000000000002c000 i6: fffff8000119f6e1 \
i7: 0000000000410114
Caller[0000000000410114]
Caller[000000007007cba4]
Instruction DUMP: 01000000 90102000 81c3e008 <c0202000> \
30680005 01000000 01000000 01000000 01000000
```

Note how the instruction dump doesn't start from the instruction that caused the fault but three instructions earlier: that's because the RISC platforms execute several instructions in parallel and may generate deferred exceptions, so one must be able to look back at the last few instructions.

This is what *ksymoops* prints when fed with input data starting at the `TSTATE` line:

```
>>TPC; 0000000001000128 <[faulty].text.start+88/a0>    <=====
>>O7; 0000000000457fb4 <sys_write+114/160>
>>I7; 0000000000410114 <linux_sparc_syscall+34/40>
Trace; 0000000000410114 <linux_sparc_syscall+34/40>
Trace; 000000007007cba4 <END_OF_CODE+6f07c40d/????>
Code;  000000000100011c <[faulty].text.start+7c/a0>
0000000000000000 <_TPC>:
Code;  000000000100011c <[faulty].text.start+7c/a0>
   0:   01 00 00 00         nop
Code;  0000000001000120 <[faulty].text.start+80/a0>
   4:   90 10 20 00         clr    %o0      ! 0 <_TPC>
Code;  0000000001000124 <[faulty].text.start+84/a0>
   8:   81 c3 e0 08         retl
Code;  0000000001000128 <[faulty].text.start+88/a0>    <=====
   c:   c0 20 20 00         clr    [ %g0 ]  <=====
Code;  000000000100012c <[faulty].text.start+8c/a0>
  10:   30 68 00 05         b,a    %xcc, 24 <_TPC+0x24> \
                            0000000001000140 <[faulty]faulty_write+0/20>
Code;  0000000001000130 <[faulty].text.start+90/a0>
  14:   01 00 00 00         nop
Code;  0000000001000134 <[faulty].text.start+94/a0>
  18:   01 00 00 00         nop
Code;  0000000001000138 <[faulty].text.start+98/a0>
  1c:   01 00 00 00         nop
Code;  000000000100013c <[faulty].text.start+9c/a0>
  20:   01 00 00 00         nop
```

To print the disassembled code shown we had to tell *ksymoops* the target file format and architecture (this is needed because the native architecture for *SPARC64* user space is 32 bit). In this case, the options *-t elf64-sparc -a sparc:v9* did the job.

You may complain that this call trace doesn't carry any interesting information; however, the *SPARC* processors don't save all the call trace on the stack: the `O7` and `I7` registers hold the instruction pointers of the last two calling functions, which is why they are shown near the call trace. In this case, the faulty instruction was in a function invoked by *sys_write*.

Note that, whatever the platform/architecture pair, the format used to show disassembled code is the same as that used by the *objdump* program. *objdump* is a powerful utility; if you want to look at the whole function that failed, you can invoke the command *objdump –d faulty.o* (once again, on *SPARC64, you need special options: —target elf64-sparc—architecture sparc:v9*). For more information on *objdump* and its command-line options, see the manpage for the command.

Learning to decode an oops message requires some practice and an understanding of the target processor you are using, as well as of the conventions used to represent assembly language, but it's worth doing. The time spent learning will be quickly repaid. Even if you have previous expertise with the PC assembly language under non-Unix operating systems, you may need to devote some time to learning, because the Unix syntax is different from Intel syntax. (A good description of the differences is in the Info documentation file for *as*, in the chapter called "i386-specific.")

System Hangs

Although most bugs in kernel code end up as oops messages, sometimes they can completely hang the system. If the system hangs, no message is printed. For example, if the code enters an endless loop, the kernel stops scheduling, and the system doesn't respond to any action, including the magic **CTRL-ALT-DEL** combination. You have two choices for dealing with system hangs—either prevent them beforehand or be able to debug them after the fact.

You can prevent an endless loop by inserting *schedule* invocations at strategic points. The *schedule* call (as you might guess) invokes the scheduler and thus allows other processes to steal CPU time from the current process. If a process is looping in kernel space due to a bug in your driver, the *schedule* calls enable you to kill the process, after tracing what is happening.

You should be aware, of course, that any call to *schedule* may create an additional source of reentrant calls to your driver, since it allows other processes to run. This reentrancy should not normally be a problem, assuming that you have used suitable locking in your driver. Be sure, however, not to call *schedule* any time that your driver is holding a spinlock.

If your driver really hangs the system, and you don't know where to insert *schedule* calls, the best way to go is to add some print messages and write them to the console (by changing the `console_loglevel` value).

Sometimes the system may appear to be hung, but it isn't. This can happen, for example, if the keyboard remains locked in some strange way. These false hangs can be detected by looking at the output of a program you keep running for just this purpose. A clock or system load meter on your display is a good status monitor; as long as it continues to update, the scheduler is working. If you are not using a graphic display, you can check the scheduler by running a program that flashes the keyboard LEDs, turns on the floppy motor every now and then, or ticks the speaker—conventional beeps are quite annoying and should be avoided; look for the KDMKTONE *ioctl* command instead. A sample program (*misc-progs/heartbeat.c*) that flashes a keyboard LED in a heartbeat fashion is available in the sources on the O'Reilly FTP site.

If the keyboard isn't accepting input, the best thing to do is log into the system through your network and kill any offending processes, or reset the keyboard (with *kbd_mode –a*). However, discovering that the hang is only a keyboard lockup is of little use if you don't have a network available to help you recover. If this is the case, you could set up alternative input devices to be able at least to reboot the system cleanly. A shutdown and reboot cycle is easier on your computer than hitting the so-called big red button, and it saves you from the lengthy *fsck* scanning of your disks.

Such an alternative input device can be, for example, the mouse. Version 1.10 or newer of the *gpm* mouse server features a command-line option to enable a similar capability, but it works only in text mode. If you don't have a network connection and run in graphics mode, we suggest running some custom solution, like a switch connected to the DCD pin of the serial line and a script that polls for status change.

An indispensable tool for these situations is the "magic SysRq key," which is available on more architectures in 2.2 and later kernels. Magic SysRq is invoked with the combination of the ALT and SysRq keys on the PC keyboard, or with the ALT and Stop keys on SPARC keyboards. A third key, pressed along with these two, performs one of a number of useful actions, as follows:

r   Turns off keyboard raw mode in situations where you cannot run *kbd_mode*.

k   Invokes the "secure attention" (SAK) function. SAK will kill all processes running on the current console, leaving you with a clean terminal.

s   Performs an emergency synchronization of all disks.

u   Attempts to remount all disks in a read-only mode. This operation, usually invoked immediately after *s*, can save a lot of filesystem checking time in cases where the system is in serious trouble.

b   Immediately reboots the system. Be sure to synchronize and remount the disks first.

p   Prints the current register information.

t   Prints the current task list.

m   Prints memory information.

Other magic SysRq functions exist; see *sysrq.txt* in the *Documentation* directory of the kernel source for the full list. Note that magic SysRq must be explicitly enabled in the kernel configuration, and that most distributions do not enable it, for obvious security reasons. For a system used to develop drivers, however, enabling magic SysRq is worth the trouble of building a new kernel in itself. Magic SysRq must be enabled at runtime with a command like the following:

```
echo 1 > /proc/sys/kernel/sysrq
```

Another precaution to use when reproducing system hangs is to mount all your disks as read-only (or unmount them). If the disks are read-only or unmounted, there's no risk of damaging the filesystem or leaving it in an inconsistent state. Another possibility is using a computer that mounts all of its filesystems via NFS, the network file system. The "NFS-Root" capability must be enabled in the kernel, and special parameters must be passed at boot time. In this case you'll avoid any filesystem corruption without even resorting to SysRq, because filesystem coherence is managed by the NFS server, which is not brought down by your device driver.

Debuggers and Related Tools

The last resort in debugging modules is using a debugger to step through the code, watching the value of variables and machine registers. This approach is time-consuming and should be avoided whenever possible. Nonetheless, the fine-grained perspective on the code that is achieved through a debugger is sometimes invaluable.

Using an interactive debugger on the kernel is a challenge. The kernel runs in its own address space on the behalf of all the processes on the system. As a result, a number of common capabilities provided by user-space debuggers, such as breakpoints and single-stepping, are harder to come by in the kernel. In this section we look at several ways of debugging the kernel; each of them has advantages and disadvantages.

Using gdb

gdb can be quite useful for looking at the system internals. Proficient use of the debugger at this level requires some confidence with *gdb* commands, some understanding of assembly code for the target platform, and the ability to match source code and optimized assembly.

The debugger must be invoked as though the kernel were an application. In addition to specifying the filename for the uncompressed kernel image, you need to provide the name of a core file on the command line. For a running kernel, that core file is the kernel core image, */proc/kcore*. A typical invocation of *gdb* looks like the following:

```
gdb /usr/src/linux/vmlinux /proc/kcore
```

The first argument is the name of the uncompressed kernel executable, not the *zImage* or *bzImage* or anything compressed.

The second argument on the *gdb* command line is the name of the core file. Like any file in */proc*, */proc/kcore* is generated when it is read. When the *read* system call executes in the */proc* filesystem, it maps to a data-generation function rather than a data-retrieval one; we've already exploited this feature in "Using the /proc Filesystem" earlier in this chapter. *kcore* is used to represent the kernel "executable" in the format of a core file; it is a huge file because it represents the whole kernel address space, which corresponds to all physical memory. From within *gdb*, you can look at kernel variables by issuing the standard *gdb* commands. For example, *p jiffies* prints the number of clock ticks from system boot to the current time.

When you print data from *gdb*, the kernel is still running, and the various data items have different values at different times; *gdb*, however, optimizes access to the core file by caching data that has already been read. If you try to look at the `jiffies` variable once again, you'll get the same answer as before. Caching values to avoid extra disk access is a correct behavior for conventional core files, but is inconvenient when a "dynamic" core image is used. The solution is to issue the command *core-file /proc/kcore* whenever you want to flush the *gdb* cache; the debugger prepares to use a new core file and discards any old information. You won't, however, always need to issue *core-file* when reading a new datum; *gdb* reads the core in chunks of a few kilobytes and caches only chunks it has already referenced.

Numerous capabilities normally provided by *gdb* are not available when you are working with the kernel. For example, *gdb* is not able to modify kernel data; it expects to be running a program to be debugged under its own control before playing with its memory image. It is also not possible to set breakpoints or watchpoints, or to single-step through kernel functions.

If you compile the kernel with debugging support (–g), the resulting *vmlinux* file turns out to work better with *gdb* than the same file compiled without –g. Note, however, that a large amount of disk space is needed to compile the kernel with the –g option (each object file and the kernel itself are three or more times bigger than usual).

On non-PC computers, the game is different. On the Alpha, *make boot* strips the kernel before creating the bootable image, so you end up with both the *vmlinux* and the *vmlinux.gz* files. The former is usable by *gdb*, and you can boot from the latter. On the SPARC, the kernel (at least the 2.0 kernel) is not stripped by default.

When you compile the kernel with –g and run the debugger using *vmlinux* together with */proc/kcore*, *gdb* can return a lot of information about the kernel internals. You can, for example, use commands such as *p *module_list*, *p *module_list->next*, and *p *chrdevs[4]->fops* to dump structures. To get the best out of *p*, you'll need to keep a kernel map and the source code handy.

Another useful task that *gdb* performs on the running kernel is disassembling functions, via the *disassemble* command (which can be abbreviated to *disass*) or the "examine instructions" (*x/i*) command. The *disassemble* command can take as its argument either a function name or a memory range, whereas *x/i* takes a single memory address, also in the form of a symbol name. You can invoke, for example, *x/20i* to disassemble 20 instructions. Note that you can't disassemble a module function, because the debugger is acting on *vmlinux*, which doesn't know about your module. If you try to disassemble a module by address, *gdb* is most likely to reply "Cannot access memory at xxxx." For the same reason, you can't look at data items belonging to a module. They can be read from */dev/mem* if you know the address of your variables, but it's hard to make sense out of raw data extracted from system RAM.

If you want to disassemble a module function, you're better off running the *objdump* utility on the module object file. Unfortunately, the tool runs on the disk copy of the file, not the running one; therefore, the addresses as shown by *objdump* will be the addresses before relocation, unrelated to the module's execution environment. Another disadvantage of disassembling an unlinked object file is that function calls are still unresolved, so you can't easily tell a call to *printk* from a call to *kmalloc*.

As you see, *gdb* is a useful tool when your aim is to peek into the running kernel, but it lacks some features that are vital to debugging device drivers.

The kdb Kernel Debugger

Many readers may be wondering why the kernel does not have any more advanced debugging features built into it. The answer, quite simply, is that Linus does not believe in interactive debuggers. He fears that they lead to poor fixes, those which patch up symptoms rather than addressing the real cause of problems. Thus, no built-in debuggers.

Other kernel developers, however, see an occasional use for interactive debugging tools. One such tool is the *kdb* built-in kernel debugger, available as a nonofficial patch from *oss.sgi.com*. To use *kdb*, you must obtain the patch (be sure to get a version that matches your kernel version), apply it, and rebuild and reinstall the kernel. Note that, as of this writing, *kdb* works only on IA-32 (x86) systems (though a version for the IA-64 existed for a while in the mainline kernel source before being removed).

Once you are running a *kdb*-enabled kernel, there are a couple of ways to enter the debugger. Hitting the Pause (or Break) key on the console will start up the debugger. *kdb* also starts up when a kernel oops happens, or when a breakpoint is hit. In any case, you will see a message that looks something like this:

```
Entering kdb (0xc1278000) on processor 1 due to Keyboard Entry
[1]kdb>
```

Note that just about everything the kernel does stops when *kdb* is running. Nothing else should be running on a system where you invoke *kdb*; in particular, you should not have networking turned on—unless, of course, you are debugging a network driver. It is generally a good idea to boot the system in single-user mode if you will be using *kdb*.

As an example, consider a quick *scull* debugging session. Assuming that the driver is already loaded, we can tell *kdb* to set a breakpoint in *scull_read* as follows:

```
[1]kdb> bp scull_read
Instruction(i) BP #0 at 0xc8833514 (scull_read)
    is enabled on cpu 1
[1]kdb> go
```

The *bp* command tells *kdb* to stop the next time the kernel enters *scull_read*. We then type **go** to continue execution. After putting something into one of the *scull* devices, we can attempt to read it by running *cat* under a shell on another terminal, yielding the following:

```
Entering kdb (0xc3108000) on processor 0 due to Breakpoint @ 0xc8833515
Instruction(i) breakpoint #0 at 0xc8833514
scull_read+0x1:    movl    %esp,%ebp
[0]kdb>
```

We are now positioned at the beginning of *scull_read*. To see how we got there, we can get a stack trace:

```
[0]kdb> bt
    EBP         EIP           Function(args)
0xc3109c5c 0xc8833515   scull_read+0x1
0xc3109fbc 0xfc458b10   scull_read+0x33c255fc( 0x3, 0x803ad78, 0x1000,
0x1000, 0x804ad78)
0xbffffc88 0xc010bec0   system_call
[0]kdb>
```

kdb attempts to print out the arguments to every function in the call trace. It gets confused, however, by optimization tricks used by the compiler. Thus it prints five arguments for *scull_read*, which only has four.

Time to look at some data. The *mds* command manipulates data; we can query the value of the `scull_devices` pointer with a command like:

```
[0]kdb> mds scull_devices 1
c8836104: c4c125c0 ....
```

Here we asked for one (four-byte) word of data starting at the location of `scull_devices`; the answer tells us that our device array was allocated starting at the address `c4c125c0`. To look at a device structure itself we need to use that address:

```
[0]kdb> mds c4c125c0
c4c125c0: c3785000   ....
c4c125c4: 00000000   ....
c4c125c8: 00000fa0   ....
c4c125cc: 000003e8   ....
c4c125d0: 0000009a   ....
c4c125d4: 00000000   ....
c4c125d8: 00000000   ....
c4c125dc: 00000001   ....
```

The eight lines here correspond to the eight fields in the `Scull_Dev` structure. Thus we see that the memory for the first device is allocated at `0xc3785000`, that there is no next item in the list, that the quantum is 4000 (hex fa0) and the array size is 1000 (hex 3e8), that there are 154 bytes of data in the device (hex 9a), and so on.

kdb can change data as well. Suppose we wanted to trim some of the data from the device:

```
[0]kdb> mm c4c125d0 0x50
0xc4c125d0 = 0x50
```

A subsequent *cat* on the device will now return less data than before.

kdb has a number of other capabilities, including single-stepping (by instructions, not lines of C source code), setting breakpoints on data access, disassembling code, stepping through linked lists, accessing register data, and more. After you have applied the *kdb* patch, a full set of manual pages can be found in the *Documentation/kdb* directory in your kernel source tree.

The Integrated Kernel Debugger Patch

A number of kernel developers have contributed to an unofficial patch called the *integrated kernel debugger*, or IKD. IKD provides a number of interesting kernel debugging facilities. The x86 is the primary platform for this patch, but much of it works on other architectures as well. As of this writing, the IKD patch can be found at *ftp://ftp.kernel.org/pub/linux/kernel/people/andrea/ikd*. It is a patch that must be applied to the source for your kernel; the patch is version specific, so be sure to download the one that matches the kernel you are working with.

One of the features of the IKD patch is a kernel stack debugger. If you turn this feature on, the kernel will check the amount of free space on the kernel stack at every function call, and force an oops if it gets too small. If something in your kernel is causing stack corruption, this tool may help you to find it. There is also a "stack meter" feature that you can use to see how close to filling up the stack you get at any particular time.

The IKD patch also includes some tools for finding kernel lockups. A "soft lockup" detector forces an oops if a kernel procedure goes for too long without scheduling. It is implemented by simply counting the number of function calls that are made and shutting things down if that number exceeds a preconfigured threshold. Another feature can continuously print the program counter on a virtual console for truly last-resort lockup tracking. The semaphore deadlock detector forces an oops if a process spends too long waiting on a *down* call.

Other debugging capabilities in IKD include the kernel trace capability, which can record the paths taken through the kernel code. There are some memory debugging tools, including a leak detector and a couple of "poisoners," that can be useful in tracking down memory corruption problems.

Finally, IKD also includes a version of the *kdb* debugger discussed in the previous section. As of this writing, however, the version of *kdb* included in the IKD patch is somewhat old. If you need *kdb*, we recommend that you go directly to the source at *oss.sgi.com* for the current version.

The kgdb Patch

kgdb is a patch that allows the full use of the *gdb* debugger on the Linux kernel, but only on x86 systems. It works by hooking into the system to be debugged via a serial line, with *gdb* running on the far end. You thus need two systems to use *kgdb*—one to run the debugger and one to run the kernel of interest. Like *kdb*, *kgdb* is currently available from *oss.sgi.com*.

Setting up *kgdb* involves installing a kernel patch and booting the modified kernel. You need to connect the two systems with a serial cable (of the null modem variety) and to install some support files on the *gdb* side of the connection. The patch places detailed instructions in the file *Documentation/i386/gdb-serial.txt*; we won't reproduce them here. Be sure to read the instructions on debugging modules: toward the end there are some nice *gdb* macros that have been written for this purpose.

Kernel Crash Dump Analyzers

Crash dump analyzers enable the system to record its state when an oops occurs, so that it may be examined at leisure afterward. They can be especially useful if you are supporting a driver for a user at a different site. Users can be somewhat reluctant to copy down oops messages for you so installing a crash dump system can let you get the information you need to track down a user's problem without requiring work from him. It is thus not surprising that the available crash dump analyzers have been written by companies in the business of supporting systems for users.

There are currently two crash dump analyzer patches available for Linux. Both were relatively new when this section was written, and both were in a state of flux. Rather than provide detailed information that is likely to go out of date, we'll restrict ourselves to providing an overview and pointers to where more information can be found.

The first analyzer is LKCD (Linux Kernel Crash Dumps). It's available, once again, from *oss.sgi.com*. When a kernel oops occurs, LKCD will write a copy of the current system state (memory, primarily) into the dump device you specified in advance. The dump device must be a system swap area. A utility called *LCRASH* is run on the next reboot (before swapping is enabled) to generate a summary of the crash, and optionally to save a copy of the dump in a conventional file. *LCRASH* can be run interactively and provides a number of debugger-like commands for querying the state of the system.

LKCD is currently supported for the Intel 32-bit architecture only, and only works with swap partitions on SCSI disks.

Another crash dump facility is available from *www.missioncriticallinux.com*. This crash dump subsystem creates crash dump files directly in */var/dumps* and does not use the swap area. That makes certain things easier, but it also means that the system will be modifying the file system while in a state where things are known to have gone wrong. The crash dumps generated are in a standard core file format, so tools like *gdb* can be used for post-mortem analysis. This package also provides a separate analyzer that is able to extract more information than *gdb* from the crash dump files.

The User-Mode Linux Port

User-Mode Linux is an interesting concept. It is structured as a separate port of the Linux kernel, with its own *arch/um* subdirectory. It does not run on a new type of hardware, however; instead, it runs on a virtual machine implemented on the Linux system call interface. Thus, User-Mode Linux allows the Linux kernel to run as a separate, user-mode process on a Linux system.

Having a copy of the kernel running as a user-mode process brings a number of advantages. Because it is running on a constrained, virtual processor, a buggy kernel cannot damage the "real" system. Different hardware and software configurations can be tried easily on the same box. And, perhaps most significantly for kernel developers, the user-mode kernel can be easily manipulated with *gdb* or another debugger. After all, it is just another process. User-Mode Linux clearly has the potential to accelerate kernel development.

As of this writing, User-Mode Linux is not distributed with the mainline kernel; it must be downloaded from its web site (*http://user-mode-linux.sourceforge.net*). The word is that it will be integrated into an early 2.4 release after 2.4.0; it may well be there by the time this book is published.

User-Mode Linux also has some significant limitations as of this writing, most of which will likely be addressed soon. The virtual processor currently works in a uniprocessor mode only; the port runs on SMP systems without a problem, but it can only emulate a uniprocessor host. The biggest problem for driver writers, though, is that the user-mode kernel has no access to the host system's hardware. Thus, while it can be useful for debugging most of the sample drivers in this book, User-Mode Linux is not yet useful for debugging drivers that have to deal with real hardware. Finally, User-Mode Linux only runs on the IA-32 architecture.

Because work is under way to fix all of these problems, User-Mode Linux will likely be an indispensable tool for Linux device driver programmers in the very near future.

The Linux Trace Toolkit

The Linux Trace Toolkit (LTT) is a kernel patch and a set of related utilities that allow the tracing of events in the kernel. The trace includes timing information and can create a reasonably complete picture of what happened over a given period of time. Thus, it can be used not only for debugging but also for tracking down performance problems.

LTT, along with extensive documentation, can be found on the Web at *www.oper-sys.com/LTT.*

Dynamic Probes

Dynamic Probes (or DProbes) is a debugging tool released (under the GPL) by IBM for Linux on the IA-32 architecture. It allows the placement of a "probe" at almost any place in the system, in both user and kernel space. The probe consists of some code (written in a specialized, stack-oriented language) that is executed when control hits the given point. This code can report information back to user space, change registers, or do a number of other things. The useful feature of DProbes is that once the capability has been built into the kernel, probes can be inserted anywhere within a running system without kernel builds or reboots. DProbes can also work with the Linux Trace Toolkit to insert new tracing events at arbitrary locations.

The DProbes tool can be downloaded from IBM's open source site: *oss.soft-ware.ibm.com.*

## CHAPTER FIVE

ENHANCED CHAR DRIVER OPERATIONS

In Chapter 3, we built a complete device driver that the user can write to and read from. But a real device usually offers more functionality than synchronous *read* and *write*. Now that we're equipped with debugging tools should something go awry, we can safely go ahead and implement new operations.

What is normally needed, in addition to reading and writing the device, is the ability to perform various types of hardware control via the device driver. Control operations are usually supported via the *ioctl* method. The alternative is to look at the data flow being written to the device and use special sequences as control commands. This latter technique should be avoided because it requires reserving some characters for controlling purposes; thus, the data flow can't contain those characters. Moreover, this technique turns out to be more complex to handle than *ioctl*. Nonetheless, sometimes it's a useful approach to device control and is used by tty's and other devices. We'll describe it later in this chapter in "Device Control Without ioctl."

As we suggested in the previous chapter, the *ioctl* system call offers a device specific entry point for the driver to handle "commands." *ioctl* is device specific in that, unlike *read* and other methods, it allows applications to access features unique to the hardware being driven, such as configuring the device and entering or exiting operating modes. These control operations are usually not available through the read/write file abstraction. For example, everything you write to a serial port is used as communication data, and you cannot change the baud rate by writing to the device. That is what *ioctl* is for: controlling the I/O channel.

Another important feature of real devices (unlike *scull*) is that data being read or written is exchanged with other hardware, and some synchronization is needed. The concepts of blocking I/O and asynchronous notification fill the gap and are introduced in this chapter by means of a modified *scull* device. The driver uses interaction between different processes to create asynchronous events. As with the original *scull*, you don't need special hardware to test the driver's workings. We *will* definitely deal with real hardware, but not until Chapter 8.

ioctl

The *ioctl* function call in user space corresponds to the following prototype:

```
int ioctl(int fd, int cmd, ...);
```

The prototype stands out in the list of Unix system calls because of the dots, which usually represent not a variable number of arguments. In a real system, however, a system call can't actually have a variable number of arguments. System calls must have a well-defined number of arguments because user programs can access them only through hardware "gates," as outlined in "User Space and Kernel Space" in Chapter 2. Therefore, the dots in the prototype represent not a variable number of arguments but a single optional argument, traditionally identified as `char *argp`. The dots are simply there to prevent type checking during compilation. The actual nature of the third argument depends on the specific control command being issued (the second argument). Some commands take no arguments, some take an integer value, and some take a pointer to other data. Using a pointer is the way to pass arbitrary data to the *ioctl* call; the device will then be able to exchange any amount of data with user space.

The *ioctl* driver method, on the other hand, receives its arguments according to this declaration:

```
int (*ioctl) (struct inode *inode, struct file *filp,
        unsigned int cmd, unsigned long arg);
```

The `inode` and `filp` pointers are the values corresponding to the file descriptor `fd` passed on by the application and are the same parameters passed to the *open* method. The `cmd` argument is passed from the user unchanged, and the optional `arg` argument is passed in the form of an `unsigned long`, regardless of whether it was given by the user as an integer or a pointer. If the invoking program doesn't pass a third argument, the `arg` value received by the driver operation has no meaningful value.

Because type checking is disabled on the extra argument, the compiler can't warn you if an invalid argument is passed to *ioctl*, and the programmer won't notice the error until runtime. This lack of checking can be seen as a minor problem with the *ioctl* definition, but it is a necessary price for the general functionality that *ioctl* provides.

As you might imagine, most *ioctl* implementations consist of a `switch` statement that selects the correct behavior according to the `cmd` argument. Different commands have different numeric values, which are usually given symbolic names to simplify coding. The symbolic name is assigned by a preprocessor definition. Custom drivers usually declare such symbols in their header files; *scull.h* declares them for *scull*. User programs must, of course, include that header file as well to have access to those symbols.

Choosing the ioctl Commands

Before writing the code for *ioctl*, you need to choose the numbers that correspond to commands. Unfortunately, the simple choice of using small numbers starting from 1 and going up doesn't work well.

The command numbers should be unique across the system in order to prevent errors caused by issuing the right command to the wrong device. Such a mismatch is not unlikely to happen, and a program might find itself trying to change the baud rate of a non-serial-port input stream, such as a FIFO or an audio device. If each *ioctl* number is unique, then the application will get an **EINVAL** error rather than succeeding in doing something unintended.

To help programmers create unique *ioctl* command codes, these codes have been split up into several bitfields. The first versions of Linux used 16-bit numbers: the top eight were the "magic" number associated with the device, and the bottom eight were a sequential number, unique within the device. This happened because Linus was "clueless" (his own word); a better division of bitfields was conceived only later. Unfortunately, quite a few drivers still use the old convention. They have to: changing the command codes would break no end of binary programs. In our sources, however, we will use the new command code convention exclusively.

To choose *ioctl* numbers for your driver according to the new convention, you should first check *include/asm/ioctl.h* and *Documentation/ioctl-number.txt*. The header defines the bitfields you will be using: type (magic number), ordinal number, direction of transfer, and size of argument. The *ioctl-number.txt* file lists the magic numbers used throughout the kernel, so you'll be able to choose your own magic number and avoid overlaps. The text file also lists the reasons why the convention should be used.

The old, and now deprecated, way of choosing an *ioctl* number was easy: authors chose a magic eight-bit number, such as "k" (hex `0x6b`), and added an ordinal number, like this:

```
#define SCULL_IOCTL1 0x6b01
#define SCULL_IOCTL2 0x6b02
/* .... */
```

If both the application and the driver agreed on the numbers, you only needed to implement the **switch** statement in your driver. However, this way of defining *ioctl* numbers, which had its foundations in Unix tradition, shouldn't be used any more. We've only shown the old way to give you a taste of what *ioctl* numbers look like.

The new way to define numbers uses four bitfields, which have the following meanings. Any new symbols we introduce in the following list are defined in `<linux/ioctl.h>`.

type
> The magic number. Just choose one number (after consulting *ioctl-number.txt*) and use it throughout the driver. This field is eight bits wide (_IOC_TYPEBITS).

number
> The ordinal (sequential) number. It's eight bits (_IOC_NRBITS) wide.

direction
> The direction of data transfer, if the particular command involves a data transfer. The possible values are _IOC_NONE (no data transfer), _IOC_READ, _IOC_WRITE, and _IOC_READ | _IOC_WRITE (data is transferred both ways). Data transfer is seen from the application's point of view; _IOC_READ means reading *from* the device, so the driver must write to user space. Note that the field is a bit mask, so _IOC_READ and _IOC_WRITE can be extracted using a logical AND operation.

size
> The size of user data involved. The width of this field is architecture dependent and currently ranges from 8 to 14 bits. You can find its value for your specific architecture in the macro _IOC_SIZEBITS. If you intend your driver to be portable, however, you can only count on a size up to 255. It's not mandatory that you use the size field. If you need larger data structures, you can just ignore it. We'll see soon how this field is used.

The header file <asm/ioctl.h>, which is included by <linux/ioctl.h>, defines macros that help set up the command numbers as follows: _IO(type,nr), _IOR(type,nr,dataitem), _IOW(type,nr,dataitem), and _IOWR(type,nr,dataitem). Each macro corresponds to one of the possible values for the direction of the transfer. The type and number fields are passed as arguments, and the size field is derived by applying *sizeof* to the dataitem argument. The header also defines macros to decode the numbers: _IOC_DIR(nr), _IOC_TYPE(nr), _IOC_NR(nr), and _IOC_SIZE(nr). We won't go into any more detail about these macros because the header file is clear, and sample code is shown later in this section.

Here is how some *ioctl* commands are defined in *scull*. In particular, these commands set and get the driver's configurable parameters.

```
/* Use 'k' as magic number */
#define SCULL_IOC_MAGIC 'k'

#define SCULL_IOCRESET _IO(SCULL_IOC_MAGIC, 0)

/*
 * S means "Set" through a ptr
 * T means "Tell" directly with the argument value
 * G means "Get": reply by setting through a pointer
 * Q means "Query": response is on the return value
```

```
 * X means "eXchange": G and S atomically
 * H means "sHift": T and Q atomically
 */
#define SCULL_IOCSQUANTUM _IOW(SCULL_IOC_MAGIC, 1, scull_quantum)
#define SCULL_IOCSQSET   _IOW(SCULL_IOC_MAGIC, 2, scull_qset)
#define SCULL_IOCTQUANTUM _IO(SCULL_IOC_MAGIC,  3)
#define SCULL_IOCTQSET   _IO(SCULL_IOC_MAGIC,  4)
#define SCULL_IOCGQUANTUM _IOR(SCULL_IOC_MAGIC, 5, scull_quantum)
#define SCULL_IOCGQSET   _IOR(SCULL_IOC_MAGIC, 6, scull_qset)
#define SCULL_IOCQQUANTUM _IO(SCULL_IOC_MAGIC,  7)
#define SCULL_IOCQQSET   _IO(SCULL_IOC_MAGIC,  8)
#define SCULL_IOCXQUANTUM _IOWR(SCULL_IOC_MAGIC, 9, scull_quantum)
#define SCULL_IOCXQSET   _IOWR(SCULL_IOC_MAGIC,10, scull_qset)
#define SCULL_IOCHQUANTUM _IO(SCULL_IOC_MAGIC, 11)
#define SCULL_IOCHQSET   _IO(SCULL_IOC_MAGIC, 12)
#define SCULL_IOCHARDRESET _IO(SCULL_IOC_MAGIC, 15) /* debugging tool */

#define SCULL_IOC_MAXNR 15
```

The last command, HARDRESET, is used to reset the module's usage count to 0 so that the module can be unloaded should something go wrong with the counter. The actual source file also defines all the commands between IOCHQSET and HARDRESET, although they're not shown here.

We chose to implement both ways of passing integer arguments—by pointer and by explicit value, although by an established convention *ioctl* should exchange values by pointer. Similarly, both ways are used to return an integer number: by pointer or by setting the return value. This works as long as the return value is a positive integer; on return from any system call, a positive value is preserved (as we saw for *read* and *write*), while a negative value is considered an error and is used to set `errno` in user space.

The "exchange" and "shift" operations are not particularly useful for *scull*. We implemented "exchange" to show how the driver can combine separate operations into a single *atomic* one, and "shift" to pair "tell" and "query." There are times when atomic* test-and-set operations like these are needed, in particular, when applications need to set or release locks.

The explicit ordinal number of the command has no specific meaning. It is used only to tell the commands apart. Actually, you could even use the same ordinal number for a read command and a write command, since the actual *ioctl* number is different in the "direction" bits, but there is no reason why you would want to do so. We chose not to use the ordinal number of the command anywhere but in the declaration, so we didn't assign a symbolic value to it. That's why explicit

---

* A fragment of program code is said to be atomic when it will always be executed as though it were a single instruction, without the possibility of the processor being interrupted and something happening in between (such as somebody else's code running).

numbers appear in the definition given previously. The example shows one way to use the command numbers, but you are free to do it differently.

The value of the *ioctl* `cmd` argument is not currently used by the kernel, and it's quite unlikely it will be in the future. Therefore, you could, if you were feeling lazy, avoid the complex declarations shown earlier and explicitly declare a set of scalar numbers. On the other hand, if you did, you wouldn't benefit from using the bitfields. The header `<linux/kd.h>` is an example of this old-fashioned approach, using 16-bit scalar values to define the *ioctl* commands. That source file relied on scalar numbers because it used the technology then available, not out of laziness. Changing it now would be a gratuitous incompatibility.

The Return Value

The implementation of *ioctl* is usually a `switch` statement based on the command number. But what should the `default` selection be when the command number doesn't match a valid operation? The question is controversial. Several kernel functions return `-EINVAL` ("Invalid argument"), which makes sense because the command argument is indeed not a valid one. The POSIX standard, however, states that if an inappropriate *ioctl* command has been issued, then `-ENOTTY` should be returned. The string associated with that value used to be "Not a typewriter" under all libraries up to and including *libc5*. Only *libc6* changed the message to "Inappropriate ioctl for device," which looks more to the point. Because most recent Linux system are *libc6* based, we'll stick to the standard and return `-ENOTTY`. It's still pretty common, though, to return `-EINVAL` in response to an invalid *ioctl* command.

The Predefined Commands

Though the *ioctl* system call is most often used to act on devices, a few commands are recognized by the kernel. Note that these commands, when applied to your device, are decoded *before* your own file operations are called. Thus, if you choose the same number for one of your *ioctl* commands, you won't ever see any request for that command, and the application will get something unexpected because of the conflict between the *ioctl* numbers.

The predefined commands are divided into three groups:

*   Those that can be issued on any file (regular, device, *FIFO*, or socket)

*   Those that are issued only on regular files

*   Those specific to the filesystem type

Commands in the last group are executed by the implementation of the hosting filesystem (see the *chattr* command). Device driver writers are interested only in the first group of commands, whose magic number is "T." Looking at the workings of the other groups is left to the reader as an exercise; *ext2_ioctl* is a most interesting function (though easier than you may expect), because it implements the append-only flag and the immutable flag.

The following *ioctl* commands are predefined for any file:

FIOCLEX

Set the close-on-exec flag (File IOctl CLose on EXec). Setting this flag will cause the file descriptor to be closed when the calling process executes a new program.

FIONCLEX

Clear the close-on-exec flag.

FIOASYNC

Set or reset asynchronous notification for the file (as discussed in "Asynchronous Notification" later in this chapter). Note that kernel versions up to Linux 2.2.4 incorrectly used this command to modify the O_SYNC flag. Since both actions can be accomplished in other ways, nobody actually uses the FIOASYNC command, which is reported here only for completeness.

FIONBIO

"File IOctl Non-Blocking I/O" (described later in this chapter in "Blocking and Nonblocking Operations"). This call modifies the O_NONBLOCK flag in filp->f_flags. The third argument to the system call is used to indicate whether the flag is to be set or cleared. We'll look at the role of the flag later in this chapter. Note that the flag can also be changed by the *fcntl* system call, using the *F_SETFL* command.

The last item in the list introduced a new system call, *fcntl*, which looks like *ioctl*. In fact, the *fcntl* call is very similar to *ioctl* in that it gets a command argument and an extra (optional) argument. It is kept separate from *ioctl* mainly for historical reasons: when Unix developers faced the problem of controlling I/O operations, they decided that files and devices were different. At the time, the only devices with *ioctl* implementations were ttys, which explains why -ENOTTY is the standard reply for an incorrect *ioctl* command. Things have changed, but *fcntl* remains in the name of backward compatibility.

Using the ioctl Argument

Another point we need to cover before looking at the *ioctl* code for the *scull* driver is how to use the extra argument. If it is an integer, it's easy: it can be used directly. If it is a pointer, however, some care must be taken.

When a pointer is used to refer to user space, we must ensure that the user address is valid and that the corresponding page is currently mapped. If kernel code tries to access an out-of-range address, the processor issues an exception.

Exceptions in kernel code are turned to oops messages by every Linux kernel up through 2.0.*x*; version 2.1 and later handle the problem more gracefully. In any case, it's the driver's responsibility to make proper checks on every user-space address it uses and to return an error if it is invalid.

Address verification for kernels 2.2.*x* and beyond is implemented by the function *access_ok*, which is declared in <asm/uaccess.h>:

```
int access_ok(int type, const void *addr, unsigned long size);
```

The first argument should be either VERIFY_READ or VERIFY_WRITE, depending on whether the action to be performed is reading the user-space memory area or writing it. The addr argument holds a user-space address, and size is a byte count. If *ioctl*, for instance, needs to read an integer value from user space, size is sizeof(int). If you need to both read and write at the given address, use VERIFY_WRITE, since it is a superset of VERIFY_READ.

Unlike most functions, *access_ok* returns a boolean value: 1 for success (access is OK) and 0 for failure (access is not OK). If it returns false, the driver will usually return −EFAULT to the caller.

There are a couple of interesting things to note about *access_ok*. First is that it does not do the complete job of verifying memory access; it only checks to see that the memory reference is in a region of memory that the process might reasonably have access to. In particular, *access_ok* ensures that the address does not point to kernel-space memory. Second, most driver code need not actually call *access_ok*. The memory-access routines described later take care of that for you. We will nonetheless demonstrate its use so that you can see how it is done, and for backward compatibility reasons that we will get into toward the end of the chapter.

The *scull* source exploits the bitfields in the *ioctl* number to check the arguments before the switch:

```
int err = 0, tmp;
int ret = 0;

/*
 * extract the type and number bitfields, and don't decode
 * wrong cmds: return ENOTTY (inappropriate ioctl) before access_ok()
 */
if (_IOC_TYPE(cmd) != SCULL_IOC_MAGIC) return -ENOTTY;
if (_IOC_NR(cmd) > SCULL_IOC_MAXNR) return -ENOTTY;

/*
 * the direction is a bitmask, and VERIFY_WRITE catches R/W
 * transfers. 'Type' is user oriented, while
 * access_ok is kernel oriented, so the concept of "read" and
 * "write" is reversed
 */
```

```
if (_IOC_DIR(cmd) & _IOC_READ)
   err = !access_ok(VERIFY_WRITE, (void *)arg, _IOC_SIZE(cmd));
else if (_IOC_DIR(cmd) & _IOC_WRITE)
   err = !access_ok(VERIFY_READ, (void *)arg, _IOC_SIZE(cmd));
if (err) return -EFAULT;
```

After calling *access_ok*, the driver can safely perform the actual transfer. In addition to the *copy_from_user* and *copy_to_user* functions, the programmer can exploit a set of functions that are optimized for the most-used data sizes (one, two, and four bytes, as well as eight bytes on 64-bit platforms). These functions are described in the following list and are defined in `<asm/uaccess.h>`.

`put_user(datum, ptr)`
`__put_user(datum, ptr)`

These macros write the datum to user space; they are relatively fast, and should be called instead of *copy_to_user* whenever single values are being transferred. Since type checking is not performed on macro expansion, you can pass any type of pointer to *put_user*, as long as it is a user-space address. The size of the data transfer depends on the type of the `ptr` argument and is determined at compile time using a special *gcc* pseudo-function that isn't worth showing here. As a result, if `ptr` is a char pointer, one byte is transferred, and so on for two, four, and possibly eight bytes.

put_user checks to ensure that the process is able to write to the given memory address. It returns 0 on success, and –**EFAULT** on error. *__put_user* performs less checking (it does not call *access_ok*), but can still fail on some kinds of bad addresses. Thus, *__put_user* should only be used if the memory region has already been verified with *access_ok*.

As a general rule, you'll call *__put_user* to save a few cycles when you are implementing a *read* method, or when you copy several items and thus call *access_ok* just once before the first data transfer.

`get_user(local, ptr)`
`__get_user(local, ptr)`

These macros are used to retrieve a single datum from user space. They behave like *put_user* and *__put_user*, but transfer data in the opposite direction. The value retrieved is stored in the local variable `local`; the return value indicates whether the operation succeeded or not. Again, *__get_user* should only be used if the address has already been verified with *access_ok*.

If an attempt is made to use one of the listed functions to transfer a value that does not fit one of the specific sizes, the result is usually a strange message from the compiler, such as "conversion to non-scalar type requested." In such cases, *copy_to_user* or *copy_from_user* must be used.

Capabilities and Restricted Operations

Access to a device is controlled by the permissions on the device file(s), and the driver is not normally involved in permissions checking. There are situations, however, where any user is granted read/write permission on the device, but some other operations should be denied. For example, not all users of a tape drive should be able to set its default block size, and the ability to work with a disk device does not mean that the user can reformat the drive. In cases like these, the driver must perform additional checks to be sure that the user is capable of performing the requested operation.

Unix systems have traditionally restricted privileged operations to the superuser account. Privilege is an all-or-nothing thing—the superuser can do absolutely anything, but all other users are highly restricted. The Linux kernel as of version 2.2 provides a more flexible system called *capabilities*. A capability-based system leaves the all-or-nothing mode behind and breaks down privileged operations into separate subgroups. In this way, a particular user (or program) can be empowered to perform a specific privileged operation without giving away the ability to perform other, unrelated operations. Capabilities are still little used in user space, but kernel code uses them almost exclusively.

The full set of capabilities can be found in `<linux/capability.h>`. A subset of those capabilities that might be of interest to device driver writers includes the following:

CAP_DAC_OVERRIDE
: The ability to override access restrictions on files and directories.

CAP_NET_ADMIN
: The ability to perform network administration tasks, including those which affect network interfaces.

CAP_SYS_MODULE
: The ability to load or remove kernel modules.

CAP_SYS_RAWIO
: The ability to perform "raw" I/O operations. Examples include accessing device ports or communicating directly with USB devices.

CAP_SYS_ADMIN
: A catch-all capability that provides access to many system administration operations.

CAP_SYS_TTY_CONFIG
: The ability to perform tty configuration tasks.

Before performing a privileged operation, a device driver should check that the calling process has the appropriate capability with the *capable* function (defined in `<sys/sched.h>`):

```
int capable(int capability);
```

In the *scull* sample driver, any user is allowed to query the quantum and quantum set sizes. Only privileged users, however, may change those values, since inappropriate values could badly affect system performance. When needed, the *scull* implementation of *ioctl* checks a user's privilege level as follows:

```
if (! capable (CAP_SYS_ADMIN))
    return -EPERM;
```

In the absence of a more specific capability for this task, **CAP_SYS_ADMIN** was chosen for this test.

The Implementation of the ioctl Commands

The *scull* implementation of *ioctl* only transfers the configurable parameters of the device and turns out to be as easy as the following:

```
    switch(cmd) {

#ifdef SCULL_DEBUG
    case SCULL_IOCHARDRESET:
      /*
       * reset the counter to 1, to allow unloading in case
       * of problems. Use 1, not 0, because the invoking
       * process has the device open.
       */
      while (MOD_IN_USE)
        MOD_DEC_USE_COUNT;
      MOD_INC_USE_COUNT;
      /* don't break: fall through and reset things */
#endif /* SCULL_DEBUG */

    case SCULL_IOCRESET:
      scull_quantum = SCULL_QUANTUM;
      scull_qset = SCULL_QSET;
      break;

    case SCULL_IOCSQUANTUM: /* Set: arg points to the value */
      if (! capable (CAP_SYS_ADMIN))
        return -EPERM;
      ret = __get_user(scull_quantum, (int *)arg);
      break;

    case SCULL_IOCTQUANTUM: /* Tell: arg is the value */
      if (! capable (CAP_SYS_ADMIN))
        return -EPERM;
      scull_quantum = arg;
      break;
```

```
case SCULL_IOCGQUANTUM: /* Get: arg is pointer to result */
  ret = __put_user(scull_quantum, (int *)arg);
  break;

case SCULL_IOCQQUANTUM: /* Query: return it (it's positive) */
  return scull_quantum;

case SCULL_IOCXQUANTUM: /* eXchange: use arg as pointer */
  if (! capable (CAP_SYS_ADMIN))
    return -EPERM;
  tmp = scull_quantum;
  ret = __get_user(scull_quantum, (int *)arg);
  if (ret == 0)
    ret = __put_user(tmp, (int *)arg);
  break;

case SCULL_IOCHQUANTUM: /* sHift: like Tell + Query */
  if (! capable (CAP_SYS_ADMIN))
    return -EPERM;
  tmp = scull_quantum;
  scull_quantum = arg;
  return tmp;

default: /* redundant, as cmd was checked against MAXNR */
  return -ENOTTY;
}
return ret;
```

scull also includes six entries that act on `scull_qset`. These entries are identical to the ones for `scull_quantum` and are not worth showing in print.

The six ways to pass and receive arguments look like the following from the caller's point of view (i.e., from user space):

```
int quantum;

ioctl(fd,SCULL_IOCSQUANTUM, &quantum);
ioctl(fd,SCULL_IOCTQUANTUM, quantum);

ioctl(fd,SCULL_IOCGQUANTUM, &quantum);
quantum = ioctl(fd,SCULL_IOCQQUANTUM);

ioctl(fd,SCULL_IOCXQUANTUM, &quantum);
quantum = ioctl(fd,SCULL_IOCHQUANTUM, quantum);
```

Of course, a normal driver would not implement such a mix of calling modes in one place. We have done so here only to demonstrate the different ways in which things could be done. Normally, however, data exchanges would be consistently performed, either through pointers (more common) or by value (less common), and mixing of the two techniques would be avoided.

Device Control Without ioctl

Sometimes controlling the device is better accomplished by writing control sequences to the device itself. This technique is used, for example, in the console driver, where so-called escape sequences are used to move the cursor, change the default color, or perform other configuration tasks. The benefit of implementing device control this way is that the user can control the device just by writing data, without needing to use (or sometimes write) programs built just for configuring the device.

For example, the *setterm* program acts on the console (or another terminal) configuration by printing escape sequences. This behavior has the advantage of permitting the remote control of devices. The controlling program can live on a different computer than the controlled device, because a simple redirection of the data stream does the configuration job. You're already used to this with ttys, but the technique is more general.

The drawback of controlling by printing is that it adds policy constraints to the device; for example, it is viable only if you are sure that the control sequence can't appear in the data being written to the device during normal operation. This is only partly true for ttys. Although a text display is meant to display only ASCII characters, sometimes control characters can slip through in the data being written and can thus affect the console setup. This can happen, for example, when you issue *grep* on a binary file; the extracted lines can contain anything, and you often end up with the wrong font on your console.*

Controlling by write *is* definitely the way to go for those devices that don't transfer data but just respond to commands, such as robotic devices.

For instance, a driver written for fun by one of your authors moves a camera on two axes. In this driver, the "device" is simply a pair of old stepper motors, which can't really be read from or written to. The concept of "sending a data stream" to a stepper motor makes little or no sense. In this case, the driver interprets what is being written as ASCII commands and converts the requests to sequences of impulses that manipulate the stepper motors. The idea is similar, somewhat, to the AT commands you send to the modem in order to set up communication, the main difference being that the serial port used to communicate with the modem must transfer real data as well. The advantage of direct device control is that you can use *cat* to move the camera without writing and compiling special code to issue the *ioctl* calls.

---

* CTRL-N sets the alternate font, which is made up of graphic symbols and thus isn't a friendly font for typing input to your shell; if you encounter this problem, echo a CTRL-O character to restore the primary font.

When writing command-oriented drivers, there's no reason to implement the *ioctl* method. An additional command in the interpreter is easier to implement and use.

Sometimes, though, you might choose to act the other way around: instead of making *write* into an interpreter and avoiding *ioctl*, you might choose to avoid *write* altogether and use *ioctl* commands exclusively, while accompanying the driver with a specific command-line tool to send those commands to the driver. This approach moves the complexity from kernel space to user space, where it may be easier to deal with, and helps keep the driver small while denying use of simple *cat* or *echo* commands.

Blocking I/O

One problem that might arise with *read* is what to do when there's no data *yet*, but we're not at end-of-file.

The default answer is "go to sleep waiting for data." This section shows how a process is put to sleep, how it is awakened, and how an application can ask if there is data without just blindly issuing a *read* call and blocking. We then apply the same concepts to *write*.

As usual, before we show actual code, we'll explain a few concepts.

Going to Sleep and Awakening

Whenever a process must wait for an event (such as the arrival of data or the termination of a process), it should go to sleep. Sleeping causes the process to suspend execution, freeing the processor for other uses. At some future time, when the event being waited for occurs, the process will be woken up and will continue with its job. This section discusses the 2.4 machinery for putting a process to sleep and waking it up. Earlier versions are discussed in "Backward Compatibility" later in this chapter.

There are several ways of handling sleeping and waking up in Linux, each suited to different needs. All, however, work with the same basic data type, a wait queue (`wait_queue_head_t`). A *wait queue* is exactly that—a queue of processes that are waiting for an event. Wait queues are declared and initialized as follows:

```
wait_queue_head_t my_queue;
init_waitqueue_head (&my_queue);
```

When a wait queue is declared statically (i.e., not as an automatic variable of a procedure or as part of a dynamically-allocated data structure), it is also possible to initialize the queue at compile time:

```
DECLARE_WAIT_QUEUE_HEAD (my_queue);
```

It is a common mistake to neglect to initialize a wait queue (especially since earlier versions of the kernel did not require this initialization); if you forget, the results will usually not be what you intended.

Once the wait queue is declared and initialized, a process may use it to go to sleep. Sleeping is accomplished by calling one of the variants of *sleep_on*, depending on how deep a sleep is called for.

`sleep_on(wait_queue_head_t *queue);`
> Puts the process to sleep on this queue. *sleep_on* has the disadvantage of not being interruptible; as a result, the process can end up being stuck (and unkillable) if the event it's waiting for never happens.

`interruptible_sleep_on(wait_queue_head_t *queue);`
> The interruptible variant works just like *sleep_on*, except that the sleep can be interrupted by a signal. This is the form that device driver writers have been using for a long time, before *wait_event_interruptible* (described later) appeared.

`sleep_on_timeout(wait_queue_head_t *queue, long timeout);`
`interruptible_sleep_on_timeout(wait_queue_head_t *queue,`
`        long timeout);`
> These two functions behave like the previous two, with the exception that the sleep will last no longer than the given timeout period. The timeout is specified in "jiffies," which are covered in Chapter 6.

`void wait_event(wait_queue_head_t queue, int condition);`
`int wait_event_interruptible(wait_queue_head_t queue, int`
`        condition);`
> These macros are the preferred way to sleep on an event. They combine waiting for an event and testing for its arrival in a way that avoids race conditions. They will sleep until the condition, which may be any boolean C expression, evaluates true. The macros expand to a *while* loop, and the condition is reevaluated over time—the behavior is different from that of a function call or a simple macro, where the arguments are evaluated only at call time. The latter macro is implemented as an expression that evaluates to 0 in case of success and `-ERESTARTSYS` if the loop is interrupted by a signal.

It is worth repeating that driver writers should almost always use the *interruptible* instances of these functions/macros. The noninterruptible version exists for the small number of situations in which signals cannot be dealt with, for example, when waiting for a data page to be retrieved from swap space. Most drivers do not present such special situations.

Of course, sleeping is only half of the problem; something, somewhere will have to wake the process up again. When a device driver sleeps directly, there is usually code in another part of the driver that performs the wakeup, once it knows that the event has occurred. Typically a driver will wake up sleepers in its interrupt handler once new data has arrived. Other scenarios are possible, however.

Just as there is more than one way to sleep, so there is also more than one way to wake up. The high-level functions provided by the kernel to wake up processes are as follows:

`wake_up(wait_queue_head_t *queue);`
This function will wake up all processes that are waiting on this event queue.

`wake_up_interruptible(wait_queue_head_t *queue);`
wake_up_interruptible wakes up only the processes that are in interruptible sleeps. Any process that sleeps on the wait queue using a noninterruptible function or macro will continue to sleep.

`wake_up_sync(wait_queue_head_t *queue);`
`wake_up_interruptible_sync(wait_queue_head_t *queue);`
Normally, a *wake_up* call can cause an immediate reschedule to happen, meaning that other processes might run before *wake_up* returns. The "synchronous" variants instead make any awakened processes runnable, but do not reschedule the CPU. This is used to avoid rescheduling when the current process is known to be going to sleep, thus forcing a reschedule anyway. Note that awakened processes could run immediately on a different processor, so these functions should not be expected to provide mutual exclusion.

If your driver is using *interruptible_sleep_on*, there is little difference between *wake_up* and *wake_up_interruptible*. Calling the latter is a common convention, however, to preserve consistency between the two calls.

As an example of wait queue usage, imagine you want to put a process to sleep when it reads your device and awaken it when someone else writes to the device. The following code does just that:

```
DECLARE_WAIT_QUEUE_HEAD(wq);

ssize_t sleepy_read (struct file *filp, char *buf, size_t count,
    loff_t *pos)
{
  printk(KERN_DEBUG "process %i (%s) going to sleep\n",
      current->pid, current->comm);
  interruptible_sleep_on(&wq);
  printk(KERN_DEBUG "awoken %i (%s)\n", current->pid, current->comm);
  return 0; /* EOF */
}
```

```
ssize_t sleepy_write (struct file *filp, const char *buf, size_t count,
                loff_t *pos)
{
  printk(KERN_DEBUG "process %i (%s) awakening the readers...\n",
      current->pid, current->comm);
  wake_up_interruptible(&wq);
  return count; /* succeed, to avoid retrial */
}
```

The code for this device is available as sleepy in the example programs and can be tested using *cat* and input/output redirection, as usual.

An important thing to remember with wait queues is that being woken up does not guarantee that the event you were waiting for has occurred; a process can be woken for other reasons, mainly because it received a signal. Any code that sleeps should do so in a loop that tests the condition after returning from the sleep, as discussed in "A Sample Implementation: scullpipe" later in this chapter.

A Deeper Look at Wait Queues

The previous discussion is all that most driver writers will need to know to get their job done. Some, however, will want to dig deeper. This section attempts to get the curious started; everybody else can skip to the next section without missing much that is important.

The `wait_queue_head_t` type is a fairly simple structure, defined in `<linux/wait.h>`. It contains only a lock variable and a linked list of sleeping processes. The individual data items in the list are of type `wait_queue_t`, and the list is the generic list defined in `<linux/list.h>` and described in "Linked Lists" in Chapter 10. Normally the `wait_queue_t` structures are allocated on the stack by functions like *interruptible_sleep_on*; the structures end up in the stack because they are simply declared as automatic variables in the relevant functions. In general, the programmer need not deal with them.

Some advanced applications, however, can require dealing with `wait_queue_t` variables directly. For these, it's worth a quick look at what actually goes on inside a function like *interruptible_sleep_on*. The following is a *simplified* version of the implementation of *interruptible_sleep_on* to put a process to sleep:

```
void simplified_sleep_on(wait_queue_head_t *queue)
{
  wait_queue_t wait;

  init_waitqueue_entry(&wait, current);
  current->state = TASK_INTERRUPTIBLE;

  add_wait_queue(queue, &wait);
  schedule();
  remove_wait_queue (queue, &wait);
}
```

The code here creates a new `wait_queue_t` variable (`wait`, which gets allocated on the stack) and initializes it. The state of the task is set to `TASK_INTER-RUPTIBLE`, meaning that it is in an interruptible sleep. The wait queue entry is then added to the queue (the `wait_queue_head_t *` argument). Then *schedule* is called, which relinquishes the processor to somebody else. *schedule* returns only when somebody else has woken up the process and set its state to `TASK_RUNNING`. At that point, the wait queue entry is removed from the queue, and the sleep is done.

Figure 5-1 shows the internals of the data structures involved in wait queues and how they are used by processes.

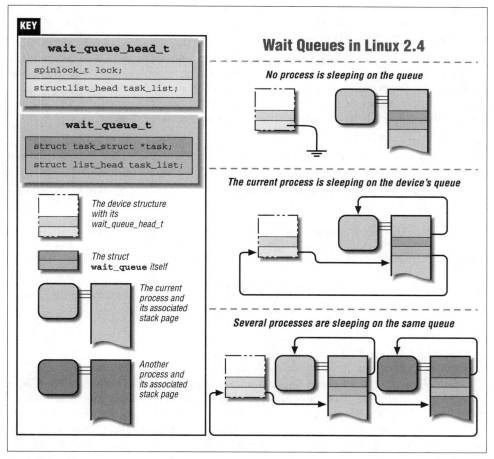

Figure 5-1. Wait queues in Linux 2.4

A quick look through the kernel shows that a great many procedures do their sleeping "manually" with code that looks like the previous example. Most of those implementations date back to kernels prior to 2.2.3, before *wait_event* was introduced. As suggested, *wait_event* is now the preferred way to sleep on an event, because *interruptible_sleep_on* is subject to unpleasant race conditions. A full description of how that can happen will have to wait until "Going to Sleep Without Races" in Chapter 9; the short version, simply, is that things can change in the time between when your driver decides to sleep and when it actually gets around to calling *interruptible_sleep_on*.

One other reason for calling the scheduler explicitly, however, is to do *exclusive* waits. There can be situations in which several processes are waiting on an event; when *wake_up* is called, all of those processes will try to execute. Suppose that the event signifies the arrival of an atomic piece of data. Only one process will be able to read that data; all the rest will simply wake up, see that no data is available, and go back to sleep.

This situation is sometimes referred to as the "thundering herd problem." In high-performance situations, thundering herds can waste resources in a big way. The creation of a large number of runnable processes that can do no useful work generates a large number of context switches and processor overhead, all for nothing. Things would work better if those processes simply remained asleep.

For this reason, the 2.3 development series added the concept of an *exclusive sleep*. If processes sleep in an exclusive mode, they are telling the kernel to wake only one of them. The result is improved performance in some situations.

The code to perform an exclusive sleep looks very similar to that for a regular sleep:

```
void simplified_sleep_exclusive(wait_queue_head_t *queue)
{
  wait_queue_t wait;

  init_waitqueue_entry(&wait, current);
  current->state = TASK_INTERRUPTIBLE | TASK_EXCLUSIVE;

  add_wait_queue_exclusive(queue, &wait);
  schedule();
  remove_wait_queue (queue, &wait);
}
```

Adding the `TASK_EXCLUSIVE` flag to the task state indicates that the process is in an exclusive wait. The call to *add_wait_queue_exclusive* is also necessary, however. That function adds the process to the *end* of the wait queue, behind all others. The purpose is to leave any processes in nonexclusive sleeps at the beginning, where they will always be awakened. As soon as *wake_up* hits the first exclusive sleeper, it knows it can stop.

The attentive reader may have noticed another reason to manipulate wait queues and the scheduler explicitly. Whereas functions like *sleep_on* will block a process on exactly one wait queue, working with the queues directly allows sleeping on multiple queues simultaneously. Most drivers need not sleep on more than one queue; if yours is the exception, you will need to use code like what we've shown.

Those wanting to dig even deeper into the wait queue code can look at <linux/sched.h> and kernel/sched.c.

Writing Reentrant Code

When a process is put to sleep, the driver is still alive and can be called by another process. Let's consider the console driver as an example. While an application is waiting for keyboard input on tty1, the user switches to tty2 and spawns a new shell. Now both shells are waiting for keyboard input within the console driver, although they sleep on different wait queues: one on the queue associated with tty1 and the other on the queue associated with tty2. Each process is blocked within the *interruptible_sleep_on* function, but the driver can still receive and answer requests from other ttys.

Of course, on SMP systems, multiple simultaneous calls to your driver can happen even when you do not sleep.

Such situations can be handled painlessly by writing *reentrant code*. Reentrant code is code that doesn't keep status information in global variables and thus is able to manage interwoven invocations without mixing anything up. If all the status information is process specific, no interference will ever happen.

If status information is needed, it can either be kept in local variables within the driver function (each process has a different stack page in kernel space where local variables are stored), or it can reside in private_data within the filp accessing the file. Using local variables is preferred because sometimes the same filp can be shared between two processes (usually parent and child).

If you need to save large amounts of status data, you can keep the pointer in a local variable and use *kmalloc* to retrieve the actual storage space. In this case you must remember to *kfree* the data, because there's no equivalent to "everything is released at process termination" when you're working in kernel space. Using local variables for large items is not good practice, because the data may not fit the single page of memory allocated for stack space.

You need to make reentrant any function that matches either of two conditions. First, if it calls *schedule*, possibly by calling *sleep_on* or *wake_up*. Second, if it copies data to or from user space, because access to user space might page-fault, and the process will be put to sleep while the kernel deals with the missing page.

Every function that calls any such functions must be reentrant as well. For example, if *sample_read* calls *sample_getdata*, which in turn can block, then *sample_read* must be reentrant as well as *sample_getdata*, because nothing prevents another process from calling it while it is already executing on behalf of a process that went to sleep.

Finally, of course, code that sleeps should always keep in mind that the state of the system can change in almost any way while a process is sleeping. The driver should be careful to check any aspect of its environment that might have changed while it wasn't paying attention.

Blocking and Nonblocking Operations

Another point we need to touch on before we look at the implementation of full-featured *read* and *write* methods is the role of the O_NONBLOCK flag in filp->f_flags. The flag is defined in <linux/fcntl.h>, which is automatically included by <linux/fs.h>.

The flag gets its name from "open-nonblock," because it can be specified at open time (and originally could only be specified there). If you browse the source code, you'll find some references to an O_NDELAY flag; this is an alternate name for O_NONBLOCK, accepted for compatibility with System V code. The flag is cleared by default, because the normal behavior of a process waiting for data is just to sleep. In the case of a blocking operation, which is the default, the following behavior should be implemented in order to adhere to the standard semantics:

- If a process calls *read* but no data is (yet) available, the process must block. The process is awakened as soon as some data arrives, and that data is returned to the caller, even if there is less than the amount requested in the count argument to the method.

- If a process calls *write* and there is no space in the buffer, the process must block, and it must be on a different wait queue from the one used for reading. When some data has been written to the hardware device, and space becomes free in the output buffer, the process is awakened and the *write* call succeeds, although the data may be only partially written if there isn't room in the buffer for the count bytes that were requested.

Both these statements assume that there are both input and output buffers; in practice, almost every device driver has them. The input buffer is required to avoid losing data that arrives when nobody is reading. In contrast, data can't be lost on *write*, because if the system call doesn't accept data bytes, they remain in the userspace buffer. Even so, the output buffer is almost always useful for squeezing more performance out of the hardware.

The performance gain of implementing an output buffer in the driver results from the reduced number of context switches and user-level/kernel-level transitions. Without an output buffer (assuming a slow device), only one or a few characters are accepted by each system call, and while one process sleeps in *write*, another process runs (that's one context switch). When the first process is awakened, it resumes (another context switch), *write* returns (kernel/user transition), and the process reiterates the system call to write more data (user/kernel transition); the call blocks, and the loop continues. If the output buffer is big enough, the *write* call succeeds on the first attempt—the buffered data will be pushed out to the device later, at interrupt time—without control needing to go back to user space for a second or third *write* call. The choice of a suitable size for the output buffer is clearly device specific.

We didn't use an input buffer in *scull*, because data is already available when *read* is issued. Similarly, no output buffer was used, because data is simply copied to the memory area associated with the device. Essentially, the device *is* a buffer, so the implementation of additional buffers would be superfluous. We'll see the use of buffers in Chapter 9, in the section titled "Interrupt-Driven I/O."

The behavior of *read* and *write* is different if O_NONBLOCK is specified. In this case, the calls simply return -EAGAIN if a process calls *read* when no data is available or if it calls *write* when there's no space in the buffer.

As you might expect, nonblocking operations return immediately, allowing the application to poll for data. Applications must be careful when using the *stdio* functions while dealing with nonblocking files, because they can easily mistake a nonblocking return for EOF. They always have to check errno.

Naturally, O_NONBLOCK is meaningful in the *open* method also. This happens when the call can actually block for a long time; for example, when opening a FIFO that has no writers (yet), or accessing a disk file with a pending lock. Usually, opening a device either succeeds or fails, without the need to wait for external events. Sometimes, however, opening the device requires a long initialization, and you may choose to support O_NONBLOCK in your *open* method by returning immediately with -EAGAIN ("try it again") if the flag is set, after initiating device initialization. The driver may also implement a blocking *open* to support access policies in a way similar to file locks. We'll see one such implementation in the section "Blocking open as an Alternative to EBUSY" later in this chapter.

Some drivers may also implement special semantics for O_NONBLOCK; for example, an open of a tape device usually blocks until a tape has been inserted. If the tape drive is opened with O_NONBLOCK, the open succeeds immediately regardless of whether the media is present or not.

Only the *read*, *write*, and *open* file operations are affected by the nonblocking flag.

A Sample Implementation: scullpipe

The */dev/scullpipe* devices (there are four of them by default) are part of the *scull* module and are used to show how blocking I/O is implemented.

Within a driver, a process blocked in a *read* call is awakened when data arrives; usually the hardware issues an interrupt to signal such an event, and the driver awakens waiting processes as part of handling the interrupt. The *scull* driver works differently, so that it can be run without requiring any particular hardware or an interrupt handler. We chose to use another process to generate the data and wake the reading process; similarly, reading processes are used to wake sleeping writer processes. The resulting implementation is similar to that of a FIFO (or named pipe) filesystem node, whence the name.

The device driver uses a device structure that embeds two wait queues and a buffer. The size of the buffer is configurable in the usual ways (at compile time, load time, or runtime).

```
typedef struct Scull_Pipe {
  wait_queue_head_t inq, outq;  /* read and write queues */
  char *buffer, *end;           /* begin of buf, end of buf */
  int buffersize;               /* used in pointer arithmetic */
  char *rp, *wp;                /* where to read, where to write */
  int nreaders, nwriters;       /* number of openings for r/w */
  struct fasync_struct *async_queue; /* asynchronous readers */
  struct semaphore sem;         /* mutual exclusion semaphore */
  devfs_handle_t handle;        /* only used if devfs is there */
} Scull_Pipe;
```

The *read* implementation manages both blocking and nonblocking input and looks like this (the puzzling first line of the function is explained later, in "Seeking a Device"):

```
ssize_t scull_p_read (struct file *filp, char *buf, size_t count,
        loff_t *f_pos)
{
  Scull_Pipe *dev = filp->private_data;

  if (f_pos != &filp->f_pos) return -ESPIPE;

  if (down_interruptible(&dev->sem))
    return -ERESTARTSYS;
  while (dev->rp == dev->wp) { /* nothing to read */
    up(&dev->sem); /* release the lock */
    if (filp->f_flags & O_NONBLOCK)
      return -EAGAIN;
    PDEBUG("\"%s\" reading: going to sleep\n", current->comm);
    if (wait_event_interruptible(dev->inq, (dev->rp != dev->wp)))
      return -ERESTARTSYS; /* signal: tell the fs layer to handle it */
    /* otherwise loop, but first reacquire the lock */
    if (down_interruptible(&dev->sem))
```

```
        return -ERESTARTSYS;
    }
    /* ok, data is there, return something */
    if (dev->wp > dev->rp)
      count = min(count, dev->wp - dev->rp);
    else /* the write pointer has wrapped, return data up to dev->end */
      count = min(count, dev->end - dev->rp);
    if (copy_to_user(buf, dev->rp, count)) {
      up (&dev->sem);
      return -EFAULT;
    }
    dev->rp += count;
    if (dev->rp == dev->end)
      dev->rp = dev->buffer; /* wrapped */
    up (&dev->sem);

    /* finally, awaken any writers and return */
    wake_up_interruptible(&dev->outq);
    PDEBUG("\"%s\" did read %li bytes\n",current->comm, (long)count);
    return count;
}
```

As you can see, we left some **PDEBUG** statements in the code. When you compile
the driver, you can enable messaging to make it easier to follow the interaction of
different processes.

Note also, once again, the use of semaphores to protect critical regions of the
code. The *scull* code has to be careful to avoid going to sleep when it holds a
semaphore—otherwise, writers would never be able to add data, and the whole
thing would deadlock. This code uses *wait_event_interruptible* to wait for data if
need be; it has to check for available data again after the wait, though. Somebody
else could grab the data between when we wake up and when we get the
semaphore back.

It's worth repeating that a process can go to sleep both when it calls *schedule*,
either directly or indirectly, and when it copies data to or from user space. In the
latter case the process may sleep if the user array is not currently present in main
memory. If *scull* sleeps while copying data between kernel and user space, it will
sleep with the device semaphore held. Holding the semaphore in this case is justi-
fied since it will not deadlock the system, and since it is important that the device
memory array not change while the driver sleeps.

The **if** statement that follows *interruptible_sleep_on* takes care of signal handling.
This statement ensures the proper and expected reaction to signals, which could
have been responsible for waking up the process (since we were in an interruptible sleep). If a signal has arrived and it has not been blocked by the process, the
proper behavior is to let upper layers of the kernel handle the event. To this aim,
the driver returns **-ERESTARTSYS** to the caller; this value is used internally by the

virtual filesystem (VFS) layer, which either restarts the system call or returns
−EINTR to user space. We'll use the same statement to deal with signal handling
for every *read* and *write* implementation. Because *signal_pending* was introduced
only in version 2.1.57 of the kernel, `sysdep.h` defines it for earlier kernels to preserve portability of source code.

The implementation for *write* is quite similar to that for *read* (and, again, its first
line will be explained later). Its only "peculiar" feature is that it never completely
fills the buffer, always leaving a hole of at least one byte. Thus, when the buffer is
empty, `wp` and `rp` are equal; when there is data there, they are always different.

```
static inline int spacefree(Scull_Pipe *dev)
{
  if (dev->rp == dev->wp)
    return dev->buffersize - 1;
  return ((dev->rp + dev->buffersize - dev->wp) % dev->buffersize) - 1;
}

ssize_t scull_p_write(struct file *filp, const char *buf, size_t count,
        loff_t *f_pos)
{
  Scull_Pipe *dev = filp->private_data;

  if (f_pos != &filp->f_pos) return -ESPIPE;

  if (down_interruptible(&dev->sem))
    return -ERESTARTSYS;

  /* Make sure there's space to write */
  while (spacefree(dev) == 0) { /* full */
    up(&dev->sem);
    if (filp->f_flags & O_NONBLOCK)
      return -EAGAIN;
    PDEBUG("\"%s\" writing: going to sleep\n",current->comm);
    if (wait_event_interruptible(dev->outq, spacefree(dev) > 0))
      return -ERESTARTSYS; /* signal: tell the fs layer to handle it */
    if (down_interruptible(&dev->sem))
      return -ERESTARTSYS;
  }
  /* ok, space is there, accept something */
  count = min(count, spacefree(dev));
  if (dev->wp >= dev->rp)
    count = min(count, dev->end - dev->wp); /* up to end-of-buffer */
  else /* the write pointer has wrapped, fill up to rp-1 */
    count = min(count, dev->rp - dev->wp - 1);
  PDEBUG("Going to accept %li bytes to %p from %p\n",
      (long)count, dev->wp, buf);
  if (copy_from_user(dev->wp, buf, count)) {
    up (&dev->sem);
    return -EFAULT;
  }
```

```
    dev->wp += count;
    if (dev->wp == dev->end)
      dev->wp = dev->buffer; /* wrapped */
    up(&dev->sem);

    /* finally, awaken any reader */
    wake_up_interruptible(&dev->inq); /* blocked in read() and select() */

    /* and signal asynchronous readers, explained later in Chapter 5 */
    if (dev->async_queue)
      kill_fasync(&dev->async_queue, SIGIO, POLL_IN);
    PDEBUG("\"%s\" did write %li bytes\n",current->comm, (long)count);
    return count;
}
```

The device, as we conceived it, doesn't implement blocking *open* and is simpler than a real FIFO. If you want to look at the real thing, you can find it in *fs/pipe.c*, in the kernel sources.

To test the blocking operation of the *scullpipe* device, you can run some programs on it, using input/output redirection as usual. Testing nonblocking activity is trickier, because the conventional programs don't perform nonblocking operations. The *misc-progs* source directory contains the following simple program, called *nbtest*, for testing nonblocking operations. All it does is copy its input to its output, using nonblocking I/O and delaying between retrials. The delay time is passed on the command line and is one second by default.

```
int main(int argc, char **argv)
{
  int delay=1, n, m=0;

  if (argc>1) delay=atoi(argv[1]);
  fcntl(0, F_SETFL, fcntl(0,F_GETFL) | O_NONBLOCK); /* stdin */
  fcntl(1, F_SETFL, fcntl(1,F_GETFL) | O_NONBLOCK); /* stdout */

  while (1) {
    n=read(0, buffer, 4096);
    if (n>=0)
      m=write(1, buffer, n);
    if ((n<0 || m<0) && (errno != EAGAIN))
      break;
    sleep(delay);
  }
  perror( n<0 ? "stdin" : "stdout");
  exit(1);
}
```

poll and select

Applications that use nonblocking I/O often use the *poll* and *select* system calls as well. *poll* and *select* have essentially the same functionality: both allow a process to determine whether it can read from or write to one or more open files without blocking. They are thus often used in applications that must use multiple input or output streams without blocking on any one of them. The same functionality is offered by two separate functions because they were implemented in Unix almost at the same time by two different groups: *select* was introduced in BSD Unix, whereas *poll* was the System V solution.

Support for either system call requires support from the device driver to function. In version 2.0 of the kernel the device method was modeled on *select* (and no *poll* was available to user programs); from version 2.1.23 onward both were offered, and the device method was based on the newly introduced *poll* system call because *poll* offered more detailed control than *select*.

Implementations of the *poll* method, implementing both the *poll* and *select* system calls, have the following prototype:

```
unsigned int (*poll) (struct file *, poll_table *);
```

The driver's method will be called whenever the user-space program performs a *poll* or *select* system call involving a file descriptor associated with the driver. The device method is in charge of these two steps:

1. Call *poll_wait* on one or more wait queues that could indicate a change in the poll status.

2. Return a bit mask describing operations that could be immediately performed without blocking.

Both of these operations are usually straightforward, and tend to look very similar from one driver to the next. They rely, however, on information that only the driver can provide, and thus must be implemented individually by each driver.

The `poll_table` structure, the second argument to the *poll* method, is used within the kernel to implement the *poll* and *select* calls; it is declared in `<linux/poll.h>`, which must be included by the driver source. Driver writers need know nothing about its internals and must use it as an opaque object; it is passed to the driver method so that every event queue that could wake up the process and change the status of the *poll* operation can be added to the `poll_table` structure by calling the function *poll_wait*:

```
void poll_wait (struct file *, wait_queue_head_t *, poll_table *);
```

The second task performed by the poll method is returning the bit mask describing which operations could be completed immediately; this is also straightforward. For example, if the device has data available, a *read* would complete without sleeping; the *poll* method should indicate this state of affairs. Several flags (defined in <linux/poll.h>) are used to indicate the possible operations:

POLLIN

This bit must be set if the device can be read without blocking.

POLLRDNORM

This bit must be set if "normal" data is available for reading. A readable device returns (POLLIN | POLLRDNORM).

POLLRDBAND

This bit indicates that out-of-band data is available for reading from the device. It is currently used only in one place in the Linux kernel (the DECnet code) and is not generally applicable to device drivers.

POLLPRI

High-priority data (out-of-band) can be read without blocking. This bit causes *select* to report that an exception condition occurred on the file, because *select* reports out-of-band data as an exception condition.

POLLHUP

When a process reading this device sees end-of-file, the driver must set POLL-HUP (hang-up). A process calling *select* will be told that the device is readable, as dictated by the *select* functionality.

POLLERR

An error condition has occurred on the device. When *poll* is invoked, the device is reported as both readable and writable, since both *read* and *write* will return an error code without blocking.

POLLOUT

This bit is set in the return value if the device can be written to without blocking.

POLLWRNORM

This bit has the same meaning as POLLOUT, and sometimes it actually is the same number. A writable device returns (POLLOUT | POLLWRNORM).

POLLWRBAND

Like POLLRDBAND, this bit means that data with nonzero priority can be written to the device. Only the datagram implementation of *poll* uses this bit, since a datagram can transmit out of band data.

It's worth noting that POLLRDBAND and POLLWRBAND are meaningful only with file descriptors associated with sockets: device drivers won't normally use these flags.

The description of *poll* takes up a lot of space for something that is relatively simple to use in practice. Consider the *scullpipe* implementation of the *poll* method:

```
unsigned int scull_p_poll(struct file *filp, poll_table *wait)
{
    Scull_Pipe *dev = filp->private_data;
    unsigned int mask = 0;

    /*
     * The buffer is circular; it is considered full
     * if "wp" is right behind "rp". "left" is 0 if the
     * buffer is empty, and it is "1" if it is completely full.
     */
    int left = (dev->rp + dev->buffersize - dev->wp) % dev->buffersize;

    poll_wait(filp, &dev->inq, wait);
    poll_wait(filp, &dev->outq, wait);
    if (dev->rp != dev->wp) mask |= POLLIN | POLLRDNORM; /* readable */
    if (left != 1)     mask |= POLLOUT | POLLWRNORM; /* writable */

    return mask;
}
```

This code simply adds the two *scullpipe* wait queues to the `poll_table`, then sets the appropriate mask bits depending on whether data can be read or written.

The *poll* code as shown is missing end-of-file support. The *poll* method should return `POLLHUP` when the device is at the end of the file. If the caller used the *select* system call, the file will be reported as readable; in both cases the application will know that it can actually issue the *read* without waiting forever, and the *read* method will return 0 to signal end-of-file.

With real FIFOs, for example, the reader sees an end-of-file when all the writers close the file, whereas in *scullpipe* the reader never sees end-of-file. The behavior is different because a FIFO is intended to be a communication channel between two processes, while *scullpipe* is a trashcan where everyone can put data as long as there's at least one reader. Moreover, it makes no sense to reimplement what is already available in the kernel.

Implementing end-of-file in the same way as FIFOs do would mean checking `dev->nwriters`, both in *read* and in *poll*, and reporting end-of-file (as just described) if no process has the device opened for writing. Unfortunately, though, if a reader opened the *scullpipe* device before the writer, it would see end-of-file without having a chance to wait for data. The best way to fix this problem would be to implement blocking within *open*; this task is left as an exercise for the reader.

Interaction with read and write

The purpose of the *poll* and *select* calls is to determine in advance if an I/O operation will block. In that respect, they complement *read* and *write*. More important, *poll* and *select* are useful because they let the application wait simultaneously for several data streams, although we are not exploiting this feature in the *scull* examples.

A correct implementation of the three calls is essential to make applications work correctly. Though the following rules have more or less already been stated, we'll summarize them here.

Reading data from the device

- If there is data in the input buffer, the *read* call should return immediately, with no noticeable delay, even if less data is available than the application requested and the driver is sure the remaining data will arrive soon. You can always return less data than you're asked for if this is convenient for any reason (we did it in *scull*), provided you return at least one byte.

- If there is no data in the input buffer, by default *read* must block until at least one byte is there. If O_NONBLOCK is set, on the other hand, *read* returns immediately with a return value of -EAGAIN (although some old versions of System V return 0 in this case). In these cases *poll* must report that the device is unreadable until at least one byte arrives. As soon as there is some data in the buffer, we fall back to the previous case.

- If we are at end-of-file, *read* should return immediately with a return value of 0, independent of O_NONBLOCK. *poll* should report POLLHUP in this case.

Writing to the device

- If there is space in the output buffer, *write* should return without delay. It can accept less data than the call requested, but it must accept at least one byte. In this case, *poll* reports that the device is writable.

- If the output buffer is full, by default *write* blocks until some space is freed. If O_NONBLOCK is set, *write* returns immediately with a return value of -EAGAIN (older System V Unices returned 0). In these cases *poll* should report that the file is not writable. If, on the other hand, the device is not able to accept any more data, *write* returns -ENOSPC ("No space left on device"), independently of the setting of O_NONBLOCK.

- Never make a *write* call wait for data transmission before returning, even if O_NONBLOCK is clear. This is because many applications use *select* to find out whether a *write* will block. If the device is reported as writable, the call must consistently not block. If the program using the device wants to ensure that the data it enqueues in the output buffer is actually transmitted, the driver must provide an *fsync* method. For instance, a removable device should have an *fsync* entry point.

Although these are a good set of general rules, one should also recognize that each device is unique and that sometimes the rules must be bent slightly. For example, record-oriented devices (such as tape drives) cannot execute partial writes.

Flushing pending output

We've seen how the *write* method by itself doesn't account for all data output needs. The *fsync* function, invoked by the system call of the same name, fills the gap. This method's prototype is

```
int (*fsync) (struct file *file, struct dentry *dentry, int datasync);
```

If some application will ever need to be assured that data has been sent to the device, the *fsync* method must be implemented. A call to *fsync* should return only when the device has been completely flushed (i.e., the output buffer is empty), even if that takes some time, regardless of whether O_NONBLOCK is set. The datasync argument, present only in the 2.4 kernel, is used to distinguish between the *fsync* and *fdatasync* system calls; as such, it is only of interest to filesystem code and can be ignored by drivers.

The *fsync* method has no unusual features. The call isn't time critical, so every device driver can implement it to the author's taste. Most of the time, char drivers just have a NULL pointer in their fops. Block devices, on the other hand, always implement the method with the general-purpose *block_fsync*, which in turn flushes all the blocks of the device, waiting for I/O to complete.

The Underlying Data Structure

The actual implementation of the *poll* and *select* system calls is reasonably simple, for those who are interested in how it works. Whenever a user application calls either function, the kernel invokes the *poll* method of all files referenced by the system call, passing the same poll_table to each of them. The structure is, for all practical purposes, an array of poll_table_entry structures allocated for a specific *poll* or *select* call. Each poll_table_entry contains the struct file pointer for the open device, a wait_queue_head_t pointer, and a wait_queue_t entry. When a driver calls *poll_wait*, one of these entries gets filled in with the information provided by the driver, and the wait queue entry gets put onto the driver's queue. The pointer to wait_queue_head_t is used to track the wait queue where the current poll table entry is registered, in order for *free_wait* to be able to dequeue the entry before the wait queue is awakened.

If none of the drivers being polled indicates that I/O can occur without blocking, the *poll* call simply sleeps until one of the (perhaps many) wait queues it is on wakes it up.

What's interesting in the implementation of *poll* is that the file operation may be called with a `NULL` pointer as `poll_table` argument. This situation can come about for a couple of reasons. If the application calling *poll* has provided a timeout value of 0 (indicating that no wait should be done), there is no reason to accumulate wait queues, and the system simply does not do it. The `poll_table` pointer is also set to `NULL` immediately after any driver being *poll*ed indicates that I/O is possible. Since the kernel knows at that point that no wait will occur, it does not build up a list of wait queues.

When the *poll* call completes, the `poll_table` structure is deallocated, and all wait queue entries previously added to the poll table (if any) are removed from the table and their wait queues.

Actually, things are somewhat more complex than depicted here, because the poll table is not a simple array but rather a set of one or more pages, each hosting an array. This complication is meant to avoid putting too low a limit (dictated by the page size) on the maximum number of file descriptors involved in a *poll* or *select* system call.

We tried to show the data structures involved in polling in Figure 5-2; the figure is a simplified representation of the real data structures because it ignores the multi-page nature of a poll table and disregards the file pointer that is part of each `poll_table_entry`. The reader interested in the actual implementation is urged to look in `<linux/poll.h>` and *fs/select.c*.

Asynchronous Notification

Though the combination of blocking and nonblocking operations and the *select* method are sufficient for querying the device most of the time, some situations aren't efficiently managed by the techniques we've seen so far.

Let's imagine, for example, a process that executes a long computational loop at low priority, but needs to process incoming data as soon as possible. If the input channel is the keyboard, you are allowed to send a signal to the application (using the 'INTR' character, usually CTRL-C), but this signaling ability is part of the tty abstraction, a software layer that isn't used for general char devices. What we need for asynchronous notification is something different. Furthermore, *any* input data should generate an interrupt, not just CTRL-C.

User programs have to execute two steps to enable asynchronous notification from an input file. First, they specify a process as the "owner" of the file. When a process invokes the `F_SETOWN` command using the *fcntl* system call, the process ID of the owner process is saved in `filp->f_owner` for later use. This step is necessary for the kernel to know just who to notify. In order to actually enable

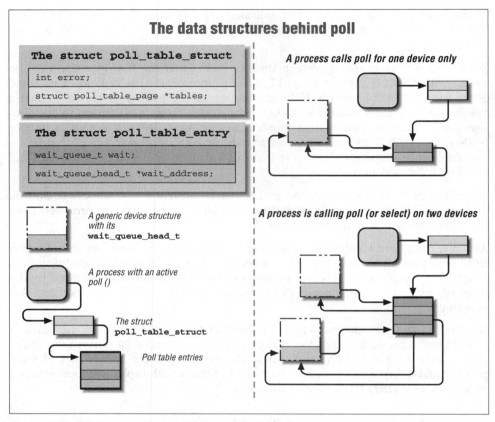

Figure 5-2. The data structures of poll

asynchronous notification, the user programs must set the **FASYNC** flag in the device by means of the **F_SETFL** *fcntl* command.

After these two calls have been executed, the input file can request delivery of a **SIGIO** signal whenever new data arrives. The signal is sent to the process (or process group, if the value is negative) stored in **filp->f_owner**.

For example, the following lines of code in a user program enable asynchronous notification to the current process for the **stdin** input file:

```
signal(SIGIO, &input_handler); /* dummy sample; sigaction() is better */
fcntl(STDIN_FILENO, F_SETOWN, getpid());
oflags = fcntl(STDIN_FILENO, F_GETFL);
fcntl(STDIN_FILENO, F_SETFL, oflags | FASYNC);
```

The program named *asynctest* in the sources is a simple program that reads stdin as shown. It can be used to test the asynchronous capabilities of *scullpipe*. The program is similar to *cat*, but doesn't terminate on end-of-file; it responds only to input, not to the absence of input.

Note, however, that not all the devices support asynchronous notification, and you can choose not to offer it. Applications usually assume that the asynchronous capability is available only for sockets and ttys. For example, pipes and FIFOs don't support it, at least in the current kernels. Mice offer asynchronous notification because some programs expect a mouse to be able to send SIGIO like a tty does.

There is one remaining problem with input notification. When a process receives a SIGIO, it doesn't know which input file has new input to offer. If more than one file is enabled to asynchronously notify the process of pending input, the application must still resort to *poll* or *select* to find out what happened.

The Driver's Point of View

A more relevant topic for us is how the device driver can implement asynchronous signaling. The following list details the sequence of operations from the kernel's point of view:

1. When **F_SETOWN** is invoked, nothing happens, except that a value is assigned to filp->f_owner.

2. When **F_SETFL** is executed to turn on **FASYNC**, the driver's *fasync* method is called. This method is called whenever the value of **FASYNC** is changed in filp->f_flags, to notify the driver of the change so it can respond properly. The flag is cleared by default when the file is opened. We'll look at the standard implementation of the driver method soon.

3. When data arrives, all the processes registered for asynchronous notification must be sent a SIGIO signal.

While implementing the first step is trivial—there's nothing to do on the driver's part—the other steps involve maintaining a dynamic data structure to keep track of the different asynchronous readers; there might be several of these readers. This dynamic data structure, however, doesn't depend on the particular device involved, and the kernel offers a suitable general-purpose implementation so that you don't have to rewrite the same code in every driver.

The general implementation offered by Linux is based on one data structure and two functions (which are called in the second and third steps described earlier). The header that declares related material is <linux/fs.h>—nothing new here—and the data structure is called struct fasync_struct. As we did with wait queues, we need to insert a pointer to the structure in the device-specific data structure. Actually, we've already seen such a field in the section "A Sample Implementation: scullpipe."

The two functions that the driver calls correspond to the following prototypes:

```
int fasync_helper(int fd, struct file *filp,
        int mode, struct fasync_struct **fa);
void kill_fasync(struct fasync_struct **fa, int sig, int band);
```

`fasync_helper` is invoked to add files to or remove files from the list of interested processes when the `FASYNC` flag changes for an open file. All of its arguments except the last are provided to the *fasync* method and can be passed through directly. `kill_fasync` is used to signal the interested processes when data arrives. Its arguments are the signal to send (usually `SIGIO`) and the band, which is almost always `POLL_IN` (but which may be used to send "urgent" or out-of-band data in the networking code).

Here's how *scullpipe* implements the *fasync* method:

```
int scull_p_fasync(fasync_file fd, struct file *filp, int mode)
{
    Scull_Pipe *dev = filp->private_data;

    return fasync_helper(fd, filp, mode, &dev->async_queue);
}
```

It's clear that all the work is performed by *fasync_helper*. It wouldn't be possible, however, to implement the functionality without a method in the driver, because the helper function needs to access the correct pointer to `struct fasync_struct *` (here `&dev->async_queue`), and only the driver can provide the information.

When data arrives, then, the following statement must be executed to signal asynchronous readers. Since new data for the *scullpipe* reader is generated by a process issuing a *write*, the statement appears in the *write* method of *scullpipe*.

```
if (dev->async_queue)
    kill_fasync(&dev->async_queue, SIGIO, POLL_IN);
```

It might appear that we're done, but there's still one thing missing. We must invoke our *fasync* method when the file is closed to remove the file from the list of active asynchronous readers. Although this call is required only if `filp->f_flags` has `FASYNC` set, calling the function anyway doesn't hurt and is the usual implementation. The following lines, for example, are part of the *close* method for *scullpipe*:

```
/* remove this filp from the asynchronously notified filp's */
scull_p_fasync(-1, filp, 0);
```

The data structure underlying asynchronous notification is almost identical to the structure `struct wait_queue`, because both situations involve waiting on an event. The difference is that `struct file` is used in place of `struct task_struct`. The `struct file` in the queue is then used to retrieve `f_owner`, in order to signal the process.

Seeking a Device

The difficult part of the chapter is over; now we'll quickly detail the *llseek* method, which is useful and easy to implement.

The llseek Implementation

The *llseek* method implements the *lseek* and *llseek* system calls. We have already stated that if the *llseek* method is missing from the device's operations, the default implementation in the kernel performs seeks from the beginning of the file and from the current position by modifying `filp->f_pos`, the current reading/writing position within the file. Please note that for the *lseek* system call to work correctly, the *read* and *write* methods must cooperate by updating the offset item they receive as argument (the argument is usually a pointer to `filp->f_pos`).

You may need to provide your own *llseek* method if the seek operation corresponds to a physical operation on the device or if seeking from end-of-file, which is not implemented by the default method, makes sense. A simple example can be seen in the *scull* driver:

```
loff_t scull_llseek(struct file *filp, loff_t off, int whence)
{
  Scull_Dev *dev = filp->private_data;
  loff_t newpos;

  switch(whence) {
   case 0: /* SEEK_SET */
    newpos = off;
    break;

   case 1: /* SEEK_CUR */
    newpos = filp->f_pos + off;
    break;

   case 2: /* SEEK_END */
    newpos = dev->size + off;
    break;

   default: /* can't happen */
    return -EINVAL;
  }
  if (newpos<0) return -EINVAL;
  filp->f_pos = newpos;
  return newpos;
}
```

The only device-specific operation here is retrieving the file length from the device. In *scull* the *read* and *write* methods cooperate as needed, as shown in "read and write" in Chapter 3.

Although the implementation just shown makes sense for *scull*, which handles a well-defined data area, most devices offer a data flow rather than a data area (just think about the serial ports or the keyboard), and seeking those devices does not make sense. If this is the case, you can't just refrain from declaring the *llseek* operation, because the default method allows seeking. Instead, you should use the following code:

```
loff_t scull_p_llseek(struct file *filp, loff_t off, int whence)
{
    return -ESPIPE; /* unseekable */
}
```

This function comes from the *scullpipe* device, which isn't seekable; the error code is translated to "Illegal seek," though the symbolic name means "is a pipe." Because the position indicator is meaningless for nonseekable devices, neither *read* nor *write* needs to update it during data transfer.

It's interesting to note that since *pread* and *pwrite* have been added to the set of supported system calls, the *lseek* device method is not the only way a user-space program can seek a file. A proper implementation of unseekable devices should allow normal *read* and *write* calls while preventing *pread* and *pwrite*. This is accomplished by the following line—the first in both the *read* and *write* methods of *scullpipe*—we didn't explain when introducing those methods:

```
if (f_pos != &filp->f_pos) return -ESPIPE;
```

Access Control on a Device File

Offering access control is sometimes vital for the reliability of a device node. Not only should unauthorized users not be permitted to use the device (a restriction is enforced by the filesystem permission bits), but sometimes only one authorized user should be allowed to open the device at a time.

The problem is similar to that of using ttys. In that case, the *login* process changes the ownership of the device node whenever a user logs into the system, in order to prevent other users from interfering with or sniffing the tty data flow. However, it's impractical to use a privileged program to change the ownership of a device every time it is opened, just to grant unique access to it.

None of the code shown up to now implements any access control beyond the filesystem permission bits. If the *open* system call forwards the request to the driver, *open* will succeed. We now introduce a few techniques for implementing some additional checks.

Every device shown in this section has the same behavior as the bare *scull* device (that is, it implements a persistent memory area) but differs from *scull* in access control, which is implemented in the *open* and *close* operations.

Single-Open Devices

The brute-force way to provide access control is to permit a device to be opened by only one process at a time (single openness). This technique is best avoided because it inhibits user ingenuity. A user might well want to run different processes on the same device, one reading status information while the other is writing data. In some cases, users can get a lot done by running a few simple programs through a shell script, as long as they can access the device concurrently. In other words, implementing a single-open behavior amounts to creating policy, which may get in the way of what your users want to do.

Allowing only a single process to open a device has undesirable properties, but it is also the easiest access control to implement for a device driver, so it's shown here. The source code is extracted from a device called *scullsingle*.

The *open* call refuses access based on a global integer flag:

```
int scull_s_open(struct inode *inode, struct file *filp)
{
    Scull_Dev *dev = &scull_s_device; /* device information */
    int num = NUM(inode->i_rdev);

    if (!filp->private_data && num > 0)
        return -ENODEV; /* not devfs: allow 1 device only */
    spin_lock(&scull_s_lock);
    if (scull_s_count) {
        spin_unlock(&scull_s_lock);
        return -EBUSY; /* already open */
    }
    scull_s_count++;
    spin_unlock(&scull_s_lock);
    /* then, everything else is copied from the bare scull device */

    if ( (filp->f_flags & O_ACCMODE) == O_WRONLY)
        scull_trim(dev);
    if (!filp->private_data)
        filp->private_data = dev;
    MOD_INC_USE_COUNT;
    return 0;       /* success */
}
```

The *close* call, on the other hand, marks the device as no longer busy.

```
int scull_s_release(struct inode *inode, struct file *filp)
{
    scull_s_count--; /* release the device */
    MOD_DEC_USE_COUNT;
    return 0;
}
```

Normally, we recommend that you put the open flag `scull_s_count` (with the accompanying spinlock, `scull_s_lock`, whose role is explained in the next subsection) within the device structure (`Scull_Dev` here) because, conceptually, it belongs to the device. The *scull* driver, however, uses standalone variables to hold the flag and the lock in order to use the same device structure and methods as the bare *scull* device and minimize code duplication.

Another Digression into Race Conditions

Consider once again the test on the variable `scull_s_count` just shown. Two separate actions are taken there: (1) the value of the variable is tested, and the open is refused if it is not 0, and (2) the variable is incremented to mark the device as taken. On a single-processor system, these tests are safe because no other process will be able to run between the two actions.

As soon as you get into the SMP world, however, a problem arises. If two processes on two processors attempt to open the device simultaneously, it is possible that they could both test the value of `scull_s_count` before either modifies it. In this scenario you'll find that, at best, the single-open semantics of the device is not enforced. In the worst case, unexpected concurrent access could create data structure corruption and system crashes.

In other words, we have another race condition here. This one could be solved in much the same way as the races we already saw in Chapter 3. Those race conditions were triggered by access to a status variable of a potentially shared data structure and were solved using semaphores. In general, however, semaphores can be expensive to use, because they can put the calling process to sleep. They are a heavyweight solution for the problem of protecting a quick check on a status variable.

Instead, *scullsingle* uses a different locking mechanism called a *spinlock*. Spinlocks will never put a process to sleep. Instead, if a lock is not available, the spinlock primitives will simply retry, over and over (i.e., "spin"), until the lock is freed. Spinlocks thus have very little locking overhead, but they also have the potential to cause a processor to spin for a long time if somebody hogs the lock. Another advantage of spinlocks over semaphores is that their implementation is empty when compiling code for a uniprocessor system (where these SMP-specific races can't happen). Semaphores are a more general resource that make sense on uniprocessor computers as well as SMP, so they don't get optimized away in the uniprocessor case.

Spinlocks can be the ideal mechanism for small critical sections. Processes should hold spinlocks for the minimum time possible, and must never sleep while holding a lock. Thus, the main *scull* driver, which exchanges data with user space and can therefore sleep, is not suitable for a spinlock solution. But spinlocks work nicely for controlling access to `scull_s_single` (even if they still are not the optimal solution, which we will see in Chapter 9).

Spinlocks are declared with a type of `spinlock_t`, which is defined in `<linux/spinlock.h>`. Prior to use, they must be initialized:

```
spin_lock_init(spinlock_t *lock);
```

A process entering a critical section will obtain the lock with **spin_lock**:

```
spin_lock(spinlock_t *lock);
```

The lock is released at the end with **spin_unlock**:

```
spin_unlock(spinlock_t *lock);
```

Spinlocks can be more complicated than this, and we'll get into the details in Chapter 9. But the simple case as shown here suits our needs for now, and all of the access-control variants of *scull* will use simple spinlocks in this manner.

The astute reader may have noticed that whereas *scull_s_open* acquires the **scull_s_lock** lock prior to incrementing the **scull_s_count** flag, *scull_s_close* takes no such precautions. This code is safe because no other code will change the value of **scull_s_count** if it is nonzero, so there will be no conflict with this particular assignment.

Restricting Access to a Single User at a Time

The next step beyond a single system-wide lock is to let a single user open a device in multiple processes but allow only one user to have the device open at a time. This solution makes it easy to test the device, since the user can read and write from several processes at once, but assumes that the user takes some responsibility for maintaining the integrity of the data during multiple accesses. This is accomplished by adding checks in the *open* method; such checks are performed *after* the normal permission checking and can only make access more restrictive than that specified by the owner and group permission bits. This is the same access policy as that used for ttys, but it doesn't resort to an external privileged program.

Those access policies are a little trickier to implement than single-open policies. In this case, two items are needed: an open count and the uid of the "owner" of the device. Once again, the best place for such items is within the device structure; our example uses global variables instead, for the reason explained earlier for *scullsingle*. The name of the device is *sculluid*.

The *open* call grants access on first open, but remembers the owner of the device. This means that a user can open the device multiple times, thus allowing cooperating processes to work concurrently on the device. At the same time, no other user can open it, thus avoiding external interference. Since this version of the function is almost identical to the preceding one, only the relevant part is reproduced here:

```
spin_lock(&scull_u_lock);
if (scull_u_count &&
    (scull_u_owner != current->uid) && /* allow user */
    (scull_u_owner != current->euid) && /* allow whoever did su */
```

```
            !capable(CAP_DAC_OVERRIDE)) { /* still allow root */
        spin_unlock(&scull_u_lock);
        return -EBUSY;  /* -EPERM would confuse the user */
    }

    if (scull_u_count == 0)
      scull_u_owner = current->uid; /* grab it */

    scull_u_count++;
    spin_unlock(&scull_u_lock);
```

We chose to return −**EBUSY** and not −**EPERM**, even though the code is performing a permission check, in order to point a user who is denied access in the right direction. The reaction to "Permission denied" is usually to check the mode and owner of the */dev* file, while "Device busy" correctly suggests that the user should look for a process already using the device.

This code also checks to see if the process attempting the open has the ability to override file access permissions; if so, the open will be allowed even if the opening process is not the owner of the device. The **CAP_DAC_OVERRIDE** capability fits the task well in this case.

The code for *close* is not shown, since all it does is decrement the usage count.

Blocking open as an Alternative to EBUSY

When the device isn't accessible, returning an error is usually the most sensible approach, but there are situations in which you'd prefer to wait for the device.

For example, if a data communication channel is used both to transmit reports on a timely basis (using *crontab*) and for casual usage according to people's needs, it's much better for the timely report to be slightly delayed rather than fail just because the channel is currently busy.

This is one of the choices that the programmer must make when designing a device driver, and the right answer depends on the particular problem being solved.

The alternative to **EBUSY**, as you may have guessed, is to implement blocking *open*.

The *scullwuid* device is a version of *sculluid* that waits for the device on *open* instead of returning −**EBUSY**. It differs from *sculluid* only in the following part of the *open* operation:

```
    spin_lock(&scull_w_lock);
    while (scull_w_count &&
      (scull_w_owner != current->uid) && /* allow user */
      (scull_w_owner != current->euid) && /* allow whoever did su */
      !capable(CAP_DAC_OVERRIDE)) {
      spin_unlock(&scull_w_lock);
```

```
    if (filp->f_flags & O_NONBLOCK) return -EAGAIN;
    interruptible_sleep_on(&scull_w_wait);
    if (signal_pending(current)) /* a signal arrived */
     return -ERESTARTSYS; /* tell the fs layer to handle it */
    /* else, loop */
    spin_lock(&scull_w_lock);
}
if (scull_w_count == 0)
  scull_w_owner = current->uid; /* grab it */
scull_w_count++;
spin_unlock(&scull_w_lock);
```

The implementation is based once again on a wait queue. Wait queues were created to maintain a list of processes that sleep while waiting for an event, so they fit perfectly here.

The *release* method, then, is in charge of awakening any pending process:

```
int scull_w_release(struct inode *inode, struct file *filp)
{
  scull_w_count--;
  if (scull_w_count == 0)
    wake_up_interruptible(&scull_w_wait); /* awaken other uid's */
  MOD_DEC_USE_COUNT;
  return 0;
}
```

The problem with a blocking-open implementation is that it is really unpleasant for the interactive user, who has to keep guessing what is going wrong. The interactive user usually invokes precompiled commands such as *cp* and *tar* and can't just add O_NONBLOCK to the *open* call. Someone who's making a backup using the tape drive in the next room would prefer to get a plain "device or resource busy" message instead of being left to guess why the hard drive is so silent today while *tar* is scanning it.

This kind of problem (different, incompatible policies for the same device) is best solved by implementing one device node for each access policy. An example of this practice can be found in the Linux tape driver, which provides multiple device files for the same device. Different device files will, for example, cause the drive to record with or without compression, or to automatically rewind the tape when the device is closed.

Cloning the Device on Open

Another technique to manage access control is creating different private copies of the device depending on the process opening it.

Clearly this is possible only if the device is not bound to a hardware object; *scull* is an example of such a "software" device. The internals of */dev/tty* use a similar technique in order to give its process a different "view" of what the */dev* entry point represents. When copies of the device are created by the software driver, we call them *virtual devices*—just as virtual consoles use a single physical tty device.

Although this kind of access control is rarely needed, the implementation can be enlightening in showing how easily kernel code can change the application's perspective of the surrounding world (i.e., the computer). The topic is quite exotic, actually, so if you aren't interested, you can jump directly to the next section.

The */dev/scullpriv* device node implements virtual devices within the *scull* package. The *scullpriv* implementation uses the minor number of the process's controlling tty as a key to access the virtual device. You can nonetheless easily modify the sources to use any integer value for the key; each choice leads to a different policy. For example, using the `uid` leads to a different virtual device for each user, while using a `pid` key creates a new device for each process accessing it.

The decision to use the controlling terminal is meant to enable easy testing of the device using input/output redirection: the device is shared by all commands run on the same virtual terminal and is kept separate from the one seen by commands run on another terminal.

The *open* method looks like the following code. It must look for the right virtual device and possibly create one. The final part of the function is not shown because it is copied from the bare *scull*, which we've already seen.

```
/* The clone-specific data structure includes a key field */
struct scull_listitem {
   Scull_Dev device;
   int key;
   struct scull_listitem *next;

};

/* The list of devices, and a lock to protect it */
struct scull_listitem *scull_c_head;
spinlock_t scull_c_lock;

/* Look for a device or create one if missing */
static Scull_Dev *scull_c_lookfor_device(int key)
{
   struct scull_listitem *lptr, *prev = NULL;

   for (lptr = scull_c_head; lptr && (lptr->key != key); lptr = lptr->next)
     prev=lptr;
   if (lptr) return &(lptr->device);

   /* not found */
   lptr = kmalloc(sizeof(struct scull_listitem), GFP_ATOMIC);
   if (!lptr) return NULL;
```

```
    /* initialize the device */
    memset(lptr, 0, sizeof(struct scull_listitem));
    lptr->key = key;
    scull_trim(&(lptr->device)); /* initialize it */
    sema_init(&(lptr->device.sem), 1);

    /* place it in the list */
    if (prev) prev->next = lptr;
    else      scull_c_head = lptr;

    return &(lptr->device);
}

int scull_c_open(struct inode *inode, struct file *filp)
{
    Scull_Dev *dev;
    int key, num = NUM(inode->i_rdev);

    if (!filp->private_data && num > 0)
        return -ENODEV; /* not devfs: allow 1 device only */

    if (!current->tty) {
        PDEBUG("Process \"%s\" has no ctl tty\n",current->comm);
        return -EINVAL;
    }
    key = MINOR(current->tty->device);

    /* look for a scullc device in the list */
    spin_lock(&scull_c_lock);
    dev = scull_c_lookfor_device(key);
    spin_unlock(&scull_c_lock);

    if (!dev) return -ENOMEM;

    /* then, everything else is copied from the bare scull device */
```

The *release* method does nothing special. It would normally release the device on last close, but we chose not to maintain an open count in order to simplify the testing of the driver. If the device were released on last close, you wouldn't be able to read the same data after writing to the device unless a background process were to keep it open. The sample driver takes the easier approach of keeping the data, so that at the next *open*, you'll find it there. The devices are released when *scull_cleanup* is called.

Here's the *release* implementation for */dev/scullpriv*, which closes the discussion of device methods.

```
int scull_c_release(struct inode *inode, struct file *filp)
{
    /*
     * Nothing to do, because the device is persistent.
     * A 'real' cloned device should be freed on last close
```

```
    */
    MOD_DEC_USE_COUNT;
    return 0;
}
```

Backward Compatibility

Many parts of the device driver API covered in this chapter have changed between the major kernel releases. For those of you needing to make your driver work with Linux 2.0 or 2.2, here is a quick rundown of the differences you will encounter.

Wait Queues in Linux 2.2 and 2.0

A relatively small amount of the material in this chapter changed in the 2.3 development cycle. The one significant change is in the area of wait queues. The 2.2 kernel had a different and simpler implementation of wait queues, but it lacked some important features, such as exclusive sleeps. The new implementation of wait queues was introduced in kernel version 2.3.1.

The 2.2 wait queue implementation used variables of the type **struct wait_queue *** instead of **wait_queue_head_t**. This pointer had to be initialized to **NULL** prior to its first use. A typical declaration and initialization of a wait queue looked like this:

```
    struct wait_queue *my_queue = NULL;
```

The various functions for sleeping and waking up looked the same, with the exception of the variable type for the queue itself. As a result, writing code that works for all 2.*x* kernels is easily done with a bit of code like the following, which is part of the **sysdep.h** header we use to compile our sample code.

```
    # define DECLARE_WAIT_QUEUE_HEAD(head) struct wait_queue *head = NULL
      typedef struct wait_queue *wait_queue_head_t;
    # define init_waitqueue_head(head) (*(head)) = NULL
```

The synchronous versions of *wake_up* were added in 2.3.29, and **sysdep.h** provides macros with the same names so that you can use the feature in your code while maintaining portability. The replacement macros expand to normal *wake_up*, since the underlying mechanisms were missing from earlier kernels. The timeout versions of *sleep_on* were added in kernel 2.1.127. The rest of the wait queue interface has remained relatively unchanged. The *sysdep.h* header defines the needed macros in order to compile and run your modules with Linux 2.2 and Linux 2.0 without cluttering the code with lots of **#ifdef**s.

The *wait_event* macro did not exist in the 2.0 kernel. For those who need it, we have provided an implementation in *sysdep.h*

Asynchronous Notification

Some small changes have been made in how asynchronous notification works for both the 2.2 and 2.4 releases.

In Linux 2.3.21, *kill_fasync* got its third argument. Prior to this release, *kill_fasync* was called as

```
kill_fasync(struct fasync_struct *queue, int signal);
```

Fortunately, *sysdep.h* takes care of the issue.

In the 2.2 release, the type of the first argument to the *fasync* method changed. In the 2.0 kernel, a pointer to the `inode` structure for the device was passed, instead of the integer file descriptor:

```
int (*fasync) (struct inode *inode, struct file *filp, int on);
```

To solve this incompatibility, we use the same approach taken for *read* and *write*: use of a wrapper function when the module is compiled under 2.0 headers.

The `inode` argument to the *fasync* method was also passed in when called from the *release* method, rather than the −1 value used with later kernels.

The fsync Method

The third argument to the *fsync* `file_operations` method (the integer `data-sync` value) was added in the 2.3 development series, meaning that portable code will generally need to include a wrapper function for older kernels. There is a trap, however, for people trying to write portable *fsync* methods: at least one distributor, which will remain nameless, patched the 2.4 *fsync* API into its 2.2 kernel. The kernel developers usually (*usually . . .*) try to avoid making API changes within a stable series, but they have little control over what the distributors do.

Access to User Space in Linux 2.0

Memory access was handled differently in the 2.0 kernels. The Linux virtual memory system was less well developed at that time, and memory access was handled a little differently. The new system was the key change that opened 2.1 development, and it brought significant improvements in performance; unfortunately, it was accompanied by yet another set of compatibility headaches for driver writers.

The functions used to access memory under Linux 2.0 were as follows:

`verify_area(int mode, const void *ptr, unsigned long size);`
This function worked similarly to *access_ok*, but performed more extensive checking and was slower. The function returned 0 in case of success and

–EFAULT in case of errors. Recent kernel headers still define the function, but it's now just a wrapper around *access_ok*. When using version 2.0 of the kernel, calling *verify_area* is never optional; no access to user space can safely be performed without a prior, explicit verification.

put_user(datum, ptr)

The *put_user* macro looks much like its modern-day equivalent. It differed, however, in that no verification was done, and there was no return value.

get_user(ptr)

This macro fetched the value at the given address, and returned it as its return value. Once again, no verification was done by the execution of the macro.

verify_area had to be called explicitly because no user-area copy function performed the check. The great news introduced by Linux 2.1, which forced the incompatible change in the *get_user* and *put_user* functions, was that the task of verifying user addresses was left to the hardware, because the kernel was now able to trap and handle processor exceptions generated during data copies to user space.

As an example of how the older calls are used, consider *scull* one more time. A version of *scull* using the 2.0 API would call *verify_area* in this way:

```
int err = 0, tmp;

/*
 * extract the type and number bitfields, and don't decode
 * wrong cmds: return ENOTTY before verify_area()
 */
if (_IOC_TYPE(cmd) != SCULL_IOC_MAGIC) return -ENOTTY;
if (_IOC_NR(cmd) > SCULL_IOC_MAXNR) return -ENOTTY;

/*
 * the direction is a bit mask, and VERIFY_WRITE catches R/W
 * transfers. 'Type' is user oriented, while
 * verify_area is kernel oriented, so the concept of "read" and
 * "write" is reversed
 */
if (_IOC_DIR(cmd) & _IOC_READ)
  err = verify_area(VERIFY_WRITE, (void *)arg, _IOC_SIZE(cmd));
else if (_IOC_DIR(cmd) & _IOC_WRITE)
  err = verify_area(VERIFY_READ, (void *)arg, _IOC_SIZE(cmd));
if (err) return err;
```

Then *get_user* and *put_user* can be used as follows:

```
case SCULL_IOCXQUANTUM: /* eXchange: use arg as pointer */
  tmp = scull_quantum;
  scull_quantum = get_user((int *)arg);
  put_user(tmp, (int *)arg);
  break;
```

```
default: /* redundant, as cmd was checked against MAXNR */
 return -ENOTTY;
}
 return 0;
```

Only a small portion of the *ioctl* switch code has been shown, since it is little different from the version for 2.2 and beyond.

Life would be relatively easy for the compatibility-conscious driver writer if it weren't for the fact that *put_user* and *get_user* are implemented as macros in all Linux versions, and their interfaces changed. As a result, a straightforward fix using macros cannot be done.

One possible solution is to define a new set of version-independent macros. The path taken by *sysdep.h* consists in defining upper-case macros: GET_USER, __GET_USER, and so on. The arguments are the same as with the kernel macros of Linux 2.4, but the caller must be sure that *verify_area* has been called first (because that call is needed when compiling for 2.0).

Capabilities in 2.0

The 2.0 kernel did not support the capabilities abstraction at all. All permissions checks simply looked to see if the calling process was running as the superuser; if so, the operation would be allowed. The function *suser* was used for this purpose; it takes no arguments and returns a nonzero value if the process has superuser privileges.

suser still exists in later kernels, but its use is strongly discouraged. It is better to define a version of *capable* for 2.0, as is done in *sysdep.h*:

```
# define capable(anything) suser()
```

In this way, code can be written that is portable but which works with modern, capability-oriented systems.

The Linux 2.0 select Method

The 2.0 kernel did not support the *poll* system call; only the BSD-style *select* call was available. The corresponding device driver method was thus called *select*, and operated in a slightly different way, though the actions to be performed are almost identical.

The *select* method is passed a pointer to a `select_table`, and must pass that pointer to *select_wait* only if the calling process should wait for the requested condition (one of `SEL_IN`, `SEL_OUT`, or `SEL_EX`).

The *scull* driver deals with the incompatibility by declaring a specific *select* method to be used when it is compiled for version 2.0 of the kernel:

```
#ifdef __USE_OLD_SELECT__
int scull_p_poll(struct inode *inode, struct file *filp,
        int mode, select_table *table)
{
    Scull_Pipe *dev = filp->private_data;

    if (mode == SEL_IN) {
        if (dev->rp != dev->wp) return 1; /* readable */
        PDEBUG("Waiting to read\n");
        select_wait(&dev->inq, table); /* wait for data */
        return 0;
    }
    if (mode == SEL_OUT) {
        /*
         * The buffer is circular; it is considered full
         * if "wp" is right behind "rp". "left" is 0 if the
         * buffer is empty, and it is "1" if it is completely full.
         */
        int left = (dev->rp + dev->buffersize - dev->wp) % dev->buffersize;
        if (left != 1) return 1; /* writable */
        PDEBUG("Waiting to write\n");
        select_wait(&dev->outq, table); /* wait for free space */
        return 0;
    }
    return 0; /* never exception-able */
}
#else /* Use poll instead, already shown */
```

The __USE_OLD_SELECT__ preprocessor symbol used here is set by the sys-dep.h include file according to kernel version.

Seeking in Linux 2.0

Prior to Linux 2.1, the *llseek* device method was called *lseek* instead, and it received different parameters from the current implementation. For that reason, under Linux 2.0 you were not allowed to seek a file, or a device, past the 2 GB limit, even though the *llseek* system call was already supported.

The prototype of the file operation in the 2.0 kernel was the following:

```
int (*lseek) (struct inode *inode, struct file *filp , off_t off,
int whence);
```

Those working to write drivers compatible with 2.0 and 2.2 usually end up defining separate implementations of the seek method for the two interfaces.

2.0 and SMP

Because Linux 2.0 only minimally supported SMP systems, race conditions of the type mentioned in this chapter did not normally come about. The 2.0 kernel *did* have a spinlock implementation, but, since only one processor could be running kernel code at a time, there was less need for locking.

Quick Reference

This chapter introduced the following symbols and header files.

#include <linux/ioctl.h>

> This header declares all the macros used to define *ioctl* commands. It is currently included by <linux/fs.h>.

_IOC_NRBITS
_IOC_TYPEBITS
_IOC_SIZEBITS
_IOC_DIRBITS

> The number of bits available for the different bitfields of *ioctl* commands. There are also four macros that specify the MASKs and four that specify the SHIFTs, but they're mainly for internal use. _IOC_SIZEBITS is an important value to check, because it changes across architectures.

_IOC_NONE
_IOC_READ
_IOC_WRITE

> The possible values for the "direction" bitfield. "Read" and "write" are different bits and can be OR'd to specify read/write. The values are 0 based.

_IOC(dir,type,nr,size)
_IO(type,nr)
_IOR(type,nr,size)
_IOW(type,nr,size)
_IOWR(type,nr,size)

> Macros used to create an *ioctl* command.

_IOC_DIR(nr)
_IOC_TYPE(nr)
_IOC_NR(nr)
_IOC_SIZE(nr)

> Macros used to decode a command. In particular, _IOC_TYPE(nr) is an OR combination of _IOC_READ and _IOC_WRITE.

#include <asm/uaccess.h>

int access_ok(int type, const void *addr, unsigned long size);

> This function checks that a pointer to user space is actually usable. *access_ok* returns a nonzero value if the access should be allowed.

VERIFY_READ
VERIFY_WRITE
The possible values for the `type` argument in *access_ok*. VERIFY_WRITE is a superset of VERIFY_READ.

```
#include <asm/uaccess.h>
int put_user(datum,ptr);
int get_user(local,ptr);
int __put_user(datum,ptr);
int __get_user(local,ptr);
```
Macros used to store or retrieve a datum to or from user space. The number of bytes being transferred depends on `sizeof(*ptr)`. The regular versions call *access_ok* first, while the qualified versions (*__put_user* and *__get_user*) assume that *access_ok* has already been called.

```
#include <linux/capability.h>
```
Defines the various `CAP_` symbols for capabilities under Linux 2.2 and later.

```
int capable(int capability);
```
Returns nonzero if the process has the given capability.

```
#include <linux/wait.h>
typedef struct { /* ... */ } wait_queue_head_t;
void init_waitqueue_head(wait_queue_head_t *queue);
DECLARE_WAIT_QUEUE_HEAD(queue);
```
The defined type for Linux wait queues. A `wait_queue_head_t` must be explicitly initialized with either *init_waitqueue_head* at runtime or *declare_wait_queue_head* at compile time.

```
#include <linux/sched.h>
void interruptible_sleep_on(wait_queue_head_t *q);
void sleep_on(wait_queue_head_t *q);
void interruptible_sleep_on_timeout(wait_queue_head_t *q,
        long timeout);
void sleep_on_timeout(wait_queue_head_t *q, long timeout);
```
Calling any of these functions puts the current process to sleep on a queue. Usually, you'll choose the *interruptible* form to implement blocking *read* and *write*.

```
void wake_up(struct wait_queue **q);
void wake_up_interruptible(struct wait_queue **q);
void wake_up_sync(struct wait_queue **q);
void wake_up_interruptible_sync(struct wait_queue **q);
```
These functions wake processes that are sleeping on the queue q. The *_interruptible* form wakes only interruptible processes. The *_sync* versions will not reschedule the CPU before returning.

```
typedef struct { /* ... */ } wait_queue_t;
init_waitqueue_entry(wait_queue_t *entry, struct task_struct
    *task);
```
The `wait_queue_t` type is used when sleeping without calling *sleep_on*. Wait queue entries must be initialized prior to use; the `task` argument used is almost always `current`.

```
void add_wait_queue(wait_queue_head_t *q, wait_queue_t
    *wait);
void add_wait_queue_exclusive(wait_queue_head_t *q,
    wait_queue_t *wait);
void remove_wait_queue(wait_queue_head_t *q, wait_queue_t
    *wait);
```
These functions add an entry to a wait queue; *add_wait_queue_exclusive* adds the entry to the end of the queue for exclusive waits. Entries should be removed from the queue after sleeping with *remove_wait_queue*.

```
void wait_event(wait_queue_head_t q, int condition);
int wait_event_interruptible(wait_queue_head_t q, int condi-
    tion);
```
These two macros will cause the process to sleep on the given queue until the given `condition` evaluates to a true value.

```
void schedule(void);
```
This function selects a runnable process from the run queue. The chosen process can be `current` or a different one. You won't usually call *schedule* directly, because the *sleep_on* functions do it internally.

```
#include <linux/poll.h>
void poll_wait(struct file *filp, wait_queue_head_t *q,
    poll_table *p)
```
This function puts the current process into a wait queue without scheduling immediately. It is designed to be used by the *poll* method of device drivers.

```
int fasync_helper(struct inode *inode, struct file *filp,
    int mode, struct fasync_struct **fa);
```
This function is a "helper" for implementing the *fasync* device method. The `mode` argument is the same value that is passed to the method, while `fa` points to a device-specific `fasync_struct *`.

```
void kill_fasync(struct fasync_struct *fa, int sig, int
    band);
```
If the driver supports asynchronous notification, this function can be used to send a signal to processes registered in `fa`.

```
#include <linux/spinlock.h>
typedef struct { /* ... */ } spinlock_t;
void spin_lock_init(spinlock_t *lock);
```
The `spinlock_t` type defines a spinlock, which must be initialized (with *spin_lock_init*) prior to use.

```
spin_lock(spinlock_t *lock);
spin_unlock(spinlock_t *lock);
```
spin_lock locks the given lock, perhaps waiting until it becomes available. The lock can then be released with *spin_unlock*.

CHAPTER SIX
FLOW OF TIME

At this point, we know the basics of how to write a full-featured char module. Real-world drivers, however, need to do more than implement the necessary operations; they have to deal with issues such as timing, memory management, hardware access, and more. Fortunately, the kernel makes a number of facilities available to ease the task of the driver writer. In the next few chapters we'll fill in information on some of the kernel resources that are available, starting with how timing issues are addressed. Dealing with time involves the following, in order of increasing complexity:

- Understanding kernel timing

- Knowing the current time

- Delaying operation for a specified amount of time

- Scheduling asynchronous functions to happen after a specified time lapse

Time Intervals in the Kernel

The first point we need to cover is the timer interrupt, which is the mechanism the kernel uses to keep track of time intervals. Interrupts are asynchronous events that are usually fired by external hardware; the CPU is interrupted in its current activity and executes special code (the Interrupt Service Routine, or ISR) to serve the interrupt. Interrupts and ISR implementation issues are covered in Chapter 9.

Timer interrupts are generated by the system's timing hardware at regular intervals; this interval is set by the kernel according to the value of HZ, which is an architecture-dependent value defined in `<linux/param.h>`. Current Linux versions define `HZ` to be 100 for most platforms, but some platforms use 1024, and the IA-64 simulator uses 20. Despite what your preferred platform uses, no driver writer should count on any specific value of `HZ`.

Every time a timer interrupt occurs, the value of the variable `jiffies` is incremented. `jiffies` is initialized to 0 when the system boots, and is thus the number of clock ticks since the computer was turned on. It is declared in `<linux/sched.h>` as `unsigned long volatile`, and will possibly overflow after a long time of continuous system operation (but no platform features jiffy overflow in less than 16 months of uptime). Much effort has gone into ensuring that the kernel operates properly when `jiffies` overflows. Driver writers do not normally have to worry about `jiffies` overflows, but it is good to be aware of the possibility.

It is possible to change the value of `HZ` for those who want systems with a different clock interrupt frequency. Some people using Linux for hard real-time tasks have been known to raise the value of `HZ` to get better response times; they are willing to pay the overhead of the extra timer interrupts to achieve their goals. All in all, however, the best approach to the timer interrupt is to keep the default value for `HZ`, by virtue of our complete trust in the kernel developers, who have certainly chosen the best value.

Processor-Specific Registers

If you need to measure very short time intervals or you need extremely high precision in your figures, you can resort to platform-dependent resources, selecting precision over portability.

Most modern CPUs include a high-resolution counter that is incremented every clock cycle; this counter may be used to measure time intervals precisely. Given the inherent unpredictability of instruction timing on most systems (due to instruction scheduling, branch prediction, and cache memory), this clock counter is the only reliable way to carry out small-scale timekeeping tasks. In response to the extremely high speed of modern processors, the pressing demand for empirical performance figures, and the intrinsic unpredictability of instruction timing in CPU designs caused by the various levels of cache memories, CPU manufacturers introduced a way to count clock cycles as an easy and reliable way to measure time lapses. Most modern processors thus include a counter register that is steadily incremented once at each clock cycle.

The details differ from platform to platform: the register may or may not be readable from user space, it may or may not be writable, and it may be 64 or 32 bits wide—in the latter case you must be prepared to handle overflows. Whether or not the register can be zeroed, we strongly discourage resetting it, even when hardware permits. Since you can always measure differences using unsigned variables, you can get the work done without claiming exclusive ownership of the register by modifying its current value.

The most renowned counter register is the TSC (timestamp counter), introduced in x86 processors with the Pentium and present in all CPU designs ever since. It is a 64-bit register that counts CPU clock cycles; it can be read from both kernel space and user space.

After including `<asm/msr.h>` (for "machine-specific registers"), you can use one of these macros:

```
rdtsc(low,high);
rdtscl(low);
```

The former atomically reads the 64-bit value into two 32-bit variables; the latter reads the low half of the register into a 32-bit variable and is sufficient in most cases. For example, a 500-MHz system will overflow a 32-bit counter once every 8.5 seconds; you won't need to access the whole register if the time lapse you are benchmarking reliably takes less time.

These lines, for example, measure the execution of the instruction itself:

```
unsigned long ini, end;
rdtscl(ini); rdtscl(end);
printk("time lapse: %li\n", end - ini);
```

Some of the other platforms offer similar functionalities, and kernel headers offer an architecture-independent function that you can use instead of *rdtsc*. It is called *get_cycles*, and was introduced during 2.1 development. Its prototype is

```
#include <linux/timex.h>
cycles_t get_cycles(void);
```

The function is defined for every platform, and it always returns 0 on the platforms that have no cycle-counter register. The `cycles_t` type is an appropriate unsigned type that can fit in a CPU register. The choice to fit the value in a single register means, for example, that only the lower 32 bits of the Pentium cycle counter are returned by *get_cycles*. The choice is a sensible one because it avoids the problems with multiregister operations while not preventing most common uses of the counter—namely, measuring short time lapses.

Despite the availability of an architecture-independent function, we'd like to take the chance to show an example of inline assembly code. To this aim, we'll implement a *rdtscl* function for MIPS processors that works in the same way as the x86 one.

We'll base the example on MIPS because most MIPS processors feature a 32-bit counter as register 9 of their internal "coprocessor 0." To access the register, only readable from kernel space, you can define the following macro that executes a "move from coprocessor 0" assembly instruction:*

```
#define rdtscl(dest) \
    __asm__ __volatile__("mfc0 %0,$9; nop" : "=r" (dest))
```

With this macro in place, the MIPS processor can execute the same code shown earlier for the x86.

What's interesting with *gcc* inline assembly is that allocation of general-purpose registers is left to the compiler. The macro just shown uses %0 as a placeholder for "argument 0," which is later specified as "any register (r) used as output (=)." The macro also states that the output register must correspond to the C expression dest. The syntax for inline assembly is very powerful but somewhat complex, especially for architectures that have constraints on what each register can do (namely, the x86 family). The complete syntax is described in the *gcc* documentation, usually available in the *info* documentation tree.

The short C-code fragment shown in this section has been run on a K7-class x86 processor and a MIPS VR4181 (using the macro just described). The former reported a time lapse of 11 clock ticks, and the latter just 2 clock ticks. The small figure was expected, since RISC processors usually execute one instruction per clock cycle.

Knowing the Current Time

Kernel code can always retrieve the current time by looking at the value of jiffies. Usually, the fact that the value represents only the time since the last boot is not relevant to the driver, because its life is limited to the system uptime. Drivers can use the current value of jiffies to calculate time intervals across events (for example, to tell double clicks from single clicks in input device drivers). In short, looking at jiffies is almost always sufficient when you need to measure time intervals, and if you need very sharp measures for short time lapses, processor-specific registers come to the rescue.

It's quite unlikely that a driver will ever need to know the wall-clock time, since this knowledge is usually needed only by user programs such as *cron* and *at*. If such a capability is needed, it will be a particular case of device usage, and the driver can be correctly instructed by a user program, which can easily do the con-

---

* The trailing *nop* instruction is required to prevent the compiler from accessing the target register in the instruction immediately following *mfc0*. This kind of interlock is typical of RISC processors, and the compiler can still schedule useful instructions in the delay slots. In this case we use *nop* because inline assembly is a black box for the compiler and no optimization can be performed.

version from wall-clock time to the system clock. Dealing directly with wall-clock time in a driver is often a sign that policy is being implemented, and should thus be looked at closely.

If your driver really needs the current time, the *do_gettimeofday* function comes to the rescue. This function doesn't tell the current day of the week or anything like that; rather, it fills a `struct timeval` pointer—the same as used in the *gettimeofday* system call—with the usual seconds and microseconds values. The prototype for *do_gettimeofday* is:

```
#include <linux/time.h>
void do_gettimeofday(struct timeval *tv);
```

The source states that *do_gettimeofday* has "near microsecond resolution" for many architectures. The precision does vary from one architecture to another, however, and can be less in older kernels. The current time is also available (though with less precision) from the `xtime` variable (a `struct timeval`); however, direct use of this variable is discouraged because you can't atomically access both the `timeval` fields `tv_sec` and `tv_usec` unless you disable interrupts. As of the 2.2 kernel, a quick and safe way of getting the time quickly, possibly with less precision, is to call *get_fast_time*:

```
void get_fast_time(struct timeval *tv);
```

Code for reading the current time is available within the *jit* ("Just In Time") module in the source files provided on the O'Reilly FTP site. *jit* creates a file called */proc/currentime*, which returns three things in ASCII when read:

- The current time as returned by *do_gettimeofday*

- The current time as found in `xtime`

- The current `jiffies` value

We chose to use a dynamic */proc* file because it requires less module code—it's not worth creating a whole device just to return three lines of text.

If you use *cat* to read the file multiple times in less than a timer tick, you'll see the difference between `xtime` and *do_gettimeofday*, reflecting the fact that `xtime` is updated less frequently:

```
morgana% cd /proc; cat currentime currentime currentime
gettime: 846157215.937221
xtime:   846157215.931188
jiffies: 1308094
gettime: 846157215.939950
xtime:   846157215.931188
jiffies: 1308094
gettime: 846157215.942465
xtime:   846157215.941188
jiffies: 1308095
```

Delaying Execution

Device drivers often need to delay the execution of a particular piece of code for a period of time—usually to allow the hardware to accomplish some task. In this section we cover a number of different techniques for achieving delays. The circumstances of each situation determine which technique is best to use; we'll go over them all and point out the advantages and disadvantages of each.

One important thing to consider is whether the length of the needed delay is longer than one clock tick. Longer delays can make use of the system clock; shorter delays typically must be implemented with software loops.

Long Delays

If you want to delay execution by a multiple of the clock tick or you don't require strict precision (for example, if you want to delay an integer number of seconds), the easiest implementation (and the most braindead) is the following, also known as *busy waiting*:

```
unsigned long j = jiffies + jit_delay * HZ;

while (jiffies < j)
    /* nothing */;
```

This kind of implementation should definitely be avoided. We show it here because on occasion you might want to run this code to understand better the internals of other code.

So let's look at how this code works. The loop is guaranteed to work because `jiffies` is declared as `volatile` by the kernel headers and therefore is reread any time some C code accesses it. Though "correct," this busy loop completely locks the processor for the duration of the delay; the scheduler never interrupts a process that is running in kernel space. Still worse, if interrupts happen to be disabled when you enter the loop, `jiffies` won't be updated, and the `while` condition remains true forever. You'll be forced to hit the big red button.

This implementation of delaying code is available, like the following ones, in the *jit* module. The */proc/jit** files created by the module delay a whole second every time they are read. If you want to test the busy wait code, you can read */proc/jitbusy*, which busy-loops for one second whenever its *read* method is called; a command such as *dd if=/proc/jitbusy bs=1* delays one second each time it reads a character.

As you may suspect, reading */proc/jitbusy* is terrible for system performance, because the computer can run other processes only once a second.

A better solution that allows other processes to run during the time interval is the following, although it can't be used in hard real-time tasks or other time-critical situations.

```
while (jiffies < j)
    schedule();
```

The variable `j` in this example and the following ones is the value of `jiffies` at the expiration of the delay and is always calculated as just shown for busy waiting.

This loop (which can be tested by reading */proc/jitsched*) still isn't optimal. The system can schedule other tasks; the current process does nothing but release the CPU, but it remains in the run queue. If it is the only runnable process, it will actually run (it calls the scheduler, which selects the same process, which calls the scheduler, which ...). In other words, the load of the machine (the average number of running processes) will be at least one, and the idle task (process number 0, also called *swapper* for historical reasons) will never run. Though this issue may seem irrelevant, running the idle task when the computer is idle relieves the processor's workload, decreasing its temperature and increasing its lifetime, as well as the duration of the batteries if the computer happens to be your laptop. Moreover, since the process is actually executing during the delay, it will be accounted for all the time it consumes. You can see this by running *time cat /proc/jitsched.*

If, instead, the system is very busy, the driver could end up waiting rather longer than expected. Once a process releases the processor with *schedule*, there are no guarantees that it will get it back anytime soon. If there is an upper bound on the acceptable delay time, calling *schedule* in this manner is not a safe solution to the driver's needs.

Despite its drawbacks, the previous loop can provide a quick and dirty way to monitor the workings of a driver. If a bug in your module locks the system solid, adding a small delay after each debugging *printk* statement ensures that every message you print before the processor hits your nasty bug reaches the system log before the system locks. Without such delays, the messages are correctly printed to the memory buffer, but the system locks before *klogd* can do its job.

The best way to implement a delay, however, is to ask the kernel to do it for you. There are two ways of setting up short-term timeouts, depending on whether your driver is waiting for other events or not.

If your driver uses a wait queue to wait for some other event, but you also want to be sure it runs within a certain period of time, it can use the timeout versions of the sleep functions, as shown in "Going to Sleep and Awakening" in Chapter 5:

```
sleep_on_timeout(wait_queue_head_t *q, unsigned long timeout);
interruptible_sleep_on_timeout(wait_queue_head_t *q,
                               unsigned long timeout);
```

Both versions will sleep on the given wait queue, but will return within the timeout period (in jiffies) in any case. They thus implement a bounded sleep that will not go on forever. Note that the timeout value represents the number of jiffies to wait, not an absolute time value. Delaying in this manner can be seen in the implementation of */proc/jitqueue*:

```
wait_queue_head_t wait;

init_waitqueue_head (&wait);
interruptible_sleep_on_timeout(&wait, jit_delay*HZ);
```

In a normal driver, execution could be resumed in either of two ways: somebody calls *wake_up* on the wait queue, or the timeout expires. In this particular implementation, nobody will ever call *wake_up* on the wait queue (after all, no other code even knows about it), so the process will always wake up when the timeout expires. That is a perfectly valid implementation, but, if there are no other events of interest to your driver, delays can be achieved in a more straightforward manner with *schedule_timeout*:

```
set_current_state(TASK_INTERRUPTIBLE);
schedule_timeout (jit_delay*HZ);
```

The previous line (for */proc/jitself*) causes the process to sleep until the given time has passed. *schedule_timeout*, too, expects a time offset, not an absolute number of jiffies. Once again, it is worth noting that an extra time interval could pass between the expiration of the timeout and when your process is actually scheduled to execute.

Short Delays

Sometimes a real driver needs to calculate very short delays in order to synchronize with the hardware. In this case, using the `jiffies` value is definitely not the solution.

The kernel functions *udelay* and *mdelay* serve this purpose.* Their prototypes are

```
#include <linux/delay.h>
void udelay(unsigned long usecs);
void mdelay(unsigned long msecs);
```

The functions are compiled inline on most supported architectures. The former uses a software loop to delay execution for the required number of microseconds, and the latter is a loop around *udelay*, provided for the convenience of the programmer. The *udelay* function is where the BogoMips value is used: its loop is based on the integer value `loops_per_second`, which in turn is the result of the BogoMips calculation performed at boot time.

The *udelay* call should be called only for short time lapses because the precision of `loops_per_second` is only eight bits, and noticeable errors accumulate when

---

* The u in *udelay* represents the Greek letter mu and stands for *micro*.

calculating long delays. Even though the maximum allowable delay is nearly one second (since calculations overflow for longer delays), the suggested maximum value for *udelay* is 1000 microseconds (one millisecond). The function *mdelay* helps in cases where the delay must be longer than one millisecond.

It's also important to remember that *udelay* is a busy-waiting function (and thus *mdelay* is too); other tasks can't be run during the time lapse. You must therefore be very careful, especially with *mdelay,* and avoid using it unless there's no other way to meet your goal.

Currently, support for delays longer than a few microseconds and shorter than a timer tick is very inefficient. This is not usually an issue, because delays need to be just long enough to be noticed by humans or by the hardware. One hundredth of a second is a suitable precision for human-related time intervals, while one millisecond is a long enough delay for hardware activities.

Although *mdelay* is not available in Linux 2.0, *sysdep.h* fills the gap.

Task Queues

One feature many drivers need is the ability to schedule execution of some tasks at a later time without resorting to interrupts. Linux offers three different interfaces for this purpose: task queues, tasklets (as of kernel 2.3.43), and kernel timers. Task queues and tasklets provide a flexible utility for scheduling execution at a later time, with various meanings for "later"; they are most useful when writing interrupt handlers, and we'll see them again in "Tasklets and Bottom-Half Processing," in Chapter 9. Kernel timers are used to schedule a task to run at a specific time in the future and are dealt with in "Kernel Timers," later in this chapter.

A typical situation in which you might use task queues or tasklets is to manage hardware that cannot generate interrupts but still allows blocking read. You need to poll the device, while taking care not to burden the CPU with unnecessary operations. Waking the reading process at fixed time intervals (for example, using `current->timeout`) isn't a suitable approach, because each poll would require two context switches (one to run the polling code in the reading process, and one to return to a process that has real work to do), and often a suitable polling mechanism can be implemented only outside of a process's context.

A similar problem is giving timely input to a simple hardware device. For example, you might need to feed steps to a stepper motor that is directly connected to the parallel port—the motor needs to be moved by single steps on a timely basis. In this case, the controlling process talks to your device driver to dispatch a movement, but the actual movement should be performed step by step at regular intervals after returning from *write.*

The preferred way to perform such floating operations quickly is to register a task for later execution. The kernel supports *task queues*, where tasks accumulate to be "consumed" when the queue is run. You can declare your own task queue and trigger it at will, or you can register your tasks in predefined queues, which are run (triggered) by the kernel itself.

This section first describes task queues, then introduces predefined task queues, which provide a good start for some interesting tests (and hang the computer if something goes wrong), and finally introduces how to run your own task queues. Following that, we look at the new *tasklet* interface, which supersedes task queues in many situations in the 2.4 kernel.

The Nature of Task Queues

A task queue is a list of tasks, each task being represented by a function pointer and an argument. When a task is run, it receives a single `void *` argument and returns `void`. The pointer argument can be used to pass along a data structure to the routine, or it can be ignored. The queue itself is a list of structures (the tasks) that are owned by the kernel module declaring and queueing them. The module is completely responsible for allocating and deallocating the structures, and static structures are commonly used for this purpose.

A queue element is described by the following structure, copied directly from `<linux/tqueue.h>`:

```
struct tq_struct {
    struct tq_struct *next;       /* linked list of active bh's */
    int sync;                     /* must be initialized to zero */
    void (*routine)(void *);      /* function to call */
    void *data;                   /* argument to function */
};
```

The "bh" in the first comment means *bottom half*. A bottom half is "half of an interrupt handler"; we'll discuss this topic thoroughly when we deal with interrupts in "Tasklets and Bottom-Half Processing," in Chapter 9. For now, suffice it to say that a bottom half is a mechanism provided by a device driver to handle asynchronous tasks which, usually, are too large to be done while handling a hardware interrupt. This chapter should make sense without an understanding of bottom halves, but we will, by necessity, refer to them occasionally.

The most important fields in the data structure just shown are `routine` and `data`. To queue a task for later execution, you need to set both these fields before queueing the structure, while `next` and `sync` should be cleared. The `sync` flag in the structure is used by the kernel to prevent queueing the same task more than once, because this would corrupt the `next` pointer. Once the task has been queued, the structure is considered "owned" by the kernel and shouldn't be modified until the task is run.

The other data structure involved in task queues is `task_queue`, which is currently just a pointer to `struct tq_struct`; the decision to `typedef` this pointer to another symbol permits the extension of `task_queue` in the future, should the need arise. `task_queue` pointers should be initialized to NULL before use.

The following list summarizes the operations that can be performed on task queues and `struct tq_struct`s.

`DECLARE_TASK_QUEUE(name);`
> This macro declares a task queue with the given `name`, and initializes it to the empty state.

`int queue_task(struct tq_struct *task, task_queue *list);`
> As its name suggests, this function queues a task. The return value is 0 if the task was already present on the given queue, nonzero otherwise.

`void run_task_queue(task_queue *list);`
> This function is used to consume a queue of accumulated tasks. You won't need to call it yourself unless you declare and maintain your own queue.

Before getting into the details of using task queues, we need to pause for a moment to look at how they work inside the kernel.

How Task Queues Are Run

A task queue, as we have already seen, is in practice a linked list of functions to call. When *run_task_queue* is asked to run a given queue, each entry in the list is executed. When you are writing functions that work with task queues, you have to keep in mind when the kernel will call *run_task_queue*; the exact context imposes some constraints on what you can do. You should also not make any assumptions regarding the order in which enqueued tasks are run; each of them must do its task independently of the other ones.

And when are task queues run? If you are using one of the predefined task queues discussed in the next section, the answer is "when the kernel gets around to it." Different queues are run at different times, but they are always run when the kernel has no other pressing work to do.

Most important, they almost certainly are *not* run when the process that queued the task is executing. They are, instead, run asynchronously. Until now, everything we have done in our sample drivers has run in the context of a process executing system calls. When a task queue runs, however, that process could be asleep, executing on a different processor, or could conceivably have exited altogether.

This asynchronous execution resembles what happens when a hardware interrupt happens (which is discussed in detail in Chapter 9). In fact, task queues are often run as the result of a "software interrupt." When running in *interrupt mode* (or *interrupt time*) in this way, your code is subject to a number of constraints. We will introduce these constraints now; they will be seen again in several places in this book. Repetition is called for in this case; the rules for interrupt mode must be followed or the system will find itself in deep trouble.

A number of actions require the context of a process in order to be executed. When you are outside of process context (i.e., in interrupt mode), you must observe the following rules:

- No access to user space is allowed. Because there is no process context, there is no path to the user space associated with any particular process.

- The `current` pointer is not valid in interrupt mode, and cannot be used.

- No sleeping or scheduling may be performed. Interrupt-mode code may not call *schedule* or *sleep_on*; it also may not call any other function that may sleep. For example, calling `kmalloc( ..., GFP_KERNEL)` is against the rules. Semaphores also may not be used since they can sleep.

Kernel code can tell if it is running in interrupt mode by calling the function *in_interrupt()*, which takes no parameters and returns nonzero if the processor is running in interrupt time.

One other feature of the current implementation of task queues is that a task can requeue itself in the same queue from which it was run. For instance, a task being run from the timer tick can reschedule itself to be run on the next tick by calling *queue_task* to put itself on the queue again. Rescheduling is possible because the head of the queue is replaced with a `NULL` pointer before consuming queued tasks; as a result, a new queue is built once the old one starts executing.

Although rescheduling the same task over and over might appear to be a pointless operation, it is sometimes useful. For example, consider a driver that moves a pair of stepper motors one step at a time by rescheduling itself on the timer queue until the target has been reached. Another example is the *jiq* module, where the printing function reschedules itself to produce its output—the result is several iterations through the timer queue.

Predefined Task Queues

The easiest way to perform deferred execution is to use the queues that are already maintained by the kernel. There are a few of these queues, but your driver can use only three of them, described in the following list. The queues are declared in `<linux/tqueue.h>`, which you should include in your source.

The scheduler queue
    The scheduler queue is unique among the predefined task queues in that it runs in process context, implying that the tasks it runs have a bit more freedom in what they can do. In Linux 2.4, this queue runs out of a dedicated

kernel thread called *keventd* and is accessed via a function called *schedule_task*. In older versions of the kernel, *keventd* was not used, and the queue (tq_scheduler) was manipulated directly.

tq_timer

> This queue is run by the timer tick. Because the tick (the function *do_timer*) runs at interrupt time, any task within this queue runs at interrupt time as well.

tq_immediate

> The immediate queue is run as soon as possible, either on return from a system call or when the scheduler is run, whichever comes first. The queue is consumed at interrupt time.

Other predefined task queues exist as well, but they are not generally of interest to driver writers.

The timeline of a driver using a task queue is represented in Figure 6-1. The figure shows a driver that queues a function in tq_immediate from an interrupt handler.

How the examples work

Examples of deferred computation are available in the *jiq* ("Just In Queue") module, from which the source in this section has been extracted. This module creates */proc* files that can be read using *dd* or other tools; this is similar to *jit*.

The process reading a *jiq* file is put to sleep until the buffer is full.* This sleeping is handled with a simple wait queue, declared as

```
DECLARE_WAIT_QUEUE_HEAD (jiq_wait);
```

The buffer is filled by successive runs of a task queue. Each pass through the queue appends a text string to the buffer being filled; each string reports the current time (in jiffies), the process that is current during this pass, and the return value of *in_interrupt*.

The code for filling the buffer is confined to the *jiq_print_tq* function, which executes at each run through the queue being used. The printing function is not interesting and is not worth showing here; instead, let's look at the initialization of the task to be inserted in a queue:

```
struct tq_struct jiq_task; /* global: initialized to zero */

    /* these lines are in jiq_init() */
    jiq_task.routine = jiq_print_tq;
    jiq_task.data = (void *)&jiq_data;
```

---

* The buffer of a */proc* file is a page of memory, 4 KB, or whatever is appropriate for the platform you use.

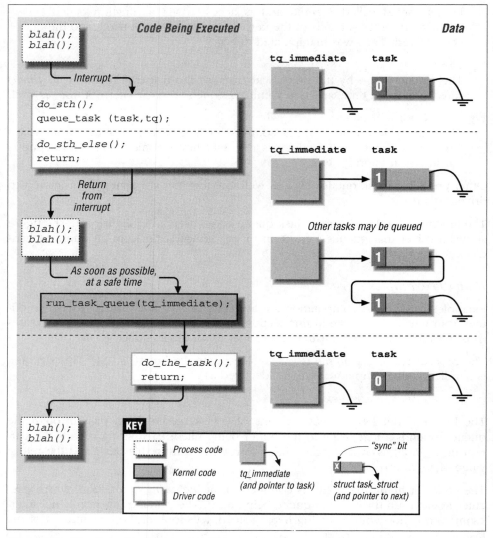

Figure 6-1. Timeline of task-queue usage

There's no need to clear the **sync** and **next** fields of **jiq_task** because static variables are initialized to 0 by the compiler.

The scheduler queue

The scheduler queue is, in some ways, the easiest to use. Because tasks executed from this queue do not run in interrupt mode, they can do more things; in particular, they can sleep. Many parts of the kernel use this queue to accomplish a wide variety of tasks.

As of kernel 2.4.0-test11, the actual task queue implementing the scheduler queue is hidden from the rest of the kernel. Rather than use *queue_task* directly, code using this queue must call *schedule_task* to put a task on the queue:

```
int schedule_task(struct tq_struct *task);
```

`task`, of course, is the task to be scheduled. The return value is directly from *queue_task*: nonzero if the task was not already on the queue.

Again, as of 2.4.0-test11, the kernel runs a special process, called *keventd*, whose sole job is running tasks from the scheduler queue. *keventd* provides a predictable process context for the tasks it runs (unlike the previous implementation, which would run tasks under an essentially random process's context).

There are a couple of implications to the *keventd* implementation that are worth keeping in mind. The first is that tasks in this queue can sleep, and some kernel code takes advantage of that freedom. Well-behaved code, however, should take care to sleep only for very short periods of time, since no other tasks will be run from the scheduler queue while *keventd* is sleeping. It is also a good idea to keep in mind that your task shares the scheduler queue with others, which can also sleep. In normal situations, tasks placed in the scheduler queue will run very quickly (perhaps even before *schedule_task* returns). If some other task sleeps, though, the time that elapses before your tasks execute could be significant. Tasks that absolutely have to run within a narrow time window should use one of the other queues.

/proc/jiqsched is a sample file that uses the scheduler queue. The *read* function for the file dispatches everything to the task queue in the following way:

```
int jiq_read_sched(char *buf, char **start, off_t offset,
                   int len, int *eof, void *data)
{

    jiq_data.len = 0;                  /* nothing printed, yet */
    jiq_data.buf = buf;                /* print in this place */
    jiq_data.jiffies = jiffies;        /* initial time */

    /* jiq_print will queue_task() again in jiq_data.queue */
    jiq_data.queue = SCHEDULER_QUEUE;

    schedule_task(&jiq_task);          /* ready to run */
    interruptible_sleep_on(&jiq_wait); /* sleep till completion */

    *eof = 1;
    return jiq_data.len;
}
```

Reading */proc/jiqsched* produces output like the following:

```
    time  delta interrupt  pid cpu command
   601687  0        0        2   1 keventd
   601687  0        0        2   1 keventd
   601687  0        0        2   1 keventd
   601687  0        0        2   1 keventd
   601687  0        0        2   1 keventd
   601687  0        0        2   1 keventd
   601687  0        0        2   1 keventd
   601687  0        0        2   1 keventd
   601687  0        0        2   1 keventd
```

In this output, the `time` field is the value of `jiffies` when the task is run, `delta` is the change in `jiffies` since the last time the task ran, `interrupt` is the output of the *in_interrupt* function, `pid` is the ID of the running process, `cpu` is the number of the CPU being used (always 0 on uniprocessor systems), and `command` is the command being run by the current process.

In this case, we see that the task is always running under the *keventd* process. It also runs very quickly—a task that resubmits itself to the scheduler queue can run hundreds or thousands of times within a single timer tick. Even on a very heavily loaded system, the latency in the scheduler queue is quite small.

The timer queue

The timer queue is different from the scheduler queue in that the queue (`tq_timer`) is directly available. Also, of course, tasks run from the timer queue are run in interrupt mode. Additionally, you're guaranteed that the queue will run at the next clock tick, thus eliminating latency caused by system load.

The sample code implements */proc/jiqtimer* with the timer queue. For this queue, it must use *queue_task* to get things going:

```
int jiq_read_timer(char *buf, char **start, off_t offset,
                   int len, int *eof, void *data)
{

    jiq_data.len = 0;          /* nothing printed, yet */
    jiq_data.buf = buf;        /* print in this place */
    jiq_data.jiffies = jiffies; /* initial time */
    jiq_data.queue = &tq_timer; /* reregister yourself here */

    queue_task(&jiq_task, &tq_timer);    /* ready to run */
    interruptible_sleep_on(&jiq_wait);   /* sleep till completion */

    *eof = 1;
    return jiq_data.len;
}
```

The following is what *head /proc/jiqtimer* returned on a system that was compiling a new kernel:

```
    time  delta interrupt   pid cpu command
45084845   1      1        8783  0  cc1
45084846   1      1        8783  0  cc1
45084847   1      1        8783  0  cc1
45084848   1      1        8783  0  cc1
45084849   1      1        8784  0  as
45084850   1      1        8758  1  cc1
45084851   1      1        8789  0  cpp
45084852   1      1        8758  1  cc1
45084853   1      1        8758  1  cc1
45084854   1      1        8758  1  cc1
45084855   1      1        8758  1  cc1
```

Note, this time, that exactly one timer tick goes by between each invocation of the task, and that an arbitrary process is running.

The immediate queue

The last predefined queue that can be used by modularized code is the immediate queue. This queue is run via the bottom-half mechanism, which means that one additional step is required to use it. Bottom halves are run only when the kernel has been told that a run is necessary; this is accomplished by "marking" the bottom half. In the case of **tq_immediate**, the necessary call is *mark_bh(IMMEDIATE_BH)*. Be sure to call *mark_bh after* the task has been queued; otherwise, the kernel may run the task queue before your task has been added.

The immediate queue is the fastest queue in the system—it's executed soonest and is run in interrupt time. The queue is consumed either by the scheduler or as soon as one process returns from its system call. Typical output can look like this:

```
    time  delta interrupt   pid cpu command
45129449   0      1        8883  0  head
45129453   4      1           0  0  swapper
45129453   0      1         601  0  X
45129453   0      1         601  0  X
45129453   0      1         601  0  X
45129453   0      1         601  0  X
45129454   1      1           0  0  swapper
45129454   0      1         601  0  X
45129454   0      1         601  0  X
45129454   0      1         601  0  X
45129454   0      1         601  0  X
45129454   0      1         601  0  X
45129454   0      1         601  0  X
```

It's clear that the queue can't be used to delay the execution of a task—it's an "immediate" queue. Instead, its purpose is to execute a task as soon as possible, but at a safe time. This feature makes it a great resource for interrupt handlers, because it offers them an entry point for executing program code outside of the actual interrupt management routine. The mechanism used to receive network packets, for example, is based on a similar mechanism.

Please note that you should not reregister your task in this queue (although we do it in *jiqimmed* for explanatory purposes). The practice gains nothing and may lock the computer hard if run on some version/platform pairs. Some implementations used to rerun the queue until it was empty. This was true, for example, for version 2.0 running on the PC platform.

Running Your Own Task Queues

Declaring a new task queue is not difficult. A driver is free to declare a new task queue, or even several of them; tasks are queued just as we've seen with the predefined queues discussed previously.

Unlike a predefined task queue, however, a custom queue is not automatically run by the kernel. The programmer who maintains a queue must arrange for a way of running it.

The following macro declares the queue and expands to a variable declaration. You'll most likely place it at the beginning of your file, outside of any function:

```
DECLARE_TASK_QUEUE(tq_custom);
```

After declaring the queue, you can invoke the usual functions to queue tasks. The call just shown pairs naturally with the following:

```
queue_task(&custom_task, &tq_custom);
```

The following line will run **tq_custom** when it is time to execute the task-queue entries that have accumulated:

```
run_task_queue(&tq_custom);
```

If you want to experiment with custom queues now, you need to register a function to trigger the queue in one of the predefined queues. Although this may look like a roundabout way to do things, it isn't. A custom queue can be useful whenever you need to accumulate jobs and execute them all at the same time, even if you use another queue to select that "same time."

Tasklets

Shortly before the release of the 2.4 kernel, the developers added a new mechanism for the deferral of kernel tasks. This mechanism, called *tasklets*, is now the preferred way to accomplish bottom-half tasks; indeed, bottom halves themselves are now implemented with tasklets.

Tasklets resemble task queues in a number of ways. They are a way of deferring a task until a safe time, and they are always run in interrupt time. Like task queues, tasklets will be run only once, even if scheduled multiple times, but tasklets may be run in parallel with other (different) tasklets on SMP systems. On SMP systems, tasklets are also guaranteed to run on the CPU that first schedules them, which provides better cache behavior and thus better performance.

Each tasklet has associated with it a function that is called when the tasklet is to be executed. The life of some kernel developer was made easier by giving that function a single argument of type **unsigned long**, which makes life a little more annoying for those who would rather pass it a pointer; casting the **long** argument to a pointer type is a safe practice on all supported architectures and pretty common in memory management (as discussed in Chapter 13). The tasklet function is of type **void**; it returns no value.

Software support for tasklets is part of **<linux/interrupt.h>**, and the tasklet itself must be declared with one of the following:

DECLARE_TASKLET(name, function, data);
> Declares a tasklet with the given name; when the tasklet is to be executed (as described later), the given function is called with the (unsigned long) data value.

DECLARE_TASKLET_DISABLED(name, function, data);
> Declares a tasklet as before, but its initial state is "disabled," meaning that it can be scheduled but will not be executed until enabled at some future time.

The sample *jiq* driver, when compiled against 2.4 headers, implements */proc/jiq-tasklet*, which works like the other *jiq* entries but uses tasklets; we didn't emulate tasklets for older kernel versions in *sysdep.h*. The module declares its tasklet as

```
void jiq_print_tasklet (unsigned long);
DECLARE_TASKLET (jiq_tasklet, jiq_print_tasklet, (unsigned long)
   &jiq_data);
```

When your driver wants to schedule a tasklet to run, it calls *tasklet_schedule*:

```
tasklet_schedule(&jiq_tasklet);
```

Once a tasklet is scheduled, it is guaranteed to be run once (if enabled) at a safe time. Tasklets may reschedule themselves in much the same manner as task queues. A tasklet need not worry about running against itself on a multiprocessor system, since the kernel takes steps to ensure that any given tasklet is only running in one place. If your driver implements multiple tasklets, however, it should be prepared for the possibility that more than one of them could run simultaneously. In that case, spinlocks must be used to protect critical sections of the code (semaphores, which can sleep, may not be used in tasklets since they run in interrupt time).

The output from */proc/jiqtasklet* looks like this:

```
     time  delta interrupt  pid cpu command
45472377  0          1     8904   0 head
45472378  1          1        0   0 swapper
45472379  1          1        0   0 swapper
45472380  1          1        0   0 swapper
45472383  3          1        0   0 swapper
45472383  0          1      601   0 X
45472383  0          1      601   0 X
45472383  0          1      601   0 X
45472383  0          1      601   0 X
45472389  6          1        0   0 swapper
```

Note that the tasklet always runs on the same CPU, even though this output was produced on a dual-CPU system.

The tasklet subsystem provides a few other functions for advanced use of tasklets:

`void tasklet_disable(struct tasklet_struct *t);`
> This function disables the given tasklet. The tasklet may still be scheduled with *tasklet_schedule*, but its execution will be deferred until a time when the tasklet has been enabled again.

`void tasklet_enable(struct tasklet_struct *t);`
> Enables a tasklet that had been previously disabled. If the tasklet has already been scheduled, it will run soon (but not directly out of *tasklet_enable*).

`void tasklet_kill(struct tasklet_struct *t);`
> This function may be used on tasklets that reschedule themselves indefinitely. *tasklet_kill* will remove the tasklet from any queue that it is on. In order to avoid race conditions with the tasklet rescheduling itself, this function waits until the tasklet executes, then pulls it from the queue. Thus, you can be sure that tasklets will not be interrupted partway through. If, however, the tasklet is not currently running and rescheduling itself, *tasklet_kill* may hang. *tasklet_kill* may not be called in interrupt time.

Kernel Timers

The ultimate resources for time keeping in the kernel are the timers. Timers are used to schedule execution of a function (a timer handler) at a particular time in the future. They thus work differently from task queues and tasklets in that you can specify *when* in the future your function will be called, whereas you can't tell exactly when a queued task will be executed. On the other hand, kernel timers are similar to task queues in that a function registered in a kernel timer is executed only once—timers aren't cyclic.

There are times when you need to execute operations detached from any process's context, like turning off the floppy motor or finishing another lengthy shutdown operation. In that case, delaying the return from *close* wouldn't be fair to the application program. Using a task queue would be wasteful, because a queued task must continually reregister itself until the requisite time has passed.

A timer is much easier to use. You register your function once, and the kernel calls it once when the timer expires. Such a functionality is used often within the kernel proper, but it is sometimes needed by the drivers as well, as in the example of the floppy motor.

The kernel timers are organized in a doubly linked list. This means that you can create as many timers as you want. A timer is characterized by its timeout value (in jiffies) and the function to be called when the timer expires. The timer handler receives an argument, which is stored in the data structure, together with a pointer to the handler itself.

The data structure of a timer looks like the following, which is extracted from `<linux/timer.h>`):

```
struct timer_list {
    struct timer_list *next;            /* never touch this */
    struct timer_list *prev;            /* never touch this */
    unsigned long expires;              /* the timeout, in jiffies */
    unsigned long data;                 /* argument to the handler */
    void (*function)(unsigned long);    /* handler of the timeout */
    volatile int running;               /* added in 2.4; don't touch */
};
```

The timeout of a timer is a value in jiffies. Thus, `timer->function` will run when `jiffies` is equal to or greater than `timer->expires`. The timeout is an absolute value; it is usually generated by taking the current value of `jiffies` and adding the amount of the desired delay.

Once a `timer_list` structure is initialized, *add_timer* inserts it into a sorted list, which is then polled more or less 100 times per second. Even systems (such as the Alpha) that run with a higher clock interrupt frequency do not check the timer list more often than that; the added timer resolution would not justify the cost of the extra passes through the list.

These are the functions used to act on timers:

`void init_timer(struct timer_list *timer);`
> This inline function is used to initialize the timer structure. Currently, it zeros the `prev` and `next` pointers (and the `running` flag on SMP systems). Programmers are strongly urged to use this function to initialize a timer and to never explicitly touch the pointers in the structure, in order to be forward compatible.

```
void add_timer(struct timer_list *timer);
```
This function inserts a timer into the global list of active timers.

```
int mod_timer(struct timer_list *timer, unsigned long
    expires);
```
Should you need to change the time at which a timer expires, *mod_timer* can be used. After the call, the new `expires` value will be used.

```
int del_timer(struct timer_list *timer);
```
If a timer needs to be removed from the list before it expires, *del_timer* should be called. When a timer expires, on the other hand, it is automatically removed from the list.

```
int del_timer_sync(struct timer_list *timer);
```
This function works like *del_timer*, but it also guarantees that, when it returns, the timer function is not running on any CPU. *del_timer_sync* is used to avoid race conditions when a timer function is running at unexpected times; it should be used in most situations. The caller of *del_timer_sync* must ensure that the timer function will not use *add_timer* to add itself again.

An example of timer usage can be seen in the *jiq* module. The file */proc/jitimer* uses a timer to generate two data lines; it uses the same printing function as the task queue examples do. The first data line is generated from the *read* call (invoked by the user process looking at */proc/jitimer*), while the second line is printed by the timer function after one second has elapsed.

The code for */proc/jitimer* is as follows:

```
struct timer_list jiq_timer;

void jiq_timedout(unsigned long ptr)
{
    jiq_print((void *)ptr);              /* print a line */
    wake_up_interruptible(&jiq_wait);  /* awaken the process */
}


int jiq_read_run_timer(char *buf, char **start, off_t offset,
                int len, int *eof, void *data)
{

    jiq_data.len = 0;        /* prepare the argument for jiq_print() */
    jiq_data.buf = buf;
    jiq_data.jiffies = jiffies;
    jiq_data.queue = NULL;        /* don't requeue */

    init_timer(&jiq_timer);                 /* init the timer structure */
    jiq_timer.function = jiq_timedout;
    jiq_timer.data = (unsigned long)&jiq_data;
    jiq_timer.expires = jiffies + HZ; /* one second */
```

```
        jiq_print(&jiq_data);     /* print and go to sleep */
        add_timer(&jiq_timer);
        interruptible_sleep_on(&jiq_wait);
        del_timer_sync(&jiq_timer);   /* in case a signal woke us up */

        *eof = 1;
        return jiq_data.len;
    }
```

Running *head /proc/jitimer* gives the following output:

```
    time  delta interrupt  pid cpu command
45584582   0          0   8920  0 head
45584682 100          1      0  1 swapper
```

From the output you can see that the timer function, which printed the last line here, was running in interrupt mode.

What can appear strange when using timers is that the timer expires at just the right time, even if the processor is executing in a system call. We suggested earlier that when a process is running in kernel space, it won't be scheduled away; the clock tick, however, is special, and it does all of its tasks independent of the current process. You can try to look at what happens when you read */proc/jitbusy* in the background and */proc/jitimer* in the foreground. Although the system appears to be locked solid by the busy-waiting system call, both the timer queue and the kernel timers continue running.

Thus, timers can be another source of race conditions, even on uniprocessor systems. Any data structures accessed by the timer function should be protected from concurrent access, either by being atomic types (discussed in Chapter 10) or by using spinlocks.

One must also be very careful to avoid race conditions with timer deletion. Consider a situation in which a module's timer function is run on one processor while a related event (a file is closed or the module is removed) happens on another. The result could be the timer function expecting a situation that is no longer valid, resulting in a system crash. To avoid this kind of race, your module should use *del_timer_sync* instead of *del_timer*. If the timer function can restart the timer itself (a common pattern), you should also have a "stop timer" flag that you set before calling *del_timer_sync*. The timer function should then check that flag and not reschedule itself with *add_timer* if the flag has been set.

Another pattern that can cause race conditions is modifying timers by deleting them with *del_timer*, then creating a new one with *add_timer*. It is better, in this situation, to simply use *mod_timer* to make the necessary change.

Backward Compatibility

Task queues and timing issues have remained relatively constant over the years. Nonetheless, a few things have changed and must be kept in mind.

The functions *sleep_on_timeout*, *interruptible_sleep_on_timeout*, and *schedule_timeout* were all added for the 2.2 kernel. In the 2.0 days, timeouts were handled with a variable (called `timeout`) in the task structure. As a result, code that now makes a call like

```
interruptible_sleep_on_timeout(my_queue, timeout);
```

used to be implemented as

```
current->timeout = jiffies + timeout;
interruptible_sleep_on(my_queue);
```

The *sysdep.h* header recreates *schedule_timeout* for pre-2.4 kernels so that you can use the new syntax and run on 2.0 and 2.2:

```
extern inline void schedule_timeout(int timeout)
{
    current->timeout = jiffies + timeout;
    current->state = TASK_INTERRUPTIBLE;
    schedule();
    current->timeout = 0;
}
```

In 2.0, there were a couple of additional functions for putting functions into task queues. *queue_task_irq* could be called instead of *queue_task* in situations in which interrupts were disabled, yielding a (very) small performance benefit. *queue_task_irq_off* is even faster, but does not function properly in situations in which the task is already queued or is running, and can thus only be used where those conditions are guaranteed not to occur. Neither of these two functions provided much in the way of performance benefits, and they were removed in kernel 2.1.30. Using *queue_task* in all cases works with all kernel versions. (It is worth noting, though, that *queue_task* had a return type of `void` in 2.2 and prior kernels.)

Prior to 2.4, the *schedule_task* function and associated *keventd* process did not exist. Instead, another predefined task queue, `tq_scheduler`, was provided. Tasks placed in `tq_scheduler` were run in the *schedule* function, and thus always ran in process context. The actual process whose context would be used was always different, however; it was whatever process was being scheduled on the CPU at the time. `tq_scheduler` typically had larger latencies, especially for tasks that resubmitted themselves. *sysdep.h* provides the following implementation for *schedule_task* on 2.0 and 2.2 systems:

```
extern inline int schedule_task(struct tq_struct *task)
{
        queue_task(task, &tq_scheduler);
        return 1;
}
```

As has been mentioned, the 2.3 development series added the tasklet mechanism; before, only task queues were available for "immediate deferred" execution. The bottom-half subsystem was implemented differently, though most of the changes are not visible to driver writers. We didn't emulate tasklets for older kernels in *sysdep.h* because they are not strictly needed for driver operation; if you want to be backward compatible you'll need to either write your own emulation or use task queues instead.

The *in_interrupt* function did not exist in Linux 2.0. Instead, a global variable `intr_count` kept track of the number of interrupt handlers running. Querying `intr_count` is semantically the same as calling *in_interrupt*, so compatibility is easily implemented in *sysdep.h*.

The *del_timer_sync* function did not exist prior to development kernel 2.4.0-test2. The usual *sysdep.h* header defines a minimal replacement when you build against older kernel headers. Kernel version 2.0 didn't have *mod_timer*, either. This gap is also filled by our compatibility header.

Quick Reference

This chapter introduced the following symbols:

`#include <linux/param.h>`
HZ The HZ symbol specifies the number of clock ticks generated per second.

`#include <linux/sched.h>`
`volatile unsigned long jiffies`
> The `jiffies` variable is incremented once for each clock tick; thus, it's incremented HZ times per second.

`#include <asm/msr.h>`
`rdtsc(low,high);`
`rdtscl(low);`
> Read the timestamp counter or its lower half. The header and macros are specific to PC-class processors; other platforms may need **asm** constructs to achieve similar results.

`extern struct timeval xtime;`
> The current time, as calculated at the last timer tick.

```
#include <linux/time.h>
void do_gettimeofday(struct timeval *tv);
void get_fast_time(struct timeval *tv);
```
The functions return the current time; the former is very high resolution, the latter may be faster while giving coarser resolution.

```
#include <linux/delay.h>
void udelay(unsigned long usecs);
void mdelay(unsigned long msecs);
```
The functions introduce delays of an integer number of microseconds and milliseconds. The former should be used to wait for no longer than one millisecond; the latter should be used with extreme care because these delays are both busy-loops.

```
int in_interrupt();
```
Returns nonzero if the processor is currently running in interrupt mode.

```
#include <linux/tqueue.h>
DECLARE_TASK_QUEUE(variablename);
```
The macro declares a new variable and initializes it.

```
void queue_task(struct tq_struct *task, task_queue *list);
```
The function registers a task for later execution.

```
void run_task_queue(task_queue *list);
```
This function consumes a task queue.

```
task_queue tq_immediate, tq_timer;
```
These predefined task queues are run as soon as possible (for `tq_immediate`), or after each timer tick (for `tq_timer`).

```
int schedule_task(struct tq_struct *task);
```
Schedules a task to be run on the scheduler queue.

```
#include <linux/interrupt.h>
DECLARE_TASKLET(name, function, data)
DECLARE_TASKLET_DISABLED(name, function, data)
```
Declare a tasklet structure that will call the given function (passing it the given `unsigned long data`) when the tasklet is executed. The second form initializes the tasklet to a disabled state, keeping it from running until it is explicitly enabled.

```
void tasklet_schedule(struct tasklet_struct *tasklet);
```
Schedules the given tasklet for running. If the tasklet is enabled, it will be run shortly on the same CPU that ran the first call to *tasklet_schedule*.

```
tasklet_enable(struct tasklet_struct *tasklet);
tasklet_disable(struct tasklet_struct *tasklet);
```
These functions respectively enable and disable the given tasklet. A disabled tasklet can be scheduled, but will not run until it has been enabled again.

```
void tasklet_kill(struct tasklet_struct *tasklet);
```
Causes an "infinitely rescheduling" tasklet to cease execution. This function can block and may not be called in interrupt time.

```
#include <linux/timer.h>
void init_timer(struct timer_list * timer);
```
This function initializes a newly allocated `timer`.

```
void add_timer(struct timer_list * timer);
```
This function inserts the `timer` into the global list of pending timers.

```
int mod_timer(struct timer_list *timer, unsigned long
        expires);
```
This function is used to change the expiration time of an already scheduled timer structure.

```
int del_timer(struct timer_list * timer);
```
del_timer removes a timer from the list of pending timers. If the timer was actually queued, *del_timer* returns 1; otherwise, it returns 0.

```
int del_timer_sync(struct timer_list *timer);
```
This function is similar to *del_timer*, but guarantees that the function is not currently running on other CPUs.

## CHAPTER SEVEN

GETTING HOLD OF MEMORY

Thus far, we have used *kmalloc* and *kfree* for the allocation and freeing of memory. The Linux kernel offers a richer set of memory allocation primitives, however. In this chapter we look at other ways of making use of memory in device drivers and at how to make the best use of your system's memory resources. We will not get into how the different architectures actually administer memory. Modules are not involved in issues of segmentation, paging, and so on, since the kernel offers a unified memory management interface to the drivers. In addition, we won't describe the internal details of memory management in this chapter, but will defer it to "Memory Management in Linux" in Chapter 13.

The Real Story of kmalloc

The *kmalloc* allocation engine is a powerful tool, and easily learned because of its similarity to *malloc*. The function is fast—unless it blocks—and it doesn't clear the memory it obtains; the allocated region still holds its previous content. The allocated region is also contiguous in physical memory. In the next few sections, we talk in detail about *kmalloc*, so you can compare it with the memory allocation techniques that we discuss later.

The Flags Argument

The first argument to *kmalloc* is the size of the block to be allocated. The second argument, the allocation flags, is much more interesting, because it controls the behavior of *kmalloc* in a number of ways.

The most-used flag, `GFP_KERNEL`, means that the allocation (internally performed by calling, eventually, *get_free_pages*, which is the source of the `GFP_` prefix) is performed on behalf of a process running in kernel space. In other words, this means that the calling function is executing a system call on behalf of a process. Using GFP_KERNEL means that *kmalloc* can put the current process to sleep waiting for a page when called in low-memory situations. A function that allocates memory using GFP_KERNEL must therefore be reentrant. While the current process sleeps, the kernel takes proper action to retrieve a memory page, either by flushing buffers to disk or by swapping out memory from a user process.

GFP_KERNEL isn't always the right allocation flag to use; sometimes *kmalloc* is called from outside a process's context. This type of call can happen, for instance, in interrupt handlers, task queues, and kernel timers. In this case, the current process should not be put to sleep, and the driver should use a flag of GFP_ATOMIC instead. The kernel normally tries to keep some free pages around in order to fulfill atomic allocation. When GFP_ATOMIC is used, *kmalloc* can use even the last free page. If that last page does not exist, however, the allocation will fail.

Other flags can be used in place of or in addition to GFP_KERNEL and GFP_ATOMIC, although those two cover most of the needs of device drivers. All the flags are defined in <linux/mm.h>: individual flags are prefixed with a double underscore, like __GFP_DMA; collections of flags lack the prefix and are sometimes called *allocation priorities*.

GFP_KERNEL

> Normal allocation of kernel memory. May sleep.

GFP_BUFFER

> Used in managing the buffer cache, this priority allows the allocator to sleep. It differs from GFP_KERNEL in that fewer attempts will be made to free memory by flushing dirty pages to disk; the purpose here is to avoid deadlocks when the I/O subsystems themselves need memory.

GFP_ATOMIC

> Used to allocate memory from interrupt handlers and other code outside of a process context. Never sleeps.

GFP_USER

> Used to allocate memory on behalf of the user. It may sleep, and is a low-priority request.

GFP_HIGHUSER

> Like GFP_USER, but allocates from high memory, if any. High memory is described in the next subsection.

__GFP_DMA

> This flag requests memory usable in DMA data transfers to/from devices. Its exact meaning is platform dependent, and the flag can be OR'd to either GFP_KERNEL or GFP_ATOMIC.

_ _GFP_HIGHMEM

> The flag requests high memory, a platform-dependent feature that has no effect on platforms that don't support it. It is part of the GFP_HIGHUSER mask and has little use elsewhere.

Memory zones

Both _ _GFP_DMA and _ _GFP_HIGHMEM have a platform-dependent role, although their use is valid for all platforms.

Version 2.4 of the kernel knows about three *memory zones:* DMA-capable memory, normal memory, and high memory. While allocation normally happens in the *normal* zone, setting either of the bits just mentioned requires memory to be allocated from a different zone. The idea is that every computer platform that must know about special memory ranges (instead of considering all RAM equivalent) will fall into this abstraction.

DMA-capable memory is the only memory that can be involved in DMA data transfers with peripheral devices. This restriction arises when the address bus used to connect peripheral devices to the processor is limited with respect to the address bus used to access RAM. For example, on the x86, devices that plug into the ISA bus can only address memory from 0 to 16 MB. Other platforms have similar needs, although usually less stringent than the ISA one.*

High memory is memory that requires special handling to be accessed. It made its appearance in kernel memory management when support for the Pentium II Virtual Memory Extension was implemented during 2.3 development to access up to 64 GB of physical memory. High memory is a concept that only applies to the x86 and SPARC platforms, and the two implementations are different.

Whenever a new page is allocated to fulfill the *kmalloc* request, the kernel builds a list of zones that can be used in the search. If _ _GFP_DMA is specified, only the DMA zone is searched: if no memory is available at low addresses, allocation fails. If no special flag is present, both normal and DMA memory is searched; if _ _GFP_HIGHMEM is set, then all three zones are used to search a free page.

If the platform has no concept of high memory or it has been disabled in the kernel configuration, _ _GFP_HIGHMEM is defined as 0 and has no effect.

The mechanism behind memory zones is implemented in *mm/page_alloc.c*, while initialization of the zone resides in platform-specific files, usually in *mm/init.c* within the *arch* tree. We'll revisit these topics in Chapter 13.

---

* It's interesting to note that the limit is only in force for the ISA bus; an x86 device that plugs into the PCI bus can perform DMA with all *normal* memory.

The Size Argument

The kernel manages the system's *physical* memory, which is available only in page-sized chunks. As a result, *kmalloc* looks rather different than a typical user-space *malloc* implementation. A simple, heap-oriented allocation technique would quickly run into trouble; it would have a hard time working around the page boundaries. Thus, the kernel uses a special page-oriented allocation technique to get the best use from the system's RAM.

Linux handles memory allocation by creating a set of pools of memory objects of fixed sizes. Allocation requests are handled by going to a pool that holds sufficiently large objects, and handing an entire memory chunk back to the requester. The memory management scheme is quite complex, and the details of it are not normally all that interesting to device driver writers. After all, the implementation can change—as it did in the 2.1.38 kernel—without affecting the interface seen by the rest of the kernel.

The one thing driver developers should keep in mind, though, is that the kernel can allocate only certain predefined fixed-size byte arrays. If you ask for an arbitrary amount of memory, you're likely to get slightly more than you asked for, up to twice as much. Also, programmers should remember that the minimum memory that *kmalloc* handles is as big as 32 or 64, depending on the page size used by the current architecture.

The data sizes available are generally powers of two. In the 2.0 kernel, the available sizes were actually slightly less than a power of two, due to control flags added by the management system. If you keep this fact in mind, you'll use memory more efficiently. For example, if you need a buffer of about 2000 bytes and run Linux 2.0, you're better off asking for 2000 bytes, rather than 2048. Requesting exactly a power of two is the worst possible case with any kernel older than 2.1.38—the kernel will allocate twice as much as you requested. This is why *scull* used 4000 bytes per quantum instead of 4096.

You can find the exact values used for the allocation blocks in *mm/kmalloc.c* (with the 2.0 kernel) or `mm/slab.c` (in current kernels), but remember that they can change again without notice. The trick of allocating less than 4 KB works well for *scull* with all 2.*x* kernels, but it's not guaranteed to be optimal in the future.

In any case, the maximum size that can be allocated by *kmalloc* is 128 KB—slightly less with 2.0 kernels. If you need more than a few kilobytes, however, there are better ways than *kmalloc* to obtain memory, as outlined next.

Lookaside Caches

A device driver often ends up allocating many objects of the same size, over and over. Given that the kernel already maintains a set of memory pools of objects that are all the same size, why not add some special pools for these high-volume objects? In fact, the kernel does implement this sort of *lookaside cache*. Device drivers normally do not exhibit the sort of memory behavior that justifies using a lookaside cache, but there can be exceptions; the USB and ISDN drivers in Linux 2.4 use caches.

Linux memory caches have a type of `kmem_cache_t` and are created with a call to *kmem_cache_create*:

```
kmem_cache_t * kmem_cache_create(const char *name, size_t size,
    size_t offset, unsigned long flags,
    void (*constructor)(void *, kmem_cache_t *,
        unsigned long flags),
    void (*destructor)(void *, kmem_cache_t *,
        unsigned long flags) );
```

The function creates a new cache object that can host any number of memory areas all of the same size, specified by the `size` argument. The `name` argument is associated with this cache and functions as housekeeping information usable in tracking problems; usually, it is set to the name of the type of structure that will be cached. The maximum length for the name is 20 characters, including the trailing terminator.

The `offset` is the offset of the first object in the page; it can be used to ensure a particular alignment for the allocated objects, but you most likely will use 0 to request the default value. `flags` controls how allocation is done, and is a bit mask of the following flags:

SLAB_NO_REAP
> Setting this flag protects the cache from being reduced when the system is looking for memory. You would not usually need to set this flag.

SLAB_HWCACHE_ALIGN
> This flag requires each data object to be aligned to a cache line; actual alignment depends on the cache layout of the host platform. This is usually a good choice.

SLAB_CACHE_DMA
> This flag requires each data object to be allocated in DMA-capable memory.

The `constructor` and `destructor` arguments to the function are optional functions (but there can be no destructor without a constructor); the former can be used to initialize newly allocated objects and the latter can be used to "clean up" objects prior to their memory being released back to the system as a whole.

Constructors and destructors can be useful, but there are a few constraints that you should keep in mind. A constructor is called when the memory for a set of objects is allocated; because that memory may hold several objects, the constructor may be called multiple times. You cannot assume that the constructor will be called as an immediate effect of allocating an object. Similarly, destructors can be called at some unknown future time, not immediately after an object has been freed. Constructors and destructors may or may not be allowed to sleep, according to whether they are passed the SLAB_CTOR_ATOMIC flag (where CTOR is short for *constructor*).

For convenience, a programmer can use the same function for both the constructor and destructor; the slab allocator always passes the SLAB_CTOR_CONSTRUCTOR flag when the callee is a constructor.

Once a cache of objects is created, you can allocate objects from it by calling *kmem_cache_alloc*:

```
void *kmem_cache_alloc(kmem_cache_t *cache, int flags);
```

Here, the `cache` argument is the cache you have created previously; the flags are the same as you would pass to *kmalloc*, and are consulted if *kmem_cache_alloc* needs to go out and allocate more memory itself.

To free an object, use *kmem_cache_free*:

```
void kmem_cache_free(kmem_cache_t *cache, const void *obj);
```

When driver code is finished with the cache, typically when the module is unloaded, it should free its cache as follows:

```
int kmem_cache_destroy(kmem_cache_t *cache);
```

The destroy option will succeed only if all objects allocated from the cache have been returned to it. A module should thus check the return status from *kmem_cache_destroy*; a failure indicates some sort of memory leak within the module (since some of the objects have been dropped).

One side benefit to using lookaside caches is that the kernel maintains statistics on cache usage. There is even a kernel configuration option that enables the collection of extra statistical information, but at a noticeable runtime cost. Cache statistics may be obtained from */proc/slabinfo*.

A scull Based on the Slab Caches: scullc

Time for an example. *scullc* is a cut-down version of the *scull* module that implements only the bare device—the persistent memory region. Unlike *scull*, which uses *kmalloc*, *scullc* uses memory caches. The size of the quantum can be modified at compile time and at load time, but not at runtime—that would require creating a new memory cache, and we didn't want to deal with these unneeded details. The sample module refuses to compile with version 2.0 of the kernel because memory caches were not there, as explained in "Backward Compatibility" later in the chapter.

scullc is a complete example that can be used to make tests. It differs from *scull* only in a few lines of code. This is how it allocates memory quanta:

```
/* Allocate a quantum using the memory cache */
if (!dptr->data[s_pos]) {
    dptr->data[s_pos] =
        kmem_cache_alloc(scullc_cache, GFP_KERNEL);
    if (!dptr->data[s_pos])
        goto nomem;
    memset(dptr->data[s_pos], 0, scullc_quantum);
}
```

And these lines release memory:

```
for (i = 0; i < qset; i++)
    if (dptr->data[i])
        kmem_cache_free(scullc_cache, dptr->data[i]);
kfree(dptr->data);
```

To support use of `scullc_cache`, these few lines are included in the file at proper places:

```
/* declare one cache pointer: use it for all devices */
kmem_cache_t *scullc_cache;

    /* init_module: create a cache for our quanta */
    scullc_cache =
        kmem_cache_create("scullc", scullc_quantum,
                          0, SLAB_HWCACHE_ALIGN,
                          NULL, NULL); /* no ctor/dtor */
    if (!scullc_cache) {
        result = -ENOMEM;
        goto fail_malloc2;
    }

    /* cleanup_module: release the cache of our quanta */
    kmem_cache_destroy(scullc_cache);
```

The main differences in passing from *scull* to *scullc* are a slight speed improvement and better memory use. Since quanta are allocated from a pool of memory fragments of exactly the right size, their placement in memory is as dense as possible, as opposed to *scull* quanta, which bring in an unpredictable memory fragmentation.

get_free_page and Friends

If a module needs to allocate big chunks of memory, it is usually better to use a page-oriented technique. Requesting whole pages also has other advantages, which will be introduced later, in "The mmap Device Operation" in Chapter 13.

To allocate pages, the following functions are available:

get_zeroed_page
Returns a pointer to a new page and fills the page with zeros.

__get_free_page
Similar to *get_zeroed_page*, but doesn't clear the page.

__get_free_pages
Allocates and returns a pointer to the first byte of a memory area that is several (physically contiguous) pages long, but doesn't zero the area.

__get_dma_pages
Similar to *get_free_pages*, but guarantees that the allocated memory is DMA capable. If you use version 2.2 or later of the kernel, you can simply use *__get_free_pages* and pass the __GFP_DMA flag; if you want backward compatibility with 2.0, you need to call this function instead.

The prototypes for the functions follow:

```
unsigned long get_zeroed_page(int flags);
unsigned long __get_free_page(int flags);
unsigned long __get_free_pages(int flags, unsigned long order);
unsigned long __get_dma_pages(int flags, unsigned long order);
```

The **flags** argument works in the same way as with *kmalloc*; usually either GFP_KERNEL or GFP_ATOMIC is used, perhaps with the addition of the __GFP_DMA flag (for memory that can be used for direct memory access operations) or __GFP_HIGHMEM when high memory can be used. **order** is the base-two logarithm of the number of pages you are requesting or freeing (i.e., $\log_2 N$). For example, **order** is 0 if you want one page and 3 if you request eight pages. If **order** is too big (no contiguous area of that size is available), the page allocation will fail. The maximum value of **order** was 5 in Linux 2.0 (corresponding to 32 pages) and 9 with later versions (corresponding to 512 pages: 2 MB on most platforms). Anyway, the bigger **order** is, the more likely it is that the allocation will fail.

When a program is done with the pages, it can free them with one of the following functions. The first function is a macro that falls back on the second:

```
void free_page(unsigned long addr);
void free_pages(unsigned long addr, unsigned long order);
```

If you try to free a different number of pages than you allocated, the memory map will become corrupted and the system will get in trouble at a later time.

It's worth stressing that *get_free_pages* and the other functions can be called at any time, subject to the same rules we saw for *kmalloc*. The functions can fail to allocate memory in certain circumstances, particularly when GFP_ATOMIC is used. Therefore, the program calling these allocation functions must be prepared to handle an allocation failure.

It has been said that if you want to live dangerously, you can assume that neither *kmalloc* nor the underlying *get_free_pages* will ever fail when called with a priority of GFP_KERNEL. This is *almost* true, but not completely: small, memory-limited systems can still run into trouble. A driver writer ignores the possibility of allocation failures at his or her peril (or that of his or her users).

Although kmalloc(GFP_KERNEL) sometimes fails when there is no available memory, the kernel does its best to fulfill allocation requests. Therefore, it's easy to degrade system responsiveness by allocating too much memory. For example, you can bring the computer down by pushing too much data into a *scull* device; the system will start crawling while it tries to swap out as much as possible in order to fulfill the *kmalloc* request. Since every resource is being sucked up by the growing device, the computer is soon rendered unusable; at that point you can no longer even start a new process to try to deal with the problem. We don't address this issue in *scull*, since it is just a sample module and not a real tool to put into a multiuser system. As a programmer, you must nonetheless be careful, because a module is privileged code and can open new security holes in the system (the most likely is a denial-of-service hole like the one just outlined).

A scull Using Whole Pages: scullp

In order to test page allocation for real, the *scullp* module is released together with other sample code. It is a reduced *scull*, just like *scullc* introduced earlier.

Memory quanta allocated by *scullp* are whole pages or page sets: the scullp_order variable defaults to 0 and can be specified at either compile time or load time.

The following lines show how it allocates memory:

```
/* Here's the allocation of a single quantum */
if (!dptr->data[s_pos]) {
    dptr->data[s_pos] =
        (void *)__get_free_pages(GFP_KERNEL, dptr->order);
    if (!dptr->data[s_pos])
        goto nomem;
    memset(dptr->data[s_pos], 0, PAGE_SIZE << dptr->order);
}
```

The code to deallocate memory in *scullp*, instead, looks like this:

```
/* This code frees a whole quantum set */
for (i = 0; i < qset; i++)
    if (dptr->data[i])
        free_pages((unsigned long)(dptr->data[i]),
                    dptr->order);
```

At the user level, the perceived difference is primarily a speed improvement and better memory use because there is no internal fragmentation of memory. We ran some tests copying four megabytes from *scull0* to *scull1* and then from *scullp0* to *scullp1*; the results showed a slight improvement in kernel-space processor usage.

The performance improvement is not dramatic, because *kmalloc* is designed to be fast. The main advantage of page-level allocation isn't actually speed, but rather more efficient memory usage. Allocating by pages wastes no memory, whereas using *kmalloc* wastes an unpredictable amount of memory because of allocation granularity.

But the biggest advantage of _ _*get_free_page* is that the page is completely yours, and you could, in theory, assemble the pages into a linear area by appropriate tweaking of the page tables. For example, you can allow a user process to *mmap* memory areas obtained as single unrelated pages. We'll discuss this kind of operation in "The mmap Device Operation" in Chapter 13, where we show how *scullp* offers memory mapping, something that *scull* cannot offer.

vmalloc and Friends

The next memory allocation function that we'll show you is *vmalloc*, which allocates a contiguous memory region in the *virtual* address space. Although the pages are not necessarily consecutive in physical memory (each page is retrieved with a separate call to _ _*get_free_page*), the kernel sees them as a contiguous range of addresses. *vmalloc* returns 0 (the NULL address) if an error occurs, otherwise, it returns a pointer to a linear memory area of size at least size.

The prototypes of the function and its relatives (*ioremap*, which is not strictly an allocation function, will be discussed shortly) are as follows:

```
#include <linux/vmalloc.h>

void * vmalloc(unsigned long size);
void vfree(void * addr);
void *ioremap(unsigned long offset, unsigned long size);
void iounmap(void * addr);
```

It's worth stressing that memory addresses returned by *kmalloc* and *get_free_pages* are also virtual addresses. Their actual value is still massaged by the MMU (memory management unit, usually part of the CPU) before it is used to address physical memory.* *vmalloc* is not different in how it uses the hardware, but rather in how the kernel performs the allocation task.

---

* Actually, some architectures define ranges of "virtual" addresses as reserved to address physical memory. When this happens, the Linux kernel takes advantage of the feature, and both the kernel and *get_free_pages* addresses lie in one of those memory ranges. The difference is transparent to device drivers and other code that is not directly involved with the memory-management kernel subsystem.

The (virtual) address range used by *kmalloc* and *get_free_pages* features a one-to-one mapping to physical memory, possibly shifted by a constant `PAGE_OFFSET` value; the functions don't need to modify the page tables for that address range. The address range used by *vmalloc* and *ioremap*, on the other hand, is completely synthetic, and each allocation builds the (virtual) memory area by suitably setting up the page tables.

This difference can be perceived by comparing the pointers returned by the allocation functions. On some platforms (for example, the x86), addresses returned by *vmalloc* are just greater than addresses that *kmalloc* addresses. On other platforms (for example, MIPS and IA-64), they belong to a completely different address range. Addresses available for *vmalloc* are in the range from `VMALLOC_START` to `VMALLOC_END`. Both symbols are defined in `<asm/pgtable.h>`.

Addresses allocated by *vmalloc* can't be used outside of the microprocessor, because they make sense only on top of the processor's MMU. When a driver needs a real physical address (such as a DMA address, used by peripheral hardware to drive the system's bus), you can't easily use *vmalloc*. The right time to call *vmalloc* is when you are allocating memory for a large sequential buffer that exists only in software. It's important to note that *vmalloc* has more overhead than _ _*get_free_pages* because it must both retrieve the memory and build the page tables. Therefore, it doesn't make sense to call *vmalloc* to allocate just one page.

An example of a function that uses *vmalloc* is the *create_module* system call, which uses *vmalloc* to get space for the module being created. Code and data of the module are later copied to the allocated space using *copy_from_user*, after *insmod* has relocated the code. In this way, the module appears to be loaded into contiguous memory. You can verify, by looking in */proc/ksyms*, that kernel symbols exported by modules lie in a different memory range than symbols exported by the kernel proper.

Memory allocated with *vmalloc* is released by *vfree*, in the same way that *kfree* releases memory allocated by *kmalloc*.

Like *vmalloc*, *ioremap* builds new page tables; unlike *vmalloc*, however, it doesn't actually allocate any memory. The return value of *ioremap* is a special virtual address that can be used to access the specified physical address range; the virtual address obtained is eventually released by calling *iounmap*. Note that the return value from *ioremap* cannot be safely dereferenced on all platforms; instead, functions like *readb* should be used. See "Directly Mapped Memory" in Chapter 8for the details.

ioremap is most useful for mapping the (physical) address of a PCI buffer to (virtual) kernel space. For example, it can be used to access the frame buffer of a PCI video device; such buffers are usually mapped at high physical addresses, outside of the address range for which the kernel builds page tables at boot time. PCI issues are explained in more detail in "The PCI Interface" in Chapter 15.

It's worth noting that for the sake of portability, you should not directly access addresses returned by *ioremap* as if they were pointers to memory. Rather, you should always use *readb* and the other I/O functions introduced in Using I/O Memory, in Chapter 8. This requirement applies because some platforms, such as the Alpha, are unable to directly map PCI memory regions to the processor address space because of differences between PCI specs and Alpha processors in how data is transferred.

There is almost no limit to how much memory *vmalloc* can allocate and *ioremap* can make accessible, although *vmalloc* refuses to allocate more memory than the amount of physical RAM, in order to detect common errors or typos made by programmers. You should remember, however, that requesting too much memory with *vmalloc* leads to the same problems as it does with *kmalloc*.

Both *ioremap* and *vmalloc* are page oriented (they work by modifying the page tables); thus the relocated or allocated size is rounded up to the nearest page boundary. In addition, the implementation of *ioremap* found in Linux 2.0 won't even consider remapping a physical address that doesn't start at a page boundary. Newer kernels allow that by "rounding down" the address to be remapped and by returning an offset into the first remapped page.

One minor drawback of *vmalloc* is that it can't be used at interrupt time because internally it uses `kmalloc(GFP_KERNEL)` to acquire storage for the page tables, and thus could sleep. This shouldn't be a problem—if the use of *__get_free_page* isn't good enough for an interrupt handler, then the software design needs some cleaning up.

A scull Using Virtual Addresses: scullv

Sample code using *vmalloc* is provided in the *scullv* module. Like *scullp*, this module is a stripped-down version of *scull* that uses a different allocation function to obtain space for the device to store data.

The module allocates memory 16 pages at a time. The allocation is done in large chunks to achieve better performance than *scullp* and to show something that takes too long with other allocation techniques to be feasible. Allocating more than one page with *__get_free_pages* is failure prone, and even when it succeeds, it can be slow. As we saw earlier, *vmalloc* is faster than other functions in allocating several pages, but somewhat slower when retrieving a single page, because of the overhead of page-table building. *scullv* is designed like *scullp*. `order` specifies the "order" of each allocation and defaults to 4. The only difference between *scullv* and *scullp* is in allocation management. These lines use *vmalloc* to obtain new memory:

```
/* Allocate a quantum using virtual addresses */
if (!dptr->data[s_pos]) {
    dptr->data[s_pos] =
        (void *)vmalloc(PAGE_SIZE << dptr->order);
```

```
    if (!dptr->data[s_pos])
        goto nomem;
    memset(dptr->data[s_pos], 0, PAGE_SIZE << dptr->order);
}
```

And these lines release memory:

```
/* Release the quantum set */
for (i = 0; i < qset; i++)
    if (dptr->data[i])
        vfree(dptr->data[i]);
```

If you compile both modules with debugging enabled, you can look at their data allocation by reading the files they create in */proc*. The following snapshots were taken on two different systems:

```
salma% cat /tmp/bigfile > /dev/scullp0; head -5 /proc/scullpmem

Device 0: qset 500, order 0, sz 1048576
  item at e00000003e641b40, qset at e000000025c60000
        0:e00000003007c000
        1:e000000024778000
salma% cat /tmp/bigfile > /dev/scullv0; head -5 /proc/scullvmem

Device 0: qset 500, order 4, sz 1048576
  item at e0000000303699c0, qset at e000000025c87000
        0:a000000000034000
        1:a000000000078000
salma% uname -m
ia64

rudo% cat /tmp/bigfile > /dev/scullp0; head -5 /proc/scullpmem

Device 0: qset 500, order 0, sz 1048576
  item at c4184780, qset at c71c4800
        0:c262b000
        1:c2193000
rudo%  cat /tmp/bigfile > /dev/scullv0; head -5 /proc/scullvmem

Device 0: qset 500, order 4, sz 1048576
  item at c4184b80, qset at c71c4000
        0:c881a000
        1:c882b000
rudo% uname -m
i686
```

The values show two different behaviors. On IA-64, physical addresses and virtual addresses are mapped to completely different address ranges (0xE and 0xA), whereas on x86 computers *vmalloc* returns virtual addresses just above the mapping used for physical memory.

Boot-Time Allocation

If you really need a huge buffer of physically contiguous memory, you need to allocate it by requesting memory at boot time. This technique is inelegant and inflexible, but it is also the least prone to failure. Needless to say, a module can't allocate memory at boot time; only drivers directly linked to the kernel can do that.

Allocation at boot time is the only way to retrieve consecutive memory pages while bypassing the limits imposed by *get_free_pages* on the buffer size, both in terms of maximum allowed size and limited choice of sizes. Allocating memory at boot time is a "dirty" technique, because it bypasses all memory management policies by reserving a private memory pool.

One noticeable problem with boot-time allocation is that it is not a feasible option for the average user: being only available for code linked in the kernel image, a device driver using this kind of allocation can only be installed or replaced by rebuilding the kernel and rebooting the computer. Fortunately, there are a pair of workarounds to this problem, which we introduce soon.

Even though we won't suggest allocating memory at boot time, it's something worth mentioning because it used to be the only way to allocate a DMA-capable buffer in the first Linux versions, before __GFP_DMA was introduced.

Acquiring a Dedicated Buffer at Boot Time

When the kernel is booted, it gains access to all the physical memory available in the system. It then initializes each of its subsystems by calling that subsystem's initialization function, allowing initialization code to allocate a memory buffer for private use by reducing the amount of RAM left for normal system operation.

With version 2.4 of the kernel, this kind of allocation is performed by calling one of these functions:

```
#include <linux/bootmem.h>
void *alloc_bootmem(unsigned long size);
void *alloc_bootmem_low(unsigned long size);
void *alloc_bootmem_pages(unsigned long size);
void *alloc_bootmem_low_pages(unsigned long size);
```

The functions allocate either whole pages (if they end with **_pages**) or non-page-aligned memory areas. They allocate either low or normal memory (see the discussion of memory zones earlier in this chapter). Normal allocation returns memory addresses that are above MAX_DMA_ADDRESS; low memory is at addresses lower than that value.

This interface was introduced in version 2.3.23 of the kernel. Earlier versions used a less refined interface, similar to the one described in Unix books. Basically, the initialization functions of several kernel subsystems received two **unsigned long** arguments, which represented the current bounds of the free memory area. Each such function could steal part of this area, returning the new lower bound. A driver allocating memory at boot time, therefore, was able to steal consecutive memory from the linear array of available RAM.

The main problem with this older mechanism of managing boot-time allocation requests was that not all initialization functions could modify the lower memory bound, so writing a driver needing such allocation usually implied providing users with a kernel patch. On the other hand, *alloc_bootmem* can be called by the initialization function of any kernel subsystem, provided it is performed at boot time.

This way of allocating memory has several disadvantages, not the least being the inability to ever free the buffer. After a driver has taken some memory, it has no way of returning it to the pool of free pages; the pool is created after all the physical allocation has taken place, and we don't recommend hacking the data structures internal to memory management. On the other hand, the advantage of this technique is that it makes available an area of consecutive physical memory that is suitable for DMA. This is currently the only safe way in the standard kernel to allocate a buffer of more than 32 consecutive pages, because the maximum value of **order** that is accepted by *get_free_pages* is 5. If, however, you need many pages and they don't have to be physically contiguous, *vmalloc* is by far the best function to use.

If you are going to resort to grabbing memory at boot time, you must modify *init/main.c* in the kernel sources. You'll find more about *main.c* in Chapter 16.

Note that this "allocation" can be performed only in multiples of the page size, though the number of pages doesn't have to be a power of two.

The bigphysarea Patch

Another approach that can be used to make large, contiguous memory regions available to drivers is to apply the *bigphysarea* patch. This unofficial patch has been floating around the Net for years; it is so renowned and useful that some distributions apply it to the kernel images they install by default. The patch basically allocates memory at boot time and makes it available to device drivers at runtime. You'll need to pass a command-line option to the kernel to specify the amount of memory that must be reserved at boot time.

The patch is currently maintained at *http://www.polyware.nl/~middelink/En/hob-v4l.html*. It includes its own documentation that describes the allocation interface it offers to device drivers. The Zoran 36120 frame grabber driver, part of the 2.4 kernel (in *drivers/char/zr36120.c*) uses the *bigphysarea* extension if it is available, and is thus a good example of how the interface is used.

Reserving High RAM Addresses

The last option for allocating contiguous memory areas, and possibly the easiest, is reserving a memory area at the *end* of physical memory (whereas *bigphysarea* reserves it at the beginning of physical memory). To this aim, you need to pass a command-line option to the kernel to limit the amount of memory being managed. For example, one of your authors uses `mem=126M` to reserve 2 megabytes in a system that actually has 128 megabytes of RAM. Later, at runtime, this memory can be allocated and used by device drivers.

The *allocator* module, part of the sample code released on the O'Reilly FTP site, offers an allocation interface to manage any high memory not used by the Linux kernel. The module is described in more detail in "Do-it-yourself allocation" in Chapter 13.

The advantage of *allocator* over the *bigphysarea* patch is that there's no need to modify official kernel sources. The disadvantage is that you must change the command-line option to the kernel whenever you change the amount of RAM in the system. Another disadvantage, which makes *allocator* unsuitable in some situations is that high memory cannot be used for some tasks, such as DMA buffers for ISA devices.

Backward Compatibility

The Linux memory management subsystem has changed dramatically since the 2.0 kernel came out. Happily, however, the changes to its programming interface have been much smaller and easier to deal with.

kmalloc and *kfree* have remained essentially constant between Linux 2.0 and 2.4. Access to high memory, and thus the `__GFP_HIGHMEM` flag, was added starting with kernel 2.3.23; *sysdep.h* fills the gaps and allows for 2.4 semantics to be used in 2.2 and 2.0.

The lookaside cache functions were introduced in Linux 2.1.23, and were simply not available in the 2.0 kernel. Code that must be portable back to Linux 2.0 should stick with *kmalloc* and *kfree*. Moreover, *kmem_destroy_cache* was introduced during 2.3 development and has only been backported to 2.2 as of 2.2.18. For this reason *scullc* refuses to compile with a 2.2 kernel older than that.

__get_free_pages in Linux 2.0 had a third, integer argument called `dma`; it served the same function that the `__GFP_DMA` flag serves in modern kernels but it was not merged in the `flags` argument. To address the problem, *sysdep.h* passes 0 as the third argument to the 2.0 function. If you want to request DMA pages and be backward compatible with 2.0, you need to call *get_dma_pages* instead of using `__GFP_DMA`.

vmalloc and *vfree* are unchanged across all 2.*x* kernels. However, the *ioremap* function was called *vremap* in the 2.0 days, and there was no *iounmap*. Instead, an I/O mapping obtained with *vremap* would be freed with *vfree*. Also, the header `<linux/vmalloc.h>` didn't exist in 2.0; the functions were declared by `<linux/mm.h>` instead. As usual, *sysdep.h* makes 2.4 code work with earlier kernels; it also includes `<linux/vmalloc.h>` if `<linux/mm.h>` is included, thus hiding this difference as well.

Quick Reference

The functions and symbols related to memory allocation follow.

```
#include <linux/malloc.h>
void *kmalloc(size_t size, int flags);
void kfree(void *obj);
```
The most frequently used interface to memory allocation.

```
#include <linux/mm.h>
GFP_KERNEL
GFP_ATOMIC
__GFP_DMA
__GFP_HIGHMEM
```
kmalloc flags. `__GFP_DMA` and `__GFP_HIGHMEM` are flags that can be OR'd to either `GFP_KERNEL` or `GFP_ATOMIC`.

```
#include <linux/malloc.h>
kmem_cache_t *kmem_cache_create(char *name, size_t size,
      size_t offset, unsigned long flags, constructor(),
      destructor());
int kmem_cache_destroy(kmem_cache_t *cache);
```
Create and destroy a slab cache. The cache can be used to allocate several objects of the same size.

```
SLAB_NO_REAP
SLAB_HWCACHE_ALIGN
SLAB_CACHE_DMA
```
Flags that can be specified while creating a cache.

```
SLAB_CTOR_ATOMIC
SLAB_CTOR_CONSTRUCTOR
```
Flags that the allocator can pass to the constructor and the destructor functions.

```
void *kmem_cache_alloc(kmem_cache_t *cache, int flags);
void kmem_cache_free(kmem_cache_t *cache, const void *obj);
```
Allocate and release a single object from the cache.

```
unsigned long get_zeroed_page(int flags);
unsigned long __get_free_page(int flags);
unsigned long __get_free_pages(int flags, unsigned long
      order);
unsigned long __get_dma_pages(int flags, unsigned long
      order);
```
The page-oriented allocation functions. *get_zeroed_page* returns a single, zero-filled page. All the other versions of the call do not initialize the contents of the returned page(s). *__get_dma_pages* is only a compatibility macro in Linux 2.2 and later (you can use __GFP_DMA instead).

```
void free_page(unsigned long addr);
void free_pages(unsigned long addr, unsigned long order);
```
These functions release page-oriented allocations.

```
#include <linux/vmalloc.h>
void * vmalloc(unsigned long size);
void vfree(void * addr);
#include <asm/io.h>
void * ioremap(unsigned long offset, unsigned long size);
void iounmap(void *addr);
```
These functions allocate or free a contiguous *virtual* address space. *ioremap* accesses physical memory through virtual addresses, while *vmalloc* allocates free pages. Regions mapped with *ioremap* are freed with *iounmap*, while pages obtained from *vmalloc* are released with *vfree*.

```
#include <linux/bootmem.h>
void *alloc_bootmem(unsigned long size);
void *alloc_bootmem_low(unsigned long size);
void *alloc_bootmem_pages(unsigned long size);
void *alloc_bootmem_low_pages(unsigned long size);
```
Only with version 2.4 of the kernel, memory can be allocated at boot time using these functions. The facility can only be used by drivers directly linked in the kernel image.

## CHAPTER EIGHT

HARDWARE MANAGEMENT

Although playing with *scull* and similar toys is a good introduction to the software interface of a Linux device driver, implementing a *real* device requires hardware. The driver is the abstraction layer between software concepts and hardware circuitry; as such, it needs to talk with both of them. Up to now, we have examined the internals of software concepts; this chapter completes the picture by showing you how a driver can access I/O ports and I/O memory while being portable across Linux platforms.

This chapter continues in the tradition of staying as independent of specific hardware as possible. However, where specific examples are needed, we use simple digital I/O ports (like the standard PC parallel port) to show how the I/O instructions work, and normal frame-buffer video memory to show memory-mapped I/O.

We chose simple digital I/O because it is the easiest form of input/output port. Also, the Centronics parallel port implements raw I/O and is available in most computers: data bits written to the device appear on the output pins, and voltage levels on the input pins are directly accessible by the processor. In practice, you have to connect LEDs to the port to actually *see* the results of a digital I/O operation, but the underlying hardware is extremely easy to use.

I/O Ports and I/O Memory

Every peripheral device is controlled by writing and reading its registers. Most of the time a device has several registers, and they are accessed at consecutive addresses, either in the memory address space or in the I/O address space.

At the hardware level, there is no conceptual difference between memory regions and I/O regions: both of them are accessed by asserting electrical signals on the address bus and control bus (i.e., the *read* and *write* signals)* and by reading from or writing to the data bus.

While some CPU manufacturers implement a single address space in their chips, some others decided that peripheral devices are different from memory and therefore deserve a separate address space. Some processors (most notably the x86 family) have separate *read* and *write* electrical lines for I/O ports, and special CPU instructions to access ports.

Because peripheral devices are built to fit a peripheral bus, and the most popular I/O buses are modeled on the personal computer, even processors that do not have a separate address space for I/O ports must fake reading and writing I/O ports when accessing some peripheral devices, usually by means of external chipsets or extra circuitry in the CPU core. The latter solution is only common within tiny processors meant for embedded use.

For the same reason, Linux implements the concept of I/O ports on all computer platforms it runs on, even on platforms where the CPU implements a single address space. The implementation of port access sometimes depends on the specific make and model of the host computer (because different models use different chipsets to map bus transactions into memory address space).

Even if the peripheral bus has a separate address space for I/O ports, not all devices map their registers to I/O ports. While use of I/O ports is common for ISA peripheral boards, most PCI devices map registers into a memory address region. This I/O memory approach is generally preferred because it doesn't require use of special-purpose processor instructions; CPU cores access memory much more efficiently, and the compiler has much more freedom in register allocation and addressing-mode selection when accessing memory.

I/O Registers and Conventional Memory

Despite the strong similarity between hardware registers and memory, a programmer accessing I/O registers must be careful to avoid being tricked by CPU (or compiler) optimizations that can modify the expected I/O behavior.

The main difference between I/O registers and RAM is that I/O operations have side effects, while memory operations have none: the only effect of a memory write is storing a value to a location, and a memory read returns the last value written there. Because memory access speed is so critical to CPU performance, the no-side-effects case has been optimized in several ways: values are cached and read/write instructions are reordered.

---

* Not all computer platform use a *read* and a *write* signal; some have different means to address external circuits. The difference is irrelevant at software level, however, and we'll assume all have *read* and *write* to simplify the discussion.

The compiler can cache data values into CPU registers without writing them to memory, and even if it stores them, both write and read operations can operate on cache memory without ever reaching physical RAM. Reordering can also happen both at compiler level and at hardware level: often a sequence of instructions can be executed more quickly if it is run in an order different from that which appears in the program text, for example, to prevent interlocks in the RISC pipeline. On CISC processors, operations that take a significant amount of time can be executed concurrently with other, quicker ones.

These optimizations are transparent and benign when applied to conventional memory (at least on uniprocessor systems), but they can be fatal to correct I/O operations because they interfere with those "side effects" that are the main reason why a driver accesses I/O registers. The processor cannot anticipate a situation in which some other process (running on a separate processor, or something happening inside an I/O controller) depends on the order of memory access. A driver must therefore ensure that no caching is performed and no read or write reordering takes place when accessing registers: the compiler or the CPU may just try to outsmart you and reorder the operations you request; the result can be strange errors that are very difficult to debug.

The problem with hardware caching is the easiest to face: the underlying hardware is already configured (either automatically or by Linux initialization code) to disable any hardware cache when accessing I/O regions (whether they are memory or port regions).

The solution to compiler optimization and hardware reordering is to place a *memory barrier* between operations that must be visible to the hardware (or to another processor) in a particular order. Linux provides four macros to cover all possible ordering needs.

```
#include <linux/kernel.h>
void barrier(void)
```
> This function tells the compiler to insert a memory barrier, but has no effect on the hardware. Compiled code will store to memory all values that are currently modified and resident in CPU registers, and will reread them later when they are needed.

```
#include <asm/system.h>
void rmb(void);
void wmb(void);
void mb(void);
```
> These functions insert hardware memory barriers in the compiled instruction flow; their actual instantiation is platform dependent. An *rmb* (read memory barrier) guarantees that any reads appearing before the barrier are completed prior to the execution of any subsequent read. *wmb* guarantees ordering in write operations, and the *mb* instruction guarantees both. Each of these functions is a superset of *barrier*.

A typical usage of memory barriers in a device driver may have this sort of form:

```
writel(dev->registers.addr, io_destination_address);
writel(dev->registers.size, io_size);
writel(dev->registers.operation, DEV_READ);
wmb();
writel(dev->registers.control, DEV_GO);
```

In this case, it is important to be sure that all of the device registers controlling a particular operation have been properly set prior to telling it to begin. The memory barrier will enforce the completion of the writes in the necessary order.

Because memory barriers affect performance, they should only be used where really needed. The different types of barriers can also have different performance characteristics, so it is worthwhile to use the most specific type possible. For example, on the x86 architecture, *wmb()* currently does nothing, since writes outside the processor are not reordered. Reads are reordered, however, so *mb()* will be slower than *wmb()*.

It is worth noting that most of the other kernel primitives dealing with synchronization, such as spinlock and **atomic_t** operations, also function as memory barriers.

Some architectures allow the efficient combination of an assignment and a memory barrier. Version 2.4 of the kernel provides a few macros that perform this combination; in the default case they are defined as follows:

```
#define set_mb(var, value)  do {var = value; mb();}  while 0
#define set_wmb(var, value) do {var = value; wmb();} while 0
#define set_rmb(var, value) do {var = value; rmb();} while 0
```

Where appropriate, `<asm/system.h>` defines these macros to use architecture-specific instructions that accomplish the task more quickly.

The header file *sysdep.h* defines macros described in this section for the platforms and the kernel versions that lack them.

Using I/O Ports

I/O ports are the means by which drivers communicate with many devices out there—at least part of the time. This section covers the various functions available for making use of I/O ports; we also touch on some portability issues.

Let us start with a quick reminder that I/O ports must be allocated before being used by your driver. As we discussed in "I/O Ports and I/O Memory" in Chapter 2, the functions used to allocate and free ports are:

```
#include <linux/ioport.h>
int check_region(unsigned long start, unsigned long len);
struct resource *request_region(unsigned long start,
        unsigned long len, char *name);
void release_region(unsigned long start, unsigned long len);
```

After a driver has requested the range of I/O ports it needs to use in its activities, it must read and/or write to those ports. To this aim, most hardware differentiates between 8-bit, 16-bit, and 32-bit ports. Usually you can't mix them like you normally do with system memory access.[*]

A C program, therefore, must call different functions to access different size ports. As suggested in the previous section, computer architectures that support only memory-mapped I/O registers fake port I/O by remapping port addresses to memory addresses, and the kernel hides the details from the driver in order to ease portability. The Linux kernel headers (specifically, the architecture-dependent header <asm/io.h>) define the following inline functions to access I/O ports.

 From now on, when we use **unsigned** without further type specifications, we are referring to an architecture-dependent definition whose exact nature is not relevant. The functions are almost always portable because the compiler automatically casts the values during assignment—their being unsigned helps prevent compile-time warnings. No information is lost with such casts as long as the programmer assigns sensible values to avoid overflow. We'll stick to this convention of "incomplete typing" for the rest of the chapter.

```
unsigned inb(unsigned port);
void outb(unsigned char byte, unsigned port);
```
>   Read or write byte ports (eight bits wide). The **port** argument is defined as **unsigned long** for some platforms and **unsigned short** for others. The return type of *inb* is also different across architectures.

```
unsigned inw(unsigned port);
void outw(unsigned short word, unsigned port);
```
>   These functions access 16-bit ports (word wide); they are not available when compiling for the M68k and S390 platforms, which support only byte I/O.

---

[*] Sometimes I/O ports are arranged like memory, and you can (for example) bind two 8-bit writes into a single 16-bit operation. This applies, for instance, to PC video boards, but in general you can't count on this feature.

```
unsigned inl(unsigned port);
void outl(unsigned longword, unsigned port);
```
These functions access 32-bit ports. `longword` is either declared as `unsigned long` or `unsigned int`, according to the platform. Like word I/O, "long" I/O is not available on M68k and S390.

Note that no 64-bit port I/O operations are defined. Even on 64-bit architectures, the port address space uses a 32-bit (maximum) data path.

The functions just described are primarily meant to be used by device drivers, but they can also be used from user space, at least on PC-class computers. The GNU C library defines them in `<sys/io.h>`. The following conditions should apply in order for *inb* and friends to be used in user-space code:

- The program must be compiled with the *-O* option to force expansion of inline functions.

- The *ioperm* or *iopl* system calls must be used to get permission to perform I/O operations on ports. *ioperm* gets permission for individual ports, while *iopl* gets permission for the entire I/O space. Both these functions are Intel specific.

- The program must run as root to invoke *ioperm* or *iopl*[*] Alternatively, one of its ancestors must have gained port access running as root.

If the host platform has no *ioperm* and no *iopl* system calls, user space can still access I/O ports by using the */dev/port* device file. Note, though, that the meaning of the file is very platform specific, and most likely not useful for anything but the PC.

The sample sources *misc-progs/inp.c* and *misc-progs/outp.c* are a minimal tool for reading and writing ports from the command line, in user space. They expect to be installed under multiple names (i.e., *inpb*, *inpw*, and *inpl* and will manipulate byte, word, or long ports depending on which name was invoked by the user. They use */dev/port* if *ioperm* is not present.

The programs can be made setuid root, if you want to live dangerously and play with your hardware without acquiring explicit privileges.

String Operations

In addition to the single-shot in and out operations, some processors implement special instructions to transfer a sequence of bytes, words, or longs to and from a single I/O port or the same size. These are the so-called *string instructions*, and they perform the task more quickly than a C-language loop can do. The following

---

[*] Technically, it must have the `CAP_SYS_RAWIO` capability, but that is the same as running as root on current systems.

macros implement the concept of string I/O by either using a single machine instruction or by executing a tight loop if the target processor has no instruction that performs string I/O. The macros are not defined at all when compiling for the M68k and S390 platforms. This should not be a portability problem, since these platforms don't usually share device drivers with other platforms, because their peripheral buses are different.

The prototypes for string functions are the following:

```
void insb(unsigned port, void *addr, unsigned long count);
void outsb(unsigned port, void *addr, unsigned long count);
```
> Read or write count bytes starting at the memory address addr. Data is read from or written to the single port port.

```
void insw(unsigned port, void *addr, unsigned long count);
void outsw(unsigned port, void *addr, unsigned long count);
```
> Read or write 16-bit values to a single 16-bit port.

```
void insl(unsigned port, void *addr, unsigned long count);
void outsl(unsigned port, void *addr, unsigned long count);
```
> Read or write 32-bit values to a single 32-bit port.

Pausing I/O

Some platforms—most notably the i386—can have problems when the processor tries to transfer data too quickly to or from the bus. The problems can arise because the processor is overclocked with respect to the ISA bus, and can show up when the device board is too slow. The solution is to insert a small delay after each I/O instruction if another such instruction follows. If your device misses some data, or if you fear it might miss some, you can use pausing functions in place of the normal ones. The pausing functions are exactly like those listed previously, but their names end in _p; they are called *inb_p*, *outb_p*, and so on. The functions are defined for most supported architectures, although they often expand to the same code as nonpausing I/O, because there is no need for the extra pause if the architecture runs with a nonobsolete peripheral bus.

Platform Dependencies

I/O instructions are, by their nature, highly processor dependent. Because they work with the details of how the processor handles moving data in and out, it is very hard to hide the differences between systems. As a consequence, much of the source code related to port I/O is platform dependent.

You can see one of the incompatibilities, data typing, by looking back at the list of functions, where the arguments are typed differently based on the architectural differences between platforms. For example, a port is `unsigned short` on the x86 (where the processor supports a 64-KB I/O space), but `unsigned long` on other platforms, whose ports are just special locations in the same address space as memory.

Other platform dependencies arise from basic structural differences in the processors and thus are unavoidable. We won't go into detail about the differences, because we assume that you won't be writing a device driver for a particular system without understanding the underlying hardware. Instead, the following is an overview of the capabilities of the architectures that are supported by version 2.4 of the kernel:

IA-32 (x86)
> The architecture supports all the functions described in this chapter. Port numbers are of type `unsigned short`.

IA-64 (Itanium)
> All functions are supported; ports are `unsigned long` (and memory-mapped). String functions are implemented in C.

Alpha
> All the functions are supported, and ports are memory-mapped. The implementation of port I/O is different in different Alpha platforms, according to the chipset they use. String functions are implemented in C and defined in *arch/alpha/lib/io.c*. Ports are `unsigned long`.

ARM
> Ports are memory-mapped, and all functions are supported; string functions are implemented in C. Ports are of type `unsigned int`.

M68k
> Ports are memory-mapped, and only byte functions are supported. No string functions are supported, and the port type is `unsigned char *`.

MIPS
MIPS64
> The MIPS port supports all the functions. String operations are implemented with tight assembly loops, because the processor lacks machine-level string I/O. Ports are memory-mapped; they are `unsigned int` in 32-bit processors and `unsigned long` in 64-bit ones.

PowerPC
> All the functions are supported; ports have type `unsigned char *`.

S390

> Similar to the M68k, the header for this platform supports only byte-wide port I/O with no string operations. Ports are `char` pointers and are memory-mapped.

Super-H

> Ports are `unsigned int` (memory-mapped), and all the functions are supported.

SPARC
SPARC64

> Once again, I/O space is memory-mapped. Versions of the port functions are defined to work with `unsigned long` ports.

The curious reader can extract more information from the *io.h* files, which sometimes define a few architecture-specific functions in addition to those we describe in this chapter. Be warned that some of these files are rather difficult reading, however.

It's interesting to note that no processor outside the x86 family features a different address space for ports, even though several of the supported families are shipped with ISA and/or PCI slots (and both buses implement different I/O and memory address spaces).

Moreover, some processors (most notably the early Alphas) lack instructions that move one or two bytes at a time.* Therefore, their peripheral chipsets simulate 8-bit and 16-bit I/O accesses by mapping them to special address ranges in the memory address space. Thus, an *inb* and an *inw* instruction that act on the same port are implemented by two 32-bit memory reads that operate on different addresses. Fortunately, all of this is hidden from the device driver writer by the internals of the macros described in this section, but we feel it's an interesting feature to note. If you want to probe further, look for examples in *include/asm-alpha/core_lca.h*.

How I/O operations are performed on each platform is well described in the programmer's manual for each platform; those manuals are usually available for download as PDF files on the Web.

---

* Single-byte I/O is not as important as one may imagine, because it is a rare operation. In order to read/write a single byte to any address space, you need to implement a data path connecting the low bits of the register-set data bus to any byte position in the external data bus. These data paths require additional logic gates that get in the way of every data transfer. Dropping byte-wide loads and stores can benefit overall system performance.

Using Digital I/O Ports

The sample code we use to show port I/O from within a device driver acts on general-purpose digital I/O ports; such ports are found in most computer systems.

A digital I/O port, in its most common incarnation, is a byte-wide I/O location, either memory-mapped or port-mapped. When you write a value to an output location, the electrical signal seen on output pins is changed according to the individual bits being written. When you read a value from the input location, the current logic level seen on input pins is returned as individual bit values.

The actual implementation and software interface of such I/O ports varies from system to system. Most of the time I/O pins are controlled by two I/O locations: one that allows selecting what pins are used as input and what pins are used as output, and one in which you can actually read or write logic levels. Sometimes, however, things are even simpler and the bits are hardwired as either input or output (but, in this case, you don't call them "general-purpose I/O" anymore); the parallel port found on all personal computers is one such not-so-general-purpose I/O port. Either way, the I/O pins are usable by the sample code we introduce shortly.

An Overview of the Parallel Port

Because we expect most readers to be using an x86 platform in the form called "personal computer," we feel it is worth explaining how the PC parallel port is designed. The parallel port is the peripheral interface of choice for running digital I/O sample code on a personal computer. Although most readers probably have parallel port specifications available, we summarize them here for your convenience.

The parallel interface, in its minimal configuration (we will overlook the ECP and EPP modes) is made up of three 8-bit ports. The PC standard starts the I/O ports for the first parallel interface at 0x378, and for the second at 0x278. The first port is a bidirectional data register; it connects directly to pins 2 through 9 on the physical connector. The second port is a read-only status register; when the parallel port is being used for a printer, this register reports several aspects of printer status, such as being online, out of paper, or busy. The third port is an output-only control register, which, among other things, controls whether interrupts are enabled.

The signal levels used in parallel communications are standard transistor-transistor logic (TTL) levels: 0 and 5 volts, with the logic threshold at about 1.2 volts; you can count on the ports at least meeting the standard TTL LS current ratings, although most modern parallel ports do better in both current and voltage ratings.

The parallel connector is not isolated from the computer's internal circuitry, which is useful if you want to connect logic gates directly to the port. But you have to be careful to do the wiring correctly; the parallel port circuitry is easily damaged when you play with your own custom circuitry unless you add optoisolators to your circuit. You can choose to use plug-in parallel ports if you fear you'll damage your motherboard.

The bit specifications are outlined in Figure 8-1. You can access 12 output bits and 5 input bits, some of which are logically inverted over the course of their signal path. The only bit with no associated signal pin is bit 4 (0x10) of port 2, which enables interrupts from the parallel port. We'll make use of this bit as part of our implementation of an interrupt handler in Chapter 9.

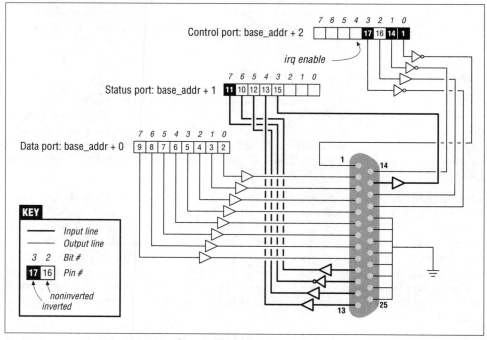

Figure 8-1. The pinout of the parallel port

A Sample Driver

The driver we will introduce is called *short* (Simple Hardware Operations and Raw Tests). All it does is read and write a few eight-bit ports, starting from the one you select at load time. By default it uses the port range assigned to the parallel interface of the PC. Each device node (with a unique minor number) accesses a different port. The *short* driver doesn't do anything useful; it just isolates for external use a single instruction acting on a port. If you are not used to port I/O, you can use *short* to get familiar with it; you can measure the time it takes to transfer data through a port or play other games.

For *short* to work on your system, it must have free access to the underlying hardware device (by default, the parallel interface); thus, no other driver may have allocated it. Most modern distributions set up the parallel port drivers as modules that are loaded only when needed, so contention for the I/O addresses is not usually a problem. If, however, you get a "can't get I/O address" error from *short* (on the console or in the system log file), some other driver has probably already taken the port. A quick look at */proc/ioports* will usually tell you which driver is getting in the way. The same caveat applies to other I/O devices if you are not using the parallel interface.

From now on, we'll just refer to "the parallel interface" to simplify the discussion. However, you can set the **base** module parameter at load time to redirect *short* to other I/O devices. This feature allows the sample code to run on any Linux platform where you have access to a digital I/O interface that is accessible via *outb* and *inb* (even though the actual hardware is memory-mapped on all platforms but the x86). Later, in "Using I/O Memory," we'll show how *short* can be used with generic memory-mapped digital I/O as well.

To watch what happens on the parallel connector, and if you have a bit of an inclination to work with hardware, you can solder a few LEDs to the output pins. Each LED should be connected in series to a 1-KΩ resistor leading to a ground pin (unless, of course, your LEDs have the resistor built in). If you connect an output pin to an input pin, you'll generate your own input to be read from the input ports.

Note that you cannot just connect a printer to the parallel port and see data sent to *short*. This driver implements simple access to the I/O ports and does not perform the handshake that printers need to operate on the data.

If you are going to view parallel data by soldering LEDs to a D-type connector, we suggest that you not use pins 9 and 10, because we'll be connecting them together later to run the sample code shown in Chapter 9.

As far as *short* is concerned, */dev/short0* writes to and reads from the eight-bit port located at the I/O address **base** (0x378 unless changed at load time). */dev/short1* writes to the eight-bit port located at **base** + 1, and so on up to **base** + 7.

The actual output operation performed by */dev/short0* is based on a tight loop using *outb*. A memory barrier instruction is used to ensure that the output operation actually takes place and is not optimized away.

```
while (count--) {
    outb(*(ptr++), address);
    wmb();
}
```

You can run the following command to light your LEDs:

```
echo  -n "any string"  > /dev/short0
```

Each LED monitors a single bit of the output port. Remember that only the last character written remains steady on the output pins long enough to be perceived by your eyes. For that reason, we suggest that you prevent automatic insertion of a trailing newline by passing the *-n* option to *echo*.

Reading is performed by a similar function, built around *inb* instead of *outb*. In order to read "meaningful" values from the parallel port, you need to have some hardware connected to the input pins of the connector to generate signals. If there is no signal, you'll read an endless stream of identical bytes. If you choose to read from an output port, you'll most likely get back the last value written to the port (this applies to the parallel interface and to most other digital I/O circuits in common use). Thus, those uninclined to get out their soldering irons can read the current output value on port 0x378 by running a command like:

```
dd if=/dev/short0 bs=1 count=1 | od -t x1
```

To demonstrate the use of all the I/O instructions, there are three variations of each *short* device: */dev/short0* performs the loop just shown, */dev/short0p* uses *outb_p* and *inb_p* in place of the "fast" functions, and */dev/short0s* uses the string instructions. There are eight such devices, from *short0* to *short7*. Although the PC parallel interface has only three ports, you may need more of them if using a different I/O device to run your tests.

The *short* driver performs an absolute minimum of hardware control, but is adequate to show how the I/O port instructions are used. Interested readers may want to look at the source for the *parport* and *parport_pc* modules to see how complicated this device can get in real life in order to support a range of devices (printers, tape backup, network interfaces) on the parallel port.

Using I/O Memory

Despite the popularity of I/O ports in the x86 world, the main mechanism used to communicate with devices is through memory-mapped registers and device memory. Both are called *I/O memory* because the difference between registers and memory is transparent to software.

I/O memory is simply a region of RAM-like locations that the device makes available to the processor over the bus. This memory can be used for a number of purposes, such as holding video data or Ethernet packets, as well as implementing device registers that behave just like I/O ports (i.e., they have side effects associated with reading and writing them).

The way used to access I/O memory depends on the computer architecture, bus, and device being used, though the principles are the same everywhere. The discussion in this chapter touches mainly on ISA and PCI memory, while trying to convey general information as well. Although access to PCI memory is introduced here, a thorough discussion of PCI is deferred to Chapter 15.

According to the computer platform and bus being used, I/O memory may or may not be accessed through page tables. When access passes though page tables, the kernel must first arrange for the physical address to be visible from your driver (this usually means that you must call *ioremap* before doing any I/O). If no page tables are needed, then I/O memory locations look pretty much like I/O ports, and you can just read and write to them using proper wrapper functions.

Whether or not *ioremap* is required to access I/O memory, direct use of pointers to I/O memory is a discouraged practice. Even though (as introduced in "I/O Ports and I/O Memory") I/O memory is addressed like normal RAM at hardware level, the extra care outlined in "I/O Registers and Conventional Memory" suggests avoiding normal pointers. The wrapper functions used to access I/O memory are both safe on all platforms and optimized away whenever straight pointer dereferencing can perform the operation.

Therefore, even though dereferencing a pointer works (for now) on the x86, failure to use the proper macros will hinder the portability and readability of the driver.

Remember from Chapter 2 that device memory regions must be allocated prior to use. This is similar to how I/O ports are registered and is accomplished by the following functions:

```
int check_mem_region(unsigned long start, unsigned long len);
void request_mem_region(unsigned long start, unsigned long len,
char *name);
void release_mem_region(unsigned long start, unsigned long len);
```

The **start** argument to pass to the functions is the physical address of the memory region, before any remapping takes place. The functions would normally be used in a manner such as the following:

```
if (check_mem_region(mem_addr, mem_size)) {
    printk("drivername: memory already in use\n");
    return -EBUSY;
}

    request_mem_region(mem_addr, mem_size, "drivername");
```

```
[...]

release_mem_region(mem_addr, mem_size);
```

Directly Mapped Memory

Several computer platforms reserve part of their memory address space for I/O locations, and automatically disable memory management for any (virtual) address in that memory range.

The MIPS processors used in personal digital assistants (PDAs) offer an interesting example of this setup. Two address ranges, 512 MB each, are directly mapped to physical addresses. Any memory access to either of those address ranges bypasses the MMU, and any access to one of those ranges bypasses the cache as well. A section of these 512 megabytes is reserved for peripheral devices, and drivers can access their I/O memory directly by using the noncached address range.

Other platforms have other means to offer directly mapped address ranges: some of them have special address spaces to dereference physical addresses (for example, SPARC64 uses a special "address space identifier" for this aim), and others use virtual addresses set up to bypass processor caches.

When you need to access a directly mapped I/O memory area, you still shouldn't dereference your I/O pointers, even though, on some architectures, you may well be able to get away with doing exactly that. To write code that will work across systems and kernel versions, however, you must avoid direct accesses and instead use the following functions.

```
unsigned readb(address);
unsigned readw(address);
unsigned readl(address);
```
> These macros are used to retrieve 8-bit, 16-bit, and 32-bit data values from I/O memory. The advantage of using macros is the typelessness of the argument: address is cast before being used, because the value "is not clearly either an integer or a pointer, and we will accept both" (from *asm-alpha/io.h*). Neither the reading nor the writing functions check the validity of address, because they are meant to be as fast as pointer dereferencing (we already know that sometimes they actually expand into pointer dereferencing).

```
void writeb(unsigned value, address);
void writew(unsigned value, address);
void writel(unsigned value, address);
```
> Like the previous functions, these functions (macros) are used to write 8-bit, 16-bit, and 32-bit data items.

```
memset_io(address, value, count);
```
> When you need to call *memset* on I/O memory, this function does what you need, while keeping the semantics of the original *memset*.

```
memcpy_fromio(dest, source, num);
memcpy_toio(dest, source, num);
```
> These functions move blocks of data to and from I/O memory and behave like the C library routine *memcpy*.

In modern versions of the kernel, these functions are available across all architectures. The implementation will vary, however; on some they are macros that expand to pointer operations, and on others they are real functions. As a driver writer, however, you need not worry about how they work, as long as you use them.

Some 64-bit platforms also offer *readq* and *writeq*, for quad-word (eight-byte) memory operations on the PCI bus. The *quad-word* nomenclature is a historical leftover from the times when all real processors had 16-bit words. Actually, the *L* naming used for 32-bit values has become incorrect too, but renaming everything would make things still more confused.

Reusing short for I/O Memory

The *short* sample module, introduced earlier to access I/O ports, can be used to access I/O memory as well. To this aim, you must tell it to use I/O memory at load time; also, you'll need to change the base address to make it point to your I/O region.

For example, this is how we used *short* to light the debug LEDs on a MIPS development board:

```
mips.root# ./short_load use_mem=1 base=0xb7ffffc0
mips.root# echo -n 7 > /dev/short0
```

Use of *short* for I/O memory is the same as it is for I/O ports; however, since no pausing or string instructions exist for I/O memory, access to */dev/short0p* and */dev/short0s* performs the same operation as */dev/short0*.

The following fragment shows the loop used by *short* in writing to a memory location:

```
while (count--) {
    writeb(*(ptr++), address);
    wmb();
}
```

Note the use of a write memory barrier here. Because *writeb* likely turns into a direct assignment on many architectures, the memory barrier is needed to ensure that the writes happen in the expected order.

Software-Mapped I/O Memory

The MIPS class of processors notwithstanding, directly mapped I/O memory is pretty rare in the current platform arena; this is especially true when a peripheral bus is used with memory-mapped devices (which is most of the time).

The most common hardware and software arrangement for I/O memory is this: devices live at well-known physical addresses, but the CPU has no predefined virtual address to access them. The well-known physical address can be either hardwired in the device or assigned by system firmware at boot time. The former is true, for example, of ISA devices, whose addresses are either burned in device logic circuits, statically assigned in local device memory, or set by means of physical jumpers. The latter is true of PCI devices, whose addresses are assigned by system software and written to device memory, where they persist only while the device is powered on.

Either way, for software to access I/O memory, there must be a way to assign a virtual address to the device. This is the role of the *ioremap* function, introduced in "vmalloc and Friends." The function, which was covered in the previous chapter because it is related to memory use, is designed specifically to assign virtual addresses to I/O memory regions. Moreover, kernel developers implemented *ioremap* so that it doesn't do anything if applied to directly mapped I/O addresses.

Once equipped with *ioremap* (and *iounmap*), a device driver can access any I/O memory address, whether it is directly mapped to virtual address space or not. Remember, though, that these addresses should not be dereferenced directly; instead, functions like *readb* should be used. We could thus arrange *short* to work with both MIPS I/O memory and the more common ISA/PCI x86 memory by equipping the module with *ioremap/iounmap* calls whenever the `use_mem` parameter is set.

Before we show how *short* calls the functions, we'd better review the prototypes of the functions and introduce a few details that we passed over in the previous chapter.

The functions are called according to the following definition:

```
#include <asm/io.h>
void *ioremap(unsigned long phys_addr, unsigned long size);
void *ioremap_nocache(unsigned long phys_addr, unsigned long size);
void iounmap(void * addr);
```

First of all, you'll notice the new function *ioremap_nocache*. We didn't cover it in Chapter 7, because its meaning is definitely hardware related. Quoting from one of the kernel headers: "It's useful if some control registers are in such an area and write combining or read caching is not desirable." Actually, the function's implementation is identical to *ioremap* on most computer platforms: in situations in which all of I/O memory is already visible through noncacheable addresses, there's no reason to implement a separate, noncaching version of *ioremap*.

Another important feature of *ioremap* is the different behavior of the 2.0 version with respect to later ones. Under Linux 2.0, the function (called, remember, *vremap* at the time) refused to remap any non-page-aligned memory region. This was a sensible choice, since at CPU level everything happens with page-sized granularity. However, sometimes you need to map small regions of I/O registers whose (physical) address is not page aligned. To fit this new need, version 2.1.131 and later of the kernel are able to remap unaligned addresses.

Our *short* module, in order to be backward portable to version 2.0 and to be able to access non-page-aligned registers, includes the following code instead of calling *ioremap* directly:

```
/* Remap a not (necessarily) aligned port region */
void *short_remap(unsigned long phys_addr)
{
    /* The code comes mainly from arch/any/mm/ioremap.c */
    unsigned long offset, last_addr, size;

    last_addr = phys_addr + SHORT_NR_PORTS - 1;
    offset = phys_addr & ~PAGE_MASK;

    /* Adjust the begin and end to remap a full page */
    phys_addr &= PAGE_MASK;
    size = PAGE_ALIGN(last_addr) - phys_addr;
    return ioremap(phys_addr, size) + offset;
}

/* Unmap a region obtained with short_remap */
void short_unmap(void *virt_add)
{
    iounmap((void *)((unsigned long)virt_add & PAGE_MASK));
}
```

ISA Memory Below 1 MB

One of the most well-known I/O memory regions is the ISA range as found on personal computers. This is the memory range between 640 KB (`0xA0000`) and 1 MB (`0x100000`). It thus appears right in the middle of regular system RAM. This positioning may seem a little strange; it is an artifact of a decision made in the early 1980s, when 640 KB of memory seemed like more than anybody would ever be able to use.

This memory range belongs to the non-directly-mapped class of memory.* You

---

* Actually, this is not completely true. The memory range is so small and so frequently used that the kernel builds page tables at boot time to access those addresses. However, the virtual address used to access them is not the same as the physical address, and thus *ioremap* is needed anyway. Moreover, version 2.0 of the kernel had that range directly mapped. See "Backward Compatibility" for 2.0 issues.

can read/write a few bytes in that memory range using the *short* module as explained previously, that is, by setting `use_mem` at load time.

Although ISA I/O memory exists only in x86-class computers, we think it's worth spending a few words and a sample driver on it.

We are not going to discuss PCI memory in this chapter, since it is the cleanest kind of I/O memory: once you know the physical address you can simply remap and access it. The "problem" with PCI I/O memory is that it doesn't lend itself to a working example for this chapter, because we can't know in advance the physical addresses your PCI memory is mapped to, nor whether it's safe to access either of those ranges. We chose to describe the ISA memory range because it's both less clean and more suitable to running sample code.

To demonstrate access to ISA memory, we will make use of yet another silly little module (part of the sample sources). In fact, this one is called *silly*, as an acronym for Simple Tool for Unloading and Printing ISA Data, or something like that.

The module supplements the functionality of *short* by giving access to the whole 384-KB memory space and by showing all the different I/O functions. It features four device nodes that perform the same task using different data transfer functions. The *silly* devices act as a window over I/O memory, in a way similar to */dev/mem*. You can read and write data, and *lseek* to an arbitrary I/O memory address.

Because *silly* provides access to ISA memory, it must start by mapping the physical ISA addresses into kernel virtual addresses. In the early days of the Linux kernel, one could simply assign a pointer to an ISA address of interest, then dereference it directly. In the modern world, though, we must work with the virtual memory system and remap the memory range first. This mapping is done with *ioremap*, as explained earlier for *short*:

```
#define ISA_BASE    0xA0000
#define ISA_MAX     0x100000  /* for general memory access */

    /* this line appears in silly_init */
    io_base = ioremap(ISA_BASE, ISA_MAX - ISA_BASE);
```

ioremap returns a pointer value that can be used with *readb* and the other functions explained in the section "Directly Mapped Memory."

Let's look back at our sample module to see how these functions might be used. */dev/sillyb*, featuring minor number 0, accesses I/O memory with *readb* and *writeb*. The following code shows the implementation for *read*, which makes the address range `0xA0000-0xFFFFF` available as a virtual file in the range `0-0x5FFFF`. The *read* function is structured as a `switch` statement over the different access modes; here is the *sillyb* `case`:

```
case M_8:
  while (count) {
      *ptr = readb(add);
      add++; count--; ptr++;
  }
  break;
```

The next two devices are */dev/sillyw* (minor number 1) and */dev/sillyl* (minor number 2). They act like */dev/sillyb*, except that they use 16-bit and 32-bit functions. Here's the *write* implementation of *sillyl*, again part of a `switch`:

```
case M_32:
  while (count >= 4) {
      writel(*(u32 *)ptr, add);
      add+=4; count-=4; ptr+=4;
  }
  break;
```

The last device is */dev/sillycp* (minor number 3), which uses the *memcpy_*io* functions to perform the same task. Here's the core of its *read* implementation:

```
case M_memcpy:
  memcpy_fromio(ptr, add, count);
  break;
```

Because *ioremap* was used to provide access to the ISA memory area, *silly* must invoke *iounmap* when the module is unloaded:

```
iounmap(io_base);
```

isa_readb and Friends

A look at the kernel source will turn up another set of routines with names like *isa_readb*. In fact, each of the functions just described has an *isa_* equivalent. These functions provide access to ISA memory without the need for a separate *ioremap* step. The word from the kernel developers, however, is that these functions are intended to be temporary driver-porting aids, and that they may go away in the future. Their use is thus best avoided.

Probing for ISA Memory

Even though most modern devices rely on better I/O bus architectures, like PCI, sometimes programmers must still deal with ISA devices and their I/O memory, so we'll spend a page on this issue. We won't touch high ISA memory (the so-called memory hole in the 14 MB to 16 MB physical address range), because that kind of I/O memory is extremely rare nowadays and is not supported by the majority of modern motherboards or by the kernel. To access that range of I/O memory you'd need to hack the kernel initialization sequence, and that is better not covered here.

When using ISA memory-mapped devices, the driver writer often ignores where relevant I/O memory is located in the physical address space, since the actual address is usually assigned by the user among a range of possible addresses. Or it may be necessary simply to see if a device is present at a given address or not.

The memory resource management scheme can be helpful in probing, since it will identify regions of memory that have already been claimed by another driver. The resource manager, however, cannot tell you about devices whose drivers have not been loaded, or whether a given region contains the device that you are interested in. Thus, it can still be necessary to actually probe memory to see what is there. There are three distinct cases that you will encounter: that RAM is mapped to the address, that ROM is there (the VGA BIOS, for example), or that the area is free.

The *skull* sample source shows a way to deal with such memory, but since *skull* is not related to any physical device, it just prints information about the 640 KB to 1 MB memory region and then exits. However, the code used to analyze memory is worth describing, since it shows how memory probes can be done.

The code to check for RAM segments makes use of *cli* to disable interrupts, because these segments can be identified only by physically writing and rereading data, and real RAM might be changed by an interrupt handler in the middle of our tests. The following code is not completely foolproof, because it might mistake RAM memory on acquisition boards for empty regions if a device is actively writing to its own memory while this code is scanning the area. However, this situation is quite unlikely to happen.

```c
unsigned char oldval, newval; /* values read from memory   */
unsigned long flags;          /* used to hold system flags */
unsigned long add, i;
void *base;

/* Use ioremap to get a handle on our region */
base = ioremap(ISA_REGION_BEGIN, ISA_REGION_END - ISA_REGION_BEGIN);
base -= ISA_REGION_BEGIN;  /* Do the offset once */

/* probe all the memory hole in 2-KB steps */
for (add = ISA_REGION_BEGIN; add < ISA_REGION_END; add += STEP) {
    /*
     * Check for an already allocated region.
     */
    if (check_mem_region (add, 2048)) {
            printk(KERN_INFO "%lx: Allocated\n", add);
            continue;
    }
    /*
     * Read and write the beginning of the region and see what happens.
     */
    save_flags(flags);
    cli();
    oldval = readb (base + add);  /* Read a byte */
```

```
    writeb (oldval^0xff, base + add);
    mb();
    newval = readb (base + add);
    writeb (oldval, base + add);
    restore_flags(flags);

    if ((oldval^newval) == 0xff) {  /* we reread our change: it's RAM */
        printk(KERN_INFO "%lx: RAM\n", add);
        continue;
    }
    if ((oldval^newval) != 0) {  /* random bits changed: it's empty */
        printk(KERN_INFO "%lx: empty\n", add);
        continue;
    }

    /*
     * Expansion ROM (executed at boot time by the BIOS)
     * has a signature where the first byte is 0x55, the second 0xaa,
     * and the third byte indicates the size of such ROM
     */
    if ( (oldval == 0x55) && (readb (base + add + 1) == 0xaa)) {
        int size = 512 * readb (base + add + 2);
        printk(KERN_INFO "%lx: Expansion ROM, %i bytes\n",
                add, size);
        add += (size & ~2048) - 2048; /* skip it */
        continue;
    }

    /*
     * If the tests above failed, we still don't know if it is ROM or
     * empty. Since empty memory can appear as 0x00, 0xff, or the low
     * address byte, we must probe multiple bytes: if at least one of
     * them is different from these three values, then this is ROM
     * (though not boot ROM).
     */
    printk(KERN_INFO "%lx: ", add);
    for (i=0; i<5; i++) {
        unsigned long radd = add + 57*(i+1);  /* a "random" value */
        unsigned char val = readb (base + radd);
        if (val && val != 0xFF && val != ((unsigned long) radd&0xFF))
            break;
    }
    printk("%s\n", i==5 ? "empty" : "ROM");
}
```

Detecting memory doesn't cause collisions with other devices, as long as you take care to restore any byte you modified while you were probing. It is worth noting that it is always possible that writing to another device's memory will cause that device to do something undesirable. In general, this method of probing memory should be avoided if possible, but it's not always possible when dealing with older hardware.

Backward Compatibility

Happily, little has changed with regard to basic hardware access. There are just a few things that need to be kept in mind when writing backward-compatible drivers.

Hardware memory barriers didn't exist in version 2.0 of the kernel. There was no need for such ordering instructions on the platforms then supported. Including *sysdep.h* in your driver will fix the problem by defining hardware barriers to be the same as software barriers.

Similarly, not all of the port-access functions (*inb* and friends) were supported on all architectures in older kernels. The string functions, in particular, tended to be absent. We don't provide the missing functions in our *sysdep.h* facility: it won't be an easy task to perform cleanly and most likely is not worth the effort, given the hardware dependency of those functions.

In Linux 2.0, *ioremap* and *iounmap* were called *vremap* and *vfree*, respectively. The parameters and the functionality were the same. Thus, a couple of definitions that map the functions to their older counterpart are often enough.

Unfortunately, while *vremap* worked just like *ioremap* for providing access to "high" memory (such as that on PCI cards), it did refuse to remap the ISA memory ranges. Back in those days, access to this memory was done via direct pointers, so there was no need to remap that address space. Thus, a more complete solution to implement *ioremap* for Linux 2.0 running on the x86 platform is as follows:

```
extern inline void *ioremap(unsigned long phys_addr, unsigned long size)
{
    if (phys_addr >= 0xA0000 && phys_addr + size <= 0x100000)
        return (void *)phys_addr;
    return vremap(phys_addr, size);
}

extern inline void iounmap(void *addr)
{
    if ((unsigned long)addr >= 0xA0000
            && (unsigned long)addr < 0x100000)
        return;
    vfree(addr);
}
```

If you include *sysdep.h* in your drivers you'll be able to use *ioremap* with no problems even when accessing ISA memory.

Allocation of memory regions (*check_mem_region* and friends) was introduced in kernel 2.3.17. In the 2.0 and 2.2 kernels, there was no central facility for the allocation of memory resources. You can use the macros anyway if you include *sysdep.h* because it nullifies the three macros when compiling for 2.0 or 2.2.

Quick Reference

This chapter introduced the following symbols related to hardware management.

`#include <linux/kernel.h>`
`void barrier(void)`
> This "software" memory barrier requests the compiler to consider all memory volatile across this instruction.

`#include <asm/system.h>`
`void rmb(void);`
`void wmb(void);`
`void mb(void);`
> Hardware memory barriers. They request the CPU (and the compiler) to checkpoint all memory reads, writes, or both, across this instruction.

`#include <asm/io.h>`
`unsigned inb(unsigned port);`
`void outb(unsigned char byte, unsigned port);`
`unsigned inw(unsigned port);`
`void outw(unsigned short word, unsigned port);`
`unsigned inl(unsigned port);`
`void outl(unsigned doubleword, unsigned port);`
> These functions are used to read and write I/O ports. They can also be called by user-space programs, provided they have the right privileges to access ports.

`unsigned inb_p(unsigned port);`
`. . .`
> The statement SLOW_DOWN_IO is sometimes needed to deal with slow ISA boards on the x86 platform. If a small delay is needed after an I/O operation, you can use the six pausing counterparts of the functions introduced in the previous entry; these pausing functions have names ending in _p.

`void insb(unsigned port, void *addr, unsigned long count);`
`void outsb(unsigned port, void *addr, unsigned long count);`
`void insw(unsigned port, void *addr, unsigned long count);`
`void outsw(unsigned port, void *addr, unsigned long count);`
`void insl(unsigned port, void *addr, unsigned long count);`
`void outsl(unsigned port, void *addr, unsigned long count);`
> The "string functions" are optimized to transfer data from an input port to a region of memory, or the other way around. Such transfers are performed by reading or writing the same port count times.

```
#include <linux/ioport.h>
int check_region(unsigned long start, unsigned long len);
void request_region(unsigned long start, unsigned long len,
     char *name);
void release_region(unsigned long start, unsigned long len);
```
Resource allocators for I/O ports. The *check* function returns 0 for success and less than 0 in case of error.

```
int check_mem_region(unsigned long start, unsigned long
     len);
void request_mem_region(unsigned long start, unsigned long
     len, char *name);
void release_mem_region(unsigned long start, unsigned long
     len);
```
These functions handle resource allocation for memory regions.

```
#include <asm/io.h>
void *ioremap(unsigned long phys_addr, unsigned long size);
void *ioremap_nocache(unsigned long phys_addr, unsigned long
     size);
void iounmap(void *virt_addr);
```
ioremap remaps a physical address range into the processor's virtual address space, making it available to the kernel. *iounmap* frees the mapping when it is no longer needed.

```
#include <linux/io.h>
unsigned readb(address);
unsigned readw(address);
unsigned readl(address);
void writeb(unsigned value, address);
void writew(unsigned value, address);
void writel(unsigned value, address);
memset_io(address, value, count);
memcpy_fromio(dest, source, nbytes);
memcpy_toio(dest, source, nbytes);
```
These functions are used to access I/O memory regions, either low ISA memory or high PCI buffers.

## CHAPTER NINE

INTERRUPT HANDLING

Although some devices can be controlled using nothing but their I/O regions, most real-world devices are a bit more complicated than that. Devices have to deal with the external world, which often includes things such as spinning disks, moving tape, wires to distant places, and so on. Much has to be done in a time frame that is different, and slower, than that of the processor. Since it is almost always undesirable to have the processor wait on external events, there must be a way for a device to let the processor know when something has happened.

That way, of course, is interrupts. An *interrupt* is simply a signal that the hardware can send when it wants the processor's attention. Linux handles interrupts in much the same way that it handles signals in user space. For the most part, a driver need only register a handler for its device's interrupts, and handle them properly when they arrive. Of course, underneath that simple picture there is some complexity; in particular, interrupt handlers are somewhat limited in the actions they can perform as a result of how they are run.

It is difficult to demonstrate the use of interrupts without a real hardware device to generate them. Thus, the sample code used in this chapter works with the parallel port. We'll be working with the *short* module from the previous chapter; with some small additions it can generate and handle interrupts from the parallel port. The module's name, *short*, actually means *short int* (it is C, isn't it?), to remind us that it handles *int*errupts.

Overall Control of Interrupts

The way that Linux handles interrupts has changed quite a bit over the years, due to changes in design and in the hardware it works with. The PC's view of interrupts in the early days was quite simple; there were just 16 interrupt lines and one processor to deal with them. Modern hardware can have many more interrupts, and can also be equipped with fancy advanced programmable interrupt controllers (APICs), which can distribute interrupts across multiple processors in an intelligent (and programmable) way.

Happily, Linux has been able to deal with all of these changes with relatively few incompatibilities at the driver level. Thus, the interface described in this chapter works, with few differences, across many kernel versions. Sometimes things do work out nicely.

Unix-like systems have used the functions *cli* and *sti* to disable and enable interrupts for many years. In modern Linux systems, however, using them directly is discouraged. It is increasingly impossible for any routine to know whether interrupts are enabled when it is called; thus, simply enabling interrupts with *sti* before return is a bad practice. Your function may be returning to a function that expects interrupts to be still disabled.

Thus, if you must disable interrupts, it is better to use the following calls:

```
unsigned long flags;

    save_flags(flags);
    cli();

    /* This code runs with interrupts disabled */

    restore_flags(flags);
```

Note that *save_flags* is a macro, and that it is passed the variable to hold the flags directly—without an & operator. There is also an important constraint on the use of these macros: *save_flags* and *restore_flags* must be called from the same function. In other words, you cannot pass the `flags` to another function, unless the other function is inlined. Code that ignores this restriction will work on some architectures but will fail on others.

Increasingly, however, even code like the previous example is discouraged wherever possible. In a multiprocessor system, critical code cannot be protected just by disabling interrupts; some sort of locking mechanism must be used. Functions such as *spin_lock_irqsave* (covered in "Using Spinlocks," later in this chapter) provide locking and interrupt control together; these functions are the only really safe way to control concurrency in the presence of interrupts.

cli, meanwhile, disables interrupts on *all* processors on the system, and can thus affect the performance of the system as a whole.[*]

---

[*] The truth is just a little more complicated than this. If you are already handling an interrupt, *cli* only disables interrupts on the current CPU.

Thus, explicit calls to *cli* and related functions are slowly disappearing from much of the kernel. There are occasions where you need them in a device driver, but they are rare. Before calling *cli*, think about whether you *really* need to disable all interrupts on the system.

Preparing the Parallel Port

Although the parallel interface is simple, it can trigger interrupts. This capability is used by the printer to notify the *lp* driver that it is ready to accept the next character in the buffer.

Like most devices, the parallel port doesn't actually generate interrupts before it's instructed to do so; the parallel standard states that setting bit 4 of port 2 (`0x37a`, `0x27a`, or whatever) enables interrupt reporting. A simple *outb* call to set the bit is performed by *short* at module initialization.

Once interrupts are enabled, the parallel interface generates an interrupt whenever the electrical signal at pin 10 (the so-called ACK bit) changes from low to high. The simplest way to force the interface to generate interrupts (short of hooking up a printer to the port) is to connect pins 9 and 10 of the parallel connector. A short length of wire inserted into the appropriate holes in the parallel port connector on the back of your system will create this connection. The pinout of the parallel port is shown in Figure 8-1.

Pin 9 is the most significant bit of the parallel data byte. If you write binary data to */dev/short0*, you'll generate several interrupts. Writing ASCII text to the port won't generate interrupts, though, because the most significant bit won't be set.

If you'd rather avoid soldering, but you do have a printer at hand, you can run the sample interrupt handler using a real printer, as shown later. Note, however, that the probing functions we are going to introduce depend on the jumper between pin 9 and 10 being in place, and you'll need it to experiment with probing using our code.

Installing an Interrupt Handler

If you want to actually "see" interrupts being generated, writing to the hardware device isn't enough; a software handler must be configured in the system. If the Linux kernel hasn't been told to expect your interrupt, it will simply acknowledge and ignore it.

Interrupt lines are a precious and often limited resource, particularly when there are only 15 or 16 of them. The kernel keeps a registry of interrupt lines, similar to the registry of I/O ports. A module is expected to request an interrupt channel (or IRQ, for interrupt request) before using it, and to release it when it's done. In many situations, modules are also expected to be able to share interrupt lines with other drivers, as we will see. The following functions, declared in `<linux/sched.h>`, implement the interface:

```
int request_irq(unsigned int irq,
    void (*handler)(int, void *, struct pt_regs *),
    unsigned long flags,
    const char *dev_name,
    void *dev_id);

void free_irq(unsigned int irq, void *dev_id);
```

The value returned from *request_irq* to the requesting function is either 0 to indicate success or a negative error code, as usual. It's not uncommon for the function to return −EBUSY to signal that another driver is already using the requested interrupt line. The arguments to the functions are as follows:

`unsigned int irq`
This is the interrupt number being requested.

`void (*handler)(int, void *, struct pt_regs *)`
The pointer to the handling function being installed. We'll discuss the arguments to this function later in this chapter.

`unsigned long flags`
As you might expect, a bit mask of options (described later) related to interrupt management.

`const char *dev_name`
The string passed to *request_irq* is used in */proc/interrupts* to show the owner of the interrupt (see the next section).

`void *dev_id`
This pointer is used for shared interrupt lines. It is a unique identifier that is used when the interrupt line is freed and that may also be used by the driver to point to its own private data area (to identify which device is interrupting). When no sharing is in force, `dev_id` can be set to NULL, but it a good idea anyway to use this item to point to the device structure. We'll see a practical use for `dev_id` in "Implementing a Handler," later in this chapter.

The bits that can be set in `flags` are as follows:

`SA_INTERRUPT`
When set, this indicates a "fast" interrupt handler. Fast handlers are executed with interrupts disabled (the topic is covered in deeper detail later in this chapter, in "Fast and Slow Handlers").

SA_SHIRQ

This bit signals that the interrupt can be shared between devices. The concept of sharing is outlined in "Interrupt Sharing," later in this chapter.

SA_SAMPLE_RANDOM

This bit indicates that the generated interrupts can contribute to the entropy pool used by */dev/random* and */dev/urandom*. These devices return truly random numbers when read and are designed to help application software choose secure keys for encryption. Such random numbers are extracted from an entropy pool that is contributed by various random events. If your device generates interrupts at truly random times, you should set this flag. If, on the other hand, your interrupts will be predictable (for example, vertical blanking of a frame grabber), the flag is not worth setting—it wouldn't contribute to system entropy anyway. Devices that could be influenced by attackers should not set this flag; for example, network drivers can be subjected to predictable packet timing from outside and should not contribute to the entropy pool. See the comments in *drivers/char/random.c* for more information.

The interrupt handler can be installed either at driver initialization or when the device is first opened. Although installing the interrupt handler from within the module's initialization function might sound like a good idea, it actually isn't. Because the number of interrupt lines is limited, you don't want to waste them. You can easily end up with more devices in your computer than there are interrupts. If a module requests an IRQ at initialization, it prevents any other driver from using the interrupt, even if the device holding it is never used. Requesting the interrupt at device open, on the other hand, allows some sharing of resources.

It is possible, for example, to run a frame grabber on the same interrupt as a modem, as long as you don't use the two devices at the same time. It is quite common for users to load the module for a special device at system boot, even if the device is rarely used. A data acquisition gadget might use the same interrupt as the second serial port. While it's not too hard to avoid connecting to your Internet service provider (ISP) during data acquisition, being forced to unload a module in order to use the modem is really unpleasant.

The correct place to call *request_irq* is when the device is first opened, *before* the hardware is instructed to generate interrupts. The place to call *free_irq* is the last time the device is closed, *after* the hardware is told not to interrupt the processor any more. The disadvantage of this technique is that you need to keep a per-device open count. Using the module count isn't enough if you control two or more devices from the same module.

This discussion notwithstanding, *short* requests its interrupt line at load time. This was done so that you can run the test programs without having to run an extra process to keep the device open. *short*, therefore, requests the interrupt from within its initialization function (*short_init*) instead of doing it in *short_open*, as a real device driver would.

The interrupt requested by the following code is `short_irq`. The actual assignment of the variable (i.e., determining which IRQ to use) is shown later, since it is not relevant to the current discussion. `short_base` is the base I/O address of the parallel interface being used; register 2 of the interface is written to enable interrupt reporting.

```
if (short_irq >= 0) {
    result = request_irq(short_irq, short_interrupt,
                         SA_INTERRUPT, "short", NULL);
    if (result) {
        printk(KERN_INFO "short: can't get assigned irq %i\n",
               short_irq);
        short_irq = -1;
    }
    else { /* actually enable it -- assume this *is* a parallel port */
        outb(0x10,short_base+2);
    }
}
```

The code shows that the handler being installed is a fast handler (`SA_INTERRUPT`), does not support interrupt sharing (`SA_SHIRQ` is missing), and doesn't contribute to system entropy (`SA_SAMPLE_RANDOM` is missing too). The *outb* call then enables interrupt reporting for the parallel port.

The /proc Interface

Whenever a hardware interrupt reaches the processor, an internal counter is incremented, providing a way to check whether the device is working as expected. Reported interrupts are shown in */proc/interrupts*. The following snapshot was taken after several days of uptime on a two-processor Pentium system:

```
           CPU0        CPU1
   0:   34584323    34936135    IO-APIC-edge    timer
   1:     224407      226473    IO-APIC-edge    keyboard
   2:          0           0        XT-PIC      cascade
   5:    5636751     5636666    IO-APIC-level   eth0
   9:          0           0    IO-APIC-level   acpi
  10:     565910      565269    IO-APIC-level   aic7xxx
  12:     889091      884276    IO-APIC-edge    PS/2 Mouse
  13:          1           0        XT-PIC      fpu
  15:    1759669     1734520    IO-APIC-edge    ide1
 NMI:   69520392    69520392
 LOC:   69513717    69513716
 ERR:          0
```

The first column is the IRQ number. You can see from the IRQs that are missing that the file shows only interrupts corresponding to installed handlers. For example, the first serial port (which uses interrupt number 4) is not shown, indicating that the modem isn't being used. In fact, even if the modem had been used earlier but wasn't in use at the time of the snapshot, it would not show up in the file; the serial ports are well behaved and release their interrupt handlers when the device is closed.

The */proc/interrupts* display shows how many interrupts have been delivered to each CPU on the system. As you can see from the output, the Linux kernel tries to divide interrupt traffic evenly across the processors, with some success. The final columns give information on the programmable interrupt controller that handles the interrupt (and which a driver writer need not worry about), and the name(s) of the device(s) that have registered handlers for the interrupt (as specified in the dev_name argument to *request_irq*).

The */proc* tree contains another interrupt-related file, */proc/stat*; sometimes you'll find one file more useful and sometimes you'll prefer the other. */proc/stat* records several low-level statistics about system activity, including (but not limited to) the number of interrupts received since system boot. Each line of *stat* begins with a text string that is the key to the line; the intr mark is what we are looking for. The following (truncated and line-broken) snapshot was taken shortly after the previous one:

```
intr 884865 695557 4527 0 3109 4907 112759 3 0 0 0 11314
     0 17747 1 0 34941 0 0 0 0 0 0 0
```

The first number is the total of all interrupts, while each of the others represents a single IRQ line, starting with interrupt 0. This snapshot shows that interrupt number 4 has been used 4907 times, even though no handler is *currently* installed. If the driver you're testing acquires and releases the interrupt at each open and close cycle, you may find */proc/stat* more useful than */proc/interrupts*.

Another difference between the two files is that *interrupts* is not architecture dependent, whereas *stat* is: the number of fields depends on the hardware underlying the kernel. The number of available interrupts varies from as few as 15 on the SPARC to as many as 256 on the IA-64 and a few other systems. It's interesting to note that the number of interrupts defined on the x86 is currently 224, not 16 as you may expect; this, as explained in *include/asm-i386/irq.h*, depends on Linux using the architectural limit instead of an implementation-specific limit (like the 16 interrupt sources of the old-fashioned PC interrupt controller).

The following is a snapshot of */proc/interrupts* taken on an IA-64 system. As you can see, besides different hardware routing of common interrupt sources, there's no platform dependency here.

```
            CPU0     CPU1
    27:     1705    34141   IO-SAPIC-level   qla1280
    40:        0        0            SAPIC   perfmon
    43:      913     6960   IO-SAPIC-level   eth0
    47:    26722      146   IO-SAPIC-level   usb-uhci
    64:        3        6    IO-SAPIC-edge   ide0
```

```
  80:          4          2   IO-SAPIC-edge  keyboard
  89:          0          0   IO-SAPIC-edge  PS/2 Mouse
 239:    5606341    5606052         SAPIC  timer
 254:      67575      52815         SAPIC  IPI
 NMI:          0          0
 ERR:          0
```

Autodetecting the IRQ Number

One of the most compelling problems for a driver at initialization time can be how to determine which IRQ line is going to be used by the device. The driver needs the information in order to correctly install the handler. Even though a programmer could require the user to specify the interrupt number at load time, this is a bad practice because most of the time the user doesn't know the number, either because he didn't configure the jumpers or because the device is jumperless. Autodetection of the interrupt number is a basic requirement for driver usability.

Sometimes autodetection depends on the knowledge that some devices feature a default behavior that rarely, if ever, changes. In this case, the driver might assume that the default values apply. This is exactly how *short* behaves by default with the parallel port. The implementation is straightforward, as shown by *short* itself:

```
if (short_irq < 0) /* not yet specified: force the default on */
    switch(short_base) {
      case 0x378: short_irq = 7; break;
      case 0x278: short_irq = 2; break;
      case 0x3bc: short_irq = 5; break;
    }
```

The code assigns the interrupt number according to the chosen base I/O address, while allowing the user to override the default at load time with something like

```
insmod ./short.o short_irq=x.
```

short_base defaults to **0x378**, so **short_irq** defaults to 7.

Some devices are more advanced in design and simply "announce" which interrupt they're going to use. In this case, the driver retrieves the interrupt number by reading a status byte from one of the device's I/O ports or PCI configuration space. When the target device is one that has the ability to tell the driver which interrupt it is going to use, autodetecting the IRQ number just means probing the device, with no additional work required to probe the interrupt.

It's interesting to note here that modern devices supply their interrupt configuration. The PCI standard solves the problem by requiring peripheral devices to declare what interrupt line(s) they are going to use. The PCI standard is discussed in Chapter 15.

Unfortunately, not every device is programmer friendly, and autodetection might require some probing. The technique is quite simple: the driver tells the device to generate interrupts and watches what happens. If everything goes well, only one interrupt line is activated.

Though probing is simple in theory, the actual implementation might be unclear. We'll look at two ways to perform the task: calling kernel-defined helper functions and implementing our own version.

Kernel-assisted probing

The Linux kernel offers a low-level facility for probing the interrupt number. It only works for nonshared interrupts, but then most hardware that is capable of working in a shared interrupt mode provides better ways of finding the configured interrupt number. The facility consists of two functions, declared in `<linux/interrupt.h>` (which also describes the probing machinery):

`unsigned long probe_irq_on(void);`
> This function returns a bit mask of unassigned interrupts. The driver must preserve the returned bit mask and pass it to *probe_irq_off* later. After this call, the driver should arrange for its device to generate at least one interrupt.

`int probe_irq_off(unsigned long);`
> After the device has requested an interrupt, the driver calls this function, passing as argument the bit mask previously returned by *probe_irq_on*. *probe_irq_off* returns the number of the interrupt that was issued after "probe_on." If no interrupts occurred, 0 is returned (thus, IRQ 0 can't be probed for, but no custom device can use it on any of the supported architectures anyway). If more than one interrupt occurred (ambiguous detection), *probe_irq_off* returns a negative value.

The programmer should be careful to enable interrupts on the device *after* the call to *probe_irq_on* and to disable them *before* calling *probe_irq_off*. Additionally, you must remember to service the pending interrupt in your device after *probe_irq_off*.

The *short* module demonstrates how to use such probing. If you load the module with **probe=1**, the following code is executed to detect your interrupt line, provided pins 9 and 10 of the parallel connector are bound together:

```
int count = 0;
do {
    unsigned long mask;

    mask = probe_irq_on();
    outb_p(0x10,short_base+2); /* enable reporting */
    outb_p(0x00,short_base);   /* clear the bit */
    outb_p(0xFF,short_base);   /* set the bit: interrupt! */
    outb_p(0x00,short_base+2); /* disable reporting */
```

```
        udelay(5);   /* give it some time */
        short_irq = probe_irq_off(mask);

        if (short_irq == 0) { /* none of them? */
            printk(KERN_INFO "short: no irq reported by probe\n");
            short_irq = -1;
        }
        /*
         * If more than one line has been activated, the result is
         * negative. We should service the interrupt (no need for lpt port)
         * and loop over again. Loop at most five times, then give up
         */
    } while (short_irq < 0 && count++ < 5);
    if (short_irq < 0)
        printk("short: probe failed %i times, giving up\n", count);
```

Note the use of *udelay* before calling *probe_irq_off*. Depending on the speed of your processor, you may have to wait for a brief period to give the interrupt time to actually be delivered.

If you dig through the kernel sources, you may stumble across references to a different pair of functions:

`void autoirq_setup(int waittime);`
>   Set up for an IRQ probe. The `waittime` argument is not used.

`int autoirq_report(int waittime);`
>   Delays for the given interval (in jiffies), then returns the number of the IRQ seen since *autoirq_setup* was called.

These functions are used primarily in the network driver code, for historical reasons. They are currently implemented with *probe_irq_on* and *probe_irq_off*; there is not usually any reason to use the *autoirq_* functions over the *probe_irq_* functions.

Probing might be a lengthy task. While this is not true for *short*, probing a frame grabber, for example, requires a delay of at least 20 ms (which is ages for the processor), and other devices might take even longer. Therefore, it's best to probe for the interrupt line only once, at module initialization, independently of whether you install the handler at device open (as you should) or within the initialization function (which is not recommended).

It's interesting to note that on some platforms (PowerPC, M68k, most MIPS implementations, and both SPARC versions), probing is unnecessary and therefore the previous functions are just empty placeholders, sometimes called "useless ISA nonsense." On other platforms, probing is only implemented for ISA devices. Anyway, most architectures define the functions (even if empty) to ease porting existing device drivers.

Generally speaking, probing is a hack, and mature architectures are like the PCI bus, which provides all the needed information.

Do-it-yourself probing

Probing can be implemented in the driver itself without too much trouble. The *short* module performs do-it-yourself detection of the IRQ line if it is loaded with `probe=2`.

The mechanism is the same as the one described earlier: enable all unused interrupts, then wait and see what happens. We can, however, exploit our knowledge of the device. Often a device can be configured to use one IRQ number from a set of three or four; probing just those IRQs enables us to detect the right one, without having to test for all possible IRQs.

The *short* implementation assumes that 3, 5, 7, and 9 are the only possible IRQ values. These numbers are actually the values that some parallel devices allow you to select.

The following code probes by testing all "possible" interrupts and looking at what happens. The `trials` array lists the IRQs to try and has 0 as the end marker; the `tried` array is used to keep track of which handlers have actually been registered by this driver.

```
int trials[] = {3, 5, 7, 9, 0};
int tried[]  = {0, 0, 0, 0, 0};
int i, count = 0;

/*
 * Install the probing handler for all possible lines. Remember
 * the result (0 for success, or -EBUSY) in order to only free
 * what has been acquired
 */
for (i=0; trials[i]; i++)
    tried[i] = request_irq(trials[i], short_probing,
                        SA_INTERRUPT, "short probe", NULL);

do {
    short_irq = 0; /* none obtained yet */
    outb_p(0x10,short_base+2); /* enable */
    outb_p(0x00,short_base);
    outb_p(0xFF,short_base); /* toggle the bit */
    outb_p(0x00,short_base+2); /* disable */
    udelay(5);   /* give it some time */

    /* the value has been set by the handler */
    if (short_irq == 0) { /* none of them? */
        printk(KERN_INFO "short: no irq reported by probe\n");
    }
    /*
     * If more than one line has been activated, the result is
     * negative. We should service the interrupt (but the lpt port
     * doesn't need it) and loop over again. Do it at most 5 times
     */
```

```
    } while (short_irq <=0 && count++ < 5);

    /* end of loop, uninstall the handler */
    for (i=0; trials[i]; i++)
        if (tried[i] == 0)
            free_irq(trials[i], NULL);

    if (short_irq < 0)
        printk("short: probe failed %i times, giving up\n", count);
```

You might not know in advance what the "possible" IRQ values are. In that case, you'll need to probe all the free interrupts, instead of limiting yourself to a few `trials[]`. To probe for all interrupts, you have to probe from IRQ 0 to IRQ `NR_IRQS-1`, where `NR_IRQS` is defined in `<asm/irq.h>` and is platform dependent.

Now we are missing only the probing handler itself. The handler's role is to update `short_irq` according to which interrupts are actually received. A 0 value in `short_irq` means "nothing yet," while a negative value means "ambiguous." These values were chosen to be consistent with *probe_irq_off* and to allow the same code to call either kind of probing within *short.c*.

```
    void short_probing(int irq, void *dev_id, struct pt_regs *regs)
    {
        if (short_irq == 0) short_irq = irq;      /* found */
        if (short_irq != irq) short_irq = -irq; /* ambiguous */
    }
```

The arguments to the handler are described later. Knowing that `irq` is the interrupt being handled should be sufficient to understand the function just shown.

Fast and Slow Handlers

Older versions of the Linux kernel took great pains to distinguish between "fast" and "slow" interrupts. Fast interrupts were those that could be handled very quickly, whereas handling slow interrupts took significantly longer. Slow interrupts could be sufficiently demanding of the processor that it was worthwhile to reenable interrupts while they were being handled. Otherwise, tasks requiring quick attention could be delayed for too long.

In modern kernels most of the differences between fast and slow interrupts have disappeared. There remains only one: fast interrupts (those that were requested with the `SA_INTERRUPT` flag) are executed with all other interrupts disabled on the current processor. Note that other processors can still handle interrupts, though you will never see two processors handling the same IRQ at the same time.

To summarize the slow and fast executing environments:

- A fast handler runs with interrupt reporting disabled in the microprocessor, and the interrupt being serviced is disabled in the interrupt controller. The handler can nonetheless enable reporting in the processor by calling *sti*.

- A slow handler runs with interrupt reporting enabled in the processor, and the interrupt being serviced is disabled in the interrupt controller.

So, which type of interrupt should your driver use? On modern systems, `SA_INTERRUPT` is only intended for use in a few, specific situations (such as timer interrupts). Unless you have a strong reason to run your interrupt handler with other interrupts disabled, you should not use `SA_INTERRUPT`.

This description should satisfy most readers, though someone with a taste for hardware and some experience with her computer might be interested in going deeper. If you don't care about the internal details, you can skip to the next section.

The internals of interrupt handling on the x86

This description has been extrapolated from *arch/i386/kernel/irq.c*, *arch/i386/kernel/i8259.c*, and *include/asm-i386/hw_irq.h* as they appear in the 2.4 kernels; although the general concepts remain the same, the hardware details differ on other platforms.

The lowest level of interrupt handling resides in assembly code declared as macros in *hw_irq.h* and expanded in *i8259.c*. Each interrupt is connected to the function *do_IRQ*, defined in *irq.c*.

The first thing *do_IRQ* does is to acknowledge the interrupt so that the interrupt controller can go on to other things. It then obtains a spinlock for the given IRQ number, thus preventing any other CPU from handling this IRQ. It clears a couple of status bits (including one called `IRQ_WAITING` that we'll look at shortly), and then looks up the handler(s) for this particular IRQ. If there is no handler, there's nothing to do; the spinlock is released, any pending tasklets and bottom halves are run, and *do_IRQ* returns.

Usually, however, if a device is interrupting there is a handler registered as well. The function *handle_IRQ_event* is called to actually invoke the handlers. It starts by testing a global interrupt lock bit; if that bit is set, the processor will spin until it is cleared. Calling *cli* sets this bit, thus blocking handling of interrupts; the normal interrupt handling mechanism does *not* set this bit, and thus allows further processing of interrupts. If the handler is of the slow variety, interrupts are reenabled in the hardware and the handler is invoked. Then it's just a matter of cleaning up, running tasklets and bottom halves, and getting back to regular work. The "regular work" may well have changed as a result of an interrupt (the handler could *wake_up* a process, for example), so the last thing that happens on return from an interrupt is a possible rescheduling of the processor.

Probing for IRQs is done by setting the `IRQ_WAITING` status bit for each IRQ that currently lacks a handler. When the interrupt happens, *do_IRQ* clears that bit and then returns, since no handler is registered. *probe_irq_off*, when called by a driver, need only search for the IRQ that no longer has `IRQ_WAITING` set.

Implementing a Handler

So far, we've learned to register an interrupt handler, but not to write one. Actually, there's nothing unusual about a handler—it's ordinary C code.

The only peculiarity is that a handler runs at interrupt time and therefore suffers some restrictions on what it can do. These restrictions are the same as those we saw with task queues. A handler can't transfer data to or from user space, because it doesn't execute in the context of a process. Handlers also cannot do anything that would sleep, such as calling *sleep_on*, allocating memory with anything other than `GFP_ATOMIC`, or locking a semaphore. Finally, handlers cannot call *schedule*.

The role of an interrupt handler is to give feedback to its device about interrupt reception and to read or write data according to the meaning of the interrupt being serviced. The first step usually consists of clearing a bit on the interface board; most hardware devices won't generate other interrupts until their "interrupt-pending" bit has been cleared. Some devices don't require this step because they don't have an "interrupt-pending" bit; such devices are a minority, although the parallel port is one of them. For that reason, *short* does not have to clear such a bit.

A typical task for an interrupt handler is awakening processes sleeping on the device if the interrupt signals the event they're waiting for, such as the arrival of new data.

To stick with the frame grabber example, a process could acquire a sequence of images by continuously reading the device; the *read* call blocks before reading each frame, while the interrupt handler awakens the process as soon as each new frame arrives. This assumes that the grabber interrupts the processor to signal successful arrival of each new frame.

The programmer should be careful to write a routine that executes in a minimum of time, independent of its being a fast or slow handler. If a long computation needs to be performed, the best approach is to use a tasklet or task queue to schedule computation at a safer time (see "Task Queues" in Chapter 6).

Our sample code in *short* makes use of the interrupt to call *do_gettimeofday* and print the current time to a page-sized circular buffer. It then awakens any reading process because there is now data available to be read.

```
void short_interrupt(int irq, void *dev_id, struct pt_regs *regs)
{
    struct timeval tv;
    int written;

    do_gettimeofday(&tv);

    /* Write a 16-byte record. Assume PAGE_SIZE is a multiple of 16 */
    written = sprintf((char *)short_head,"%08u.%06u\n",
                      (int)(tv.tv_sec % 100000000), (int)(tv.tv_usec));
    short_incr_bp(&short_head, written);
    wake_up_interruptible(&short_queue); /* wake any reading process */
}
```

This code, though simple, represents the typical job of an interrupt handler. It, in turn, calls *short_incr_bp*, which is defined as follows:

```
static inline void short_incr_bp(volatile unsigned long *index,
                                 int delta)
{
    unsigned long new = *index + delta;
    barrier ();  /* Don't optimize these two together */
    *index = (new >= (short_buffer + PAGE_SIZE)) ? short_buffer : new;
}
```

This function has been carefully written to wrap a pointer into the circular buffer without ever exposing an incorrect value. By assigning only the final value and placing a barrier to keep the compiler from optimizing things, it is possible to manipulate the circular buffer pointers safely without locks.

The device file used to read the buffer being filled at interrupt time is */dev/shortint*. This device special file, together with */dev/shortprint*, wasn't introduced in Chapter 8, because its use is specific to interrupt handling. The internals of */dev/shortint* are specifically tailored for interrupt generation and reporting. Writing to the device generates one interrupt every other byte; reading the device gives the time when each interrupt was reported.

If you connect together pins 9 and 10 of the parallel connector, you can generate interrupts by raising the high bit of the parallel data byte. This can be accomplished by writing binary data to */dev/short0* or by writing anything to */dev/shortint*.*

The following code implements *read* and *write* for */dev/shortint*.

---

* The *shortint* device accomplishes its task by alternately writing 0x00 and 0xff to the parallel port.

```
ssize_t short_i_read (struct file *filp, char *buf, size_t count,
                      loff_t *f_pos)
{
    int count0;

    while (short_head == short_tail) {
        interruptible_sleep_on(&short_queue);
        if (signal_pending (current))  /* a signal arrived */
          return -ERESTARTSYS; /* tell the fs layer to handle it */
        /* else, loop */
    }
    /* count0 is the number of readable data bytes */
    count0 = short_head - short_tail;
    if (count0 < 0) /* wrapped */
        count0 = short_buffer + PAGE_SIZE - short_tail;
    if (count0 < count) count = count0;

    if (copy_to_user(buf, (char *)short_tail, count))
        return -EFAULT;
    short_incr_bp (&short_tail, count);
    return count;
}

ssize_t short_i_write (struct file *filp, const char *buf, size_t count,
                   loff_t *f_pos)
{
    int written = 0, odd = *f_pos & 1;
    unsigned long address = short_base; /* output to the parallel
                                            data latch */

    if (use_mem) {
        while (written < count)
            writeb(0xff * ((++written + odd) & 1), address);
    } else {
        while (written < count)
            outb(0xff * ((++written + odd) & 1), address);
    }

    *f_pos += count;
    return written;
}
```

The other device special file, */dev/shortprint*, uses the parallel port to drive a printer, and you can use it if you want to avoid soldering a wire between pin 9 and 10 of a D-25 connector. The *write* implementation of *shortprint* uses a circular buffer to store data to be printed, while the *read* implementation is the one just shown (so you can read the time your printer takes to eat each character).

In order to support printer operation, the interrupt handler has been slightly modified from the one just shown, adding the ability to send the next data byte to the printer if there is more data to transfer.

Using Arguments

Though *short* ignores them, three arguments are passed to an interrupt handler: `irq`, `dev_id`, and `regs`. Let's look at the role of each.

The interrupt number (`int irq`) is useful as information you may print in your log messages, if any. Although it had a role in pre-2.0 kernels, when no `dev_id` existed, `dev_id` serves that role much better.

The second argument, `void *dev_id`, is a sort of ClientData; a `void *` argument is passed to *request_irq*, and this same pointer is then passed back as an argument to the handler when the interrupt happens.

You'll usually pass a pointer to your device data structure in `dev_id`, so a driver that manages several instances of the same device doesn't need any extra code in the interrupt handler to find out which device is in charge of the current interrupt event. Typical use of the argument in an interrupt handler is as follows:

```
static void sample_interrupt(int irq, void *dev_id, struct pt_regs
                             *regs)
{
    struct sample_dev *dev = dev_id;

    /* now 'dev' points to the right hardware item */
    /* .... */
}
```

The typical *open* code associated with this handler looks like this:

```
static void sample_open(struct inode *inode, struct file *filp)
{
    struct sample_dev *dev = hwinfo + MINOR(inode->i_rdev);
    request_irq(dev->irq, sample_interrupt,
    0 /* flags */, "sample", dev /* dev_id */);
    /*....*/
    return 0;
}
```

The last argument, `struct pt_regs *regs`, is rarely used. It holds a snapshot of the processor's context before the processor entered interrupt code. The registers can be used for monitoring and debugging; they are not normally needed for regular device driver tasks.

Enabling and Disabling Interrupts

We have already seen the *sti* and *cli* functions, which can enable and disable all interrupts. Sometimes, however, it's useful for a driver to enable and disable interrupt reporting for its own IRQ line only. The kernel offers three functions for this purpose, all declared in `<asm/irq.h>`:

```
void disable_irq(int irq);
void disable_irq_nosync(int irq);
void enable_irq(int irq);
```

Calling any of these functions may update the mask for the specified `irq` in the programmable interrupt controller (PIC), thus disabling or enabling IRQs across all processors. Calls to these functions can be nested—if *disable_irq* is called twice in succession, two *enable_irq* calls will be required before the IRQ is truly reenabled. It is possible to call these functions from an interrupt handler, but enabling your own IRQ while handling it is not usually good practice.

disable_irq will not only disable the given interrupt, but will also wait for a currently executing interrupt handler, if any, to complete. *disable_irq_nosync*, on the other hand, returns immediately. Thus, using the latter will be a little faster, but may leave your driver open to race conditions.

But why disable an interrupt? Sticking to the parallel port, let's look at the *plip* network interface. A *plip* device uses the bare-bones parallel port to transfer data. Since only five bits can be read from the parallel connector, they are interpreted as four data bits and a clock/handshake signal. When the first four bits of a packet are transmitted by the initiator (the interface sending the packet), the clock line is raised, causing the receiving interface to interrupt the processor. The *plip* handler is then invoked to deal with newly arrived data.

After the device has been alerted, the data transfer proceeds, using the handshake line to clock new data to the receiving interface (this might not be the best implementation, but it is necessary for compatibility with other packet drivers using the parallel port). Performance would be unbearable if the receiving interface had to handle two interrupts for every byte received. The driver therefore disables the interrupt during the reception of the packet; instead, a poll-and-delay loop is used to bring in the data.

Similarly, since the handshake line from the receiver to the transmitter is used to acknowledge data reception, the transmitting interface disables its IRQ line during packet transmission.

Finally, it's interesting to note that the SPARC and M68k implementations define both the *disable_irq* and *enable_irq* symbols as pointers rather than functions. This trick allows the kernel to assign the pointers at boot time according to the actual platform being run. The C-language semantics to use the function are the same on all Linux systems, independent of whether this trick is used or not, which helps avoid some tedious coding of conditionals.

Tasklets and Bottom-Half Processing

One of the main problems with interrupt handling is how to perform longish tasks within a handler. Often a substantial amount of work must be done in response to a device interrupt, but interrupt handlers need to finish up quickly and not keep interrupts blocked for long. These two needs (work and speed) conflict with each other, leaving the driver writer in a bit of a bind.

Linux (along with many other systems) resolves this problem by splitting the interrupt handler into two halves. The so-called top half is the routine that actually responds to the interrupt—the one you register with *request_irq*. The bottom half is a routine that is scheduled by the top half to be executed later, at a safer time. The use of the term bottom half in the 2.4 kernel can be a bit confusing, in that it can mean either the second half of an interrupt handler or one of the mechanisms used to implement this second half, or both. When we refer to a *bottom half* we are speaking generally about a bottom half; the old Linux bottom-half implementation is referred to explicitly with the acronym BH.

But what is a bottom half useful for?

The big difference between the top-half handler and the bottom half is that all interrupts are enabled during execution of the bottom half—that's why it runs at a safer time. In the typical scenario, the top half saves device data to a device-specific buffer, schedules its bottom half, and exits: this is very fast. The bottom half then performs whatever other work is required, such as awakening processes, starting up another I/O operation, and so on. This setup permits the top half to service a new interrupt while the bottom half is still working.

Every serious interrupt handler is split this way. For instance, when a network interface reports the arrival of a new packet, the handler just retrieves the data and pushes it up to the protocol layer; actual processing of the packet is performed in a bottom half.

One thing to keep in mind with bottom-half processing is that all of the restrictions that apply to interrupt handlers also apply to bottom halves. Thus, bottom halves cannot sleep, cannot access user space, and cannot invoke the scheduler.

The Linux kernel has two different mechanisms that may be used to implement bottom-half processing. Tasklets were introduced late in the 2.3 development series; they are now the preferred way to do bottom-half processing, but they are not portable to earlier kernel versions. The older bottom-half (BH) implementation exists in even very old kernels, though it is implemented with tasklets in 2.4. We'll look at both mechanisms here. In general, device drivers writing new code should choose tasklets for their bottom-half processing if possible, though portability considerations may determine that the BH mechanism needs to be used instead.

The following discussion works, once again, with the *short* driver. When loaded with a module option, *short* can be told to do interrupt processing in a top/bottom-half mode, with either a tasklet or bottom-half handler. In this case, the top half executes quickly; it simply remembers the current time and schedules the bottom half processing. The bottom half is then charged with encoding this time and awakening any user processes that may be waiting for data.

Tasklets

We have already had an introduction to tasklets in Chapter 6, so a quick review should suffice here. Remember that tasklets are a special function that may be scheduled to run, in interrupt context, at a system-determined safe time. They may be scheduled to run multiple times, but will only run once. No tasklet will ever run in parallel with itself, since they only run once, but tasklets can run in parallel with other tasklets on SMP systems. Thus, if your driver has multiple tasklets, they must employ some sort of locking to avoid conflicting with each other.

Tasklets are also guaranteed to run on the same CPU as the function that first schedules them. An interrupt handler can thus be secure that a tasklet will not begin executing before the handler has completed. However, another interrupt can certainly be delivered while the tasklet is running, so locking between the tasklet and the interrupt handler may still be required.

Tasklets must be declared with the **DECLARE_TASKLET** macro:

```
DECLARE_TASKLET(name, function, data);
```

name is the name to be given to the tasklet, **function** is the function that is called to execute the tasklet (it takes one **unsigned long** argument and returns **void**), and **data** is an unsigned long value to be passed to the tasklet function.

The *short* driver declares its tasklet as follows:

```
void short_do_tasklet (unsigned long);
DECLARE_TASKLET (short_tasklet, short_do_tasklet, 0);
```

The function *tasklet_schedule* is used to schedule a tasklet for running. If *short* is loaded with **tasklet=1**, it installs a different interrupt handler that saves data and schedules the tasklet as follows:

```
void short_tl_interrupt(int irq, void *dev_id, struct pt_regs *regs)
{
    do_gettimeofday((struct timeval *) tv_head); /* cast to stop
    'volatile' warning */
    short_incr_tv(&tv_head);
    tasklet_schedule(&short_tasklet);
    short_bh_count++; /* record that an interrupt arrived */
}
```

The actual tasklet routine, *short_do_tasklet*, will be executed shortly at the system's convenience. As mentioned earlier, this routine performs the bulk of the work of handling the interrupt; it looks like this:

```
void short_do_tasklet (unsigned long unused)
{
    int savecount = short_bh_count, written;
    short_bh_count = 0; /* we have already been removed from queue */
    /*
     * The bottom half reads the tv array, filled by the top half,
     * and prints it to the circular text buffer, which is then consumed
     * by reading processes
     */

    /* First write the number of interrupts that occurred before
       this bh */

    written = sprintf((char *)short_head,"bh after %6i\n",savecount);
    short_incr_bp(&short_head, written);

    /*
     * Then, write the time values. Write exactly 16 bytes at a time,
     * so it aligns with PAGE_SIZE
     */

    do {
        written = sprintf((char *)short_head,"%08u.%06u\n",
                    (int)(tv_tail->tv_sec % 100000000),
                    (int)(tv_tail->tv_usec));
        short_incr_bp(&short_head, written);
        short_incr_tv(&tv_tail);
    } while (tv_tail != tv_head);

    wake_up_interruptible(&short_queue); /* wake any reading process */
}
```

Among other things, this tasklet makes a note of how many interrupts have arrived since it was last called. A device like *short* can generate a great many interrupts in a brief period, so it is not uncommon for several to arrive before the bottom half is executed. Drivers must always be prepared for this possibility, and must be able to determine how much work there is to perform from the information left by the top half.

The BH Mechanism

Unlike tasklets, old-style BH bottom halves have been around almost as long as the Linux kernel itself. They show their age in a number of ways. For example, all BH bottom halves are predefined in the kernel, and there can be a maximum of 32 of them. Since they are predefined, bottom halves cannot be used directly by modules, but that is not actually a problem, as we will see.

Whenever some code wants to schedule a bottom half for running, it calls *mark_bh*. In the older BH implemention, *mark_bh* would set a bit in a bit mask, allowing the corresponding bottom-half handler to be found quickly at runtime. In modern kernels, it just calls *tasklet_schedule* to schedule the bottom-half routine for execution.

Marking bottom halves is defined in `<linux/interrupt.h>` as

```
void mark_bh(int nr);
```

Here, `nr` is the "number" of the BH to activate. The number is a symbolic constant defined in `<linux/interrupt.h>` that identifies the bottom half to run. The function that corresponds to each bottom half is provided by the driver that owns the bottom half. For example, when `mark_bh(SCSI_BH)` is called, the function being scheduled for execution is *scsi_bottom_half_handler*, which is part of the SCSI driver.

As mentioned earlier, bottom halves are static objects, so a modularized driver won't be able to register its *own* BH. There's no support for dynamic allocation of BH bottom halves, and it's unlikely there ever will be. Fortunately, the immediate task queue can be used instead.

The rest of this section lists some of the most interesting bottom halves. It then describes how the kernel runs a BH bottom half, which you should understand in order to use bottom halves properly.

Several BH bottom halves declared by the kernel are interesting to look at, and a few can even be used by a driver, as introduced earlier. These are the most interesting BHs:

IMMEDIATE_BH

This is the most important bottom half for driver writers. The function being scheduled runs (with *run_task_queue*) the `tq_immediate` task queue. A driver (like a custom module) that doesn't own a bottom half can use the immediate queue as if it were its own BH. After registering a task in the queue, the driver must mark the BH in order to have its code actually executed; how to do this was introduced in "The immediate queue," in Chapter 6.

TQUEUE_BH

This BH is activated at each timer tick *if* a task is registered in `tq_timer`. In practice, a driver can implement its own BH using `tq_timer`. The timer queue introduced in "The timer queue" in Chapter 6 is a BH, but there's no need to call *mark_bh* for it.

TIMER_BH

This BH is marked by *do_timer*, the function in charge of the clock tick. The function that this BH executes is the one that drives the kernel timers. There is no way to use this facility for a driver short of using *add_timer*.

The remaining BH bottom halves are used by specific kernel drivers. There are no entry points in them for a module, and it wouldn't make sense for there to be any. The list of these other bottom halves is steadily shrinking as the drivers are converted to using tasklets.

Once a BH has been marked, it is executed when *bh_action* (*kernel/softirq.c*) is invoked, which happens when tasklets are run. This happens whenever a process exits from a system call or when an interrupt handler exits. Tasklets are always executed as part of the timer interrupt, so a driver can usually expect that a bottom-half routine will be executed at most 10 ms after it has been scheduled.

Writing a BH Bottom Half

It's quite apparent from the list of available bottom halves in "The BH Mechanism" that a driver implementing a bottom half should attach its code to `IMMEDIATE_BH` by using the immediate queue.

When `IMMEDIATE_BH` is marked, the function in charge of the immediate bottom half just consumes the immediate queue. If your interrupt handler queues its BH handler to `tq_immediate` and marks the `IMMEDIATE_BH` bottom half, the queued task will be called at just the right time. Because in all kernels we are interested in you can queue the same task multiple times without trashing the task queue, you can queue your bottom half every time the top-half handler runs. We'll see this behavior in a while.

Drivers with exotic configurations—multiple bottom halves or other setups that can't easily be handled with a plain `tq_immediate`—can be satisfied by using a custom task queue. The interrupt handler queues the tasks in its own queue, and when it's ready to run them, a simple queue-consuming function is inserted into the immediate queue. See "Running Your Own Task Queues" in Chapter 6 for details.

Let's now look at the *short* BH implementation. When loaded with `bh=1`, the module installs an interrupt handler that uses a BH bottom half:

```
void short_bh_interrupt(int irq, void *dev_id, struct pt_regs *regs)
{
    /* cast to stop 'volatile' warning */
    do_gettimeofday((struct timeval *) tv_head);
    short_incr_tv(&tv_head);

    /* Queue the bh. Don't care about multiple enqueueing */
    queue_task(&short_task, &tq_immediate);
    mark_bh(IMMEDIATE_BH);

    short_bh_count++; /* record that an interrupt arrived */
}
```

As expected, this code calls *queue_task* without checking whether the task is already enqueued.

The BH, then, performs the rest of the work. This BH is, in fact, the same *short_do_tasklet* that was shown previuosly.

Here's an example of what you see when loading *short* by specifying `bh=1`:

```
morgana% echo 1122334455 > /dev/shortint ; cat /dev/shortint
bh after       5
50588804.876653
50588804.876693
50588804.876720
50588804.876747
50588804.876774
```

The actual timings that you will see will vary, of course, depending on your particular system.

Interrupt Sharing

The notion of an IRQ conflict is almost synonymous with the PC architecture. In general, IRQ lines on the PC have not been able to serve more than one device, and there have never been enough of them. As a result, frustrated users have often spent much time with their computer case open, trying to find a way to make all of their hardware play well together.

But, in fact, there is nothing in the design of the hardware itself that says that interrupt lines cannot be shared. The problems are on the software side. With the arrival of the PCI bus, the writers of system software have had to work a little harder, since all PCI interrupts can explicitly be shared. So Linux supports shared interrupts—and on all buses where it makes any sense, not just the PCI. Thus, suitably aware drivers for ISA devices can also share an IRQ line.

The question of interrupt sharing under the ISA bus brings in the issue of level-triggered versus edge-triggered interrupt lines. Although the former kind of interrupt reporting is safe with regard to sharing, it may lead to software lockup if not handled correctly. Edge-triggered interrupts, on the other hand, are not safe with regard to sharing; ISA is edge triggered, because this signaling is easier to implement at hardware level and therefore was the common choice in the 1980s. This issue is unrelated to electrical signal levels; in order to support sharing, the line must be able to be driven active by multiple sources whether it is level triggered or edge triggered.

With a level-triggered interrupt line, the peripheral device asserts the IRQ signal until software clears the pending interrupt (usually by writing to a device register); therefore, if several devices pull the line active, the CPU will signal an interrupt as soon as the IRQ is enabled until all drivers have serviced their devices. This behavior is safe with regard to sharing but may lead to lockup if a driver fails to clear its interrupt source.

When using edge-triggered interrupts, on the other hand, interrupts may be lost: if one device pulls the line active for too long a time, when another device pulls the line active no edge will be generated, and the processor will ignore the second request. A shared handler may just not see the interrupt, and if its hardware doesn't deassert the IRQ line no other interrupt will be notified for either shared device.

For this reason, even if interrupt sharing is supported under ISA, it may not function properly; while some devices pull the IRQ line active for a single clock cycle, other devices are not so well behaved and may cause great pains to the driver writer who tries to share the IRQ. We won't go any deeper into this issue; for the rest of this section we assume that either the host bus supports sharing or that you know what you are doing.

To develop a driver that can manage a shared interrupt line, some details need to be considered. As discussed later, some of the features described in this chapter are not available for devices using interrupt sharing. Whenever possible, it's better to support sharing because it presents fewer problems for the final user. In some cases (e.g., when working with the PCI bus), interrupt sharing is mandatory.

Installing a Shared Handler

Shared interrupts are installed through *request_irq* just like nonshared ones, but there are two differences:

- The `SA_SHIRQ` bit must be specified in the `flags` argument when requesting the interrupt.

- The `dev_id` argument *must* be unique. Any pointer into the module's address space will do, but `dev_id` definitely cannot be set to `NULL`.

The kernel keeps a list of shared handlers associated with the interrupt, like a driver's signature, and `dev_id` differentiates between them. If two drivers were to register `NULL` as their signature on the same interrupt, things might get mixed up at unload time, causing the kernel to oops when an interrupt arrived. For this reason, modern kernels will complain loudly if passed a `NULL` `dev_id` when registering shared interrupts.

When a shared interrupt is requested, *request_irq* succeeds if either the interrupt line is free or any handlers already registered for that line have also specified that the IRQ is to be shared. With 2.0 kernels, it was also necessary that all handlers for a shared interrupt were either fast or slow—the two modes could not be mixed.

Whenever two or more drivers are sharing an interrupt line and the hardware interrupts the processor on that line, the kernel invokes every handler registered for that interrupt, passing each its own `dev_id`. Therefore, a shared handler must be able to recognize its own interrupts, and should quickly exit when its own device has not interrupted.

If you need to probe for your device before requesting the IRQ line, the kernel can't help you. No probing function is available for shared handlers. The standard probing mechanism works if the line being used is free, but if the line is already held by another driver with sharing capabilities, the probe will fail, even if your driver would have worked perfectly.

The only available technique for probing shared lines, then, is the do-it-yourself way. The driver should request every possible IRQ line as a shared handler and then see where interrupts are reported. The difference between that and do-it-yourself probing is that the probing handler must check with the device to see that the interrupt actually occurred, because it could have been called in response to another device interrupting on a shared line.

Releasing the handler is performed in the normal way, using *release_irq*. Here the `dev_id` argument is used to select the correct handler to release from the list of shared handlers for the interrupt. That's why the `dev_id` pointer must be unique.

A driver using a shared handler needs to be careful about one more thing: it can't play with *enable_irq* or *disable_irq*. If it does, things might go haywire for other devices sharing the line. In general, the programmer must remember that his driver doesn't own the IRQ, and its behavior should be more "social" than is necessary if one owns the interrupt line.

Running the Handler

As suggested earlier, when the kernel receives an interrupt, all the registered handlers are invoked. A shared handler must be able to distinguish between interrupts that it needs to handle and interrupts generated by other devices.

Loading *short* with the option `shared=1` installs the following handler instead of the default:

```
void short_sh_interrupt(int irq, void *dev_id, struct pt_regs *regs)
{
    int value, written;
    struct timeval tv;

    /* If it wasn't short, return immediately */
    value = inb(short_base);
    if (!(value & 0x80)) return;

    /* clear the interrupting bit */
    outb(value & 0x7F, short_base);
```

```
        /* the rest is unchanged */

        do_gettimeofday(&tv);
        written = sprintf((char *)short_head,"%08u.%06u\n",
                            (int)(tv.tv_sec % 100000000), (int)(tv.tv_usec));
        short_incr_bp(&short_head, written);
        wake_up_interruptible(&short_queue); /* wake any reading process */
    }
```

An explanation is due here. Since the parallel port has no "interrupt-pending" bit to check, the handler uses the ACK bit for this purpose. If the bit is high, the interrupt being reported is for *short*, and the handler clears the bit.

The handler resets the bit by zeroing the high bit of the parallel interface's data port—*short* assumes that pins 9 and 10 are connected together. If one of the other devices sharing the IRQ with *short* generates an interrupt, *short* sees that its own line is still inactive and does nothing.

A full-featured driver probably splits the work into top and bottom halves, of course, but that's easy to add and does not have any impact on the code that implements sharing. A real driver would also likely use the `dev_id` argument to determine which, of possibly many, devices might be interrupting.

Note that if you are using a printer (instead of the jumper wire) to test interrupt management with *short*, this shared handler won't work as advertised, because the printer protocol doesn't allow for sharing, and the driver can't know whether the interrupt was from the printer or not.

The /proc Interface

Installing shared handlers in the system doesn't affect */proc/stat*, which doesn't even know about handlers. However, */proc/interrupts* changes slightly.

All the handlers installed for the same interrupt number appear on the same line of */proc/interrupts*. The following output shows how shared interrupt handlers are displayed:

```
              CPU0        CPU1
    0:    22114216    22002860    IO-APIC-edge    timer
    1:      135401      136582    IO-APIC-edge    keyboard
    2:           0           0         XT-PIC    cascade
    5:     5162076     5160039    IO-APIC-level   eth0
    9:           0           0    IO-APIC-level   acpi, es1370
   10:      310450      312222    IO-APIC-level   aic7xxx
   12:      460372      471747    IO-APIC-edge    PS/2 Mouse
   13:           1           0         XT-PIC    fpu
   15:     1367555     1322398    IO-APIC-edge    ide1
  NMI:    44117004    44117004
  LOC:    44116987    44116986
  ERR:           0
```

The shared interrupt line here is IRQ 9; the active handlers are listed on one line, separated by commas. Here the power management subsystem ("acpi") is sharing this IRQ with the sound card ("es1370"). The kernel is unable to distinguish interrupts from these two sources, and will invoke each interrupt handlers in the driver for each interrupt.

Interrupt-Driven I/O

Whenever a data transfer to or from the managed hardware might be delayed for any reason, the driver writer should implement buffering. Data buffers help to detach data transmission and reception from the *write* and *read* system calls, and overall system performance benefits.

A good buffering mechanism leads to *interrupt-driven I/O*, in which an input buffer is filled at interrupt time and is emptied by processes that read the device; an output buffer is filled by processes that write to the device and is emptied at interrupt time. An example of interrupt-driven output is the implementation of */dev/shortint*.

For interrupt-driven data transfer to happen successfully, the hardware should be able to generate interrupts with the following semantics:

- For input, the device interrupts the processor when new data has arrived and is ready to be retrieved by the system processor. The actual actions to perform depend on whether the device uses I/O ports, memory mapping, or DMA.

- For output, the device delivers an interrupt either when it is ready to accept new data or to acknowledge a successful data transfer. Memory-mapped and DMA-capable devices usually generate interrupts to tell the system they are done with the buffer.

The timing relationships between a *read* or *write* and the actual arrival of data were introduced in "Blocking and Nonblocking Operations", in Chapter 5. But interrupt-driven I/O introduces the problem of synchronizing concurrent access to shared data items and all the issues related to race conditions. The next section covers this related topic in some depth.

Race Conditions

We have already seen race conditions come up a number of times in the previous chapters. Whereas race conditions can happen at any time on SMP systems, uniprocessor systems, to this point, have had to worry about them rather less.*

---

* Note, however, that the kernel developers are seriously considering making *all* kernel code preemptable at almost any time, making locking mandatory even on uniprocessor systems.

Interrupts, however, can bring with them a whole new set of race conditions, even on uniprocessor systems. Since an interrupt can happen at any time, it can cause the interrupt handler to be executed in the middle of an arbitrary piece of driver code. Thus, any device driver that is working with interrupts—and that is most of them—must be very concerned with race conditions. For this reason, we look more closely at race conditions and their prevention in this chapter.

Dealing with race conditions is one of the trickiest aspects of programming, because the related bugs are subtle and very difficult to reproduce, and it's hard to tell when there is a race condition between interrupt code and the driver methods. The programmer must take great care to avoid corruption of data or metadata.

Different techniques can be employed to prevent data corruption, and we will introduce the most common ones. We won't show complete code because the best code for each situation depends on the operating mode of the device being driven, and on the programmer's taste. All of the drivers in this book, however, protect themselves against race conditions, so examples can be found in the sample code.

The most common ways of protecting data from concurrent access are as follows:

- Using a circular buffer and avoiding shared variables

- Using spinlocks to enforce mutual exclusion

- Using lock variables that are atomically incremented and decremented

Note that semaphores are not listed here. Because locking a semaphore can put a process to sleep, semaphores may not be used in interrupt handlers.

Whatever approach you choose, you still need to decide what to do when accessing a variable that can be modified at interrupt time. In simple cases, such a variable can simply be declared as `volatile` to prevent the compiler from optimizing access to its value (for example, it prevents the compiler from holding the value in a register for the whole duration of a function). However, the compiler generates suboptimal code whenever `volatile` variables are involved, so you might choose to resort to some sort of locking instead. In more complicated situations, there is no choice but to use some sort of locking.

Using Circular Buffers

Using a circular buffer is an effective way of handling concurrent-access problems; the best way to deal with concurrent access is to perform no concurrent access whatsoever.

The circular buffer uses an algorithm called "producer and consumer": one player pushes data in and the other pulls data out. Concurrent access is avoided if there is exactly one producer and exactly one consumer. There are two examples of producer and consumer in *short*. In one case, the reading process is waiting to consume data that is produced at interrupt time; in the other, the bottom half consumes data produced by the top half.

Two pointers are used to address a circular buffer: `head` and `tail`. `head` is the point at which data is being written and is updated only by the producer of the data. Data is being read from `tail`, which is updated only by the consumer. As mentioned earlier, if data is written at interrupt time, you must be careful when accessing `head` multiple times. You should either declare it as `volatile` or use some sort of locking.

The circular buffer runs smoothly, except when it fills up. If that happens, things become hairy, and you can choose among different possible solutions. The *short* implementation just loses data; there's no check for overflow, and if `head` goes beyond `tail`, a whole buffer of data is lost. Some alternative implementations are to drop the last item; to overwrite the buffer tail, as *printk* does (see "How Messages Get Logged" in Chapter 4); to hold up the producer, as *scullpipe* does; or to allocate a temporary extra buffer to back up the main buffer. The best solution depends on the importance of your data and other situation-specific questions, so we won't cover it here.

Although the circular buffer appears to solve the problem of concurrent access, there is still the possibility of a race condition when the *read* function goes to sleep. This code shows where the problem appears in *short*:

```
while (short_head == short_tail) {
    interruptible_sleep_on(&short_queue);
    /* ... */
    }
```

When executing this statement, it is possible that new data will arrive *after* the `while` condition is evaluated as true and *before* the process goes to sleep. Information carried in by the interrupt won't be read by the process; the process goes to sleep even though `head != tail`, and it isn't awakened until the next data item arrives.

We didn't implement correct locking for *short* because the source of *short_read* is included in "A Sample Driver" in Chapter 8, and at that point this discussion was not worth introducing. Also, the data involved is not worth the effort.

Although the data that *short* collects is not vital, and the likelihood of getting an interrupt in the time lapse between two successive instructions is often negligible, sometimes you just can't take the risk of going to sleep when data is pending. This problem is general enough to deserve special treatment and is delayed to "Going to Sleep Without Races" later in this chapter, where we'll discuss it in detail.

It's interesting to note that only a producer-and-consumer situation can be addressed with a circular buffer. A programmer must often deal with more complex data structures to solve the concurrent-access problem. The producer/consumer situation is actually the simplest class of these problems; other structures, such as linked lists, simply don't lend themselves to a circular buffer implementation.

Using Spinlocks

We have seen spinlocks before, for example, in the *scull* driver. The discussion thus far has looked only at a few uses of spinlocks; in this section we cover them in rather more detail.

A spinlock, remember, works through a shared variable. A function may acquire the lock by setting the variable to a specific value. Any other function needing the lock will query it and, seeing that it is not available, will "spin" in a busy-wait loop until it is available. Spinlocks thus need to be used with care. A function that holds a spinlock for too long can waste much time because other CPUs are forced to wait.

Spinlocks are represented by the type `spinlock_t`, which, along with the various spinlock functions, is declared in `<asm/spinlock.h>`. Normally, a spinlock is declared and initialized to the unlocked state with a line like:

```
spinlock_t my_lock = SPIN_LOCK_UNLOCKED;
```

If, instead, it is necessary to initialize a spinlock at runtime, use *spin_lock_init*:

```
spin_lock_init(&my_lock);
```

There are a number of functions (actually macros) that work with spinlocks:

`spin_lock(spinlock_t *lock);`
> Acquire the given lock, spinning if necessary until it is available. On return from *spin_lock*, the calling function owns the lock.

`spin_lock_irqsave(spinlock_t *lock, unsigned long flags);`
> This version also acquires the lock; in addition, it disables interrupts on the local processor and stores the current interrupt state in `flags`. Note that all of the spinlock primitives are defined as macros, and that the `flags` argument is passed directly, not as a pointer.

`spin_lock_irq(spinlock_t *lock);`
> This function acts like *spin_lock_irqsave*, except that it does not save the current interrupt state. This version is slightly more efficient than *spin_lock_irqsave*, but it should only be used in situations in which you know that interrupts will not have already been disabled.

```
spin_lock_bh(spinlock_t *lock);
```
Obtains the given lock and prevents the execution of bottom halves.

```
spin_unlock(spinlock_t *lock);
spin_unlock_irqrestore(spinlock_t *lock, unsigned long
      flags);
spin_unlock_irq(spinlock_t *lock);
spin_unlock_bh(spinlock_t *lock);
```
These functions are the counterparts of the various locking primitives described previously. *spin_unlock* unlocks the given lock and nothing else. *spin_unlock_irqrestore* possibly enables interrupts, depending on the **flags** value (which should have come from *spin_lock_irqsave*). *spin_unlock_irq* enables interrupts unconditionally, and *spin_unlock_bh* reenables bottom-half processing. In each case, your function should be in possession of the lock before calling one of the unlocking primitives, or serious disorder will result.

```
spin_is_locked(spinlock_t *lock);
spin_trylock(spinlock_t *lock)
spin_unlock_wait(spinlock_t *lock);
```
spin_is_locked queries the state of a spinlock without changing it. It returns nonzero if the lock is currently busy. To attempt to acquire a lock without waiting, use *spin_trylock*, which returns nonzero if the operation failed (the lock was busy). *spin_unlock_wait* waits until the lock becomes free, but does not take possession of it.

Many users of spinlocks stick to *spin_lock* and *spin_unlock*. If you are using spin-locks in interrupt handlers, however, you must use the IRQ-disabling versions (usually *spin_lock_irqsave* and *spin_unlock_irqsave*) in the noninterrupt code. To do otherwise is to invite a deadlock situation.

It is worth considering an example here. Assume that your driver is running in its *read* method, and it obtains a lock with *spin_lock*. While the *read* method is holding the lock, your device interrupts, and your interrupt handler is executed on the same processor. If it attempts to use the same lock, it will go into a busy-wait loop, since your *read* method already holds the lock. But, since the interrupt routine has preempted that method, the lock will never be released and the processor deadlocks, which is probably not what you wanted.

This problem can be avoided by using *spin_lock_irqsave* to disable interrupts on the local processor while the lock is held. When in doubt, use the *_irqsave* versions of the primitives and you will not need to worry about deadlocks. Remember, though, that the **flags** value from *spin_lock_irqsave* must not be passed to other functions.

Regular spinlocks work well for most situations encountered by device driver writers. In some cases, however, there is a particular pattern of access to critical data that is worth treating specially. If you have a situation in which numerous threads (processes, interrupt handlers, bottom-half routines) need to access critical data in a read-only mode, you may be worried about the overhead of using spinlocks. Numerous readers cannot interfere with each other; only a writer can create problems. In such situations, it is far more efficient to allow all readers to access the data simultaneously.

Linux has a different type of spinlock, called a *reader-writer spinlock* for this case. These locks have a type of `rwlock_t` and should be initialized to `RW_LOCK_UNLOCKED`. Any number of threads can hold the lock for reading at the same time. When a writer comes along, however, it waits until it can get exclusive access.

The functions for working with reader-writer locks are as follows:

```
read_lock(rwlock_t *lock);
read_lock_irqsave(rwlock_t *lock, unsigned long flags);
read_lock_irq(rwlock_t *lock);
read_lock_bh(rwlock_t *lock);
```
   function in the same way as regular spinlocks.

```
read_unlock(rwlock_t *lock);
read_unlock_irqrestore(rwlock_t *lock, unsigned long flags);
read_unlock_irq(rwlock_t *lock);
read_unlock_bh(rwlock_t *lock);
```
   These are the various ways of releasing a read lock.

```
write_lock(rwlock_t *lock);
write_lock_irqsave(rwlock_t *lock, unsigned long flags);
write_lock_irq(rwlock_t *lock);
write_lock_bh(rwlock_t *lock);
```
   Acquire a lock as a writer.

```
write_unlock(rwlock_t *lock);
write_unlock_irqrestore(rwlock_t *lock, unsigned long
      flags);
write_unlock_irq(rwlock_t *lock);
write_unlock_bh(rwlock_t *lock);
```
   Release a lock that was acquired as a writer.

If your interrupt handler uses read locks only, then all of your code may acquire read locks with *read_lock* and not disable interrupts. Any write locks must be acquired with *write_lock_irqsave*, however, to avoid deadlocks.

It is worth noting that in kernels built for uniprocessor systems, the spinlock functions expand to nothing. They thus have no overhead (other than possibly disabling interrupts) on those systems, where they are not needed.

Using Lock Variables

The kernel provides a set of functions that may be used to provide atomic (noninterruptible) access to variables. Use of these functions can occasionally eliminate the need for a more complicated locking scheme, when the operations to be performed are very simple. The atomic operations may also be used to provide a sort of "poor person's spinlock" by manually testing and looping. It is usually better, however, to use spinlocks directly, since they have been optimized for this purpose.

The Linux kernel exports two sets of functions to deal with locks: bit operations and access to the "atomic" data type.

Bit operations

It's quite common to have single-bit lock variables or to update device status flags at interrupt time—while a process may be accessing them. The kernel offers a set of functions that modify or test single bits atomically. Because the whole operation happens in a single step, no interrupt (or other processor) can interfere.

Atomic bit operations are very fast, since they perform the operation using a single machine instruction without disabling interrupts whenever the underlying platform can do that. The functions are architecture dependent and are declared in `<asm/bitops.h>`. They are guaranteed to be atomic even on SMP computers and are useful to keep coherence across processors.

Unfortunately, data typing in these functions is architecture dependent as well. The `nr` argument is mostly defined as `int` but is `unsigned long` for a few architectures. Here is the list of bit operations as they appear in 2.1.37 and later:

`void set_bit(nr, void *addr);`
> This function sets bit number `nr` in the data item pointed to by `addr`. The function acts on an `unsigned long`, even though `addr` is a pointer to `void`.

`void clear_bit(nr, void *addr);`
> The function clears the specified bit in the `unsigned long` datum that lives at `addr`. Its semantics are otherwise the same as *set_bit*.

`void change_bit(nr, void *addr);`
> This function toggles the bit.

`test_bit(nr, void *addr);`
> This function is the only bit operation that doesn't need to be atomic; it simply returns the current value of the bit.

```
int test_and_set_bit(nr, void *addr);
int test_and_clear_bit(nr, void *addr);
int test_and_change_bit(nr, void *addr);
```

These functions behave atomically like those listed previously, except that they also return the previous value of the bit.

When these functions are used to access and modify a shared flag, you don't have to do anything except call them. Using bit operations to manage a lock variable that controls access to a shared variable, on the other hand, is more complicated and deserves an example. Most modern code will not use bit operations in this way, but code like the following still exists in the kernel.

A code segment that needs to access a shared data item tries to atomically acquire a lock using either *test_and_set_bit* or *test_and_clear_bit*. The usual implementation is shown here; it assumes that the lock lives at bit `nr` of address `addr`. It also assumes that the bit is either 0 when the lock is free or nonzero when the lock is busy.

```
/* try to set lock */
while (test_and_set_bit(nr, addr) != 0)
    wait_for_a_while();

/* do your work */

/* release lock, and check... */
if (test_and_clear_bit(nr, addr) == 0)
    something_went_wrong(); /* already released: error */
```

If you read through the kernel source, you will find code that works like this example. As mentioned before, however, it is better to use spinlocks in new code, unless you need to perform useful work while waiting for the lock to be released (e.g., in the `wait_for_a_while()` instruction of this listing).

Atomic integer operations

Kernel programmers often need to share an integer variable between an interrupt handler and other functions. A separate set of functions has been provided to facilitate this sort of sharing; they are defined in `<asm/atomic.h>`.

The facility offered by *atomic.h* is much stronger than the bit operations just described. *atomic.h* defines a new data type, `atomic_t`, which can be accessed only through atomic operations. An `atomic_t` holds an `int` value on all supported architectures. Because of the way this type works on some processors, however, the full integer range may not be available; thus, you should not count on an `atomic_t` holding more than 24 bits. The following operations are defined for the type and are guaranteed to be atomic with respect to all processors of an SMP computer. The operations are very fast because they compile to a single machine instruction whenever possible.

```
void atomic_set(atomic_t *v, int i);
```
    Set the atomic variable v to the integer value i.

```
int atomic_read(atomic_t *v);
```
    Return the current value of v.

```
void atomic_add(int i, atomic_t *v);
```
    Add i to the atomic variable pointed to by v. The return value is void, because most of the time there's no need to know the new value. This function is used by the networking code to update statistics about memory usage in sockets.

```
void atomic_sub(int i, atomic_t *v);
```
    Subtract i from *v.

```
void atomic_inc(atomic_t *v);
void atomic_dec(atomic_t *v);
```
    Increment or decrement an atomic variable.

```
int atomic_inc_and_test(atomic_t *v);
int atomic_dec_and_test(atomic_t *v);
int atomic_add_and_test(int i, atomic_t *v);
int atomic_sub_and_test(int i, atomic_t *v);
```
    These functions behave like their counterparts listed earlier, but they also return the previous value of the atomic data type.

As stated earlier, atomic_t data items must be accessed only through these functions. If you pass an atomic item to a function that expects an integer argument, you'll get a compiler error.

Going to Sleep Without Races

The one race condition that has been omitted so far in this discussion is the problem of going to sleep. Generally stated, things can happen in the time between when your driver decides to sleep and when the *sleep_on* call is actually performed. Occasionally, the condition you are sleeping for may come about before you actually go to sleep, leading to a longer sleep than expected. It is a problem far more general than interrupt-driven I/O, and an efficient solution requires a little knowledge of the internals of *sleep_on*.

As an example, consider again the following code from the *short* driver:

```
while (short_head == short_tail) {
    interruptible_sleep_on(&short_queue);
    /* ... */
}
```

In this case, the value of short_head could change between the test in the while statement and the call to *interruptible_sleep_on*. In that case, the driver will sleep even though new data is available; this condition leads to delays in the best case, and a lockup of the device in the worst.

The way to solve this problem is to go halfway to sleep before performing the test. The idea is that the process can add itself to the wait queue, declare itself to be sleeping, and *then* perform its tests. This is the typical implementation:

```
wait_queue_t wait;
init_waitqueue_entry(&wait, current);

add_wait_queue(&short_queue, &wait);
while (1) {
    set_current_state(TASK_INTERRUPTIBLE);
    if (short_head != short_tail) /* whatever test your driver needs */
    break;
    schedule();
}
set_current_state(TASK_RUNNING);
remove_wait_queue(&short_queue, &wait);
```

This code is somewhat like an unrolling of the internals of *sleep_on*; we'll step through it here.

The code starts by declaring a `wait_queue_t` variable, initializing it, and adding it to the driver's wait queue (which, as you may remember, is of type `wait_queue_head_t`). Once these steps have been performed, a call to *wake_up* on `short_queue` will wake this process.

The process is not yet asleep, however. It gets closer to that state with the call to *set_current_state*, which sets the process's state to `TASK_INTERRUPTIBLE`. The rest of the system now thinks that the process is asleep, and the scheduler will not try to run it. This is an important step in the "going to sleep" process, but things still are not done.

What happens now is that the code tests for the condition for which it is waiting, namely, that there is data in the buffer. If no data is present, a call to *schedule* is made, causing some other process to run and truly putting the current process to sleep. Once the process is woken up, it will test for the condition again, and possibly exit from the loop.

Beyond the loop, there is just a bit of cleaning up to do. The current state is set to `TASK_RUNNING` to reflect the fact that we are no longer asleep; this is necessary because if we exited the loop without ever sleeping, we may still be in `TASK_INTERRUPTIBLE`. Then *remove_wait_queue* is used to take the process off the wait queue.

So why is this code free of race conditions? When new data comes in, the interrupt handler will call *wake_up* on `short_queue`, which has the effect of setting the state of every sleeping process on the queue to `TASK_RUNNING`. If the *wake_up* call happens after the buffer has been tested, the state of the task will be changed and *schedule* will cause the current process to continue running—after a short delay, if not immediately.

This sort of "test while half asleep" pattern is so common in the kernel source that a pair of macros was added during 2.1 development to make life easier:

```
wait_event(wq, condition);
wait_event_interruptible(wq, condition);
```
> Both of these macros implement the code just discussed, testing the `condition` (which, since this is a macro, is evaluated at each iteration of the loop) in the middle of the "going to sleep" process.

Backward Compatibility

As we stated at the beginning of this chapter, interrupt handling in Linux presents relatively few compatibility problems with older kernels. There are a few, however, which we discuss here. Most of the changes occurred between versions 2.0 and 2.2 of the kernel; interrupt handling has been remarkably stable since then.

Differences in the 2.2 Kernel

The biggest change since the 2.2 series has been the addition of tasklets in kernel 2.3.43. Prior to this change, the BH bottom-half mechanism was the only way for interrupt handlers to schedule deferred work.

The *set_current_state* function did not exist in Linux 2.2 (but *sysdep.h* implements it). To manipulate the current process state, it was necessary to manipulate the task structure directly. For example:

```
current->state = TASK_INTERRUPTIBLE;
```

Further Differences in the 2.0 Kernel

In Linux 2.0, there were many more differences between fast and slow handlers. Slow handlers were slower even before they began to execute, because of extra setup costs in the kernel. Fast handlers saved time not only by keeping interrupts disabled, but also by not checking for bottom halves before returning from the interrupt. Thus, the delay before the execution of a bottom half marked in an interrupt handler could be longer in the 2.0 kernel. Finally, when an IRQ line was being shared in the 2.0 kernel, all of the registered handlers had to be either fast or slow; the two modes could not be mixed.

Most of the SMP issues did not exist in 2.0, of course. Interrupt handlers could only execute on one CPU at a time, so there was no distinction between disabling interrupts locally or globally.

The *disable_irq_nosync* function did not exist in 2.0; in addition, calls to *disable_irq* and *enable_irq* did not nest.

The atomic operations were different in 2.0. The functions *test_and_set_bit*, *test_and_clear_bit*, and *test_and_change_bit* did not exist; instead, *set_bit*, *clear_bit*, and *change_bit* returned a value and functioned like the modern *test_and_* versions. For the integer operations, `atomic_t` was just a `typedef` for `int`, and variables of type `atomic_t` could be manipulated like `int`s. The *atomic_set* and *atomic_read* functions did not exist.

The *wait_event* and *wait_event_interruptible* macros did not exist in Linux 2.0.

Quick Reference

These symbols related to interrupt management were introduced in this chapter.

```
#include <linux/sched.h>
int request_irq(unsigned int irq, void (*handler)(),
      unsigned long flags, const char *dev_name, void
      *dev_id);
void free_irq(unsigned int irq, void *dev_id);
```
These calls are used to register and unregister an interrupt handler.

```
SA_INTERRUPT
SA_SHIRQ
SA_SAMPLE_RANDOM
```
Flags for *request_irq*. `SA_INTERRUPT` requests installation of a fast handler (as opposed to a slow one). `SA_SHIRQ` installs a shared handler, and the third flag asserts that interrupt timestamps can be used to generate system entropy.

```
/proc/interrupts
/proc/stat
```
These filesystem nodes are used to report information about hardware interrupts and installed handlers.

```
unsigned long probe_irq_on(void);
int probe_irq_off(unsigned long);
```
These functions are used by the driver when it has to probe to determine what interrupt line is being used by a device. The result of *probe_irq_on* must be passed back to *probe_irq_off* after the interrupt has been generated. The return value of *probe_irq_off* is the detected interrupt number.

```
void disable_irq(int irq);
void disable_irq_nosync(int irq);
void enable_irq(int irq);
```
A driver can enable and disable interrupt reporting. If the hardware tries to generate an interrupt while interrupts are disabled, the interrupt is lost forever. A driver using a shared handler must not use these functions.

```
DECLARE_TASKLET(name, function, arg);
tasklet_schedule(struct tasklet_struct *);
```
Utilities for dealing with tasklets. *DECLARE_TASKLET* declares a tasklet with the given name; when run, the given function will be called with **arg**. Use *tasklet_schedule* to schedule a tasklet for execution.

```
#include <linux/interrupt.h>
void mark_bh(int nr);
```
This function marks a bottom half for execution.

```
#include <linux/spinlock.h>
spinlock_t my_lock = SPINLOCK_UNLOCKED;
spin_lock_init(spinlock_t *lock);
spin_lock(spinlock_t *lock);
spin_lock_irqsave(spinlock_t *lock, unsigned long flags);
spin_lock_irq(spinlock_t *lock);
spin_lock_bh(spinlock_t *lock);
spin_unlock(spinlock_t *lock);
spin_unlock_irqrestore(spinlock_t *lock, unsigned long
      flags);
spin_unlock_irq(spinlock_t *lock);
spin_unlock_bh(spinlock_t *lock);
spin_is_locked(spinlock_t *lock);
spin_trylock(spinlock_t *lock)
spin_unlock_wait(spinlock_t *lock);
```
Various utilities for using spinlocks.

```
rwlock_t my_lock = RW_LOCK_UNLOCKED;
read_lock(rwlock_t *lock);
read_lock_irqsave(rwlock_t *lock, unsigned long flags);
read_lock_irq(rwlock_t *lock);
read_lock_bh(rwlock_t *lock);
read_unlock(rwlock_t *lock);
read_unlock_irqrestore(rwlock_t *lock, unsigned long flags);
read_unlock_irq(rwlock_t *lock);
read_unlock_bh(rwlock_t *lock);
```

```
write_lock(rwlock_t *lock);
write_lock_irqsave(rwlock_t *lock, unsigned long flags);
write_lock_irq(rwlock_t *lock);
write_lock_bh(rwlock_t *lock);
write_unlock(rwlock_t *lock);
write_unlock_irqrestore(rwlock_t *lock, unsigned long
        flags);
write_unlock_irq(rwlock_t *lock);
write_unlock_bh(rwlock_t *lock);
```
The variations on locking and unlocking for reader-writer spinlocks.

```
#include <asm/bitops.h>
void set_bit(nr, void *addr);
void clear_bit(nr, void *addr);
void change_bit(nr, void *addr);
test_bit(nr, void *addr);
int test_and_set_bit(nr, void *addr);
int test_and_clear_bit(nr, void *addr);
int test_and_change_bit(nr, void *addr);
```
These functions atomically access bit values; they can be used for flags or lock variables. Using these functions prevents any race condition related to concurrent access to the bit.

```
#include <asm/atomic.h>
void atomic_add(atomic_t i, atomic_t *v);
void atomic_sub(atomic_t i, atomic_t *v);
void atomic_inc(atomic_t *v);
void atomic_dec(atomic_t *v);
int atomic_dec_and_test(atomic_t *v);
```
These functions atomically access integer variables. To achieve a clean compile, the atomic_t variables must be accessed only through these functions.

```
#include <linux/sched.h>
TASK_RUNNING
TASK_INTERRUPTIBLE
TASK_UNINTERRUPTIBLE
```
The most commonly used values for the state of the current task. They are used as hints for *schedule*.

```
set_current_state(int state);
```
Sets the current task state to the given value.

```
void add_wait_queue(struct wait_queue ** p, struct
    wait_queue * wait)
void remove_wait_queue(struct wait_queue ** p, struct
    wait_queue * wait)
void __add_wait_queue(struct wait_queue ** p, struct
    wait_queue * wait)
void __remove_wait_queue(struct wait_queue ** p, struct
    wait_queue * wait)
```
The lowest-level functions that use wait queues. The leading underscores indicate a lower-level functionality. In this case, interrupt reporting must already be disabled in the processor.

```
wait_event(wait_queue_head_t queue, condition);
wait_event_interruptible(wait_queue_head_t queue, condi-
    tion);
```
These macros wait on the given queue until the given condition evaluates true.

## CHAPTER TEN

JUDICIOUS USE OF DATA TYPES

Before we go on to more advanced topics, we need to stop for a quick note on portability issues. Modern versions of the Linux kernel are highly portable, running on several very different architectures. Given the multiplatform nature of Linux, drivers intended for serious use should be portable as well.

But a core issue with kernel code is being able both to access data items of known length (for example, filesystem data structures or registers on device boards) and to exploit the capabilities of different processors (32-bit and 64-bit architectures, and possibly 16 bit as well).

Several of the problems encountered by kernel developers while porting x86 code to new architectures have been related to incorrect data typing. Adherence to strict data typing and compiling with the *-Wall -Wstrict-prototypes* flags can prevent most bugs.

Data types used by kernel data are divided into three main classes: standard C types such as `int`, explicitly sized types such as `u32`, and types used for specific kernel objects, such as `pid_t`. We are going to see when and how each of the three typing classes should be used. The final sections of the chapter talk about some other typical problems you might run into when porting driver code from the x86 to other platforms, and introduce the generalized support for linked lists exported by recent kernel headers.

If you follow the guidelines we provide, your driver should compile and run even on platforms on which you are unable to test it.

Use of Standard C Types

Although most programmers are accustomed to freely using standard types like `int` and `long`, writing device drivers requires some care to avoid typing conflicts and obscure bugs.

The problem is that you can't use the standard types when you need "a two-byte filler" or "something representing a four-byte string" because the normal C data types are not the same size on all architectures. To show the data size of the various C types, the *datasize* program has been included in the sample files provided on the O'Reilly FTP site, in the directory *misc-progs*. This is a sample run of the program on a PC (the last four types shown are introduced in the next section):

```
morgana% misc-progs/datasize
arch    Size:  char  shor   int   long   ptr  long-long  u8 u16 u32 u64
i686              1     2     4      4     4      8        1   2   4   8
```

The program can be used to show that **long** integers and pointers feature a different size on 64-bit platforms, as demonstrated by running the program on different Linux computers:

```
arch    Size:  char  shor   int   long   ptr  long-long  u8 u16 u32 u64
i386              1     2     4      4     4      8        1   2   4   8
alpha             1     2     4      8     8      8        1   2   4   8
armv4l            1     2     4      4     4      8        1   2   4   8
ia64              1     2     4      8     8      8        1   2   4   8
m68k              1     2     4      4     4      8        1   2   4   8
mips              1     2     4      4     4      8        1   2   4   8
ppc               1     2     4      4     4      8        1   2   4   8
sparc             1     2     4      4     4      8        1   2   4   8
sparc64           1     2     4      4     4      8        1   2   4   8
```

It's interesting to note that the user space of *Linux-sparc64* runs 32-bit code, so pointers are 32 bits wide in user space, even though they are 64 bits wide in kernel space. This can be verified by loading the *kdatasize* module (available in the directory *misc-modules* within the sample files). The module reports size information at load time using *printk* and returns an error (so there's no need to unload it):

```
kernel: arch   Size:   char short int long   ptr long-long u8 u16 u32 u64
kernel: sparc64          1     2    4    8     8     8       1   2   4   8
```

Although you must be careful when mixing different data types, sometimes there are good reasons to do so. One such situation is for memory addresses, which are special as far as the kernel is concerned. Although conceptually addresses are pointers, memory administration is better accomplished by using an unsigned integer type; the kernel treats physical memory like a huge array, and a memory address is just an index into the array. Furthermore, a pointer is easily dereferenced; when dealing directly with memory addresses you almost never want to dereference them in this manner. Using an integer type prevents this dereferencing, thus avoiding bugs. Therefore, addresses in the kernel are **unsigned long**, exploiting the fact that pointers and **long** integers are always the same size, at least on all the platforms currently supported by Linux.

The C99 standard defines the `intptr_t` and `uintptr_t` types for an integer variable which can hold a pointer value. These types are almost unused in the 2.4 kernel, but it would not be surprising to see them show up more often as a result of future development work.

Assigning an Explicit Size to Data Items

Sometimes kernel code requires data items of a specific size, either to match pre-defined binary structures* or to align data within structures by inserting "filler" fields (but please refer to "Data Alignment" later in this chapter for information about alignment issues).

The kernel offers the following data types to use whenever you need to know the size of your data. All the types are declared in `<asm/types.h>`, which in turn is included by `<linux/types.h>`:

```
u8;     /* unsigned byte (8 bits) */
u16;    /* unsigned word (16 bits) */
u32;    /* unsigned 32-bit value */
u64;    /* unsigned 64-bit value */
```

These data types are accessible only from kernel code (i.e., `__KERNEL__` must be defined before including `<linux/types.h>`). The corresponding signed types exist, but are rarely needed; just replace `u` with `s` in the name if you need them.

If a user-space program needs to use these types, it can prefix the names with a double underscore: `__u8` and the other types are defined independent of `__KERNEL__`. If, for example, a driver needs to exchange binary structures with a program running in user space by means of *ioctl*, the header files should declare 32-bit fields in the structures as `__u32`.

It's important to remember that these types are Linux specific, and using them hinders porting software to other Unix flavors. Systems with recent compilers will support the C99-standard types, such as `uint8_t` and `uint32_t`; when possible, those types should be used in favor of the Linux-specific variety. If your code must work with 2.0 kernels, however, use of these types will not be possible (since only older compilers work with 2.0).

You might also note that sometimes the kernel uses conventional types, such as `unsigned int`, for items whose dimension is architecture independent. This is usually done for backward compatibility. When `u32` and friends were introduced in version 1.1.67, the developers couldn't change existing data structures to the

---

* This happens when reading partition tables, when executing a binary file, or when decoding a network packet.

new types because the compiler issues a warning when there is a type mismatch between the structure field and the value being assigned to it.* Linus didn't expect the OS he wrote for his own use to become multiplatform; as a result, old structures are sometimes loosely typed.

Interface-Specific Types

Most of the commonly used data types in the kernel have their own `typedef` statements, thus preventing any portability problems. For example, a process identifier (pid) is usually `pid_t` instead of `int`. Using `pid_t` masks any possible difference in the actual data typing. We use the expression *interface-specific* to refer to a type defined by a library in order to provide an interface to a specific data structure.

Even when no interface-specific type is defined, it's always important to use the proper data type in a way consistent with the rest of the kernel. A jiffy count, for instance, is always `unsigned long`, independent of its actual size, so the `unsigned long` type should always be used when working with jiffies. In this section we concentrate on use of "_t" types.

The complete list of `_t` types appears in `<linux/types.h>`, but the list is rarely useful. When you need a specific type, you'll find it in the prototype of the functions you need to call or in the data structures you use.

Whenever your driver uses functions that require such "custom" types and you don't follow the convention, the compiler issues a warning; if you use the -*Wall* compiler flag and are careful to remove all the warnings, you can feel confident that your code is portable.

The main problem with `_t` data items is that when you need to print them, it's not always easy to choose the right *printk* or *printf* format, and warnings you resolve on one architecture reappear on another. For example, how would you print a `size_t`, which is `unsigned long` on some platforms and `unsigned int` on some others?

Whenever you need to print some interface-specific data, the best way to do it is by casting the value to the biggest possible type (usually `long` or `unsigned long`) and then printing it through the corresponding format. This kind of tweaking won't generate errors or warnings because the format matches the type, and you won't lose data bits because the cast is either a null operation or an extension of the item to a bigger data type.

In practice, the data items we're talking about aren't usually meant to be printed, so the issue applies only to debugging messages. Most often, the code needs only

---

* As a matter of fact, the compiler signals type inconsistencies even if the two types are just different names for the same object, like `unsigned long` and `u32` on the PC.

to store and compare the interface-specific types, in addition to passing them as arguments to library or kernel functions.

Although _t types are the correct solution for most situations, sometimes the right type doesn't exist. This happens for some old interfaces that haven't yet been cleaned up.

The one ambiguous point we've found in the kernel headers is data typing for I/O functions, which is loosely defined (see the section "Platform Dependencies" in Chapter 8). The loose typing is mainly there for historical reasons, but it can create problems when writing code. For example, one can get into trouble by swapping the arguments to functions like *outb*; if there were a port_t type, the compiler would find this type of error.

Other Portability Issues

In addition to data typing, there are a few other software issues to keep in mind when writing a driver if you want it to be portable across Linux platforms.

A general rule is to be suspicious of explicit constant values. Usually the code has been parameterized using preprocessor macros. This section lists the most important portability problems. Whenever you encounter other values that have been parameterized, you'll be able to find hints in the header files and in the device drivers distributed with the official kernel.

Time Intervals

When dealing with time intervals, don't assume that there are 100 jiffies per second. Although this is currently true for Linux-x86, not every Linux platform runs at 100 Hz (as of 2.4 you find values ranging from 20 to 1200, although 20 is only used in the IA-64 simulator). The assumption can be false even for the x86 if you play with the HZ value (as some people do), and nobody knows what will happen in future kernels. Whenever you calculate time intervals using jiffies, scale your times using HZ (the number of timer interrupts per second). For example, to check against a timeout of half a second, compare the elapsed time against HZ/2. More generally, the number of jiffies corresponding to msec milliseconds is always msec*HZ/1000. This detail had to be fixed in many network drivers when porting them to the Alpha; some of them didn't work on that platform because they assumed HZ to be 100.

Page Size

When playing games with memory, remember that a memory page is PAGE_SIZE bytes, not 4 KB. Assuming that the page size is 4 KB and hard-coding the value is a common error among PC programmers—instead, supported platforms show page sizes from 4 KB to 64 KB, and sometimes they differ between different implementations of the same platform. The relevant macros are **PAGE_SIZE** and **PAGE_SHIFT**. The latter contains the number of bits to shift an address to get its page number. The number currently is 12 or greater, for 4 KB and bigger pages. The macros are defined in **<asm/page.h>**; user-space programs can use *getpagesize* if they ever need the information.

Let's look at a nontrivial situation. If a driver needs 16 KB for temporary data, it shouldn't specify an **order** of 2 to *get_free_pages*. You need a portable solution. Using an array of **#ifdef** conditionals may work, but it only accounts for platforms you care to list and would break on other architectures, such as one that might be supported in the future. We suggest that you use this code instead:

```
int order = (14 - PAGE_SHIFT > 0) ? 14 - PAGE_SHIFT : 0;
buf = get_free_pages(GFP_KERNEL, order);
```

The solution depends on the knowledge that 16 KB is **1<<14**. The quotient of two numbers is the difference of their logarithms (orders), and both **14** and **PAGE_SHIFT** are orders. The value of **order** is calculated at compile time, and the implementation shown is a safe way to allocate memory for any power of two, independent of **PAGE_SIZE**.

Byte Order

Be careful not to make assumptions about byte ordering. Whereas the PC stores multibyte values low-byte first (little end first, thus little-endian), most high-level platforms work the other way (big-endian). Modern processors can operate in either mode, but most of them prefer to work in big-endian mode; support for little-endian memory access has been added to interoperate with PC data and Linux usually prefers to run in the native processor mode. Whenever possible, your code should be written such that it does not care about byte ordering in the data it manipulates. However, sometimes a driver needs to build an integer number out of single bytes or do the opposite.

You'll need to deal with endianness when you fill in network packet headers, for example, or when you are dealing with a peripheral that operates in a specific byte ordering mode. In that case, the code should include **<asm/byteorder.h>** and should check whether **__BIG_ENDIAN** or **__LITTLE_ENDIAN** is defined by the header.

You could code a bunch of **#ifdef __LITTLE_ENDIAN** conditionals, but there is a better way. The Linux kernel defines a set of macros that handle conversions between the processor's byte ordering and that of the data you need to store or load in a specific byte order. For example:

```
u32 __cpu_to_le32 (u32);
u32 __le32_to_cpu (u32);
```

These two macros convert a value from whatever the CPU uses to an unsigned, little-endian, 32-bit quantity and back. They work whether your CPU is big-endian or little-endian, and, for that matter, whether it is a 32-bit processor or not. They return their argument unchanged in cases where there is no work to be done. Use of these macros makes it easy to write portable code without having to use a lot of conditional compilation constructs.

There are dozens of similar routines; you can see the full list in `<linux/byte-order/big_endian.h>` and `<linux/byteorder/little_endian.h>`. After a while, the pattern is not hard to follow. *__be64_to_cpu* converts an unsigned, big-endian, 64-bit value to the internal CPU representation. *__le16_to_cpus*, instead, handles signed, little-endian, 16-bit quantities. When dealing with pointers, you can also use functions like *__cpu_to_le32p*, which take a pointer to the value to be converted rather than the value itself. See the include file for the rest.

Not all Linux versions defined all the macros that deal with byte ordering. In particular, the *linux/byteorder* directory appeared in version 2.1.72 to make order in the various `<asm/byteorder.h>` files and remove duplicate definitions. If you use our *sysdep.h*, you'll be able to use all of the macros available in Linux 2.4 when compiling code for 2.0 or 2.2.

Data Alignment

The last problem worth considering when writing portable code is how to access unaligned data—for example, how to read a four-byte value stored at an address that isn't a multiple of four bytes. PC users often access unaligned data items, but few architectures permit it. Most modern architectures generate an exception every time the program tries unaligned data transfers; data transfer is handled by the exception handler, with a great performance penalty. If you need to access unaligned data, you should use the following macros:

```
#include <asm/unaligned.h>
get_unaligned(ptr);
put_unaligned(val, ptr);
```

These macros are typeless and work for every data item, whether it's one, two, four, or eight bytes long. They are defined with any kernel version.

Another issue related to alignment is portability of data structures across platforms. The same data structure (as defined in the C-language source file) can be compiled differently on different platforms. The compiler arranges structure fields to be aligned according to conventions that differ from platform to platform. At least in theory, the compiler can even reorder structure fields in order to optimize memory usage.*

---

* Field reordering doesn't happen in currently supported architectures because it could break interoperability with existing code, but a new architecture may define field reordering rules for structures with holes due to alignment restrictions.

In order to write data structures for data items that can be moved across architectures, you should always enforce natural alignment of the data items in addition to standardizing on a specific endianness. *Natural alignment* means storing data items at an address that is a multiple of their size (for instance, 8-byte items go in an address multiple of 8). To enforce natural alignment while preventing the compiler from moving fields around, you should use filler fields that avoid leaving holes in the data structure.

To show how alignment is enforced by the compiler, the *dataalign* program is distributed in the *misc-progs* directory of the sample code, and an equivalent *kdataalign* module is part of *misc-modules*. This is the output of the program on several platforms and the output of the module on the SPARC64:

```
arch   Align:  char  short  int  long   ptr long-long  u8 u16 u32 u64
i386              1     2     4    4     4      4        1   2   4   4
i686              1     2     4    4     4      4        1   2   4   4
alpha             1     2     4    8     8      8        1   2   4   8
armv4l            1     2     4    4     4      4        1   2   4   4
ia64              1     2     4    8     8      8        1   2   4   8
mips              1     2     4    4     4      8        1   2   4   8
ppc               1     2     4    4     4      8        1   2   4   8
sparc             1     2     4    4     4      8        1   2   4   8
sparc64           1     2     4    4     4      8        1   2   4   8

kernel: arch  Align: char short int long  ptr long-long u8 u16 u32 u64
kernel: sparc64         1    2    4    8    8     8       1   2   4   8
```

It's interesting to note that not all platforms align 64-bit values on 64-bit boundaries, so you'll need filler fields to enforce alignment and ensure portability.

Linked Lists

Operating system kernels, like many other programs, often need to maintain lists of data structures. The Linux kernel has, at times, been host to several linked list implementations at the same time. To reduce the amount of duplicated code, the kernel developers have created a standard implementation of circular, doubly-linked lists; others needing to manipulate lists are encouraged to use this facility, introduced in version 2.1.45 of the kernel.

To use the list mechanism, your driver must include the file <linux/list.h>. This file defines a simple structure of type list_head:

```
struct list_head {
    struct list_head *next, *prev;
};
```

Linked lists used in real code are almost invariably made up of some type of structure, each one describing one entry in the list. To use the Linux list facility in your code, you need only embed a `list_head` inside the structures that make up the list. If your driver maintains a list of things to do, say, its declaration would look something like this:

```
struct todo_struct {
    struct list_head list;
    int priority; /* driver specific */
    /* ... add other driver-specific fields */
};
```

The head of the list must be a standalone `list_head` structure. List heads must be initialized prior to use with the `INIT_LIST_HEAD` macro. A "things to do" list head could be declared and initialized with:

```
struct list_head todo_list;

INIT_LIST_HEAD(&todo_list);
```

Alternatively, lists can be initialized at compile time as follows:

```
LIST_HEAD(todo_list);
```

Several functions are defined in `<linux/list.h>` that work with lists:

`list_add(struct list_head *new, struct list_head *head);`
> This function adds the **new** entry immediately after the list head—normally at the beginning of the list. It can thus be used to build stacks. Note, however, that the **head** need not be the nominal head of the list; if you pass a `list_head` structure that happens to be in the middle of the list somewhere, the new entry will go immediately after it. Since Linux lists are circular, the head of the list is not generally different from any other entry.

`list_add_tail(struct list_head *new, struct list_head *head);`
> Add a new entry just before the given list head—at the end of the list, in other words. *list_add_tail* can thus be used to build first-in first-out queues.

`list_del(struct list_head *entry);`
> The given entry is removed from the list.

`list_empty(struct list_head *head);`
> Returns a nonzero value if the given list is empty.

`list_splice(struct list_head *list, struct list_head *head);`
> This function joins two lists by inserting `list` immediately after `head`.

The `list_head` structures are good for implementing a list of like structures, but the invoking program is usually more interested in the larger structures that make up the list as a whole. A macro, *list_entry*, is provided that will map a `list_head` structure pointer back into a pointer to the structure that contains it. It is invoked as follows:

```
list_entry(struct list_head *ptr, type_of_struct, field_name);
```

where `ptr` is a pointer to the `struct list_head` being used, `type_of_struct` is the type of the structure containing the `ptr`, and `field_name` is the name of the list field within the structure. In our `todo_struct` structure from before, the list field is called simply `list`. Thus, we would turn a list entry into its containing structure with a line like this:

```
struct todo_struct *todo_ptr =
    list_entry(listptr, struct todo_struct, list);
```

The *list_entry* macro takes a little getting used to, but is not that hard to use.

The traversal of linked lists is easy: one need only follow the `prev` and `next` pointers. As an example, suppose we want to keep the list of `todo_struct` items sorted in descending priority order. A function to add a new entry would look something like this:

```
void todo_add_entry(struct todo_struct *new)
{
    struct list_head *ptr;
    struct todo_struct *entry;

    for (ptr = todo_list.next; ptr != &todo_list; ptr = ptr->next) {
        entry = list_entry(ptr, struct todo_struct, list);
        if (entry->priority < new->priority) {
            list_add_tail(&new->list, ptr);
            return;
        }
    }
    list_add_tail(&new->list, &todo_struct)
}
```

The `<linux/list.h>` file also defines a macro *list_for_each* that expands to the `for` loop used in this code. As you may suspect, you must be careful when modifying the list while traversing it.

Figure 10-1 shows how the simple `struct list_head` is used to maintain a list of data structures.

Although not all features exported by the *list.h* as it appears in Linux 2.4 are available with older kernels, our *sysdep.h* fills the gap by declaring all macros and functions for use in older kernels.

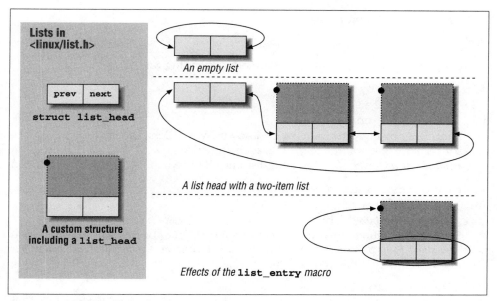

Figure 10-1. The list_head data structure

Quick Reference

The following symbols were introduced in this chapter.

```
#include <linux/types.h>
typedef u8;
typedef u16;
typedef u32;
typedef u64;
```
These types are guaranteed to be 8-, 16-, 32-, and 64-bit unsigned integer values. The equivalent signed types exist as well. In user space, you can refer to the types as __u8, __u16, and so forth.

```
#include <asm/page.h>
PAGE_SIZE
PAGE_SHIFT
```
These symbols define the number of bytes per page for the current architecture and the number of bits in the page offset (12 for 4-KB pages and 13 for 8-KB pages).

```
#include <asm/byteorder.h>
__LITTLE_ENDIAN
__BIG_ENDIAN
```
Only one of the two symbols is defined, depending on the architecture.

```
#include <asm/byteorder.h>
u32 __cpu_to_le32 (u32);
u32 __le32_to_cpu (u32);
```
Functions for converting between known byte orders and that of the processor. There are more than 60 such functions; see the various files in *include/linux/byteorder/* for a full list and the ways in which they are defined.

```
#include <asm/unaligned.h>
get_unaligned(ptr);
put_unaligned(val, ptr);
```
Some architectures need to protect unaligned data access using these macros. The macros expand to normal pointer dereferencing for architectures that permit you to access unaligned data.

```
#include <linux/list.h>
list_add(struct list_head *new, struct list_head *head);
list_add_tail(struct list_head *new, struct list_head
      *head);
list_del(struct list_head *entry);
list_empty(struct list_head *head);
list_entry(entry, type, member);
list_splice(struct list_head *list, struct list_head *head);
```
Functions for manipulating circular, doubly linked lists.

## CHAPTER ELEVEN

KMOD AND ADVANCED MODULARIZATION

In this second part of the book, we discuss more advanced topics than we've seen up to now. Once again, we start with modularization.

The introduction to modularization in Chapter 2 was only part of the story; the kernel and the *modutils* package support some advanced features that are more complex than we needed earlier to get a basic driver up and running. The features that we talk about in this chapter include the *kmod* process and version support inside modules (a facility meant to save you from recompiling your modules each time you upgrade your kernel). We also touch on how to run user-space helper programs from within kernel code.

The implementation of demand loading of modules has changed significantly over time. This chapter discusses the 2.4 implementation, as usual. The sample code works, as far as possible, on the 2.0 and 2.2 kernels as well; we cover the differences at the end of the chapter.

Loading Modules on Demand

To make it easier for users to load and unload modules, to avoid wasting kernel memory by keeping drivers in core when they are not in use, and to allow the creation of "generic" kernels that can support a wide variety of hardware, Linux offers support for automatic loading and unloading of modules. To exploit this feature, you need to enable *kmod* support when you configure the kernel before you compile it; most kernels from distributors come with *kmod* enabled. This ability to request additional modules when they are needed is particularly useful for drivers using module stacking.

The idea behind *kmod* is simple, yet effective. Whenever the kernel tries to access certain types of resources and finds them unavailable, it makes a special kernel call to the *kmod* subsystem instead of simply returning an error. If *kmod* succeeds in making the resource available by loading one or more modules, the kernel continues working; otherwise, it returns the error. Virtually any resource can be requested this way: char and block drivers, filesystems, line disciplines, network protocols, and so on.

One example of a driver that benefits from demand loading is the Advanced Linux Sound Architecture (ALSA) sound driver suite, which should (someday) replace the current sound implementation (Open Sound System, or OSS) in the Linux kernel.* ALSA is split into many pieces. The set of core code that every system needs is loaded first. Additional pieces get loaded depending on both the installed hardware (which sound card is present) and the desired functionality (MIDI sequencer, synthesizer, mixer, OSS compatibility, etc.). Thus, a large and complicated system can be broken down into components, with only the necessary parts being actually present in the running system.

Another common use of automatic module loading is to make a "one size fits all" kernel to package with distributions. Distributors want their kernels to support as much hardware as possible. It is not possible, however, to simply configure in every conceivable driver; the resulting kernel would be too large to load (and very wasteful of system memory), and having that many drivers trying to probe for hardware would be a near-certain way to create conflicts and confusion. With automatic loading, the kernel can adapt itself to the hardware it finds on each individual system.

Requesting Modules in the Kernel

Any kernel-space code can request the loading of a module when needed, by invoking a facility known as *kmod*. *kmod* was initially implemented as a separate, standalone kernel process that handled module loading requests, but it has long since been simplified by not requiring the separate process context. To use *kmod*, you must include <linux/kmod.h> in your driver source.

To request the loading of a module, call *request_module*:

```
int request_module(const char *module_name);
```

The **module_name** can either be the name of a specific module file or the name of a more generic capability; we'll look more closely at module names in the next section. The return value from *request_module* will be 0, or one of the usual negative error codes if something goes wrong.

Note that *request_module* is synchronous—it will sleep until the attempt to load the module has completed. This means, of course, that *request_module* cannot be called from interrupt context. Note also that a successful return from *request_module* does not guarantee that the capability you were after is now available. The return value indicates that *request_module* was successful in running *modprobe*,

---

* The ALSA drivers can be found at *www.alsa-project.org*.

but does not reflect the success status of *modprobe* itself. Any number of problems or configuration errors can lead *request_module* to return a success status when it has not loaded the module you needed.

Thus the proper usage of *request_module* usually requires testing for the existence of a needed capability twice:

```
if ( (ptr = look_for_feature()) == NULL) {
    /* if feature is missing, create request string */
    sprintf(modname, "fmt-for-feature-%i\n", featureid);
    request_module(modname); /* and try lo load it */
}
/* Check for existence of the feature again; error if missing */
if ( (ptr = look_for_feature()) == NULL)
    return -ENODEV;
```

The first check avoids redundant calls to *request_module*. If the feature is not available in the running kernel, a request string is generated and *request_module* is used to look for it. The final check makes sure that the required feature has become available.

The User-Space Side

The actual task of loading a module requires help from user space, for the simple reason that it is far easier to implement the required degree of configurability and flexibility in that context. When the kernel code calls *request_module*, a new "kernel thread" process is created, which runs a helper program in the user context. This program is called *modprobe*; we have seen it briefly earlier in this book.

modprobe can do a great many things. In the simplest case, it just calls *insmod* with the name of a module as passed to *request_module*. Kernel code, however, will often call *request_module* with a more abstract name representing a needed capability, such as `scsi_hostadapter`; *modprobe* will then find and load the correct module. *modprobe* can also handle module dependencies; if a requested module requires yet another module to function, *modprobe* will load both— assuming that *depmod -a* was run after the modules have been installed.[*]

The *modprobe* utility is configured by the file */etc/modules.conf*.[†] See the *modules.conf* manpage for the full list of things that can appear in this file. Here is an overview of the most common sorts of entries:

---

[*] Most distributions run *depmod -a* automatically at boot time, so you don't need to worry about that unless you installed new modules after you rebooted. See the *modprobe* documentation for more details.

[†] On older systems, this file is often called */etc/conf.modules* instead. That name still works, but its use is deprecated.

`path[misc]=`*`directory`*

> This directive tells *modprobe* that miscellaneous modules can be found in the *misc* subdirectory under the given *`directory`*. Other paths worth setting include `boot`, which points to a directory of modules that should be loaded at boot time, and `toplevel`, which gives a top-level directory under which a tree of module subdirectories may be found. You almost certainly want to include a separate `keep` directive as well.

`keep`

> Normally, a `path` directive will cause *modprobe* to discard all other paths (including the defaults) that it may have known about. By placing a `keep` *before* any `path` directives, you can cause *modprobe* to add new paths to the list instead of replacing it.

`alias `*`alias_name real_name`*

> Causes *modprobe* to load the module *`real_name`* when asked to load *`alias_name`*. The alias name usually identifies a specific capability; it has values such as `scsi_hostadapter`, `eth0`, or `sound`. This is the means by which generic requests ("a driver for the first Ethernet card") get mapped into specific modules. Alias lines are usually created by the system installation process; once it has figured out what hardware a specific system has, it generates the appropriate `alias` entries to get the right drivers loaded.

`options [-k] `*`module opts`*

> Provides a set of options (*opts*) for the given *`module`* when it is loaded. If the *-k* flag is provided, the module will not be automatically removed by a *modprobe -r* run.

`pre-install `*`module command`*
`post-install `*`module command`*
`pre-remove `*`module command`*
`post-remove `*`module command`*

> The first two specify a *`command`* to be run either before or after the given *`module`* is installed; the second two run the command before or after module removal. These directives are useful for causing extra user-space processing to happen or for running a required daemon process. The command should be given as a full pathname to avoid possible problems.
>
> Note that, for the removal commands to be run, the module must be removed with *modprobe*. They will not be run if the module is removed with *rmmod*, or if the system goes down (gracefully or otherwise).

modprobe supports far more directives than we have listed here, but the others are generally only needed in complicated situations.

A typical */etc/modules.conf* looks like this:

```
alias scsi_hostadapter aic7xxx
alias eth0 eepro100
pre-install pcmcia_core /etc/rc.d/init.d/pcmcia start
options short irq=1
alias sound es1370
```

This file tells *modprobe* which drivers to load to make the SCSI system, Ethernet, and sound cards work. It also ensures that if the PCMCIA drivers are loaded, a startup script is invoked to run the card services daemon. Finally, an option is provided to be passed to the *short* driver.

Module Loading and Security

The loading of a module into the kernel has obvious security implications, since the loaded code runs at the highest possible privilege level. For this reason, it is important to be very careful in how you work with the module-loading system.

When editing the *modules.conf* file, one should always keep in mind that anybody who can load kernel modules has complete control over the system. Thus, for example, any directories added to the load path should be very carefully protected, as should the *modules.conf* file itself.

Note that *insmod* will normally refuse to load any modules that are not owned by the root account; this behavior is an attempt at a defense against an attacker who obtains write access to a module directory. You can override this check with an option to *insmod* (or a *modules.conf* line), but doing so reduces the security of your system.

One other thing to keep in mind is that the module name parameter that you pass to *request_module* eventually ends up on the *modprobe* command line. If that module name is provided by a user-space program in any way, it must be very carefully validated before being handed off to *request_module*. Consider, for example, a system call that configures network interfaces. In response to an invocation of *ifconfig*, this system call tells *request_module* to load the driver for the (user-specified) interface. A hostile user can then carefully choose a fictitious interface name that will cause *modprobe* to do something improper. This is a real vulnerability that was discovered late in the 2.4.0-test development cycle; the worst problems have been cleaned up, but the system is still vulnerable to malicious module names.

Module Loading Example

Let's now try to use the demand-loading functions in practice. To this end, we'll use two modules called *master* and *slave*, found in the directory *misc-modules* in the source files provided on the O'Reilly FTP site.

In order to run this test code without installing the modules in the default module search path, you can add something like the following lines to your */etc/modules.conf*:

```
keep
path[misc]=~rubini/driverBook/src/misc-modules
```

The slave module performs no function; it just takes up space until removed. The master module, on the other hand, looks like this:

```
#include <linux/kmod.h>
#include "sysdep.h"


int master_init_module(void)
{
    int r[2]; /* results */

    r[0]=request_module("slave");
    r[1]=request_module("nonexistent");
    printk(KERN_INFO "master: loading results are %i, %i\n", r[0],r[1]);
    return 0; /* success */
}

void master_cleanup_module(void)
{ }
```

At load time, *master* tries to load two modules: the slave module and one that doesn't exist. The *printk* messages reach your system logs and possibly the console. This is what happens in a system configured for *kmod* support when the daemon is active and the commands are issued on the text console:

```
morgana.root# depmod -a
morgana.root# insmod ./master.o
master: loading results are 0, 0
morgana.root# cat /proc/modules
slave                248    0  (autoclean)
master               740    0  (unused)
es1370             34832    1
```

Both the return value from *request_module* and the */proc/modules* file (described in "Initialization and Shutdown" in Chapter 2) show that the slave module has been correctly loaded. Note, however, that the attempt to load nonexistent also shows a successful return value. Because *modprobe* was run, *request_module* returns success, regardless of what happened to *modprobe*.

A subsequent removal of *master* will produce results like the following:

```
morgana.root# rmmod master
morgana.root# cat /proc/modules
slave                248    0  (autoclean)
es1370             34832    1
```

The *slave* module has been left behind in the kernel, where it will remain until the next module cleanup pass is done (which is often never on modern systems).

Running User-Mode Helper Programs

As we have seen, the *request_module* function runs a program in user mode (i.e., running as a separate process, in an unprivileged processor mode, and in user space) to help it get its job done. In the 2.3 development series, the kernel developers made the "run a user-mode helper" capability available to the rest of the kernel code. Should your driver need to run a user-mode program to support its operations, this mechanism is the way to do it. Since it's part of the *kmod* implementation, we'll look at it here. If you are interested in this capability, a look at *kernel/kmod.c* is recommended; it's not much code and illustrates nicely the use of user-mode helpers.

The interface for running helper programs is fairly simple. As of kernel 2.4.0-test9, there is a function *call_usermodehelper*; it is used primarily by the hot-plug subsystem (i.e., for USB devices and such) to perform module loading and configuration tasks when a new device is attached to the system. Its prototype is:

```
int call_usermodehelper(char *path, char **argv, char **envp);
```

The arguments will be familiar: they are the name of the executable to run, arguments to pass to it (`argv[0]`, by convention, is the name of the program itself), and the values of any environment variables. Both arrays must be terminated by NULL values, just like with the *execve* system call. *call_usermodehelper* will sleep until the program has been started, at which point it returns the status of the operation.

Helper programs run in this mode are actually run as children of a kernel thread called *keventd*. An important implication of this design is that there is no way for your code to know when the helper program has finished or what its exit status is. Running helper programs is thus a bit of an act of faith.

It is worth pointing out that truly legitimate uses of user-mode helper programs are rare. In most cases, it is better to set up a script to be run at module installation time that does all needed work as part of loading the module rather than to wire invocations of user-mode programs into kernel code. This sort of policy is best left to the user whenever possible.

Intermodule Communication

Very late in the pre-2.4.0 development series, the kernel developers added a new interface providing limited communication between modules. This intermodule scheme allows modules to register strings pointing to data of interest, which can be retrieved by other modules. We'll look briefly at this interface, using a variation of our *master* and *slave* modules.

We use the same *master* module, but introduce a new slave module called *inter*. All *inter* does is to make a string and a function available under the name ime_string (ime means "intermodule example") and ime_function; it looks, in its entirety, as follows:

```
static char *string = "inter says 'Hello World'";

void ime_function(const char *who)
{
    printk(KERN_INFO "inter: ime_function called by %s\n", who);
}

int ime_init(void)
{
    inter_module_register("ime_string", THIS_MODULE, string);
    inter_module_register("ime_function", THIS_MODULE, ime_function);
    return 0;
}

void ime_cleanup(void)
{
    inter_module_unregister("ime_string");
    inter_module_unregister("ime_function");
}
```

This code uses *inter_module_register*, which has this prototype:

```
void inter_module_register(const char *string, struct module *module,
                           const void *data);
```

string is the string other modules will use to find the data; module is a pointer to the module owning the data, which will almost always be THIS_MODULE; and data is a pointer to whatever data is to be shared. Note the use of a const pointer for the data; it is assumed that it will be exported in a read-only mode. *inter_module_register* will complain (via *printk*) if the given string is already registered.

When the data is no longer to be shared, the module should call *inter_module_unregister* to clean it up:

```
void inter_module_unregister(const char *string);
```

Two functions are exported that can access data shared via *inter_module_register*:

const void *inter_module_get(const char *string);
   This function looks up the given string and returns the associated data pointer. If the string has not been registered, NULL is returned.

```
const void *inter_module_get_request(const char *string,
    const char *module);
```

This function is like *inter_module_get* with the added feature that, if the given `string` is not found, it will call *request_module* with the given `module` name and then will try again.

Both functions also increment the usage count for the module that registered the data. Thus, a pointer obtained with *inter_module_get* or *inter_module_get_request* will remain valid until it is explicitly released. At least, the module that created that pointer will not be unloaded during that time; it is still possible for the module itself to do something that will invalidate the pointer.

When you are done with the pointer, you must release it so that the other module's usage count will be decremented properly. A simple call to

```
void inter_module_put(const char *string);
```

will release the pointer, which should not be used after this call.

In our sample *master* module, we call *inter_module_get_request* to cause the *inter* module to be loaded and to obtain the two pointers. The string is simply printed, and the function pointer is used to make a call from *master* into *inter*. The additional code in *master* looks like this:

```
static const char *ime_string = NULL;
static void master_test_inter();

void master_test_inter()
{
    void (*ime_func)();
    ime_string = inter_module_get_request("ime_string", "inter");
    if (ime_string)
        printk(KERN_INFO "master: got ime_string '%s'\n", ime_string);
    else
        printk(KERN_INFO "master: inter_module_get failed");
    ime_func = inter_module_get("ime_function");
    if (ime_func) {
        (*ime_func)("master");
        inter_module_put("ime_function");
    }
}

void master_cleanup_module(void)
{
    if (ime_string)
        inter_module_put("ime_string");
}
```

Note that one of the calls to *inter_module_put* is deferred until module cleanup time. This will cause the usage count of *inter* to be (at least) 1 until *master* is unloaded.

There are a few other worthwhile details to keep in mind when using the inter-module functions. First, they are available even in kernels that have been configured without support for loadable modules, so there is no need for a bunch of `#ifdef` lines to test for that case. The namespace implemented by the intermodule communication functions is global, so names should be chosen with care or conflicts will result. Finally, intermodule data is stored in a simple linked list; performance will suffer if large numbers of lookups are made or many strings are stored. This facility is intended for light use, not as a general dictionary subsystem.

Version Control in Modules

One of the main problems with modules is their version dependency, which was introduced in Chapter 2. The need to recompile the module against the headers of each kernel version being used can become a real pain when you run several custom modules, and recompiling is not even possible if you run a commercial module distributed in binary form.

Fortunately, the kernel developers found a flexible way to deal with version problems. The idea is that a module is incompatible with a different kernel version only if the software interface offered by the kernel has changed. The software interface, then, can be represented by a function prototype and the exact definition of all the data structures involved in the function call. Finally, a CRC algorithm* can be used to map all the information about the software interface to a single 32-bit number.

The issue of version dependencies is thus handled by mangling the name of each symbol exported by the kernel to include the checksum of all the information related to that symbol. This information is obtained by parsing the header files and extracting the information from them. This facility is optional and can be enabled at compilation time. Modular kernels shipped by Linux distributors usually have versioning support enabled.

For example, the symbol `printk` is exported to modules as something like `printk_R12345678` when version support is enabled, where `12345678` is the hexadecimal representation of the checksum of the software interface used by the function. When a module is loaded into the kernel, *insmod* (or *modprobe*) can accomplish its task only if the checksum added to each symbol in the kernel matches the one added to the same symbol in the module.

There are some limitations to this scheme. A common source of surprises has been loading a module compiled for SMP systems into a uniprocessor kernel, or vice

---

* CRC means "cyclic redundancy check," a way of generating a short, unique number from an arbitrary amount of data.

versa. Because numerous inline functions (e.g., spinlock operations) and symbols are defined differently for SMP kernels, it is important that modules and the kernel agree on whether they are built for SMP. Version 2.4 and recent 2.2 kernels throw an extra `smp_` string onto each symbol when compiling for SMP to catch this particular case. There are still potential traps, however. Modules and the kernel can differ in which version of the compiler was used to build them, which view of memory they take, which version of the processor they were built for, and more. The version support scheme can catch the most common problems, but it still pays to be careful.

But let's see what happens in both the kernel and the module when version support is enabled:

- In the kernel itself, the symbol is not modified. The linking process happens in the usual way, and the symbol table of the *vmlinux* file looks the same as before.

- The public symbol table is built using the versioned names, and this is what appears in */proc/ksyms.*

- The module must be compiled using the mangled names, which appear in the object files as undefined symbols.

- The loading program (*insmod*) matches the undefined symbols in the module with the public symbols in the kernel, thus using the version information.

Note that the kernel and the module must both agree on whether versioning is in use. If one is built for versioned symbols and the other isn't, *insmod* will refuse to load the module.

Using Version Support in Modules

Driver writers must add some explicit support if their modules are to work with versioning. Version control can be inserted in one of two places: in the makefile or in the source itself. Since the documentation of the *modutils* package describes how to do it in the makefile, we'll show you how to do it in the C source. The *master* module used to demonstrate how *kmod* works is able to support versioned symbols. The capability is automatically enabled if the kernel used to compile the module exploits version support.

The main facility used to mangle symbol names is the header `<linux/modver-sions.h>`, which includes preprocessor definitions for all the public kernel symbols. This file is generated as part of the kernel compilation (actually, "make depend") process; if your kernel has never been built, or is built without version support, there will be little of interest inside. `<linux/modversions.h>` must be included before any other header file, so place it first if you put it directly in your driver source. The usual technique, however, is to tell *gcc* to prepend the file with a compilation command like:

```
gcc -DMODVERSIONS -include /usr/src/linux/include/linux/modversions.h...
```

After the header is included, whenever the module uses a kernel symbol, the compiler sees the mangled version.

To enable versioning in the module if it has been enabled in the kernel, we must make sure that `CONFIG_MODVERSIONS` has been defined in `<linux/config.h>`. That header controls what features are enabled (compiled) in the current kernel. Each `CONFIG_` macro defined states that the corresponding option is active.*

The initial part of *master.c*, therefore, consists of the following lines:

```
#include <linux/config.h> /* retrieve the CONFIG_* macros */
#if defined(CONFIG_MODVERSIONS) && !defined(MODVERSIONS)
#  define MODVERSIONS /* force it on */
#endif

#ifdef MODVERSIONS
#  include <linux/modversions.h>
#endif
```

When compiling the file against a versioned kernel, the symbol table in the object file refers to versioned symbols, which match the ones exported by the kernel itself. The following screendump shows the symbol names stored in *master.o*. In the output of *nm*, T means "text," D means "data," and U means "undefined." The "undefined" tag denotes symbols that the object file references but doesn't declare.

```
00000034 T cleanup_module
00000000 t gcc2_compiled.
00000000 T init_module
00000034 T master_cleanup_module
00000000 T master_init_module
         U printk_Rsmp_1b7d4074
         U request_module_Rsmp_27e4dc04
morgana% fgrep 'printk' /proc/ksyms
c011b8b0 printk_Rsmp_1b7d4074
```

Because the checksums added to the symbol names in *master.o* are derived from the entire prototypes of *printk* and *request_module*, the module is compatible with a wide range of kernel versions. If, however, the data structures related to either function get modified, *insmod* will refuse to load the module because of its incompatibility with the kernel.

---

* The `CONFIG_` macros are defined in `<linux/autoconf.h>`. You should, however, include `<linux/config.h>` instead, because the latter is protected from double inclusion, and sources `<linux/autoconf.h>` internally.

Exporting Versioned Symbols

The one thing not covered by the previous discussion is what happens when a module exports symbols to be used by other modules. If we rely on version information to achieve module portability, we'd like to be able to add a CRC code to our own symbols. This subject is slightly trickier than just linking to the kernel, because we need to export the mangled symbol name to other modules; we need a way to build the checksums.

The task of parsing the header files and building the checksums is performed by *genksyms*, a tool released with the *modutils* package. This program receives the output of the C preprocessor on its own standard input and prints a new header file on standard output. The output file defines the checksummed version of each symbol exported by the original source file. The output of *genksyms* is usually saved with a `.ver` suffix; it is a good idea to stay consistent with this practice.

To show you how symbols are exported, we have created two dummy modules called *export.c* and *import.c. export* exports a simple function called *export_function*, which is used by the second module, *import.c*. This function receives two integer arguments and returns their sum—we are not interested in the function, but rather in the linking process.

The makefile in the *misc-modules* directory has a rule to build an *export.ver* file from *export.c*, so that the checksummed symbol for *export_function* can be used by the *import* module:

```
ifdef CONFIG_MODVERSIONS
export.o import.o: export.ver
endif

export.ver: export.c
        $(CC) -I$(INCLUDEDIR) $(CFLAGS) -E -D__GENKSYMS__ $^ | \
            $(GENKSYMS) -k 2.4.0 > $@
```

These lines demonstrate how to build *export.ver* and add it to the dependencies of both object files, but only if **MODVERSIONS** is defined. A few lines added to *Makefile* take care of defining **MODVERSIONS** if version support is enabled in the kernel, but they are not worth showing here. The *-k* option must be used to tell *genksyms* which version of the kernel you are working with. Its purpose is to determine the format of the output file; it need not match the kernel you are using exactly.

One thing that is worth showing, however, is the definition of the **GKSMP** symbol. As mentioned above, a prefix (`-p smp_`) is added to every checksum if the kernel is built for SMP systems. The *genksyms* utility does not add this prefix itself; it must be told explicitly to do so. The following makefile code will cause the prefix to be set appropriately:

```
ifdef CONFIG_SMP
        GENKSYMS += -p smp_
endif
```

The source file, then, must declare the right preprocessor symbols for every conceivable preprocessor pass: the input to *genksyms* and the actual compilation, both with version support enabled and with it disabled. Moreover, *export.c* should be able to autodetect version support in the kernel, as *master.c* does. The following lines show you how to do this successfully:

```
#include <linux/config.h> /* retrieve the CONFIG_* macros */
#if defined(CONFIG_MODVERSIONS) && !defined(MODVERSIONS)
#    define MODVERSIONS
#endif

/*
 * Include the versioned definitions for both kernel symbols and our
 * symbol, *unless* we are generating checksums (__GENKSYMS__
 * defined) */
#if defined(MODVERSIONS) && !defined(__GENKSYMS__)
#    include <linux/modversions.h>
#    include "export.ver" /* redefine "export_function" to include CRC */
#endif
```

The code, though hairy, has the advantage of leaving the makefile in a clean state. Passing the correct flags from *make*, on the other hand, involves writing long command lines for the various cases, which we won't do here.

The simple *import* module calls *export_function* by passing the numbers 2 and 2 as arguments; the expected result is therefore 4. The following example shows that *import* actually links to the versioned symbol of *export* and calls the function. The versioned symbol appears in */proc/ksyms*.

```
morgana.root# insmod ./export.o
morgana.root# grep export /proc/ksyms
c883605c export_function_Rsmp_888cb211   [export]
morgana.root# insmod ./import.o
import: my mate tells that 2+2 = 4
morgana.root# cat /proc/modules
import                   312    0   (unused)
export                   620    0   [import]
```

Backward Compatibility

The demand-loading capability was entirely reimplemented in the 2.1 development series. Fortunately, very few modules need to be aware of the change in any way. For completeness, however, we will describe the old implementation here.

In the 2.0 days, demand loading was handled by a separate, user-space daemon process called *kerneld*. This process connected into the kernel via a special interface and received module load (and unload) requests as they were generated by kernel code. There were numerous disadvantages to this scheme, including the fact that no modules could be loaded until the system initialization process had gotten far enough to start *kerneld*.

The *request_module* function, however, remained unchanged, as did all aspects of the modules themselves. It was, however, necessary to include `<linux/kerneld.h>` instead of `<linux/kmod.h>`.

Symbol versioning in the 2.0 kernel did not use the `smp_` prefix on SMP systems. As a result, *insmod* would happily load an SMP module into a uniprocessor kernel, or vice versa. The usual result of such a mismatch was extreme chaos.

The ability to run user-mode helper programs and the intermodule communication mechanism did not exist until Linux 2.4.

Quick Reference

This chapter introduced the following kernel symbols.

`/etc/modules.conf`
> This is the configuration file for *modprobe* and *depmod*. It is used to configure demand loading and is described in the manpages for the two programs.

`#include <linux/kmod.h>`
`int request_module(const char *name);`
> This function performs demand loading of modules.

`void inter_module_register(const char *string, struct module`
`        *module, const void *data);`
`void inter_module_unregister(const char *);`
> *inter_module_register* makes data available to other modules via the intermodule communication system. When the data is no longer to be shared, *inter_module_unregister* will end that availability.

`const void *inter_module_get(const char *string);`
`const void *inter_module_get_request(const char *string,`
`        const char *module);`
` void inter_module_put(const char *string);`
> The first two functions look up a string in the intermodule communication system; *inter_module_get_request* also attempts to load the given `module` if the string is not found. Both increment the usage count of the module that exported the string; *inter_module_put* should be called to decrement it when the data pointer is no longer needed.

```
#include <linux/config.h>
```
CONFIG_MODVERSIONS

This macro is defined only if the current kernel has been compiled to support versioned symbols.

```
#ifdef MODVERSIONS
#include <linux/modversions.h>
```

This header, which exists only if CONFIG_MODVERSIONS is valid, contains the versioned names for all the symbols exported by the kernel.

_ _GENKSYMS_ _

This macro is defined by *make* when preprocessing files to be read by *genksyms* to build new version codes. It is used to conditionally prevent inclusion of `<linux/modversions.h>` when building new checksums.

```
int call_usermodehelper(char *path, char *argv[], char
      *envp[]);
```

This function runs a user-mode program in the *keventd* process context.

CHAPTER TWELVE
LOADING BLOCK DRIVERS

Our discussion thus far has been limited to char drivers. As we have already mentioned, however, char drivers are not the only type of driver used in Linux systems. Here we turn our attention to block drivers. Block drivers provide access to block-oriented devices—those that transfer data in randomly accessible, fixed-size blocks. The classic block device is a disk drive, though others exist as well.

The char driver interface is relatively clean and easy to use; the block interface, unfortunately, is a little messier. Kernel developers like to complain about it. There are two reasons for this state of affairs. The first is simple history—the block interface has been at the core of every version of Linux since the first, and it has proved hard to change. The other reason is performance. A slow char driver is an undesirable thing, but a slow block driver is a drag on the entire system. As a result, the design of the block interface has often been influenced by the need for speed.

The block driver interface has evolved significantly over time. As with the rest of the book, we cover the 2.4 interface in this chapter, with a discussion of the changes at the end. The example drivers work on all kernels between 2.0 and 2.4, however.

This chapter explores the creation of block drivers with two new example drivers. The first, *sbull* (Simple Block Utility for Loading Localities) implements a block device using system memory—a RAM-disk driver, essentially. Later on, we'll introduce a variant called *spull* as a way of showing how to deal with partition tables.

As always, these example drivers gloss over many of the issues found in real block drivers; their purpose is to demonstrate the interface that such drivers must work with. Real drivers will have to deal with hardware, so the material covered in Chapter 8 and Chapter 9 will be useful as well.

One quick note on terminology: the word *block* as used in this book refers to a block of data as determined by the kernel. The size of blocks can be different in different disks, though they are always a power of two. A *sector* is a fixed-size unit of data as determined by the underlying hardware. Sectors are almost always 512 bytes long.

Registering the Driver

Like char drivers, block drivers in the kernel are identified by major numbers. Block major numbers are entirely distinct from char major numbers, however. A block device with major number 32 can coexist with a char device using the same major number since the two ranges are separate.

The functions for registering and unregistering block devices look similar to those for char devices:

```
#include <linux/fs.h>
int register_blkdev(unsigned int major, const char *name,
    struct block_device_operations *bdops);
int unregister_blkdev(unsigned int major, const char *name);
```

The arguments have the same general meaning as for char devices, and major numbers can be assigned dynamically in the same way. So the *sbull* device registers itself in almost exactly the same way as *scull* did:

```
result = register_blkdev(sbull_major, "sbull", &sbull_bdops);
if (result < 0) {
    printk(KERN_WARNING "sbull: can't get major %d\n",sbull_major);
    return result;
}
if (sbull_major == 0) sbull_major = result; /* dynamic */
major = sbull_major; /* Use 'major' later on to save typing */
```

The similarity stops here, however. One difference is already evident: *register_chrdev* took a pointer to a `file_operations` structure, but *register_blkdev* uses a structure of type `block_device_operations` instead—as it has since kernel version 2.3.38. The structure is still sometimes referred to by the name `fops` in block drivers; we'll call it `bdops` to be more faithful to what the structure is and to follow the suggested naming. The definition of this structure is as follows:

```
struct block_device_operations {
    int (*open) (struct inode *inode, struct file *filp);
    int (*release) (struct inode *inode, struct file *filp);
    int (*ioctl) (struct inode *inode, struct file *filp,
                    unsigned command, unsigned long argument);
    int (*check_media_change) (kdev_t dev);
    int (*revalidate) (kdev_t dev);
};
```

The *open*, *release*, and *ioctl* methods listed here are exactly the same as their char device counterparts. The other two methods are specific to block devices and are discussed later in this chapter. Note that there is no **owner** field in this structure; block drivers must still maintain their usage count manually, even in the 2.4 kernel.

The **bdops** structure used in *sbull* is as follows:

```
struct block_device_operations sbull_bdops = {
    open:                 sbull_open,
    release:              sbull_release,
    ioctl:                sbull_ioctl,
    check_media_change:   sbull_check_change,
    revalidate:           sbull_revalidate,
};
```

Note that there are no read or write operations provided in the **block_device_operations** structure. All I/O to block devices is normally buffered by the system (the only exception is with "raw" devices, which we cover in the next chapter); user processes do not perform direct I/O to these devices. User-mode access to block devices usually is implicit in filesystem operations they perform, and those operations clearly benefit from I/O buffering. However, even "direct" I/O to a block device, such as when a filesystem is created, goes through the Linux buffer cache.* As a result, the kernel provides a single set of read and write functions for block devices, and drivers do not need to worry about them.

Clearly, a block driver must eventually provide some mechanism for actually doing block I/O to a device. In Linux, the method used for these I/O operations is called *request*; it is the equivalent of the "strategy" function found on many Unix systems. The *request* method handles both read and write operations and can be somewhat complex. We will get into the details of *request* shortly.

For the purposes of block device registration, however, we must tell the kernel where our *request* method is. This method is not kept in the **block_device_operations** structure, for both historical and performance reasons; instead, it is associated with the queue of pending I/O operations for the device. By default, there is one such queue for each major number. A block driver must initialize that queue with *blk_init_queue*. Queue initialization and cleanup is defined as follows:

```
#include <linux/blkdev.h>
blk_init_queue(request_queue_t *queue, request_fn_proc *request);
blk_cleanup_queue(request_queue_t *queue);
```

---

* Actually, the 2.3 development series added the raw I/O capability, allowing user processes to write to block devices without involving the buffer cache. Block drivers, however, are entirely unaware of raw I/O, so we defer the discussion of that facility to the next chapter.

The *init* function sets up the queue, and associates the driver's *request* function (passed as the second parameter) with the queue. It is necessary to call *blk_cleanup_queue* at module cleanup time. The *sbull* driver initializes its queue with this line of code:

```
blk_init_queue(BLK_DEFAULT_QUEUE(major), sbull_request);
```

Each device has a request queue that it uses by default; the macro `BLK_DEFAULT_QUEUE(major)` is used to indicate that queue when needed. This macro looks into a global array of `blk_dev_struct` structures called `blk_dev`, which is maintained by the kernel and indexed by major number. The structure looks like this:

```
struct blk_dev_struct {
    request_queue_t    request_queue;
    queue_proc         *queue;
    void               *data;
};
```

The `request_queue` member contains the I/O request queue that we have just initialized. We will look at the `queue` member shortly. The `data` field may be used by the driver for its own data—but few drivers do so.

Figure 12-1 visualizes the main steps a driver module performs to register with the kernel proper and deregister. If you compare this figure with Figure 2-1, similarities and differences should be clear.

In addition to `blk_dev`, several other global arrays hold information about block drivers. These arrays are indexed by the major number, and sometimes also the minor number. They are declared and described in *drivers/block/ll_rw_block.c*.

`int blk_size[][];`
> This array is indexed by the major and minor numbers. It describes the size of each device, in kilobytes. If `blk_size[major]` is `NULL`, no checking is performed on the size of the device (i.e., the kernel might request data transfers past end-of-device).

`int blksize_size[][];`
> The size of the block used by each device, in bytes. Like the previous one, this bidimensional array is indexed by both major and minor numbers. If `blksize_size[major]` is a null pointer, a block size of `BLOCK_SIZE` (currently 1 KB) is assumed. The block size for the device must be a power of two, because the kernel uses bit-shift operators to convert offsets to block numbers.

`int hardsect_size[][];`
> Like the others, this data structure is indexed by the major and minor numbers. The default value for the hardware sector size is 512 bytes. With the 2.2 and 2.4 kernels, different sector sizes are supported, but they must always be a power of two greater than or equal to 512 bytes.

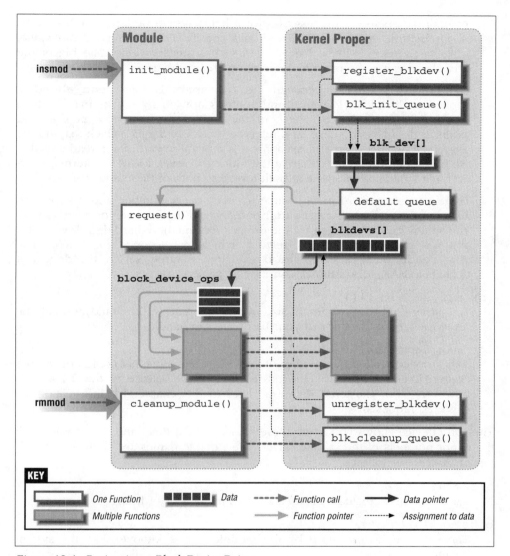

Figure 12-1. Registering a Block Device Driver

```
int read_ahead[];
int max_readahead[][];
```
These arrays define the number of sectors to be read in advance by the kernel when a file is being read sequentially. `read_ahead` applies to all devices of a given type and is indexed by major number; `max_readahead` applies to individual devices and is indexed by both the major and minor numbers.

Reading data before a process asks for it helps system performance and over-all throughput. A slower device should specify a bigger read-ahead value, while fast devices will be happy even with a smaller value. The bigger the read-ahead value, the more memory the buffer cache uses.

The primary difference between the two arrays is this: `read_ahead` is applied at the block I/O level and controls how many blocks may be read sequentially *from the disk* ahead of the current request. `max_readahead` works at the filesystem level and refers to blocks *in the file*, which may not be sequential on disk. Kernel development is moving toward doing read ahead at the filesystem level, rather than at the block I/O level. In the 2.4 kernel, how-ever, read ahead is still done at both levels, so both of these arrays are used.

There is one `read_ahead[]` value for each major number, and it applies to all its minor numbers. `max_readahead`, instead, has a value for every device. The values can be changed via the driver's *ioctl* method; hard-disk drivers usu-ally set `read_ahead` to 8 sectors, which corresponds to 4 KB. The `max_readahead` value, on the other hand, is rarely set by the drivers; it defaults to `MAX_READAHEAD`, currently 31 pages.

`int max_sectors[][];`
This array limits the maximum size of a single request. It should normally be set to the largest transfer that your hardware can handle.

`int max_segments[];`
This array controlled the number of individual segments that could appear in a clustered request; it was removed just before the release of the 2.4 kernel, however. (See "Clustered Requests" later in this chapter for information on clustered requests).

The *sbull* device allows you to set these values at load time, and they apply to all the minor numbers of the sample driver. The variable names and their default val-ues in *sbull* are as follows:

`size=2048` *(kilobytes)*
Each RAM disk created by *sbull* takes two megabytes of RAM.

`blksize=1024` *(bytes)*
The software "block" used by the module is one kilobyte, like the system default.

`hardsect=512` *(bytes)*
The *sbull* sector size is the usual half-kilobyte value.

`rahead=2` *(sectors)*
Because the RAM disk is a fast device, the default read-ahead value is small.

The *sbull* device also allows you to choose the number of devices to install. `devs`, the number of devices, defaults to 2, resulting in a default memory usage of four megabytes—two disks at two megabytes each.

The initialization of these arrays in *sbull* is done as follows:

```
read_ahead[major] = sbull_rahead;
result = -ENOMEM; /* for the possible errors */

sbull_sizes = kmalloc(sbull_devs * sizeof(int), GFP_KERNEL);
if (!sbull_sizes)
    goto fail_malloc;
for (i=0; i < sbull_devs; i++) /* all the same size */
    sbull_sizes[i] = sbull_size;
blk_size[major]=sbull_sizes;

sbull_blksizes = kmalloc(sbull_devs * sizeof(int), GFP_KERNEL);
if (!sbull_blksizes)
    goto fail_malloc;
for (i=0; i < sbull_devs; i++) /* all the same blocksize */
    sbull_blksizes[i] = sbull_blksize;
blksize_size[major]=sbull_blksizes;

sbull_hardsects = kmalloc(sbull_devs * sizeof(int), GFP_KERNEL);
if (!sbull_hardsects)
    goto fail_malloc;
for (i=0; i < sbull_devs; i++) /* all the same hardsect */
    sbull_hardsects[i] = sbull_hardsect;
hardsect_size[major]=sbull_hardsects;
```

For brevity, the error handling code (the target of the `fail_malloc goto`) has been omitted; it simply frees anything that was successfully allocated, unregisters the device, and returns a failure status.

One last thing that must be done is to register every "disk" device provided by the driver. *sbull* calls the necessary function (*register_disk*) as follows:

```
for (i = 0; i < sbull_devs; i++)
        register_disk(NULL, MKDEV(major, i), 1, &sbull_bdops,
                        sbull_size << 1);
```

In the 2.4.0 kernel, *register_disk* does nothing when invoked in this manner. The real purpose of *register_disk* is to set up the partition table, which is not supported by *sbull*. All block drivers, however, make this call whether or not they support partitions, indicating that it may become necessary for all block devices in the future. A block driver without partitions will work without this call in 2.4.0, but it is safer to include it. We revisit *register_disk* in detail later in this chapter, when we cover partitions.

The cleanup function used by *sbull* looks like this:

```
for (i=0; i<sbull_devs; i++)
    fsync_dev(MKDEV(sbull_major, i)); /* flush the devices */
unregister_blkdev(major, "sbull");
/*
 * Fix up the request queue(s)
```

```
     */
    blk_cleanup_queue(BLK_DEFAULT_QUEUE(major));

    /* Clean up the global arrays */
    read_ahead[major] = 0;
    kfree(blk_size[major]);
    blk_size[major] = NULL;
    kfree(blksize_size[major]);
    blksize_size[major] = NULL;
    kfree(hardsect_size[major]);
    hardsect_size[major] = NULL;
```

Here, the call to *fsync_dev* is needed to free all references to the device that the kernel keeps in various caches. *fsync_dev* is the implementation of *block_fsync*, which is the *fsync* "method" for block devices.

The Header File blk.h

All block drivers should include the header file `<linux/blk.h>`. This file defines much of the common code that is used in block drivers, and it provides functions for dealing with the I/O request queue.

Actually, the *blk.h* header is quite unusual, because it defines several symbols based on the symbol `MAJOR_NR`, which must be declared by the driver *before* it includes the header. This convention was developed in the early days of Linux, when all block devices had preassigned major numbers and modular block drivers were not supported.

If you look at *blk.h*, you'll see that several device-dependent symbols are declared according to the value of `MAJOR_NR`, which is expected to be known in advance. However, if the major number is dynamically assigned, the driver has no way to know its assigned number at compile time and cannot correctly define `MAJOR_NR`. If `MAJOR_NR` is undefined, *blk.h* can't set up some of the macros used with the request queue. Fortunately, `MAJOR_NR` can be defined as an integer variable and all will work fine for add-on block drivers.

blk.h makes use of some other predefined, driver-specific symbols as well. The following list describes the symbols in `<linux/blk.h>` that must be defined in advance; at the end of the list, the code used in *sbull* is shown.

MAJOR_NR
>   This symbol is used to access a few arrays, in particular `blk_dev` and `blk-size_size`. A custom driver like *sbull*, which is unable to assign a constant value to the symbol, should `#define` it to the variable holding the major number. For *sbull*, this is `sbull_major`.

DEVICE_NAME

The name of the device being created. This string is used in printing error messages.

DEVICE_NR(kdev_t device)

This symbol is used to extract the ordinal number of the physical device from the kdev_t device number. This symbol is used in turn to declare CUR-RENT_DEV, which can be used within the *request* function to determine which hardware device owns the minor number involved in a transfer request.

The value of this macro can be MINOR(device) or another expression, according to the convention used to assign minor numbers to devices and partitions. The macro should return the same device number for all partitions on the same physical device—that is, DEVICE_NR represents the disk number, not the partition number. Partitionable devices are introduced later in this chapter.

DEVICE_INTR

This symbol is used to declare a pointer variable that refers to the current bottom-half handler. The macros SET_INTR(intr) and CLEAR_INTR are used to assign the variable. Using multiple handlers is convenient when the device can issue interrupts with different meanings.

DEVICE_ON(kdev_t device)
DEVICE_OFF(kdev_t device)

These macros are intended to help devices that need to perform processing before or after a set of transfers is performed; for example, they could be used by a floppy driver to start the drive motor before I/O and to stop it afterward. Modern drivers no longer use these macros, and DEVICE_ON does not even get called anymore. Portable drivers, though, should define them (as empty symbols), or compilation errors will result on 2.0 and 2.2 kernels.

DEVICE_NO_RANDOM

By default, the function *end_request* contributes to system entropy (the amount of collected "randomness"), which is used by */dev/random*. If the device isn't able to contribute significant entropy to the random device, DEVICE_NO_RANDOM should be defined. */dev/random* was introduced in "Installing an Interrupt Handler" in Chapter 9, where SA_SAMPLE_RANDOM was explained.

DEVICE_REQUEST

Used to specify the name of the *request* function used by the driver. The only effect of defining DEVICE_REQUEST is to cause a forward declaration of the *request* function to be done; it is a holdover from older times, and most (or all) drivers can leave it out.

The *sbull* driver declares the symbols in the following way:

```
#define MAJOR_NR sbull_major /* force definitions on in blk.h */
static int sbull_major; /* must be declared before including blk.h */

#define DEVICE_NR(device) MINOR(device)    /* has no partition bits */
#define DEVICE_NAME "sbull"                /* name for messaging */
#define DEVICE_INTR sbull_intrptr          /* pointer to bottom half */
#define DEVICE_NO_RANDOM                   /* no entropy to contribute */
#define DEVICE_REQUEST sbull_request
#define DEVICE_OFF(d) /* do-nothing */

#include <linux/blk.h>

#include "sbull.h"          /* local definitions */
```

The *blk.h* header uses the macros just listed to define some additional macros usable by the driver. We'll describe those macros in the following sections.

Handling Requests: A Simple Introduction

The most important function in a block driver is the *request* function, which performs the low-level operations related to reading and writing data. This section discusses the basic design of the *request* procedure.

The Request Queue

When the kernel schedules a data transfer, it queues the request in a list, ordered in such a way that it maximizes system performance. The queue of requests is then passed to the driver's *request* function, which has the following prototype:

```
void request_fn(request_queue_t *queue);
```

The *request* function should perform the following tasks for each request in the queue:

1. Check the validity of the request. This test is performed by the macro INIT_REQUEST, defined in *blk.h*; the test consists of looking for problems that could indicate a bug in the system's request queue handling.

2. Perform the actual data transfer. The CURRENT variable (a macro, actually) can be used to retrieve the details of the current request. CURRENT is a pointer to struct request, whose fields are described in the next section.

3. Clean up the request just processed. This operation is performed by *end_request*, a static function whose code resides in *blk.h*. *end_request* handles the management of the request queue and wakes up processes waiting on the I/O operation. It also manages the CURRENT variable, ensuring that it points to the next unsatisfied request. The driver passes the function a single argument, which is 1 in case of success and 0 in case of failure. When *end_request* is called with an argument of 0, an "I/O error" message is delivered to the system logs (via *printk*).

4. Loop back to the beginning, to consume the next request.

Based on the previous description, a minimal *request* function, which does not actually transfer any data, would look like this:

```
void sbull_request(request_queue_t *q)
{
    while(1) {
        INIT_REQUEST;
        printk("<1>request %p: cmd %i sec %li (nr. %li)\n", CURRENT,
                CURRENT->cmd,
                CURRENT->sector,
                CURRENT->current_nr_sectors);
        end_request(1); /* success */
    }
}
```

Although this code does nothing but print messages, running this function provides good insight into the basic design of data transfer. It also demonstrates a couple of features of the macros defined in <linux/blk.h>. The first is that, although the while loop looks like it will never terminate, the fact is that the INIT_REQUEST macro performs a return when the request queue is empty. The loop thus iterates over the queue of outstanding requests and then returns from the *request* function. Second, the CURRENT macro always describes the request to be processed. We get into the details of CURRENT in the next section.

A block driver using the *request* function just shown will actually work—for a short while. It is possible to make a filesystem on the device and access it for as long as the data remains in the system's buffer cache.

This empty (but verbose) function can still be run in *sbull* by defining the symbol SBULL_EMPTY_REQUEST at compile time. If you want to understand how the kernel handles different block sizes, you can experiment with blksize= on the *insmod* command line. The empty *request* function shows the internal workings of the kernel by printing the details of each request.

The *request* function has one very important constraint: it must be atomic. *request* is not usually called in direct response to user requests, and it is not running in the context of any particular process. It can be called at interrupt time, from tasklets, or from any number of other places. Thus, it must not sleep while carrying out its tasks.

Performing the Actual Data Transfer

To understand how to build a working *request* function for *sbull*, let's look at how the kernel describes a request within a `struct request`. The structure is defined in `<linux/blkdev.h>`. By accessing the fields in the `request` structure, usually by way of `CURRENT`, the driver can retrieve all the information needed to transfer data between the buffer cache and the physical block device.* `CURRENT` is just a pointer into `blk_dev[MAJOR_NR].request_queue`. The following fields of a request hold information that is useful to the *request* function:

`kdev_t rq_dev;`
> The device accessed by the request. By default, the same *request* function is used for every device managed by the driver. A single *request* function deals with all the minor numbers; `rq_dev` can be used to extract the minor device being acted upon. The `CURRENT_DEV` macro is simply defined as `DEVICE_NR(CURRENT->rq_dev)`.

`int cmd;`
> This field describes the operation to be performed; it is either `READ` (from the device) or `WRITE` (to the device).

`unsigned long sector;`
> The number of the first sector to be transferred in this request.

`unsigned long current_nr_sectors;`
`unsigned long nr_sectors;`
> The number of sectors to transfer for the current request. The driver should refer to `current_nr_sectors` and ignore `nr_sectors` (which is listed here just for completeness). See "Clustered Requests" later in this chapter for more detail on `nr_sectors`.

`char *buffer;`
> The area in the buffer cache to which data should be written (`cmd==READ`) or from which data should be read (`cmd==WRITE`).

`struct buffer_head *bh;`
> The structure describing the first buffer in the list for this request. Buffer heads are used in the management of the buffer cache; we'll look at them in detail shortly in "The request structure and the buffer cache."

There are other fields in the structure, but they are primarily meant for internal use in the kernel; the driver is not expected to use them.

---

* Actually, not all blocks passed to a block driver need be in the buffer cache, but that's a topic beyond the scope of this chapter.

The implementation for the working *request* function in the *sbull* device is shown here. In the following code, the `Sbull_Dev` serves the same function as `Scull_Dev`, introduced in "scull's Memory Usage" in Chapter 3.

```
void sbull_request(request_queue_t *q)
{
    Sbull_Dev *device;
    int status;

    while(1) {
        INIT_REQUEST;   /* returns when queue is empty */

        /* Which "device" are we using? */
        device = sbull_locate_device (CURRENT);
        if (device == NULL) {
            end_request(0);
            continue;
        }

        /* Perform the transfer and clean up. */
        spin_lock(&device->lock);
        status = sbull_transfer(device, CURRENT);
        spin_unlock(&device->lock);
        end_request(status);
    }
}
```

This code looks little different from the empty version shown earlier; it concerns itself with request queue management and pushes off the real work to other functions. The first, *sbull_locate_device*, looks at the device number in the request and finds the right `Sbull_Dev` structure:

```
static Sbull_Dev *sbull_locate_device(const struct request *req)
{
    int devno;
    Sbull_Dev *device;

    /* Check if the minor number is in range */
    devno = DEVICE_NR(req->rq_dev);
    if (devno >= sbull_devs) {
        static int count = 0;
        if (count++ < 5) /* print the message at most five times */
            printk(KERN_WARNING "sbull: request for unknown device\n");
        return NULL;
    }
    device = sbull_devices + devno; /* Pick it out of device array */
    return device;
}
```

The only "strange" feature of the function is the conditional statement that limits it to reporting five errors. This is intended to avoid clobbering the system logs with too many messages, since `end_request(0)` already prints an "I/O error" message when the request fails. The `static` counter is a standard way to limit message reporting and is used several times in the kernel.

The actual I/O of the request is handled by *sbull_transfer*.

```
static int sbull_transfer(Sbull_Dev *device, const struct request *req)
{
    int size;
    u8 *ptr;

    ptr = device->data + req->sector * sbull_hardsect;
    size = req->current_nr_sectors * sbull_hardsect;

    /* Make sure that the transfer fits within the device. */
    if (ptr + size > device->data + sbull_blksize*sbull_size) {
        static int count = 0;
        if (count++ < 5)
            printk(KERN_WARNING "sbull: request past end of device\n");
        return 0;
    }

    /* Looks good, do the transfer. */
    switch(req->cmd) {
        case READ:
            memcpy(req->buffer, ptr, size); /* from sbull to buffer */
            return 1;
        case WRITE:
            memcpy(ptr, req->buffer, size); /* from buffer to sbull */
            return 1;
        default:
            /* can't happen */
            return 0;
    }
}
```

Since *sbull* is just a RAM disk, its "data transfer" reduces to a *memcpy* call.

Handling Requests: The Detailed View

The *sbull* driver as described earlier works very well. In simple situations (as with *sbull*), the macros from `<linux/blk.h>` can be used to easily set up a *request* function and get a working driver. As has already been mentioned, however, block drivers are often a performance-critical part of the kernel. Drivers based on the simple code shown earlier will likely not perform very well in many situations, and can also be a drag on the system as a whole. In this section we get into the details of how the I/O request queue works with an eye toward writing a faster, more efficient driver.

The I/O Request Queue

Each block driver works with at least one I/O request queue. This queue contains, at any given time, all of the I/O operations that the kernel would like to see done on the driver's devices. The management of this queue is complicated; the performance of the system depends on how it is done.

The queue is designed with physical disk drives in mind. With disks, the amount of time required to transfer a block of data is typically quite small. The amount of time required to position the head (*seek*) to do that transfer, however, can be very large. Thus the Linux kernel works to minimize the number and extent of the seeks performed by the device.

Two things are done to achieve those goals. One is the clustering of requests to adjacent sectors on the disk. Most modern filesystems will attempt to lay out files in consecutive sectors; as a result, requests to adjoining parts of the disk are common. The kernel also applies an "elevator" algorithm to the requests. An elevator in a skyscraper is either going up or down; it will continue to move in those directions until all of its "requests" (people wanting on or off) have been satisfied. In the same way, the kernel tries to keep the disk head moving in the same direction for as long as possible; this approach tends to minimize seek times while ensuring that all requests get satisfied eventually.

A Linux I/O request queue is represented by a structure of type `request_queue`, declared in `<linux/blkdev.h>`. The `request_queue` structure looks somewhat like `file_operations` and other such objects, in that it contains pointers to a number of functions that operate on the queue—for example, the driver's *request* function is stored there. There is also a queue head (using the functions from `<linux/list.h>` described in "Linked Lists" in Chapter 10), which points to the list of outstanding requests to the device.

These requests are, of course, of type `struct request`; we have already looked at some of the fields in this structure. The reality of the `request` structure is a little more complicated, however; understanding it requires a brief digression into the structure of the Linux buffer cache.

The request structure and the buffer cache

The design of the `request` structure is driven by the Linux memory management scheme. Like most Unix-like systems, Linux maintains a *buffer cache*, a region of memory that is used to hold copies of blocks stored on disk. A great many "disk" operations performed at higher levels of the kernel—such as in the filesystem code—act only on the buffer cache and do not generate any actual I/O operations. Through aggressive caching the kernel can avoid many read operations altogether, and multiple writes can often be merged into a single physical write to disk.

One unavoidable aspect of the buffer cache, however, is that blocks that are adjacent on disk are almost certainly *not* adjacent in memory. The buffer cache is a dynamic thing, and blocks end up being scattered widely. In order to keep track of everything, the kernel manages the buffer cache through `buffer_head` structures. One `buffer_head` is associated with each data buffer. This structure contains a great many fields, most of which do not concern a driver writer. There are a few that are important, however, including the following:

`char *b_data;`
  The actual data block associated with this buffer head.

`unsigned long b_size;`
  The size of the block pointed to by `b_data`.

`kdev_t b_rdev;`
  The device holding the block represented by this buffer head.

`unsigned long b_rsector;`
  The sector number where this block lives on disk.

`struct buffer_head *b_reqnext;`
  A pointer to a linked list of buffer head structures in the request queue.

`void (*b_end_io)(struct buffer_head *bh, int uptodate);`
  A pointer to a function to be called when I/O on this buffer completes. `bh` is the buffer head itself, and `uptodate` is nonzero if the I/O was successful.

Every block passed to a driver's *request* function either lives in the buffer cache, or, on rare occasion, lives elsewhere but has been made to look as if it lived in the buffer cache.* As a result, every request passed to the driver deals with one or more `buffer_head` structures. The `request` structure contains a member (called simply `bh`) that points to a linked list of these structures; satisfying the request requires performing the indicated I/O operation on each buffer in the list. Figure 12-2 shows how the request queue and `buffer_head` structures fit together.

Requests are not made of random lists of buffers; instead, all of the buffer heads attached to a single request will belong to a series of adjacent blocks on the disk. Thus a request is, in a sense, a single operation referring to a (perhaps long) group of blocks on the disk. This grouping of blocks is called *clustering*, and we will look at it in detail after completing our discussion of how the request list works.

---

* The RAM-disk driver, for example, makes its memory look as if it were in the buffer cache. Since the "disk" buffer is already in system RAM, there's no need to keep a copy in the buffer cache. Our sample code is thus much less efficient than a properly implemented RAM disk, not being concerned with RAM-disk-specific performance issues.

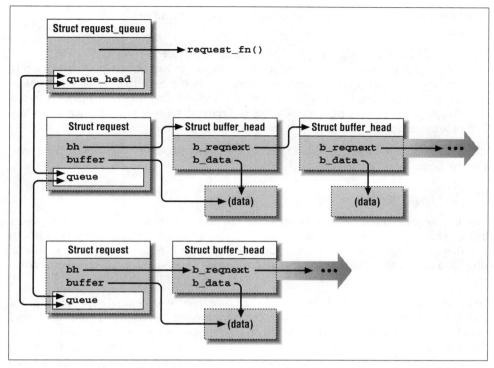

Figure 12-2. Buffers in the I/O Request Queue

Request queue manipulation

The header `<linux/blkdev.h>` defines a small number of functions that manipulate the request queue, most of which are implemented as preprocessor macros. Not all drivers will need to work with the queue at this level, but a familiarity with how it all works can be helpful. Most request queue functions will be introduced as we need them, but a few are worth mentioning here.

```
struct request *blkdev_entry_next_request(struct list_head
    *head);
```
> Returns the next entry in the request list. Usually the `head` argument is the `queue_head` member of the `request_queue` structure; in this case the function returns the first entry in the queue. The function uses the *list_entry* macro to look in the list.

```
struct request *blkdev_next_request(struct request *req);
struct request *blkdev_prev_request(struct request *req);
```
> Given a request structure, return the next or previous structure in the request queue.

`blkdev_dequeue_request(struct request *req);`

Removes a request from its request queue.

`blkdev_release_request(struct request *req);`

Releases a request structure back to the kernel when it has been completely executed. Each request queue maintains its own free list of request structures (two, actually: one for reads and one for writes); this function places a structure back on the proper free list. *blkdev_release_request* will also wake up any processes that are waiting on a free request structure.

All of these functions require that the `io_request_lock` be held, which we will discuss next.

The I/O request lock

The I/O request queue is a complex data structure that is accessed in many places in the kernel. It is entirely possible that the kernel needs to add more requests to the queue at the same time that your driver is taking requests off. The queue is thus subject to the usual sort of race conditions, and must be protected accordingly.

In Linux 2.2 and 2.4, all request queues are protected with a single global spinlock called `io_request_lock`. Any code that manipulates a request queue must hold that lock *and* disable interrupts, with one small exception: the very first entry in the request queue is (by default) considered to be owned by the driver. Failure to acquire the `io_request_lock` prior to working with the request queue can cause the queue to be corrupted, with a system crash following shortly thereafter.

The simple *request* function shown earlier did not need to worry about this lock because the kernel always calls the *request* function with the `io_request_lock` held. A driver is thus protected against corrupting the request queue; it is also protected against reentrant calls to the *request* function. This scheme was designed to enable drivers that are not SMP aware to function on multiprocessor systems.

Note, however, that the `io_request_lock` is an expensive resource to hold. As long as your driver holds this lock, no other requests may be queued to any block driver in the system, and no other *request* functions may be called. A driver that holds this lock for a long time may well slow down the system as a whole.

Thus, well-written block drivers often drop this lock as soon as possible. We will see an example of how this can be done shortly. Block drivers that drop the `io_request_lock` must be written with a couple of important things in mind, however. First is that the *request* function must always reacquire this lock before returning, since the calling code expects it to still be held. The other concern is that, as soon as the `io_request_lock` is dropped, the possibility of reentrant calls to the *request* function is very real; the function must be written to handle that eventuality.

A variant of this latter case can also occur if your *request* function returns while an I/O request is still active. Many drivers for real hardware will start an I/O operation, then return; the work is completed in the driver's interrupt handler. We will look at interrupt-driven block I/O in detail later in this chapter; for now it is worth mentioning, however, that the *request* function can be called while these operations are still in progress.

Some drivers handle *request* function reentrancy by maintaining an internal request queue. The *request* function simply removes any new requests from the I/O request queue and adds them to the internal queue, which is then processed through a combination of tasklets and interrupt handlers.

How the blk.h macros and functions work

In our simple *request* function earlier, we were not concerned with `buffer_head` structures or linked lists. The macros and functions in `<linux/blk.h>` hide the structure of the I/O request queue in order to make the task of writing a block driver simpler. In many cases, however, getting reasonable performance requires a deeper understanding of how the queue works. In this section we look at the actual steps involved in manipulating the request queue; subsequent sections show some more advanced techniques for writing block *request* functions.

The fields of the `request` structure that we looked at earlier—`sector`, `current_nr_sectors`, and `buffer`—are really just copies of the analogous information stored in the first `buffer_head` structure on the list. Thus, a *request* function that uses this information from the `CURRENT` pointer is just processing the first of what might be many buffers within the request. The task of splitting up a multibuffer request into (seemingly) independent, single-buffer requests is handled by two important definitions in `<linux/blk.h>`: the `INIT_REQUEST` macro and the *end_request* function.

Of the two, `INIT_REQUEST` is the simpler; all it really does is make a couple of consistency checks on the request queue and cause a return from the *request* function if the queue is empty. It is simply making sure that there is still work to do.

The bulk of the queue management work is done by *end_request*. This function, remember, is called when the driver has processed a single "request" (actually one buffer); it has several tasks to perform:

1. Complete the I/O processing on the current buffer; this involves calling the *b_end_io* function with the status of the operation, thus waking any process that may be sleeping on the buffer.

2. Remove the buffer from the request's linked list. If there are further buffers to be processed, the `sector`, `current_nr_sectors`, and `buffer` fields in the request structure are updated to reflect the contents of the next `buffer_head` structure in the list. In this case (there are still buffers to be transferred), *end_request* is finished for this iteration and steps 3 to 5 are not executed.

3. Call *add_blkdev_randomness* to update the entropy pool, unless `DEVICE_NO_RANDOM` has been defined (as is done in the *sbull* driver).

4. Remove the finished request from the request queue by calling *blkdev_dequeue_request*. This step modifies the request queue, and thus must be performed with the `io_request_lock` held.

5. Release the finished request back to the system; `io_request_lock` is required here too.

The kernel defines a couple of helper functions that are used by *end_request* to do most of this work. The first one is called *end_that_request_first*, which handles the first two steps just described. Its prototype is

```
int end_that_request_first(struct request *req, int status, char *name);
```

`status` is the status of the request as passed to *end_request*; the `name` parameter is the device name, to be used when printing error messages. The return value is nonzero if there are more buffers to be processed in the current request; in that case the work is done. Otherwise, the request is dequeued and released with *end_that_request_last*:

```
void end_that_request_last(struct request *req);
```

In *end_request* this step is handled with this code:

```
struct request *req = CURRENT;
blkdev_dequeue_request(req);
end_that_request_last(req);
```

That is all there is to it.

Clustered Requests

The time has come to look at how to apply all of that background material to the task of writing better block drivers. We'll start with a look at the handling of clustered requests. Clustering, as mentioned earlier, is simply the practice of joining together requests that operate on adjacent blocks on the disk. There are two advantages to doing things this way. First, clustering speeds up the transfer; clustering can also save some memory in the kernel by avoiding allocation of redundant `request` structures.

As we have seen, block drivers need not be aware of clustering at all; <linux/blk.h> transparently splits each clustered request into its component pieces. In many cases, however, a driver can do better by explicitly acting on clustering. It is often possible to set up the I/O for several consecutive blocks at the same time, with an improvement in throughput. For example, the Linux floppy driver attempts to write an entire track to the diskette in a single operation. Most high-performance disk controllers can do "scatter/gather" I/O as well, leading to large performance gains.

To take advantage of clustering, a block driver must look directly at the list of buffer_head structures attached to the request. This list is pointed to by CURRENT->bh; subsequent buffers can be found by following the b_reqnext pointers in each buffer_head structure. A driver performing clustered I/O should follow roughly this sequence of operations with each buffer in the cluster:

1. Arrange to transfer the data block at address bh->b_data, of size bh->b_size bytes. The direction of the data transfer is CURRENT->cmd (i.e., either READ or WRITE).

2. Retrieve the next buffer head in the list: bh->b_reqnext. Then detach the buffer just transferred from the list, by zeroing its b_reqnext—the pointer to the new buffer you just retrieved.

3. Update the request structure to reflect the I/O done with the buffer that has just been removed. Both CURRENT->hard_nr_sectors and CURRENT->nr_sectors should be decremented by the number of sectors (not blocks) transferred from the buffer. The sector numbers CURRENT->hard_sector and CURRENT->sector should be incremented by the same amount. Performing these operations keeps the request structure consistent.

4. Loop back to the beginning to transfer the next adjacent block.

When the I/O on each buffer completes, your driver should notify the kernel by calling the buffer's I/O completion routine:

```
bh->b_end_io(bh, status);
```

status is nonzero if the operation was successful. You also, of course, need to remove the request structure for the completed operations from the queue. The processing steps just described can be done without holding the io_request_lock, but that lock must be reacquired before changing the queue itself.

Your driver can still use *end_request* (as opposed to manipulating the queue directly) at the completion of the I/O operation, as long as it takes care to set the CURRENT->bh pointer properly. This pointer should either be NULL or it should point to the last `buffer_head` structure that was transferred. In the latter case, the *b_end_io* function should *not* have been called on that last buffer, since *end_request* will make that call.

A full-featured implementation of clustering appears in *drivers/block/floppy.c*, while a summary of the operations required appears in *end_request*, in *blk.h*. Neither *floppy.c* nor *blk.h* are easy to understand, but the latter is a better place to start.

The active queue head

One other detail regarding the behavior of the I/O request queue is relevant for block drivers that are dealing with clustering. It has to do with the queue head— the first request on the queue. For historical compatibility reasons, the kernel (almost) always assumes that a block driver is processing the first entry in the request queue. To avoid corruption resulting from conflicting activity, the kernel will never modify a request once it gets to the head of the queue. No further clustering will happen on that request, and the elevator code will not put other requests in front of it.

Many block drivers remove requests from the queue entirely before beginning to process them. If your driver works this way, the request at the head of the queue should be fair game for the kernel. In this case, your driver should inform the kernel that the head of the queue is not active by calling *blk_queue_headactive*:

```
blk_queue_headactive(request_queue_t *queue, int active);
```

If `active` is 0, the kernel will be able to make changes to the head of the request queue.

Multiqueue Block Drivers

As we have seen, the kernel, by default, maintains a single I/O request queue for each major number. The single queue works well for devices like *sbull*, but it is not always optimal for real-world situations.

Consider a driver that is handling real disk devices. Each disk is capable of operating independently; the performance of the system is sure to be better if the drives could be kept busy in parallel. A simple driver based on a single queue will not achieve that—it will perform operations on a single device at a time.

It would not be all that hard for a driver to walk through the request queue and pick out requests for independent drives. But the 2.4 kernel makes life easier by allowing the driver to set up independent queues for each device. Most high-performance drivers take advantage of this multiqueue capability. Doing so is not difficult, but it does require moving beyond the simple `<linux/blk.h>` definitions.

The *sbull* driver, when compiled with the SBULL_MULTIQUEUE symbol defined, operates in a multiqueue mode. It works without the <linux/blk.h> macros, and demonstrates a number of the features that have been described in this section.

To operate in a multiqueue mode, a block driver must define its own request queues. *sbull* does this by adding a queue member to the Sbull_Dev structure:

```
request_queue_t queue;
int busy;
```

The busy flag is used to protect against *request* function reentrancy, as we will see.

Request queues must be initialized, of course. *sbull* initializes its device-specific queues in this manner:

```
for (i = 0; i < sbull_devs; i++) {
    blk_init_queue(&sbull_devices[i].queue, sbull_request);
    blk_queue_headactive(&sbull_devices[i].queue, 0);
}
blk_dev[major].queue = sbull_find_queue;
```

The call to *blk_init_queue* is as we have seen before, only now we pass in the device-specific queues instead of the default queue for our major device number. This code also marks the queues as not having active heads.

You might be wondering how the kernel manages to find the request queues, which are buried in a device-specific, private structure. The key is the last line just shown, which sets the queue member in the global blk_dev structure. This member points to a function that has the job of finding the proper request queue for a given device number. Devices using the default queue have no such function, but multiqueue devices must implement it. *sbull*'s queue function looks like this:

```
request_queue_t *sbull_find_queue(kdev_t device)
{
    int devno = DEVICE_NR(device);

    if (devno >= sbull_devs) {
        static int count = 0;
        if (count++ < 5) /* print the message at most five times */
            printk(KERN_WARNING "sbull: request for unknown device\n");
        return NULL;
    }
    return &sbull_devices[devno].queue;
}
```

Like the *request* function, *sbull_find_queue* must be atomic (no sleeping allowed).

Each queue has its own *request* function, though usually a driver will use the same function for all of its queues. The kernel passes the actual request queue into the *request* function as a parameter, so the function can always figure out which device is being operated on. The multiqueue *request* function used in *sbull* looks a little different from the ones we have seen so far because it manipulates the request queue directly. It also drops the `io_request_lock` while performing transfers to allow the kernel to execute other block operations. Finally, the code must take care to avoid two separate perils: multiple calls of the *request* function and conflicting access to the device itself.

```
void sbull_request(request_queue_t *q)
{
    Sbull_Dev *device;
    struct request *req;
    int status;

    /* Find our device */
    device = sbull_locate_device (blkdev_entry_next_request(&q->queue_head));
    if (device->busy) /* no race here - io_request_lock held */
        return;
    device->busy = 1;

    /* Process requests in the queue */
    while(! list_empty(&q->queue_head)) {

    /* Pull the next request off the list. */
        req = blkdev_entry_next_request(&q->queue_head);
        blkdev_dequeue_request(req);
        spin_unlock_irq (&io_request_lock);
        spin_lock(&device->lock);

    /* Process all of the buffers in this (possibly clustered) request. */
        do {
            status = sbull_transfer(device, req);
        } while (end_that_request_first(req, status, DEVICE_NAME));
        spin_unlock(&device->lock);
        spin_lock_irq (&io_request_lock);
        end_that_request_last(req);
    }
    device->busy = 0;
}
```

Instead of using `INIT_REQUEST`, this function tests its specific request queue with the list function *list_empty*. As long as requests exist, it removes each one in turn from the queue with *blkdev_dequeue_request*. Only then, once the removal is complete, is it able to drop `io_request_lock` and obtain the device-specific lock. The actual transfer is done using *sbull_transfer*, which we have already seen.

Each call to *sbull_transfer* handles exactly one `buffer_head` structure attached to the request. The function then calls *end_that_request_first* to dispose of that buffer, and, if the request is complete, goes on to *end_that_request_last* to clean up the request as a whole.

The management of concurrency here is worth a quick look. The `busy` flag is used to prevent multiple invocations of *sbull_request*. Since *sbull_request* is always called with the `io_request_lock` held, it is safe to test and set the `busy` flag with no additional protection. (Otherwise, an `atomic_t` could have been used). The `io_request_lock` is dropped before the device-specific lock is acquired. It is possible to acquire multiple locks without risking deadlock, but it is harder; when the constraints allow, it is better to release one lock before obtaining another.

end_that_request_first is called without the `io_request_lock` held. Since this function operates only on the given request structure, calling it this way is safe—as long as the request is not on the queue. The call to *end_that_request_last*, however, requires that the lock be held, since it returns the request to the request queue's free list. The function also always exits from the outer loop (and the function as a whole) with the `io_request_lock` held and the device lock released.

Multiqueue drivers must, of course, clean up all of their queues at module removal time:

```
for (i = 0; i < sbull_devs; i++)
        blk_cleanup_queue(&sbull_devices[i].queue);
blk_dev[major].queue = NULL;
```

It is worth noting, briefly, that this code could be made more efficient. It allocates a whole set of request queues at initialization time, even though some of them may never be used. A request queue is a large structure, since many (perhaps thousands) of `request` structures are allocated when the queue is initialized. A more clever implementation would allocate a request queue when needed in either the *open* method or the *queue* function. We chose a simpler implementation for *sbull* in order to avoid complicating the code.

That covers the mechanics of multiqueue drivers. Drivers handling real hardware may have other issues to deal with, of course, such as serializing access to a controller. But the basic structure of multiqueue drivers is as we have seen here.

Doing Without the Request Queue

Much of the discussion to this point has centered around the manipulation of the I/O request queue. The purpose of the request queue is to improve performance by allowing the driver to act asynchronously and, crucially, by allowing the merging of contiguous (on the disk) operations. For normal disk devices, operations on contiguous blocks are common, and this optimization is necessary.

Not all block devices benefit from the request queue, however. *sbull*, for example, processes requests synchronously and has no problems with seek times. For *sbull*, the request queue actually ends up slowing things down. Other types of block devices also can be better off without a request queue. For example, RAID devices, which are made up of multiple disks, often spread "contiguous" blocks across multiple physical devices. Block devices implemented by the logical volume manager (LVM) capability (which first appeared in 2.4) also have an implementation that is more complex than the block interface that is presented to the rest of the kernel.

In the 2.4 kernel, block I/O requests are placed on the queue by the function _ _*make_request*, which is also responsible for invoking the driver's *request* function. Block drivers that need more control over request queueing, however, can replace that function with their own "make request" function. The RAID and LVM drivers do so, providing their own variant that, eventually, requeues each I/O request (with different block numbers) to the appropriate low-level device (or devices) that make up the higher-level device. A RAM-disk driver, instead, can execute the I/O operation directly.

sbull, when loaded with the `noqueue=1` option on 2.4 systems, will provide its own "make request" function and operate without a request queue. The first step in this scenario is to replace _ _*make_request*. The "make request" function pointer is stored in the request queue, and can be changed with *blk_queue_make_request*:

```
void blk_queue_make_request(request_queue_t *queue,
make_request_fn *func);
```

The `make_request_fn` type, in turn, is defined as follows:

```
typedef int (make_request_fn) (request_queue_t *q, int rw,
        struct buffer_head *bh);
```

The "make request" function must arrange to transfer the given block, and see to it that the *b_end_io* function is called when the transfer is done. The kernel does *not* hold the `io_request_lock` lock when calling the *make_request_fn* function, so the function must acquire the lock itself if it will be manipulating the request queue. If the transfer has been set up (not necessarily completed), the function should return 0.

The phrase "arrange to transfer" was chosen carefully; often a driver-specific make request function will not actually transfer the data. Consider a RAID device. What the function really needs to do is to map the I/O operation onto one of its constituent devices, then invoke that device's driver to actually do the work. This mapping is done by setting the `b_rdev` member of the `buffer_head` structure to the number of the "real" device that will do the transfer, then signaling that the block still needs to be written by returning a nonzero value.

When the kernel sees a nonzero return value from the make request function, it concludes that the job is not done and will try again. But first it will look up the make request function for the device indicated in the **b_rdev** field. Thus, in the RAID case, the RAID driver's "make request" function will *not* be called again; instead, the kernel will pass the block to the appropriate function for the underlying device.

sbull, at initialization time, sets up its make request function as follows:

```
if (noqueue)
    blk_queue_make_request(BLK_DEFAULT_QUEUE(major), sbull_make_request);
```

It does not call *blk_init_queue* when operating in this mode, because the request queue will not be used.

When the kernel generates a request for an *sbull* device, it will call *sbull_make_request*, which is as follows:

```
int sbull_make_request(request_queue_t *queue, int rw,
                       struct buffer_head *bh)
{
    u8 *ptr;

    /* Figure out what we are doing */
    Sbull_Dev *device = sbull_devices + MINOR(bh->b_rdev);
    ptr = device->data + bh->b_rsector * sbull_hardsect;

    /* Paranoid check; this apparently can really happen */
    if (ptr + bh->b_size > device->data + sbull_blksize*sbull_size) {
        static int count = 0;
        if (count++ < 5)
            printk(KERN_WARNING "sbull: request past end of device\n");
        bh->b_end_io(bh, 0);
        return 0;
    }

    /* This could be a high-memory buffer; shift it down */
#if CONFIG_HIGHMEM
    bh = create_bounce(rw, bh);
#endif

    /* Do the transfer */
    switch(rw) {
    case READ:
    case READA:  /* Read ahead */
        memcpy(bh->b_data, ptr, bh->b_size); /* from sbull to buffer */
        bh->b_end_io(bh, 1);
        break;
    case WRITE:
        refile_buffer(bh);
        memcpy(ptr, bh->b_data, bh->b_size); /* from buffer to sbull */
        mark_buffer_uptodate(bh, 1);
```

```
            bh->b_end_io(bh, 1);
            break;
        default:
            /* can't happen */
            bh->b_end_io(bh, 0);
            break;
        }

        /* Nonzero return means we're done */
        return 0;
    }
```

For the most part, this code should look familiar. It contains the usual calculations to determine where the block lives within the *sbull* device and uses *memcpy* to perform the operation. Because the operation completes immediately, it is able to call `bh->b_end_io` to indicate the completion of the operation, and it returns 0 to the kernel.

There is, however, one detail that the "make request" function must take care of. The buffer to be transferred could be resident in high memory, which is not directly accessible by the kernel. High memory is covered in detail in Chapter 13. We won't repeat the discussion here; suffice it to say that one way to deal with the problem is to replace a high-memory buffer with one that is in accessible memory. The function *create_bounce* will do so, in a way that is transparent to the driver. The kernel normally uses *create_bounce* before placing buffers in the driver's request queue; if the driver implements its own *make_request_fn*, however, it must take care of this task itself.

How Mounting and Unmounting Works

Block devices differ from char devices and normal files in that they can be mounted on the computer's filesystem. Mounting provides a level of indirection not seen with char devices, which are accessed through a `struct file` pointer that is held by a specific process. When a filesystem is mounted, there is no process holding that `file` structure.

When the kernel mounts a device in the filesystem, it invokes the normal *open* method to access the driver. However, in this case both the `filp` and `inode` arguments to *open* are dummy variables. In the `file` structure, only the `f_mode` and `f_flags` fields hold anything meaningful; in the `inode` structure only `i_rdev` may be used. The remaining fields hold random values and should not be used. The value of `f_mode` tells the driver whether the device is to be mounted read-only (`f_mode == FMODE_READ`) or read/write (`f_mode == (FMODE_READ|FMODE_WRITE)`).

This interface may seem a little strange; it is done this way for two reasons. First is that the *open* method can still be called normally by a process that accesses the device directly—the *mkfs* utility, for example. The other reason is a historical artifact: block devices once used the same `file_operations` structure as char devices, and thus had to conform to the same interface.

Other than the limitations on the arguments to the *open* method, the driver does not really see anything unusual when a filesystem is mounted. The device is opened, and then the *request* method is invoked to transfer blocks back and forth. The driver cannot really tell the difference between operations that happen in response to an individual process (such as *fsck*) and those that originate in the filesystem layers of the kernel.

As far as *umount* is concerned, it just flushes the buffer cache and calls the *release* driver method. Since there is no meaningful `filp` to pass to the *release* method, the kernel uses NULL. Since the *release* implementation of a block driver can't use `filp->private_data` to access device information, it uses `inode->i_rdev` to differentiate between devices instead. This is how *sbull* implements *release*:

```
int sbull_release (struct inode *inode, struct file *filp)
{
    Sbull_Dev *dev = sbull_devices + MINOR(inode->i_rdev);

    spin_lock(&dev->lock);
    dev->usage--;
    MOD_DEC_USE_COUNT;
    spin_unlock(&dev->lock);
    return 0;
}
```

Other driver functions are not affected by the "missing `filp`" problem because they aren't involved with mounted filesystems. For example, *ioctl* is issued only by processes that explicitly *open* the device.

The ioctl Method

Like char devices, block devices can be acted on by using the *ioctl* system call. The only relevant difference between block and char *ioctl* implementations is that block drivers share a number of common *ioctl* commands that most drivers are expected to support.

The commands that block drivers usually handle are the following, declared in `<linux/fs.h>`.

BLKGETSIZE
> Retrieve the size of the current device, expressed as the number of sectors. The value of `arg` passed in by the system call is a pointer to a `long` value

and should be used to copy the size to a user-space variable. This *ioctl* command is used, for instance, by *mkfs* to know the size of the filesystem being created.

BLKFLSBUF

Literally, "flush buffers." The implementation of this command is the same for every device and is shown later with the sample code for the whole *ioctl* method.

BLKRRPART

Reread the partition table. This command is meaningful only for partitionable devices, introduced later in this chapter.

BLKRAGET
BLKRASET

Used to get and change the current block-level read-ahead value (the one stored in the `read_ahead` array) for the device. For `GET`, the current value should be written to user space as a `long` item using the pointer passed to *ioctl* in `arg`; for `SET`, the new value is passed as an argument.

BLKFRAGET
BLKFRASET

Get and set the filesystem-level read-ahead value (the one stored in `max_readahead`) for this device.

BLKROSET
BLKROGET

These commands are used to change and check the read-only flag for the device.

BLKSECTGET
BLKSECTSET

These commands retrieve and set the maximum number of sectors per request (as stored in `max_sectors`).

BLKSSZGET

Returns the sector size of this block device in the integer variable pointed to by the caller; this size comes directly from the `hardsect_size` array.

BLKPG

The `BLKPG` command allows user-mode programs to add and delete partitions. It is implemented by *blk_ioctl* (described shortly), and no drivers in the mainline kernel provide their own implementation.

BLKELVGET

BLKELVSET

These commands allow some control over how the elevator request sorting algorithm works. As with `BLKPG`, no driver implements them directly.

HDIO_GETGEO

Defined in `<linux/hdreg.h>` and used to retrieve the disk geometry. The geometry should be written to user space in a `struct hd_geometry`, which is declared in *hdreg.h* as well. *sbull* shows the general implementation for this command.

The `HDIO_GETGEO` command is the most commonly used of a series of `HDIO_` commands, all defined in `<linux/hdreg.h>`. The interested reader can look in *ide.c* and *hd.c* for more information about these commands.

Almost all of these *ioctl* commands are implemented in the same way for all block devices. The 2.4 kernel has provided a function, *blk_ioctl*, that may be called to implement the common commands; it is declared in `<linux/blkpg.h>`. Often the only ones that must be implemented in the driver itself are `BLKGETSIZE` and `HDIO_GETGEO`. The driver can then safely pass any other commands to *blk_ioctl* for handling.

The *sbull* device supports only the general commands just listed, because implementing device-specific commands is no different from the implementation of commands for char drivers. The *ioctl* implementation for *sbull* is as follows:

```
int sbull_ioctl (struct inode *inode, struct file *filp,
                 unsigned int cmd, unsigned long arg)
{
    int err;
    long size;
    struct hd_geometry geo;

    PDEBUG("ioctl 0x%x 0x%lx\n", cmd, arg);
    switch(cmd) {

      case BLKGETSIZE:
        /* Return the device size, expressed in sectors */
        if (!arg) return -EINVAL; /* NULL pointer: not valid */
        err = ! access_ok (VERIFY_WRITE, arg, sizeof(long));
        if (err) return -EFAULT;
        size = blksize*sbull_sizes[MINOR(inode->i_rdev)]
               / sbull_hardsects[MINOR(inode->i_rdev)];
        if (copy_to_user((long *) arg, &size, sizeof (long)))
            return -EFAULT;
        return 0;

      case BLKRRPART: /* reread partition table: can't do it */
        return -ENOTTY;

      case HDIO_GETGEO:
```

```
        /*
         * Get geometry: since we are a virtual device, we have to make
         * up something plausible. So we claim 16 sectors, four heads,
         * and calculate the corresponding number of cylinders. We set
         * the start of data at sector four.
         */
        err = ! access_ok(VERIFY_WRITE, arg, sizeof(geo));
        if (err) return -EFAULT;
        size = sbull_size * blksize / sbull_hardsect;
        geo.cylinders = (size & ~0x3f) >> 6;
        geo.heads = 4;
        geo.sectors = 16;
        geo.start = 4;
        if (copy_to_user((void *) arg, &geo, sizeof(geo)))
            return -EFAULT;
        return 0;

    default:
        /*
         * For ioctls we don't understand, let the block layer
         * handle them.
         */
        return blk_ioctl(inode->i_rdev, cmd, arg);
    }

    return -ENOTTY; /* unknown command */
}
```

The PDEBUG statement at the beginning of the function has been left in so that when you compile the module, you can turn on debugging to see which *ioctl* commands are invoked on the device.

Removable Devices

Thus far, we have ignored the final two file operations in the block_device_operations structure, which deal with devices that support removable media. It's now time to look at them; *sbull* isn't actually removable but it pretends to be, and therefore it implements these methods.

The operations in question are *check_media_change* and *revalidate*. The former is used to find out if the device has changed since the last access, and the latter re-initializes the driver's status after a disk change.

As far as *sbull* is concerned, the data area associated with a device is released half a minute after its usage count drops to zero. Leaving the device unmounted (or closed) long enough simulates a disk change, and the next access to the device allocates a new memory area.

This kind of "timely expiration" is implemented using a kernel timer.

check_media_change

The checking function receives kdev_t as a single argument that identifies the device. The return value is 1 if the medium has been changed and 0 otherwise. A block driver that doesn't support removable devices can avoid declaring the function by setting bdops->check_media_change to NULL.

It's interesting to note that when the device is removable but there is no way to know if it changed, returning 1 is a safe choice. This is the behavior of the IDE driver when dealing with removable disks.

The implementation in *sbull* returns 1 if the device has already been removed from memory due to the timer expiration, and 0 if the data is still valid. If debugging is enabled, it also prints a message to the system logger; the user can thus verify when the method is called by the kernel.

```
int sbull_check_change(kdev_t i_rdev)
{
    int minor = MINOR(i_rdev);
    Sbull_Dev *dev = sbull_devices + minor;

    PDEBUG("check_change for dev %i\n",minor);
    if (dev->data)
        return 0; /* still valid */
    return 1; /* expired */
}
```

Revalidation

The validation function is called when a disk change is detected. It is also called by the various *stat* system calls implemented in version 2.1 of the kernel. The return value is currently unused; to be safe, return 0 to indicate success and a negative error code in case of error.

The action performed by *revalidate* is device specific, but *revalidate* usually updates the internal status information to reflect the new device.

In *sbull*, the *revalidate* method tries to allocate a new data area if there is not already a valid area.

```
int sbull_revalidate(kdev_t i_rdev)
{
    Sbull_Dev *dev = sbull_devices + MINOR(i_rdev);

    PDEBUG("revalidate for dev %i\n",MINOR(i_rdev));
    if (dev->data)
        return 0;
```

```
        dev->data = vmalloc(dev->size);
        if (!dev->data)
            return -ENOMEM;
        return 0;
    }
```

Extra Care

Drivers for removable devices should also check for a disk change when the device is opened. The kernel provides a function to cause this check to happen:

```
    int check_disk_change(kdev_t dev);
```

The return value is nonzero if a disk change was detected. The kernel automatically calls *check_disk_change* at *mount* time, but not at *open* time.

Some programs, however, directly access disk data without mounting the device: *fsck*, *mcopy*, and *fdisk* are examples of such programs. If the driver keeps status information about removable devices in memory, it should call the kernel *check_disk_change* function when the device is first opened. This function uses the driver methods (*check_media_change* and *revalidate*), so nothing special has to be implemented in *open* itself.

Here is the *sbull* implementation of *open*, which takes care of the case in which there's been a disk change:

```
    int sbull_open (struct inode *inode, struct file *filp)
    {
        Sbull_Dev *dev; /* device information */
        int num = MINOR(inode->i_rdev);

        if (num >= sbull_devs) return -ENODEV;
        dev = sbull_devices + num;

        spin_lock(&dev->lock);
        /* revalidate on first open and fail if no data is there */
        if (!dev->usage) {
            check_disk_change(inode->i_rdev);
            if (!dev->data)
            {
                spin_unlock (&dev->lock);
                return -ENOMEM;
            }
        }
        dev->usage++;
        spin_unlock(&dev->lock);
        MOD_INC_USE_COUNT;
        return 0;              /* success */
    }
```

Nothing else needs to be done in the driver for a disk change. Data is corrupted anyway if a disk is changed while its open count is greater than zero. The only way the driver can prevent this problem from happening is for the usage count to control the door lock in those cases where the physical device supports it. Then *open* and *close* can disable and enable the lock appropriately.

Partitionable Devices

Most block devices are not used in one large chunk. Instead, the system administrator expects to be able to *partition* the device—to split it into several independent pseudodevices. If you try to create partitions on an *sbull* device with *fdisk*, you'll run into problems. The *fdisk* program calls the partitions */dev/sbull01*, */dev/sbull02*, and so on, but those names don't exist on the filesystem. More to the point, there is no mechanism in place for binding those names to partitions in the *sbull* device. Something more must be done before a block device can be partitioned.

To demonstrate how partitions are supported, we introduce a new device called *spull*, a "Simple Partitionable Utility." It is far simpler than *sbull*, lacking the request queue management and some flexibility (like the ability to change the hard-sector size). The device resides in the *spull* directory and is completely detached from *sbull*, even though they share some code.

To be able to support partitions on a device, we must assign several minor numbers to each physical device. One number is used to access the whole device (for example, */dev/hda*), and the others are used to access the various partitions (such as */dev/hda1*). Since *fdisk* creates partition names by adding a numerical suffix to the whole-disk device name, we'll follow the same naming convention in the *spull* driver.

The device nodes implemented by *spull* are called pd, for "partitionable disk." The four whole devices (also called *units*) are thus named */dev/pda* through */dev/pdd*; each device supports at most 15 partitions. Minor numbers have the following meaning: the least significant four bits represent the partition number (where 0 is the whole device), and the most significant four bits represent the unit number. This convention is expressed in the source file by the following macros:

```
#define MAJOR_NR spull_major /* force definitions on in blk.h */
int spull_major; /* must be declared before including blk.h */

#define SPULL_SHIFT 4                          /* max 16 partitions  */
#define SPULL_MAXNRDEV 4                       /* max 4 device units */
#define DEVICE_NR(device) (MINOR(device)>>SPULL_SHIFT)
#define DEVICE_NAME "pd"                       /* name for messaging */
```

The *spull* driver also hardwires the value of the hard-sector size in order to simplify the code:

```
#define SPULL_HARDSECT 512   /* 512-byte hardware sectors */
```

The Generic Hard Disk

Every partitionable device needs to know how it is partitioned. The information is available in the partition table, and part of the initialization process consists of decoding the partition table and updating the internal data structures to reflect the partition information.

This decoding isn't easy, but fortunately the kernel offers "generic hard disk" support usable by all block drivers. Such support considerably reduces the amount of code needed in the driver for handling partitions. Another advantage of the generic support is that the driver writer doesn't need to understand how the partitioning is done, and new partitioning schemes can be supported in the kernel without requiring changes to driver code.

A block driver that supports partitions must include `<linux/genhd.h>` and should declare a `struct gendisk` structure. This structure describes the layout of the disk(s) provided by the driver; the kernel maintains a global list of such structures, which may be queried to see what disks and partitions are available on the system.

Before we go further, let's look at some of the fields in `struct gendisk`. You'll need to understand them in order to exploit generic device support.

`int major`
> The major number for the device that the structure refers to.

`const char *major_name`
> The base name for devices belonging to this major number. Each device name is derived from this name by adding a letter for each unit and a number for each partition. For example, "hd" is the base name that is used to build */dev/hda1* and */dev/hdb3*. In modern kernels, the full length of the disk name can be up to 32 characters; the 2.0 kernel, however, was more restricted. Drivers wishing to be backward portable to 2.0 should limit the `major_name` field to five characters. The name for *spull* is **pd** ("partitionable disk").

`int minor_shift`
> The number of bit shifts needed to extract the drive number from the device minor number. In *spull* the number is 4. The value in this field should be consistent with the definition of the macro `DEVICE_NR(device)` (see "The Header File blk.h"). The macro in *spull* expands to `device>>4`.

int max_p
> The maximum number of partitions. In our example, `max_p` is 16, or more generally, `1 << minor_shift`.

struct hd_struct *part
> The decoded partition table for the device. The driver uses this item to determine what range of the disk's sectors is accessible through each minor number. The driver is responsible for allocation and deallocation of this array, which most drivers implement as a static array of `max_nr << minor_shift` structures. The driver should initialize the array to zeros before the kernel decodes the partition table.

int *sizes
> An array of integers with the same information as the global `blk_size` array. In fact, they are usually the same array. The driver is responsible for allocating and deallocating the `sizes` array. Note that the partition check for the device copies this pointer to `blk_size`, so a driver handling partitionable devices doesn't need to allocate the latter array.

int nr_real
> The number of real devices (units) that exist.

void *real_devices
> A private area that may be used by the driver to keep any additional required information.

void struct gendisk *next
> A pointer used to implement the linked list of generic hard-disk structures.

struct block_device_operations *fops;
> A pointer to the block operations structure for this device.

Many of the fields in the `gendisk` structure are set up at initialization time, so the compile-time setup is relatively simple:

```
struct gendisk spull_gendisk = {
    major:          0,              /* Major number assigned later */
    major_name:     "pd",          /* Name of the major device */
    minor_shift:    SPULL_SHIFT,    /* Shift to get device number */
    max_p:          1 << SPULL_SHIFT, /* Number of partitions */
    fops:           &spull_bdops,  /* Block dev operations */
    /* everything else is dynamic */
};
```

Partition Detection

When a module initializes itself, it must set things up properly for partition detection. Thus, *spull* starts by setting up the `spull_sizes` array for the `gendisk` structure (which also gets stored in `blk_size[MAJOR_NR]` and in the **sizes** field of the **gendisk** structure) and the **spull_partitions** array, which holds the actual partition information (and gets stored in the **part** member of the **gendisk** structure). Both of these arrays are initialized to zeros at this time. The code looks like this:

```
spull_sizes = kmalloc( (spull_devs << SPULL_SHIFT) * sizeof(int),
                GFP_KERNEL);
if (!spull_sizes)
    goto fail_malloc;

/* Start with zero-sized partitions, and correctly sized units */
memset(spull_sizes, 0, (spull_devs << SPULL_SHIFT) * sizeof(int));
for (i=0; i< spull_devs; i++)
    spull_sizes[i<<SPULL_SHIFT] = spull_size;
blk_size[MAJOR_NR] = spull_gendisk.sizes = spull_sizes;

/* Allocate the partitions array. */
spull_partitions = kmalloc( (spull_devs << SPULL_SHIFT) *
                            sizeof(struct hd_struct), GFP_KERNEL);
if (!spull_partitions)
    goto fail_malloc;

memset(spull_partitions, 0, (spull_devs << SPULL_SHIFT) *
        sizeof(struct hd_struct));
/* fill in whole-disk entries */
for (i=0; i < spull_devs; i++)
    spull_partitions[i << SPULL_SHIFT].nr_sects =
        spull_size*(blksize/SPULL_HARDSECT);
spull_gendisk.part = spull_partitions;
spull_gendisk.nr_real = spull_devs;
```

The driver should also include its **gendisk** structure on the global list. There is no kernel-supplied function for adding **gendisk** structures; it must be done by hand:

```
spull_gendisk.next = gendisk_head;
gendisk_head = &spull_gendisk;
```

In practice, the only thing the system does with this list is to implement */proc/partitions.*

The *register_disk* function, which we have already seen briefly, handles the job of reading the disk's partition table.

```
register_disk(struct gendisk *gd, int drive, unsigned minors,
            struct block_device_operations *ops, long size);
```

Here, **gd** is the **gendisk** structure that we built earlier, **drive** is the device number, **minors** is the number of partitions supported, **ops** is the **block_device_operations** structure for the driver, and **size** is the size of the device in sectors.

Fixed disks might read the partition table only at module initialization time and when BLKRRPART is invoked. Drivers for removable drives will also need to make this call in the *revalidate* method. Either way, it is important to remember that *register_disk* will call your driver's *request* function to read the partition table, so the driver must be sufficiently initialized at that point to handle requests. You should also not have any locks held that will conflict with locks acquired in the *request* function. *register_disk* must be called for each disk actually present on the system.

spull sets up partitions in the *revalidate* method:

```
int spull_revalidate(kdev_t i_rdev)
{
    /* first partition, # of partitions */
    int part1 = (DEVICE_NR(i_rdev) << SPULL_SHIFT) + 1;
    int npart = (1 << SPULL_SHIFT) -1;

    /* first clear old partition information */
    memset(spull_gendisk.sizes+part1, 0, npart*sizeof(int));
    memset(spull_gendisk.part +part1, 0, npart*sizeof(struct hd_struct));
    spull_gendisk.part[DEVICE_NR(i_rdev) << SPULL_SHIFT].nr_sects =
            spull_size << 1;

    /* then fill new info */
    printk(KERN_INFO "Spull partition check: (%d) ", DEVICE_NR(i_rdev));
    register_disk(&spull_gendisk, i_rdev, SPULL_MAXNRDEV, &spull_bdops,
                spull_size << 1);
    return 0;
}
```

It's interesting to note that *register_disk* prints partition information by repeatedly calling

```
printk(" %s", disk_name(hd, minor, buf));
```

That's why *spull* prints a leading string. It's meant to add some context to the information that gets stuffed into the system log.

When a partitionable module is unloaded, the driver should arrange for all the partitions to be flushed, by calling *fsync_dev* for every supported major/minor pair. All of the relevant memory should be freed as well, of course. The cleanup function for *spull* is as follows:

```
for (i = 0; i < (spull_devs << SPULL_SHIFT); i++)
    fsync_dev(MKDEV(spull_major, i)); /* flush the devices */
blk_cleanup_queue(BLK_DEFAULT_QUEUE(major));
read_ahead[major] = 0;
kfree(blk_size[major]); /* which is gendisk->sizes as well */
blk_size[major] = NULL;
kfree(spull_gendisk.part);
kfree(blksize_size[major]);
blksize_size[major] = NULL;
```

It is also necessary to remove the `gendisk` structure from the global list. There is no function provided to do this work, so it's done by hand:

```
for (gdp = &gendisk_head; *gdp; gdp = &((*gdp)->next))
    if (*gdp == &spull_gendisk) {
        *gdp = (*gdp)->next;
        break;
    }
```

Note that there is no *unregister_disk* to complement the *register_disk* function. Everything done by *register_disk* is stored in the driver's own arrays, so there is no additional cleanup required at unload time.

Partition Detection Using initrd

If you want to mount your root filesystem from a device whose driver is available only in modularized form, you must use the *initrd* facility offered by modern Linux kernels. We won't introduce *initrd* here; this subsection is aimed at readers who know about *initrd* and wonder how it affects block drivers. More information on *initrd* can be found in *Documentation/initrd.txt* in the kernel source.

When you boot a kernel with *initrd*, it establishes a temporary running environment before it mounts the real root filesystem. Modules are usually loaded from within the RAM disk being used as the temporary root file system.

Because the *initrd* process is run after all boot-time initialization is complete (but before the real root filesystem has been mounted), there's no difference between loading a normal module and loading one living in the *initrd* RAM disk. If a driver can be correctly loaded and used as a module, all Linux distributions that have *initrd* available can include the driver on their installation disks without requiring you to hack in the kernel source.

The Device Methods for spull

We have seen how to initialize partitionable devices, but not yet how to access data within the partitions. To do that, we need to make use of the partition information stored in the `gendisk->part` array by *register_disk*. This array is made up of `hd_struct` structures, and is indexed by the minor number. The `hd_struct` has two fields of interest: `start_sect` tells where a given partition starts on the disk, and `nr_sects` gives the size of that partition.

Here we will show how *spull* makes use of that information. The following code includes only those parts of *spull* that differ from *sbull*, because most of the code is exactly the same.

First of all, *open* and *close* must keep track of the usage count for each device. Because the usage count refers to the physical device (unit), the following declaration and assignment is used for the **dev** variable:

```
Spull_Dev *dev = spull_devices + DEVICE_NR(inode->i_rdev);
```

The **DEVICE_NR** macro used here is the one that must be declared before `<linux/blk.h>` is included; it yields the physical device number without taking into account which partition is being used.

Although almost every device method works with the physical device as a whole, *ioctl* should access specific information for each partition. For example, when *mkfs* calls *ioctl* to retrieve the size of the device on which it will build a filesystem, it should be told the size of the partition of interest, not the size of the whole device. Here is how the **BLKGETSIZE** *ioctl* command is affected by the change from one minor number per device to multiple minor numbers per device. As you might expect, **spull_gendisk->part** is used as the source of the partition size.

```
    case BLKGETSIZE:
        /* Return the device size, expressed in sectors */
        err = ! access_ok (VERIFY_WRITE, arg, sizeof(long));
        if (err) return -EFAULT;
        size = spull_gendisk.part[MINOR(inode->i_rdev)].nr_sects;
        if (copy_to_user((long *) arg, &size, sizeof (long)))
        return -EFAULT;
        return 0;
```

The other *ioctl* command that is different for partitionable devices is **BLKRRPART**. Rereading the partition table makes sense for partitionable devices and is equivalent to revalidating a disk after a disk change:

```
    case BLKRRPART: /* re-read partition table */
        return spull_revalidate(inode->i_rdev);
```

But the major difference between *sbull* and *spull* is in the *request* function. In *spull*, the *request* function needs to use the partition information in order to correctly transfer data for the different minor numbers. Locating the transfer is done by simply adding the starting sector to that provided in the request; the partition size information is then used to be sure the request fits within the partition. Once that is done, the implementation is the same as for *sbull*.

Here are the relevant lines in *spull_request*:

```
ptr = device->data +
        (spull_partitions[minor].start_sect + req->sector)*SPULL_HARDSECT;
size = req->current_nr_sectors*SPULL_HARDSECT;
/*
 * Make sure that the transfer fits within the device.
 */
if (req->sector + req->current_nr_sectors >
                spull_partitions[minor].nr_sects) {
```

```
      static int count = 0;
      if (count++ < 5)
        printk(KERN_WARNING "spull: request past end of partition\n");
      return 0;
    }
```

The number of sectors is multiplied by the hardware sector size (which, remember, is hardwired in *spull*) to get the size of the partition in bytes.

Interrupt-Driven Block Drivers

When a driver controls a real hardware device, operation is usually interrupt driven. Using interrupts helps system performance by releasing the processor during I/O operations. In order for interrupt-driven I/O to work, the device being controlled must be able to transfer data asynchronously and to generate interrupts.

When the driver is interrupt driven, the *request* function spawns a data transfer and returns immediately without calling *end_request*. However, the kernel doesn't consider a request fulfilled unless *end_request* (or its component parts) has been called. Therefore, the top-half or the bottom-half interrupt handler calls *end_request* when the device signals that the data transfer is complete.

Neither *sbull* nor *spull* can transfer data without using the system microprocessor; however, *spull* is equipped with the capability of simulating interrupt-driven operation if the user specifies the `irq=1` option at load time. When `irq` is not 0, the driver uses a kernel timer to delay fulfillment of the current request. The length of the delay is the value of `irq`: the greater the value, the longer the delay.

As always, block transfers begin when the kernel calls the driver's *request* function. The *request* function for an interrupt-driven device instructs the hardware to perform the transfer and then returns; it does not wait for the transfer to complete. The *spull request* function performs the usual error checks and then calls *spull_transfer* to transfer the data (this is the task that a driver for real hardware performs asynchronously). It then delays acknowledgment until interrupt time:

```
    void spull_irqdriven_request(request_queue_t *q)
    {
        Spull_Dev *device;
        int status;
        long flags;

        /* If we are already processing requests, don't do any more now. */
        if (spull_busy)
                return;

        while(1) {
            INIT_REQUEST;   /* returns when queue is empty */

            /* Which "device" are we using? */
            device = spull_locate_device (CURRENT);
```

```
        if (device == NULL) {
            end_request(0);
            continue;
        }
        spin_lock_irqsave(&device->lock, flags);

        /* Perform the transfer and clean up. */
        status = spull_transfer(device, CURRENT);
        spin_unlock_irqrestore(&device->lock, flags);
        /* ... and wait for the timer to expire -- no end_request(1) */
        spull_timer.expires = jiffies + spull_irq;
        add_timer(&spull_timer);
        spull_busy = 1;
        return;
    }
}
```

New requests can accumulate while the device is dealing with the current one. Because reentrant calls are almost guaranteed in this scenario, the *request* function sets a `spull_busy` flag so that only one transfer happens at any given time. Since the entire function runs with the `io_request_lock` held (the kernel, remember, obtains this lock before calling the *request* function), there is no need for particular care in testing and setting the `busy` flag. Otherwise, an `atomic_t` item should have been used instead of an `int` variable in order to avoid race conditions.

The interrupt handler has a couple of tasks to perform. First, of course, it must check the status of the outstanding transfer and clean up the request. Then, if there are further requests to be processed, the interrupt handler is responsible for getting the next one started. To avoid code duplication, the handler usually just calls the *request* function to start the next transfer. Remember that the *request* function expects the caller to hold the `io_request_lock`, so the interrupt handler will have to obtain it. The *end_request* function also requires this lock, of course.

In our sample module, the role of the interrupt handler is performed by the function invoked when the timer expires. That function calls *end_request* and schedules the next data transfer by calling the *request* function. In the interest of code simplicity, the *spull* interrupt handler performs all this work at "interrupt" time; a real driver would almost certainly defer much of this work and run it from a task queue or tasklet.

```
/* this is invoked when the timer expires */
void spull_interrupt(unsigned long unused)
{
    unsigned long flags

    spin_lock_irqsave(&io_request_lock, flags);
    end_request(1);     /* This request is done - we always succeed */
```

```
    spull_busy = 0;   /* We have io_request_lock, no request conflict */
    if (! QUEUE_EMPTY) /* more of them? */
        spull_irqdriven_request(NULL);   /* Start the next transfer */
    spin_unlock_irqrestore(&io_request_lock, flags);
}
```

If you try to run the interrupt-driven flavor of the *spull* module, you'll barely notice the added delay. The device is almost as fast as it was before because the buffer cache avoids most data transfers between memory and the device. If you want to perceive how a slow device behaves, you can specify a bigger value for `irq=` when loading *spull*.

Backward Compatibility

Much has changed with the block device layer, and most of those changes happened between the 2.2 and 2.4 stable releases. Here is a quick summary of what was different before. As always, you can look at the drivers in the sample source, which work on 2.0, 2.2, and 2.4, to see how the portability challenges have been handled.

The `block_device_operations` structure did not exist in Linux 2.2. Instead, block drivers used a `file_operations` structure just like char drivers. The *check_media_change* and *revalidate* methods used to be a part of that structure. The kernel also provided a set of generic functions— *block_read*, *block_write*, and *block_fsync*—which most drivers used in their `file_operations` structures. A typical 2.2 or 2.0 `file_operations` initialization looked like this:

```
struct file_operations sbull_bdops = {
    read:       block_read,
    write:      block_write,
    ioctl:      sbull_ioctl,
    open:       sbull_open,
    release:    sbull_release,
    fsync:      block_fsync,
    check_media_change: sbull_check_change,
    revalidate: sbull_revalidate
};
```

Note that block drivers are subject to the same changes in the `file_operations` prototypes between 2.0 and 2.2 as char drivers.

In 2.2 and previous kernels, the *request* function was stored in the `blk_dev` global array. Initialization required a line like

```
blk_dev[major].request_fn = sbull_request;
```

Because this method allows for only one queue per major number, the multiqueue capability of 2.4 kernels is not present in earlier releases. Because there was only one queue, the *request* function did not need the queue as an argument, so it took none. Its prototype was as follows:

```
void (*request) (void);
```

Also, all queues had active heads, so `blk_queue_headactive` did not exist.

There was no *blk_ioctl* function in 2.2 and prior releases. There was, however, a macro called RO_IOCTLS, which could be inserted in a `switch` statement to implement BLKROSET and BLKROGET. *sysdep.h* in the sample source includes an implementation of *blk_ioctl* that uses RO_IOCTLS and implements a few other of the standard *ioctl* commands as well:

```
#ifdef RO_IOCTLS
static inline int blk_ioctl(kdev_t dev, unsigned int cmd,
                            unsigned long arg)
{
    int err;

    switch (cmd) {
    case BLKRAGET: /* return the read-ahead value */
        if (!arg)  return -EINVAL;
        err = ! access_ok(VERIFY_WRITE, arg, sizeof(long));
        if (err) return -EFAULT;
        PUT_USER(read_ahead[MAJOR(dev)],(long *) arg);
        return 0;

    case BLKRASET: /* set the read-ahead value */
        if (!capable(CAP_SYS_ADMIN)) return -EACCES;
        if (arg > 0xff) return -EINVAL; /* limit it */
        read_ahead[MAJOR(dev)] = arg;
        return 0;

    case BLKFLSBUF: /* flush */
        if (! capable(CAP_SYS_ADMIN)) return -EACCES; /* only root */
        fsync_dev(dev);
        invalidate_buffers(dev);
        return 0;

        RO_IOCTLS(dev, arg);
    }
    return -ENOTTY;
}
#endif  /* RO_IOCTLS */
```

The BLKFRAGET, BLKFRASET, BLKSECTGET, BLKSECTSET, BLKELVGET, and BLKELVSET commands were added with Linux 2.2, and BLKPG was added in 2.4.

Linux 2.0 did not have the `max_readahead` array. The `max_segments` array, instead, existed and was used in Linux 2.0 and 2.2, but device drivers did not normally need to set it.

Finally, *register_disk* did not exist until Linux 2.4. There was, instead, a function called *resetup_one_dev*, which performed a similar function:

```
resetup_one_dev(struct gendisk *gd, int drive);
```

register_disk is emulated in *sysdep.h* with the following code:

```
static inline void register_disk(struct gendisk *gdev, kdev_t dev,
            unsigned minors, struct file_operations *ops, long size)
{
    if (! gdev)
        return;
    resetup_one_dev(gdev, MINOR(dev) >> gdev->minor_shift);
}
```

Linux 2.0 was different, of course, in not supporting any sort of fine-grained SMP. Thus, there was no `io_request_lock` and much less need to worry about concurrent access to the I/O request queue.

One final thing worth keeping in mind: although nobody really knows what will happen in the 2.5 development series, a major block device overhaul is almost certain. Many people are unhappy with the design of this layer, and there is a lot of pressure to redo it.

Quick Reference

The most important functions and macros used in writing block drivers are summarized here. To save space, however, we do not list the fields of **struct request**, **struct buffer_head**, or **struct genhd**, and we omit the predefined *ioctl* commands.

```
#include <linux/fs.h>
int register_blkdev(unsigned int major, const char *name,
     struct block_device_operations *bdops);
int unregister_blkdev(unsigned int major, const char *name);
```
These functions are in charge of device registration in the module's initialization function and device removal in the cleanup function.

```
#include <linux/blkdev.h>
blk_init_queue(request_queue_t *queue, request_fn_proc
     *request);
blk_cleanup_queue(request_queue_t *queue);
```
The first function initializes a queue and establishes the *request* function; the second is used at cleanup time.

`BLK_DEFAULT_QUEUE(major)`
> This macro returns a default I/O request queue for a given major number.

`struct blk_dev_struct blk_dev[MAX_BLKDEV];`
> This array is used by the kernel to find the proper queue for a given request.

`int read_ahead[];`
`int max_readahead[][];`
> `read_ahead` contains block-level read-ahead values for every major number. A value of 8 is reasonable for devices like hard disks; the value should be greater for slower media. `max_readahead` contains filesystem-level read-ahead values for every major and minor number, and is not usually changed from the system default.

`int max_sectors[][];`
> This array, indexed by both major and minor number, holds the maximum number of sectors that should be merged into a single I/O request.

`int blksize_size[][];`
`int blk_size[][];`
`int hardsect_size[][];`
> These two-dimensional arrays are indexed by major and minor number. The driver is responsible for allocating and deallocating the row in the matrix associated with its major number. The arrays represent the size of device blocks in bytes (it usually is 1 KB), the size of each minor device in kilobytes (not blocks), and the size of the hardware sector in bytes.

`MAJOR_NR`
`DEVICE_NAME`
`DEVICE_NR(kdev_t device)`
`DEVICE_INTR`
`#include <linux/blk.h>`
> These macros must be defined by the driver *before* it includes `<linux/blk.h>`, because they are used within that file. `MAJOR_NR` is the major number for the device, `DEVICE_NAME` is the name of the device to be used in error messages, `DEVICE_NR` returns the minor number of the *physical* device referred to by a device number, and `DEVICE_INTR` is a little-used symbol that points to the device's bottom-half interrupt handler.

`spinlock_t io_request_lock;`
> The spinlock that must be held whenever an I/O request queue is being manipulated.

```
struct request *CURRENT;
```
This macro points to the current request when the default queue is being used. The request structure describes a data chunk to be transferred and is used by the driver's *request* function.

```
INIT_REQUEST;
end_request(int status);
```
INIT_REQUEST checks the next request on the queue and returns if there are no more requests to execute. *end_request* is called at the completion of a block request.

```
spinlock_t io_request_lock;
```
The I/O request lock must be held any time that the request queue is being manipulated.

```
struct request *blkdev_entry_next_request(struct list_head
    *head);
struct request *blkdev_next_request(struct request *req);
struct request *blkdev_prev_request(struct request *req);
blkdev_dequeue_request(struct request *req);
blkdev_release_request(struct request *req);
```
Various functions for working with the I/O request queue.

```
blk_queue_headactive(request_queue_t *queue, int active);
```
Indicates whether the first request in the queue is being actively processed by the driver or not.

```
void blk_queue_make_request(request_queue_t *queue,
    make_request_fn *func);
```
Provides a function to handle block I/O requests directly out of the kernel.

```
end_that_request_first(struct request *req, int status, char
    *name);
end_that_request_last(struct request *req);
```
Handle the stages of completing a block I/O request. *end_that_request_last* is only called when all buffers in the request have been processed—that is, when *end_that_request_first* returns 0.

```
bh->b_end_io(struct buffer_head *bh, int status);
```
Signals the completion of I/O on the given buffer.

```
int blk_ioctl(kdev_t dev, unsigned int cmd, unsigned long
    arg);
```
A utility function that implements most of the standard block device *ioctl* commands.

`int check_disk_change(kdev_t dev);`
> This function checks to see if a media change has occurred on the given device, and calls the driver's *revalidate* method if a change is detected.

`#include<linux/gendisk.h>`
`struct gendisk;`
`struct gendisk *gendisk_head;`
> The generic hard disk allows Linux to support partitionable devices easily. The `gendisk` structure describes a generic disk; `gendisk_head` is the beginning of a linked list of structures describing all of the disks on the system.

`void register_disk(struct gendisk *gd, int drive, unsigned`
`    minors, struct block_device_operations *ops, long`
`    size);`
> This function scans the partition table of the disk and rewrites `genhd->part` to reflect the new partitioning.

## CHAPTER THIRTEEN

MMAP AND DMA

This chapter delves into the area of Linux memory management, with an emphasis on techniques that are useful to the device driver writer. The material in this chapter is somewhat advanced, and not everybody will need a grasp of it. Nonetheless, many tasks can only be done through digging more deeply into the memory management subsystem; it also provides an interesting look into how an important part of the kernel works.

The material in this chapter is divided into three sections. The first covers the implementation of the *mmap* system call, which allows the mapping of device memory directly into a user process's address space. We then cover the kernel `kiobuf` mechanism, which provides direct access to user memory from kernel space. The `kiobuf` system may be used to implement "raw I/O" for certain kinds of devices. The final section covers direct memory access (DMA) I/O operations, which essentially provide peripherals with direct access to system memory.

Of course, all of these techniques require an understanding of how Linux memory management works, so we start with an overview of that subsystem.

Memory Management in Linux

Rather than describing the theory of memory management in operating systems, this section tries to pinpoint the main features of the Linux implementation of the theory. Although you do not need to be a Linux virtual memory guru to implement *mmap*, a basic overview of how things work is useful. What follows is a fairly lengthy description of the data structures used by the kernel to manage memory. Once the necessary background has been covered, we can get into working with these structures.

Address Types

Linux is, of course, a virtual memory system, meaning that the addresses seen by user programs do not directly correspond to the physical addresses used by the hardware. Virtual memory introduces a layer of indirection, which allows a number of nice things. With virtual memory, programs running on the system can allocate far more memory than is physically available; indeed, even a single process can have a virtual address space larger than the system's physical memory. Virtual memory also allows playing a number of tricks with the process's address space, including mapping in device memory.

Thus far, we have talked about virtual and physical addresses, but a number of the details have been glossed over. The Linux system deals with several types of addresses, each with its own semantics. Unfortunately, the kernel code is not always very clear on exactly which type of address is being used in each situation, so the programmer must be careful.

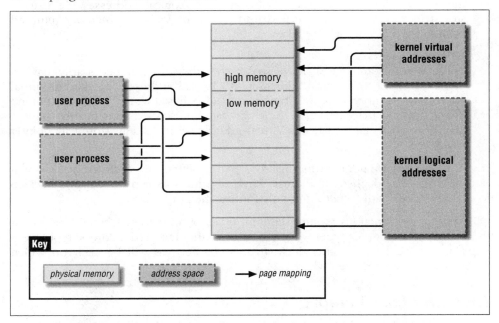

Figure 13-1. Address types used in Linux

The following is a list of address types used in Linux. Figure 13-1 shows how these address types relate to physical memory.

User virtual addresses

These are the regular addresses seen by user-space programs. User addresses are either 32 or 64 bits in length, depending on the underlying hardware architecture, and each process has its own virtual address space.

Physical addresses

The addresses used between the processor and the system's memory. Physical addresses are 32- or 64-bit quantities; even 32-bit systems can use 64-bit physical addresses in some situations.

Bus addresses

The addresses used between peripheral buses and memory. Often they are the same as the physical addresses used by the processor, but that is not necessarily the case. Bus addresses are highly architecture dependent, of course.

Kernel logical addresses

These make up the normal address space of the kernel. These addresses map most or all of main memory, and are often treated as if they were physical addresses. On most architectures, logical addresses and their associated physical addresses differ only by a constant offset. Logical addresses use the hardware's native pointer size, and thus may be unable to address all of physical memory on heavily equipped 32-bit systems. Logical addresses are usually stored in variables of type `unsigned long` or `void *`. Memory returned from *kmalloc* has a logical address.

Kernel virtual addresses

These differ from logical addresses in that they do not necessarily have a direct mapping to physical addresses. All logical addresses are kernel virtual addresses; memory allocated by *vmalloc* also has a virtual address (but no direct physical mapping). The function *kmap*, described later in this chapter, also returns virtual addresses. Virtual addresses are usually stored in pointer variables.

If you have a logical address, the macro *__pa()* (defined in `<asm/page.h>`) will return its associated physical address. Physical addresses can be mapped back to logical addresses with *__va()*, but only for low-memory pages.

Different kernel functions require different types of addresses. It would be nice if there were different C types defined so that the required address type were explicit, but we have no such luck. In this chapter, we will be clear on which types of addresses are used where.

High and Low Memory

The difference between logical and kernel virtual addresses is highlighted on 32-bit systems that are equipped with large amounts of memory. With 32 bits, it is possible to address 4 GB of memory. Linux on 32-bit systems has, until recently, been limited to substantially less memory than that, however, because of the way it sets up the virtual address space. The system was unable to handle more memory than it could set up logical addresses for, since it needed directly mapped kernel addresses for all memory.

Recent developments have eliminated the limitations on memory, and 32-bit systems can now work with well over 4 GB of system memory (assuming, of course, that the processor itself can address that much memory). The limitation on how much memory can be directly mapped with logical addresses remains, however. Only the lowest portion of memory (up to 1 or 2 GB, depending on the hardware and the kernel configuration) has logical addresses; the rest (high memory) does not. High memory can require 64-bit physical addresses, and the kernel must set up explicit virtual address mappings to manipulate it. Thus, many kernel functions are limited to low memory only; high memory tends to be reserved for user-space process pages.

The term "high memory" can be confusing to some, especially since it has other meanings in the PC world. So, to make things clear, we'll define the terms here:

Low memory
> Memory for which logical addresses exist in kernel space. On almost every system you will likely encounter, all memory is low memory.

High memory
> Memory for which logical addresses do not exist, because the system contains more physical memory than can be addressed with 32 bits.

On i386 systems, the boundary between low and high memory is usually set at just under 1 GB. This boundary is not related in any way to the old 640 KB limit found on the original PC. It is, instead, a limit set by the kernel itself as it splits the 32-bit address space between kernel and user space.

We will point out high-memory limitations as we come to them in this chapter.

The Memory Map and struct page

Historically, the kernel has used logical addresses to refer to explicit pages of memory. The addition of high-memory support, however, has exposed an obvious problem with that approach—logical addresses are not available for high memory. Thus kernel functions that deal with memory are increasingly using pointers to `struct page` instead. This data structure is used to keep track of just about everything the kernel needs to know about physical memory; there is one `struct page` for each physical page on the system. Some of the fields of this structure include the following:

`atomic_t count;`
> The number of references there are to this page. When the count drops to zero, the page is returned to the free list.

`wait_queue_head_t wait;`
> A list of processes waiting on this page. Processes can wait on a page when a kernel function has locked it for some reason; drivers need not normally worry about waiting on pages, though.

`void *virtual;`
> The kernel virtual address of the page, if it is mapped; `NULL`, otherwise. Low-memory pages are always mapped; high-memory pages usually are not.

`unsigned long flags;`
> A set of bit flags describing the status of the page. These include `PG_locked`, which indicates that the page has been locked in memory, and `PG_reserved`, which prevents the memory management system from working with the page at all.

There is much more information within `struct page`, but it is part of the deeper black magic of memory management and is not of concern to driver writers.

The kernel maintains one or more arrays of `struct page` entries, which track all of the physical memory on the system. On most systems, there is a single array, called `mem_map`. On some systems, however, the situation is more complicated. Nonuniform memory access (NUMA) systems and those with widely discontiguous physical memory may have more than one memory map array, so code that is meant to be portable should avoid direct access to the array whenever possible. Fortunately, it is usually quite easy to just work with `struct page` pointers without worrying about where they come from.

Some functions and macros are defined for translating between `struct page` pointers and virtual addresses:

`struct page *virt_to_page(void *kaddr);`
> This macro, defined in `<asm/page.h>`, takes a kernel logical address and returns its associated `struct page` pointer. Since it requires a logical address, it will not work with memory from *vmalloc* or high memory.

`void *page_address(struct page *page);`
> Returns the kernel virtual address of this page, if such an address exists. For high memory, that address exists only if the page has been mapped.

`#include <linux/highmem.h>`
`void *kmap(struct page *page);`
`void kunmap(struct page *page);`
> *kmap* returns a kernel virtual address for any page in the system. For low-memory pages, it just returns the logical address of the page; for high-memory pages, *kmap* creates a special mapping. Mappings created with *kmap* should always be freed with *kunmap*; a limited number of such mappings is available, so it is better not to hold on to them for too long. *kmap* calls are

additive, so if two or more functions both call *kmap* on the same page the right thing happens. Note also that *kmap* can sleep if no mappings are available.

We will see some uses of these functions when we get into the example code later in this chapter.

Page Tables

When a program looks up a virtual address, the CPU must convert the address to a physical address in order to access physical memory. The step is usually performed by splitting the address into bitfields. Each bitfield is used as an index into an array, called a *page table*, to retrieve either the address of the next table or the address of the physical page that holds the virtual address.

The Linux kernel manages three levels of page tables in order to map virtual addresses to physical addresses. The multiple levels allow the memory range to be sparsely populated; modern systems will spread a process out across a large range of virtual memory. It makes sense to do things that way; it allows for runtime flexibility in how things are laid out.

Note that Linux uses a three-level system even on hardware that only supports two levels of page tables or hardware that uses a different way to map virtual addresses to physical ones. The use of three levels in a processor-independent implementation allows Linux to support both two-level and three-level processors without clobbering the code with a lot of `#ifdef` statements. This kind of conservative coding doesn't lead to additional overhead when the kernel runs on two-level processors, because the compiler actually optimizes out the unused level.

It is time to take a look at the data structures used to implement the paging system. The following list summarizes the implementation of the three levels in Linux, and Figure 13-2 depicts them.

Page Directory (PGD)
> The top-level page table. The PGD is an array of `pgd_t` items, each of which points to a second-level page table. Each process has its own page directory, and there is one for kernel space as well. You can think of the page directory as a page-aligned array of `pgd_ts`.

Page mid-level Directory (PMD)
> The second-level table. The PMD is a page-aligned array of `pmd_t` items. A `pmd_t` is a pointer to the third-level page table. Two-level processors have no physical PMD; they declare their PMD as an array with a single element, whose value is the PMD itself—we'll see in a while how this is handled in C and how the compiler optimizes this level away.

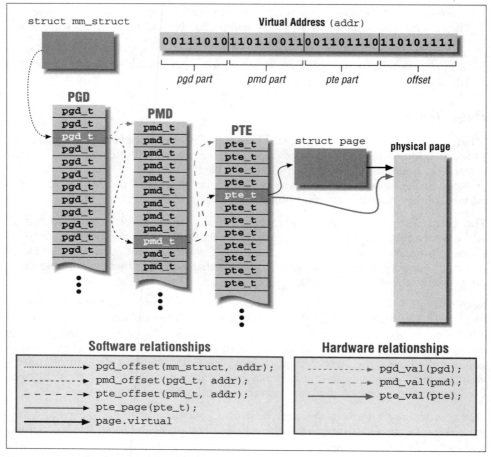

Figure 13-2. The three levels of Linux page tables

Page Table

A page-aligned array of items, each of which is called a Page Table Entry. The kernel uses the `pte_t` type for the items. A `pte_t` contains the physical address of the data page.

The types introduced in this list are defined in `<asm/page.h>`, which must be included by every source file that plays with paging.

The kernel doesn't need to worry about doing page-table lookups during normal program execution, because they are done by the hardware. Nonetheless, the kernel must arrange things so that the hardware can do its work. It must build the page tables and look them up whenever the processor reports a page fault, that is, whenever the page associated with a virtual address needed by the processor is not present in memory. Device drivers, too, must be able to build page tables and handle faults when implementing *mmap*.

It's interesting to note how software memory management exploits the same page tables that are used by the CPU itself. Whenever a CPU doesn't implement page tables, the difference is only hidden in the lowest levels of architecture-specific code. In Linux memory management, therefore, you always talk about three-level page tables irrespective of whether they are known to the hardware or not. An example of a CPU family that doesn't use page tables is the PowerPC. PowerPC designers implemented a hash algorithm that maps virtual addresses into a one-level page table. When accessing a page that is already in memory but whose physical address has expired from the CPU caches, the CPU needs to read memory only once, as opposed to the two or three accesses required by a multilevel page table approach. The hash algorithm, like multilevel tables, makes it possible to reduce use of memory in mapping virtual addresses to physical ones.

Irrespective of the mechanisms used by the CPU, the Linux software implementation is based on three-level page tables, and the following symbols are used to access them. Both `<asm/page.h>` and `<asm/pgtable.h>` must be included for all of them to be accessible.

`PTRS_PER_PGD`
`PTRS_PER_PMD`
`PTRS_PER_PTE`
> The size of each table. Two-level processors set `PTRS_PER_PMD` to 1, to avoid dealing with the middle level.

`unsigned pgd_val(pgd_t pgd)`
`unsigned pmd_val(pmd_t pmd)`
`unsigned pte_val(pte_t pte)`
> These three macros are used to retrieve the `unsigned` value from the typed data item. The actual type used varies depending on the underlying architecture and kernel configuration options; it is usually either `unsigned long` or, on 32-bit processors supporting high memory, `unsigned long long`. SPARC64 processors use `unsigned int`. The macros help in using strict data typing in source code without introducing computational overhead.

`pgd_t * pgd_offset(struct mm_struct * mm, unsigned long address)`
`pmd_t * pmd_offset(pgd_t * dir, unsigned long address)`
`pte_t * pte_offset(pmd_t * dir, unsigned long address)`
> These inline functions* are used to retrieve the `pgd`, `pmd`, and `pte` entries

---

* On 32-bit SPARC processors, the functions are not `inline` but rather real `extern` functions, which are not exported to modularized code. Therefore you won't be able to use these functions in a module running on the SPARC, but you won't usually need to.

associated with `address`. Page-table lookup begins with a pointer to `struct mm_struct`. The pointer associated with the memory map of the current process is `current->mm`, while the pointer to kernel space is described by `&init_mm`. Two-level processors define `pmd_offset(dir,add)` as `(pmd_t *)dir`, thus folding the `pmd` over the `pgd`. Functions that scan page tables are always declared as `inline`, and the compiler optimizes out any `pmd` lookup.

`struct page *pte_page(pte_t pte)`

This function returns a pointer to the `struct page` entry for the page in this page-table entry. Code that deals with page-tables will generally want to use *pte_page* rather than *pte_val*, since *pte_page* deals with the processor-dependent format of the page-table entry and returns the `struct page` pointer, which is usually what's needed.

`pte_present(pte_t pte)`

This macro returns a boolean value that indicates whether the data page is currently in memory. This is the most used of several functions that access the low bits in the `pte`—the bits that are discarded by *pte_page*. Pages may be absent, of course, if the kernel has swapped them to disk (or if they have never been loaded). The page tables themselves, however, are always present in the current Linux implementation. Keeping page tables in memory simplifies the kernel code because *pgd_offset* and friends never fail; on the other hand, even a process with a "resident storage size" of zero keeps its page tables in real RAM, wasting some memory that might be better used elsewhere.

Each process in the system has a `struct mm_struct` structure, which contains its page tables and a great many other things. It also contains a spinlock called `page_table_lock`, which should be held while traversing or modifying the page tables.

Just seeing the list of these functions is not enough for you to be proficient in the Linux memory management algorithms; real memory management is much more complex and must deal with other complications, like cache coherence. The previous list should nonetheless be sufficient to give you a feel for how page management is implemented; it is also about all that you will need to know, as a device driver writer, to work occasionally with page tables. You can get more information from the *include/asm* and *mm* subtrees of the kernel source.

Virtual Memory Areas

Although paging sits at the lowest level of memory management, something more is necessary before you can use the computer's resources efficiently. The kernel needs a higher-level mechanism to handle the way a process sees its memory. This mechanism is implemented in Linux by means of virtual memory areas, which are typically referred to as areas or VMAs.

An area is a homogeneous region in the virtual memory of a process, a contiguous range of addresses with the same permission flags. It corresponds loosely to the concept of a "segment," although it is better described as "a memory object with its own properties." The memory map of a process is made up of the following:

- An area for the program's executable code (often called text).

- One area each for data, including initialized data (that which has an explicitly assigned value at the beginning of execution), uninitialized data (BSS),* and the program stack.

- One area for each active memory mapping.

The memory areas of a process can be seen by looking in */proc/pid/maps* (where *pid*, of course, is replaced by a process ID). */proc/self* is a special case of */proc/pid*, because it always refers to the current process. As an example, here are a couple of memory maps, to which we have added short comments after a sharp sign:

```
morgana.root# cat /proc/1/maps    # look at init
08048000-0804e000 r-xp 00000000 08:01 51297    /sbin/init  # text
0804e000-08050000 rw-p 00005000 08:01 51297    /sbin/init  # data
08050000-08054000 rwxp 00000000 00:00 0        # zero-mapped bss
40000000-40013000 r-xp 00000000 08:01 39003    /lib/ld-2.1.3.so # text
40013000-40014000 rw-p 00012000 08:01 39003    /lib/ld-2.1.3.so # data
40014000-40015000 rw-p 00000000 00:00 0        # bss for ld.so
4001b000-40108000 r-xp 00000000 08:01 39006    /lib/libc-2.1.3.so # text
40108000-4010c000 rw-p 000ec000 08:01 39006    /lib/libc-2.1.3.so # data
4010c000-40110000 rw-p 00000000 00:00 0        # bss for libc.so
bfffe000-c0000000 rwxp fffff000 00:00 0        # zero-mapped stack

morgana.root# rsh wolf head /proc/self/maps   #### alpha-axp: static ecoff
000000011fffe000-0000000120000000 rwxp 0000000000000000 00:00 0    # stack
0000000120000000-0000000120014000 r-xp 0000000000000000 08:03 2844 # text
0000000140000000-0000000140002000 rwxp 0000000000014000 08:03 2844 # data
0000000140002000-0000000140008000 rwxp 0000000000000000 00:00 0    # bss
```

The fields in each line are as follows:

> *start-end perm offset major:minor inode image.*

Each field in */proc/*/maps* (except the image name) corresponds to a field in struct vm_area_struct, and is described in the following list.

start
end
 The beginning and ending virtual addresses for this memory area.

---

* The name *BSS* is a historical relic, from an old assembly operator meaning "Block started by symbol." The BSS segment of executable files isn't stored on disk, and the kernel maps the zero page to the BSS address range.

`perm`

> A bit mask with the memory area's read, write, and execute permissions. This field describes what the process is allowed to do with pages belonging to the area. The last character in the field is either p for "private" or s for "shared."

`offset`

> Where the memory area begins in the file that it is mapped to. An offset of zero, of course, means that the first page of the memory area corresponds to the first page of the file.

`major`
`minor`

> The major and minor numbers of the device holding the file that has been mapped. Confusingly, for device mappings, the major and minor numbers refer to the disk partition holding the device special file that was opened by the user, and not the device itself.

`inode`

> The inode number of the mapped file.

`image`

> The name of the file (usually an executable image) that has been mapped.

A driver that implements the *mmap* method needs to fill a VMA structure in the address space of the process mapping the device. The driver writer should therefore have at least a minimal understanding of VMAs in order to use them.

Let's look at the most important fields in `struct vm_area_struct` (defined in `<linux/mm.h>`). These fields may be used by device drivers in their *mmap* implementation. Note that the kernel maintains lists and trees of VMAs to optimize area lookup, and several fields of `vm_area_struct` are used to maintain this organization. VMAs thus can't be created at will by a driver, or the structures will break. The main fields of VMAs are as follows (note the similarity between these fields and the */proc* output we just saw):

`unsigned long vm_start;`
`unsigned long vm_end;`

> The virtual address range covered by this VMA. These fields are the first two fields shown in */proc/*/maps*.

`struct file *vm_file;`

> A pointer to the `struct file` structure associated with this area (if any).

`unsigned long vm_pgoff;`

> The offset of the area in the file, in pages. When a file or device is mapped, this is the file position of the first page mapped in this area.

`unsigned long vm_flags;`
> A set of flags describing this area. The flags of the most interest to device driver writers are `VM_IO` and `VM_RESERVED`. `VM_IO` marks a VMA as being a memory-mapped I/O region. Among other things, the `VM_IO` flag will prevent the region from being included in process core dumps. `VM_RESERVED` tells the memory management system not to attempt to swap out this VMA; it should be set in most device mappings.

`struct vm_operations_struct *vm_ops;`
> A set of functions that the kernel may invoke to operate on this memory area. Its presence indicates that the memory area is a kernel "object" like the `struct file` we have been using throughout the book.

`void *vm_private_data;`
> A field that may be used by the driver to store its own information.

Like `struct vm_area_struct`, the `vm_operations_struct` is defined in `<linux/mm.h>`; it includes the operations listed next. These operations are the only ones needed to handle the process's memory needs, and they are listed in the order they are declared. Later in this chapter, some of these functions will be implemented; they will be described more completely at that point.

`void (*open)(struct vm_area_struct *vma);`
> The *open* method is called by the kernel to allow the subsystem implementing the VMA to initialize the area, adjust reference counts, and so forth. This method will be invoked any time that a new reference to the VMA is made (when a process forks, for example). The one exception happens when the VMA is first created by *mmap*; in this case, the driver's *mmap* method is called instead.

`void (*close)(struct vm_area_struct *vma);`
> When an area is destroyed, the kernel calls its *close* operation. Note that there's no usage count associated with VMAs; the area is opened and closed exactly once by each process that uses it.

`void (*unmap)(struct vm_area_struct *vma, unsigned long`
`    addr, size_t len);`
> The kernel calls this method to "unmap" part or all of an area. If the entire area is unmapped, then the kernel calls *vm_ops->close* as soon as *vm_ops->unmap* returns.

`void (*protect)(struct vm_area_struct *vma, unsigned long,`
`    size_t, unsigned int newprot);`
> This method is intended to change the protection on a memory area, but is currently not used. Memory protection is handled by the page tables, and the kernel sets up the page-table entries separately.

```
int (*sync)(struct vm_area_struct *vma, unsigned long,
       size_t, unsigned int flags);
```
> This method is called by the *msync* system call to save a dirty memory region to the storage medium. The return value is expected to be 0 to indicate success and negative if there was an error.

```
struct page *(*nopage)(struct vm_area_struct *vma, unsigned
       long address, int write_access);
```
> When a process tries to access a page that belongs to a valid VMA, but that is currently not in memory, the *nopage* method is called (if it is defined) for the related area. The method returns the `struct page` pointer for the physical page, after, perhaps, having read it in from secondary storage. If the *nopage* method isn't defined for the area, an empty page is allocated by the kernel. The third argument, `write_access`, counts as "no-share": a nonzero value means the page must be owned by the current process, whereas 0 means that sharing is possible.

```
struct page *(*wppage)(struct vm_area_struct *vma, unsigned
       long address, struct page *page);
```
> This method handles write-protected page faults but is currently unused. The kernel handles attempts to write over a protected page without invoking the area-specific callback. Write-protect faults are used to implement copy-on-write. A private page can be shared across processes until one process writes to it. When that happens, the page is cloned, and the process writes on its own copy of the page. If the whole area is marked as read-only, a `SIGSEGV` is sent to the process, and the copy-on-write is not performed.

```
int (*swapout)(struct page *page, struct file *file);
```
> This method is called when a page is selected to be swapped out. A return value of 0 signals success; any other value signals an error. In case of error, the process owning the page is sent a `SIGBUS`. It is highly unlikely that a driver will ever need to implement *swapout*; device mappings are not something that the kernel can just write to disk.

That concludes our overview of Linux memory management data structures. With that out of the way, we can now proceed to the implementation of the *mmap* system call.

The mmap Device Operation

Memory mapping is one of the most interesting features of modern Unix systems. As far as drivers are concerned, memory mapping can be used to provide user programs with direct access to device memory.

A definitive example of *mmap* usage can be seen by looking at a subset of the virtual memory areas for the X Window System server:

```
cat /proc/731/maps
08048000-08327000 r-xp 00000000 08:01 55505    /usr/X11R6/bin/XF86_SVGA
08327000-08369000 rw-p 002de000 08:01 55505    /usr/X11R6/bin/XF86_SVGA
40015000-40019000 rw-s fe2fc000 08:01 10778    /dev/mem
40131000-40141000 rw-s 000a0000 08:01 10778    /dev/mem
40141000-40941000 rw-s f4000000 08:01 10778    /dev/mem
     . . .
```

The full list of the X server's VMAs is lengthy, but most of the entries are not of interest here. We do see, however, three separate mappings of */dev/mem*, which give some insight into how the X server works with the video card. The first mapping shows a 16 KB region mapped at `fe2fc000`. This address is far above the highest RAM address on the system; it is, instead, a region of memory on a PCI peripheral (the video card). It will be a control region for that card. The middle mapping is at `a0000`, which is the standard location for video RAM in the 640 KB ISA hole. The last */dev/mem* mapping is a rather larger one at `f4000000` and is the video memory itself. These regions can also be seen in */proc/iomem*:

```
000a0000-000bffff : Video RAM area
f4000000-f4ffffff : Matrox Graphics, Inc. MGA G200 AGP
fe2fc000-fe2fffff : Matrox Graphics, Inc. MGA G200 AGP
```

Mapping a device means associating a range of user-space addresses to device memory. Whenever the program reads or writes in the assigned address range, it is actually accessing the device. In the X server example, using *mmap* allows quick and easy access to the video card's memory. For a performance-critical application like this, direct access makes a large difference.

As you might suspect, not every device lends itself to the *mmap* abstraction; it makes no sense, for instance, for serial ports and other stream-oriented devices. Another limitation of *mmap* is that mapping is `PAGE_SIZE` grained. The kernel can dispose of virtual addresses only at the level of page tables; therefore, the mapped area must be a multiple of `PAGE_SIZE` and must live in physical memory starting at an address that is a multiple of `PAGE_SIZE`. The kernel accommodates for size granularity by making a region slightly bigger if its size isn't a multiple of the page size.

These limits are not a big constraint for drivers, because the program accessing the device is device dependent anyway. It needs to know how to make sense of the memory region being mapped, so the `PAGE_SIZE` alignment is not a problem. A bigger constraint exists when ISA devices are used on some non-x86 platforms, because their hardware view of ISA may not be contiguous. For example, some Alpha computers see ISA memory as a scattered set of 8-bit, 16-bit, or 32-bit items, with no direct mapping. In such cases, you can't use *mmap* at all. The inability to perform direct mapping of ISA addresses to Alpha addresses is due to the incompatible data transfer specifications of the two systems. Whereas early Alpha processors could issue only 32-bit and 64-bit memory accesses, ISA can do only 8-bit and 16-bit transfers, and there's no way to transparently map one protocol onto the other.

There are sound advantages to using *mmap* when it's feasible to do so. For instance, we have already looked at the X server, which transfers a lot of data to and from video memory; mapping the graphic display to user space dramatically improves the throughput, as opposed to an *lseek/write* implementation. Another typical example is a program controlling a PCI device. Most PCI peripherals map their control registers to a memory address, and a demanding application might prefer to have direct access to the registers instead of repeatedly having to call *ioctl* to get its work done.

The *mmap* method is part of the `file_operations` structure and is invoked when the *mmap* system call is issued. With *mmap*, the kernel performs a good deal of work before the actual method is invoked, and therefore the prototype of the method is quite different from that of the system call. This is unlike calls such as *ioctl* and *poll*, where the kernel does not do much before calling the method.

The system call is declared as follows (as described in the *mmap(2)* manual page):

```
mmap (caddr_t addr, size_t len, int prot, int flags, int fd,
off_t offset)
```

On the other hand, the file operation is declared as

```
int (*mmap) (struct file *filp, struct vm_area_struct *vma);
```

The `filp` argument in the method is the same as that introduced in Chapter 3, while `vma` contains the information about the virtual address range that is used to access the device. Much of the work has thus been done by the kernel; to implement *mmap*, the driver only has to build suitable page tables for the address range and, if necessary, replace `vma->vm_ops` with a new set of operations.

There are two ways of building the page tables: doing it all at once with a function called *remap_page_range*, or doing it a page at a time via the *nopage* VMA method. Both methods have their advantages. We'll start with the "all at once" approach, which is simpler. From there we will start adding the complications needed for a real-world implementation.

Using remap_page_range

The job of building new page tables to map a range of physical addresses is handled by *remap_page_range*, which has the following prototype:

```
int remap_page_range(unsigned long virt_add, unsigned long phys_add,
                     unsigned long size, pgprot_t prot);
```

The value returned by the function is the usual 0 or a negative error code. Let's look at the exact meaning of the function's arguments:

`virt_add`

> The user virtual address where remapping should begin. The function builds page tables for the virtual address range between `virt_add` and `virt_add+size`.

`phys_add`

> The physical address to which the virtual address should be mapped. The function affects physical addresses from `phys_add` to `phys_add+size`.

`size`

> The dimension, in bytes, of the area being remapped.

`prot`

> The "protection" requested for the new VMA. The driver can (and should) use the value found in `vma->vm_page_prot`.

The arguments to *remap_page_range* are fairly straightforward, and most of them are already provided to you in the VMA when your *mmap* method is called. The one complication has to do with caching: usually, references to device memory should not be cached by the processor. Often the system BIOS will set things up properly, but it is also possible to disable caching of specific VMAs via the protection field. Unfortunately, disabling caching at this level is highly processor dependent. The curious reader may wish to look at the function *pgprot_noncached* from *drivers/char/mem.c* to see what's involved. We won't discuss the topic further here.

A Simple Implementation

If your driver needs to do a simple, linear mapping of device memory into a user address space, *remap_page_range* is almost all you really need to do the job. The following code comes from *drivers/char/mem.c* and shows how this task is performed in a typical module called *simple* (Simple Implementation Mapping Pages with Little Enthusiasm):

```
#include <linux/mm.h>

int simple_mmap(struct file *filp, struct vm_area_struct *vma)
{
    unsigned long offset = vma->vm_pgoff << PAGE_SHIFT;

    if (offset >= __pa(high_memory) || (filp->f_flags & O_SYNC))
        vma->vm_flags |= VM_IO;
    vma->vm_flags |= VM_RESERVED;

    if (remap_page_range(vma->vm_start, offset,
            vma->vm_end-vma->vm_start, vma->vm_page_prot))
        return -EAGAIN;
    return 0;
}
```

The */dev/mem* code checks to see if the requested offset (stored in `vma->vm_pgoff`) is beyond physical memory; if so, the `VM_IO` VMA flag is set to mark the area as being I/O memory. The `VM_RESERVED` flag is always set to keep the system from trying to swap this area out. Then it is just a matter of calling *remap_page_range* to create the necessary page tables.

Adding VMA Operations

As we have seen, the `vm_area_struct` structure contains a set of operations that may be applied to the VMA. Now we'll look at providing those operations in a simple way; a more detailed example will follow later on.

Here, we will provide *open* and *close* operations for our VMA. These operations will be called anytime a process opens or closes the VMA; in particular, the *open* method will be invoked anytime a process forks and creates a new reference to the VMA. The *open* and *close* VMA methods are called in addition to the processing performed by the kernel, so they need not reimplement any of the work done there. They exist as a way for drivers to do any additional processing that they may require.

We'll use these methods to increment the module usage count whenever the VMA is opened, and to decrement it when it's closed. In modern kernels, this work is not strictly necessary; the kernel will not call the driver's *release* method as long as a VMA remains open, so the usage count will not drop to zero until all references to the VMA are closed. The 2.0 kernel, however, did not perform this tracking, so portable code will still want to be able to maintain the usage count.

So, we will override the default `vma->vm_ops` with operations that keep track of the usage count. The code is quite simple—a complete *mmap* implementation for a modularized */dev/mem* looks like the following:

```
void simple_vma_open(struct vm_area_struct *vma)
{ MOD_INC_USE_COUNT; }

void simple_vma_close(struct vm_area_struct *vma)
{ MOD_DEC_USE_COUNT; }

static struct vm_operations_struct simple_remap_vm_ops = {
    open:   simple_vma_open,
    close:  simple_vma_close,
};

int simple_remap_mmap(struct file *filp, struct vm_area_struct *vma)
{
    unsigned long offset = VMA_OFFSET(vma);

    if (offset >= __pa(high_memory) || (filp->f_flags & O_SYNC))
        vma->vm_flags |= VM_IO;
    vma->vm_flags |= VM_RESERVED;
```

```
if (remap_page_range(vma->vm_start, offset, vma->vm_end-vma->vm_start,
        vma->vm_page_prot))
    return -EAGAIN;

vma->vm_ops = &simple_remap_vm_ops;
simple_vma_open(vma);
return 0;
}
```

This code relies on the fact that the kernel initializes to NULL the vm_ops field in the newly created area before calling f_op->mmap. The code just shown checks the current value of the pointer as a safety measure, should something change in future kernels.

The strange VMA_OFFSET macro that appears in this code is used to hide a difference in the vma structure across kernel versions. Since the offset is a number of pages in 2.4 and a number of bytes in 2.2 and earlier kernels, <sysdep.h> declares the macro to make the difference transparent (and the result is expressed in bytes).

Mapping Memory with nopage

Although *remap_page_range* works well for many, if not most, driver *mmap* implementations, sometimes it is necessary to be a little more flexible. In such situations, an implementation using the *nopage* VMA method may be called for.

The *nopage* method, remember, has the following prototype:

```
struct page (*nopage)(struct vm_area_struct *vma,
              unsigned long address, int write_access);
```

When a user process attempts to access a page in a VMA that is not present in memory, the associated *nopage* function is called. The address parameter will contain the virtual address that caused the fault, rounded down to the beginning of the page. The *nopage* function must locate and return the struct page pointer that refers to the page the user wanted. This function must also take care to increment the usage count for the page it returns by calling the *get_page* macro:

```
get_page(struct page *pageptr);
```

This step is necessary to keep the reference counts correct on the mapped pages. The kernel maintains this count for every page; when the count goes to zero, the kernel knows that the page may be placed on the free list. When a VMA is unmapped, the kernel will decrement the usage count for every page in the area. If your driver does not increment the count when adding a page to the area, the usage count will become zero prematurely and the integrity of the system will be compromised.

One situation in which the *nopage* approach is useful can be brought about by the *mremap* system call, which is used by applications to change the bounding addresses of a mapped region. If the driver wants to be able to deal with *mremap*, the previous implementation won't work correctly, because there's no way for the driver to know that the mapped region has changed.

The Linux implementation of *mremap* doesn't notify the driver of changes in the mapped area. Actually, it *does* notify the driver if the size of the area is reduced via the *unmap* method, but no callback is issued if the area increases in size.

The basic idea behind notifying the driver of a reduction is that the driver (or the filesystem mapping a regular file to memory) needs to know when a region is unmapped in order to take the proper action, such as flushing pages to disk. Growth of the mapped region, on the other hand, isn't really meaningful for the driver until the program invoking *mremap* accesses the new virtual addresses. In real life, it's quite common to map regions that are never used (unused sections of program code, for example). The Linux kernel, therefore, doesn't notify the driver if the mapped region grows, because the *nopage* method will take care of pages one at a time as they are actually accessed.

In other words, the driver isn't notified when a mapping grows because *nopage* will do it later, without having to use memory before it is actually needed. This optimization is mostly aimed at regular files, whose mapping uses real RAM.

The *nopage* method, therefore, must be implemented if you want to support the *mremap* system call. But once you have *nopage*, you can choose to use it extensively, with some limitations (described later). This method is shown in the next code fragment. In this implementation of *mmap*, the device method only replaces vma->vm_ops. The *nopage* method takes care of "remapping" one page at a time and returning the address of its `struct page` structure. Because we are just implementing a window onto physical memory here, the remapping step is simple—we need only locate and return a pointer to the `struct page` for the desired address.

An implementation of */dev/mem* using *nopage* looks like the following:

```
struct page *simple_vma_nopage(struct vm_area_struct *vma,
            unsigned long address, int write_access)
{
    struct page *pageptr;
    unsigned long physaddr = address - vma->vm_start + VMA_OFFSET(vma);
    pageptr = virt_to_page(__va(physaddr));
    get_page(pageptr);
    return pageptr;
}

int simple_nopage_mmap(struct file *filp, struct vm_area_struct *vma)
{
    unsigned long offset = VMA_OFFSET(vma);
```

```
    if (offset >= __pa(high_memory) || (filp->f_flags & O_SYNC))
        vma->vm_flags |= VM_IO;
    vma->vm_flags |= VM_RESERVED;

    vma->vm_ops = &simple_nopage_vm_ops;
    simple_vma_open(vma);
    return 0;
}
```

Since, once again, we are simply mapping main memory here, the *nopage* function need only find the correct **struct page** for the faulting address and increment its reference count. The required sequence of events is thus to calculate the desired physical address, turn it into a logical address with _ _*va*, and then finally to turn it into a **struct page** with *virt_to_page*. It would be possible, in general, to go directly from the physical address to the **struct page**, but such code would be difficult to make portable across architectures. Such code might be necessary, however, if one were trying to map high memory, which, remember, has no logical addresses. *simple*, being simple, does not worry about that (rare) case.

If the *nopage* method is left **NULL**, kernel code that handles page faults maps the zero page to the faulting virtual address. The zero page is a copy-on-write page that reads as zero and that is used, for example, to map the BSS segment. Therefore, if a process extends a mapped region by calling *mremap*, and the driver hasn't implemented *nopage*, it will end up with zero pages instead of a segmentation fault.

The *nopage* method normally returns a pointer to a **struct page**. If, for some reason, a normal page cannot be returned (e.g., the requested address is beyond the device's memory region), **NOPAGE_SIGBUS** can be returned to signal the error. *nopage* can also return **NOPAGE_OOM** to indicate failures caused by resource limitations.

Note that this implementation will work for ISA memory regions but not for those on the PCI bus. PCI memory is mapped above the highest system memory, and there are no entries in the system memory map for those addresses. Because there is thus no **struct page** to return a pointer to, *nopage* cannot be used in these situations; you must, instead, use *remap_page_range*.

Remapping Specific I/O Regions

All the examples we've seen so far are reimplementations of */dev/mem*; they remap physical addresses into user space. The typical driver, however, wants to map only the small address range that applies to its peripheral device, not all of memory. In order to map to user space only a subset of the whole memory range, the driver needs only to play with the offsets. The following lines will do the trick for a driver mapping a region of **simple_region_size** bytes, beginning at physical address **simple_region_start** (which should be page aligned).

```
unsigned long off = vma->vm_pgoff << PAGE_SHIFT;
unsigned long physical = simple_region_start + off;
unsigned long vsize = vma->vm_end - vma->vm_start;
unsigned long psize = simple_region_size - off;

if (vsize > psize)
    return -EINVAL; /*  spans too high */
remap_page_range(vma_>vm_start, physical, vsize, vma->vm_page_prot);
```

In addition to calculating the offsets, this code introduces a check that reports an error when the program tries to map more memory than is available in the I/O region of the target device. In this code, **psize** is the physical I/O size that is left after the offset has been specified, and **vsize** is the requested size of virtual memory; the function refuses to map addresses that extend beyond the allowed memory range.

Note that the user process can always use *mremap* to extend its mapping, possibly past the end of the physical device area. If your driver has no *nopage* method, it will never be notified of this extension, and the additional area will map to the zero page. As a driver writer, you may well want to prevent this sort of behavior; mapping the zero page onto the end of your region is not an explicitly bad thing to do, but it is highly unlikely that the programmer wanted that to happen.

The simplest way to prevent extension of the mapping is to implement a simple *nopage* method that always causes a bus signal to be sent to the faulting process. Such a method would look like this:

```
struct page *simple_nopage(struct vm_area_struct *vma,
                       unsigned long address, int write_access);
{ return NOPAGE_SIGBUS; /* send a SIGBUS */}
```

Remapping RAM

Of course, a more thorough implementation could check to see if the faulting address is within the device area, and perform the remapping if that is the case. Once again, however, *nopage* will not work with PCI memory areas, so extension of PCI mappings is not possible. In Linux, a page of physical addresses is marked as "reserved" in the memory map to indicate that it is not available for memory management. On the PC, for example, the range between 640 KB and 1 MB is marked as reserved, as are the pages that host the kernel code itself.

An interesting limitation of *remap_page_range* is that it gives access only to reserved pages and physical addresses above the top of physical memory. Reserved pages are locked in memory and are the only ones that can be safely mapped to user space; this limitation is a basic requirement for system stability.

Therefore, *remap_page_range* won't allow you to remap conventional addresses—which include the ones you obtain by calling *get_free_page*. Instead, it will map in the zero page. Nonetheless, the function does everything that most hardware drivers need it to, because it can remap high PCI buffers and ISA memory.

The limitations of *remap_page_range* can be seen by running *mapper*, one of the sample programs in *misc-progs* in the files provided on the O'Reilly FTP site. *mapper* is a simple tool that can be used to quickly test the *mmap* system call; it maps read-only parts of a file based on the command-line options and dumps the mapped region to standard output. The following session, for instance, shows that */dev/mem* doesn't map the physical page located at address 64 KB—instead we see a page full of zeros (the host computer in this examples is a PC, but the result would be the same on other platforms):

```
morgana.root# ./mapper /dev/mem 0x10000 0x1000 | od -Ax -t x1
mapped "/dev/mem" from 65536 to 69632
000000 00 00 00 00 00 00 00 00 00 00 00 00 00 00 00 00
*
001000
```

The inability of *remap_page_range* to deal with RAM suggests that a device like *scullp* can't easily implement *mmap*, because its device memory is conventional RAM, not I/O memory. Fortunately, a relatively easy workaround is available to any driver that needs to map RAM into user space; it uses the *nopage* method that we have seen earlier.

Remapping RAM with the nopage method

The way to map real RAM to user space is to use `vm_ops->nopage` to deal with page faults one at a time. A sample implementation is part of the *scullp* module, introduced in Chapter 7.

scullp is the page oriented char device. Because it is page oriented, it can implement *mmap* on its memory. The code implementing memory mapping uses some of the concepts introduced earlier in "Memory Management in Linux."

Before examining the code, let's look at the design choices that affect the *mmap* implementation in *scullp*.

- *scullp* doesn't release device memory as long as the device is mapped. This is a matter of policy rather than a requirement, and it is different from the behavior of *scull* and similar devices, which are truncated to a length of zero when opened for writing. Refusing to free a mapped *scullp* device allows a process to overwrite regions actively mapped by another process, so you can test and see how processes and device memory interact. To avoid releasing a mapped device, the driver must keep a count of active mappings; the `vmas` field in the device structure is used for this purpose.

- Memory mapping is performed only when the *scullp* `order` parameter is 0. The parameter controls how *get_free_pages* is invoked (see Chapter 7, "get_free_page and Friends"). This choice is dictated by the internals of *get_free_pages*, the allocation engine exploited by *scullp*. To maximize allocation performance, the Linux kernel maintains a list of free pages for each allocation order, and only the page count of the first page in a cluster is incremented by *get_free_pages* and decremented by *free_pages*. The *mmap* method is disabled for a *scullp* device if the allocation order is greater than zero, because *nopage* deals with single pages rather than clusters of pages. (Return to "A scull Using Whole Pages: scullp" in Chapter 7 if you need a refresher on *scullp* and the memory allocation order value.)

The last choice is mostly intended to keep the code simple. It *is* possible to correctly implement *mmap* for multipage allocations by playing with the usage count of the pages, but it would only add to the complexity of the example without introducing any interesting information.

Code that is intended to map RAM according to the rules just outlined needs to implement *open*, *close*, and *nopage*; it also needs to access the memory map to adjust the page usage counts.

This implementation of *scullp_mmap* is very short, because it relies on the *nopage* function to do all the interesting work:

```
int scullp_mmap(struct file *filp, struct vm_area_struct *vma)
{
    struct inode *inode = INODE_FROM_F(filp);

    /* refuse to map if order is not 0 */
    if (scullp_devices[MINOR(inode->i_rdev)].order)
        return -ENODEV;

    /* don't do anything here: "nopage" will fill the holes */
    vma->vm_ops = &scullp_vm_ops;
    vma->vm_flags |= VM_RESERVED;
    vma->vm_private_data = scullp_devices + MINOR(inode->i_rdev);
    scullp_vma_open(vma);
    return 0;
}
```

The purpose of the leading conditional is to avoid mapping devices whose allocation order is not 0. *scullp*'s operations are stored in the **vm_ops** field, and a pointer to the device structure is stashed in the **vm_private_data** field. At the end, **vm_ops->open** is called to update the usage count for the module and the count of active mappings for the device.

open and *close* simply keep track of these counts and are defined as follows:

```
void scullp_vma_open(struct vm_area_struct *vma)
{
    ScullP_Dev *dev = scullp_vma_to_dev(vma);

    dev->vmas++;
    MOD_INC_USE_COUNT;
}

void scullp_vma_close(struct vm_area_struct *vma)
{
    ScullP_Dev *dev = scullp_vma_to_dev(vma);

    dev->vmas--;
    MOD_DEC_USE_COUNT;
}
```

The function *sculls_vma_to_dev* simply returns the contents of the **vm_private_data** field. It exists as a separate function because kernel versions prior to 2.4 lacked that field, requiring that other means be used to get that pointer. See "Backward Compatibility" at the end of this chapter for details.

Most of the work is then performed by *nopage*. In the *scullp* implementation, the **address** parameter to *nopage* is used to calculate an offset into the device; the offset is then used to look up the correct page in the *scullp* memory tree.

```
struct page *scullp_vma_nopage(struct vm_area_struct *vma,
                               unsigned long address, int write)
{
    unsigned long offset;
    ScullP_Dev *ptr, *dev = scullp_vma_to_dev(vma);
    struct page *page = NOPAGE_SIGBUS;
    void *pageptr = NULL; /* default to "missing" */

    down(&dev->sem);
    offset = (address - vma->vm_start) + VMA_OFFSET(vma);
    if (offset >= dev->size) goto out; /* out of range */

    /*
     * Now retrieve the scullp device from the list, then the page.
     * If the device has holes, the process receives a SIGBUS when
     * accessing the hole.
     */
    offset >>= PAGE_SHIFT; /* offset is a number of pages */
    for (ptr = dev; ptr && offset >= dev->qset;) {
        ptr = ptr->next;
        offset -= dev->qset;
    }
    if (ptr && ptr->data) pageptr = ptr->data[offset];
    if (!pageptr) goto out; /* hole or end-of-file */
    page = virt_to_page(pageptr);

    /* got it, now increment the count */
```

```
        get_page(page);
out:
        up(&dev->sem);
        return page;
}
```

scullp uses memory obtained with *get_free_pages*. That memory is addressed using logical addresses, so all *scullp_nopage* has to do to get a `struct page` pointer is to call *virt_to_page*.

The *scullp* device now works as expected, as you can see in this sample output from the *mapper* utility. Here we send a directory listing of */dev* (which is long) to the *scullp* device, and then use the *mapper* utility to look at pieces of that listing with *mmap*.

```
morgana% ls -l /dev > /dev/scullp
morgana% ./mapper /dev/scullp 0 140
mapped "/dev/scullp" from 0 to 140
total 77
-rwxr-xr-x    1 root      root        26689 Mar   2   2000 MAKEDEV
crw-rw-rw-    1 root      root      14,   14 Aug 10 20:55 admmidi0
morgana% ./mapper /dev/scullp 8192 200
mapped "/dev/scullp" from 8192 to 8392
0
crw-----      1 root      root      113,   1 Mar 26   1999 cum1
crw-----      1 root      root      113,   2 Mar 26   1999 cum2
crw-----      1 root      root      113,   3 Mar 26   1999 cum3
```

Remapping Virtual Addresses

Although it's rarely necessary, it's interesting to see how a driver can map a virtual address to user space using *mmap*. A true virtual address, remember, is an address returned by a function like *vmalloc* or *kmap*—that is, a virtual address mapped in the kernel page tables. The code in this section is taken from *scullv*, which is the module that works like *scullp* but allocates its storage through *vmalloc*.

Most of the *scullv* implementation is like the one we've just seen for *scullp*, except that there is no need to check the `order` parameter that controls memory allocation. The reason for this is that *vmalloc* allocates its pages one at a time, because single-page allocations are far more likely to succeed than multipage allocations. Therefore, the allocation order problem doesn't apply to *vmalloc*ed space.

Most of the work of *vmalloc* is building page tables to access allocated pages as a continuous address range. The *nopage* method, instead, must pull the page tables back apart in order to return a `struct page` pointer to the caller. Therefore, the *nopage* implementation for *scullv* must scan the page tables to retrieve the page map entry associated with the page.

The function is similar to the one we saw for *scullp*, except at the end. This code excerpt only includes the part of *nopage* that differs from *scullp*:

```
pgd_t *pgd; pmd_t *pmd; pte_t *pte;
unsigned long lpage;

/*
 * After scullv lookup, "page" is now the address of the page
 * needed by the current process. Since it's a vmalloc address,
 * first retrieve the unsigned long value to be looked up
 * in page tables.
 */
lpage = VMALLOC_VMADDR(pageptr);
spin_lock(&init_mm.page_table_lock);
pgd = pgd_offset(&init_mm, lpage);
pmd = pmd_offset(pgd, lpage);
pte = pte_offset(pmd, lpage);
page = pte_page(*pte);
spin_unlock(&init_mm.page_table_lock);

/* got it, now increment the count */
get_page(page);
out:
up(&dev->sem);
return page;
```

The page tables are looked up using the functions introduced at the beginning of this chapter. The page directory used for this purpose is stored in the memory structure for kernel space, `init_mm`. Note that *scullv* obtains the `page_table_lock` prior to traversing the page tables. If that lock were not held, another processor could make a change to the page table while *scullv* was halfway through the lookup process, leading to erroneous results.

The macro `VMALLOC_VMADDR(pageptr)` returns the correct `unsigned long` value to be used in a page-table lookup from a *vmalloc* address. A simple cast of the value wouldn't work on the x86 with kernels older than 2.1, because of a glitch in memory management. Memory management for the x86 changed in version 2.1.1, and `VMALLOC_VMADDR` is now defined as the identity function, as it has always been for the other platforms. Its use is still suggested, however, as a way of writing portable code.

Based on this discussion, you might also want to map addresses returned by *ioremap* to user space. This mapping is easily accomplished because you can use *remap_page_range* directly, without implementing methods for virtual memory areas. In other words, *remap_page_range* is already usable for building new page tables that map I/O memory to user space; there's no need to look in the kernel page tables built by *vremap* as we did in *scullv*.

The kiobuf Interface

As of version 2.3.12, the Linux kernel supports an I/O abstraction called the *kernel I/O buffer*, or `kiobuf`. The kiobuf interface is intended to hide much of the complexity of the virtual memory system from device drivers (and other parts of the system that do I/O). Many features are planned for kiobufs, but their primary use in the 2.4 kernel is to facilitate the mapping of user-space buffers into the kernel.

The kiobuf Structure

Any code that works with kiobufs must include `<linux/iobuf.h>`. This file defines `struct kiobuf`, which is the heart of the kiobuf interface. This structure describes an array of pages that make up an I/O operation; its fields include the following:

`int nr_pages;`
　　The number of pages in this kiobuf

`int length;`
　　The number of bytes of data in the buffer

`int offset;`
　　The offset to the first valid byte in the buffer

`struct page **maplist;`
　　An array of `page` structures, one for each page of data in the kiobuf

The key to the kiobuf interface is the `maplist` array. Functions that operate on pages stored in a kiobuf deal directly with the `page` structures—all of the virtual memory system overhead has been moved out of the way. This implementation allows drivers to function independent of the complexities of memory management, and in general simplifies life greatly.

Prior to use, a kiobuf must be initialized. It is rare to initialize a single kiobuf in isolation, but, if need be, this initialization can be performed with *kiobuf_init*:

```
void kiobuf_init(struct kiobuf *iobuf);
```

Usually kiobufs are allocated in groups as part of a *kernel I/O vector*, or *kiovec*. A kiovec can be allocated and initialized in one step with a call to *alloc_kiovec*:

```
int alloc_kiovec(int nr, struct kiobuf **iovec);
```

The return value is 0 or an error code, as usual. When your code has finished with the kiovec structure, it should, of course, return it to the system:

```
void free_kiovec(int nr, struct kiobuf **);
```

The kernel provides a pair of functions for locking and unlocking the pages mapped in a kiovec:

```
int lock_kiovec(int nr, struct kiobuf *iovec[], int wait);
int unlock_kiovec(int nr, struct kiobuf *iovec[]);
```

Locking a kiovec in this manner is unnecessary, however, for most applications of kiobufs seen in device drivers.

Mapping User-Space Buffers and Raw I/O

Unix systems have long provided a "raw" interface to some devices—block devices in particular—which performs I/O directly from a user-space buffer and avoids copying data through the kernel. In some cases much improved performance can be had in this manner, especially if the data being transferred will not be used again in the near future. For example, disk backups typically read a great deal of data from the disk exactly once, then forget about it. Running the backup via a raw interface will avoid filling the system buffer cache with useless data.

The Linux kernel has traditionally not provided a raw interface, for a number of reasons. As the system gains in popularity, however, more applications that expect to be able to do raw I/O (such as large database management systems) are being ported. So the 2.3 development series finally added raw I/O; the driving force behind the kiobuf interface was the need to provide this capability.

Raw I/O is not always the great performance boost that some people think it should be, and driver writers should not rush out to add the capability just because they can. The overhead of setting up a raw transfer can be significant, and the advantages of buffering data in the kernel are lost. For example, note that raw I/O operations almost always must be synchronous—the *write* system call cannot return until the operation is complete. Linux currently lacks the mechanisms that user programs need to be able to safely perform asynchronous raw I/O on a user buffer.

In this section, we add a raw I/O capability to the *sbull* sample block driver. When kiobufs are available, *sbull* actually registers two devices. The block *sbull* device was examined in detail in Chapter 12. What we didn't see in that chapter was a second, char device (called *sbullr*), which provides raw access to the RAM-disk device. Thus, */dev/sbull0* and */dev/sbullr0* access the same memory; the former using the traditional, buffered mode and the second providing raw access via the kiobuf mechanism.

It is worth noting that in Linux systems, there is no need for block drivers to provide this sort of interface. The raw device, in *drivers/char/raw.c*, provides this capability in an elegant, general way for all block devices. The block drivers need not even know they are doing raw I/O. The raw I/O code in *sbull* is essentially a simplification of the raw device code for demonstration purposes.

Raw I/O to a block device must always be sector aligned, and its length must be a multiple of the sector size. Other kinds of devices, such as tape drives, may not have the same constraints. *sbullr* behaves like a block device and enforces the alignment and length requirements. To that end, it defines a few symbols:

```
#   define SBULLR_SECTOR 512   /* insist on this */
#   define SBULLR_SECTOR_MASK (SBULLR_SECTOR - 1)
#   define SBULLR_SECTOR_SHIFT 9
```

The *sbullr* raw device will be registered only if the hard-sector size is equal to SBULLR_SECTOR. There is no real reason why a larger hard-sector size could not be supported, but it would complicate the sample code unnecessarily.

The *sbullr* implementation adds little to the existing *sbull* code. In particular, the *open* and *close* methods from *sbull* are used without modification. Since *sbullr* is a char device, however, it needs *read* and *write* methods. Both are defined to use a single transfer function as follows:

```
ssize_t sbullr_read(struct file *filp, char *buf, size_t size,
                    loff_t *off)
{
    Sbull_Dev *dev = sbull_devices +
                    MINOR(filp->f_dentry->d_inode->i_rdev);
    return sbullr_transfer(dev, buf, size, off, READ);
}

ssize_t sbullr_write(struct file *filp, const char *buf, size_t size,
                    loff_t *off)
{
    Sbull_Dev *dev = sbull_devices +
                    MINOR(filp->f_dentry->d_inode->i_rdev);
    return sbullr_transfer(dev, (char *) buf, size, off, WRITE);
}
```

The *sbullr_transfer* function handles all of the setup and teardown work, while passing off the actual transfer of data to yet another function. It is written as follows:

```
static int sbullr_transfer (Sbull_Dev *dev, char *buf, size_t count,
                    loff_t *offset, int rw)
{
    struct kiobuf *iobuf;
    int result;

    /* Only block alignment and size allowed */
    if ((*offset & SBULLR_SECTOR_MASK) || (count & SBULLR_SECTOR_MASK))
        return -EINVAL;
    if ((unsigned long) buf & SBULLR_SECTOR_MASK)
        return -EINVAL;

    /* Allocate an I/O vector */
    result = alloc_kiovec(1, &iobuf);
```

```
    if (result)
        return result;

    /* Map the user I/O buffer and do the I/O. */
    result = map_user_kiobuf(rw, iobuf, (unsigned long) buf, count);
    if (result) {
        free_kiovec(1, &iobuf);
        return result;
    }
    spin_lock(&dev->lock);
    result = sbullr_rw_iovec(dev, iobuf, rw,
                    *offset >> SBULLR_SECTOR_SHIFT,
                    count >> SBULLR_SECTOR_SHIFT);
    spin_unlock(&dev->lock);

    /* Clean up and return. */
    unmap_kiobuf(iobuf);
    free_kiovec(1, &iobuf);
    if (result > 0)
        *offset += result << SBULLR_SECTOR_SHIFT;
    return result << SBULLR_SECTOR_SHIFT;
}
```

After doing a couple of sanity checks, the code creates a kiovec (containing a single kiobuf) with *alloc_kiovec*. It then uses that kiovec to map in the user buffer by calling *map_user_kiobuf*:

```
int map_user_kiobuf(int rw, struct kiobuf *iobuf,
                    unsigned long address, size_t len);
```

The result of this call, if all goes well, is that the buffer at the given (user virtual) **address** with length **len** is mapped into the given **iobuf**. This operation can sleep, since it is possible that part of the user buffer will need to be faulted into memory.

A kiobuf that has been mapped in this manner must eventually be unmapped, of course, to keep the reference counts on the pages straight. This unmapping is accomplished, as can be seen in the code, by passing the kiobuf to *unmap_kiobuf*.

So far, we have seen how to prepare a kiobuf for I/O, but not how to actually perform that I/O. The last step involves going through each page in the kiobuf and doing the required transfers; in *sbullr*, this task is handled by *sbullr_rw_iovec*. Essentially, this function passes through each page, breaks it up into sector-sized pieces, and passes them to *sbull_transfer* via a fake **request** structure:

```
static int sbullr_rw_iovec(Sbull_Dev *dev, struct kiobuf *iobuf, int rw,
                int sector, int nsectors)
{
    struct request fakereq;
    struct page *page;
    int offset = iobuf->offset, ndone = 0, pageno, result;
```

```
            /* Perform I/O on each sector */
            fakereq.sector = sector;
            fakereq.current_nr_sectors = 1;
            fakereq.cmd = rw;

            for (pageno = 0; pageno < iobuf->nr_pages; pageno++) {
                page = iobuf->maplist[pageno];
                while (ndone < nsectors) {
                    /* Fake up a request structure for the operation */
                    fakereq.buffer = (void *) (kmap(page) + offset);
                    result = sbull_transfer(dev, &fakereq);
                    kunmap(page);
                    if (result == 0)
                        return ndone;
                    /* Move on to the next one */
                    ndone++;
                    fakereq.sector++;
                    offset += SBULLR_SECTOR;
                    if (offset >= PAGE_SIZE) {
                        offset = 0;
                        break;
                    }
                }
            }
        }
        return ndone;
    }
```

Here, the `nr_pages` member of the `kiobuf` structure tells us how many pages need to be transferred, and the `maplist` array gives us access to each page. Thus it is just a matter of stepping through them all. Note, however, that *kmap* is used to get a kernel virtual address for each page; in this way, the function will work even if the user buffer is in high memory.

Some quick tests copying data show that a copy to or from an *sbullr* device takes roughly two-thirds the system time as the same copy to the block *sbull* device. The savings is gained by avoiding the extra copy through the buffer cache. Note that if the same data is read several times over, that savings will evaporate—especially for a real hardware device. Raw device access is often not the best approach, but for some applications it can be a major improvement.

Although kiobufs remain controversial in the kernel development community, there is interest in using them in a wider range of contexts. There is, for example, a patch that implements Unix pipes with kiobufs—data is copied directly from one process's address space to the other with no buffering in the kernel at all. A patch also exists that makes it easy to use a kiobuf to map kernel virtual memory into a process's address space, thus eliminating the need for a *nopage* implementation as shown earlier.

Direct Memory Access and Bus Mastering

Direct memory access, or DMA, is the advanced topic that completes our overview of memory issues. DMA is the hardware mechanism that allows peripheral components to transfer their I/O data directly to and from main memory without the need for the system processor to be involved in the transfer. Use of this mechanism can greatly increase throughput to and from a device, because a great deal of computational overhead is eliminated.

To exploit the DMA capabilities of its hardware, the device driver needs to be able to correctly set up the DMA transfer and synchronize with the hardware. Unfortunately, because of its hardware nature, DMA is very system dependent. Each architecture has its own techniques to manage DMA transfers, and the programming interface is different for each. The kernel can't offer a unified interface, either, because a driver can't abstract too much from the underlying hardware mechanisms. Some steps have been made in that direction, however, in recent kernels.

This chapter concentrates mainly on the PCI bus, since it is currently the most popular peripheral bus available. Many of the concepts are more widely applicable, though. We also touch on how some other buses, such as ISA and SBus, handle DMA.

Overview of a DMA Data Transfer

Before introducing the programming details, let's review how a DMA transfer takes place, considering only input transfers to simplify the discussion.

Data transfer can be triggered in two ways: either the software asks for data (via a function such as *read*) or the hardware asynchronously pushes data to the system.

In the first case, the steps involved can be summarized as follows:

1. When a process calls *read*, the driver method allocates a DMA buffer and instructs the hardware to transfer its data. The process is put to sleep.

2. The hardware writes data to the DMA buffer and raises an interrupt when it's done.

3. The interrupt handler gets the input data, acknowledges the interrupt, and awakens the process, which is now able to read data.

The second case comes about when DMA is used asynchronously. This happens, for example, with data acquisition devices that go on pushing data even if nobody is reading them. In this case, the driver should maintain a buffer so that a subsequent *read* call will return all the accumulated data to user space. The steps involved in this kind of transfer are slightly different:

1. The hardware raises an interrupt to announce that new data has arrived.

2. The interrupt handler allocates a buffer and tells the hardware where to transfer its data.

3. The peripheral device writes the data to the buffer and raises another interrupt when it's done.

4. The handler dispatches the new data, wakes any relevant process, and takes care of housekeeping.

A variant of the asynchronous approach is often seen with network cards. These cards often expect to see a circular buffer (often called a *DMA ring buffer*) established in memory shared with the processor; each incoming packet is placed in the next available buffer in the ring, and an interrupt is signaled. The driver then passes the network packets to the rest of the kernel, and places a new DMA buffer in the ring.

The processing steps in all of these cases emphasize that efficient DMA handling relies on interrupt reporting. While it is possible to implement DMA with a polling driver, it wouldn't make sense, because a polling driver would waste the performance benefits that DMA offers over the easier processor-driven I/O.

Another relevant item introduced here is the DMA buffer. To exploit direct memory access, the device driver must be able to allocate one or more special buffers, suited to DMA. Note that many drivers allocate their buffers at initialization time and use them until shutdown—the word *allocate* in the previous lists therefore means "get hold of a previously allocated buffer."

Allocating the DMA Buffer

This section covers the allocation of DMA buffers at a low level; we will introduce a higher-level interface shortly, but it is still a good idea to understand the material presented here.

The main problem with the DMA buffer is that when it is bigger than one page, it must occupy contiguous pages in physical memory because the device transfers data using the ISA or PCI system bus, both of which carry physical addresses. It's interesting to note that this constraint doesn't apply to the SBus (see "SBus" in Chapter 15), which uses virtual addresses on the peripheral bus. Some architectures *can* also use virtual addresses on the PCI bus, but a portable driver cannot count on that capability.

Although DMA buffers can be allocated either at system boot or at runtime, modules can only allocate their buffers at runtime. Chapter 7 introduced these techniques: "Boot-Time Allocation" talked about allocation at system boot, while "The Real Story of kmalloc" and "get_free_page and Friends" described allocation at runtime. Driver writers must take care to allocate the right kind of memory when it will be used for DMA operations—not all memory zones are suitable. In particular, high memory will not work for DMA on most systems—the peripherals simply cannot work with addresses that high.

Most devices on modern buses can handle 32-bit addresses, meaning that normal memory allocations will work just fine for them. Some PCI devices, however, fail to implement the full PCI standard and cannot work with 32-bit addresses. And ISA devices, of course, are limited to 16-bit addresses only.

For devices with this kind of limitation, memory should be allocated from the DMA zone by adding the `GFP_DMA` flag to the *kmalloc* or *get_free_pages* call. When this flag is present, only memory that can be addressed with 16 bits will be allocated.

Do-it-yourself allocation

We have seen how *get_free_pages* (and therefore *kmalloc*) can't return more than 128 KB (or, more generally, 32 pages) of consecutive memory space. But the request is prone to fail even when the allocated buffer is less than 128 KB, because system memory becomes fragmented over time.*

When the kernel cannot return the requested amount of memory, or when you need more than 128 KB (a common requirement for PCI frame grabbers, for example), an alternative to returning `-ENOMEM` is to allocate memory at boot time or reserve the top of physical RAM for your buffer. We described allocation at boot time in "Boot-Time Allocation" in Chapter 7, but it is not available to modules. Reserving the top of RAM is accomplished by passing a `mem=` argument to the kernel at boot time. For example, if you have 32 MB, the argument `mem=31M` keeps the kernel from using the top megabyte. Your module could later use the following code to gain access to such memory:

```
dmabuf = ioremap( 0x1F00000 /* 31M */, 0x100000 /* 1M */);
```

Actually, there is another way to allocate DMA space: perform aggressive allocation until you are able to get enough consecutive pages to make a buffer. We strongly discourage this allocation technique if there's any other way to achieve your goal. Aggressive allocation results in high machine load, and possibly in a system lockup if your aggressiveness isn't correctly tuned. On the other hand, sometimes there is no other way available.

In practice, the code invokes `kmalloc(GFP_ATOMIC)` until the call fails; it then waits until the kernel frees some pages, and then allocates everything once again.

---

* The word *fragmentation* is usually applied to disks, to express the idea that files are not stored consecutively on the magnetic medium. The same concept applies to memory, where each virtual address space gets scattered throughout physical RAM, and it becomes difficult to retrieve consecutive free pages when a DMA buffer is requested.

If you keep an eye on the pool of allocated pages, sooner or later you'll find that your DMA buffer of consecutive pages has appeared; at this point you can release every page but the selected buffer. This kind of behavior is rather risky, though, because it may lead to a deadlock. We suggest using a kernel timer to release every page in case allocation doesn't succeed before a timeout expires.

We're not going to show the code here, but you'll find it in *misc-modules/allocator.c*; the code is thoroughly commented and designed to be called by other modules. Unlike every other source accompanying this book, the allocator is covered by the GPL. The reason we decided to put the source under the GPL is that it is neither particularly beautiful nor particularly clever, and if someone is going to use it, we want to be sure that the source is released with the module.

Bus Addresses

A device driver using DMA has to talk to hardware connected to the interface bus, which uses physical addresses, whereas program code uses virtual addresses.

As a matter of fact, the situation is slightly more complicated than that. DMA-based hardware uses *bus*, rather than *physical*, addresses. Although ISA and PCI addresses are simply physical addresses on the PC, this is not true for every platform. Sometimes the interface bus is connected through bridge circuitry that maps I/O addresses to different physical addresses. Some systems even have a page-mapping scheme that can make arbitrary pages appear contiguous to the peripheral bus.

At the lowest level (again, we'll look at a higher-level solution shortly), the Linux kernel provides a portable solution by exporting the following functions, defined in <asm/io.h>:

```
unsigned long virt_to_bus(volatile void * address);
void * bus_to_virt(unsigned long address);
```

The *virt_to_bus* conversion must be used when the driver needs to send address information to an I/O device (such as an expansion board or the DMA controller), while *bus_to_virt* must be used when address information is received from hardware connected to the bus.

DMA on the PCI Bus

The 2.4 kernel includes a flexible mechanism that supports PCI DMA (also known as *bus mastering*). It handles the details of buffer allocation and can deal with setting up the bus hardware for multipage transfers on hardware that supports them. This code also takes care of situations in which a buffer lives in a non-DMA-capable zone of memory, though only on some platforms and at a computational cost (as we will see later).

The functions in this section require a `struct pci_dev` structure for your device. The details of setting up a PCI device are covered in Chapter 15. Note, however, that the routines described here can also be used with ISA devices; in that case, the `struct pci_dev` pointer should simply be passed in as `NULL`.

Drivers that use the following functions should include `<linux/pci.h>`.

Dealing with difficult hardware

The first question that must be answered before performing DMA is whether the given device is capable of such operation on the current host. Many PCI devices fail to implement the full 32-bit bus address space, often because they are modified versions of old ISA hardware. The Linux kernel will attempt to work with such devices, but it is not always possible.

The function *pci_dma_supported* should be called for any device that has addressing limitations:

```
int pci_dma_supported(struct pci_dev *pdev, dma_addr_t mask);
```

Here, `mask` is a simple bit mask describing which address bits the device can successfully use. If the return value is nonzero, DMA is possible, and your driver should set the `dma_mask` field in the PCI device structure to the mask value. For a device that can only handle 16-bit addresses, you might use a call like this:

```
if (pci_dma_supported (pdev, 0xffff))
    pdev->dma_mask = 0xffff;
else {
    card->use_dma = 0;    /* We'll have to live without DMA */
    printk (KERN_WARN, "mydev: DMA not supported\n");
}
```

As of kernel 2.4.3, a new function, *pci_set_dma_mask*, has been provided. This function has the following prototype:

```
int pci_set_dma_mask(struct pci_dev *pdev, dma_addr_t mask);
```

If DMA can be supported with the given mask, this function returns 0 and sets the `dma_mask` field; otherwise, `-EIO` is returned.

For devices that can handle 32-bit addresses, there is no need to call *pci_dma_supported*.

DMA mappings

A *DMA mapping* is a combination of allocating a DMA buffer and generating an address for that buffer that is accessible by the device. In many cases, getting that address involves a simple call to *virt_to_bus*; some hardware, however, requires that *mapping registers* be set up in the bus hardware as well. Mapping registers are an equivalent of virtual memory for peripherals. On systems where these registers are used, peripherals have a relatively small, dedicated range of addresses to which they may perform DMA. Those addresses are remapped, via the mapping registers, into system RAM. Mapping registers have some nice features, including the ability to make several distributed pages appear contiguous in the device's address space. Not all architectures have mapping registers, however; in particular, the popular PC platform has no mapping registers.

Setting up a useful address for the device may also, in some cases, require the establishment of a *bounce buffer*. Bounce buffers are created when a driver attempts to perform DMA on an address that is not reachable by the peripheral device—a high-memory address, for example. Data is then copied to and from the bounce buffer as needed. Making code work properly with bounce buffers requires adherence to some rules, as we will see shortly.

The DMA mapping sets up a new type, `dma_addr_t`, to represent bus addresses. Variables of type `dma_addr_t` should be treated as opaque by the driver; the only allowable operations are to pass them to the DMA support routines and to the device itself.

The PCI code distinguishes between two types of DMA mappings, depending on how long the DMA buffer is expected to stay around:

Consistent DMA mappings
> These exist for the life of the driver. A consistently mapped buffer must be simultaneously available to both the CPU and the peripheral (other types of mappings, as we will see later, can be available only to one or the other at any given time). The buffer should also, if possible, not have caching issues that could cause one not to see updates made by the other.

Streaming DMA mappings
> These are set up for a single operation. Some architectures allow for significant optimizations when streaming mappings are used, as we will see, but these mappings also are subject to a stricter set of rules in how they may be accessed. The kernel developers recommend the use of streaming mappings over consistent mappings whenever possible. There are two reasons for this recommendation. The first is that, on systems that support them, each DMA mapping uses one or more mapping registers on the bus. Consistent mappings, which have a long lifetime, can monopolize these registers for a long time, even when they are not being used. The other reason is that, on some hardware, streaming mappings can be optimized in ways that are not available to consistent mappings.

The two mapping types must be manipulated in different ways; it's time to look at the details.

Setting up consistent DMA mappings

A driver can set up a consistent mapping with a call to *pci_alloc_consistent*:

```
void *pci_alloc_consistent(struct pci_dev *pdev, size_t size,
                           dma_addr_t *bus_addr);
```

This function handles both the allocation and the mapping of the buffer. The first two arguments are our PCI device structure and the size of the needed buffer. The function returns the result of the DMA mapping in two places. The return value is a kernel virtual address for the buffer, which may be used by the driver; the associated bus address, instead, is returned in **bus_addr**. Allocation is handled in this function so that the buffer will be placed in a location that works with DMA; usually the memory is just allocated with *get_free_pages* (but note that the size is in bytes, rather than an order value).

Most architectures that support PCI perform the allocation at the **GFP_ATOMIC** priority, and thus do not sleep. The ARM port, however, is an exception to this rule.

When the buffer is no longer needed (usually at module unload time), it should be returned to the system with *pci_free_consistent*:

```
void pci_free_consistent(struct pci_dev *pdev, size_t size,
                         void *cpu_addr, dma_handle_t bus_addr);
```

Note that this function requires that both the CPU address and the bus address be provided.

Setting up streaming DMA mappings

Streaming mappings have a more complicated interface than the consistent variety, for a number of reasons. These mappings expect to work with a buffer that has already been allocated by the driver, and thus have to deal with addresses that they did not choose. On some architectures, streaming mappings can also have multiple, discontiguous pages and multipart "scatter-gather" buffers.

When setting up a streaming mapping, you must tell the kernel in which direction the data will be moving. Some symbols have been defined for this purpose:

PCI_DMA_TODEVICE
PCI_DMA_FROMDEVICE
These two symbols should be reasonably self-explanatory. If data is being sent to the device (in response, perhaps, to a *write* system call), **PCI_DMA_TODEVICE** should be used; data going to the CPU, instead, will be marked with **PCI_DMA_FROMDEVICE**.

PCI_DMA_BIDIRECTIONAL

If data can move in either direction, use **PCI_DMA_BIDIRECTIONAL**.

PCI_DMA_NONE

This symbol is provided only as a debugging aid. Attempts to use buffers with this "direction" will cause a kernel panic.

For a number of reasons that we will touch on shortly, it is important to pick the right value for the direction of a streaming DMA mapping. It may be tempting to just pick **PCI_DMA_BIDIRECTIONAL** at all times, but on some architectures there will be a performance penalty to pay for that choice.

When you have a single buffer to transfer, map it with *pci_map_single*:

```
dma_addr_t pci_map_single(struct pci_dev *pdev, void *buffer,
                          size_t size, int direction);
```

The return value is the bus address that you can pass to the device, or **NULL** if something goes wrong.

Once the transfer is complete, the mapping should be deleted with *pci_unmap_single*:

```
void pci_unmap_single(struct pci_dev *pdev, dma_addr_t bus_addr,
                      size_t size, int direction);
```

Here, the **size** and **direction** arguments must match those used to map the buffer.

There are some important rules that apply to streaming DMA mappings:

- The buffer must be used only for a transfer that matches the direction value given when it was mapped.

- Once a buffer has been mapped, it belongs to the device, not the processor. Until the buffer has been unmapped, the driver should not touch its contents in any way. Only after *pci_unmap_single* has been called is it safe for the driver to access the contents of the buffer (with one exception that we'll see shortly). Among other things, this rule implies that a buffer being written to a device cannot be mapped until it contains all the data to write.

- The buffer must not be unmapped while DMA is still active, or serious system instability is guaranteed.

You may be wondering why the driver can no longer work with a buffer once it has been mapped. There are actually two reasons why this rule makes sense. First, when a buffer is mapped for DMA, the kernel must ensure that all of the data in that buffer has actually been written to memory. It is likely that some data will remain in the processor's cache, and must be explicitly flushed. Data written to the buffer by the processor after the flush may not be visible to the device.

Second, consider what happens if the buffer to be mapped is in a region of memory that is not accessible to the device. Some architectures will simply fail in this case, but others will create a bounce buffer. The bounce buffer is just a separate region of memory that *is* accessible to the device. If a buffer is mapped with a direction of PCI_DMA_TODEVICE, and a bounce buffer is required, the contents of the original buffer will be copied as part of the mapping operation. Clearly, changes to the original buffer after the copy will not be seen by the device. Similarly, PCI_DMA_FROMDEVICE bounce buffers are copied back to the original buffer by *pci_unmap_single*; the data from the device is not present until that copy has been done.

Incidentally, bounce buffers are one reason why it is important to get the direction right. PCI_DMA_BIDIRECTIONAL bounce buffers are copied before and after the operation, which is often an unnecessary waste of CPU cycles.

Occasionally a driver will need to access the contents of a streaming DMA buffer without unmapping it. A call has been provided to make this possible:

```
void pci_sync_single(struct pci_dev *pdev, dma_handle_t bus_addr,
                     size_t size, int direction);
```

This function should be called *before* the processor accesses a PCI_DMA_FROMDEVICE buffer, and *after* an access to a PCI_DMA_TODEVICE buffer.

Scatter-gather mappings

Scatter-gather mappings are a special case of streaming DMA mappings. Suppose you have several buffers, all of which need to be transferred to or from the device. This situation can come about in several ways, including from a *readv* or *writev* system call, a clustered disk I/O request, or a list of pages in a mapped kernel I/O buffer. You could simply map each buffer in turn and perform the required operation, but there are advantages to mapping the whole list at once.

One reason is that some smart devices can accept a *scatterlist* of array pointers and lengths and transfer them all in one DMA operation; for example, "zero-copy" networking is easier if packets can be built in multiple pieces. Linux is likely to take much better advantage of such devices in the future. Another reason to map scatterlists as a whole is to take advantage of systems that have mapping registers in the bus hardware. On such systems, physically discontiguous pages can be assembled into a single, contiguous array from the device's point of view. This technique works only when the entries in the scatterlist are equal to the page size in length (except the first and last), but when it does work it can turn multiple operations into a single DMA and speed things up accordingly.

Finally, if a bounce buffer must be used, it makes sense to coalesce the entire list into a single buffer (since it is being copied anyway).

So now you're convinced that mapping of scatterlists is worthwhile in some situations. The first step in mapping a scatterlist is to create and fill in an array of `struct scatterlist` describing the buffers to be transferred. This structure is architecture dependent, and is described in `<linux/scatterlist.h>`. It will always contain two fields, however:

`char *address;`
> The address of a buffer used in the scatter/gather operation

`unsigned int length;`
> The length of that buffer

To map a scatter/gather DMA operation, your driver should set the `address` and `length` fields in a `struct scatterlist` entry for each buffer to be transferred. Then call:

```
int pci_map_sg(struct pci_dev *pdev, struct scatterlist *list,
               int nents, int direction);
```

The return value will be the number of DMA buffers to transfer; it may be less than `nents`, the number of scatterlist entries passed in.

Your driver should transfer each buffer returned by *pci_map_sg*. The bus address and length of each buffer will be stored in the `struct scatterlist` entries, but their location in the structure varies from one architecture to the next. Two macros have been defined to make it possible to write portable code:

`dma_addr_t sg_dma_address(struct scatterlist *sg);`
> Returns the bus (DMA) address from this scatterlist entry

`unsigned int sg_dma_len(struct scatterlist *sg);`
> Returns the length of this buffer

Again, remember that the address and length of the buffers to transfer may be different from what was passed in to *pci_map_sg*.

Once the transfer is complete, a scatter-gather mapping is unmapped with a call to *pci_unmap_sg*:

```
void pci_unmap_sg(struct pci_dev *pdev, struct scatterlist *list,
                  int nents, int direction);
```

Note that `nents` must be the number of entries that you originally passed to *pci_map_sg*, and not the number of DMA buffers that function returned to you.

Scatter-gather mappings are streaming DMA mappings, and the same access rules apply to them as to the single variety. If you must access a mapped scatter-gather list, you must synchronize it first:

```
void pci_dma_sync_sg(struct pci_dev *pdev, struct scatterlist *sg,
                     int nents, int direction);
```

How different architectures support PCI DMA

As we stated at the beginning of this section, DMA is a very hardware-specific operation. The PCI DMA interface we have just described attempts to abstract out as many hardware dependencies as possible. There are still some things that show through, however.

M68K
S/390
Super-H

These architectures do not support the PCI bus as of 2.4.0.

IA-32 (x86)
MIPS
PowerPC
ARM

These platforms support the PCI DMA interface, but it is mostly a false front. There are no mapping registers in the bus interface, so scatterlists cannot be combined and virtual addresses cannot be used. There is no bounce buffer support, so mapping of high-memory addresses cannot be done. The mapping functions on the ARM architecture can sleep, which is not the case for the other platforms.

IA-64

The Itanium architecture also lacks mapping registers. This 64-bit architecture can easily generate addresses that PCI peripherals cannot use, though. The PCI interface on this platform thus implements bounce buffers, allowing any address to be (seemingly) used for DMA operations.

Alpha
MIPS64
SPARC

These architectures support an I/O memory management unit. As of 2.4.0, the MIPS64 port does not actually make use of this capability, so its PCI DMA implementation looks like that of the IA-32. The Alpha and SPARC ports, though, can do full-buffer mapping with proper scatter-gather support.

The differences listed will not be problems for most driver writers, as long as the interface guidelines are followed.

A simple PCI DMA example

The actual form of DMA operations on the PCI bus is very dependent on the device being driven. Thus, this example does not apply to any real device; instead, it is part of a hypothetical driver called *dad* (DMA Acquisition Device). A driver for this device might define a transfer function like this:

```
int dad_transfer(struct dad_dev *dev, int write, void *buffer,
                 size_t count)
{
    dma_addr_t bus_addr;
    unsigned long flags;

    /* Map the buffer for DMA */
    dev->dma_dir = (write ? PCI_DMA_TODEVICE : PCI_DMA_FROMDEVICE);
    dev->dma_size = count;
    bus_addr = pci_map_single(dev->pci_dev, buffer, count,
                              dev->dma_dir);
    dev->dma_addr = bus_addr;

    /* Set up the device */
    writeb(dev->registers.command, DAD_CMD_DISABLEDMA);
    writeb(dev->registers.command, write ? DAD_CMD_WR : DAD_CMD_RD);
    writel(dev->registers.addr, cpu_to_le32(bus_addr));
    writel(dev->registers.len, cpu_to_le32(count));

    /* Start the operation */
    writeb(dev->registers.command, DAD_CMD_ENABLEDMA);
    return 0;
}
```

This function maps the buffer to be transferred and starts the device operation. The other half of the job must be done in the interrupt service routine, which would look something like this:

```
void dad_interrupt(int irq, void *dev_id, struct pt_regs *regs)
{
    struct dad_dev *dev = (struct dad_dev *) dev_id;

    /* Make sure it's really our device interrupting */

    /* Unmap the DMA buffer */
    pci_unmap_single(dev->pci_dev, dev->dma_addr, dev->dma_size,
                     dev->dma_dir);

    /* Only now is it safe to access the buffer, copy to user, etc. */
    ...
}
```

Obviously a great deal of detail has been left out of this example, including whatever steps may be required to prevent attempts to start multiple simultaneous DMA operations.

A quick look at SBus

SPARC-based systems have traditionally included a Sun-designed bus called the SBus. This bus is beyond the scope of this chapter, but a quick mention is worthwhile. There is a set of functions (declared in <asm/sbus.h>) for performing DMA mappings on the SBus; they have names like *sbus_alloc_consistent* and *sbus_map_sg.* In other words, the SBus DMA API looks almost exactly like the PCI interface. A detailed look at the function definitions will be required before working with DMA on the SBus, but the concepts will match those discussed earlier for the PCI bus.

DMA for ISA Devices

The ISA bus allows for two kinds of DMA transfers: native DMA and ISA bus master DMA. Native DMA uses standard DMA-controller circuitry on the motherboard to drive the signal lines on the ISA bus. ISA bus master DMA, on the other hand, is handled entirely by the peripheral device. The latter type of DMA is rarely used and doesn't require discussion here because it is similar to DMA for PCI devices, at least from the driver's point of view. An example of an ISA bus master is the 1542 SCSI controller, whose driver is *drivers/scsi/aha1542.c* in the kernel sources.

As far as native DMA is concerned, there are three entities involved in a DMA data transfer on the ISA bus:

The 8237 DMA controller (DMAC)
> The controller holds information about the DMA transfer, such as the direction, the memory address, and the size of the transfer. It also contains a counter that tracks the status of ongoing transfers. When the controller receives a DMA request signal, it gains control of the bus and drives the signal lines so that the device can read or write its data.

The peripheral device
> The device must activate the DMA request signal when it's ready to transfer data. The actual transfer is managed by the DMAC; the hardware device sequentially reads or writes data onto the bus when the controller strobes the device. The device usually raises an interrupt when the transfer is over.

The device driver
> The driver has little to do: it provides the DMA controller with the direction, bus address, and size of the transfer. It also talks to its peripheral to prepare it for transferring the data and responds to the interrupt when the DMA is over.

The original DMA controller used in the PC could manage four "channels," each associated with one set of DMA registers. Four devices could store their DMA information in the controller at the same time. Newer PCs contain the equivalent of two DMAC devices:* the second controller (master) is connected to the system processor, and the first (slave) is connected to channel 0 of the second controller.†

---

* These circuits are now part of the motherboard's chipset, but a few years ago they were two separate 8237 chips.

† The original PCs had only one controller; the second was added in 286-based platforms. However, the second controller is connected as the master because it handles 16-bit transfers; the first transfers only 8 bits at a time and is there for backward compatibility.

The channels are numbered from 0 to 7; channel 4 is not available to ISA peripherals because it is used internally to cascade the slave controller onto the master. The available channels are thus 0 to 3 on the slave (the 8-bit channels) and 5 to 7 on the master (the 16-bit channels). The size of any DMA transfer, as stored in the controller, is a 16-bit number representing the number of bus cycles. The maximum transfer size is therefore 64 KB for the slave controller and 128 KB for the master.

Because the DMA controller is a system-wide resource, the kernel helps deal with it. It uses a DMA registry to provide a request-and-free mechanism for the DMA channels and a set of functions to configure channel information in the DMA controller.

Registering DMA usage

You should be used to kernel registries—we've already seen them for I/O ports and interrupt lines. The DMA channel registry is similar to the others. After `<asm/dma.h>` has been included, the following functions can be used to obtain and release ownership of a DMA channel:

```
int request_dma(unsigned int channel, const char *name);
void free_dma(unsigned int channel);
```

The `channel` argument is a number between 0 and 7 or, more precisely, a positive number less than `MAX_DMA_CHANNELS`. On the PC, `MAX_DMA_CHANNELS` is defined as 8, to match the hardware. The `name` argument is a string identifying the device. The specified name appears in the file */proc/dma*, which can be read by user programs.

The return value from *request_dma* is 0 for success and `-EINVAL` or `-EBUSY` if there was an error. The former means that the requested channel is out of range, and the latter means that another device is holding the channel.

We recommend that you take the same care with DMA channels as with I/O ports and interrupt lines; requesting the channel at *open* time is much better than requesting it from the module initialization function. Delaying the request allows some sharing between drivers; for example, your sound card and your analog I/O interface can share the DMA channel as long as they are not used at the same time.

We also suggest that you request the DMA channel *after* you've requested the interrupt line and that you release it *before* the interrupt. This is the conventional order for requesting the two resources; following the convention avoids possible deadlocks. Note that every device using DMA needs an IRQ line as well; otherwise, it couldn't signal the completion of data transfer.

In a typical case, the code for *open* looks like the following, which refers to our hypothetical *dad* module. The *dad* device as shown uses a fast interrupt handler without support for shared IRQ lines.

```
int dad_open (struct inode *inode, struct file *filp)
{
    struct dad_device *my_device;

    /* ... */
    if ( (error = request_irq(my_device.irq, dad_interrupt,
                             SA_INTERRUPT, "dad", NULL)) )
        return error; /* or implement blocking open */

    if ( (error = request_dma(my_device.dma, "dad")) ) {
        free_irq(my_device.irq, NULL);
        return error; /* or implement blocking open */
    }
    /* ... */
    return 0;
}
```

The *close* implementation that matches the *open* just shown looks like this:

```
void dad_close (struct inode *inode, struct file *filp)
{
    struct dad_device *my_device;

    /* ... */
    free_dma(my_device.dma);
    free_irq(my_device.irq, NULL);
    /* ... */
}
```

As far as */proc/dma* is concerned, here's how the file looks on a system with the sound card installed:

```
merlino% cat /proc/dma
 1: Sound Blaster8
 4: cascade
```

It's interesting to note that the default sound driver gets the DMA channel at system boot and never releases it. The `cascade` entry shown is a placeholder, indicating that channel 4 is not available to drivers, as explained earlier.

Talking to the DMA controller

After registration, the main part of the driver's job consists of configuring the DMA controller for proper operation. This task is not trivial, but fortunately the kernel exports all the functions needed by the typical driver.

The driver needs to configure the DMA controller either when *read* or *write* is called, or when preparing for asynchronous transfers. This latter task is performed either at *open* time or in response to an *ioctl* command, depending on the driver and the policy it implements. The code shown here is the code that is typically called by the *read* or *write* device methods.

This subsection provides a quick overview of the internals of the DMA controller so you will understand the code introduced here. If you want to learn more, we'd urge you to read <asm/dma.h> and some hardware manuals describing the PC architecture. In particular, we don't deal with the issue of 8-bit versus 16-bit data transfers. If you are writing device drivers for ISA device boards, you should find the relevant information in the hardware manuals for the devices.

The DMA controller is a shared resource, and confusion could arise if more than one processor attempts to program it simultaneously. For that reason, the controller is protected by a spinlock, called **dma_spin_lock**. Drivers should not manipulate the lock directly, however; two functions have been provided to do that for you:

unsigned long claim_dma_lock();
> Acquires the DMA spinlock. This function also blocks interrupts on the local processor; thus the return value is the usual "flags" value, which must be used when reenabling interrupts.

void release_dma_lock(unsigned long flags);
> Returns the DMA spinlock and restores the previous interrupt status.

The spinlock should be held when using the functions described next. It should *not* be held during the actual I/O, however. A driver should never sleep when holding a spinlock.

The information that must be loaded into the controller is made up of three items: the RAM address, the number of atomic items that must be transferred (in bytes or words), and the direction of the transfer. To this end, the following functions are exported by <asm/dma.h>:

void set_dma_mode(unsigned int channel, char mode);
> Indicates whether the channel must read from the device (DMA_MODE_READ) or write to it (DMA_MODE_WRITE). A third mode exists, DMA_MODE_CAS-CADE, which is used to release control of the bus. Cascading is the way the first controller is connected to the top of the second, but it can also be used by true ISA bus-master devices. We won't discuss bus mastering here.

void set_dma_addr(unsigned int channel, unsigned int addr);
> Assigns the address of the DMA buffer. The function stores the 24 least significant bits of addr in the controller. The addr argument must be a *bus* address (see "Bus Addresses" earlier in this chapter).

```
void set_dma_count(unsigned int channel, unsigned int
     count);
```
Assigns the number of bytes to transfer. The count argument represents bytes for 16-bit channels as well; in this case, the number *must* be even.

In addition to these functions, there are a number of housekeeping facilities that must be used when dealing with DMA devices:

```
void disable_dma(unsigned int channel);
```
A DMA channel can be disabled within the controller. The channel should be disabled before the controller is configured, to prevent improper operation (the controller is programmed via eight-bit data transfers, and thus none of the previous functions is executed atomically).

```
void enable_dma(unsigned int channel);
```
This function tells the controller that the DMA channel contains valid data.

```
int get_dma_residue(unsigned int channel);
```
The driver sometimes needs to know if a DMA transfer has been completed. This function returns the number of bytes that are still to be transferred. The return value is 0 after a successful transfer and is unpredictable (but not 0) while the controller is working. The unpredictability reflects the fact that the residue is a 16-bit value, which is obtained by two 8-bit input operations.

```
void clear_dma_ff(unsigned int channel)
```
This function clears the DMA flip-flop. The flip-flop is used to control access to 16-bit registers. The registers are accessed by two consecutive 8-bit operations, and the flip-flop is used to select the least significant byte (when it is clear) or the most significant byte (when it is set). The flip-flop automatically toggles when 8 bits have been transferred; the programmer must clear the flip-flop (to set it to a known state) before accessing the DMA registers.

Using these functions, a driver can implement a function like the following to prepare for a DMA transfer:

```
int dad_dma_prepare(int channel, int mode, unsigned int buf,
                    unsigned int count)
{
    unsigned long flags;

    flags = claim_dma_lock();
    disable_dma(channel);
    clear_dma_ff(channel);
    set_dma_mode(channel, mode);
    set_dma_addr(channel, virt_to_bus(buf));
    set_dma_count(channel, count);
    enable_dma(channel);
    release_dma_lock(flags);
```

```
        return 0;
    }
```

A function like the next one, then, is used to check for successful completion of DMA:

```
int dad_dma_isdone(int channel)
{
    int residue;
    unsigned long flags = claim_dma_lock ();
    residue = get_dma_residue(channel);
    release_dma_lock(flags);
    return (residue == 0);
}
```

The only thing that remains to be done is to configure the device board. This device-specific task usually consists of reading or writing a few I/O ports. Devices differ in significant ways. For example, some devices expect the programmer to tell the hardware how big the DMA buffer is, and sometimes the driver has to read a value that is hardwired into the device. For configuring the board, the hardware manual is your only friend.

Backward Compatibility

As with other parts of the kernel, both memory mapping and DMA have seen a number of changes over the years. This section describes the things a driver writer must take into account in order to write portable code.

Changes to Memory Management

The 2.3 development series saw major changes in the way memory management worked. The 2.2 kernel was quite limited in the amount of memory it could use, especially on 32-bit processors. With 2.4, those limits have been lifted; Linux is now able to manage all the memory that the processor is able to address. Some things have had to change to make all this possible; overall, however, the scale of the changes at the API level is surprisingly small.

As we have seen, the 2.4 kernel makes extensive use of pointers to **struct page** to refer to specific pages in memory. This structure has been present in Linux for a long time, but it was not previously used to refer to the pages themselves; instead, the kernel used logical addresses.

Thus, for example, *pte_page* returned an **unsigned long** value instead of **struct page ***. The *virt_to_page* macro did not exist at all; if you needed to find a **struct page** entry you had to go directly to the memory map to get it. The macro **MAP_NR** would turn a logical address into an index in **mem_map**; thus, the current *virt_to_page* macro could be defined (and, in *sysdep.h* in the sample code, is defined) as follows:

```
#ifdef MAP_NR
#define virt_to_page(page) (mem_map + MAP_NR(page))
#endif
```

The **MAP_NR** macro went away when *virt_to_page* was introduced. The *get_page* macro also didn't exist prior to 2.4, so *sysdep.h* defines it as follows:

```
#ifndef get_page
#  define get_page(p) atomic_inc(&(p)->count)
#endif
```

struct page has also changed with time; in particular, the **virtual** field is present in Linux 2.4 only.

The **page_table_lock** was introduced in 2.3.10. Earlier code would obtain the "big kernel lock" (by calling *lock_kernel* and *unlock_kernel*) before traversing page tables.

The **vm_area_struct** structure saw a number of changes in the 2.3 development series, and more in 2.1. These included the following:

- The **vm_pgoff** field was called **vm_offset** in 2.2 and before. It was an offset in bytes, not pages.

- The **vm_private_data** field did not exist in Linux 2.2, so drivers had no way of storing their own information in the VMA. A number of them did so anyway, using the **vm_pte** field, but it would be safer to obtain the minor device number from **vm_file** and use it to retrieve the needed information.

- The 2.4 kernel initializes the **vm_file** pointer before calling the *mmap* method. In 2.2, drivers had to assign that value themselves, using the **file** structure passed in as an argument.

- The **vm_file** pointer did not exist at all in 2.0 kernels; instead, there was a **vm_inode** pointer pointing to the **inode** structure. This field needed to be assigned by the driver; it was also necessary to increment **inode->i_count** in the *mmap* method.

- The **VM_RESERVED** flag was added in kernel 2.4.0-test10.

There have also been changes to the the various **vm_ops** methods stored in the VMA:

- 2.2 and earlier kernels had a method called *advise*, which was never actually used by the kernel. There was also a *swapin* method, which was used to bring in memory from backing store; it was not generally of interest to driver writers.

- The *nopage* and *wppage* methods returned **unsigned long** (i.e., a logical address) in 2.2, rather than **struct page ***.

- The `NOPAGE_SIGBUS` and `NOPAGE_OOM` return codes for *nopage* did not exist. *nopage* simply returned 0 to indicate a problem and send a bus signal to the affected process.

Because *nopage* used to return `unsigned long`, its job was to return the logical address of the page of interest, rather than its `mem_map` entry.

There was, of course, no high-memory support in older kernels. All memory had logical addresses, and the *kmap* and *kunmap* functions did not exist.

In the 2.0 kernel, the `init_mm` structure was not exported to modules. Thus, a module that wished to access `init_mm` had to dig through the task table to find it (as part of the *init* process). When running on a 2.0 kernel, *scullp* finds `init_mm` with this bit of code:

```
static struct mm_struct *init_mm_ptr;
#define init_mm (*init_mm_ptr) /* to avoid ifdefs later */

static void retrieve_init_mm_ptr(void)
{
    struct task_struct *p;

    for (p = current ; (p = p->next_task) != current ; )
        if (p->pid == 0)
            break;

    init_mm_ptr = p->mm;
}
```

The 2.0 kernel also lacked the distinction between logical and physical addresses, so the `__va` and `__pa` macros did not exist. There was no need for them at that time.

Another thing the 2.0 kernel did not have was maintenance of the module's usage count in the presence of memory-mapped areas. Drivers that implement *mmap* under 2.0 need to provide *open* and *close* VMA operations to adjust the usage count themselves. The sample source modules that implement *mmap* provide these operations.

Finally, the 2.0 version of the driver *mmap* method, like most others, had a `struct inode` argument; the method's prototype was

```
int (*mmap)(struct inode *inode, struct file *filp,
        struct vm_area_struct *vma);
```

Changes to DMA

The PCI DMA interface as described earlier did not exist prior to kernel 2.3.41. Before then, DMA was handled in a more direct—and system-dependent—way. Buffers were "mapped" by calling *virt_to_bus*, and there was no general interface for handling bus-mapping registers.

For those who need to write portable PCI drivers, *sysdep.h* in the sample code includes a simple implementation of the 2.4 DMA interface that may be used on older kernels.

The ISA interface, on the other hand, is almost unchanged since Linux 2.0. ISA is an old architecture, after all, and there have not been a whole lot of changes to keep up with. The only addition was the DMA spinlock in 2.2; prior to that kernel, there was no need to protect against conflicting access to the DMA controller. Versions of these functions have been defined in *sysdep.h*; they disable and restore interrupts, but perform no other function.

Quick Reference

This chapter introduced the following symbols related to memory handling. The list doesn't include the symbols introduced in the first section, as that section is a huge list in itself and those symbols are rarely useful to device drivers.

`#include <linux/mm.h>`
All the functions and structures related to memory management are prototyped and defined in this header.

`int remap_page_range(unsigned long virt_add, unsigned long`
`        phys_add, unsigned long size, pgprot_t prot);`
This function sits at the heart of *mmap*. It maps `size` bytes of physical addresses, starting at `phys_addr`, to the virtual address `virt_add`. The protection bits associated with the virtual space are specified in `prot`.

`struct page *virt_to_page(void *kaddr);`
`void *page_address(struct page *page);`
These macros convert between kernel logical addresses and their associated memory map entries. *page_address* only works for low-memory pages, or high-memory pages that have been explicitly mapped.

`void *__va(unsigned long physaddr);`
`unsigned long __pa(void *kaddr);`
These macros convert between kernel logical addresses and physical addresses.

`unsigned long kmap(struct page *page);`
`void kunmap(struct page *page);`
kmap returns a kernel virtual address that is mapped to the given page, creating the mapping if need be. *kunmap* deletes the mapping for the given page.

```
#include <linux/iobuf.h>
void kiobuf_init(struct kiobuf *iobuf);
int alloc_kiovec(int number, struct kiobuf **iobuf);
void free_kiovec(int number, struct kiobuf **iobuf);
```
These functions handle the allocation, initialization, and freeing of kernel I/O buffers. *kiobuf_init* initializes a single kiobuf, but is rarely used; *alloc_kiovec*, which allocates and initializes a vector of kiobufs, is usually used instead. A vector of kiobufs is freed with *free_kiovec*.

```
int lock_kiovec(int nr, struct kiobuf *iovec[], int wait);
int unlock_kiovec(int nr, struct kiobuf *iovec[]);
```
These functions lock a kiovec in memory, and release it. They are unnecessary when using kiobufs for I/O to user-space memory.

```
int map_user_kiobuf(int rw, struct kiobuf *iobuf, unsigned
     long address, size_t len);
void unmap_kiobuf(struct kiobuf *iobuf);
```
map_user_kiobuf maps a buffer in user space into the given kernel I/O buffer; *unmap_kiobuf* undoes that mapping.

```
#include <asm/io.h>
unsigned long virt_to_bus(volatile void * address);
void * bus_to_virt(unsigned long address);
```
These functions convert between kernel virtual and bus addresses. Bus addresses must be used to talk to peripheral devices.

```
#include <linux/pci.h>
```
The header file required to define the following functions.

```
int pci_dma_supported(struct pci_dev *pdev, dma_addr_t
     mask);
```
For peripherals that cannot address the full 32-bit range, this function determines whether DMA can be supported at all on the host system.

```
void *pci_alloc_consistent(struct pci_dev *pdev, size_t
     size, dma_addr_t *bus_addr)
void pci_free_consistent(struct pci_dev *pdev, size_t size,
     void *cpuaddr, dma_handle_t bus_addr);
```
These functions allocate and free consistent DMA mappings, for a buffer that will last the lifetime of the driver.

```
PCI_DMA_TODEVICE
PCI_DMA_FROMDEVICE
PCI_DMA_BIDIRECTIONAL
PCI_DMA_NONE
```
These symbols are used to tell the streaming mapping functions the direction in which data will be moving to or from the buffer.

```
dma_addr_t pci_map_single(struct pci_dev *pdev, void
     *buffer, size_t size, int direction);
void pci_unmap_single(struct pci_dev *pdev, dma_addr_t
     bus_addr, size_t size, int direction);
```
Create and destroy a single-use, streaming DMA mapping.

```
void pci_sync_single(struct pci_dev *pdev, dma_handle_t
     bus_addr, size_t size, int direction)
```
Synchronizes a buffer that has a streaming mapping. This function must be used if the processor must access a buffer while the streaming mapping is in place (i.e., while the device owns the buffer).

```
struct scatterlist { /* ... */ };
dma_addr_t sg_dma_address(struct scatterlist *sg);
unsigned int sg_dma_len(struct scatterlist *sg);
```
The `scatterlist` structure describes an I/O operation that involves more than one buffer. The macros *sg_dma_address* and *sg_dma_len* may be used to extract bus addresses and buffer lengths to pass to the device when implementing scatter-gather operations.

```
pci_map_sg(struct pci_dev *pdev, struct scatterlist *list,
     int nents, int direction);
pci_unmap_sg(struct pci_dev *pdev, struct scatterlist *list,
     int nents, int direction);
pci_dma_sync_sg(struct pci_dev *pdev, struct scatterlist
     *sg, int nents, int direction)
```
pci_map_sg maps a scatter-gather operation, and *pci_unmap_sg* undoes that mapping. If the buffers must be accessed while the mapping is active, *pci_dma_sync_sg* may be used to synchronize things.

```
/proc/dma
```
This file contains a textual snapshot of the allocated channels in the DMA controllers. PCI-based DMA is not shown because each board works independently, without the need to allocate a channel in the DMA controller.

```
#include <asm/dma.h>
```
This header defines or prototypes all the functions and macros related to DMA. It must be included to use any of the following symbols.

```
int request_dma(unsigned int channel, const char *name);
void free_dma(unsigned int channel);
```
These functions access the DMA registry. Registration must be performed before using ISA DMA channels.

```
unsigned long claim_dma_lock();
void release_dma_lock(unsigned long flags);
```
These functions acquire and release the DMA spinlock, which must be held prior to calling the other ISA DMA functions described later in this list. They also disable and reenable interrupts on the local processor.

```
void set_dma_mode(unsigned int channel, char mode);
void set_dma_addr(unsigned int channel, unsigned int addr);
void set_dma_count(unsigned int channel, unsigned int
    count);
```
These functions are used to program DMA information in the DMA controller. addr is a bus address.

```
void disable_dma(unsigned int channel);
void enable_dma(unsigned int channel);
```
A DMA channel must be disabled during configuration. These functions change the status of the DMA channel.

```
int get_dma_residue(unsigned int channel);
```
If the driver needs to know how a DMA transfer is proceeding, it can call this function, which returns the number of data transfers that are yet to be completed. After successful completion of DMA, the function returns 0; the value is unpredictable while data is being transferred.

```
void clear_dma_ff(unsigned int channel)
```
The DMA flip-flop is used by the controller to transfer 16-bit values by means of two 8-bit operations. It must be cleared before sending any data to the controller.

CHAPTER FOURTEEN
NETWORK DRIVERS

We are now through discussing char and block drivers and are ready to move on to the fascinating world of networking. Network interfaces are the third standard class of Linux devices, and this chapter describes how they interact with the rest of the kernel.

The role of a network interface within the system is similar to that of a mounted block device. A block device registers its features in the `blk_dev` array and other kernel structures, and it then "transmits" and "receives" blocks on request, by means of its *request* function. Similarly, a network interface must register itself in specific data structures in order to be invoked when packets are exchanged with the outside world.

There are a few important differences between mounted disks and packet-delivery interfaces. To begin with, a disk exists as a special file in the */dev* directory, whereas a network interface has no such entry point. The normal file operations (read, write, and so on) do not make sense when applied to network interfaces, so it is not possible to apply the Unix "everything is a file" approach to them. Thus, network interfaces exist in their own namespace and export a different set of operations.

Although you may object that applications use the *read* and *write* system calls when using sockets, those calls act on a software object that is distinct from the interface. Several hundred sockets can be multiplexed on the same physical interface.

But the most important difference between the two is that block drivers operate only in response to requests from the kernel, whereas network drivers receive packets asynchronously from the outside. Thus, while a block driver *is asked* to send a buffer toward the kernel, the network device *asks* to push incoming packets toward the kernel. The kernel interface for network drivers is designed for this different mode of operation.

Network drivers also have to be prepared to support a number of administrative tasks, such as setting addresses, modifying transmission parameters, and maintaining traffic and error statistics. The API for network drivers reflects this need, and thus looks somewhat different from the interfaces we have seen so far.

The network subsystem of the Linux kernel is designed to be completely protocol independent. This applies to both networking protocols (IP versus IPX or other protocols) and hardware protocols (Ethernet versus token ring, etc.). Interaction between a network driver and the kernel proper deals with one network packet at a time; this allows protocol issues to be hidden neatly from the driver and the physical transmission to be hidden from the protocol.

This chapter describes how the network interfaces fit in with the rest of the Linux kernel and shows a memory-based modularized network interface, which is called (you guessed it) *snull*. To simplify the discussion, the interface uses the Ethernet hardware protocol and transmits IP packets. The knowledge you acquire from examining *snull* can be readily applied to protocols other than IP, and writing a non-Ethernet driver is only different in tiny details related to the actual network protocol.

This chapter doesn't talk about IP numbering schemes, network protocols, or other general networking concepts. Such topics are not (usually) of concern to the driver writer, and it's impossible to offer a satisfactory overview of networking technology in less than a few hundred pages. The interested reader is urged to refer to other books describing networking issues.

The networking subsystem has seen many changes over the years as the kernel developers have striven to provide the best performance possible. The bulk of this chapter describes network drivers as they are implemented in the 2.4 kernel. Once again, the sample code works on the 2.0 and 2.2 kernels as well, and we cover the differences between those kernels and 2.4 at the end of the chapter.

One note on terminology is called for before getting into network devices. The networking world uses the term *octet* to refer to a group of eight bits, which is generally the smallest unit understood by networking devices and protocols. The term byte is almost never encountered in this context. In keeping with standard usage, we will use octet when talking about networking devices.

How snull Is Designed

This section discusses the design concepts that led to the *snull* network interface. Although this information might appear to be of marginal use, failing to understand this driver might lead to problems while playing with the sample code.

The first, and most important, design decision was that the sample interfaces should remain independent of real hardware, just like most of the sample code used in this book. This constraint led to something that resembles the loopback interface. *snull* is not a loopback interface, however; it simulates conversations with real remote hosts in order to better demonstrate the task of writing a network driver. The Linux loopback driver is actually quite simple; it can be found in *drivers/net/loopback.c.*

Another feature of *snull* is that it supports only IP traffic. This is a consequence of the internal workings of the interface—*snull* has to look inside and interpret the packets to properly emulate a pair of hardware interfaces. Real interfaces don't depend on the protocol being transmitted, and this limitation of *snull* doesn't affect the fragments of code that are shown in this chapter.

Assigning IP Numbers

The *snull* module creates two interfaces. These interfaces are different from a simple loopback in that whatever you transmit through one of the interfaces loops back to the other one, not to itself. It looks like you have two external links, but actually your computer is replying to itself.

Unfortunately, this effect can't be accomplished through IP-number assignment alone, because the kernel wouldn't send out a packet through interface A that was directed to its own interface B. Instead, it would use the loopback channel without passing through *snull.* To be able to establish a communication through the *snull* interfaces, the source and destination addresses need to be modified during data transmission. In other words, packets sent through one of the interfaces should be received by the other, but the receiver of the outgoing packet shouldn't be recognized as the local host. The same applies to the source address of received packets.

To achieve this kind of "hidden loopback," the *snull* interface toggles the least significant bit of the third octet of both the source and destination addresses; that is, it changes both the network number and the host number of class C IP numbers. The net effect is that packets sent to network A (connected to `sn0`, the first interface) appear on the `sn1` interface as packets belonging to network B.

To avoid dealing with too many numbers, let's assign symbolic names to the IP numbers involved:

- `snullnet0` is the class C network that is connected to the `sn0` interface. Similarly, `snullnet1` is the network connected to `sn1`. The addresses of these networks should differ only in the least significant bit of the third octet.

- `local0` is the IP address assigned to the `sn0` interface; it belongs to `snullnet0`. The address associated with `sn1` is `local1`. `local0` and `local1` must differ in the least significant bit of their third octet and in the fourth octet.

- remote0 is a host in snullnet0, and its fourth octet is the same as that of local1. Any packet sent to remote0 will reach local1 after its class C address has been modified by the interface code. The host remote1 belongs to snullnet1, and its fourth octet is the same as that of local0.

The operation of the *snull* interfaces is depicted in Figure 14-1, in which the host-name associated with each interface is printed near the interface name.

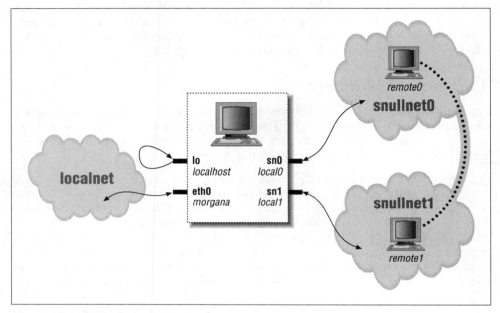

Figure 14-1. How a host sees its interfaces

Here are possible values for the network numbers. Once you put these lines in */etc/networks*, you can call your networks by name. The values shown were chosen from the range of numbers reserved for private use.

```
snullnet0        192.168.0.0
snullnet1        192.168.1.0
```

The following are possible host numbers to put into */etc/hosts*:

```
192.168.0.1      local0
192.168.0.2      remote0
192.168.1.2      local1
192.168.1.1      remote1
```

The important feature of these numbers is that the host portion of local0 is the same as that of remote1, and the host portion of local1 is the same as that of remote0. You can use completely different numbers as long as this relationship applies.

Be careful, however, if your computer is already connected to a network. The numbers you choose might be real Internet or intranet numbers, and assigning them to your interfaces will prevent communication with the real hosts. For example, although the numbers just shown are not routable Internet numbers, they could already be used by your private network if it lives behind a firewall.

Whatever numbers you choose, you can correctly set up the interfaces for operation by issuing the following commands:

```
ifconfig sn0 local0
ifconfig sn1 local1
case "`uname -r`" in 2.0.*)
    route add -net snullnet0 dev sn0
    route add -net snullnet1 dev sn1
esac
```

There is no need to invoke *route* with 2.2 and later kernels because the route is automatically added. Also, you may need to add the `netmask 255.255.255.0` parameter if the address range chosen is not a class C range.

At this point, the "remote" end of the interface can be reached. The following screendump shows how a host reaches `remote0` and `remote1` through the *snull* interface.

```
morgana% ping -c 2 remote0
64 bytes from 192.168.0.99: icmp_seq=0 ttl=64 time=1.6 ms
64 bytes from 192.168.0.99: icmp_seq=1 ttl=64 time=0.9 ms
2 packets transmitted, 2 packets received, 0% packet loss

morgana% ping -c 2 remote1
64 bytes from 192.168.1.88: icmp_seq=0 ttl=64 time=1.8 ms
64 bytes from 192.168.1.88: icmp_seq=1 ttl=64 time=0.9 ms
2 packets transmitted, 2 packets received, 0% packet loss
```

Note that you won't be able to reach any other "host" belonging to the two networks because the packets are discarded by your computer after the address has been modified and the packet has been received. For example, a packet aimed at 192.168.0.32 will leave through `sn0` and reappear at `sn1` with a destination address of 192.168.1.32, which is not a local address for the host computer.

The Physical Transport of Packets

As far as data transport is concerned, the *snull* interfaces belong to the Ethernet class.

snull emulates Ethernet because the vast majority of existing networks—at least the segments that a workstation connects to—are based on Ethernet technology, be it 10baseT, 100baseT, or gigabit. Additionally, the kernel offers some generalized support for Ethernet devices, and there's no reason not to use it. The advantage of being an Ethernet device is so strong that even the *plip* interface (the interface that uses the printer ports) declares itself as an Ethernet device.

The last advantage of using the Ethernet setup for *snull* is that you can run *tcp-dump* on the interface to see the packets go by. Watching the interfaces with *tcp-dump* can be a useful way to see how the two interfaces work. (Note that on 2.0 kernels, *tcpdump* will not work properly unless *snull*'s interfaces show up as `ethx`. Load the driver with the `eth=1` option to use the regular Ethernet names, rather than the default `snx` names.)

As was mentioned previously, *snull* only works with IP packets. This limitation is a result of the fact that *snull* snoops in the packets and even modifies them, in order for the code to work. The code modifies the source, destination, and check-sum in the IP header of each packet without checking whether it actually conveys IP information. This quick-and-dirty data modification destroys non-IP packets. If you want to deliver other protocols through *snull*, you must modify the module's source code.

Connecting to the Kernel

We'll start looking at the structure of network drivers by dissecting the *snull* source. Keeping the source code for several drivers handy might help you follow the discussion and to see how real-world Linux network drivers operate. As a place to start, we suggest *loopback.c*, *plip.c*, and *3c509.c*, in order of increasing complexity. Keeping *skeleton.c* handy might help as well, although this sample driver doesn't actually run. All these files live in *drivers/net*, within the kernel source tree.

Module Loading

When a driver module is loaded into a running kernel, it requests resources and offers facilities; there's nothing new in that. And there's also nothing new in the way resources are requested. The driver should probe for its device and its hard-ware location (I/O ports and IRQ line)—but without registering them—as described in "Installing an Interrupt Handler" in Chapter 9. The way a network driver is registered by its module initialization function is different from char and block drivers. Since there is no equivalent of major and minor numbers for net-work interfaces, a network driver does not request such a number. Instead, the driver inserts a data structure for each newly detected interface into a global list of network devices.

Each interface is described by a `struct net_device` item. The structures for `sn0` and `sn1`, the two *snull* interfaces, are declared like this:

```
struct net_device snull_devs[2] = {
    { init: snull_init, },  /* init, nothing more */
    { init: snull_init, }
};
```

The initialization shown seems quite simple—it sets only one field. In fact, the `net_device` structure is huge, and we will be filling in other pieces of it later on. But it is not helpful to cover the entire structure at this point; instead, we will explain each field as it is used. For the interested reader, the definition of the structure may be found in `<linux/netdevice.h>`.

The first `struct net_device` field we will look at is `name`, which holds the interface name (the string identifying the interface). The driver can hardwire a name for the interface or it can allow dynamic assignment, which works like this: if the name contains a `%d` format string, the first available name found by replacing that string with a small integer is used. Thus, `eth%d` is turned into the first available `eth`*n* name; the first Ethernet interface is called `eth0`, and the others follow in numeric order. The *snull* interfaces are called `sn0` and `sn1` by default. However, if `eth=1` is specified at load time (causing the integer variable `snull_eth` to be set to 1), *snull_init* uses dynamic assignment, as follows:

```
if (!snull_eth) { /* call them "sn0" and "sn1" */
    strcpy(snull_devs[0].name, "sn0");
    strcpy(snull_devs[1].name, "sn1");
} else { /* use automatic assignment */
    strcpy(snull_devs[0].name, "eth%d");
    strcpy(snull_devs[1].name, "eth%d");
}
```

The other field we initialized is `init`, a function pointer. Whenever you register a device, the kernel asks the driver to initialize itself. Initialization means probing for the physical interface and filling the `net_device` structure with the proper values, as described in the following section. If initialization fails, the structure is not linked to the global list of network devices. This peculiar way of setting things up is most useful during system boot; every driver tries to register its own devices, but only devices that exist are linked to the list.

Because the real initialization is performed elsewhere, the initialization function has little to do, and a single statement does it:

```
for (i=0; i<2;  i++)
    if ( (result = register_netdev(snull_devs + i)) )
        printk("snull: error %i registering device \"%s\"\n",
                result, snull_devs[i].name);
    else device_present++;
```

Initializing Each Device

Probing for the device should be performed in the *init* function for the interface (which is often called the "probe" function). The single argument received by *init* is a pointer to the device being initialized; its return value is either 0 or a negative error code, usually −ENODEV.

No real probing is performed for the *snull* interface, because it is not bound to any hardware. When you write a real driver for a real interface, the usual rules for probing devices apply, depending on the peripheral bus you are using. Also, you should avoid registering I/O ports and interrupt lines at this point. Hardware registration should be delayed until device open time; this is particularly important if interrupt lines are shared with other devices. You don't want your interface to be called every time another device triggers an IRQ line just to reply "no, it's not mine."

The main role of the initialization routine is to fill in the `dev` structure for this device. Note that for network devices, this structure is always put together at runtime. Because of the way the network interface probing works, the `dev` structure cannot be set up at compile time in the same manner as a `file_operations` or `block_device_operations` structure. So, on exit from `dev->init`, the `dev` structure should be filled with correct values. Fortunately, the kernel takes care of some Ethernet-wide defaults through the function *ether_setup*, which fills several fields in `struct net_device`.

The core of *snull_init* is as follows:

```
ether_setup(dev); /* assign some of the fields */

dev->open            = snull_open;
dev->stop            = snull_release;
dev->set_config      = snull_config;
dev->hard_start_xmit = snull_tx;
dev->do_ioctl        = snull_ioctl;
dev->get_stats       = snull_stats;
dev->rebuild_header  = snull_rebuild_header;
dev->hard_header     = snull_header;
#ifdef HAVE_TX_TIMEOUT
dev->tx_timeout      = snull_tx_timeout;
dev->watchdog_timeo  = timeout;
#endif
/* keep the default flags, just add NOARP */
dev->flags          |= IFF_NOARP;
dev->hard_header_cache = NULL;      /* Disable caching */
SET_MODULE_OWNER(dev);
```

The single unusual feature of the code is setting IFF_NOARP in the flags. This specifies that the interface cannot use ARP, the Address Resolution Protocol. ARP is a low-level Ethernet protocol; its job is to turn IP addresses into Ethernet Medium Access Control (MAC) addresses. Since the "remote" systems simulated by *snull* do not really exist, there is nobody available to answer ARP requests for them. Rather than complicate *snull* with the addition of an ARP implementation, we chose to mark the interface as being unable to handle that protocol. The assignment to hard_header_cache is there for a similar reason: it disables the caching of the (nonexistent) ARP replies on this interface. This topic is discussed in detail later in this chapter in "MAC Address Resolution."

The initialization code also sets a couple of fields (tx_timeout and watch-dog_timeo) that relate to the handling of transmission timeouts. We will cover this topic thoroughly later in this chapter in "Transmission Timeouts."

Finally, this code calls SET_MODULE_OWNER, which initializes the owner field of the net_device structure with a pointer to the module itself. The kernel uses this information in exactly the same way it uses the owner field of the file_operations structure—to maintain the module's usage count.

We'll look now at one more struct net_device field, priv. Its role is similar to that of the private_data pointer that we used for char drivers. Unlike fops->private_data, this priv pointer is allocated at initialization time instead of open time, because the data item pointed to by priv usually includes the statistical information about interface activity. It's important that statistical information always be available, even when the interface is down, because users may want to display the statistics at any time by calling *ifconfig*. The memory wasted by allocating priv during initialization instead of on open is irrelevant because most probed interfaces are constantly up and running in the system. The *snull* module declares a snull_priv data structure to be used for priv:

```
struct snull_priv {
    struct net_device_stats stats;
    int status;
    int rx_packetlen;
    u8 *rx_packetdata;
    int tx_packetlen;
    u8 *tx_packetdata;
    struct sk_buff *skb;
    spinlock_t lock;
};
```

The structure includes an instance of struct net_device_stats, which is the standard place to hold interface statistics. The following lines in *snull_init* allocate and initialize dev->priv:

```
dev->priv = kmalloc(sizeof(struct snull_priv), GFP_KERNEL);
if (dev->priv == NULL)
    return -ENOMEM;
memset(dev->priv, 0, sizeof(struct snull_priv));
spin_lock_init(& ((struct snull_priv *) dev->priv)->lock);
```

Module Unloading

Nothing special happens when the module is unloaded. The module cleanup function simply unregisters the interfaces from the list after releasing memory associated with the private structure:

```
void snull_cleanup(void)
{
    int i;

    for (i=0; i<2;  i++) {
        kfree(snull_devs[i].priv);
        unregister_netdev(snull_devs + i);
    }
    return;
}
```

Modularized and Nonmodularized Drivers

Although char and block drivers are the same regardless of whether they're modular or linked into the kernel, that's not the case for network drivers.

When a driver is linked directly into the Linux kernel, it doesn't declare its own net_device structures; the structures declared in *drivers/net/Space.c* are used instead. *Space.c* declares a linked list of all the network devices, both driver-specific structures like plip1 and general-purpose eth devices. Ethernet drivers don't care about their net_device structures at all, because they use the general-purpose structures. Such general eth device structures declare *ethif_probe* as their *init* function. A programmer inserting a new Ethernet interface in the mainstream kernel needs only to add a call to the driver's initialization function to *ethif_probe*. Authors of non-eth drivers, on the other hand, insert their net_device structures in *Space.c*. In both cases only the source file *Space.c* has to be modified if the driver must be linked to the kernel proper.

At system boot, the network initialization code loops through all the net_device structures and calls their probing (dev->init) functions by passing them a pointer to the device itself. If the probe function succeeds, the kernel initializes the next available net_device structure to use that interface. This way of setting up drivers permits incremental assignment of devices to the names eth0, eth1, and so on, without changing the name field of each device.

When a modularized driver is loaded, on the other hand, it declares its own net_device structures (as we have seen in this chapter), even if the interface it controls is an Ethernet interface.

The curious reader can learn more about interface initialization by looking at *Space.c* and *net_init.c*.

The net_device Structure in Detail

The `net_device` structure is at the very core of the network driver layer and deserves a complete description. At a first reading, however, you can skip this section, because you don't need a thorough understanding of the structure to get started. This list describes all the fields, but more to provide a reference than to be memorized. The rest of this chapter briefly describes each field as soon as it is used in the sample code, so you don't need to keep referring back to this section.

`struct net_device` can be conceptually divided into two parts: visible and invisible. The visible part of the structure is made up of the fields that can be explicitly assigned in static `net_device` structures. All structures in *drivers/net/Space.c* are initialized in this way, without using the tagged syntax for structure initialization. The remaining fields are used internally by the network code and usually are not initialized at compilation time, not even by tagged initialization. Some of the fields are accessed by drivers (for example, the ones that are assigned at initialization time), while some shouldn't be touched.

The Visible Head

The first part of `struct net_device` is composed of the following fields, in this order:

`char name[IFNAMSIZ];`
> The name of the device. If the name contains a `%d` format string, the first available device name with the given base is used; assigned numbers start at zero.

`unsigned long rmem_end;`
`unsigned long rmem_start;`
`unsigned long mem_end;`
`unsigned long mem_start;`
> Device memory information. These fields hold the beginning and ending addresses of the shared memory used by the device. If the device has different receive and transmit memories, the `mem` fields are used for transmit memory and the `rmem` fields for receive memory. `mem_start` and `mem_end` can be specified on the kernel command line at system boot, and their values are retrieved by *ifconfig*. The `rmem` fields are never referenced outside of the driver itself. By convention, the `end` fields are set so that `end - start` is the amount of available on-board memory.

`unsigned long base_addr;`
> The I/O base address of the network interface. This field, like the previous ones, is assigned during device probe. The *ifconfig* command can be used to display or modify the current value. The `base_addr` can be explicitly assigned on the kernel command line at system boot or at load time. The field is not used by the kernel, like the memory fields shown previously.

`unsigned char irq;`
> The assigned interrupt number. The value of `dev->irq` is printed by *ifconfig* when interfaces are listed. This value can usually be set at boot or load time and modified later using *ifconfig*.

`unsigned char if_port;`
> Which port is in use on multiport devices. This field is used, for example, with devices that support both coaxial (`IF_PORT_10BASE2`) and twisted-pair (`IF_PORT_10BASET`) Ethernet connections. The full set of known port types is defined in `<linux/netdevice.h>`.

`unsigned char dma;`
> The DMA channel allocated by the device. The field makes sense only with some peripheral buses, like ISA. It is not used outside of the device driver itself, but for informational purposes (in *ifconfig*).

`unsigned long state;`
> Device state. The field includes several flags. Drivers do not normally manipulate these flags directly; instead, a set of utility functions has been provided. These functions will be discussed shortly when we get into driver operations.

`struct net_device *next;`
> Pointer to the next device in the global linked list. This field shouldn't be touched by the driver.

`int (*init)(struct net_device *dev);`
> The initialization function, described earlier.

The Hidden Fields

The `net_device` structure includes many additional fields, which are usually assigned at device initialization. Some of these fields convey information about the interface, while some exist only for the benefit of the driver (i.e., they are not used by the kernel); other fields, most notably the device methods, are part of the kernel-driver interface.

We will list the three groups separately, independent of the actual order of the fields, which is not significant.

Interface information

Most of the information about the interface is correctly set up by the function *ether_setup*. Ethernet cards can rely on this general-purpose function for most of these fields, but the `flags` and `dev_addr` fields are device specific and must be explicitly assigned at initialization time.

Some non-Ethernet interfaces can use helper functions similar to *ether_setup*. *drivers/net/net_init.c* exports a number of such functions, including the following:

`void ltalk_setup(struct net_device *dev);`
> Sets up the fields for a LocalTalk device.

`void fc_setup(struct net_device *dev);`
> Initializes for fiber channel devices.

`void fddi_setup(struct net_device *dev);`
> Configures an interface for a Fiber Distributed Data Interface (FDDI) network.

`void hippi_setup(struct net_device *dev);`
> Prepares fields for a High-Performance Parallel Interface (HIPPI) high-speed interconnect driver.

`void tr_configure(struct net_device *dev);`
> Handles setup for token ring network interfaces. Note that the 2.4 kernel also exports a function *tr_setup*, which, interestingly, does nothing at all.

Most devices will be covered by one of these classes. If yours is something radically new and different, however, you will need to assign the following fields by hand.

`unsigned short hard_header_len;`
> The hardware header length, that is, the number of octets that lead the transmitted packet before the IP header, or other protocol information. The value of `hard_header_len` is 14 (`ETH_HLEN`) for Ethernet interfaces.

`unsigned mtu;`
> The maximum transfer unit (MTU). This field is used by the network layer to drive packet transmission. Ethernet has an MTU of 1500 octets (`ETH_DATA_LEN`).

`unsigned long tx_queue_len;`
> The maximum number of frames that can be queued on the device's transmission queue. This value is set to 100 by *ether_setup*, but you can change it. For example, *plip* uses 10 to avoid wasting system memory (*plip* has a lower throughput than a real Ethernet interface).

`unsigned short type;`
> The hardware type of the interface. The `type` field is used by ARP to determine what kind of hardware address the interface supports. The proper value for Ethernet interfaces is `ARPHRD_ETHER`, and that is the value set by *ether_setup*. The recognized types are defined in `<linux/if_arp.h>`.

`unsigned char addr_len;`
`unsigned char broadcast[MAX_ADDR_LEN];`
`unsigned char dev_addr[MAX_ADDR_LEN];`
> Hardware (MAC) address length and device hardware addresses. The Ethernet address length is six octets (we are referring to the hardware ID of the

interface board), and the broadcast address is made up of six `0xff` octets; *ether_setup* arranges for these values to be correct. The device address, on the other hand, must be read from the interface board in a device-specific way, and the driver should copy it to `dev_addr`. The hardware address is used to generate correct Ethernet headers before the packet is handed over to the driver for transmission. The *snull* device doesn't use a physical interface, and it invents its own hardware address.

`unsigned short flags;`
Interface flags, detailed next.

The `flags` field is a bit mask including the following bit values. The `IFF_` prefix stands for "interface flags." Some flags are managed by the kernel, and some are set by the interface at initialization time to assert various capabilities and other features of the interface. The valid flags, which are defined in `<linux/if.h>`, are as follows:

`IFF_UP`
This flag is read-only for the driver. The kernel turns it on when the interface is active and ready to transfer packets.

`IFF_BROADCAST`
This flag states that the interface allows broadcasting. Ethernet boards do.

`IFF_DEBUG`
This marks debug mode. The flag can be used to control the verbosity of your *printk* calls or for other debugging purposes. Although no official driver currently uses this flag, it can be set and reset by user programs via *ioctl*, and your driver can use it. The *misc-progs/netifdebug* program can be used to turn the flag on and off.

`IFF_LOOPBACK`
This flag should be set only in the loopback interface. The kernel checks for `IFF_LOOPBACK` instead of hardwiring the `lo` name as a special interface.

`IFF_POINTOPOINT`
This flag signals that the interface is connected to a point-to-point link. It is set by *ifconfig*. For example, *plip* and the PPP driver have it set.

`IFF_NOARP`
This means that the interface can't perform ARP. For example, point-to-point interfaces don't need to run ARP, which would only impose additional traffic without retrieving useful information. *snull* runs without ARP capabilities, so it sets the flag.

IFF_PROMISC

This flag is set to activate promiscuous operation. By default, Ethernet interfaces use a hardware filter to ensure that they receive broadcast packets and packets directed to that interface's hardware address only. Packet sniffers such as *tcpdump* set promiscuous mode on the interface in order to retrieve all packets that travel on the interface's transmission medium.

IFF_MULTICAST

This flag is set by interfaces that are capable of multicast transmission. *ether_setup* sets IFF_MULTICAST by default, so if your driver does not support multicast, it must clear the flag at initialization time.

IFF_ALLMULTI

This flag tells the interface to receive all multicast packets. The kernel sets it when the host performs multicast routing, only if IFF_MULTICAST is set. IFF_ALLMULTI is read-only for the interface. We'll see the multicast flags used in "Multicasting" later in this chapter.

IFF_MASTER
IFF_SLAVE

These flags are used by the load equalization code. The interface driver doesn't need to know about them.

IFF_PORTSEL
IFF_AUTOMEDIA

These flags signal that the device is capable of switching between multiple media types, for example, unshielded twisted pair (UTP) versus coaxial Ethernet cables. If IFF_AUTOMEDIA is set, the device selects the proper medium automatically.

IFF_DYNAMIC

This flag indicates that the address of this interface can change; used with dialup devices.

IFF_RUNNING

This flag indicates that the interface is up and running. It is mostly present for BSD compatibility; the kernel makes little use of it. Most network drivers need not worry about IFF_RUNNING.

IFF_NOTRAILERS

This flag is unused in Linux, but it exists for BSD compatibility.

When a program changes IFF_UP, the *open* or *stop* device method is called. When IFF_UP or any other flag is modified, the *set_multicast_list* method is invoked. If the driver needs to perform some action because of a modification in the flags, it must take that action in *set_multicast_list*. For example, when IFF_PROMISC is set or reset, *set_multicast_list* must notify the onboard hardware filter. The responsibilities of this device method are outlined in "Multicasting."

The device methods

As happens with the char and block drivers, each network device declares the functions that act on it. Operations that can be performed on network interfaces are listed in this section. Some of the operations can be left NULL, and some are usually untouched because *ether_setup* assigns suitable methods to them.

Device methods for a network interface can be divided into two groups: fundamental and optional. Fundamental methods include those that are needed to be able to use the interface; optional methods implement more advanced functionalities that are not strictly required. The following are the fundamental methods:

int (*open)(struct net_device *dev);
> Opens the interface. The interface is opened whenever *ifconfig* activates it. The *open* method should register any system resource it needs (I/O ports, IRQ, DMA, etc.), turn on the hardware, and increment the module usage count.

int (*stop)(struct net_device *dev);
> Stops the interface. The interface is stopped when it is brought down; operations performed at open time should be reversed.

int (*hard_start_xmit) (struct sk_buff *skb, struct
    net_device *dev);
> This method initiates the transmission of a packet. The full packet (protocol headers and all) is contained in a socket buffer (sk_buff) structure. Socket buffers are introduced later in this chapter.

int (*hard_header) (struct sk_buff *skb, struct net_device
    *dev, unsigned short type, void *daddr, void *saddr,
    unsigned len);
> This function builds the hardware header from the source and destination hardware addresses that were previously retrieved; its job is to organize the information passed to it as arguments into an appropriate, device-specific hardware header. *eth_header* is the default function for Ethernet-like interfaces, and *ether_setup* assigns this field accordingly.

int (*rebuild_header)(struct sk_buff *skb);
> This function is used to rebuild the hardware header before a packet is transmitted. The default function used by Ethernet devices uses ARP to fill the packet with missing information. The *rebuild_header* method is used rarely in the 2.4 kernel; *hard_header* is used instead.

void (*tx_timeout)(struct net_device *dev);
> This method is called when a packet transmission fails to complete within a reasonable period, on the assumption that an interrupt has been missed or the interface has locked up. It should handle the problem and resume packet transmission.

```
struct net_device_stats *(*get_stats)(struct net_device
    *dev);
```
Whenever an application needs to get statistics for the interface, this method is called. This happens, for example, when *ifconfig* or *netstat -i* is run. A sample implementation for *snull* is introduced in "Statistical Information" later in this chapter.

```
int (*set_config)(struct net_device *dev, struct ifmap
    *map);
```
Changes the interface configuration. This method is the entry point for configuring the driver. The I/O address for the device and its interrupt number can be changed at runtime using *set_config*. This capability can be used by the system administrator if the interface cannot be probed for. Drivers for modern hardware normally do not need to implement this method.

The remaining device operations may be considered optional.

```
int (*do_ioctl)(struct net_device *dev, struct ifreq *ifr,
    int cmd);
```
Perform interface-specific *ioctl* commands. Implementation of those commands is described later in "Custom ioctl Commands." The corresponding field in `struct net_device` can be left as `NULL` if the interface doesn't need any interface-specific commands.

```
void (*set_multicast_list)(struct net_device *dev);
```
This method is called when the multicast list for the device changes and when the flags change. See "Multicasting" for further details and a sample implementation.

```
int (*set_mac_address)(struct net_device *dev, void *addr);
```
This function can be implemented if the interface supports the ability to change its hardware address. Many interfaces don't support this ability at all. Others use the default *eth_mac_addr* implementation (from *drivers/net/net_init.c*). *eth_mac_addr* only copies the new address into `dev->dev_addr`, and it will only do so if the interface is not running. Drivers that use *eth_mac_addr* should set the hardware MAC address from `dev->dev_addr` when they are configured.

```
int (*change_mtu)(struct net_device *dev, int new_mtu);
```
This function is in charge of taking action if there is a change in the MTU (maximum transfer unit) for the interface. If the driver needs to do anything particular when the MTU is changed, it should declare its own function; otherwise, the default will do the right thing. *snull* has a template for the function if you are interested.

```
int (*header_cache) (struct neighbour *neigh, struct
    hh_cache *hh);
```
header_cache is called to fill in the hh_cache structure with the results of an ARP query. Almost all drivers can use the default *eth_header_cache* implementation.

```
int (*header_cache_update) (struct hh_cache *hh, struct
    net_device *dev, unsigned char *haddr);
```
This method updates the destination address in the hh_cache structure in response to a change. Ethernet devices use *eth_header_cache_update*.

```
int (*hard_header_parse) (struct sk_buff *skb, unsigned char
    *haddr);
```
The *hard_header_parse* method extracts the source address from the packet contained in skb, copying it into the buffer at haddr. The return value from the function is the length of that address. Ethernet devices normally use *eth_header_parse*.

Utility fields

The remaining struct net_device data fields are used by the interface to hold useful status information. Some of the fields are used by *ifconfig* and *netstat* to provide the user with information about the current configuration. An interface should thus assign values to these fields.

```
unsigned long trans_start;
unsigned long last_rx;
```
Both of these fields are meant to hold a jiffies value. The driver is responsible for updating these values when transmission begins and when a packet is received, respectively. The trans_start value is used by the networking subsystem to detect transmitter lockups. last_rx is currently unused, but the driver should maintain this field anyway to be prepared for future use.

```
int watchdog_timeo;
```
The minimum time (in jiffies) that should pass before the networking layer decides that a transmission timeout has occurred and calls the driver's *tx_timeout* function.

```
void *priv;
```
The equivalent of filp->private_data. The driver owns this pointer and can use it at will. Usually the private data structure includes a struct net_device_stats item. The field is used in "Initializing Each Device," later in this chapter.

```
struct dev_mc_list *mc_list;
int mc_count;
```
These two fields are used in handling multicast transmission. `mc_count` is the count of items in `mc_list`. See "Multicasting" for further details.

```
spinlock_t xmit_lock;
int xmit_lock_owner;
```
The `xmit_lock` is used to avoid multiple simultaneous calls to the driver's *hard_start_xmit* function. `xmit_lock_owner` is the number of the CPU that has obtained `xmit_lock`. The driver should make no changes to these fields.

```
struct module *owner;
```
The module that "owns" this device structure; it is used to maintain the use count for the module.

There are other fields in `struct net_device`, but they are not used by network drivers.

Opening and Closing

Our driver can probe for the interface at module load time or at kernel boot. Before the interface can carry packets, however, the kernel must open it and assign an address to it. The kernel will open or close an interface in response to the *ifconfig* command.

When *ifconfig* is used to assign an address to the interface, it performs two tasks. First, it assigns the address by means of `ioctl(SIOCSIFADDR)` (Socket I/O Control Set Interface Address). Then it sets the `IFF_UP` bit in `dev->flag` by means of `ioctl(SIOCSIFFLAGS)` (Socket I/O Control Set Interface Flags) to turn the interface on.

As far as the device is concerned, `ioctl(SIOCSIFADDR)` does nothing. No driver function is invoked—the task is device independent, and the kernel performs it. The latter command (`ioctl(SIOCSIFFLAGS)`), though, calls the *open* method for the device.

Similarly, when the interface is shut down, *ifconfig* uses `ioctl(SIOCSIFFLAGS)` to clear `IFF_UP`, and the *stop* method is called.

Both device methods return 0 in case of success and the usual negative value in case of error.

As far as the actual code is concerned, the driver has to perform many of the same tasks as the char and block drivers do. *open* requests any system resources it needs and tells the interface to come up; *stop* shuts down the interface and releases system resources. There are a couple of additional steps to be performed, however.

First, the hardware address needs to be copied from the hardware device to `dev->dev_addr` before the interface can communicate with the outside world. The hardware address can be assigned at probe time or at open time, at the driver's will. The *snull* software interface assigns it from within *open*; it just fakes a hardware number using an ASCII string of length `ETH_ALEN`, the length of Ethernet hardware addresses.

The *open* method should also start the interface's transmit queue (allow it to accept packets for transmission) once it is ready to start sending data. The kernel provides a function to start the queue:

```
void netif_start_queue(struct net_device *dev);
```

The *open* code for *snull* looks like the following:

```
int snull_open(struct net_device *dev)
{
    MOD_INC_USE_COUNT;

    /* request_region(), request_irq(), .... (like fops->open) */

    /*
     * Assign the hardware address of the board: use "\0SNULx", where
     * x is 0 or 1. The first byte is '\0' to avoid being a multicast
     * address (the first byte of multicast addrs is odd).
     */
    memcpy(dev->dev_addr, "\0SNUL0", ETH_ALEN);
    dev->dev_addr[ETH_ALEN-1] += (dev - snull_devs); /* the number */

    netif_start_queue(dev);
    return 0;
}
```

As you can see, in the absence of real hardware, there is little to do in the *open* method. The same is true of the *stop* method; it just reverses the operations of *open*. For this reason the function implementing *stop* is often called *close* or *release*.

```
int snull_release(struct net_device *dev)
{
    /* release ports, irq and such -- like fops->close */

    netif_stop_queue(dev); /* can't transmit any more */
    MOD_DEC_USE_COUNT;
    return 0;
}
```

The function:

```
void netif_stop_queue(struct net_device *dev);
```

is the opposite of *netif_start_queue*; it marks the device as being unable to transmit any more packets. The function must be called when the interface is closed (in the *stop* method) but can also be used to temporarily stop transmission, as explained in the next section.

Packet Transmission

The most important tasks performed by network interfaces are data transmission and reception. We'll start with transmission because it is slightly easier to understand.

Whenever the kernel needs to transmit a data packet, it calls the *hard_start_transmit* method to put the data on an outgoing queue. Each packet handled by the kernel is contained in a socket buffer structure (`struct sk_buff`), whose definition is found in `<linux/skbuff.h>`. The structure gets its name from the Unix abstraction used to represent a network connection, the *socket*. Even if the interface has nothing to do with sockets, each network packet belongs to a socket in the higher network layers, and the input/output buffers of any socket are lists of `struct sk_buff` structures. The same `sk_buff` structure is used to host network data throughout all the Linux network subsystems, but a socket buffer is just a packet as far as the interface is concerned.

A pointer to `sk_buff` is usually called `skb`, and we follow this practice both in the sample code and in the text.

The socket buffer is a complex structure, and the kernel offers a number of functions to act on it. The functions are described later in "The Socket Buffers;" for now a few basic facts about `sk_buff` are enough for us to write a working driver.

The socket buffer passed to *hard_start_xmit* contains the physical packet as it should appear on the media, complete with the transmission-level headers. The interface doesn't need to modify the data being transmitted. `skb->data` points to the packet being transmitted, and `skb->len` is its length, in octets.

The *snull* packet transmission code is follows; the physical transmission machinery has been isolated in another function because every interface driver must implement it according to the specific hardware being driven.

```
int snull_tx(struct sk_buff *skb, struct net_device *dev)
{
    int len;
    char *data;
    struct snull_priv *priv = (struct snull_priv *) dev->priv;
    len = skb->len < ETH_ZLEN ? ETH_ZLEN : skb->len;
    data = skb->data;
    dev->trans_start = jiffies; /* save the timestamp */

    /* Remember the skb, so we can free it at interrupt time */
    priv->skb = skb;
```

```
    /* actual delivery of data is device specific, and not shown here */
    snull_hw_tx(data, len, dev);

    return 0; /* Our simple device cannot fail */
}
```

The transmission function thus performs only some sanity checks on the packet and transmits the data through the hardware-related function. That function (*snull_hw_tx*) is omitted here since it is entirely occupied with implementing the trickery of the *snull* device (including manipulating the source and destination addresses) and has little of interest to authors of real network drivers. It is present, of course, in the sample source for those who want to go in and see how it works.

Controlling Transmission Concurrency

The *hard_start_xmit* function is protected from concurrent calls by a spinlock (`xmit_lock`) in the `net_device` structure. As soon as the function returns, however, it may be called again. The function returns when the software is done instructing the hardware about packet transmission, but hardware transmission will likely not have been completed. This is not an issue with *snull*, which does all of its work using the CPU, so packet transmission is complete before the transmission function returns.

Real hardware interfaces, on the other hand, transmit packets asynchronously and have a limited amount of memory available to store outgoing packets. When that memory is exhausted (which, for some hardware, will happen with a single outstanding packet to transmit), the driver will need to tell the networking system not to start any more transmissions until the hardware is ready to accept new data.

This notification is accomplished by calling *netif_stop_queue*, the function introduced earlier to stop the queue. Once your driver has stopped its queue, it *must* arrange to restart the queue at some point in the future, when it is again able to accept packets for transmission. To do so, it should call:

```
    void netif_wake_queue(struct net_device *dev);
```

This function is just like *netif_start_queue*, except that it also pokes the networking system to make it start transmitting packets again.

Most modern network interfaces maintain an internal queue with multiple packets to transmit; in this way they can get the best performance from the network. Network drivers for these devices support having multiple transmisions outstanding at any given time, but device memory can fill up whether or not the hardware supports multiple outstanding transmission. Whenever device memory fills to the point that there is no room for the largest possible packet, the driver should stop the queue until space becomes available again.

Transmission Timeouts

Most drivers that deal with real hardware have to be prepared for that hardware to fail to respond occasionally. Interfaces can forget what they are doing, or the system can lose an interrupt. This sort of problem is common with some devices designed to run on personal computers.

Many drivers handle this problem by setting timers; if the operation has not completed by the time the timer expires, something is wrong. The network system, as it happens, is essentially a complicated assembly of state machines controlled by a mass of timers. As such, the networking code is in a good position to detect transmission timeouts automatically.

Thus, network drivers need not worry about detecting such problems themselves. Instead, they need only set a timeout period, which goes in the `watchdog_timeo` field of the `net_device` structure. This period, which is in jiffies, should be long enough to account for normal transmission delays (such as collisions caused by congestion on the network media).

If the current system time exceeds the device's `trans_start` time by at least the timeout period, the networking layer will eventually call the driver's *tx_timeout* method. That method's job is to do whatever is needed to clear up the problem and to ensure the proper completion of any transmissions that were already in progress. It is important, in particular, that the driver not lose track of any socket buffers that have been entrusted to it by the networking code.

snull has the ability to simulate transmitter lockups, which is controlled by two load-time parameters:

```
static int lockup = 0;
MODULE_PARM(lockup, "i");

#ifdef HAVE_TX_TIMEOUT
static int timeout = SNULL_TIMEOUT;
MODULE_PARM(timeout, "i");
#endif
```

If the driver is loaded with the parameter `lockup=n`, a lockup will be simulated once every n packets transmitted, and the `watchdog_timeo` field will be set to the given `timeout` value. When simulating lockups, *snull* also calls *netif_stop_queue* to prevent other transmission attempts from occurring.

The *snull* transmission timeout handler looks like this:

```
void snull_tx_timeout (struct net_device *dev)
{
    struct snull_priv *priv = (struct snull_priv *) dev->priv;

    PDEBUG("Transmit timeout at %ld, latency %ld\n", jiffies,
                jiffies - dev->trans_start);
```

```
        priv->status = SNULL_TX_INTR;
        snull_interrupt(0, dev, NULL);
        priv->stats.tx_errors++;
        netif_wake_queue(dev);
        return;
    }
```

When a transmission timeout happens, the driver must mark the error in the interface statistics and arrange for the device to be reset to a sane state so that new packets can be transmitted. When a timeout happens in *snull*, the driver calls *snull_interrupt* to fill in the "missing" interrupt and restarts the transmit queue with *netif_wake_queue*.

Packet Reception

Receiving data from the network is trickier than transmitting it because an `sk_buff` must be allocated and handed off to the upper layers from within an interrupt handler. The usual way to receive a packet is through an interrupt, unless the interface is a purely software one like *snull* or the loopback interface. Although it is possible to write polling drivers, and a few exist in the official kernel, interrupt-driven operation is much better, both in terms of data throughput and computational demands. Because most network interfaces are interrupt driven, we won't talk about the polling implementation, which just exploits kernel timers.

The implementation of *snull* separates the "hardware" details from the device-independent housekeeping. The function *snull_rx* is thus called after the hardware has received the packet and it is already in the computer's memory. *snull_rx* receives a pointer to the data and the length of the packet; its sole responsibility is to send the packet and some additional information to the upper layers of networking code. This code is independent of the way the data pointer and length are obtained.

```
    void snull_rx(struct net_device *dev, int len, unsigned char *buf)
    {
        struct sk_buff *skb;
        struct snull_priv *priv = (struct snull_priv *) dev->priv;

        /*
         * The packet has been retrieved from the transmission
         * medium. Build an skb around it, so upper layers can handle it
         */
        skb = dev_alloc_skb(len+2);
        if (!skb) {
            printk("snull rx: low on mem - packet dropped\n");
            priv->stats.rx_dropped++;
            return;
        }
        memcpy(skb_put(skb, len), buf, len);
```

```
        /* Write metadata, and then pass to the receive level */
        skb->dev = dev;
        skb->protocol = eth_type_trans(skb, dev);
        skb->ip_summed = CHECKSUM_UNNECESSARY; /* don't check it */
        priv->stats.rx_packets++;
        priv->stats.rx_bytes += len;
        netif_rx(skb);
        return;
    }
```

The function is sufficiently general to act as a template for any network driver, but some explanation is necessary before you can reuse this code fragment with confidence.

The first step is to allocate a buffer to hold the packet. Note that the buffer allocation function (*dev_alloc_skb*) needs to know the data length. The information is used by the function to allocate space for the buffer. *dev_alloc_skb* calls *kmalloc* with atomic priority; it can thus be used safely at interrupt time. The kernel offers other interfaces to socket-buffer allocation, but they are not worth introducing here; socket buffers are explained in detail in "The Socket Buffers," later in this chapter.

Once there is a valid **skb** pointer, the packet data is copied into the buffer by calling *memcpy*; the *skb_put* function updates the end-of-data pointer in the buffer and returns a pointer to the newly created space.

If you are writing a high-performance driver for an interface that can do full bus-mastering I/O, there is a possible optimization that is worth considering here. Some drivers allocate socket buffers for incoming packets prior to their reception, then instruct the interface to place the packet data directly into the socket buffer's space. The networking layer cooperates with this strategy by allocating all socket buffers in DMA-capable space. Doing things this way avoids the need for a separate copy operation to fill the socket buffer, but requires being careful with buffer sizes because you won't know in advance how big the incoming packet is. The implementation of a *change_mtu* method is also important in this situation, since it allows the driver to respond to a change in the maximum packet size.

The network layer needs to have some information spelled out before it will be able to make sense of the packet. To this end, the **dev** and **protocol** fields must be assigned before the buffer is passed upstairs. Then we need to specify how checksumming is to be performed or has been performed on the packet (*snull* does not need to perform any checksums). The possible policies for **skb->ip_summed** are as follows:

CHECKSUM_HW
    The device has already performed checksums in hardware. An example of a hardware checksum is the SPARC HME interface.

CHECKSUM_NONE

Checksums are still to be verified, and the task must be accomplished by system software. This is the default in newly allocated buffers.

CHECKSUM_UNNECESSARY

Don't do any checksums. This is the policy in *snull* and in the loopback interface.

Finally, the driver updates its statistics counter to record that a packet has been received. The statistics structure is made up of several fields; the most important are `rx_packets`, `rx_bytes`, `tx_packets`, and `tx_bytes`, which contain the number of packets received and transmitted and the total number of octets transferred. All the fields are thoroughly described in "Statistical Information" later in this chpater.

The last step in packet reception is performed by *netif_rx*, which hands off the socket buffer to the upper layers.

The Interrupt Handler

Most hardware interfaces are controlled by means of an interrupt handler. The interface interrupts the processor to signal one of two possible events: a new packet has arrived or transmission of an outgoing packet is complete. This generalization doesn't always apply, but it does account for all the problems related to asynchronous packet transmission. Parallel Line Internet Protocol (PLIP) and Point-to-Point Protocol (PPP) are examples of interfaces that don't fit this generalization. They deal with the same events, but the low-level interrupt handling is slightly different.

The usual interrupt routine can tell the difference between a new-packet-arrived interrupt and a done-transmitting notification by checking a status register found on the physical device. The *snull* interface works similarly, but its status word is implemented in software and lives in `dev->priv`. The interrupt handler for a network interface looks like this:

```
void snull_interrupt(int irq, void *dev_id, struct pt_regs *regs)
{
    int statusword;
    struct snull_priv *priv;
    /*
     * As usual, check the "device" pointer for shared handlers.
     * Then assign "struct device *dev"
     */
    struct net_device *dev = (struct net_device *)dev_id;
    /* ... and check with hw if it's really ours */

    if (!dev /*paranoid*/ ) return;

    /* Lock the device */
```

```
    priv = (struct snull_priv *) dev->priv;
    spin_lock(&priv->lock);

    /* retrieve statusword: real netdevices use I/O instructions */
    statusword = priv->status;
    if (statusword & SNULL_RX_INTR) {
        /* send it to snull_rx for handling */
        snull_rx(dev, priv->rx_packetlen, priv->rx_packetdata);
    }
    if (statusword & SNULL_TX_INTR) {
        /* a transmission is over: free the skb */
        priv->stats.tx_packets++;
        priv->stats.tx_bytes += priv->tx_packetlen;
        dev_kfree_skb(priv->skb);
    }

    /* Unlock the device and we are done */
    spin_unlock(&priv->lock);
    return;
}
```

The handler's first task is to retrieve a pointer to the correct `struct net_device`. This pointer usually comes from the `dev_id` pointer received as an argument.

The interesting part of this handler deals with the "transmission done" situation. In this case, the statistics are updated, and *dev_kfree_skb* is called to return the (no longer needed) socket buffer to the system. If your driver has temporarily stopped the transmission queue, this is the place to restart it with *netif_wake_queue*.

Packet reception, on the other hand, doesn't need any special interrupt handling. Calling *snull_rx* (which we have already seen) is all that's required.

Changes in Link State

Network connections, by definition, deal with the world outside the local system. They are thus often affected by outside events, and they can be transient things. The networking subsystem needs to know when network links go up or down, and it provides a few functions that the driver may use to convey that information.

Most networking technologies involving an actual, physical connection provide a *carrier* state; the presence of the carrier means that the hardware is present and ready to function. Ethernet adapters, for example, sense the carrier signal on the wire; when a user trips over the cable, that carrier vanishes, and the link goes down. By default, network devices are assumed to have a carrier signal present. The driver can change that state explicitly, however, with these functions:

```
    void netif_carrier_off(struct net_device *dev);
    void netif_carrier_on(struct net_device *dev);
```

If your driver detects a lack of carrier on one of its devices, it should call *netif_carrier_off* to inform the kernel of this change. When the carrier returns, *netif_carrier_on* should be called. Some drivers also call *netif_carrier_off* when making major configuration changes (such as media type); once the adapter has finished resetting itself, the new carrier will be detected and traffic can resume.

An integer function also exsists:

```
int netif_carrier_ok(struct net_device *dev);
```

This can be used to test the current carrier state (as reflected in the device structure).

The Socket Buffers

We've now discussed most of the issues related to network interfaces. What's still missing is some more detailed discussion of the `sk_buff` structure. The structure is at the core of the network subsystem of the Linux kernel, and we now introduce both the main fields of the structure and the functions used to act on it.

Although there is no strict need to understand the internals of `sk_buff`, the ability to look at its contents can be helpful when you are tracking down problems and when you are trying to optimize the code. For example, if you look in *loopback.c*, you'll find an optimization based on knowledge of the `sk_buff` internals. The usual warning applies here: if you write code that takes advantage of knowledge of the `sk_buff` structure, you should be prepared to see it break with future kernel releases. Still, sometimes the performance advantages justify the additional maintenance cost.

We are not going to describe the whole structure here, just the fields that might be used from within a driver. If you want to see more, you can look at <linux/skbuff.h>, where the structure is defined and the functions are prototyped. Additional details about how the fields and functions are used can be easily retrieved by grepping in the kernel sources.

The Important Fields

The fields introduced here are the ones a driver might need to access. They are listed in no particular order.

```
struct net_device *rx_dev;
struct net_device *dev;
```
    The devices receiving and sending this buffer, respectively.

```
union { /* ... */ } h;
union { /* ... */ } nh;
union { /* ... */} mac;
```
Pointers to the various levels of headers contained within the packet. Each field of the unions is a pointer to a different type of data structure. `h` hosts pointers to transport layer headers (for example, `struct tcphdr *th`); `nh` includes network layer headers (such as `struct iphdr *iph`); and `mac` collects pointers to link layer headers (such as `struct ethdr *ethernet`).

If your driver needs to look at the source and destination addresses of a TCP packet, it can find them in `skb->h.th`. See the header file for the full set of header types that can be accessed in this way.

Note that network drivers are responsible for setting the `mac` pointer for incoming packets. This task is normally handled by *ether_type_trans*, but non-Ethernet drivers will have to set `skb->mac.raw` directly, as shown later in "Non-Ethernet Headers."

```
unsigned char *head;
unsigned char *data;
unsigned char *tail;
unsigned char *end;
```
Pointers used to address the data in the packet. `head` points to the beginning of the allocated space, `data` is the beginning of the valid octets (and is usually slightly greater than `head`), `tail` is the end of the valid octets, and `end` points to the maximum address `tail` can reach. Another way to look at it is that the *available* buffer space is `skb->end - skb->head`, and the *currently used* data space is `skb->tail - skb->data`.

```
unsigned long len;
```
The length of the data itself (`skb->tail - skb->data`).

```
unsigned char ip_summed;
```
The checksum policy for this packet. The field is set by the driver on incoming packets, as was described in "Packet Reception."

```
unsigned char pkt_type;
```
Packet classification used in delivering it. The driver is responsible for setting it to `PACKET_HOST` (this packet is for me), `PACKET_BROADCAST`, `PACKET_MULTICAST`, or `PACKET_OTHERHOST` (no, this packet is not for me). Ethernet drivers don't modify `pkt_type` explicitly because *eth_type_trans* does it for them.

The remaining fields in the structure are not particularly interesting. They are used to maintain lists of buffers, to account for memory belonging to the socket that owns the buffer, and so on.

Functions Acting on Socket Buffers

Network devices that use a `sock_buff` act on the structure by means of the official interface functions. Many functions operate on socket buffers; here are the most interesting ones:

```
struct sk_buff *alloc_skb(unsigned int len, int priority);
struct sk_buff *dev_alloc_skb(unsigned int len);
```
> Allocate a buffer. The *alloc_skb* function allocates a buffer and initializes both `skb->data` and `skb->tail` to `skb->head`. The *dev_alloc_skb* function is a shortcut that calls *alloc_skb* with `GFP_ATOMIC` priority and reserves some space between `skb->head` and `skb->data`. This data space is used for optimizations within the network layer and should not be touched by the driver.

```
void kfree_skb(struct sk_buff *skb);
void dev_kfree_skb(struct sk_buff *skb);
```
> Free a buffer. The *kfree_skb* call is used internally by the kernel. A driver should use *dev_kfree_skb* instead, which is intended to be safe to call from driver context.

```
unsigned char *skb_put(struct sk_buff *skb, int len);
unsigned char *__skb_put(struct sk_buff *skb, int len);
```
> These inline functions update the `tail` and `len` fields of the `sk_buff` structure; they are used to add data to the end of the buffer. Each function's return value is the previous value of `skb->tail` (in other words, it points to the data space just created). Drivers can use the return value to copy data by invoking `ins(ioaddr, skb_put(...))` or `memcpy(skb_put(...), data, len)`. The difference between the two functions is that *skb_put* checks to be sure that the data will fit in the buffer, whereas *__skb_put* omits the check.

```
unsigned char *skb_push(struct sk_buff *skb, int len);
unsigned char *__skb_push(struct sk_buff *skb, int len);
```
> These functions decrement `skb->data` and increment `skb->len`. They are similar to *skb_put*, except that data is added to the beginning of the packet instead of the end. The return value points to the data space just created. The functions are used to add a hardware header before transmitting a packet. Once again, *__skb_push* differs in that it does not check for adequate available space.

```
int skb_tailroom(struct sk_buff *skb);
```
> This function returns the amount of space available for putting data in the buffer. If a driver puts more data into the buffer than it can hold, the system panics. Although you might object that a *printk* would be sufficient to tag the

error, memory corruption is so harmful to the system that the developers decided to take definitive action. In practice, you shouldn't need to check the available space if the buffer has been correctly allocated. Since drivers usually get the packet size before allocating a buffer, only a severely broken driver will put too much data in the buffer, and a panic might be seen as due punishment.

`int skb_headroom(struct sk_buff *skb);`
> Returns the amount of space available in front of `data`, that is, how many octets one can "push" to the buffer.

`void skb_reserve(struct sk_buff *skb, int len);`
> This function increments both `data` and `tail`. The function can be used to reserve headroom before filling the buffer. Most Ethernet interfaces reserve 2 bytes in front of the packet; thus, the IP header is aligned on a 16-byte boundary, after a 14-byte Ethernet header. *snull* does this as well, although the instruction was not shown in "Packet Reception" to avoid introducing extra concepts at that point.

`unsigned char *skb_pull(struct sk_buff *skb, int len);`
> Removes data from the head of the packet. The driver won't need to use this function, but it is included here for completeness. It decrements `skb->len` and increments `skb->data`; this is how the hardware header (Ethernet or equivalent) is stripped from the beginning of incoming packets.

The kernel defines several other functions that act on socket buffers, but they are meant to be used in higher layers of networking code, and the driver won't need them.

MAC Address Resolution

An interesting issue with Ethernet communication is how to associate the MAC addresses (the interface's unique hardware ID) with the IP number. Most protocols have a similar problem, but we concentrate on the Ethernet-like case here. We'll try to offer a complete description of the issue, so we will show three situations: ARP, Ethernet headers without ARP (like *plip*), and non-Ethernet headers.

Using ARP with Ethernet

The usual way to deal with address resolution is by using ARP, the Address Resolution Protocol. Fortunately, ARP is managed by the kernel, and an Ethernet interface doesn't need to do anything special to support ARP. As long as `dev->addr` and `dev->addr_len` are correctly assigned at open time, the driver doesn't need to worry about resolving IP numbers to physical addresses; *ether_setup* assigns the correct device methods to `dev->hard_header` and `dev->rebuild_header`.

Although the kernel normally handles the details of address resolution (and caching of the results), it calls upon the interface driver to help in the building of the packet. After all, the driver knows about the details of the physical layer header, while the authors of the networking code have tried to insulate the rest of the kernel from that knowledge. To this end, the kernel calls the driver's *hard_header* method to lay out the packet with the results of the ARP query. Normally, Ethernet driver writers need not know about this process—the common Ethernet code takes care of everything.

Overriding ARP

Simple point-to-point network interfaces such as *plip* might benefit from using Ethernet headers, while avoiding the overhead of sending ARP packets back and forth. The sample code in *snull* also falls into this class of network devices. *snull* cannot use ARP because the driver changes IP addresses in packets being transmitted, and ARP packets exchange IP addresses as well. Although we could have implemented a simple ARP reply generator with little trouble, it is more illustrative to show how to handle physical-layer headers directly.

If your device wants to use the usual hardware header without running ARP, you need to override the default `dev->hard_header` method. This is how *snull* implements it, as a very short function.

```
int snull_header(struct sk_buff *skb, struct net_device *dev,
                 unsigned short type, void *daddr, void *saddr,
                 unsigned int len)
{
    struct ethhdr *eth = (struct ethhdr *)skb_push(skb,ETH_HLEN);

    eth->h_proto = htons(type);
    memcpy(eth->h_source, saddr ? saddr : dev->dev_addr, dev->addr_len);
    memcpy(eth->h_dest,   daddr ? daddr : dev->dev_addr, dev->addr_len);
    eth->h_dest[ETH_ALEN-1]   ^= 0x01;   /* dest is us xor 1 */
    return (dev->hard_header_len);
}
```

The function simply takes the information provided by the kernel and formats it into a standard Ethernet header. It also toggles a bit in the destination Ethernet address, for reasons described later.

When a packet is received by the interface, the hardware header is used in a couple of ways by *eth_type_trans*. We have already seen this call in *snull_rx*:

```
skb->protocol = eth_type_trans(skb, dev);
```

The function extracts the protocol identifier (`ETH_P_IP` in this case) from the Ethernet header; it also assigns `skb->mac.raw`, removes the hardware header from packet data (with *skb_pull*), and sets `skb->pkt_type`. This last item defaults to `PACKET_HOST` at `skb` allocation (which indicates that the packet is directed to this host), and *eth_type_trans* changes it according to the Ethernet destination address. If that address does not match the address of the interface that received it, the `pkt_type` field will be set to `PACKET_OTHERHOST`. Subsequently, unless the interface is in promiscuous mode, *netif_rx* will drop any packet of type `PACKET_OTHERHOST`. For this reason, *snull_header* is careful to make the destination hardware address match that of the "receiving" interface.

If your interface is a point-to-point link, you won't want to receive unexpected multicast packets. To avoid this problem, remember that a destination address whose first octet has 0 as the least significant bit (LSB) is directed to a single host (i.e., it is either `PACKET_HOST` or `PACKET_OTHERHOST`). The *plip* driver uses 0xfc as the first octet of its hardware address, while *snull* uses 0x00. Both addresses result in a working Ethernet-like point-to-point link.

Non-Ethernet Headers

We have just seen that the hardware header contains some information in addition to the destination address, the most important being the communication protocol. We now describe how hardware headers can be used to encapsulate relevant information. If you need to know the details, you can extract them from the kernel sources or the technical documentation for the particular transmission medium. Most driver writers will be able to ignore this discussion and just use the Ethernet implementation.

It's worth noting that not all information has to be provided by every protocol. A point-to-point link such as *plip* or *snull* could avoid transferring the whole Ethernet header without losing generality. The *hard_header* device method, shown earlier as implemented by *snull_header*, receives the delivery information—both protocol-level and hardware addresses—from the kernel. It also receives the 16-bit protocol number in the `type` argument; IP, for example, is identified by `ETH_P_IP`. The driver is expected to correctly deliver both the packet data and the protocol number to the receiving host. A point-to-point link could omit addresses from its hardware header, transferring only the protocol number, because delivery is guaranteed independent of the source and destination addresses. An IP-only link could even avoid transmitting any hardware header whatsoever.

When the packet is picked up at the other end of the link, the receiving function in the driver should correctly set the fields `skb->protocol`, `skb->pkt_type`, and `skb->mac.raw`.

`skb->mac.raw` is a char pointer used by the address-resolution mechanism implemented in higher layers of the networking code (for instance, *net/ipv4/arp.c*).

It must point to a machine address that matches `dev->type`. The possible values for the device type are defined in `<linux/if_arp.h>`; Ethernet interfaces use `ARPHRD_ETHER`. For example, here is how *eth_type_trans* deals with the Ethernet header for received packets:

```
skb->mac.raw = skb->data;
skb_pull(skb, dev->hard_header_len);
```

In the simplest case (a point-to-point link with no headers), `skb->mac.raw` can point to a static buffer containing the hardware address of this interface, `proto-col` can be set to `ETH_P_IP`, and `packet_type` can be left with its default value of `PACKET_HOST`.

Because every hardware type is unique, it is hard to give more specific advice than already discussed. The kernel is full of examples, however. See, for example, the AppleTalk driver (*drivers/net/appletalk/cops.c*), the infrared drivers (such as *drivers/net/irda/smc_ircc.c*), or the PPP driver (*drivers/net/ppp_generic.c*).

Custom ioctl Commands

We have seen that the *ioctl* system call is implemented for sockets; `SIOCSIFADDR` and `SIOCSIFMAP` are examples of "socket *ioctls*." Now let's see how the third argument of the system call is used by networking code.

When the *ioctl* system call is invoked on a socket, the command number is one of the symbols defined in `<linux/sockios.h>`, and the function *sock_ioctl* directly invokes a protocol-specific function (where "protocol" refers to the main network protocol being used, for example, IP or AppleTalk).

Any *ioctl* command that is not recognized by the protocol layer is passed to the device layer. These device-related *ioctl* commands accept a third argument from user space, a `struct ifreq *`. This structure is defined in `<linux/if.h>`. The `SIOCSIFADDR` and `SIOCSIFMAP` commands actually work on the `ifreq` structure. The extra argument to `SIOCSIFMAP`, although defined as `ifmap`, is just a field of `ifreq`.

In addition to using the standardized calls, each interface can define its own *ioctl* commands. The *plip* interface, for example, allows the interface to modify its internal timeout values via *ioctl*. The *ioctl* implementation for sockets recognizes 16 commands as private to the interface: `SIOCDEVPRIVATE` through `SIOCDEVPRI-VATE+15`.

When one of these commands is recognized, `dev->do_ioctl` is called in the relevant interface driver. The function receives the same `struct ifreq *` pointer that the general-purpose *ioctl* function uses:

```
int (*do_ioctl)(struct net_device *dev, struct ifreq *ifr, int cmd);
```

The `ifr` pointer points to a kernel-space address that holds a copy of the structure passed by the user. After *do_ioctl* returns, the structure is copied back to user space; the driver can thus use the private commands to both receive and return data.

The device-specific commands can choose to use the fields in `struct ifreq`, but they already convey a standardized meaning, and it's unlikely that the driver can adapt the structure to its needs. The field `ifr_data` is a `caddr_t` item (a pointer) that is meant to be used for device-specific needs. The driver and the program used to invoke its *ioctl* commands should agree about the use of `ifr_data`. For example, *pppstats* uses device-specific commands to retrieve information from the *ppp* interface driver.

It's not worth showing an implementation of *do_ioctl* here, but with the information in this chapter and the kernel examples, you should be able to write one when you need it. Note, however, that the *plip* implementation uses `ifr_data` incorrectly and should not be used as an example for an *ioctl* implementation.

Statistical Information

The last method a driver needs is *get_stats*. This method returns a pointer to the statistics for the device. Its implementation is pretty easy; the one shown works even when several interfaces are managed by the same driver, because the statistics are hosted within the device data structure.

```
struct net_device_stats *snull_stats(struct net_device *dev)
{
    struct snull_priv *priv = (struct snull_priv *) dev->priv;
    return &priv->stats;
}
```

The real work needed to return meaningful statistics is distributed throughout the driver, where the various fields are updated. The following list shows the most interesting fields in `struct net_device_stats`.

`unsigned long rx_packets;`
`unsigned long tx_packets;`
These fields hold the total number of incoming and outgoing packets successfully transferred by the interface.

`unsigned long rx_bytes;`
`unsigned long tx_bytes;`
The number of bytes received and transmitted by the interface. These fields were added in the 2.2 kernel.

`unsigned long rx_errors;`
`unsigned long tx_errors;`
> The number of erroneous receptions and transmissions. There's no end of things that can go wrong with packet transmission, and the `net_device_stats` structure includes six counters for specific receive errors and five for transmit errors. See `<linux/netdevice.h>` for the full list. If possible, your driver should maintain detailed error statistics, because they can be most helpful to system administrators trying to track down a problem.

`unsigned long rx_dropped;`
`unsigned long tx_dropped;`
> The number of packets dropped during reception and transmission. Packets are dropped when there's no memory available for packet data. `tx_dropped` is rarely used.

`unsigned long collisions;`
> The number of collisions due to congestion on the medium.

`unsigned long multicast;`
> The number of multicast packets received.

It is worth repeating that the *get_stats* method can be called at any time—even when the interface is down—so the driver should not release statistic information when running the *stop* method.

Multicasting

A *multicast* packet is a network packet meant to be received by more than one host, but not by all hosts. This functionality is obtained by assigning special hardware addresses to groups of hosts. Packets directed to one of the special addresses should be received by all the hosts in that group. In the case of Ethernet, a multicast address has the least significant bit of the first address octet set in the destination address, while every device board has that bit clear in its own hardware address.

The tricky part of dealing with host groups and hardware addresses is performed by applications and the kernel, and the interface driver doesn't need to deal with these problems.

Transmission of multicast packets is a simple problem because they look exactly like any other packets. The interface transmits them over the communication medium without looking at the destination address. It's the kernel that has to assign a correct hardware destination address; the *hard_header* device method, if defined, doesn't need to look in the data it arranges.

The kernel handles the job of tracking which multicast addresses are of interest at any given time. The list can change frequently, since it is a function of the applications that are running at any given time and the user's interest. It is the driver's job to accept the list of interesting multicast addresses and deliver to the kernel any packets sent to those addresses. How the driver implements the multicast list is somewhat dependent on how the underlying hardware works. Typically, hardware belongs to one of three classes, as far as multicast is concerned:

- Interfaces that cannot deal with multicast. These interfaces either receive packets directed specifically to their hardware address (plus broadcast packets), or they receive every packet. They can receive multicast packets only by receiving every packet, thus potentially overwhelming the operating system with a huge number of "uninteresting" packets. You don't usually count these interfaces as multicast capable, and the driver won't set IFF_MULTICAST in dev->flags.

  Point-to-point interfaces are a special case, because they always receive every packet without performing any hardware filtering.

- Interfaces that can tell multicast packets from other packets (host-to-host or broadcast). These interfaces can be instructed to receive every multicast packet and let the software determine if this host is a valid recipient. The overhead introduced in this case is acceptable, because the number of multicast packets on a typical network is low.

- Interfaces that can perform hardware detection of multicast addresses. These interfaces can be passed a list of multicast addresses for which packets are to be received, and they will ignore other multicast packets. This is the optimum case for the kernel, because it doesn't waste processor time dropping "uninteresting" packets received by the interface.

The kernel tries to exploit the capabilities of high-level interfaces by supporting at its best the third device class, which is the most versatile. Therefore, the kernel notifies the driver whenever the list of valid multicast addresses is changed, and it passes the new list to the driver so it can update the hardware filter according to the new information.

Kernel Support for Multicasting

Support for multicast packets is made up of several items: a device method, a data structure and device flags.

```
void (*dev->set_multicast_list)(struct net_device *dev);
```
This device method is called whenever the list of machine addresses associated with the device changes. It is also called when dev->flags is modified, because some flags (e.g., IFF_PROMISC) may also require you to reprogram the hardware filter. The method receives a pointer to struct net_device as an argument and returns void. A driver not interested in implementing this

method can leave the field set to NULL.

`struct dev_mc_list *dev->mc_list;`

> This is a linked list of all the multicast addresses associated with the device. The actual definition of the structure is introduced at the end of this section.

`int dev->mc_count;`

> The number of items in the linked list. This information is somewhat redundant, but checking `mc_count` against 0 is a useful shortcut for checking the list.

`IFF_MULTICAST`

> Unless the driver sets this flag in `dev->flags`, the interface won't be asked to handle multicast packets. The *set_multicast_list* method will nonetheless be called when `dev->flags` changes, because the multicast list may have changed while the interface was not active.

`IFF_ALLMULTI`

> This flag is set in `dev->flags` by the networking software to tell the driver to retrieve all multicast packets from the network. This happens when multicast routing is enabled. If the flag is set, `dev->mc_list` shouldn't be used to filter multicast packets.

`IFF_PROMISC`

> This flag is set in `dev->flags` when the interface is put into promiscuous mode. Every packet should be received by the interface, independent of `dev->mc_list`.

The last bit of information needed by the driver developer is the definition of `struct dev_mc_list`, which lives in *<linux/netdevice.h>*.

```
struct dev_mc_list {
    struct dev_mc_list   *next;                  /* Next address in list */
    __u8                 dmi_addr[MAX_ADDR_LEN]; /* Hardware address */
    unsigned char        dmi_addrlen;            /* Address length */
    int                  dmi_users;              /* Number of users */
    int                  dmi_gusers;             /* Number of groups */
};
```

Because multicasting and hardware addresses are independent of the actual transmission of packets, this structure is portable across network implementations, and each address is identified by a string of octets and a length, just like `dev->dev_addr`.

A Typical Implementation

The best way to describe the design of *set_multicast_list* is to show you some pseudocode.

The following function is a typical implementation of the function in a full-featured (ff) driver. The driver is full featured in that the interface it controls has a complex hardware packet filter, which can hold a table of multicast addresses to be received by this host. The maximum size of the table is FF_TABLE_SIZE.

All the functions prefixed with ff_ are placeholders for hardware-specific operations.

```
void ff_set_multicast_list(struct net_device *dev)
{
    struct dev_mc_list *mcptr;

    if (dev->flags & IFF_PROMISC) {
        ff_get_all_packets();
        return;
    }
    /* If there's more addresses than we handle, get all multicast
    packets and sort them out in software. */
    if (dev->flags & IFF_ALLMULTI || dev->mc_count > FF_TABLE_SIZE) {
        ff_get_all_multicast_packets();
        return;
    }
    /* No multicast?  Just get our own stuff */
    if (dev->mc_count == 0) {
        ff_get_only_own_packets();
        return;
    }
    /* Store all of the multicast addresses in the hardware filter */
    ff_clear_mc_list();
    for (mc_ptr = dev->mc_list; mc_ptr; mc_ptr = mc_ptr->next)
        ff_store_mc_address(mc_ptr->dmi_addr);
    ff_get_packets_in_multicast_list();
}
```

This implementation can be simplified if the interface cannot store a multicast table in the hardware filter for incoming packets. In that case, FF_TABLE_SIZE reduces to 0 and the last four lines of code are not needed.

As was mentioned earlier, even interfaces that can't deal with multicast packets need to implement the *set_multicast_list* method to be notified about changes in dev->flags. This approach could be called a "nonfeatured" (nf) implementation. The implementation is very simple, as shown by the following code:

```
void nf_set_multicast_list(struct net_device *dev)
{
    if (dev->flags & IFF_PROMISC)
        nf_get_all_packets();
    else
        nf_get_only_own_packets();
}
```

Implementing IFF_PROMISC is important, because otherwise the user won't be able to run *tcpdump* or any other network analyzers. If the interface runs a point-to-point link, on the other hand, there's no need to implement *set_multicast_list* at all, because users receive every packet anyway.

Backward Compatibility

Version 2.3.43 of the kernel saw a major rework of the networking subsystem. The new "softnet" implementation was a great improvement in terms of performance and clean design. It also, of course, brought changes to the network driver interface—though fewer than one might have expected.

Differences in Linux 2.2

First of all, Linux 2.3.14 renamed the network device structure, which had always been struct device, to struct net_device. The new name is certainly more appropriate, since the structure was never meant to describe devices in general.

Prior to version 2.3.43, the functions *netif_start_queue*, *netif_stop_queue*, and *netif_wake_queue* did not exist. Packet transmission was, instead, controlled by three fields in the device structure, and *sysdep.h* implements the three functions using the three fields when compiling for 2.2 or 2.0.

unsigned char start;
:   This variable indicated that the interface was ready for operations; it was normally set to 1 in the driver's *open* method. The current implementation is to call *netif_start_queue* instead.

unsigned long interrupt;
:   interrupt was used to indicate that the device was servicing an interrupt—accordingly, it was set to 1 at the beginning of the interrupt handler and to 0 before returning. It was never a substitute for proper locking, and its use has been replaced with internal spinlocks.

unsigned long tbusy;
:   When nonzero, this variable indicated that the device could handle no more outgoing packets. Where a 2.4 driver will call *netif_stop_queue*, older drivers would set tbusy to 1. Restarting the queue required setting tbusy back to 0 and calling mark_bh(NET_BH).

Normally, setting tbusy was sufficient to ensure that the driver's *hard_start_xmit* method would not be called. However, if the networking system decided that a transmitter lockup must have occurred, it would call that method anyway. There was no *tx_timeout* method before softnet was integrated. Thus, pre-softnet drivers had to explicitly check for a call to *hard_start_xmit* when tbusy was set and react accordingly.

The type of the **name** field in **struct device** was different. The 2.2 version was simply

```
char *name;
```

Thus, the storage for the interface name had to be allocated separately, and **name** assigned to point to that storage. Usually the device name was stored in a static variable within the driver. The **%d** notation for dynamically assigned interface names was not present in 2.2; instead, if the name began with a null byte or a space character, the kernel would allocate the next **eth** name. The 2.4 kernel still implements this behavior, but its use is deprecated. Starting with 2.5, only the **%d** format is likely to be recognized.

The **owner** field (and the **SET_MODULE_OWNER** macro) were added in kernel 2.4.0-test11, just before the official stable release. Previously, network driver modules had to maintain their own use counts. *sysdep.h* defines an empty **SET_MODULE_OWNER** for kernels that do not have it; portable code should also continue to manage its use count manually (in addition to letting the networking system do it).

The link state functions (*netif_carrier_on* and *netif_carrier_off*) did not exist in the 2.2 kernel. The kernel simply did without that information in those days.

Further Differences in Linux 2.0

The 2.1 development series also saw its share of changes to the network driver interface. Most took the form of small changes to function prototypes, rather than sweeping changes to the network code as a whole.

Interface statistics were kept in a structure called **struct 1enet_statistics**, defined in **<linux/if_ether.h>**. Even non-Ethernet drivers used this structure. The field names were all the same as the current **struct net_device_stats**, but the **rx_bytes** and **tx_bytes** fields were not present.

The 2.0 kernel handled transmitter lockups in the same way as 2.2 did. There was, however, an additional function:

```
void dev_tint(struct device *dev);
```

This function would be called by the driver after a lockup had been cleared to restart the transmission of packets.

A couple of functions had different prototypes. *dev_kfree_skb* had a second, integer argument that was either **FREE_READ** for incoming packets (i.e., **skb**s allocated by the driver) or **FREE_WRITE** for outgoing packets (**skb**s allocated by the networking code). Almost all calls to *dev_kfree_skb* in network driver code used **FREE_WRITE**. The nonchecking versions of the **skb** functions (such as *__skb_push*) did not exist; *sysdep.h* in the sample code provides emulation for these functions under 2.0.

The *rebuild_header* method had a different set of arguments:

```
int (*rebuild_header) (void *eth, struct device *dev,
unsigned long raddr, struct sk_buff *skb);
```

The Linux kernel also made heavier use of *rebuild_header*; it did most of the work that *hard_header* does now. When *snull* is compiled under Linux 2.0, it builds hardware headers as follows:

```
int snull_rebuild_header(void *buff, struct net_device *dev, unsigned long dst,
                    struct sk_buff *skb)
{
    struct ethhdr *eth = (struct ethhdr *)buff;

    memcpy(eth->h_source, dev->dev_addr, dev->addr_len);
    memcpy(eth->h_dest, dev->dev_addr, dev->addr_len);
    eth->h_dest[ETH_ALEN-1]   ^= 0x01;   /* dest is us xor 1 */
    return 0;
}
```

The device methods for header caching were also significantly different in this kernel. If your driver needs to implement these functions directly (very few do), and it also needs to work with the 2.0 kernel, see the definitions in `<linux/netdevice.h>` to see how things were done in those days.

Probing and HAVE_DEVLIST

If you look at the source for almost any network driver in the kernel, you will find some boilerplate that looks like this:

```
#ifdef HAVE_DEVLIST
/*
 * Support for an alternate probe manager,
 * which will eliminate the boilerplate below.
 */
struct netdev_entry netcard_drv =
{cardname, netcard_probe1, NETCARD_IO_EXTENT, netcard_portlist};
#else
/* Regular probe routine defined here */
```

Interestingly, this code has been around since the 1.1 development series, but we are still waiting for the promised alternate probe manager. It is probably safe to not worry about being prepared for this great change, especially since ideas for how to implement it will likely have changed in the intervening years.

Quick Reference

This section provides a reference for the concepts introduced in this chapter. It also explains the role of each header file that a driver needs to include. The lists of fields in the `net_device` and `sk_buff` structures, however, are not repeated here.

`#include <linux/netdevice.h>`
> This header hosts the definitions of `struct net_device` and `struct net_device_stats`, and includes a few other headers that are needed by network drivers.

`int register_netdev(struct net_device *dev);`
`void unregister_netdev(struct net_device *dev);`
> Register and unregister a network device.

`SET_MODULE_OWNER(struct net_device *dev);`
> This macro will store a pointer to the current module in the device structure (or in any structure with an **owner** field, actually); it is used to enable the networking subsystem to manage the module's use count.

`netif_start_queue(struct net_device *dev);`
`netif_stop_queue(struct net_device *dev);`
`netif_wake_queue(struct net_device *dev);`
> These functions control the passing of packets to the driver for transmission. No packets will be transmitted until *netif_start_queue* has been called. *netif_stop_queue* suspends transmission, and *netif_wake_queue* restarts the queue and pokes the network layer to restart transmitting packets.

`void netif_rx(struct sk_buff *skb);`
> This function can be called (including at interrupt time) to notify the kernel that a packet has been received and encapsulated into a socket buffer.

`#include <linux/if.h>`
> Included by *netdevice.h*, this file declares the interface flags (`IFF_` macros) and `struct ifmap`, which has a major role in the *ioctl* implementation for network drivers.

`void netif_carrier_off(struct net_device *dev);`
`void netif_carrier_on(struct net_device *dev);`
`int netif_carrier_ok(struct net_device *dev);`
> The first two functions may be used to tell the kernel whether a carrier signal is currently present on the given interface. *netif_carrier_ok* will test the carrier state as reflected in the device structure.

```
#include <linux/if_ether.h>
ETH_ALEN
ETH_P_IP
struct ethhdr;
```
Included by *netdevice.h*, *if_ether.h* defines all the ETH_ macros used to represent octet lengths (such as the address length) and network protocols (such as IP). It also defines the ethhdr structure.

```
#include <linux/skbuff.h>
```
The definition of struct sk_buff and related structures, as well as several inline functions to act on the buffers. This header is included by *netdevice.h*.

```
struct sk_buff *alloc_skb(unsigned int len, int priority);
struct sk_buff *dev_alloc_skb(unsigned int len);
void kfree_skb(struct sk_buff *skb);
void dev_kfree_skb(struct sk_buff *skb);
```
These functions handle the allocation and freeing of socket buffers. Drivers should normally use the dev_ variants, which are intended for that purpose.

```
unsigned char *skb_put(struct sk_buff *skb, int len);
unsigned char *__skb_put(struct sk_buff *skb, int len);
unsigned char *skb_push(struct sk_buff *skb, int len);
unsigned char *__skb_push(struct sk_buff *skb, int len);
```
These functions add data to an skb; *skb_put* puts the data at the end of the skb, while *skb_push* puts it at the beginning. The regular versions perform checking to ensure that adequate space is available; double-underscore versions leave those tests out.

```
int skb_headroom(struct sk_buff *skb);
int skb_tailroom(struct sk_buff *skb);
void skb_reserve(struct sk_buff *skb, int len);
```
These functions perform management of space within an skb. *skb_headroom* and *skb_tailroom* tell how much space is available at the beginning and end, respectively, of an skb. *skb_reserve* may be used to reserve space at the beginning of an skb, which must be empty.

```
unsigned char *skb_pull(struct sk_buff *skb, int len);
```
skb_pull will "remove" data from an skb by adjusting the internal pointers.

```
#include <linux/etherdevice.h>
void ether_setup(struct net_device *dev);
```
This function sets most device methods to the general-purpose implementation for Ethernet drivers. It also sets dev->flags and assigns the next available ethx name to dev->name if the first character in the name is a blank space or the null character.

```
unsigned short eth_type_trans(struct sk_buff *skb, struct
    net_device *dev);
```
When an Ethernet interface receives a packet, this function can be called to set `skb->pkt_type`. The return value is a protocol number that is usually stored in `skb->protocol`.

```
#include <linux/sockios.h>
```
SIOCDEVPRIVATE

This is the first of 16 *ioctl* commands that can be implemented by each driver for its own private use. All the network *ioctl* commands are defined in *sockios.h*.

## CHAPTER FIFTEEN

OVERVIEW OF PERIPHERAL BUSES

Whereas Chapter 8 introduced the lowest levels of hardware control, this chapter provides an overview of the higher-level bus architectures. A bus is made up of both an electrical interface and a programming interface. In this chapter, we deal with the programming interface.

This chapter covers a number of bus architectures. However, the primary focus is on the kernel functions that access PCI peripherals, because these days the PCI bus is the most commonly used peripheral bus on desktops and bigger computers, and the one that is best supported by the kernel. ISA is still common for electronic hobbyists and is described later, although it is pretty much a bare-metal kind of bus and there isn't much to say in addition to what is covered in Chapter 8 and Chapter 9.

The PCI Interface

Although many computer users think of PCI (Peripheral Component Interconnect) as a way of laying out electrical wires, it is actually a complete set of specifications defining how different parts of a computer should interact.

The PCI specification covers most issues related to computer interfaces. We are not going to cover it all here; in this section we are mainly concerned with how a PCI driver can find its hardware and gain access to it. The probing techniques discussed in "Automatic and Manual Configuration" in Chapter 2, and "Autodetecting the IRQ Number" in Chapter 9 can be used with PCI devices, but the specification offers a preferable alternative to probing.

The PCI architecture was designed as a replacement for the ISA standard, with three main goals: to get better performance when transferring data between the computer and its peripherals, to be as platform independent as possible, and to simplify adding and removing peripherals to the system.

The PCI bus achieves better performance by using a higher clock rate than ISA; its clock runs at 25 or 33 MHz (its actual rate being a factor of the system clock), and 66-MHz and even 133-MHz implementations have recently been deployed as well. Moreover, it is equipped with a 32-bit data bus, and a 64-bit extension has been included in the specification (although only 64-bit platforms implement it). Platform independence is often a goal in the design of a computer bus, and it's an especially important feature of PCI because the PC world has always been dominated by processor-specific interface standards. PCI is currently used extensively on IA-32, Alpha, PowerPC, SPARC64, and IA-64 systems, and some other platforms as well.

What is most relevant to the driver writer, however, is the support for autodetection of interface boards. PCI devices are jumperless (unlike most older peripherals) and are automatically configured at boot time. The device driver, then, must be able to access configuration information in the device in order to complete initialization. This happens without the need to perform any probing.

PCI Addressing

Each PCI peripheral is identified by a *bus* number, a *device* number, and a *function* number. The PCI specification permits a system to host up to 256 buses. Each bus hosts up to 32 devices, and each device can be a multifunction board (such as an audio device with an accompanying CD-ROM drive) with a maximum of eight functions. Each function can thus be identified at hardware level by a 16-bit address, or key. Device drivers written for Linux, though, don't need to deal with those binary addresses as they use a specific data structure, called `pci_dev`, to act on the devices. (We have already seen `struct pci_dev`, of course, in Chapter 13.)

Most recent workstations feature at least two PCI buses. Plugging more than one bus in a single system is accomplished by means of *bridges*, special-purpose PCI peripherals whose task is joining two buses. The overall layout of a PCI system is organized as a tree, where each bus is connected to an upper-layer bus up to bus 0. The CardBus PC-card system is also connected to the PCI system via bridges. A typical PCI system is represented in Figure 15-1, where the various bridges are highlighted.

The 16-bit hardware addresses associated with PCI peripherals, although mostly hidden in the `struct pci_dev` object, are still visible occasionally, especially when lists of devices are being used. One such situation is the output of *lspci* (part of the *pciutils* package, available with most distributions) and the layout of information in */proc/pci* and */proc/bus/pci*.* When the hardware address is displayed, it can either be shown as a 16-bit value, as two values (an 8-bit bus number and an

---

* Please note that the discussion, as usual, is based on the 2.4 version of the kernel, relegating backward compatibility issues to the end of the chapter.

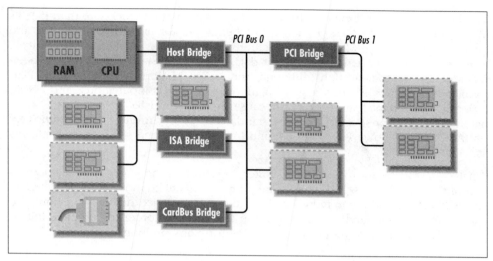

Figure 15-1. Layout of a Typical PCI System

8-bit device and function number), or as three values (bus, device, and function); all the values are usually displayed in hexadecimal.

For example, */proc/bus/pci/devices* uses a single 16-bit field (to ease parsing and sorting), while */proc/bus/busnumber* splits the address into three fields. The following shows how those addresses appear, showing only the beginning of the output lines:

```
rudo% lspci | cut -d: -f1-2
00:00.0 Host bridge
00:01.0 PCI bridge
00:07.0 ISA bridge
00:07.1 IDE interface
00:07.3 Bridge
00:07.4 USB Controller
00:09.0 SCSI storage controller
00:0b.0 Multimedia video controller
01:05.0 VGA compatible controller
rudo% cat /proc/bus/pci/devices | cut -d\      -f1,3
0000    0
0008    0
0038    0
0039    0
003b    0
003c    b
0048    a
0058    b
0128    a
```

The two lists of devices are sorted in the same order, since *lspci* uses the */proc* files as its source of information. Taking the VGA video controller as an example, 0x128 means 01:05.0 when split into bus (eight bits), device (five bits) and function (three bits). The second field in the two listings shown shows the class of device and the interrupt number, respectively.

The hardware circuitry of each peripheral board answers queries pertaining to three address spaces: memory locations, I/O ports, and configuration registers. The first two address spaces are shared by all the devices on a PCI bus (i.e., when you access a memory location, all the devices see the bus cycle at the same time). The configuration space, on the other hand, exploits *geographical addressing*. Configuration transactions (i.e., bus accesses that insist on the configuration space) address only one slot at a time. Thus, there are no collisions at all with configuration access.

As far as the driver is concerned, memory and I/O regions are accessed in the usual ways via *inb*, *readb*, and so forth. Configuration transactions, on the other hand, are performed by calling specific kernel functions to access configuration registers. With regard to interrupts, every PCI slot has four interrupt pins, and each device function can use one of them without being concerned about how those pins are routed to the CPU. Such routing is the responsibility of the computer platform and is implemented outside of the PCI bus. Since the PCI specification requires interrupt lines to be shareable, even a processor with a limited number of IRQ lines, like the x86, can host many PCI interface boards (each with four interrupt pins).

The I/O space in a PCI bus uses a 32-bit address bus (leading to 4 GB of I/O ports), while the memory space can be accessed with either 32-bit or 64-bit addresses. However, 64-bit addresses are available only on a few platforms. Addresses are supposed to be unique to one device, but software may erroneously configure two devices to the same address, making it impossible to access either one; the problem never occurs unless a driver is willingly playing with registers it shouldn't touch. The good news is that every memory and I/O address region offered by the interface board can be remapped by means of configuration transactions. That is, the firmware initializes PCI hardware at system boot, mapping each region to a different address to avoid collisions.* The addresses to which these regions are currently mapped can be read from the configuration space, so the Linux driver can access its devices without probing. After reading the configuration registers the driver can safely access its hardware.

The PCI configuration space consists of 256 bytes for each device function, and the layout of the configuration registers is standardized. Four bytes of the

---

* Actually, that configuration is not restricted to the time the system boots; hot-pluggable devices, for example, cannot be available at boot time and appear later instead. The main point here is that the device driver need not change the address of I/O or memory regions.

configuration space hold a unique function ID, so the driver can identify its device by looking for the specific ID for that peripheral.* In summary, each device board is geographically addressed to retrieve its configuration registers; the information in those registers can then be used to perform normal I/O access, without the need for further geographic addressing.

It should be clear from this description that the main innovation of the PCI interface standard over ISA is the configuration address space. Therefore, in addition to the usual driver code, a PCI driver needs the ability to access configuration space, in order to save itself from risky probing tasks.

For the remainder of this chapter, we'll use the word *device* to refer to a device function, because each function in a multifunction board acts as an independent entity. When we refer to a device, we mean the tuple "bus number, device number, function number," which can be represented by a 16-bit number or two 8-bit numbers (usually called bus and devfn).

Boot Time

To see how PCI works, we'll start from system boot, since that's when the devices are configured.

When power is applied to a PCI device, the hardware remains inactive. In other words, the device will respond only to configuration transactions. At power on, the device has no memory and no I/O ports mapped in the computer's address space; every other device-specific feature, such as interrupt reporting, is disabled as well.

Fortunately, every PCI motherboard is equipped with PCI-aware firmware, called the BIOS, NVRAM, or PROM, depending on the platform. The firmware offers access to the device configuration address space by reading and writing registers in the PCI controller.

At system boot, the firmware (or the Linux kernel, if so configured) performs configuration transactions with every PCI peripheral in order to allocate a safe place for any address region it offers. By the time a device driver accesses the device, its memory and I/O regions have already been mapped into the processor's address space. The driver can change this default assignment, but it will never need to do that.

As suggested, the user can look at the PCI device list and the devices' configuration registers by reading */proc/bus/pci/devices* and */proc/bus/pci/*/**. The former is a text file with (hexadecimal) device information, and the latter are binary files that report a snapshot of the configuration registers of each device, one file per device.

---

* You'll find the ID of any device in its own hardware manual. A list is included in the file *pci.ids*, part of the *pciutils* package and of the kernel sources; it doesn't pretend to be complete, but just lists the most renowned vendors and devices.

Configuration Registers and Initialization

As mentioned earlier, the layout of the configuration space is device independent. In this section, we look at the configuration registers that are used to identify the peripherals.

PCI devices feature a 256-byte address space. The first 64 bytes are standardized, while the rest are device dependent. Figure 15-2 shows the layout of the device-independent configuration space.

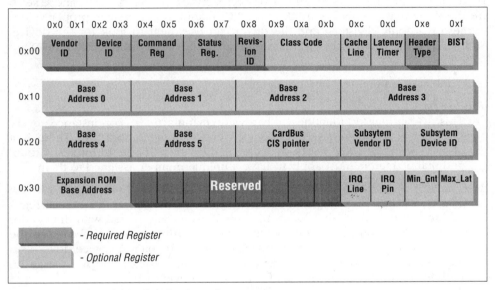

Figure 15-2. *The standardized PCI configuration registers*

As the figure shows, some of the PCI configuration registers are required and some are optional. Every PCI device must contain meaningful values in the required registers, whereas the contents of the optional registers depend on the actual capabilities of the peripheral. The optional fields are not used unless the contents of the required fields indicate that they are valid. Thus, the required fields assert the board's capabilities, including whether the other fields are usable or not.

It's interesting to note that the PCI registers are always little-endian. Although the standard is designed to be architecture independent, the PCI designers sometimes show a slight bias toward the PC environment. The driver writer should be careful about byte ordering when accessing multibyte configuration registers; code that works on the PC might not work on other platforms. The Linux developers have taken care of the byte-ordering problem (see the next section, "Accessing the Configuration Space"), but the issue must be kept in mind. If you ever need to convert data from host order to PCI order or vice versa, you can resort to the functions defined in `<asm/byteorder.h>`, introduced in Chapter 10, knowing that PCI byte order is little-endian.

Describing all the configuration items is beyond the scope of this book. Usually, the technical documentation released with each device describes the supported registers. What we're interested in is how a driver can look for its device and how it can access the device's configuration space.

Three or five PCI registers identify a device: `vendorID`, `deviceID`, and `class` are the three that are always used. Every PCI manufacturer assigns proper values to these read-only registers, and the driver can use them to look for the device. Additionally, the fields `subsystem vendorID` and `subsystem deviceID` are sometimes set by the vendor to further differentiate similar devices.

Let's look at these registers in more detail.

`vendorID`

> This 16-bit register identifies a hardware manufacturer. For instance, every Intel device is marked with the same vendor number, `0x8086`. There is a global registry of such numbers, maintained by the PCI Special Interest Group, and manufacturers must apply to have a unique number assigned to them.

`deviceID`

> This is another 16-bit register, selected by the manufacturer; no official registration is required for the device ID. This ID is usually paired with the vendor ID to make a unique 32-bit identifier for a hardware device. We'll use the word *signature* to refer to the vendor and device ID pair. A device driver usually relies on the signature to identify its device; you can find what value to look for in the hardware manual for the target device.

`class`

> Every peripheral device belongs to a *class*. The `class` register is a 16-bit value whose top 8 bits identify the "base class" (or *group*). For example, "ethernet" and "token ring" are two classes belonging to the "network" group, while the "serial" and "parallel" classes belong to the "communication" group. Some drivers can support several similar devices, each of them featuring a different signature but all belonging to the same class; these drivers can rely on the `class` register to identify their peripherals, as shown later.

`subsystem vendorID`
`subsystem deviceID`

> These fields can be used for further identification of a device. If the chip in itself is a generic interface chip to a local (onboard) bus, it is often used in several completely different roles, and the driver must identify the actual device it is talking with. The subsystem identifiers are used to this aim.

Using those identifiers, you can detect and get hold of your device. With version 2.4 of the kernel, the concept of a *PCI driver* and a specialized initialization interface have been introduced. While that interface is the preferred one for new drivers, it is not available for older kernel versions. As an alternative to the PCI driver interface, the following headers, macros, and functions can be used by a PCI module to look for its hardware device. We chose to introduce this backward-compatible interface first because it is portable to all kernel versions we cover in this book. Moreover, it is somewhat more immediate by virtue of being less abstracted from direct hardware management.

`#include <linux/config.h>`

The driver needs to know if the PCI functions are available in the kernel. By including this header, the driver gains access to the `CONFIG_` macros, including `CONFIG_PCI`, described next. But note that every source file that includes `<linux/module.h>` already includes this one as well.

`CONFIG_PCI`

This macro is defined if the kernel includes support for PCI calls. Not every computer includes a PCI bus, so the kernel developers chose to make PCI support a compile-time option to save memory when running Linux on non-PCI computers. If `CONFIG_PCI` is not enabled, every PCI function call is defined to return a failure status, so the driver may or may not use a preprocessor conditional to mask out PCI support. If the driver can only handle PCI devices (as opposed to both PCI and non-PCI device implementations), it should issue a compile-time error if the macro is undefined.

`#include <linux/pci.h>`

This header declares all the prototypes introduced in this section, as well as the symbolic names associated with PCI registers and bits; it should always be included. This header also defines symbolic values for the error codes returned by the functions.

`int pci_present(void);`

Because the PCI-related functions don't make sense on non-PCI computers, the *pci_present* function allows one to check if PCI functionality is available or not. The call is discouraged as of 2.4, because it now just checks if some PCI device is there. With 2.0, however, a driver had to call the function to avoid unpleasant errors when looking for its device. Recent kernels just report that no device is there, instead. The function returns a boolean value of true (nonzero) if the host is PCI aware.

`struct pci_dev;`

The data structure is used as a software object representing a PCI device. It is at the core of every PCI operation in the system.

```
struct pci_dev *pci_find_device (unsigned int vendor,
        unsigned int device, const struct pci_dev *from);
```
If CONFIG_PCI is defined and *pci_present* is true, this function is used to scan the list of installed devices looking for a device featuring a specific signature. The from argument is used to get hold of multiple devices with the same signature; the argument should point to the last device that has been found, so that the search can continue instead of restarting from the head of the list. To find the first device, from is specified as NULL. If no (further) device is found, NULL is returned.

```
struct pci_dev *pci_find_class (unsigned int class, const
        struct pci_dev *from);
```
This function is similar to the previous one, but it looks for devices belonging to a specific class (a 16-bit class: both the base class and subclass). It is rarely used nowadays except in very low-level PCI drivers. The from argument is used exactly like in *pci_find_device*.

```
int pci_enable_device(struct pci_dev *dev);
```
This function actually enables the device. It wakes up the device and in some cases also assigns its interrupt line and I/O regions. This happens, for example, with CardBus devices (which have been made completely equivalent to PCI at driver level).

```
struct pci_dev *pci_find_slot (unsigned int bus, unsigned
        int devfn);
```
This function returns a PCI device structure based on a bus/device pair. The devfn argument represents both the *device* and *function* items. Its use is extremely rare (drivers should not care about which slot their device is plugged into); it is listed here just for completeness.

Based on this information, initialization for a typical device driver that handles a single device type will look like the following code. The code is for a hypothetical device *jail* and is Just Another Instruction List:

```
#ifndef CONFIG_PCI
#  error "This driver needs PCI support to be available"
#endif

int jail_find_all_devices(void)
{
    struct pci_dev *dev = NULL;
    int found;

    if (!pci_present())
    return -ENODEV;

    for (found=0; found < JAIL_MAX_DEV;) {
        dev = pci_find_device(JAIL_VENDOR, JAIL_ID, dev);
        if (!dev) /* no more devices are there */
```

```
        break;
        /* do device-specific actions and count the device */
        found += jail_init_one(dev);
    }
    return  (index == 0) ? -ENODEV : 0;
}
```

The role of *jail_init_one* is very device specific and thus not shown here. There are, nonetheless, a few things to keep in mind when writing that function:

- The function may need to perform additional probing to ensure that the device is really one of those it supports. Some PCI peripherals contain a general-purpose PCI interface chip and device-specific circuitry. Every peripheral board that uses the same interface chip has the same signature. Further probing can either be performed by reading the subsystem identifiers or reading specific device registers (in the device I/O regions, introduced later).

- Before accessing any device resource (I/O region or interrupt), the driver must call *pci_enable_device*. If the additional probing just discussed requires accessing device I/O or memory space, the function must be called before such probing takes place.

- A network interface driver should make `dev->driver_data` point to the `struct net_device` associated with this interface.

The function shown in the previous code excerpt returns 0 if it rejects the device and 1 if it accepts it (possibly based on the further probing just described).

The code excerpt shown is correct if the driver deals with only one kind of PCI device, identified by `JAIL_VENDOR` and `JAIL_ID`. If you need to support more vendor/device pairs, your best bet is using the technique introduced later in "Hardware Abstractions," unless you need to support older kernels than 2.4, in which case *pci_find_class* is your friend.

Using *pci_find_class* requires that *jail_find_all_devices* perform a little more work than in the example. The function should check the newly found device against a list of vendor/device pairs, possibly using `dev->vendor` and `dev->device`. Its core should look like this:

```
struct devid {unsigned short vendor, device} devlist[] = {
    {JAIL_VENDOR1, JAIL_DEVICE1},
    {JAIL_VENDOR2, JAIL_DEVICE2},
    /* ... */
    { 0, 0 }
};

    /* ... */

    for (found=0; found < JAIL_MAX_DEV;) {
        struct devid *idptr;
        dev = pci_find_class(JAIL_CLASS, dev);
```

```
            if (!dev) /* no more devices are there */
                break;
            for (idptr = devlist; idptr->vendor; idptr++) {
                if (dev->vendor != idptr->vendor) continue;
                if (dev->device != idptr->device) continue;
                break;
            }
            if (!idptr->vendor) continue; /* not one of ours */
            jail_init_one(dev); /* device-specific initialization */
            found++;
    }
```

Accessing the Configuration Space

After the driver has detected the device, it usually needs to read from or write to the three address spaces: memory, port, and configuration. In particular, accessing the configuration space is vital to the driver because it is the only way it can find out where the device is mapped in memory and in the I/O space.

Because the microprocessor has no way to access the configuration space directly, the computer vendor has to provide a way to do it. To access configuration space, the CPU must write and read registers in the PCI controller, but the exact implementation is vendor dependent and not relevant to this discussion because Linux offers a standard interface to access the configuration space.

As far as the driver is concerned, the configuration space can be accessed through 8-bit, 16-bit, or 32-bit data transfers. The relevant functions are prototyped in `<linux/pci.h>`:

```
int pci_read_config_byte(struct pci_dev *dev, int where, u8
    *ptr);
int pci_read_config_word(struct pci_dev *dev, int where, u16
    *ptr);
int pci_read_config_dword(struct pci_dev *dev, int where,
    u32 *ptr);
```

Read one, two, or four bytes from the configuration space of the device identified by `dev`. The `where` argument is the byte offset from the beginning of the configuration space. The value fetched from the configuration space is returned through `ptr`, and the return value of the functions is an error code. The *word* and *dword* functions convert the value just read from little-endian to the native byte order of the processor, so you need not deal with byte ordering.

```
int pci_write_config_byte (struct pci_dev *dev, int where,
    u8 val);
int pci_write_config_word (struct pci_dev *dev, int where,
    u16 val);
int pci_write_config_dword (struct pci_dev *dev, int where,
    u32 val);
```

Write one, two, or four bytes to the configuration space. The device is identified by dev as usual, and the value being written is passed as val. The *word* and *dword* functions convert the value to little-endian before writing to the peripheral device.

The preferred way to read the configuration variables you need is using the fields of the struct pci_dev that refers to your device. Nonetheless, you'll need the functions just listed if you need to write and read back a configuration variable. Also, you'll need the *pci_read_* functions if you want to keep backward compatibility with kernels older than 2.4.*

The best way to address the configuration variables using the *pci_read_* functions is by means of the symbolic names defined in <linux/pci.h>. For example, the following two-line function retrieves the revision ID of a device by passing the symbolic name for where to *pci_read_config_byte*:

```
unsigned char jail_get_revision(unsigned char bus, unsigned char fn)
{
    unsigned char *revision;

    pci_read_config_byte(bus, fn, PCI_REVISION_ID, &revision);
    return revision;
}
```

As suggested, when accessing multibyte values as single bytes the programmer must remember to watch out for byte-order problems.

Looking at a configuration snapshot

If you want to browse the configuration space of the PCI devices on your system, you can proceed in one of two ways. The easier path is using the resources that Linux already offers via */proc/bus/pci*, although these were not available in version 2.0 of the kernel. The alternative that we follow here is, instead, writing some code of our own to perform the task; such code is both portable across all known 2.*x* kernel releases and a good way to look at the tools in action. The source file *pci/pcidata.c* is included in the sample code provided on the O'Reilly FTP site.

---

* The field names in struct pci_dev changed from version 2.2 and 2.4 because the first layout proved suboptimal. As for 2.0, there was no pci_dev structure, and the one you use is a light emulation offered by the *pci-compat.h* header.

This module creates a dynamic */proc/pcidata* file that contains a binary snapshot of the configuration space for your PCI devices. The snapshot is updated every time the file is read. The size of */proc/pcidata* is limited to `PAGE_SIZE` bytes (to avoid dealing with multipage */proc* files, as introduced in "Using the /proc Filesystem" in Chapter 4). Thus, it lists only the configuration memory for the first `PAGE_SIZE/256` devices, which means 16 or 32 devices according to the platform you are running on. We chose to make */proc/pcidata* a binary file to keep the code simple, instead of making it a text file like most */proc* files. Note that the files in */proc/bus/pci* are binary as well.

Another limitation of *pcidata* is that it scans only the first PCI bus on the system. If your computer includes bridges to other PCI buses, *pcidata* ignores them. This should not be an issue for sample code not meant to be of real use.

Devices appear in */proc/pcidata* in the same order used by */proc/bus/pci/devices* (but in the opposite order from the one used by */proc/pci* in version 2.0).

For example, our frame grabber appears fifth in */proc/pcidata* and (currently) has the following configuration registers:

```
morgana% dd bs=256 skip=4 count=1 if=/proc/pcidata | od -Ax -t x1
1+0 records in
1+0 records out
000000 86 80 23 12 06 00 00 02 00 00 00 04 00 20 00 00
000010 00 00 00 f1 00 00 00 00 00 00 00 00 00 00 00 00
000020 00 00 00 00 00 00 00 00 00 00 00 00 00 00 00 00
000030 00 00 00 00 00 00 00 00 00 00 00 00 0a 01 00 00
000040 00 00 00 00 00 00 00 00 00 00 00 00 00 00 00 00
*
000100
```

The numbers in this dump represent the PCI registers. Using Figure 15-2 as a reference, you can look at the meaning of the numbers shown. Alternatively, you can use the *pcidump* program, also found on the FTP site, which formats and labels the output listing.

The *pcidump* code is not worth including here because the program is simply a long table, plus 10 lines of code that scan the table. Instead, let's look at some selected output lines:

```
morgana% dd bs=256 skip=4 count=1 if=/proc/pcidata | ./pcidump
1+0 records in
1+0 records out
        Compulsory registers:
Vendor id: 8086
Device id: 1223
I/O space enabled: n
Memory enabled: y
Master enabled: y
Revision id (decimal): 0
Programmer Interface: 00
```

```
Class of device: 0400
Header type: 00
Multi function device: n
        Optional registers:
Base Address 0: f1000000
Base Address 0 Is I/O: n
Base Address 0 is 64-bits: n
Base Address 0 is below-1M: n
Base Address 0 is prefetchable: n
Does generate interrupts: y
Interrupt line (decimal): 10
Interrupt pin (decimal): 1
```

pcidata and *pcidump*, used with *grep*, can be useful tools for debugging a driver's initialization code, even though their task is in part already available in the *pciutils* package, included in all recent Linux distributions. Note that, unlike other sample code accompanying the book, the *pcidata.c* module is subject to the GPL because we took the PCI scanning loop from the kernel sources. This shouldn't matter to you as a driver writer, because we've included the module in the source files only as a support utility, not as a template to be reused in new drivers.

Accessing the I/O and Memory Spaces

A PCI device implements up to six I/O address regions. Each region consists of either memory or I/O locations. Most devices implement their I/O registers in memory regions, because it's generally a saner approach (as explained in "I/O Ports and I/O Memory," in Chapter 8). However, unlike normal memory, I/O registers should not be cached by the CPU because each access can have side effects. The PCI device that implements I/O registers as a memory region marks the difference by setting a "memory-is-prefetchable" bit in its configuration register.* If the memory region is marked as prefetchable, the CPU can cache its contents and do all sorts of optimization with it; nonprefetchable memory access, on the other hand, can't be optimized because each access can have side effects, exactly like I/O ports usually have. Peripherals that map their control registers to a memory address range declare that range as nonprefetchable, whereas something like video memory on PCI boards is prefetchable. In this section, we use the word *region* to refer to a generic I/O address space, either memory-mapped or port-mapped.

An interface board reports the size and current location of its regions using configuration registers—the six 32-bit registers shown in Figure 15-2, whose symbolic names are PCI_BASE_ADDRESS_0 through PCI_BASE_ADDRESS_5. Since the I/O space defined by PCI is a 32-bit address space, it makes sense to use the same configuration interface for memory and I/O. If the device uses a 64-bit address

---

* The information lives in one of the low-order bits of the base address PCI registers. The bits are defined in <linux/pci.h>.

bus, it can declare regions in the 64-bit memory space by using two consecutive PCI_BASE_ADDRESS registers for each region, low bits first. It is possible for one device to offer both 32-bit regions and 64-bit regions.

PCI I/O resources in Linux 2.4

In Linux 2.4, the I/O regions of PCI devices have been integrated in the generic resource management. For this reason, you don't need to access the configuration variables in order to know where your device is mapped in memory or I/O space. The preferred interface for getting region information consists of the following functions:

unsigned long pci_resource_start(struct pci_dev *dev, int
    bar);
> The function returns the first address (memory address or I/O port number) associated with one of the six PCI I/O regions. The region is selected by the integer bar (the base address register), ranging from 0 to 5, inclusive.

unsigned long pci_resource_end(struct pci_dev *dev, int
    bar);
> The function returns the last address that is part of the I/O region number bar. Note that this is the last usable address, not the first address after the region.

unsigned long pci_resource_flags(struct pci_dev *dev, int
    bar);
> This function returns the flags associated with this resource.

Resource flags are used to define some features of the individual resource. For PCI resources associated with PCI I/O regions, the information is extracted from the base address registers, but can come from elsewhere for resources not associated with PCI devices.

All resource flags are defined in <linux/ioport.h>; the most important of them are listed here.

IORESOURCE_IO
IORESOURCE_MEM
> If the associated I/O region exists, one and only one of these flags is set.

IORESOURCE_PREFETCH
IORESOURCE_READONLY
> The flags tell whether a memory region is prefetchable and/or write protected. The latter flag is never set for PCI resources.

By making use of the *pci_resource_* functions, a device driver can completely ignore the underlying PCI registers, since the system already used them to structure resource information.

Peeking at the base address registers

By avoiding direct access to the PCI registers, you gain a better hardware abstraction and forward portability but can get no backward portability. If you want your device driver to work with Linux versions older than 2.4, you can't use the beautiful resource interface and must access the PCI registers directly.

In this section we look at how base address registers behave and how they can be accessed. All of this is obviously superfluous if you can exploit resource management as shown previously.

We won't go into much detail here about the base address registers, because if you're going to write a PCI driver, you will need the hardware manual for the device anyway. In particular, we are not going to use either the prefetchable bit or the two "type" bits of the registers, and we'll limit the discussion to 32-bit peripherals. It's nonetheless interesting to see how things are usually implemented and how Linux drivers deal with PCI memory.

The PCI specs state that manufacturers must map each valid region to a configurable address. This means that the device must be equipped with a programmable 32-bit address decoder for each region it implements, and a 64-bit programmable decoder must be present in any board that exploits the 64-bit PCI extension.

The actual implementation and use of a programmable decoder is simplified by the fact that usually the number of bytes in a region is a power of two, for example, 32 bytes, 4 KB, or 2 MB. Moreover, it wouldn't make much sense to map a region to an unaligned address; 1 MB regions naturally align at an address that is a multiple of 1 MB, and 32-byte regions at a multiple of 32. The PCI specification exploits this alignment; it states that the address decoder must look only at the high bits of the address bus and that only the high bits are programmable. This convention also means that the size of any region must be a power of two.

Mapping a PCI region in the physical address space is thus performed by setting a suitable value in the high bits of a configuration register. For example, a 1-MB region, which has 20 bits of address space, is remapped by setting the high 12 bits of the register; thus, to make the board respond to the 64-MB to 65-MB address range, you can write to the register any address in the 0x040*xxxxx* range. In practice, only very high addresses are used to map PCI regions.

This "partial decoding" technique has the additional advantage that the software can determine the size of a PCI region by checking the number of nonprogrammable bits in the configuration register. To this end, the PCI standard states that unused bits must always read as 0. By imposing a minimum size of 8 bytes for I/O regions and 16 bytes for memory regions, the standard can fit some extra information into the low bits of the base address registers:

- Bit 0 is the "space" bit. It is set to 0 if the region maps to the memory address space, and 1 if it maps to the I/O address space.

- Bits 1 and 2 are the "type" bits: memory regions can be marked as 32-bit regions, 64-bit regions, or "32-bit regions that must be mapped below 1 MB" (an obsolete x86-specific idea, now unused).

- Bit 3 is the "prefetchable" bit, used for memory regions.

It's apparent from whence information for the resource flags comes.

Detecting the size of a PCI region is simplified by using several bit masks defined in `<linux/pci.h>`: the `PCI_BASE_ADDRESS_SPACE` bit mask is set to `PCI_BASE_ADDRESS_SPACE_MEMORY` if this is a memory region, and to `PCI_BASE_ADDRESS_SPACE_IO` if it is an I/O region. To know the actual address where a memory region is mapped, you can AND the PCI register with `PCI_BASE_ADDRESS_MEM_MASK` to discard the low bits listed earlier. Use `PCI_BASE_ADDRESS_IO_MASK` for I/O regions. Please note that PCI regions may be allocated in any order by device manufacturers; it's not uncommon to find devices that use the first and third regions, leaving the second unused.

Typical code for reporting the current location and size of the PCI regions looks like the following. This code is part of the *pciregions* module, distributed in the same directory as *pcidata*; the module creates a */proc/pciregions* file, using the code shown earlier to generate data. The program writes a value of all 1s to the configuration register and reads it back to know how many bits of the registers can be programmed. Note that while the program probes the configuration register, the device is actually remapped to the top of the physical address space, which is why interrupt reporting is disabled during the probe (to prevent a driver from accessing the region while it is mapped to the wrong place).

Despite the PCI specs stating that the I/O address space is 32 bits wide, a few manufacturers, clearly x86 biased, pretend that it is 64 KB and do not implement all 32 bits of the base address register. That's why the following code (and the kernel proper) ignores high bits of the address mask for I/O regions.

```
static u32 addresses[] = {
    PCI_BASE_ADDRESS_0,
    PCI_BASE_ADDRESS_1,
    PCI_BASE_ADDRESS_2,
    PCI_BASE_ADDRESS_3,
    PCI_BASE_ADDRESS_4,
    PCI_BASE_ADDRESS_5,
    0
};

int pciregions_read_proc(char *buf, char **start, off_t offset,
                int len, int *eof, void *data)
{
    /* this macro helps in keeping the following lines short */
```

```
#define PRINTF(fmt, args...) sprintf(buf+len, fmt, ## args)
    len=0;

    /* Loop through the devices (code not printed in the book) */

        /* Print the address regions of this device */
        for (i=0; addresses[i]; i++) {
            u32 curr, mask, size;
            char *type;

            pci_read_config_dword(dev, addresses[i],&curr);
            cli();
            pci_write_config_dword(dev, addresses[i],~0);
            pci_read_config_dword(dev, addresses[i],&mask);
            pci_write_config_dword(dev, addresses[i],curr);
            sti();

            if (!mask)
                continue; /* there may be other regions */

            /*
             * apply the I/O or memory mask to current position.
             * note that I/O is limited to 0xffff, and 64-bit is not
             * supported by this simple implementation
             */
            if (curr & PCI_BASE_ADDRESS_SPACE_IO) {
                curr &= PCI_BASE_ADDRESS_IO_MASK;
            } else {
                curr &= PCI_BASE_ADDRESS_MEM_MASK;
            }

            len += PRINTF("\tregion %i: mask 0x%08lx, now at 0x%08lx\n",
                        i, (unsigned long)mask,
                           (unsigned long)curr);
            /* extract the type, and the programmable bits */
            if (mask & PCI_BASE_ADDRESS_SPACE_IO) {
                type = "I/O"; mask &= PCI_BASE_ADDRESS_IO_MASK;
                size = (~mask + 1) & 0xffff; /* Bleah */
            } else {
                type = "mem"; mask &= PCI_BASE_ADDRESS_MEM_MASK;
                size = ~mask + 1;
            }
            len += PRINTF("\tregion %i: type %s, size %i (%i%s)\n", i,
                        type, size,
                        (size & 0xfffff) == 0 ? size >> 20 :
                          (size & 0x3ff) == 0 ? size >> 10 : size,
                        (size & 0xfffff) == 0 ? "MB" :
                          (size & 0x3ff) == 0 ? "KB" : "B");
```

```
            if (len > PAGE_SIZE / 2) {
                len += PRINTF("... more info skipped ...\n");
                *eof = 1; return len;
            }
        }
    return len;
}
```

Here, for example, is what */proc/pciregions* reports for our frame grabber:

```
Bus 0, device 13, fun  0 (id 8086-1223)
        region 0: mask 0xfffff000, now at 0xf1000000
        region 0: type mem, size 4096 (4KB)
```

It's interesting to note that the memory size reported by the program just listed can be overstated. For instance, */proc/pciregions* reported that a video device had 16 MB of memory when it actually had only 1. This lie is acceptable because the size information is used only by the firmware to allocate address ranges; region over-sizing is not a problem for the driver writer who knows the internals of the device and can correctly deal with the address range assigned by the firmware. In this case, device RAM could be added later without the need to change the behavior of PCI registers while upgrading the RAM.

Such overstating, when present, is reflected in the resource interface, and *pci_resource_size* will report the overstated size.

PCI Interrupts

As far as interrupts are concerned, PCI is easy to handle. By the time Linux boots, the computer's firmware has already assigned a unique interrupt number to the device, and the driver just needs to use it. The interrupt number is stored in configuration register 60 (`PCI_INTERRUPT_LINE`), which is one byte wide. This allows for as many as 256 interrupt lines, but the actual limit depends on the CPU being used. The driver doesn't need to bother checking the interrupt number, because the value found in `PCI_INTERRUPT_LINE` is guaranteed to be the right one.

If the device doesn't support interrupts, register 61 (`PCI_INTERRUPT_PIN`) is 0; otherwise, it's nonzero. However, since the driver knows if its device is interrupt driven or not, it doesn't usually need to read `PCI_INTERRUPT_PIN`.

Thus, PCI-specific code for dealing with interrupts just needs to read the configuration byte to obtain the interrupt number that is saved in a local variable, as shown in the following code. Otherwise, the information in Chapter 9 applies.

```
result = pci_read_config_byte(dev, PCI_INTERRUPT_LINE, &myirq);
if (result) { /* deal with error */ }
```

The rest of this section provides additional information for the curious reader, but isn't needed for writing drivers.

A PCI connector has four interrupt pins, and peripheral boards can use any or all of them. Each pin is individually routed to the motherboard's interrupt controller, so interrupts can be shared without any electrical problems. The interrupt controller is then responsible for mapping the interrupt wires (pins) to the processor's hardware; this platform-dependent operation is left to the controller in order to achieve platform independence in the bus itself.

The read-only configuration register located at `PCI_INTERRUPT_PIN` is used to tell the computer which single pin is actually used. It's worth remembering that each device board can host up to eight devices; each device uses a single interrupt pin and reports it in its own configuration register. Different devices on the same device board can use different interrupt pins or share the same one.

The `PCI_INTERRUPT_LINE` register, on the other hand, is read/write. When the computer is booted, the firmware scans its PCI devices and sets the register for each device according to how the interrupt pin is routed for its PCI slot. The value is assigned by the firmware because only the firmware knows how the motherboard routes the different interrupt pins to the processor. For the device driver, however, the `PCI_INTERRUPT_LINE` register is read-only. Interestingly, recent versions of the Linux kernel under some circumstances can assign interrupt lines without resorting to the BIOS.

Handling Hot-Pluggable Devices

During the 2.3 development cycle, the kernel developers overhauled the PCI programming interface in order to simplify things and support hot-pluggable devices, that is, those devices that can be added to or removed from the system while the system runs (such as CardBus devices). The material introduced in this section is not available in 2.2 and earlier kernels, but is the preferred way to go for newer drivers.

The basic idea being exploited is that whenever a new device appears during the system's lifetime, all available device drivers must check whether the new device is theirs or not. Therefore, instead of using the classic *init* and *cleanup* entry points for the driver, the hot-plug-aware device driver must register an object with the kernel, and the *probe* function for the object will be asked to check any device in the system to take hold of it or leave it alone.

This approach has no downside: the usual case of a static device list is handled by scanning the device list once for each device at system boot; modularized drivers will just unload as usual if no device is there, and an external process devoted to monitoring the bus will arrange for them to be loaded if the need arises. This is exactly how the PCMCIA subsystem has always worked, and having it integrated in the kernel proper allows for more coherent handling of similar issues with different hardware environments.

While you may object that hot-pluggable PCI is not common these days, the new driver-object technique proves very useful even for non-hot-plug drivers that must handle a number of alternative devices. The initialization code is simplified and streamlined because it just needs to check the *current* device against a list of known devices, instead of actively searching the PCI bus by looping once around *pci_find_class* or looping several times around *pci_find_device*.

But let's show some code. The design is built around struct pci_driver, defined in <linux/pci.h> as usual. The structure defines the operations it implements, and also includes a list of devices it supports (in order to avoid unneeded calls to its code). In short, here's how initialization and cleanup are handled, for a hypothetical "hot plug PCI module" (HPPM):

```
struct pci_driver hppm_driver = { /* .... */ };

int hppm_init_module(void)
{
    return pci_module_init(&hppm_driver);
}

int hppm_cleanup_module(void)
{
    pci_unregister_driver(&hppm_driver);
}

module_init(hppm);
module_exit(hppm);
```

That's all. It's incredibly easy. The hidden magic is split between the implementation of *pci_module_init* and the internals of the driver structure. We'd better follow a top-down path and start by introducing the relevant functions:

int pci_register_driver(struct pci_driver *drv);
> This function inserts the driver in a linked list that is maintained by the system. That's how compiled-in device drivers perform their initialization; it is not used directly by modularized code. The return value is a count of devices being handled by the driver.

int pci_module_init(struct pci_driver *drv);
> This function is a wrapper over the previous one and is meant to be called by modularized initialization code. It returns 0 for success and -ENODEV if no device has been found. This is meant to prevent a module from staying in memory if no device is currently there (expecting the module to be auto-loaded later if a matching device appears). Since this function is defined as inline, its behavior actually changes depending on whether MODULE is defined or not; it can thus be used as a drop-in replacement for *pci_register_driver* even for nonmodularized code.

`void pci_unregister_driver(struct pci_driver *drv);`
> This function removes the driver from the linked list of known drivers.

`void pci_insert_device(struct pci_dev *dev, struct pci_bus`
> `*bus);`
`void pci_remove_device(struct pci_dev *dev);`
> These two functions implement the flip side of the hot-plug system; they are called by the event handlers associated with plug/unplug events reported by a bus. The `dev` structure is used to scan the list of registered drivers. There is no need for device drivers to call them, and they are listed here to help give a complete view of the design around PCI drivers.

`struct pci_driver *pci_dev_driver(const struct pci_dev`
> `*dev);`
> This is a utility function to look up the driver associated with a device (if any). It's used by */proc/bus* support functions and is not meant to be called by device drivers.

The pci_driver structure

The `pci_driver` data structure is the core of hot-plug support, and we'll describe it in detail to complete the whole picture. The structure is pretty small, being made of just a few methods and a device ID list.

`struct list_head node;`
> Used to manage a list of drivers. It's an example of generic lists, which were introduced in "Linked Lists" in Chapter 10; it's not meant to be used by device drivers.

`char *name;`
> The name of the driver; it has informational value.

`const struct pci_device_id *id_table;`
> An array that lists which devices are supported by this driver. The *probe* method will be called only for devices that match one of the items in the array. If the field is specified as NULL, the *probe* function will be called for every device in the system. If the field is not NULL, the last item in the array must be set to 0.

`int (*probe)(struct pci_dev *dev, const struct pci_device_id`
> `*id);`
> The function must initialize the device it is passed and return 0 in case of success or a negative error code (actually, the error code is not currently used, but it's safe to return an `errno` value anyway instead of just -1).

```
void (*remove)(struct pci_dev *dev);
```
The *remove* method is used to tell the device driver that it should shut down the device and stop dealing with it, releasing any associated storage. The function is called either when the device is removed from the system or when the driver calls *pci_unregister_driver* in order to be unloaded from the system. Unlike *probe*, this method is specific to one PCI device, not to the whole set handled by this driver; the specific device is passed as an argument.

```
int (*suspend)(struct pci_dev *dev, u32 state);
int (*resume)(struct pci_dev *dev);
```
These are the power-management functions for PCI devices. If the device driver supports power-management features, these two methods should be implemented to shut down and reactivate the device; they are called by higher layers at proper times.

The PCI driver object is quite straightforward and a pleasure to use. We think there's little to add to the field enumeration, because normal hardware-handling code fits well in this abstraction without the need to tweak it in any way.

The only missing piece left to describe is the struct pci_device_id object. The structure includes several ID fields, and the actual device that needs to be driven is matched against all of the fields. Any field can be set to PCI_ANY_ID to tell the system to effectively ignore it.

unsigned int vendor, device;
> The vendor and device IDs of the device this driver is interested in. The values are matched against registers 0x00 and 0x02 of the PCI configuration space.

unsigned int subvendor, subdevice;
> The sub-IDs, matched against registers 0x2C and 0x2E of the PCI configuration space. They are used in matching the device because sometimes a vendor/device ID pair identifies a group of devices and the driver can only work with a few items in the group.

unsigned int class, class_mask;
> If the device driver wants to deal with an entire class or a subset thereof, it can set the previous fields to PCI_ANY_ID and use class identifiers instead. The class_mask is present to allow both for drivers that want to deal with a base class and for drivers that are only interested in a subclass. If device selection is performed using vendor/device identifiers, both these fields must be set to 0 (not to PCI_ANY_ID, since the check is performed through a logical AND with the mask field).

`unsigned long driver_data;`
> A field left for use by the device driver. It can, for example, differentiate between the various devices at compilation time, avoiding tedious arrays of conditional tests at runtime.

It's interesting to note that the `pci_device_id` data structure is just a hint to the system; the actual device driver is still free to return 0 from its *probe* method, thus refusing the device even if it matched the array of device identifiers. Thus if, for example, there exist several devices with the same signature, the driver can look for further information before choosing whether it is able to drive the peripheral or not.

Hardware Abstractions

We complete the discussion of PCI by taking a quick look at how the system handles the plethora of PCI controllers available on the marketplace. This is just an informative section, meant to show to the curious reader how the object-oriented layout of the kernel extends down to the lowest levels.

The mechanism used to implement hardware abstraction is the usual structure containing methods. It's a powerful technique that adds just the minimal overhead of dereferencing a pointer to the normal overhead of a function call. In the case of PCI management, the only hardware-dependent operations are the ones that read and write configuration registers, because everything else in the PCI world is accomplished by directly reading and writing the I/O and memory address spaces, and those are under direct control of the CPU.

The relevant structure for hardware abstraction, thus, includes only six fields:

```
struct pci_ops {
    int (*read_byte)(struct pci_dev *, int where, u8 *val);
    int (*read_word)(struct pci_dev *, int where, u16 *val);
    int (*read_dword)(struct pci_dev *, int where, u32 *val);
    int (*write_byte)(struct pci_dev *, int where, u8 val);
    int (*write_word)(struct pci_dev *, int where, u16 val);
    int (*write_dword)(struct pci_dev *, int where, u32 val);
};
```

The structure is defined in `<linux/pci.h>` and used by *drivers/pci/pci.c*, where the actual public functions are defined.

The six functions that act on the PCI configuration space have more overhead than dereferencing a pointer, because they use cascading pointers due to the high object-orientedness of the code, but the overhead is not an issue in operations that are performed quite rarely and never in speed-critical paths. The actual implementation of *pci_read_config_byte(dev)*, for instance, expands to:

```
dev->bus->ops->read_byte();
```

The various PCI buses in the system are detected at system boot, and that's when the `struct pci_bus` items are created and associated with their features, including the `ops` field.

Implementing hardware abstraction via "hardware operations" data structures is typical in the Linux kernel. One important example is the `struct alpha_machine_vector` data structure. It is defined in `<asm-alpha/machvec.h>` and it takes care of everything that may change across different Alpha-based computers.

A Look Back: ISA

The ISA bus is quite old in design and is a notoriously poor performer, but it still holds a good part of the market for extension devices. If speed is not important and you want to support old motherboards, an ISA implementation is preferable to PCI. An additional advantage of this old standard is that if you are an electronic hobbyist, you can easily build your own ISA devices, something definitely not possible with PCI.

On the other hand, a great disadvantage of ISA is that it's tightly bound to the PC architecture; the interface bus has all the limitations of the 80286 processor and causes endless pain to system programmers. The other great problem with the ISA design (inherited from the original IBM PC) is the lack of geographical addressing, which has led to many problems and lengthy unplug-rejumper-plug-test cycles to add new devices. It's interesting to note that even the oldest Apple II computers were already exploiting geographical addressing, and they featured jumperless expansion boards.

Despite its great disadvantages, ISA is still used in several unexpected places. For example, the VR41xx series of MIPS processors used in several palmtops features an ISA-compatible expansion bus, strange as it seems. The reason behind these unexpected uses of ISA is the extreme low cost of some legacy hardware, like 8390-based Ethernet cards, so a CPU with ISA electrical signaling can easily exploit the awful but cheap PC devices.

Hardware Resources

An ISA device can be equipped with I/O ports, memory areas, and interrupt lines.

Even though the x86 processors support 64 kilobytes of I/O port memory (i.e., the processor asserts 16 address lines), some old PC hardware decodes only the lowest 10 address lines. This limits the usable address space to 1024 ports, because any address in the range 1 KB to 64 KB will be mistaken for a low address by any device that decodes only the low address lines. Some peripherals circumvent this limitation by mapping only one port into the low kilobyte and using the high address lines to select between different device registers. For example, a device mapped at `0x340` can safely use port `0x740`, `0xB40`, and so on.

If the availability of I/O ports is limited, memory access is still worse. An ISA device can use only the memory range between 640 KB and 1 MB and between 15 MB and 16 MB. The 640-KB to 1-MB range is used by the PC BIOS, by VGA-compatible video boards, and by various other devices, leaving little space available for new devices. Memory at 15 MB, on the other hand, is not directly supported by Linux, and hacking the kernel to support it is a waste of programming time nowadays.

The third resource available to ISA device boards is interrupt lines. A limited number of interrupt lines are routed to the ISA bus, and they are shared by all the interface boards. As a result, if devices aren't properly configured, they can find themselves using the same interrupt lines.

Although the original ISA specification doesn't allow interrupt sharing across devices, most device boards allow it.* Interrupt sharing at the software level is described in "Interrupt Sharing," in Chapter 9.

ISA Programming

As far as programming is concerned, there's no specific aid in the kernel or the BIOS to ease access to ISA devices (like there is, for example, for PCI). The only facilities you can use are the registries of I/O ports and IRQ lines, described in "Using Resources" (Chapter 2) and "Installing an Interrupt Handler" (Chapter 9).

The programming techniques shown throughout the first part of this book apply to ISA devices; the driver can probe for I/O ports, and the interrupt line must be autodetected with one of the techniques shown in "Autodetecting the IRQ Number," in Chapter 9.

The helper functions *isa_readb* and friends have been briefly introduced in "Using I/O Memory" in Chapter 8 and there's nothing more to say about them.

---

* The problem with interrupt sharing is a matter of electrical engineering: if a device drives the signal line inactive—by applying a low-impedance voltage level—the interrupt can't be shared. If, on the other hand, the device uses a pull-up resistor to the inactive logic level, then sharing is possible. This is nowadays the norm. However, there's still a potential risk of losing interrupt events since ISA interrupts are edge triggered instead of level triggered. Edge-triggered interrupts are easier to implement in hardware but don't lend themselves to safe sharing.

The Plug-and-Play Specification

Some new ISA device boards follow peculiar design rules and require a special initialization sequence intended to simplify installation and configuration of add-on interface boards. The specification for the design of these boards is called *Plug and Play* (PnP) and consists of a cumbersome rule set for building and configuring jumperless ISA devices. PnP devices implement relocatable I/O regions; the PC's BIOS is responsible for the relocation—reminiscent of PCI.

In short, the goal of PnP is to obtain the same flexibility found in PCI devices without changing the underlying electrical interface (the ISA bus). To this end, the specs define a set of device-independent configuration registers and a way to geographically address the interface boards, even though the physical bus doesn't carry per-board (geographical) wiring—every ISA signal line connects to every available slot.

Geographical addressing works by assigning a small integer, called the *Card Select Number* (CSN), to each PnP peripheral in the computer. Each PnP device features a unique serial identifier, 64 bits wide, that is hardwired into the peripheral board. CSN assignment uses the unique serial number to identify the PnP devices. But the CSNs can be assigned safely only at boot time, which requires the BIOS to be PnP aware. For this reason, old computers require the user to obtain and insert a specific configuration diskette even if the device is PnP capable.

Interface boards following the PnP specs are complicated at the hardware level. They are much more elaborate than PCI boards and require complex software. It's not unusual to have difficulty installing these devices, and even if the installation goes well, you still face the performance constraints and the limited I/O space of the ISA bus. It's much better in our opinion to install PCI devices whenever possible and enjoy the new technology instead.

If you are interested in the PnP configuration software, you can browse *drivers/net/3c509.c*, whose probing function deals with PnP devices. Linux 2.1.33 added some initial support for PnP as well, in the directory *drivers/pnp*.

PC/104 and PC/104+

In the industrial world, two bus architectures are quite fashionable currently: PC/104 and PC/104+. Both are standard in PC-class single-board computers.

Both standards refer to specific form factors for printed circuit boards as well as electrical/mechanical specifications for board interconnections. The practical advantage of these buses is that they allow circuit boards to be stacked vertically using a plug-and-socket kind of connector on one side of the device.

The electrical and logical layout of the two buses is identical to ISA (PC/104) and PCI (PC/104+), so software won't notice any difference between the usual desktop buses and these two.

Other PC Buses

PCI and ISA are the most commonly used peripheral interfaces in the PC world, but they aren't the only ones. Here's a summary of the features of other buses found in the PC market.

MCA

Micro Channel Architecture (MCA) is an IBM standard used in PS/2 computers and some laptops. The main problem with Micro Channel is the lack of documentation, which has resulted in a lack of Linux support for MCA up until recently.

At the hardware level, Micro Channel has more features than ISA. It supports multimaster DMA, 32-bit address and data lines, shared interrupt lines, and geographical addressing to access per-board configuration registers. Such registers are called *Programmable Option Select*, or POS, but they don't have all the features of the PCI registers. Linux support for Micro Channel includes functions that are exported to modules.

A device driver can read the integer value `MCA_bus` to see if it is running on a Micro Channel computer, similar to how it uses *pci_present* if it's interested in PCI support. If the symbol is a preprocessor macro, the macro `MCA_bus__is_a_macro` is defined as well. If `MCA_bus__is_a_macro` is undefined, then `MCA_bus` is an integer variable exported to modularized code. Both `MCA_BUS` and `MCA_bus__is_a_macro` are defined in `<asm/processor.h>`.

EISA

The Extended ISA (EISA) bus is a 32-bit extension to ISA, with a compatible interface connector; ISA device boards can be plugged into an EISA connector. The additional wires are routed under the ISA contacts.

Like PCI and MCA, the EISA bus is designed to host jumperless devices, and it has the same features as MCA: 32-bit address and data lines, multimaster DMA, and shared interrupt lines. EISA devices are configured by software, but they don't need any particular operating system support. EISA drivers already exist in the Linux kernel for Ethernet devices and SCSI controllers.

An EISA driver checks the value `EISA_bus` to determine if the host computer carries an EISA bus. Like `MCA_bus`, `EISA_bus` is either a macro or a variable, depending on whether `EISA_bus__is_a_macro` is defined. Both symbols are defined in `<asm/processor.h>`.

As far as the driver is concerned, there is no special support for EISA in the kernel, and the programmer must deal with ISA extensions by himself. The driver uses standard EISA I/O operations to access the EISA registers. The drivers that are already in the kernel can be used as sample code.

VLB

Another extension to ISA is the VESA Local Bus (VLB) interface bus, which extends the ISA connectors by adding a third lengthwise slot. A device can just plug into this extra connector (without plugging in the two associated ISA connectors), because the VLB slot duplicates all important signals from the ISA connectors. Such "standalone" VLB peripherals not using the ISA slot are rare, because most devices need to reach the back panel so that their external connectors are available.

The VESA bus is much more limited in its capabilities than the EISA, MCA, and PCI buses and is disappearing from the market. No special kernel support exists for VLB. However, both the Lance Ethernet driver and the IDE disk driver in Linux 2.0 can deal with VLB versions of their devices.

SBus

While most computers nowadays are equipped with a PCI or ISA interface bus, most not-so-recent SPARC-based workstations use SBus to connect their peripherals.

SBus is quite an advanced design, although it has been around for a long time. It is meant to be processor independent (even though only SPARC computers use it) and is optimized for I/O peripheral boards. In other words, you can't plug additional RAM into SBus slots (RAM expansion boards have long been forgotten even in the ISA world, and PCI does not support them either). This optimization is meant to simplify the design of both hardware devices and system software, at the expense of some additional complexity in the motherboard.

This I/O bias of the bus results in peripherals using *virtual* addresses to transfer data, thus bypassing the need to allocate a contiguous DMA buffer. The motherboard is responsible for decoding the virtual addresses and mapping them to physical addresses. This requires attaching an MMU (memory management unit) to the bus; the chipset in charge of the task is called IOMMU. Although somehow more complex than using physical addresses on the interface bus, this design is greatly simplified by the fact that SPARC processors have always been designed by keeping the MMU core separate from the CPU core (either physically or at least conceptually). Actually, this design choice is shared by other smart processor designs and is beneficial overall. Another feature of this bus is that device boards exploit massive geographical addressing, so there's no need to implement an address decoder in every peripheral or to deal with address conflicts.

SBus peripherals use the Forth language in their PROMs to initialize themselves. Forth was chosen because the interpreter is lightweight and therefore can be easily implemented in the firmware of any computer system. In addition, the SBus specification outlines the boot process, so that compliant I/O devices fit easily into the system and are recognized at system boot. This was a great step to support multiplatform devices; it's a completely different world from the PC-centric ISA stuff we were used to. However, it didn't succeed for a variety of commercial reasons.

Although current kernel versions offer quite full-featured support for SBus devices, the bus is so little used nowadays that it's not worth covering in detail here. Interested readers can look at source files in *arch/sparc/kernel* and *arch/sparc/mm*.

NuBus

Another interesting but forgotten interface bus is NuBus. It is found on older Mac computers (those with the M68k family of CPUs).

All of the bus is memory-mapped (like everything with the M68k), and the devices are only geographically addressed. This is good and typical of Apple, as the much older Apple II already had a similar bus layout. What is bad is that it's almost impossible to find documentation on NuBus, due to the close-everything policy Apple has always followed with its Mac computers (and unlike the previous Apple II, whose source code and schematics were available at little cost).

The file *drivers/nubus/nubus.c* includes almost everything we know about this bus, and it's interesting reading; it shows how much hard reverse engineering developers had to do.

External Buses

One of the most recent entries in the field of interface buses is the whole class of external buses. This includes USB, FireWire, and IEEE1284 (parallel-port-based external bus). These interfaces are somewhat similar to older and not-so-external technology such as PCMCIA/CardBUS and even SCSI.

Conceptually, these buses are neither full-featured interface buses (like PCI is) nor dumb communication channels (like the serial ports are). It's hard to classify the software that is needed to exploit their features, as it's usually split into two levels: the driver for the hardware controller (like drivers for PCI SCSI adaptors or PCI controllers introduced earlier in "The PCI Interface") and the driver for the specific "client" device (like *sd.c* handles generic SCSI disks and so-called PCI drivers deal with cards plugged in the bus).

But there's another problem with these new buses. With the exception of USB, their support is either not mature or is somehow in need of a revision (the latter condition applies especially to the SCSI kernel subsystem, which is reported to be far from optimal by several of the best kernel hackers).

USB

USB, the Universal Serial Bus, is the only external bus that is currently mature enough to deserve some discussion. Topologically, a USB subsystem is not laid out as a bus; it is rather a tree built out of several point-to-point links. The links are four-wire cables (ground, power, and two signal wires) that connect a device and a hub (just like twisted pair Ethernet). Usually, PC-class computers are equipped with a "root hub" and offer two plugs for external connections. You can connect either devices or additional hubs to the plugs.

The bus is nothing exciting at the technological level, as it's a single-master implementation in which the host computer polls the various devices. Despite this intrinsic limit of the bus, it has interesting features, such as the ability for a device to request a fixed bandwidth for its data transfers in order to reliably support video and audio I/O. Another important feature of USB is that it acts merely as a communication channel between the device and the host, without requiring specific meaning or structure in the data it delivers.*

This is unlike SCSI communication and like standard serial media.

These features, together with the inherent hot-plug capability of the design, make USB a handy low-cost mechanism to connect (and disconnect) several devices to the computer without the need to shut the system down, open the cover, and swear over screws and wires. USB is becoming popular in the PC market but remains unsuitable for high-speed devices because its maximum transfer rate is 12 Mb per second.

USB is supported by version 2.2.18 (and later) and 2.4.*x* of the Linux kernel. The USB controller in any computer belongs to one of two kinds, and both drivers are part of the standard kernel.

Writing a USB Driver

As far as "client" device drivers are concerned, the approach to USB is similar to the `pci_driver` layout: the device driver registers its driver object with the USB subsystem, and it later uses vendor and device identifiers to identify insertion of its hardware.

The relevant data structure is `struct usb_driver`, and its typical use is as follows:

```
#include <linux/usb.h>

static struct usb_driver sample_usb_driver = {
```

---

* Actually, some structuring is there, but it mostly reduces to the requirement for the communication to fit into one of a few predefined classes: a keyboard won't allocate bandwidth, for example, while a camera will.

```
        name:          "sample",
        probe:         sample_probe,
        disconnect:    sample_disconnect,
};

int init_module(void)
{
    /* just register it; returns 0 or error code */
    return usb_register(&sample_usb_driver);
}

void cleanup_module(void)
{
    usb_deregister(&sample_usb_driver);
}
```

The *probe* function declared in the data structure is called by the USB kernel subsystem whenever a new device is connected to the system (or when the driver is loaded if any unclaimed devices are already connected to the bus).

Each device identifies itself by providing the system with vendor, device, and class identifiers, similar to what PCI devices do. The task of *sample_probe*, therefore, is looking into the information it receives and claiming ownership of the device if suitable.

To claim ownership, the function returns a non-**NULL** pointer that will be used to identify the device. This will usually be a pointer to the device-specific data structure that is at the core of the device driver as a whole.

To exchange information with the device, you'll then need to tell the USB subsystem how to communicate. This task is performed by filling a **struct urb** (for *USB request block*) and by passing it to *usb_submit_urb*. This step is usually performed by the *open* method associated with the device special file, or an equivalent function.

Note that not every USB driver needs to implement its own device special files by requesting a major number and so on. Devices that fall within a class for which the kernel offers generalized support won't have their own device files and will report their information through other means.

An example of generalized management is input handling. If your USB device is an input device (such as a graphic tablet), you won't allocate a major number but rather will register your hardware by calling *input_register_device*. In this case, the *open* callback of your input device is in charge of establishing communication by calling *usb_submit_urb*.

A USB input driver, therefore, must rely on several other system blocks, and most of them can be modules as well. The module-stacking architecture for USB input device drivers is shown in Figure 15-3.

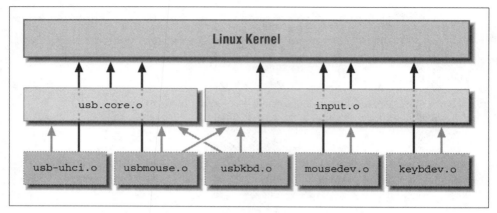

Figure 15-3. Modules involved in USB input management

You'll find a complete USB device driver in the sample files available on the O'Reilly FTP site. It is a very simplified keyboard and mouse driver that shows how to lay out a complete USB driver. To keep it simple, it doesn't use the input subsystem to report events but rather posts messages about them using *printk.* You'll need at least a USB keyboard or a USB mouse to test the driver.

There's quite a lot of documentation on USB available currently, including two articles by one of your authors, whose style and technical level resembles that of *Linux Device Drivers.* These articles even include a more complete USB sample device driver that uses the input kernel subsystem and can be run by alternative means if you have no USB devices handy. You can find them at *http://www.linux.it/kerneldocs.*

Backward Compatibility

The current implementation of PCI support in the kernel was not available with version 2.0 of the kernel. With 2.0 the support API was much more raw, because it lacked the various objects that have been described in this chapter.

The six functions to access the configuration space received as arguments the 16-bit low-level key to the PCI device instead of using a pointer to `struct pci_dev`. Also, you had to include `<asm/pcibios.h>` before being able to read or write to the configuration space.

Fortunately, dealing with the difference is not a big problem, and if you include *sysdep.h* you'll be able to use 2.4 semantics even when compiling under 2.0. PCI support for version 2.0 is available in the header *pci-compat.h*, automatically included by *sysdep.h* when you compile under 2.0. The header, as distributed, implements the most important functions used to work with the PCI bus.

If you use *pci-compat.h* to develop drivers that work all the way from 2.0 through 2.4, you must call *pci_release_device* when you are done with a `pci_dev` item. This happens because the fake `pci_dev` structures created by the header are allocated with *kmalloc*, whereas the real structures of 2.2 and 2.4 are static resources in the kernel proper. The extra function is defined to do nothing by *sysdep.h* whenever compiling for 2.2 or 2.4, so it does no harm. Feel free to look at *pciregions.c* or *pcidata.c* to see portable code in action.

Another relevant difference in 2.0 is */proc* support for PCI. There was no */proc/bus/pci* file hierarchy (and no */proc/bus* at all, actually), only a single */proc/pci* file. It was meant more for human reading than for machine reading, and it was not very readable anyway. Under 2.2 it was possible to select a "backward-compatible */proc/pci*" at compile time, but the obsolete file was completely removed in version 2.4.

The concept of hot-pluggable PCI drivers (and `struct pci_driver`) is new as of version 2.4. We do not offer backward-compatible macros to use the feature on older kernels.

Quick Reference

This section, as usual, summarizes the symbols introduced in the chapter.

`#include <linux/config.h>`
`CONFIG_PCI`
> This macro should be used to conditionally compile PCI-related code. When a PCI module is loaded to a non-PCI kernel, *insmod* complains about several symbols being unresolved.

`#include <linux/pci.h>`
> This header includes symbolic names for the PCI registers and several vendor and device ID values.

`int pci_present(void);`
> This function returns a boolean value that tells whether the computer we're running on has PCI capabilities or not.

`struct pci_dev;`
`struct pci_bus;`
`struct pci_driver;`
`struct pci_device_id;`
> These structures represent the objects involved in PCI management. The concept of `pci_driver` is new as of Linux 2.4, and `struct pci_device_id` is central to it.

```
struct pci_dev *pci_find_device(unsigned int vendor,
    unsigned int device, struct pci_dev *from);
struct pci_dev *pci_find_class(unsigned int class, struct
    pci_dev *from);
```
These functions are used to look up the device list looking for devices with a specific signature or belonging to a specific class. The return value is NULL if none is found. from is used to continue a search; it must be NULL the first time you call either function, and it must point to the device just found if you are searching for more devices.

```
int pci_read_config_byte(struct pci_dev *dev, int where, u8
    *val);
int pci_read_config_word(struct pci_dev *dev, int where, u16
    *val);
int pci_read_config_dword(struct pci_dev *dev, int where,
    u32 *val);
int pci_write_config_byte (struct pci_dev *dev, int where,
    u8 *val);
int pci_write_config_word (struct pci_dev *dev, int where,
    u16 *val);
int pci_write_config_dword (struct pci_dev *dev, int where,
    u32 *val);
```
These functions are used to read or write a PCI configuration register. Although the Linux kernel takes care of byte ordering, the programmer must be careful about byte ordering when assembling multibyte values from individual bytes. The PCI bus is little-endian.

```
int pci_register_driver(struct pci_driver *drv);
int pci_module_init(struct pci_driver *drv);
void pci_unregister_driver(struct pci_driver *drv);
```
These functions support the concept of a PCI driver. Whereas compiled-in code uses *pci_register_driver* (which returns the number of devices that are managed by this driver), modularized code should call *pci_module_init* instead (which returns 0 if one or more devices are there and −ENODEV if no suitable device is plugged into the system).

```
#include <linux/usb.h>
#include <linux/input.h>
```
The former header is where everything related to USB resides and must be included by USB device drivers. The latter defines the core of the input subsystem. Neither of them is available in Linux 2.0.

```
struct usb_driver;
int usb_register(struct usb_driver *d);
void usb_deregister(struct usb_driver *d);
```
usb_driver is the main building block of USB device drivers. It must be registered and unregistered at module load and unload time.

## CHAPTER SIXTEEN

PHYSICAL LAYOUT OF THE KERNEL SOURCE

So far, we've talked about the Linux kernel from the perspective of writing device drivers. Once you begin playing with the kernel, however, you may find that you want to "understand it all." In fact, you may find yourself passing whole days navigating through the source code and grepping your way through the source tree to uncover the relationships among the different parts of the kernel.

This kind of "heavy grepping" is one of the tasks your authors perform quite often, and it is an efficient way to retrieve information from the source code. Nowadays you can even exploit Internet resources to understand the kernel source tree; some of them are listed in the Preface. But despite Internet resources, wise use of *grep*,* *less*, and possibly *ctags* or *etags* can still be the best way to extract information from the kernel sources.

In our opinion, acquiring a bit of a knowledge base before sitting down in front of your preferred shell prompt can be helpful. Therefore, this chapter presents a quick overview of the Linux kernel source files based on version 2.4.2. If you're interested in other versions, some of the descriptions may not apply literally. Whole sections may be missing (like the *drivers/media* directory that was introduced in 2.4.0-test6 by moving various preexisting drivers to this new directory). We hope the following information is useful, even if not authoritative, for browsing other versions of the kernel.

Every pathname is given relative to the source root (usually */usr/src/linux*), while filenames with no directory component are assumed to reside in the "current" directory—the one being discussed. Header files (when named with < and > angle brackets) are given relative to the *include* directory of the source tree. We won't dissect the *Documentation* directory, as its role is self-explanatory.

---

* Usually, *find* and *xargs* are needed to build a command line for *grep.* Although not trivial, proficient use of Unix tools is outside of the scope of this book.

Booting the Kernel

The usual way to look at a program is to start where execution begins. As far as Linux is concerned, it's hard to tell *where* execution begins—it depends on how you define "begins."

The architecture-independent starting point is *start_kernel* in *init/main.c*. This function is invoked from architecture-specific code, to which it never returns. It is in charge of spinning the wheel and can thus be considered the "mother of all functions," the first breath in the computer's life. Before *start_kernel*, there was chaos.

By the time *start_kernel* is invoked, the processor has been initialized, protected mode* has been entered, the processor is executing at the highest privilege level (sometimes called *supervisor mode*), and interrupts are disabled. The *start_kernel* function is in charge of initializing all the kernel data structures. It does this by calling external functions to perform subtasks, since each setup function is defined in the appropriate kernel subsystem.

The first function called by *start_kernel*, after acquiring the kernel lock and printing the Linux banner string, is *setup_arch*. This allows platform-specific C-language code to run; *setup_arch* receives a pointer to the local `command_line` pointer in *start_kernel*, so it can make it point to the real (platform-dependent) location where the command line is stored. As the next step, *start_kernel* passes the command line to *parse_options* (defined in the same *init/main.c* file) so that the boot options can be honored.

Command-line parsing is performed by calling handler functions associated with each kernel argument (for example, `video=` is associated with *video_setup*). Each function usually ends up setting variables that are used later, when the associated facility is initialized. The internal organization of command-line parsing is similar to the init calls mechanism, described later.

After parsing, *start_kernel* activates the various basic functionalities of the system. This includes setting up interrupt tables, activating the timer interrupt, and initializing the console and memory management. All of this is performed by functions declared elsewhere in platform-specific code. The function continues by initializing less basic kernel subsystems, including buffer management, signal handling, and file and inode management.

Finally, *start_kernel* forks the *init* kernel thread (which gets 1 as a process ID) and executes the *idle* function (again, defined in architecture-specific code).

The initial boot sequence can thus be summarized as follows:

---

* This concept only makes sense on the x86 architecture. More mature architectures don't find themselves in a limited backward-compatible mode when they power up.

1. System firmware or a boot loader arranges for the kernel to be placed at the proper address in memory. This code is usually external to Linux source code.

2. Architecture-specific assembly code performs very low-level tasks, like initializing memory and setting up CPU registers so that C code can run flawlessly. This includes selecting a stack area and setting the stack pointer accordingly. The amount of such code varies from platform to platform; it can range from a few dozen lines up to a few thousand lines.

3. *start_kernel* is called. It acquires the kernel lock, prints the banner, and calls *setup_arch*.

4. Architecture-specific C-language code completes low-level initialization and retrieves a command line for *start_kernel* to use.

5. *start_kernel* parses the command line and calls the handlers associated with the keyword it identifies.

6. *start_kernel* initializes basic facilities and forks the *init* thread.

It is the task of the *init* thread to perform all other initialization. The thread is part of the same *init/main.c* file, and the bulk of the initialization (init) calls are performed by *do_basic_setup*. The function initializes all bus subsystems that it finds (PCI, SBus, and so on). It then invokes *do_initcalls*; device driver initialization is performed as part of the *initcall* processing.

The idea of init calls was added in version 2.3.13 and is not available in older kernels; it is designed to avoid hairy #ifdef conditionals all over the initialization code. Every optional kernel feature (device driver or whatever) must be initialized only if configured in the system, so the call to initialization functions used to be surrounded by #ifdef CONFIG_*FEATURE* and #endif. With init calls, each optional feature declares its own initialization function; the compilation process then places a reference to the function in a special ELF section. At boot time, *do_initcalls* scans the ELF section to invoke all the relevant initialization functions.

The same idea is applied to command-line arguments. Each driver that can receive a command-line argument at boot time defines a data structure that associates the argument with a function. A pointer to the data structure is placed into a separate ELF section, so *parse_option* can scan this section for each command-line option and invoke the associated driver function, if a match is found. The remaining arguments end up in either the environment or the command line of the *init* process. All the magic for init calls and ELF sections is part of <linux/init.h>.

Unfortunately, this init call idea works only when no ordering is required across the various initialization functions, so a few #ifdefs are still present in *init/main.c*.

It's interesting to see how the idea of init calls and its application to the list of command-line arguments helped reduce the amount of conditional compilation in the code:

```
morgana% grep -c ifdef linux-2.[024]/init/main.c
linux-2.0/init/main.c:120
linux-2.2/init/main.c:246
linux-2.4/init/main.c:35
```

Despite the huge addition of new features over time, the amount of conditional compilation dropped significantly in 2.4 with the adoption of init calls. Another advantage of this technique is that device driver maintainers don't need to patch *main.c* every time they add support for a new command-line argument. The addition of new features to the kernel has been greatly facilitated by this technique and there are no more hairy cross references all over the boot code. But as a side effect, 2.4 can't be compiled into older file formats that are less flexible than ELF. For this reason, *uClinux** developers switched from COFF to ELF while porting their system from 2.0 to 2.4.

Another side effect of extensive use of ELF sections is that the final pass in compiling the kernel is not a conventional link pass as it used to be. Every platform now defines exactly how to link the kernel image (the *vmlinux* file) by means of an *ldscript* file; the file is called *vmlinux.lds* in the source tree of each platform. Use of *ld* scripts is described in the standard documentation for the *binutils* package.

There is yet another advantage to putting the initialization code into a special section. Once initialization is complete, that code is no longer needed. Since this code has been isolated, the kernel is able to dump it and reclaim the memory it occupies.

Before Booting

In the previous section, we treated *start_kernel* as the first kernel function. However, you might be interested in what happens *before* that point, so we'll step back to take a quick look at that topic. The uninterested reader can jump directly to the next section.

As suggested, the code that runs before *start_kernel* is, for the most part, assembly code, but several platforms call library C functions from there (most commonly, *inflate*, the core of *gunzip*).

On most common platforms, the code that runs before *start_kernel* is mainly devoted to moving the kernel around after the computer's firmware (possibly with

---

* *uClinux* is a version of the Linux kernel that can run on processors without an MMU. This is typical in the embedded world, and several M68k and ARM processors have no hardware memory management. *uClinux* stands for microcontroller Linux, since it's meant to run on microcontrollers rather than full-fledged computers.

the help of a boot loader) has loaded it into RAM from some other storage, such as a local disk or a remote workstation over the network.

It's not uncommon, though, to find some rudimentary boot loader code inside the *boot* directory of an architecture-specific tree. For example, *arch/i386/boot* includes code that can load the rest of the kernel off a floppy disk and activate it. The file *bootsect.S* that you will find there, however, can run only off a floppy disk and is by no means a complete boot loader (for example, it is unable to pass a command line to the kernel it loads). Nonetheless, copying a new kernel to a floppy is still a handy way to quickly boot it on the PC.

A known limitation of the x86 platform is that the CPU can see only 640 KB of system memory when it is powered on, no matter how large your installed memory is. Dealing with the limitation requires the kernel to be compressed, and support for decompression is available in *arch/i386/boot* together with other code such as VGA mode setting. On the PC, because of this limit, you can't do anything with a *vmlinux* kernel image, and the file you actually boot is called *zImage* or *bzImage*; the boot sector described earlier is actually prepended to this file rather than to *vmlinux*. We won't spend more time on the booting process on the x86 platform, since you can choose from several boot loaders, and the topic is generally well discussed elsewhere.

Some platforms differ greatly in the layout of their boot code from the PC. Sometimes the code must deal with several variations of the same architecture. This is the case, for example, with ARM, MIPS, and M68k. These platforms cover a wide variety of CPU and system types, ranging from powerful servers and workstations down to PDAs or embedded appliances. Different environments require different boot code and sometimes even different *ld* scripts to compile the kernel image. Some of this support is not included in the official kernel tree published by Linus and is available only from third-party Concurrent Versions System (CVS) trees that closely track the official tree but have not yet been merged. Current examples include the SGI CVS tree for MIPS workstations and the LinuxCE CVS tree for MIPS-based palm computers. Nonetheless, we'd like to spend a few words on this topic because we feel it's an interesting one. Everything from *start_kernel* onward is based on this extra complexity but doesn't notice it.

Specific *ld* scripts and makefile rules are needed especially for embedded systems, and particularly for variants without a memory management unit, which are supported by *uClinux*. When you have no hardware MMU that maps virtual addresses to physical ones, you must link the kernel to be executed from the physical address where it will be loaded in the target platform. It's not uncommon in small systems to link the kernel so that it is loaded into read-only memory (usually flash memory), where it is directly activated at power-on time without the help of any boot loader.

When the kernel is executed directly from flash memory, the makefiles, *ld* scripts, and boot code work in tight cooperation. The *ld* rules place the code and read-only segments (such as the init calls information) into flash memory, while placing the data segments (data and block started by symbol (BSS)) in system RAM. The result is that the two sets are not consecutive. The makefile, then, offers special rules to coalesce all these sections into consecutive addresses and convert them to a format suitable for upload to the target system. Coalescing is mandatory because the data segment contains initialized data structures that must get written to read-only memory or otherwise be lost. Finally, assembly code that runs before *start_kernel* must copy over the data segment from flash memory to RAM (to the address where the linker placed it) and zero out the address range associated with the BSS segment. Only after this remapping has taken place can C-language code run.

When you upload a new kernel to the target system, the firmware there retrieves the data file from the network or from a serial channel and writes it to flash memory. The intermediate format used to upload the kernel to a target computer varies from system to system, because it depends on how the actual upload takes place. But in each case, this format is a generic container of binary data used to transfer the compiled image using standardized tools. For example, the BIN format is meant to be transferred over a network, while the S3 format is a hexadecimal ASCII file sent to the target system through a serial cable.* Most of the time, when powering on the system, the user can select whether to boot Linux or to type firmware commands.

The init Process

When *start_kernel* forks out the *init* thread (implemented by the *init* function in *init/main.c*), it is still running in kernel mode, and so is the *init* thread. When all initializations described earlier are complete, the thread drops the kernel lock and prepares to execute the user-space *init* process. The file being executed resides in */sbin/init*, */etc/init*, or */bin/init*. If none of those are found, */bin/sh* is run as a recovery measure in case the real *init* got lost or corrupted. As an alternative, the user can specify on the kernel command line which file the *init* thread should execute.

The procedure to enter user space is simple. The code opens */dev/console* as standard input by calling the *open* system call and connects the console to *stdout* and *stderr* by calling *dup*; it finally calls *execve* to execute the user-space program.

The thread is able to invoke system calls while running in kernel mode because *init/main.c* has declared `__KERNEL_SYSCALLS__` before including `<asm/unistd.h>`. The header defines special code that allows kernel code to

---

* We are not describing the formats or the tools in detail, because the information is readily available to people researching embedded Linux.

invoke a limited number of system calls just as if it were running in user space. More information about kernel system calls can be found in *http://www.linux.it/kerneldocs/ksys.*

The final call to *execve* finalizes the transition to user space. There is no magic involved in this transition. As with any *execve* call in Unix, this one replaces the memory maps of the current process with new memory maps defined by the binary file being executed (you should remember how executing a file means mapping it to the virtual address space of the current process). It doesn't matter that, in this case, the calling process is running in kernel space. That's transparent to the implementation of *execve*, which just finds that there are no previous memory maps to release before activating the new ones.

Whatever the system setup or command line, the *init* process is now executing in user space and any further kernel operation takes place in response to system calls coming from *init* itself or from the processes it forks out.

More information about how the *init* process brings up the whole system can be found in *http://www.linux.it/kerneldocs/init.* We'll now proceed on our tour by looking at the system calls implemented in each source directory, and then at how device drivers are laid out and organized in the source tree.

The kernel Directory

Some kernel facilities—those associated with filesystems, memory management, and networking—live in their own source trees. The *kernel* directory of the source tree includes all other basic facilities.

The most important such facility is scheduling. Thus, *sched.c*, together with `<linux/sched.h>`, can be considered the most important source file in the Linux kernel. In addition to the scheduler proper, implemented by *schedule*, the file defines the system calls that control process priorities and all the mechanisms for sleeping and waking.

The *fork* and *exit* system calls are implemented by two files that are named after them. They are comprehensive and well-structured files that deal with everything related to process creation and destruction.

The delivery of kernel messages is implemented in *printk.c*, which is also concerned with console management. Console code is not trivial, since the concept of "console" is pretty abstract nowadays and includes the text screen (either native or based on the frame buffer), the serial port, and even the printer port.

Other facilities that are implemented in this directory are time handling (*time.c*), kernel timers (*timer.c*), signal delivery and handling (*signal.c*), module management and related system calls (*module.c*), the *kmod* thread (*kmod.c*), systemwide power management (*pm.c*), tasklets (*softirq.c*), and the panic function (*panic.c*).

The fs Directory

File handling is at the core of any Unix system, and the *fs* directory in Linux is the fattest of all directories. It includes all the filesystems supported by the current Linux version, each in its own subdirectory, as well as the most important system calls after *fork* and *exit*.

The *execve* system call lives in *exec.c* and relies on the various available binary formats to actually interpret the binary data found in the executable files. The most important binary format nowadays is ELF, implemented by *binfmt_elf.c*. *binfmt_script.c* supports the execution of interpreted files. After detecting the need for an interpreter (usually on the #! or "shebang" line), the file relies on the other binary formats to load the interpreter.

Miscellaneous binary formats (such as the Java executable format) can be defined by the user with a */proc* interface defined in *binfmt_misc.c*. The *misc* binary format is able to identify an interpreted binary format based on the contents of the executable file, and fire the appropriate interpreter with appropriate arguments. The tool is configured via */proc/sys/fs/binfmt_misc*.

The fundamental system calls for file access are defined in *open.c* and *read_write.c*. The former also defines *close* and several other file-access system calls (*chown*, for instance). *select.c* implements *select* and *poll*. *pipe.c* and *fifo.c* implement pipes and named pipes. *readdir.c* implements the *getdents* system call, which is how user-space programs read directories (the name stands for "get directory entries"). Other programming interfaces to access directory data (such as the *readdir* interface) are all implemented in user space as library functions, based on the *getdents* system call.

Most system calls related to moving files around, such as *mkdir*, *rmdir*, *rename*, *link*, *symlink*, and *mknod*, are implemented in *namei.c*, which in turn lays its foundations on the directory entry cache that lives in *dcache.c*.

Mounting and unmounting filesystems, as well as support for the use of a temporary root for *initrd*, are implemented in *super.c*.

Of particular interest to device driver writers is *devices.c*, which implements the char and block driver registries and acts as dispatcher for all devices. It does so by implementing the generic *open* method that is used before the device-specific `file_operations` structure is fetched and used. *read* and *write* for block devices are implemented in *block_dev.c*, which in turn delegates to *buffer.c* everything related to buffer management.

There are several other files in this directory, but they are less interesting. The most important ones are *inode.c* and *file.c*, which manage the internal organization of file and inode data structures; *ioctl.c*, which implements *ioctl*; and *dquot.c*, which implements quotas.

As we suggested, most of the subdirectories of *fs* host individual filesystem implementations. However, *fs/partitions* is not a filesystem type but rather a container for partition management code. Some files in there are always compiled, regardless of kernel configuration, while other files that implement support for specific partitioning schemes can be individually enabled or disabled.

The mm Directory

The last major directory of kernel source files is devoted to memory management. The files in this directory implement all the data structures that are used throughout the system to manage memory-related issues. While memory management is founded on registers and features specific to a given CPU, we've already seen in Chapter 13 how most of the code has been made platform independent. Interested users can check how *asm/arch-arch/mm* implements the lowest level for a specific computer platform.

The *kmalloc/kfree* memory allocation engine is defined in *slab.c*. This file is a completely new implementation that replaces what used to live in *kmalloc.c*. The latter file doesn't exist anymore after version 2.0.

While most programmers are familiar with how an operating system manages memory in blocks and pages, Linux (taking an idea from Sun Microsystem's Solaris) uses an additional, more flexible concept called a *slab*. Each slab is a cache that contains multiple memory objects of the same size. Some slabs are specialized and contain structs of a certain type used by a certain part of the kernel; others are more general and contain memory regions of 32 bytes, 64 bytes, and so on. The advantage of using slabs is that structs or other regions of memory can be cached and reused with very little overhead; the more ponderous technique of allocating and freeing pages is invoked less often.

The other important allocation tool, *vmalloc*, and the function that lies behind them all, *get_free_pages*, are defined in *vmalloc.c* and *page_alloc.c* respectively. Both are pretty straightforward and make interesting reading.

In addition to allocation services, a memory management system must offer memory mappings. After all, *mmap* is the foundation of many system activities, including the execution of a file. The actual *sys_mmap* function doesn't live here, though. It is buried in architecture-specific code, because system calls with more than five arguments need special handling in relation to CPU registers. The function that implements *mmap* for all platforms is *do_mmap_pgoff*, defined in *mmap.c*. The same file implements *sys_sendfile* and *sys_brk*. The latter may look unrelated, because *brk* is used to raise the maximum virtual address usable by a process. Actually, Linux (and most current Unices) creates new virtual address space for a process by mapping pages from */dev/zero*.

The mechanisms for mapping a regular file into memory have been placed in *filemap.c*; the file acts on pretty low-level data structures within the memory management system. *mprotect* and *remap* are implemented in two files of the same names; memory locking appears in *mlock.c*.

When a process has several memory maps active, you need an efficient way to look for free areas in its memory address space. To this end, all memory maps of a process are laid out in an Adelson-Velski-Landis (AVL) tree. The software structure is implemented in *mmap_avl.c*.

Swap file initialization and removal (i.e., the *swapon* and *swapoff* system calls) are in *swapfile.c*. The scope of *swap_state.c* is the swap cache, and page aging is in *swap.c*. What is known as *swapping* is not defined here. Instead, it is part of managing memory pages, implemented by the *kswapd* thread.

The lowest level of page-table management is implemented by the *memory.c* file, which still carries the original notes by Linus when he implemented the first real memory management features in December 1991. Everything that happens at lower levels is part of architecture-specific code (often hidden as macros in the header files).

Code specific to high-memory management (the memory beyond that which can be addressed directly by the kernel, especially used in the x86 world to accommodate more than 4 GB of RAM without abandoning the 32-bit architecture) is in *highmem.c*, as you may imagine.

vmscan.c implements the *kswapd* kernel thread. This is the procedure that looks for unused and old pages in order to free them or send them to swap space, as already suggested. It's a well-commented source file because fine-tuning these algorithms is the key factor to overall system performance. Every design choice in this nontrivial and critical section needs to be well motivated, which explains the good amount of comments.

The rest of the source files found in the *mm* directory deal with minor but sometimes important details, like the *oom_killer*, a procedure that elects which process to kill when the system runs out of memory.

Interestingly, the *uClinux* port of the Linux kernel to MMU-less processors introduces a separate *mmnommu* directory. It closely replicates the official *mm* while leaving out any MMU-related code. The developers chose this path to avoid adding a mess of conditional code in the *mm* source tree. Since *uClinux* is not (yet) integrated with the mainstream kernel, you'll need to download a *uClinux* CVS tree or tar ball if you want to compare the two directories (both included in the *uClinux* tree).

The net directory

The *net* directory in the Linux file hierarchy is the repository for the socket abstraction and the network protocols; these features account for a lot of code, since Linux supports several different network protocols. Each protocol (IP, IPX, and so on) lives in its own subdirectory; the directory for IP is called *ipv4* because it represents version 4 of the protocol. The new standard (not yet in wide use as we write this) is called *ipv6* and is implemented in Linux as well. Unix-domain sockets are treated as just another network protocol; their implementation can be found in the *unix* subdirectory.

The network implementation in Linux is based on the same file operations that act on device files. This is natural, because network connections (sockets) are described by normal file descriptors. The file *socket.c* is the locus of the socket file operations. It dispatches the system calls to one of the network protocols via a `struct proto_ops` structure. This structure is defined by each network protocol to map system calls to its specific, low-level data handling operations.

Not every subdirectory of *net* is used to define a protocol family. There are a few notable exceptions: *core, bridge, ethernet, sunrpc,* and *khttpd.*

Files in *core* implement generic network features such as device handling, firewalls, multicasting, and aliases; this includes the handling of socket buffers (*core/skbuff.c*) and socket operations that remain independent of the underlying protocol (*core/sock.c*). The device-independent data management that sits near device-specific code is defined in *core/dev.c.*

The *ethernet* and *bridge* directories are used to implement specific low-level functionalities, specifically, the Ethernet-related helper functions described in Chapter 14, and bridging functionality.

sunrpc and *khttpd* are peculiar because they include kernel-level implementations of tasks that are usually carried out in user space.

In *sunrpc* you can find support functions for the kernel-level NFS server (which is an RPC-based service), while *khttpd* implements a kernel-space web server. Those services have been brought to kernel space to avoid the overhead of system calls and context switches during time-critical tasks. Both have demonstrated good performance in this mode. The *khttpd* subsystem, however, has already been rendered obsolete by *TUX,* which, as of this writing, holds the record for the world's fastest web server. *TUX* will likely be integrated into the 2.5 kernel series.

The two remaining source files within *net* are *sysctl_net.c* and *netsyms.c.* The former is the back end of the *sysctl* mechanism,* and the latter is just a list of

---

* *sysctl* has not been described in this book; interested readers can have a look at Alessandro's description of this mechanism at *http://www.linux.it/kerneldocs/sysctl.*

EXPORT_SYMBOL declarations. There are several such files all over the kernel, usually one in each major directory.

ipc and lib

The smallest directories (in size) in the Linux source tree are *ipc* and *lib*. The former is an implementation of the System V interprocess communication primitives, namely semaphores, message queues, and shared memory; they often get forgotten, but many applications use them (especially shared memory). The latter directory includes generic support functions, similar to the ones available in the standard C library.

The generic library functions are a very small subset of those available in user space, but cover the indispensable things you generally need to write code: string functions (including *simple_atol* to convert a string to a **long** integer with error checking) and <ctype.h> functions. The most important file in this directory is *vsprintf.c*; it implements the function by the same name, which sits at the core of *sprintf* and *printk*. Another important file is *inflate.c*, which includes the decompressing code of *gzip*.

include and arch

In a quick overview of the kernel source code, there's little to say about headers and architecture-specific code. Header files have been introduced all over the book, so their role (and the separation between *include/linux* and *include/asm*) should already be clear.

Architecture-specific code, on the other hand, has never been introduced in detail, but it doesn't easily lend itself to discussion. Inside each architecture's directory you usually find a file hierarchy similar to the top-level one (i.e., there are *mm* and *kernel* subdirectories), but also boot-related code and assembly source files. The most important assembly file within each supported architecture is called *kernel/entry.S*; it's the back end of the system call mechanism (i.e., the place where user processes enter kernel mode). Besides that, however, there's little in common across the various architectures, and describing them all would make no sense.

Drivers

Current Linux kernels support a huge number of devices. Device drivers account for half of the size of the source tree (actually two-thirds if you exclude architecture-specific code that you are not using). They account for almost 1500 C-language files and more than 800 headers.

The *drivers* directory itself doesn't host any source file, only subdirectories (and, obviously, a makefile).

Structuring the huge amount of source code is not easy, and the developers haven't followed any strict rules. The original division between *drivers/char* and *drivers/block* is inefficient nowadays, and more directories have been created according to several different requirements. Still, the most generic char and block drivers are found in *drivers/char* and *drivers/block*, so we'll start by visiting those two.

drivers/char

The *drivers/char* directory is perhaps the most important in the *drivers* hierarchy, because it hosts a lot of driver-independent code.

The generic tty layer (as well as line disciplines, tty software drivers, and similar features) is implemented in this directory. *console.c* defines the `linux` terminal type (by implementing its specific escape sequences and keyboard encoding). *vt.c* defines the virtual consoles, including code for switching from one virtual console to another. Selection support (the cut-and-paste capability of the Linux text console) is implemented by *selection.c*; the default line discipline is implemented by *n_tty.c*.

There are other files that, despite what you might expect, are device independent. *lp.c* implements a generic parallel port printer driver that includes a console-on-line-printer capability. It remains device independent by using the *parport* device driver to map operations to actual hardware (as seen in Figure 2-2). Similarly, *keyboard.c* implements the higher levels of keyboard handling; it exports the *handle_scancode* function so that platform-specific keyboard drivers (like *pc_keyb.c*, in the same directory) can benefit from generalized management. *mem.c* implements */dev/mem*, */dev/null*, and */dev/zero*, basic resources you can't do without.

Actually, since *mem.c* is never left out of the compilation process, it has been elected as the home of *chr_dev_init*, which in turn initializes several other device drivers if they have been selected for compilation.

There are other device-independent and platform-independent source files in *drivers/char*. If you are interested in looking at the role of each source file, the best place to start is the makefile for this directory, an interesting and pretty much self-explanatory file.

drivers/block

Like the preceding *drivers/char* directory, *drivers/block* has been present in Linux development for a long time. It used to host all block device drivers, and for this reason it included some device-independent code that is still present.

The most important file is *ll_rw_blk.c* (low-level read-write block). It implements all the request management functions that we described in Chapter 12.

A relatively new entry in this directory is *blkpg.c* (added as of 2.3.3). The file implements generic code for partition and geometry handling in block devices. Its code, together with the *fs/partitions* directory described earlier, replaces what was earlier part of "generic hard disk" support. The file called *genhd.c* still exists, but now includes only the generic initialization function for block drivers (similar to the one for char drivers that is part of *mem.c*). One of the public functions exported by *blkpg.c* is *blk_ioctl*, covered by "The ioctl Method" in Chapter 12.

The last device-independent file found in *drivers/block* is *elevator.o*. This file implements the mechanism to change the elevator function associated with a block device driver. The functionality can be exploited by means of *ioctl* commands briefly introduced in "The ioctl Method."

In addition to the hardware-dependent device drivers you would expect to find in *drivers/block*, the directory also includes software device drivers that are inherently cross-platform, just like the *sbull* and *spull* drivers that we introduced in this book. They are the RAM disk *rd.c*, the "network block device" *nbd.c*, and the loopback block device *loop.c*. The loopback device is used to mount files as if they were block devices. (See the manpage for *mount*, where it describes the *-o loop* option.) The network block device can be used to access remote resources as block devices (thus allowing, for example, a remote swap device).

Other files in the directory implement drivers for specific hardware, such as the various different floppy drives, the old-fashioned x86 XT disk controller, and a few more. Most of the important families of block drivers have been moved to a separate directory.

drivers/ide

The IDE family of device drivers used to live in *drivers/block* but has expanded to the point where they were moved into a separate directory. As a matter of fact, the IDE interface has been enhanced and extended over time in order to support more than just conventional hard disks. For example, IDE tapes are now supported as well.

The *drivers/ide* directory is a whole world of its own, with some generalized code and its own programming interface. You'll note in the directory some files that are just a few kilobytes long; they include only the IDE controller detection code, and rely on the generalized IDE driver for everything else. They are interesting reading if you are curious about IDE drivers.

drivers/md

This directory is concerned with implementing RAID functionality and the Logical Volume Manager abstraction. The code registers its own char and block major numbers, so it can be considered a driver just like those traditional drivers; nonetheless, the code has been kept separate because it has nothing to do with direct hardware management.

drivers/cdrom

This directory hosts the generic CD-ROM interface. Both the IDE and SCSI *cdrom* drivers rely on *drivers/cdrom/cdrom.c* for some of their functionality. The main entry points to the file are *register_cdrom* and *unregister_cdrom*; the caller passes them a pointer to `struct cdrom_device_info` as the main object involved in CD-ROM management.

Other files in this directory are concerned with specific hardware drives that are neither IDE nor SCSI. Those devices are pretty rare nowadays, as they have been made obsolete by modern IDE controllers.

drivers/scsi

Everything related to the SCSI bus has always been placed in this directory. This includes both controller-independent support for specific devices (such as hard drives and tapes) and drivers for specific SCSI controller boards.

Management of the SCSI bus interface is scattered in several files: *scsi.c*, *hosts.c*, *scsi_ioctl.c*, and a dozen more. If you are interested in the whole list, you'd better browse the makefile, where `scsi_mod-objs` is defined. All public entry points to this group of files have been collected in *scsi_syms.c*.

Code that supports a specific type of hardware drive plugs into the SCSI core system by calling *scsi_register_module* with an argument of `MODULE_SCSI_DEV`. This is how disk support is added to the core system by *sd.c*, CD-ROM support by *sr.c* (which, internally, refers to the *cdrom_* class of functions), tape support by *st.c*, and generic devices by *sg.c*.

The "generic" driver is used to provide user-space programs with direct access to SCSI devices. The underlying device can be virtually anything; currently both CD burners and scanner programs rely on the SCSI generic device to access the hardware they drive. By opening the */dev/sg* devices, a user-space driver can do anything it needs without specific support in the kernel.

Host adapters (i.e., SCSI controller hardware) can be plugged into the core system by calling *scsi_register_module* with an argument of `MODULE_SCSI_HA`. Most drivers currently do that by using the *scsi_module.c* facility to register themselves: the driver's source file defines its (static) data structures and then includes *scsi_module.c*. This file defines standard initialization and cleanup functions, based on `<linux/init.h>` and the init calls mechanisms. This technique allows drivers to serve as either modules or compiled-in functions without any `#ifdef` lines.

Interestingly, one of the host adapters supported in *drivers/scsi* is the IDE SCSI emulation code, a software host adapter that maps to IDE devices. It is used, as an example, for CD mastering: the system sees all of the drives as SCSI devices, and the user-space program need only be SCSI aware.

Please note that several SCSI drivers have been contributed to Linux by the manufacturers rather than by your preferred hacker community; therefore not all of them are fun reading.

drivers/net

As you might expect, this directory is the home for most interface adapters. Unlike *drivers/scsi*, this directory doesn't include the actual communication protocols, which live in the top-level *net* directory tree. Nonetheless, there's still some bit of software abstraction implemented in *drivers/net*, namely, the implementation of the various line disciplines used by serial-based network communication.

The line discipline is the software layer responsible for the data that traverses the communication line. Every tty device has a line discipline attached. Each line discipline is identified by a number, and the number, as usual, is specified using a symbolic name. The default Linux line discipline is N_TTY, that is, the normal tty management routines, defined in *drivers/char/n_tty.c*.

When PPP, SLIP, or other communication protocols are concerned, however, the default line discipline must be replaced. User-space programs switch the discipline to N_PPP or N_SLIP, and the default will be restored when the device is finally closed. The reason that *pppd* and *slattach* don't exit, after setting up the communication link is just this: as soon as they exit, the device is closed and the default line discipline gets restored.

The job of initializing network drivers hasn't yet been transferred to the init calls mechanism, because some subtle technical details prevent the switch. Initialization is therefore still performed the old way: the *Space.c* file performs the initialization by scanning a list of known hardware and probing for it. The list is controlled by #ifdef directives that select which devices are actually included at compile time.

drivers/sound

Like *drivers/scsi* and *drivers/net*, this directory includes all the drivers for sound cards. The contents of the directory are somewhat similar to the SCSI directory: a few files make up the core sound system, and individual device drivers stack on top of it. The core sound system is in charge of requesting the major number SOUND_MAJOR and dispatching any use of it to the underlying device drivers. A hardware driver plugs into the core by calling *sound_install_audiodrv*, declared in *dev_table.c*.

The list of device-independent files in this directory is pretty long, since it includes generic support for mixers, generic support for sequencers, and so on. To those who want to probe further, we suggest using the makefile as a reference to what is what.

drivers/video

Here you find all the frame buffer video devices. The directory is concerned with video output, not video input. Like */drivers/sound*, the whole directory implements a single char device driver; a core frame buffer system dispatches actual access to the various frame buffers available on the computer.

The entry point to */dev/fb* devices is in *fbmem.c*. The file registers the major number and maintains an internal list of which frame buffer device is in charge of each minor number. A hardware driver registers itself by calling *register_framebuffer*, passing a pointer to `struct fb_info`. The data structure includes everything that's needed for specific device management. It includes the *open* and *release* methods, but no *read*, *write*, or *mmap*; these methods are implemented in a generalized way in *fbmem.c* itself.

In addition to frame buffer memory, this directory is in charge of frame buffer consoles. Because the layout of pixels in frame buffer memory is standardized to some extent, kernel developers have been able to implement generic console support for the various layouts of display memory. Once a hardware driver registers its own `struct fb_info`, it automatically gets a text console attached to it, according to its declared layout of video memory.

Unfortunately, there is no real standardization in this area, so the kernel currently supports 17 different screen layouts; they range from the fairly standard 16-bit and 32-bit color displays to the hairy VGA and Mac pixel placements. The files concerned with placing text on frame buffers are called *fbcon-name.c*.

When the first frame buffer device is registered, the function *register_framebuffer* calls *take_over_console* (exported by *drivers/char/console.c*) in order to actually set up the current frame buffer as the system console. At boot time, before frame buffer initialization, the console is either the native text screen or, if none is there, the first serial port. The command line starting the kernel, of course, can override the default by selecting a specific console device. Kernel developers created *take_over_console* to add support for frame buffer consoles without complicating the boot code. (Usually frame buffer drivers depend on PCI or equivalent support, so they can't be active too early during the boot process.) The *take_over_console* feature, however, is not limited to frame buffers; it's available to any code involving any hardware. If you want to transmit kernel messages using a Morse beeper or UDP network packets, you can do that by calling *take_over_console* from your kernel module.

drivers/input

Input management is another facility meant to simplify and standardize activities that are common to several drivers, and to offer a unified interface to user space. The core file here is called *input.c*. It registers itself as a char driver using `INPUT_MAJOR` as its major number. Its role is collecting events from low-level device drivers and dispatching them to higher layers.

The input interface is defined in `<linux/input.h>`. Each low-level driver registers itself by calling *input_register_device*. After registration, users are able to feed new events to the system by calling *input_event*.

Higher-level modules can register with *input.c* by calling *input_register_handler* and specifying what kind of events they are interested in. This is, for example, how *keybdev.c* expresses its interest in keyboard events (which it ultimately feeds to *driver/char/keyboard.c*).

A high-level module can also register its own minor numbers so it can use its own file operations and become the owner of an input-related special file in */dev*. Currently, however, third-party modules can't easily register minor numbers, and the feature can be used reliably only by the files in *drivers/input*. Minor numbers can currently be used to support mice, joysticks, and generic even channels in user space.

drivers/media

This directory, introduced as of version 2.4.0-test7, collects other communication media, currently radio and video input devices. Both the *media/radio* and *media/video* drivers currently stack on *video/videodev.c*, which implements the "Video For Linux" API.

video/videodev.c is a generic container. It requests a major number and makes it available to hardware drivers. Individual low-level drivers register by calling *video_register_device*. They pass a pointer to their own `struct video_device` and an integer that specifies the type of device. Supported devices are frame grabbers (`VFL_TYPE_GRABBER`), radios (`VFL_TYPE_RADIO`), teletext devices (`VFL_TYPE_VTX`), and undecoded vertical-blank information (`VFL_TYPE_VBI`).

Bus-Specific Directories

Some of the subdirectories of *drivers* are specific to devices that plug into a particular bus architecture. They have been separated from the generic *char* and *block* directories because quite a good deal of code is generic to the bus architecture (as opposed to specific to the hardware device).

The least populated of these directories is *drivers/pci*. It contains only code that talks with PCI controllers (or to system BIOS), whereas PCI hardware drivers are scattered all over the place. The PCI interface is so widespread that it makes no sense to relegate PCI cards to a specific place.

If you are wondering whether ISA has a specific directory, the answer is no. There are no specific ISA support files because the bus offers no resource management or standardization to build a software layer over it. ISA hardware drivers fit best in *drivers/char* or *drivers/sound* or elsewhere.

Other bus-specific directories range from less known internal computer buses to widely used external interface standards.

The former class includes *drivers/sbus*, *drivers/nubus*, *drivers/zorro* (the bus used in Amiga computers), *drivers/dio* (the bus of the HP300 class of computers), and *drivers/tc* (Turbo Channel, used in MIPS DECstations). Whereas *sbus* includes both SBus support functions and drivers for some SBus devices, the others include only support functions. Hardware drivers based on all of these buses live in *drivers/net*, *drivers/scsi*, or wherever is appropriate for the actual hardware (with the exception of a few SBus drivers, as noted). A few of these buses are currently used by just one driver.

Directories devoted to external buses include *drivers/usb*, *drivers/pcmcia*, *drivers/parport* (generic cross-platform parallel port support, which defines a whole new class of device drivers), *drivers/isdn* (all ISDN controllers supported by Linux and their common support functions), *drivers/atm* (the same, for ATM network connections), and *drivers/ieee1394* (FireWire).

Platform-Specific Directories

Sometimes, a computer platform has its own directory tree in the *drivers* hierarchy. This has tended to happen when kernel development for that platform has proceeded alongside the main source tree without being merged for a while. In these cases, keeping the directory tree separate helped in maintaining the code. Examples include *drivers/acorn* (old ARM-based computers), *drivers/macintosh*, *drivers/sgi* (Silicon Graphics workstations), and *drivers/s390* (IBM mainframes). There is little of value, usually, in looking at that code, unless you are interested in the specific platform.

Other Subdirectories

There are other subdirectories in *drivers*, but they are, in our opinion, currently of minor interest and very specific use. *drivers/mtd* implements a Memory Technology Device layer, which is used to manage solid-state disks (flash memories and other kinds of EEPROM). *drivers/i2c* offers an implementation of the i2c protocol, which is the "Inter Integrated Circuit" two-wire bus used internally by several modern peripherals, especially frame grabbers. *drivers/i2o*, similarly, handles I2O devices (a proprietary high-speed communication standard for certain PCI devices, which has been unveiled under pressure from the free software community). *drivers/pnp* is a collection of common ISA Plug-and-Play code from various drivers, but fortunately the PnP hack is not really used nowadays by manufacturers.

Under *drivers/* you also find initial support for new device classes that are currently implemented by a very small range of devices.

That's the case for fiber channel support (*drivers/fc4*) and *drivers/telephony*. There's even an empty directory *drivers/misc*, which claims to be "for misc devices that really don't fit anywhere else." The directory is empty of code, but hosts an (empty) makefile with the comment just quoted.

The Linux kernel is so huge that it's impossible to cover it all in a few pages. Moreover, it is a moving target, and once you think you are finished, you find that the new patch released by your preferred hackers includes a whole lot of new material. It may well be that the *misc* directory in 2.4 is not empty anymore as you read this.

Although we consider it unlikely, it may even happen that 2.6 or 3.0 will turn out to be pretty different from 2.4; unfortunately, this edition of the book won't automatically update itself to cover the new releases and will become obsolete over time. Despite our best efforts to cover the current version of the kernel, both in this chapter and in the whole book, there's no substitute for direct reference to the source code.

BIBLIOGRAPHY

Most of the information in this book has been extracted from the kernel sources, which are the best documentation about the Linux kernel.

Kernel sources can be retrieved from hundreds of FTP sites around the world, so we won't list them here.

Version dependencies are best checked by looking at the patches, which are available from the same places where you get the whole source. The program called *repatch* might help you in checking how a single file has been modified throughout the different kernel patches; it is available in the source files provided on the O'Reilly FTP site.

On *sunsite.unc.edu* and all its mirrors you can also find several device drivers, which can surely help in writing your own.

Linux Kernel Books

Bar, Moshe. *Linux Internals*. McGraw-Hill. 2000. This terse book by *Byte* columnist Moshe Bar covers much of how the Linux kernel works, and includes a number of 2.4 features.

Bovet, Daniel P., and Marco Cesati. *Understanding the Linux Kernel*. O'Reilly & Associates. 2000. Covers the design and implementation of the Linux kernel in great detail. It is more oriented toward providing an understanding of the algorithms used than documenting the kernel API.

Maxwell, Scott. *Linux Core Kernel Commentary*. Coriolis. 1999. Mostly a large listing of the core kernel code, with 150 pages of commentary at the end. It can be useful for trying to figure out what is happening in a particular part of the kernel.

Nutt, Gary J. *Kernel Projects for Linux*. Addison-Wesley. 2000. Written to be used in college-level classrooms; as such, it is not a full introduction to the Linux kernel in its own right. For those looking to play with the kernel, though, this book can be a good aid.

Unix Design and Internals

Bach, Maurice. *The Design of the Unix Operating System*. Prentice Hall. 1987. This book, though quite old, covers all the issues related to Unix implementations. It was the main source of inspiration for Linus in the first Linux versions.

Stevens, Richard. *Unix Network Programming*. P T R Prentice-Hall. 1990. Perhaps the definitive book on the Unix network programming API.

Stevens, Richard. *Advanced Programming in the UNIX Environment*. Addison-Wesley. 1992. Every detail of Unix system calls is described herein, making it a good companion when implementing advanced features in the device methods.

INDEX

We'd like to hear your suggestions for improving our indexes. Send email to *index@oreilly.com.*

D

About the Author

Alessandro Rubini installed Linux 0.99.14 soon after getting his degree as an electronic engineer. He then received a Ph.D. in computer science at the University of Pavia. He left the University soon afterward because he didn't want to write articles. He now works as a freelancer writing device drivers and, um...articles. He used to be a young hacker before his babies were born; he's now an old advocate of free software who developed a bias for non-PC computer platforms.

Jonathan Corbet got his first look at the BSD Unix source back in 1981, when an instructor at the University of Colorado let him "fix" the paging algorithm. He has been digging around inside every system he could get his hands on ever since, working on drivers for VAX, Sun, Ardent, and x86 systems on the way. He got his first Linux system in 1993, and has never looked back. Mr. Corbet is the cofounder and executive editor of *Linux Weekly News* (*http://LWN.net*); he lives in Boulder, Colorado with his wife and two children.

Colophon

Our look is the result of reader comments, our own experimentation, and feedback from distribution channels. Distinctive covers complement our distinctive approach to technical topics, breathing personality and life into potentially dry subjects.

The image on the cover of *Linux Device Drivers* is of a bucking horse. A colorful description of this appears in *Marvels of the New West: A Vivid Portrayal of the Stupendous Marvels in the Vast Wonderland West of the Missouri River*, by William Thayer (The Henry Bill Publishing Co., Norwich, CT, 1888). Thayer quotes a stockman, who gives this description of a bucking horse: "When a horse bucks he puts his head down between his legs, arches his back like an angry cat, and springs into the air with all his legs at once, coming down again with a frightful jar, and he sometimes keeps on repeating the performance until he is completely worn out with the excursion. The rider is apt to feel rather worn out too by that time, if he has kept his seat, which is not a very easy matter, especially if the horse is a real scientific bucker, and puts a kind of side action into every jump. The double girth commonly attached to these Mexican saddles is useful for keeping the saddle in its place during one of those bouts, but there is no doubt that they frequently make a horse buck who would not do so with a single girth. With some animals you can never draw up the flank girth without setting them bucking."

Darren Kelly was the production editor, Cynthia Kogut was the copyeditor, and Susan Carlson Greene was the proofreader for *Linux Device Drivers*, Second Edition. Catherine Morris and Claire Cloutier provided quality control. Judy Hoer wrote the index. Matt Hutchinson, Lucy Muellner, and Joe Wizda provided production support.

Edie Freedman designed the cover of this book. The cover image is a 19th-century engraving from the Dover Pictorial Archive. Emma Colby produced the cover layout with QuarkXPress 4.1, using Adobe's ITC Garamond font.

David Futato designed the interior layout based on a series design by Nancy Priest. Chapter opener images are taken from the Dover Pictorial Archive, the book *Marvels of the New West: A Vivid Portrayal of the Stupendous Marvels in the Vast Wonderland West of the Missouri River* (by William M. Thayer, The Henry Bill Publishing Company, Norwich, CT, 1888), and *The Pioneer History of America: A Popular Account of the Heroes and Adventures* (by Augustus Lynch Mason, A.M., The Jones Brothers Publishing Company, Cincinnati, OH, 1884). The print version of this book was created by translating the DocBook XML markup of its source files into a set of gtroff macros, using a filter developed at O'Reilly & Associates by Norman Walsh. Steve Talbott designed and wrote the underlying macro set on the basis of the GNU *troff –gs* macros; Lenny Muellner adapted them to XML and implemented the book design. The GNU groff text formatter version 1.11.1 was used to generate PostScript output. The text and heading fonts are ITC Garamond Light and Garamond Book. The illustrations that appear in the book were produced by Robert Romano and Jessamyn Read using Macromedia FreeHand 9 and Adobe Photoshop 6.

Whenever possible, our books use a durable and flexible lay-flat binding. If the page count exceeds this binding's limit, perfect binding is used.

Linux

Free as in Freedom

By Sam Williams
1st Edition, March 2002
240 pages, ISBN 0-596-00287-4

Free as in Freedom interweaves biographical snapshots of GNU project founder Richard Stallman with the political, social and economic history of the free software movement. *Free as in Freedom* looks at how the latest twists and turns in the software marketplace have done little to throw Stallman off his pedestal. If anything, they have made his logic-based rhetoric and immovable personality more persuasive.

LPI Linux Certification in a Nutshell

By Jeff Dean
1st Edition May 2001
570 pages, ISBN 1-56592-748-6

LPI Linux Certification in a Nutshell prepares system administrators for the basic LPI General Linux 101 exam and the more advanced 102 exam. The book is divided into two parts, one for each of the LPI exams. Each part features a summary of the exam, a Highlighter's Index, labs, suggested exercises, and practice exams to help you pass the LPI exams with flying colors.

The Linux Web Server CD Bookshelf

By O'Reilly & Associates, Inc.
1st Edition September 2001
(Includes CD-ROM)
812 pages, ISBN 0-59600-208-4

Six best selling O'Reilly Animal Guides are now available on CD-ROM, easily accessible and searchable with your favorite web browser: *Running Linux*, 3rd Edition; *Linux in a Nutshell*, 3rd Edition; *Apache: The Definitive Guide*, 2nd Edition; *MySQL & mSQL*; *Programming the Perl DBI*; and *CGI Programming with Perl*, 2nd Edition. As a bonus, you get the new paperback version of *Linux in a Nutshell*.

CVS Pocket Reference

By Gregor N. Purdy
1st Edition August 2000
78 pages, ISBN 0-596-00003-0

The *CVS Pocket Reference* is a quick reference guide to help administrators and users set up and manage source code development. This small book, the ultimate companion for open source developers, covers CVS Version 1.10.8 and delivers the core concepts of version control, along with a complete command reference and guide to configuration and repository setup.

Web Database Applications with PHP & MySQL

By Hugh E. Williams & David Lane
1st Edition March 2002
582 pages, ISBN 0-596-00041-3

This book offers both theoretical and practical guidance for creating web database applications. The detailed information on designing relational databases and the web application architectures that interact with them will be especially useful to readers who have worked with or built database-backed web sites before. The book implements a sample web application using PHP and MySQL on the Apache platform.

Linux Network Administrator's Guide, 2nd Edition

By Olaf Kirch & Terry Dawson
2nd Edition June 2000
506 pages, ISBN 1-56592-400-2

Fully updated, this comprehensive, impressive introduction to networking on Linux now covers firewalls, including the use of ipchains and iptables (netfilter), masquerading, and accounting. Other new topics include Novell (NCP/IPX) support and INN (news administration). Original material on serial connections, UUCP, routing and DNS, mail and News, SLIP and PPP, NFS, and NIS has been thoroughly updated.

Linux

Using Samba

By Peter Kelly, Perry Donham &
David Collier-Brown
1st Edition November 1999
416 pages, Includes CD-ROM
ISBN 1-56592-449-5

Samba turns a Unix or Linux system into a
file and print server for Microsoft Windows
network clients. This complete guide to
Samba administration covers basic 2.0 con-
figuration, security, logging, and troubleshooting. Whether you're
playing on one note or a full three-octave range, this book will
help you maintain an efficient and secure server. Includes a
CD-ROM of sources and ready-to-install binaries.

Managing & Using MySQL, 2nd Edition

By George Reese, Randy Jay Yarger & Tim King
2nd Edition April 2002
448 pages, ISBN 0-596-00211-4

This edition retains the best features of the
first edition, while adding the latest on
MySQL and the relevant programming language interfaces, with more complete reference information. The administration section
is greatly enhanced; the programming lan-
guage chapters have been updated—especially the Perl and PHP
chapters—and new additions include chapters on security and
extending MySQL and a system tables reference.

Understanding the Linux Kernel

By Daniel P. Bovet & Marco Cesati
1st Edition October 2000
650 pages, ISBN 0-596-00002-2

Understanding the Linux Kernel helps readers understand how Linux performs best and
how it meets the challenge of different environments. The authors introduce each topic
by explaining its importance, and show how
kernel operations relate to the utilities that
are familiar to Unix programmers and users.

UNIX Power Tools, 2nd Edition

By Jerry Peek, Tim O'Reilly & Mike Loukides
2nd Edition August 1997
1120 pages, Includes CD-ROM
ISBN 1-56592-260-3

Loaded with practical advice about almost
every aspect of Unix, this second edition of
UNIX Power Tools addresses the technology
that Unix users face today. You'll find thorough coverage of POSIX utilities, including
GNU versions, detailed bash and tcsh shell coverage, a strong
emphasis on Perl, and a CD-ROM that contains the best freeware
available.

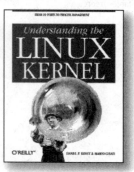

How to stay in touch with O'Reilly

1. Visit our award-winning web site

http://www.oreilly.com/

★ "Top 100 Sites on the Web"—PC Magazine
★ CIO Magazine's Web Business 50 Awards

Our web site contains a library of comprehensive product information (including book excerpts and tables of contents), downloadable software, background articles, interviews with technology leaders, links to relevant sites, book cover art, and more. File us in your bookmarks or favorites!

2. Join our email mailing lists

Sign up to get email announcements of new books and conferences, special offers, and O'Reilly Network technology newsletters at:

http://www.elists.oreilly.com

It's easy to customize your free elists subscription so you'll get exactly the O'Reilly news you want.

3. Get examples from our books

To find example files for a book, go to:

http://www.oreilly.com/catalog

select the book, and follow the "Examples" link.

4. Work with us

Check out our web site for current employment opportunites:

http://jobs.oreilly.com/

5. Register your book

Register your book at:

http://register.oreilly.com

6. Contact us

O'Reilly & Associates, Inc.
1005 Gravenstein Hwy North
Sebastopol, CA 95472 USA
TEL: 707-827-7000 or 800-998-9938
       (6am to 5pm PST)
FAX: 707-829-0104

order@oreilly.com
For answers to problems regarding your order or our products. To place a book order online visit:

http://www.oreilly.com/order_new/

catalog@oreilly.com
To request a copy of our latest catalog.

booktech@oreilly.com
For book content technical questions or corrections.

proposals@oreilly.com
To submit new book proposals to our editors and product managers.

international@oreilly.com
For information about our international distributors or translation queries. For a list of our distributors outside of North America check out:

http://international.oreilly.com/distributors.html

O'REILLY®

Notes